IN TANDEM

READING AND WRITING FOR COLLEGE STUDENTS

Deanne Spears
City College of San Francisco

with a
BRIEF GUIDE TO GRAMMAR AND USAGE

David Spears
City College of San Francisco

Boston Burr Ridge, IL Dubuque, IA New York San Francisco St. Louis
Bangkok Bogotá Caracas Kuala Lumpur Lisbon London Madrid Mexico City
Milan Montreal New Delhi Santiago Seoul Singapore Sydney Taipei Toronto

The McGraw·Hill Companies

Published by McGraw-Hill, an imprint of The McGraw-Hill Companies, Inc., 1221 Avenue of the Americas, New York, NY 10020.

This book is printed on acid-free paper.

1 2 3 4 5 6 7 8 9 0 DOC/DOC 0 9 8 7

SE ISBN: 978-0-07-338570-9
SE MHID: 0-07-338570-0
AIE ISBN: 978-0-07-333171-3
AIE MHID: 0-07-333171-6

Sponsoring Editor: *John Kindler*
Marketing Manager: *Tamara Wederbrand*
Editorial Assistant: *Jesse Hassenger*
Production Editor: *Chanda Feldman*
Manuscript Editor: *Jennifer Gordon*
Design Manager: *Kim Menning*
Text Designer: *Glenda King*
Cover Designer: *Ross Carson*
Photo Research: *Editorial Image, LLC.*
Production Supervisor: *Dennis Fitzgerald*
Composition: *10/12 Stone Serif by ICC Macmillan Inc.*
Printing: *PMS 293, 45# New Era Matte, R. R. Donnelley & Sons, Inc.*
Cover: Keyboard: © Mark Harwood/Getty Images; Book: © Stockbyte/Getty Images

Credits: The credits section for this book begins on page 630 and is considered an extension of the copyright page.

Library of Congress Control Number: 2007030441

www.mhhe.com

Dedication

With love to Charlotte—
and to Ellen, Bill, and Sarah

Brief Contents

Contents

Readings Arranged by Theme

Social Issues and Social Currents

The Immigration Dilemma

Science, Nature, and Technology

Saving and Destroying The Environment

Preface

In Tandem comes out of our shared experience in teaching composition, reading, and grammar at City College of San Francisco, a large urban community college with a diverse student population. Indeed, the book is a distillation what we have learned about teaching these difficult subjects through the years.

Teaching composition is more of an art than a science. And it is also an evolving art. In the face of declining literacy and verbal test scores, we English instructors struggle to help college students master critical reading skills and write clear and comprehensible academic prose. In the thirty-plus years that we have taught, we have seen trends come and go. Despite these shifting trends, all of them have had in common the central purpose of teaching students first to think, and then to read and to write well.

Recently, college English instructors have been putting more emphasis on tying writing assignments to students' reading, even in basic skills composition courses. In addition, many colleges across the country are offering linked composition and reading courses in their curricula. We all give credence to the observation that good readers tend to be better writers than poor readers. The rationale for this book, then, is to exploit this symbiosis—the idea that good reading skills promote good writing skills—by treating them as twin undertakings, one reinforcing the other. The book's title, *In Tandem*, and the structure imposed on the material throughout, reflect this linked approach.

The Introduction to Instructors on the following pages explains the content and structure of the book in detail.

Several people deserve thanks for their help as we prepared *In Tandem* for publication. Among them are three colleagues at City College of San Francisco: Eleanor Brown, Andrea Sanelli, and Joan Wilson. Deanne's daughter, Charlotte Milan, advised us on current trends in the food industry, which guided our choice of some of the reading selections in Part 5.

David would like to thank his sixth grade English teacher, Lenore Larney, for introducing him to grammar; Paul Roberts, whose book *Understanding Grammar* showed him how truly interesting the subject could be; and Bruce Hannah, a City College colleague and dear friend with whom he spent many afternoons sipping vodka martinis and discussing the intricacies of grammar.

Many reviewers saw this project in its various stages, offering their comments and suggestions—along with their encouraging words. They were invaluable as we trimmed and shaped the manuscript, and we thank them:

Lori Allen, Florida Community College at Jacksonville
Audrey Antee, Florida Community College at Jacksonville
John Bagnole, Ohio University
Annmarie Chiarini, Community College of Baltimore County–Essex
Dean Cooledge, University of Maryland–Eastern Shore
Fawcett Dunstan, Community College of Baltimore County–Essex
David Glaud, University of Wisconsin–Parkside
Paul Haeder, Spokane Falls Community College
Alexander Howe, University of D.C.
Raymond Marafino, Capital Community College
Barbara McLay, University of South Florida
Angela Medina, Rio Hondo College
Melinda Morrow, DeVry University
Julie Peluso, Northern Virginia Community College
Linda Piccirillo-Smith, Kent State University
Bradley Waltman, Community College of Southern Nevada

We also want to thank several people at McGraw-Hill for their help with this text: Jennifer Gordon's expertise in copyediting significantly improved the manuscript; Emily and David Tietz were invaluable in locating photographs; Marty Moga secured reprint permissions in a timely and efficient fashion; Chanda Feldman exercised careful oversight on all aspects of the project. Jesse Hassenger was, as always, adept at handling the little details that inevitably bedevil even the most organized writer. And finally, special thanks to John Kindler, our editor, for believing in us.

We welcome suggestions, comments, or questions. Please feel free to contact Deanne at dkspears@gmail.com for general matters concerning the text and David at dspears@stanfordalumni.org for matters concerning grammar and usage. We will do our best to reply within a day or two.

Deanne Spears and David Spears

Introduction—To The Instructor

A RATIONALE FOR A NEW TEXT—READING AND WRITING IN TANDEM

College writing assignments most frequently require analysis, synthesis, and argumentation. However, these assignments, which make up so much of the required writing in college classes, are often quite difficult for students, especially when their reading and writing skills may not be up to par. My goal in the Parts 1–8 of the text, then, is to give students realistic instruction in some essential reading skills and then to provide practical and realistic suggestions for writing various types of essays. The reading and writing sections move from the simple to the complex, from personal experience to more difficult analytical assignments, all on accessible and engaging subjects. By the end of the course, students should have a good foundation for writing more complex analytical essays in their lower-division courses. Along the way, they will gain more confidence in comprehending college-level prose.

THE STRUCTURE OF THE BOOK

We want the structure of the book to be clean and uncluttered. A glance at the table of contents shows the organization and the progression of skills. Part 1, An Overview of the Writing Process, explains the process of writing an essay from start to finish along with a sample student essay. This section also includes an explanation of the steps required for writing a good essay, brainstorming techniques, writing the thesis, and a sample student essay. The section ends with an explanation of how to integrate and cite quoted material, how to construct a Works Cited page using MLA format, and how to format an essay.

Parts 2–7 have a uniform structure: Each is divided into three sections. Section 1 presents a specific reading skill followed by a practice essay. Section 2 contains reading selections and exercises, which look back to the skill under discussion in Section 1 and ahead to the writing assignments in Section 3. Section 3 includes instruction in writing skills and writing topics pertaining both to the readings and to the particular type of essay discussed. Specific and realistic suggestions help students learn how to write each particular type of essay. The number of reading selections varies from part to part. Because Part 5 takes up the most crucial skills for good reading and writing skills (making inferences and writing analysis and synthesis essays), this section has more readings than the others. This tripartite structure is discussed in more detail below.

Section 1: Reading Instruction

Central to the book are good quality, high-interest readings on a variety of contemporary topics and issues. The reading skills, as with the writing skills, move from basic to more complex. Beginning with the fundamental skills of identifying the main idea and the writer's purpose, Part 2 establishes the foundation. Other skills covered in Parts 3–7 are techniques for improving reading vocabulary, suggestions for annotating (reading with a pencil in your hand), making inferences and drawing conclusions, identifying common patterns of development, taking note of transitional devices, and finally evaluating argumentative prose. These sections offer enough instruction to get students started and some practice exercises or illustrative examples before they turn to the main readings.

If instructors wish to assign material outside the text, the accompanying website includes several extra readings and exercises as well as two pairs of editorials arguing for and against a particular controversial issue.

My aim is to help students to undo their poor reading habits, to promote good ones in their place, and to move them from being passive readers who read only to get through their required assignments with minimal interaction with the text to being active and confident readers. The exercises and discussion questions following the readings will help them explore the implications embedded in a text. Writing assignments tied to these readings will give them a chance to explore a particular idea from the readings that has resonance.

Section 2: The Readings and Exercise Apparatus

The book contains 39 readings of varying lengths for analysis. In addition, the readings reflect a range of difficulty, allowing the instructor to choose from easy, moderate, or more difficult readings, depending on the students' abilities and the course syllabus. This structure allows a sensible progression from relatively simple to complex. Interspersed throughout the text, where appropriate, are visual elements to analyze—photographs, cartoons, charts and graphs, and public service announcements. In Part 8, students are provided with paired editorials—three on the impact of immigration on American society and the economy and two on global warming.

Each reading begins with a short biographical headnote Then, because all students need to improve their store of vocabulary words and to learn useful prefixes, roots, and suffixes, there is a brief section on word analysis, using one or two words from the selection as examples. For example, the student might learn the prefix *circum-* as well as a few words containing it, like *circumspect, circumlocution,* or *circumnavigate.*

Each reading selection ends with multiple-choice questions on the writer's main idea and purpose, followed by different types of exercises in locating supporting details, sequencing, inferences, interpreting meaning, and vocabulary. To avoid monotony, these exercises, particularly the vocabulary ones, vary from selection to selection. Some exercises are specific to the particular skill taken up in the first part; for example, in Part 3 the discussion of improving vocabulary and using the dictionary is complemented by exercises requiring students to use the dictionary. Practice in making inferences, taken up in Part 5, is similarly reinforced in the exercise material in Parts 5–7.

Each selection ends with some discussion questions and a section called "Explore the Web," where students are directed to relevant websites for further exploration of the topic under discussion.

Section 3: Writing Instruction

Section 3 in Parts 2–8 contains a brief explanation of how to write a particular kind of essay, with the emphasis on writing about one or more of the readings. This requires the student to annotate the text carefully and then to correctly use quotations and to paraphrase and summarize material from the reading. The student will therefore have extensive practice in integrating a writer's ideas in defense of his or her thesis. Throughout, the *process* of writing is explained and illustrated with a judicious number of student paragraphs and essays.

The types of writing, as noted before, begin with the relatively simple personal experience essay, where students analyze either a personal experience described in one of the readings or an experience of their own. The next type of writing is one I devised as an accessible way to teach analysis: a profile of a person or a community (New Orleans is the example here), either based on the subject of one of the readings or perhaps a profile of the student's own devising. Subsequent types of writing assignments include paraphrase and summary (Part 4), analysis and synthesis (Part 5), comparison and contrast (Part 6), cause-and-effect (Part 7), and argumentation (Part 8).

Section 3 ends with a variety of topics for two kinds of writing assignments—first, generic topics where the student is asked to write a particular type of paper based on his own ideas, observations, and experience, and second, more academic topics where the student is asked to respond to, to assess, and to analyze one or more readings. Thus instructors have a range of topics—some easy, some more challenging—from which to choose.

The Tell-Show-Share Method

The pivotal section of the book is Section 3 at the end of Part 5, which takes up instruction on how to write an analysis and a synthesis essay. After years of experimenting with various ways to teach students how to write analytical essays, my colleagues and I began using the system devised by Jeff Rackham and Olivia Bertagnolli and published in a fine textbook, *Windows* (HarperCollins, 1994). Unfortunately, this book is no longer in print, but my colleagues and I have adapted their tell-show-share method to teach analysis for several years. I reprint Rackham and Bertagnolli's explanation. Then I demonstrate the process of writing an analysis using the T-S-S method—beginning with the first step of inspiration/invention, followed by note-taking, writing the thesis, and finally organization and development of supporting ideas. This section also includes examples of student-written introductory and body paragraphs.

I hope that this section of the book will be greatly useful to other composition teachers who, like me and my colleagues, grapple with the inherent difficulties of teaching students what a college essay should look like without overwhelming them with jargon or with unrealistic expectations. The tell-show-share method can be used to analyze other material besides essays, for example, short stories, films, speeches, or even paintings. The possibilities are limitless. In short, it serves as useful starting point for writing assignments beyond lower-division composition courses.

In Tandem, then, derives from many years of teaching students to write well enough to survive in their college courses (not just in freshman English). The coverage of quotation, paraphrase, summary, analysis, and synthesis—all requiring students to use ideas from the readings in support of the thesis—will appeal to other instructors as well.

Deanne Spears
Half Moon Bay, California

GUIDE TO GRAMMAR AND USAGE

In the grammar section of this book I cover what I have found to be the areas of greatest concern to the student writer: subject-verb agreement, fragments, pronoun case, pronoun agreement, punctuation (including the dreaded comma splice), modification problems, and parallel structure. I have found that an understanding of the principles of accepted usage gives the writer a confidence in his ability to form more or less error-free sentences, a confidence that allows him the freedom to concentrate on what he wants to say rather than how he is saying it.*

Of course, it is impossible to explain subject-verb agreement if the student can't recognize a subject or a verb; It is impossible to explain when to use he if he has no idea of the cases in English. So, to make the explanations of acceptable usage understandable, I begin the section with a review of basic grammar and cover parts of speech, clauses and phrases, and sentence patterns.

Throughout the grammar section there are brief exercises to test students' mastery of each concept and a few proofreading exercises adapted from sample student paragraphs used earlier in the book.

*In my section on pronouns, I explain why I use the masculine pronoun. I am a male. When Deanne writes, I encourage her to use "she."

I have taught grammar for many years and feel that it is well within the grasp of almost every student to improve significantly his use of the language in a short period of time if he is sufficiently motivated. I hope that my section of this book will encourage students to solve the usage problems that make writing a chore. I also hope that the freedom from worry about errors will reveal, at least to some students, the pleasure one feels when he discovers he is able to express himself clearly. Few things are as exciting as finding one's voice. Learning the fundamentals of accepted usage seems to me to be the first step in this process.

David Spears
Half Moon Bay, California

Introduction—To The Student

"Only connect! That was the whole of her sermon.
Only connect the prose and the passion, and
both will be exalted . . ."

—E. M. Forster, *Howards End* (1910)

MAKING CONNECTIONS—LINKING READING AND WRITING

The title of this book, *In Tandem*, implies a shared connection between reading and writing—the two activities most central to college study. The underlying principle of this book is that good reading promotes good writing. They are twin undertakings, one reinforcing the other. If the reader/writer does the job right, a mutual exchange takes place—something like a symbiotic relationship. As the British novelist E. M. Forster suggests when he wrote "Only connect," the prose (what you read) embodies the passion (what you feel about what you read), thus connecting you, the reader, and the unseen writer.

When you read, you internalize the writer's words. You take in and absorb the experiences, feelings, perceptions, and observations a piece of writing conveys. Then the magical part begins. Through the prism of your mind, you connect with these elements, making them your own and shaping them according to your own experience and beliefs. Anne Fadiman, writer in residence at Yale University, recently reaffirmed this relationship between reader and writer: "The act of reading is collaborative, conversational."[1] She continues by saying that this engagement works with any piece of writing that requires an emotional investment of ourselves.

Of course, we can't connect in this way to everything we read. It's pretty hard to feel the passion Forster refers to when you read your biology text or when you consult Craigslist on the web to find a used car to buy. Making connections is best suited to essays and articles, and also fiction—writing that examines issues and problems that affect us all or that reflect new cultural directions. For example, you will encounter these questions in this text:

[1]Quoted in David L. Ulin, "Literature, Now More Than Ever," *Los Angeles Times*, October 16, 2005, E4.

- What Images of summer do I carry in my memory?
- What do American soldiers have to say about fighting in the Iraq War?
- If I observed a person of Middle Eastern descent acting suspiciously on an airplane, what would I do?
- In what way is Internet dating like an arranged marriage?
- Why did the Easter Islanders build those huge statues?
- Why do so many people cheat, and is it true that cheaters never prosper?
- Is it possible to survive on a minimum-wage salary in the United States today?
- Is torture ever ethical?
- What is Intelligent Design, and should it be taught in high school biology classes?

The underlying principle of the book, then, regards reading and writing as twin activities that complement and reinforce each other. Your writing assignments will ask you to make connections. As you read the selections in Parts 1–7 of this text, you will practice annotating the readings in the margin; on paper, you will jot down your impressions and reactions as you go. During this process, you may begin to see links, perhaps between an idea embedded in the text and something you yourself have experienced or observed, or perhaps links between an idea as articulated by two or more writers. Careful and critical reading will lead you to make connections that you can then set down in an essay of your own.

LINKING READING AND WRITING—AN ILLUSTRATION

Let us illustrate how this process might work with one reader's response to a prose passage. The first selection in Part 1 is titled "Girls of Summer: Lazy Days from a Gen X Childhood" by Kristie Helms. The title and subtitle invite reflection. What should a kid's summers be like? What were your summers like? What does the term "Gen X" mean? Does your generation have a label?

Helms' article starts off like this:

> We lived on the banks of the Tennessee River, and we owned the summers when we were girls. We ran wild through humid summer days that never ended but only melted one into the other. We floated down rivers of week-days with no school, no rules, no parents, and no constructs other than our fantasies.

When I first read Helms' article in the magazine where it was originally published, I was immediately drawn into her world. Some questions occurred to me: What's the Tennessee River like? Who are the "we" she mentions? How does one "own" a summer? What did they do when they "ran wild" through the days? What does she mean by the word "constructs"? What is the dominant impression she wants to convey in this opening paragraph?

Yet there was my world, too, quite different from hers. In my mind I could see all the childhood summers spent with my grandparents in a little farm town in Iowa, so unlike my school-year life in Chicago or, later, in Los Angeles. I can transport myself instantly in my mind to that little town, and in my mind's eye I can see the red Keds I used to wear and how my siblings, numerous cousins, and I spent our days. I can feel the humidity of a July Iowa afternoon and the way my shorts and T-shirt always stuck to my skin when we played softball or rode our bikes on the dusty, unpaved country roads. I can see the peanut butter jars full of fireflies that we caught on hot summer nights.

If I were to write an essay after making these connections, I would have a couple of choices: I could examine my reactions by comparing my summer to Kristie Helms' summers, or I could write about a particular idea from her article that I found significant. Whichever approach one takes, it is a twin process: We learn to read accurately to make sure that we clearly understand what the writer is saying. But just as important, we learn to connect to that writing—to discover what we think about it, to see how—or perhaps to see *if*—it relates to our experience, our values, and our way of looking at the world. I connected easily with Helms' article that first time, even though I didn't grow up on the banks of the Tennessee River, and I am more of a Baby Boomer than a Generation Xer. Still, the connection is there, waiting to be made. Other readers of different generations and from different parts of the world would undoubtedly have completely different reactions.

THE ORGANIZATION OF THE TEXT

The organization of *In Tandem* affords you ample practice in making the kinds of connections described above. Each of the book's seven parts is divided into two sections: Each begins with a discussion of a particular reading skill followed by a short sample reading selection. For further practice, each part has a selection of readings, accompanied by comprehension and other exercises to measure your understanding. The last section explains how to write a specific kind of essay, followed by a series of writing assignments.

Many of these writing assignments pertain to the readings, giving you necessary practice in writing about what you have read. Others are more open-ended, giving you the opportunity, for example, to write a comparison and contrast essay on a subject of your own choosing. As the book progresses, the writing assignments gradually become more complex and challenging. We begin with a personal experience essay, then move to writing a profile of a person, and from there to the practical assignment of writing paraphrases and a summary. In Parts 4–7, the assignments become more academic, and you will learn to organize and develop an analysis, a synthesis essay, a comparison-contrast essay, a cause-effect essay, and finally, an argument. As you work through the text, then, you will gradually acquire the skills so necessary to writing other papers in college: This means learning to select information from a reading to write about, to gather evidence and support using paraphrase and direct quotation, and to learn the correct ways to document these ideas.

About the Authors

Deanne Spears is originally from Portland, Oregon. She now considers herself a native Californian, having moved to Los Angeles as a child when there were orange groves and smog was a new word. During her childhood, she spent carefree summers in a small farming community in northwest Iowa. After receiving a B.A. and M.A. in comparative literature from the University of Southern California, she began teaching composition and reading at City College of San Francisco. She continues to tutor students in reading and to conduct teacher-preparation workshops for the college. In addition to her primary interests—reading and studying Italian—she and David enjoy cooking, watching movies (we have almost 100 titles in our Netflix queue), kayaking in Princeton Harbor, camping (especially in Kings Canyon and Yosemite Creek), and exploring the wealth of inexpensive ethnic restaurants in the Bay Area. Deanne is the author of *Developing Critical Reading Skills*, the eighth edition of which will be published in 2008.

Born in Evansville, Indiana, David Spears moved (was moved, to be precise) to San Francisco when he was ten and never left the Bay Area. He received a B.A. from Stanford University in comparative literature and, after teaching junior high school for three years, spent a year at the University of Chicago, receiving an M.A., also in comparative lit. Since then he has taught English at City College of San Francisco. For sixteen years of that time he was a single dad, raising a daughter, Sarah, who is now teaching English at a middle school in the area. About ten years ago, thanks to Sarah's interest in the show when she was growing up, he won the one and only Brady Bunch trivia contest held at City College.

Dave (the name he calls himself) is also a professional jazz musician. He plays vibes at various clubs and restaurants in a group with Dick Fregulia and George Martin, friends from Stanford, and Brandon Robinson, a friend from Half Moon Bay. CDs are available upon request.

David and Deanne and their friend Mac enjoy walking the bluffs and beaches of Half Moon Bay with Katie, David's Australian cattle dog.

IN TANDEM

READING AND WRITING FOR COLLEGE STUDENTS

PART ONE

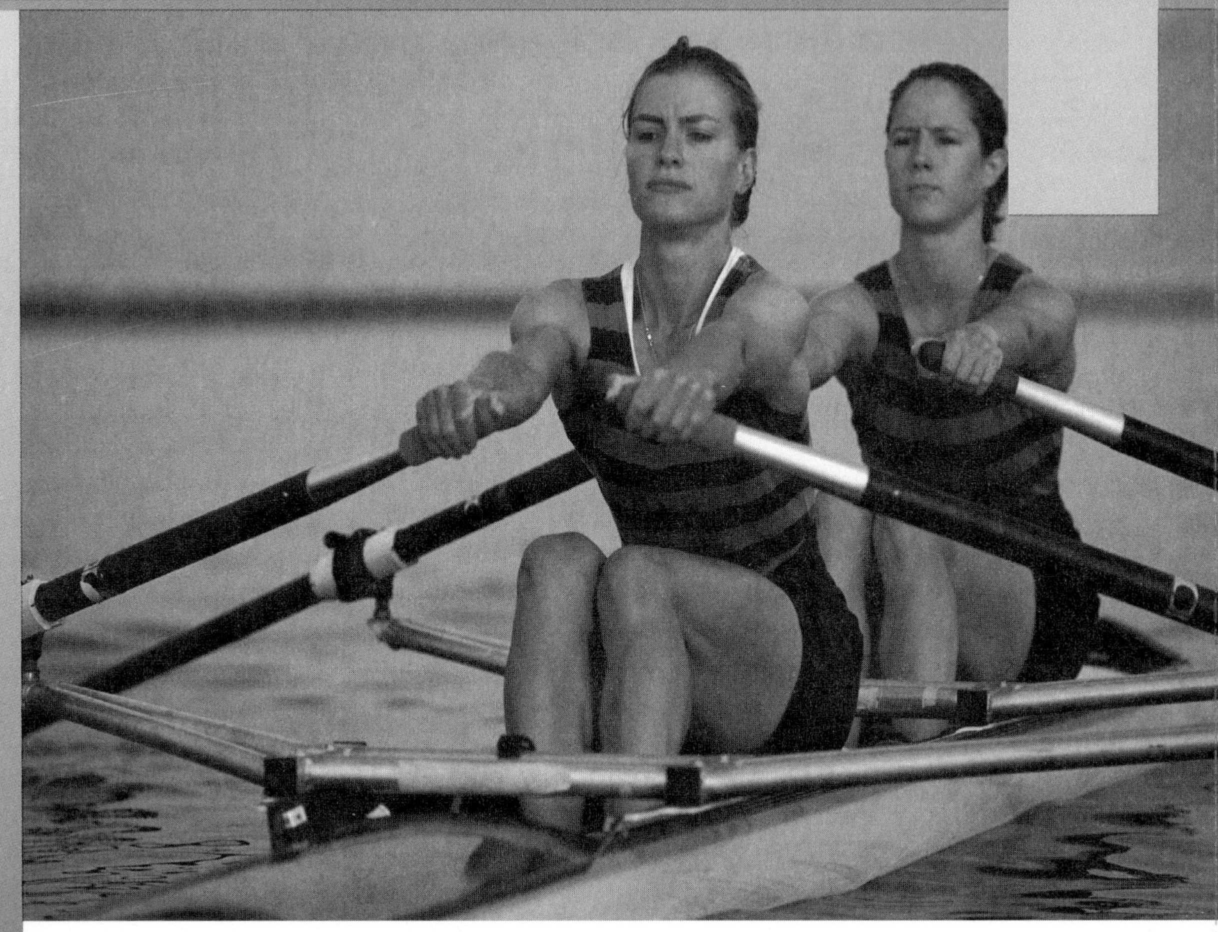

An Overview of the Writing Process

Several years ago, when I first began teaching composition classes, I remember thinking about the challenges faced by writers as they begin to learn more about their own writing processes. Two observations made by Winston Churchill—prime minister of England during World War II—struck me as relevant and helpful to the students I was teaching.

Writing, Thinking, and Persistence

In addition to being a prominent statesman and a respected writer, Churchill was also a talented amateur painter. He wrote, "When I get to heaven I mean to spend a considerable portion of my first million years in painting, and so get to the bottom of the subject." This wise saying relates as much to writing as it does to painting, and it implies two things about these activities:

1. It takes a long time to get good at something.
2. Through writing (or painting), one can get to the heart of a matter.

Like painting for Churchill, writing allows you to clarify your thinking about a subject and to set that thinking down for others to read. Writing reveals the inner workings of your mind, but not in the haphazard way that often characterizes spontaneous thought patterns. Instead, writing leads to the creation of a sustained whole, made coherent by deliberate, careful preplanning and by extensive revision.

This textbook invites you to read widely, to complete comprehension and analysis exercises on your assigned readings, and then to write about what you have read—to get to the heart of the subject. You are encouraged to explore your feelings, reactions, judgments, perceptions, and observations about a variety of topics addressed by contemporary writers. Reading analytically and writing in response to what you have read are processes that lead to new ways of seeing and understanding the world in which we live and then presenting your view of that world to others.

Fear of the Blank Canvas

Although the quotation from Churchill regarding his longing to paint for "a million years" suggests his love of the process, he also recognized the difficulty and challenges of art. For example, he described the fear he experienced when he began a new painting with this telling phrase: "the terror of the blank canvas." To connect this phrase to writing, we might refer to the terror of the blank piece of paper, or since today most writers compose on a computer, the terror of the blank screen. As the phrase suggests, writing is a lonely, often tedious process. How does one begin to put down the thoughts skittering around in the brain? The cursor sits there—blinking and waiting for words and phrases that make sense to fill the screen.

And of course, unlike Churchill in his hypothetical heaven, you do not have a million years to perfect each writing assignment. Often, you have only a week, ten days, or perhaps two weeks to compose a paper that is intelligent and readable. In the next section we will look at the definition of a well-written paper and at a sample paper written by a first-year student. Through exploring her process, we will look at some strategies to make facing the blank screen a bit less daunting and to help you successfully complete writing assignments (whether for college classes or later in your professional life).

A WELL-WRITTEN PAPER

To begin the discussion of a well-written paper—whether it is a report for a business course, a case study for an education or nursing seminar, or a proposal for a change in safety regulations at work—I'd like to consider briefly a classic form of writing: the essay. Understanding the essay form leads to understanding the basic patterns and processes for any coherent, intelligent piece of writing.

The Classic Essay

The essay form derives from the short pieces written by sixteenth-century French writer Michel de Montaigne. He called his little writings *essaies* (which translates as "attempts") to explain his observations of human behavior and customs. Montaigne's essay titles are quite revealing of his purpose and show how carefully he focused on a specific topic: "On the Custom of Wearing Clothes," "Cowardice the Mother of Cruelty," "Of Cannibals," and "On the Resemblance of Children to Their Fathers," just to cite a few titles.

For most college courses and for the workplace, the genre used for writing assignments is the same as the essay—*nonfiction*. Like the topics of Montaigne's essays, your subjects will relate to real events, individuals, and facts, as opposed to fiction, where individuals and events are created from the writer's imagination, or to the ideas in nonfiction writing.

Modern Nonfiction Writing

In the centuries since Montaigne wrote, the essay has evolved into open and varied forms of nonfiction writing. Nevertheless, we can define common characteristics that many of today's well-written nonfictional forms share with the traditional essay form. Like the classic essay, most modern writing assignments should lead to a sustained piece of writing that takes up and explores a single, rather narrow subject. Modern papers often attempt, like Montaigne's *essaies*, to provide new insights and observations on the topic the writer addresses.

Like the classic essay, the well-written modern paper is usually composed of several paragraphs unified around a common theme, called the *thesis*. The *thesis statement* (which will be discussed later in this chapter) provides readers with an overview of the paper's subject and of the writer's approach to that subject. Composing and revising the thesis statement also help the writer to define, clarify, and narrow the paper's subject.

The length of a classic essay can vary, just as can a paper or report you are asked to write for a college course or for the workplace. For example, many typical assignments for college classes ask you to write papers between 500 and 1,500 words, or roughly two to five double-spaced, typewritten pages in length. On the other hand you might be asked to write a much longer paper requiring research. For papers that use sources other than your own observations and ideas, you will find the section "Using Quotations" an excellent resource.

INTRODUCTION TO THE WRITING PROCESS

Whether we are considering an essay composed by Montaigne, an editorial argument constructed by a contemporary journalist, or a paper written by a college student, understanding the process that leads to the final product is essential. Each writer's process must be developed as a unique path to follow—a path that differs for each writer and for each writing project undertaken. The writing process, then, is not simple or easily defined. However, it is useful to think of the journey toward a finished paper as having three stages: prewriting, writing, revising. To examine these stages and to learn more about developing your own writing process, I am providing a step-by-step discussion of the way one student, Luisa Hernandez, a business major enrolled in an introductory college writing class, approached her first assignment.

THE WRITING PROCESS AND A SAMPLE STUDENT ESSAY

Here is the topic assigned by Luisa's instructor.

> What behavior have you observed among contemporary college students that you find either commendable or troubling? Support your ideas with examples from your own observation and experience. Length: 750–1,000 words

Prewriting

Before she could even begin writing—facing the blank screen—Luisa needed to prepare in several ways. Her process indicates important steps in the prewriting process.

Understand the Writing Task

To begin thinking about this paper, Luisa first read the assignment carefully and then asked for clarification. She was not sure whether the paper requirements would allow her to observe only students from her own classes or whether she needed to observe more widely. I told her that for this short paper, she should focus on student behavior she had already observed in her own college classes.

Use Brainstorming Strategies to Find and Narrow the Topic

At a conference during my office hours, Luisa and I discussed her approach to the topic. One behavior she had noted that disturbed her was cheating. She used various strategies to explore this subject, including these approaches:

- *Freewriting:* After returning from an exam where she saw students using cell phones to cheat, Luisa sat at her computer and let her thoughts flow. She wrote without stopping for about five minutes to see where her writing would take her. Her freewriting led her to see how many forms of cheating existed, and that insight led to her next strategy.
- *Listing:* Luisa made lists of the various forms of cheating she had observed, trying to decide whether she wanted to address just one form of cheating or whether she wanted to treat the subject more broadly.
- *Clustering:* Using her lists and her notes from freewriting, Luisa made clusters of her ideas. For example, one cluster related to electronically aided cheating, while another cluster noted the various excuses students used to justify their cheating.
- *Reading:* While she knew she was not writing a research paper, Luisa also sought out and read several articles she found in the college library's online databases to help her think about the effects of cheating on both students and instructors.
- *Talking:* Sometimes, talking with others can help a writer to formulate ideas. For example, Luisa came to my office and expressed concern that the discussion she had in mind about cheating on college campuses was dull. During our conversation, she revealed that, as a business major, she had been following the trials of corporate executives accused of fraudulent accounting practices in preparation for her course in business ethics.

  Suddenly, a lightbulb clicked on in her head, and she wondered if she could somehow link that subject to cheating on campus. Making this connection, she realized, might bring something fresh to the topic. In addition, this comparison between business cheating and college cheating provided a narrowed, specific focus for her paper.

While you might not use every step Luisa followed during the brainstorming part of your prewriting, these approaches are useful tools to have in your "writing vocabulary." It is also important to remember that these approaches are not the only ways to brainstorm. For instance some people prefer to draw diagrams or to make informal outlines as ways of exploring their initial thoughts about a writing task. Throughout this text, you will see examples of student papers that demonstrate many different brainstorming strategies.

Consider the Audience

Before moving further along in writing her paper, Luisa knew she needed to spend some time thinking about her audience. She knew that in addition to considering the instructor, she also needed to think about her classmates who would be reading her ideas during peer editing workshops and other group discussions. She was not writing this paper just to vent her frustration, as she might in a private journal. Nor was she writing as she might in an e-mail to a close friend whom she knew shared her views. Instead, she was writing for a larger audience, and she knew she needed to consider the following:

- *The readers' knowledge about the subject:* For example, would she need to explain how cell phones could be used to pass information silently through text messaging or would all of her readers know about this capacity?
- *The readers' values:* Might some of her audience believe that cheating is justified under some circumstances? Should she change her approach to the subject if this were true?
- *The readers' interests:* Other business majors might be particularly interested in her comparison between business cheating and college cheating, but would students in other majors be equally interested? How could she appeal to a broader audience?
- *The readers' diversity:* For example, Luisa knew her paper would be read by both her classmates and her instructor. These readers would have widely varying ways of thinking about the way the paper was written, and she knew she needed to consider all of her audience members—not just her classmates or just her instructor.

Writing

Now that Luisa had spent time making sure she understood the writing assignment—brainstorming to find a specific, narrowed subject and thinking about her audience—she was ready to take the first step toward composing the first draft of her essay.

Writing the Thesis Statement

The thesis is the heart of the essay. Without a clear, well-thought-out thesis, it is hard to rescue an essay no matter how many hours you put into it. The thesis has three functions:

- It tells the reader the subject of your paper.
- It indicates what your approach to that subject will be.
- It helps you, the writer, to organize the supporting ideas.

Before she started to write her first draft, Luisa revised her thesis many times until she was satisfied with it. Here are three of her early attempts at a thesis. Study these trial thesis statements. What problem does each one present?

- Corporate executives caught in many recent scandals cheated because they thought they could get away with it, and that's probably why students cheat, too.
- Should corporate executives be prosecuted when they are caught cooking the books? In the same way, should students be expelled when they cheat?
- Corporate executives started their life of crime by cheating in small ways when they were younger before moving on to ever-larger and more damaging deceptions, just as many students do.

None of these trial thesis statements provided sufficient direction for a sustained piece of writing, nor did they emphasize the cause-effect pattern she wanted to impose on her observation that college students who cheat and then justify their behavior may lead to more serious criminal behavior later in adulthood. After many false starts, Luisa came up with this thesis:

> Although most college students are serious about their studies, in many of my classes at Danbury Community College, I have observed that many classmates, like the corporate executives involved in the recent scandals, routinely cheat and then justify their behavior.

Let's examine the structure of her thesis in more detail.

The first phrase, "Although most college students are serious about their studies," prevents her from generalizing about her subject, since obviously not all students cheat. The second part, "I have observed that many classmates," both establishes her credibility and shows that she is writing from personal observation rather than just inventing examples and making unjust accusations. Thus she is both narrowing her topic and paying attention to the responses of her audience. She makes sure readers will understand what she says and will give her discussion a fair hearing.

The next part, "like the corporate executives involved in the recent scandals," maintains thematic unity. With this phrase, Luisa promises that by the time the reader reaches the concluding paragraphs, he or she will see how the fraud committed by corporate executives connects to cheating in college.

The last phrase, "routinely cheat and then justify their behavior," provides a structure for the three body paragraphs Luisa is planning. The first two will show examples of cheating, while the third will give examples of typical rationalizations. Study the final draft of Luisa's paper (pages 13–16) in relation to the thesis to see how it embeds the architecture of the final draft.

Planning the Structure

Before she began writing her first draft, Luisa knew she needed to think about how she was going to organize her ideas, reasons, and examples. She had learned in her writing class that, like Montaigne's essays, a well-written paper must have a structure. In the simplest terms, a coherent piece of writing is usually characterized as having a beginning, a middle, and an end—in other words, an introduction, supporting paragraphs (the body), and a conclusion. Readers of a paper should be able to begin by skimming through it quickly, to get an overview of its architecture.[1]

For example, Luisa knew she needed to state the thesis clearly in the introductory paragraph(s) of her essay and to identify the main supporting points at the beginning of each body paragraph. Through this way of organizing her thoughts, Luisa allows her readers to understand the direction of the paper before giving it a careful reading and evaluation.

The visibility of Luisa's thesis and of her main points shows the audience that Luisa is mindful of her audience. She knows that her paper exists to be read; it inhabits a wider world than her own universe. Luisa's paper also proceeds in an organized fashion—in this case, as a series of paragraphs providing examples that lead to a demonstration of cause and effect (the way college cheating may lead to unethical decisions later in life).

Introduction The opening should draw the reader into the world of the paper by showing him or her what you are going to discuss. The thesis should be clearly stated in the introduction, which does not have to be only one paragraph. For a complicated subject, the introduction might stretch over two or three paragraphs.

Luisa decided to use a two-paragraph introduction (see page 13) because she wanted to provide an explanation in the first paragraph to make clear the basis for her thesis, which appears in the second paragraph.

In addition to Luisa's approach, there are many ways to capture the readers' attention in your introduction. Here are some possibilities:

- *Tell a brief story:* Luisa might have described a particular incident of cheating that she observed.
- *Provide an intriguing statistic:* Luisa might have researched the changing percentages of colleges and universities that report cheating to be a serious problem on their campuses.
- *Define a key term:* If Luisa had decided to focus on technology-assisted cheating, she might have defined that phrase.
- *Ask a thoughtful question:* Luisa might have asked, "How does college cheating relate to the corporate scandals we hear about with increasing frequency on the evening news?"

Of course, there are many other ways to begin a paper; these are just a few possibilities. As you read the selections in this textbook, as well as the

[1]For the term "architecture" to describe the structure of an essay, I am indebted to James Sauvé, a colleague at City College of San Francisco.

student-written sample papers, pay particular attention to introductions that get your attention. Perhaps the approaches you admire could be included in the repertoire of possibilities for your own opening paragraphs.

Body As she planned her draft, Luisa knew she needed a method of organizing her information. She decided to provide a series of examples of cheating behaviors. Her first informal outline of the body looked like this:

Luisa's First Informal Outline of the Body of her Paper

A. Examples of cheating I have observed at Danbury
B. Examples of the rationalizations students use to justify their cheating
C. Examples of Internet-related cheating

As she thought about the second set of examples, she realized that they would provide a perfect way to lead into her discussion of corporate cheating, so she revised her informal outline to look like this:

Luisa's Revised Informal Outline of the Body of her Paper

A. Examples of cheating I have observed at Danbury
B. Examples of Internet-related cheating
C. Examples of the rationalizations students use to justify their cheating and ways this behavior might relate to later unethical behavior

Reordering her examples allowed Luisa to support effectively a *cause-and-effect* exploration of her topic, which is what her thesis promises. The third example specifically provides her argument for asking readers to accept her thesis that college cheating may relate to and even cause corporate cheating.

There are many ways to organize a paper and to make sure that organization supports the paper's purpose. Using examples to demonstrate cause and effect is just one of many possible approaches. Later in this book you will learn to write papers for the purpose of comparing and contrasting, synthesizing or analyzing ideas, or making an argument.

Once Luisa had thought about organizing and developing the body paragraphs to provide evidence, reinforcement, and support for her thesis, she wondered how long each body paragraph should be. While there is no definite rule, a typical college paper has two or three paragraphs per typed, double-spaced page. This means that each paragraph should be roughly five to eight sentences long. A page consisting of one long paragraph looks too dense and formidable for the reader to tackle.

As you revise your early drafts, watch for long paragraphs that seem to wander around, addressing many different topics. Once you carefully consider a long, unwieldy paragraph, you will probably see ways to divide it logically into two or three shorter paragraphs. Conversely, too many short paragraphs on a page create the impression that your ideas are skimpily developed, which means that you should amplify them with more supporting details.

Conclusion Once Luisa had thought about, planned, and drafted the introduction and body of her paper, she read the draft through and then put it away so that she could think about it for a few days before drafting the conclusion. While deadlines do not always allow the luxury of waiting a day or two between the stages of writing, taking even a few hours away from a writing project can give you the distance you need revise effectively and objectively.

Luisa knew that there were many approaches she might consider for the final paragraph or paragraphs of her paper. Here are several we discussed in class:

- Sum up the examples, details, and reasons offered in the body to support the thesis.
- Present a solution to the problem posed.
- Leave the reader with something challenging to think about.
- Indicate future possibilities related to the topic.
- Ask a thought-provoking question.

Most of all, as Luisa considered the scope of the essay, she kept in mind this important maxim: "No insight, no essay."[2] Whether or not a paper successfully communicates to the reader depends wholly on an insight, a perception, a unique observation that belongs solely to the writer. A successful paper does not just rehash the obvious or state what everyone else in the crowd thinks about a subject.

Luisa had discovered the insight that connected college and corporate cheating during the brainstorming process that was part of her prewriting for this paper. She knew she had to make sure that her conclusion led her readers to understand this insight. In addition to explaining the reasons she has offered to support the relationship between school ethics and business ethics, she also ends her concluding paragraph with a question that invites readers to develop their own insights about the topic.

Revision

Once she had completed her draft, Luisa again put her paper away for a day. She knew that she was now facing the most challenging part of her writing process. For Luisa, finding ideas and writing the draft took time, energy, and commitment, but revision took even more time and a great deal of courage. She knew that she would need to "re-see" (the literal meaning of *revision*)

[2]Douglas Hunt, *The Dolphin Reader*, 2nd ed. Boston: Houghton Mifflin, 1990, 3.

with a highly critical eye. She would have to put herself in the place of her readers and try to identify ways her paper could be made even stronger, clearer, and more interesting.

As she faced the revision process, Luisa kept in mind another useful maxim: "Thou shalt not confuse the reader." A careful writer tries to ensure that each paragraph and each sentence are transparent and understandable on the first reading and that the connections among ideas are logically explained. In addition, unclear, muddled, or ambiguous sentences and improperly used words annoy readers and make them lose interest in your paper.

As Luisa reviewed her paper in preparation for revision, she kept in mind three steps to this process:

- Identify any large changes, such as additions to content (such as new examples or statistics) or organization (see, for example, the change to paragraph order Luisa made during her drafting, page 10).
- Identify any stylistic changes, such as the need to revise unclear sentence structure or overuse of a descriptive word.
- Identify any grammatical, spelling, or typographical errors. (Note: An early draft of Luisa's two opening paragraphs are reprinted in Part 9 as a proofreading exercise. See page 623 to compare her draft with her final paper.)

Luisa knew that the first step, identifying large changes, was the most difficult, so she was grateful to have the help of a peer editing group in her class for this stage of the process.

Suggestions from the Peer Editing Group

When two students in Luisa's peer group examined her first draft, they expressed some doubts about her thesis—the risky linking of corporate misbehavior to cheating in college. In her final revision, she solved this problem by adding the phrase "one might speculate" in paragraph 2 and also by adding the central observations that one does not engage in criminal activity all of a sudden and that deceptive behavior can easily develop into a pattern. She also deleted a supporting paragraph about students who pretend to have done their assignments because this idea did not fit the thesis. These changes strengthened her essay and created a more logical connection between rationalizing financial fraud and cheating in college classes.

For additional suggestions relating to the revision process, see the checklist on pages 22–23.

Luisa's Final Paper

Here in Luisa's final paper, which she wrote, rewrote, and polished over a ten-day period:

1st introductory paragraph gives background and prepares the reader for the real subject, taken up in the 2nd intro paragraph.

2nd paragraph connects the ideas expressed in paragraph 1. The final sentence states her thesis. Notice that Luisa guards against generalizing by using the phrases "might speculate" and "might have started."

Lying and Cheating as a Way of Life

I have been following some of the corporate scandals of the 1990s and thinking about their effect on American culture. For several months, the dominant story in the business media has been the financial mismanagement and accounting fraud of corporate executives at companies like Enron, Tyco, Health-South, Adelphia Communications, and WorldCom. In each case, executives created false financial statements to keep their companies' stock prices high, while at the same time they were stealing from the company's assets for their own personal profit. These criminal actions ruined lives, damaged reputations, and endangered their employees' livelihoods.

As the number of these ugly stories multiplied, it occurred to me that these scandals were just an extension of a trend that has been gaining strength over the past decade: Deception and cheating are acceptable ways to get ahead in life. While it might seem like an exaggeration to link the serious criminal activity associated with these accounting scandals with cheating on a quiz, still a person does not become a criminal overnight. Just as it's hard to eat only one potato chip, it's hard just to tell one lie. Also, small lies, if undetected, lead to bigger lies. It is possible that some of these corrupt executives might have started on their path to criminality with smaller deceptions from their student days. I have observed that many classmates, like the corporate executives involved in the recent scandals, routinely cheat and then justify their behavior.

1st body paragraph starts with a clear topic sentence developing the thesis. Paragraph is unified because all support relates to types of cheating on tests. The essay's architecture reveals itself clearly.

In all of my classes at Danbury Community College, I have observed obvious cheating by students who have devised several clever ways to pass tests without studying. Their methods range from old-fashioned crib notes or writing down math formulas on the palms of their hands to deliberate copying from another student's exam when the instructor isn't looking. But more sophisticated techniques for cheating are now possible with Internet-equipped cell phones, which allow students to look up answers online, and PDA's, which allow students to program answers for retrieval during tests. However, my biology professor, Dr. Mathes, caught on to this new method of cheating during the first exam and banned all electronic devices from the classroom. She also announced that any student caught with a PDA or cell phone during an exam would receive an automatic grade of F.

2nd body paragraph supports the thesis with a second example.

Communication over the Internet has led to an increase in another kind of cheating—plagiarism. In high school, I knew a girl who routinely asked her best friend to e-mail copies of papers the friend wrote for her classes. This girl just printed out a copy of the friend's files and then turned them in as her own work. She got away with it because they were taking different sections of English with different teachers. Copying someone else's paper is one type of plagiarism. But with the Internet, college papers are available with the click of a mouse, often for free or for a small charge, so that a student doesn't even have to bother asking a friend for help. Websites like collegesucks.com, essaysrus.com, and essayexpress.com offer papers on every conceivable subject; other sites offer custom-made essays for a fee. Our English teacher, Mr. Ramirez, warned us about plagiarizing from the Internet, and he told us a couple of stories about students whom he caught turning in papers from Internet sites and who received F's. Still, the threat of being caught or of flunking doesn't seem to be stopping students from downloading papers.

The third body paragraph supports the last part of the thesis statement by listing typical excuses to justify both corporate and academic cheating. Note that "perhaps" in the last sentence guards against the charge of Luisa's making unfair accusations.

Students justify their cheating by rationalizing. One friend who programs answers into his cell phone to retrieve during calculus tests told me that he finds it impossible to keep up with all of their reading assignments because he has to work part-time to pay his college expenses. A single mom told me that she is going through a personal crisis and just can't seem to find the strength to study. An old boyfriend told me that he can't afford to get a low grade, which will look bad on his record (he hopes to go to law school), making cheating or plagiarizing his only option. Another rationalization is the everybody-does-it argument, so that students argue that they have to cheat to compete. Similarly, corporate executives accused in the various business scandals justified their deception by saying that an inflated stock price, even one based on fraudulent accounting, made money for their shareholders or that they used their stolen money to help their communities. But cheating is cheating, and no amount of rationalization can justify it. Perhaps these executives themselves cheated in college and got away with it, leading them to engage in more serious kinds of deception. Maybe they thought they could get away with illegal business dealings just as they had gotten away with cheating in their academic lives.

Conclusion establishes thematic unity by returning to the thesis. Note that the concluding sentence ends with a rhetorical question, leaving the reader with something to think about.

Although students who cheat and plagiarize may not see the connection between the corporate scandals and their own behavior, from my perspective, they are different only in degree. Such deceptions have a way of multiplying, just as telling one lie leads to telling another and another, until pretty soon, it's impossible to keep all the lies straight. It seems short-sighted for students to go to all the trouble and expense of enrolling in college and then to sabotage their own education by engaging in such pretenses. After all, their prospective employers will expect their new hires actually to know something when they're on the job. As the corporate scandals suggest, if students justify their cheating in school, what kinds of bigger deceptions will they engage in when they go out into the big world?

TYING THE ELEMENTS TOGETHER: THE FINISHED ESSAY

Luisa's paper varies the conventional five-paragraph model by taking two paragraphs to orient the reader to the subject. Her introduction works well because she takes sufficient time to connect the two elements, thus drawing the reader into the world of her essay. Finally, the length of her paper, 877 words, is well within the assignment's requirements of 750–1,000 words, making it sufficiently developed.

Now that you have followed the process of a student writer, we can review the steps involved. For example, if you have seven days to complete a major writing assignment, you can follow these steps, which will be explained in more detail below.

Steps to Writing a Good Essay

DAY 1

- Start early.
- Have a plan.
- Be sure you understand what the assignment is asking you to do.

- Brainstorm the topic.
- Consider your audience.
- Annotate your readings if necessary.
- Write your thesis statement.

DAYS 2 AND 3

- Organize your information and decide on a structure that will support the purpose of your paper.
- Write a rough draft.
- Evaluate your rough draft and write the second draft.

DAY 4

- Put your drafts away and don't look at them.

DAY 5

- Evaluate the second draft.
- Make necessary changes.
- Edit for spelling and grammar errors.
- Revise and prepare a third or fourth draft, as necessary.

DAY 6

- Do a final edit for clarity, grammar, and usage.
- Put the paper through spell check.
- Do a final proofreading (spell check does not catch all errors).
- Evaluate the paper using the checklist on pages 22–23.
- Print out the final copy.

If you have more than a week to complete the assignment, simply expand this schedule to fit the extra time. The important point to remember is that writing takes time, and it cannot be rushed, so do not try to write for hours at a time or try to complete these steps in one day. Let us expand on these steps in a bit more detail.

Explaining the Steps in More Detail

1. ***Start early and don't procrastinate.***

   Procrastination results in self-sabotage. Starting a complicated paper the night before it is due almost always ensures a poorly written paper and no feeling of satisfaction or accomplishment for a job well done. Start right away.

   If you are unsure about the assignment, ask your instructor for help, or if your college has a writing center, take the assignment to a tutor for help. Be sure you understand what type of paper you are being asked to write. For example, if you are assigned to write a paper analyzing a reading, do not summarize it. Each writing section in this text will address a different purpose for writing and will explain ways of writing for these purposes.

2. ***Have a plan.***

   If your assignment requires you to respond to any readings, be sure to annotate the material carefully, following the models in Part 4 of this text. As you work on the prewriting stage, consider the brainstorming techniques discussed on page 6. Some common brainstorming techniques are freewriting, clustering, listing, or even making an old-fashioned outline. For her paper, Luisa used the free-association technique by sitting at the computer and jotting down words and phrases pertaining to the topic. She then organized the ideas into the two related subjects that she introduces in her first two body paragraphs.

   Some writers prefer to brainstorm in their head, letting the ideas float around in the brain until they come together into something cohesive and supportable. There is no one way to brainstorm, however, and you simply have to try various methods until you find one that works for you. Whatever technique you do use, the process should yield an insight into your subject, a point of view uniquely your own that will sustain you through the essay, just as Luisa eventually hit upon the idea of connecting corporate fraud to college cheating.

3. ***Write a thesis statement.***

   Your thesis statement should be appropriate for the length of the paper. Refine and revise it until you are satisfied. Be sure that the thesis statement is supportable. Some teachers suggest writing the thesis statement on an index card and keeping it front of you while you write each draft, just to ensure that you do not drift away into something irrelevant to the thesis. For suggestions and examples of thesis statements, refer to the writing sections in this book.

4. ***Write a rough draft.***

   The rough or first draft is a chance for you to get your initial ideas down on paper without regard for form or structure. During this stage, it is important to get your ideas down without worrying if you are using correct punctuation or spelling or if you are using the most logical order to present your ideas. You can shape your thoughts and make corrections later. Do all of your drafts on a computer or word processor. Writing a draft in longhand and then typing it into the computer is inefficient and does not take advantage of the computer's capabilities.

5. ***Evaluate the rough draft and write the second draft.***

   Cast a critical eye on your rough draft. Ask yourself these questions:

   - Have I followed the requirements of the assignment?
   - Does every part of the paper show that I evaluated and considered my audience effectively?
   - Have I written a thesis that gives the reader an overview of what I will say about my subject and of the organization I will use in the paper?
   - Have I developed the body of the paper with sufficient examples, reasons, and observations?
   - Does the body of the paper have unity and coherence and does it relate clearly to the introduction and conclusion?
   - Does the conclusion follow logically from the evidence provided in the body of the paper and does it fulfill the promise of the thesis?

   After considering these points, make necessary changes in your text to produce a second draft. These steps—brainstorming, writing a thesis, and writing and revising a rough draft—might take 2 or 3 hours over a couple of days, depending, of course, on the complexity of the assignment.

6. ***Put the essay aside for a day or two.***

   You will usually have the luxury of putting the paper aside if you start the assignment on time. A day off gives you the chance to put some distance between yourself and the paper, giving you a fresh perspective when you do return to it.

7. ***Write your second, third, or even fourth drafts.***

   A day or two before the essay is due, re-evaluate the paper using the criteria above. Check your supporting paragraphs for sufficient development and adequate support to bolster your thesis. Use quotations if appropriate or required, and check to ensure your quotations are correctly cited and formatted, as explained later in the section on using quoted material. Add examples and details if your paragraphs seem too short and sketchy.

   While your essay was sitting in the drawer, some new ideas or insights probably occurred to you. Add these and make any necessary changes. Rework each paragraph until you are sure that each one says exactly what you want to say. Do not be afraid to tinker with your sentences or to move ideas around, which can be done speedily on the computer. All of these changes will constitute your third or perhaps your fourth draft.

   Some writers like to use a sort of looping technique, which involves writing, clarifying, and revising at the same time. It works like this: Write the introduction, admittedly the hardest paragraph to write, and rework it until you are more or less satisfied with it. Then write the second paragraph and perhaps the third paragraph. Return to the first paragraph and revise it again. Then do the same with the second paragraph, and so on.

While this back-and-forth style of writing sounds inefficient, it actually allows you to progress through the paper writing down ideas as they occur to you and then polishing those ideas until you are satisfied with them. Keep adding paragraphs and looping back until the paper is finished. I used this technique to write this section of the book, because while I had taught students about the writing process for years, I had not written about it before. Over a period of about ten days, I kept circling back to the introduction and the explanation section, making changes and tinkering with each paragraph until each one said exactly what I wanted to say. It is time-consuming but eminently worthwhile.

8. ***Do the final edit and proofreading.***

Put your essay through a final spell check on the computer—remember, though, that spell checkers will not find all errors. For example, the spell check will not know the difference between *their* and *there*.

Edit for errors, consulting Part 9 on grammar and editing if necessary. Then go through the checklist on pages 22–23, do a final proofreading, print out your final draft, and pat yourself on the back for a job well done.

MISCELLANEOUS OBSERVATIONS ABOUT THE WRITING PROCESS

Of course, not every writer is going to be comfortable with these strategies; not everyone likes to work within the confines of such a rigid schedule. It may take a bit of experimenting over the first year or two of college to find the system that works best for you. So consider these steps as suggestions only. Also, do not be discouraged, because writing a successful paper takes a great deal of time and effort. Even very experienced writers often take many hours just to write a few solid pages.

Besides the actual writing of the paper in its various drafts, the editing process—moving sentences around, changing words, cutting to avoid wordiness and repetition, correcting grammar errors—also takes time. The American essayist and writer of children's books, E. B. White, was a master of elegant and careful writing. In a letter to a friend, he once apologized for writing such a long letter, saying that he didn't have time to write a short one.

THE AFTERMATH: GETTING THE PAPER BACK

When you receive the paper back from your instructor, go over his or her remarks and corrections carefully. Remember that the instructor is an important part of your audience. There are many reasons you want your paper to be clear to your instructor. Consider, also, that it is very discouraging for an instructor when a student simply looks at the grade and ignores the hard work that has gone into the paper's evaluation.

If you do not understand a comment (or if you cannot read the instructor's handwriting), make an appointment for a conference. If your college has a writing center, you could also take the paper there for an objective appraisal and suggestions for improvement on the next assignment. If your instructor allows students to rewrite papers for a higher grade, take advantage of this policy, but you may want to schedule a conference first to discuss your plans for revision.

Here is another technique that has worked for me: For the past two years I have been taking intermediate Italian courses where we are required to write essays. Writing is hard enough, but it is even harder to write in a language one doesn't know very well. Despite my best efforts and despite consulting a grammar book and a dictionary, mistakes abounded in my papers. One technique that helped me avoid making the same mistakes in subsequent papers was to copy, paste, and open a new copy of the essay I had turned in. Then using either boldface or red typeface, I corrected each error the instructor marked. I kept all my returned and revised papers in a folder so that I could refer easily to past errors and ways to correct them when tackling a new assignment.

Let's say that your instructor has noted on your first two essays, for example, that you are consistently writing fragments (incomplete sentences) like this one:

> Although students who cheat and plagiarize may not see the connection between the corporate scandals and their own behavior.

You can be sure that your instructor will not be happy with your progress if your third, fourth, and fifth papers also contain sentence fragments. In this case, rewrite the sentence in your new copy using boldface and make it complete. Then study these corrections before writing your next paper.

If you are unsure how to correct the error, look at the section on fragments at the end of this text. If you still do not know how to fix the problem, go to your instructor for help or go to a writing tutor. Still other students find it helpful to keep an error log. To do this, copy down the sentence with the error and write it in the left column of a notebook; then write the correct version in the right column. Whatever method you find most appealing, use it.

Finally, take advantage of one or more of the various OWLs available on the World Wide Web. The acronym OWL stands for online writing lab. Purdue University sponsors one of the most respected and comprehensive OWLs at this address: http://owl.English.purdue.edu. This site contains an abundance of information, for example, how to write a thesis statement, how to develop a paragraph, how to write concise sentences, how to avoid plagiarism, and much more—all for free. When you access the home page, pull down from "Handouts and Materials" to either "Complete Handouts Index" or "Printer-Friendly Handouts."

A CHECKLIST FOR WRITING AND REVISING ESSAYS

Use the questions in this checklist to evaluate your final draft before you hand it in.

CONTENT

- Does the title indicate that I have a point of view about the topic? Will the title arouse the reader's curiosity?
- Does my introduction invite the reader into the world of the essay?
- Do I have a clear, properly limited, and interesting thesis?
- Is my thesis conspicuous? Will the reader be able to locate it easily?
- Have I adequately supported my thesis?
- Have I dealt with probable objections to my thesis?
- Does my last paragraph give a sense of completion?
- Are my voice, tone, and stance appropriate for the audience and for my purpose?

STRUCTURE

- Is the architecture of the essay readily apparent?
- Have I provided clear and helpful transitions between paragraphs?
- Are the body paragraphs unified and fully developed?
- Does each supporting paragraph relate to the thesis?

SENTENCE STYLE

- Are my sentences concise?
- Do my sentences show enough variety in structure?
- Are my sentences written in standard idiomatic form?
- Is every sentence clear and understandable upon the first reading?
- Do all of the words I use mean what I think they mean?
- Is my word choice free of clichés, jargon, euphemisms, and needless abstraction?

GRAMMAR AND MECHANICS

- Have I edited to correct grammatical errors that I have made in past papers?
- Did I put the paper through spell check?

- Have I followed correct form for punctuation?
- Are all of my quotations introduced with a signal phrase or some other device?
- Are my quotations typed accurately, and are all the page references correct, according to MLA rules?
- Have I included page numbers?
- Is the first page of my paper formatted correctly following MLA rules?
- Have I included a Works Cited page, if needed, using MLA rules?

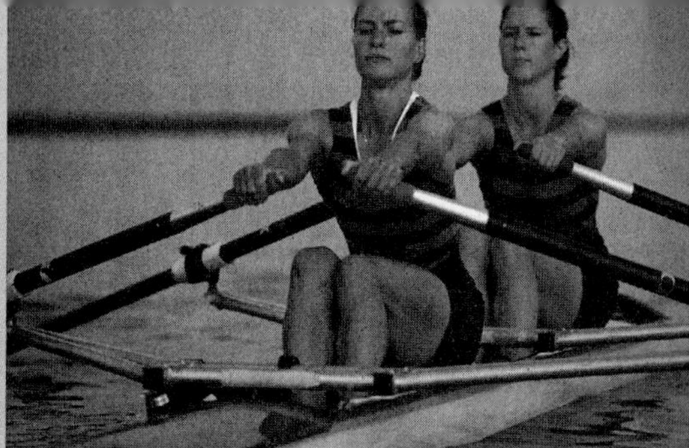

Using Quotations

CORRECT TECHNIQUES OF DOCUMENTATION

Although quotations are not typically required in writing personal experience or personal response essays, they are necessary in academic writing assignments. Whether you are asked to write an analytical essay, a synthesis essay, a comparison and contest essay, or an argumentative essay, you will need to incorporate ideas from one reading, or perhaps from several readings, into your paragraphs as support for your thesis. These ideas can either be paraphrased (see Part 4) or quoted directly, although most college academic essays usually employ a balanced mix of the two.

USING QUOTATIONS: ACADEMIC WRITING

The ability to document quotations correctly and the ability to integrate quotations logically and gracefully into your writing will be useful for many projects you will encounter in college and later in the professional world.

Typical Academic Assignments Requiring the Use of Quotations

- Research papers
- Reviews of books or of articles in professional journals
- Statistical studies
- Response papers (assignments asking you to respond to the ideas of other writers)

This section outlines the rules for correctly integrating quoted material into your supporting paragraphs, following the guidelines established by the Modern Language Association. MLA is the organization that determines the rules for preparing scholarly manuscripts and college research papers in English and the humanities. If you write a paper for your English class or for any other humanities course, more than likely you will be asked to follow MLA format. (Social science disciplines—such as psychology, anthropology, sociology, economics, and speech—follow slightly different guidelines established by the American Psychological Association, APA.) Any good grammar and usage handbook explains both systems. If you are in doubt about which system to use for class, ask your instructor which method to use.

A *quotation* refers to another writer's material—phrases, sentences, or occasionally an entire paragraph—that you insert into your own paragraphs to reinforce your supporting ideas. Putting quotation marks around the material indicates that you are taking the material from an outside source. It is not necessary to memorize these rules, although with time they will most likely become second nature. You might put a bookmark in this section for ease of reference when you begin to use quotations.

FOURTEEN RULES FOR USING QUOTATIONS

1. ***Copy quoted material exactly.***

   Since the whole idea of a quotation is to reproduce a writer's words faithfully, you must be careful to copy the quoted material exactly as it is written and, of course, indicate that the material is a quotation by using double quotation marks around all the words. Here is a sentence from Anjula Razdan's article, "What's Love Got to Do with It?" reprinted in Part 6 of this text. We will use this quotation to make several points about using quoted material.

Original Material

The point of the Western romantic ideal is to live "happily ever after," yet nearly half of all marriages in this country end in divorce, and the number of never-married adults grows each year.

2. ***Choose appropriate quotations and use them as evidence to support your point, not as a substitute for evidence or as padding.***

   For example, if you are writing an essay analyzing the differences between arranged marriages and Western-style marriages, you migh want to discuss what Americans think about arranged marriages. In Razdan's article, one student found that the foregoing quotation sums up the problem with the Western ideal. Study this student's supporting paragraph and the placement of the quotation carefully.

Main idea

1st supporting idea

2nd supporting idea

3rd supporting idea

Reinforcing quotation

> Most Americans would resist the notion of an arranged marriage. Our culture reinforces our freedom to choose our own marriage partner, and the idea of our parents making that choice for us is horrifying. We want to be the masters of our own destiny, and if our parents were to make such an important choice for us, the concept of marrying for love would be destroyed. We look for "Mr. Right" or "Miss Perfect," certain that any future spouse our parents might choose would be someone completely unsuitable, someone we could probably never imagine spending even one evening with, much less the rest of our lives. Yet as Anjula Razdan, herself the product of an arranged marriage, observes, "The point of the Western romantic ideal is to live 'happily ever after,' yet nearly half of all marriages in this country end in divorce, and the number of never-married adults grows each year" (395).

In Part 5 of this text, you will be shown a method of developing body paragraphs using quotations called the tell-show-share method. For now, note that the quotation is used as *reinforcement* to counter the writer's three supporting points. Also it comes relatively late in the paragraph, after the writer has offered her own ideas.

3. ***Be sparing in your use of quotations.***

   Choose your quotations carefully, and resist the temptation to fill your paragraphs with quotations. Paragraphs with excessive quotations look sketchy and say to the reader that you have simply strung quotations together with a few words of your own. In the sample above, one quotation is sufficient. Also do not refer to quotations as quotations. Do not write, "As this quotation shows. . . ." It is better to use an introductory phrase like "Yet as Razdan observes . . . ."

4. ***Cite the page number properly and use correct punctuation.***

   In the sample above, the page number (referring to the page number where the quotation is printed in this text) is cited in parentheses after the final quotation marks. The period goes *outside* the parentheses. Following current MLA practice, the page number alone is sufficient; do not add "p.," "pg.," or "page."

If the writer had omitted the author's name in her lead-in sentence, then the citation would look like this:

> Yet as one writer observes, "The point of the Western romantic ideal is to live 'happily ever after,' yet nearly half of all marriages in this country end in divorce, and the number of never-married adults grows each year" (Razdan 395).

In this case the citation uses only the writer's last name, and there is no comma between the name and the page number. (Again, no "p." or "page"!)

Finally, note that in the original quotation in the box above, the phrase "happily ever after" was printed with double quotation marks. To indicate correctly a quotation within a larger quotation, change the double marks in the original phrase to single quotation marks.

5. ***Generally, introduce quotations with a signal phrase.***

A *signal* or *lead-in phrase* alerts the reader that a quotation is to follow. If you are using an entire sentence or more as quoted material, do not abruptly drop the writer's words into your paragraph. Some teachers called these "dropped" or "naked" quotations. In most cases, your signal phrase should include the name of the person you are quoting. In the above paragraph, the signal phrase in the sample paragraph is "Yet as Anjula Razdan observes." Here are some other examples of signal phrases used to introduce quoted material. Notice that the question of whether or not to use punctuation depends on how you word the signal phrase.

Signal Phrases Requiring a Comma

- According to Anjula Razdan, "Online dating services attracted some 20 million people last year." (But try to vary your signal phrases so you do not fall into the pattern of overusing the "according to" phrase.)
- Anjula Razdan states, "I was born and raised in Illinois by parents who emigrated from India 35 years ago."
- As Anjula Razdan points out, "yet I grew up under the spell of Western romantic love."

- Anjula Razdan examines the phenomenon of romantic love and concludes, "Boundless choice notwithstanding, what does it mean when the marital success rate is the statistical equivalent of a coin toss?"

  Note that in these four examples, a comma separates the signal phrase from the quotation because none of these signal phrases can stand alone grammatically as a sentence, in which case a colon would be used. (See rule 6 below.)

  Signal Phrases Not Requiring a Comma

- Anjula Razdan concedes that "the very idea of an arranged marriage offended my ideas of both love and liberty."
- Robert Epstein, editor of *Psychology Today*, argues that "it is our myths of 'love at first sight' and 'a knight in a shining Porsche' that get so many of us into trouble."

  In these two examples, no comma is necessary because the quotation is preceded by the word *that*, making the lead-in phrase unable to stand alone.

6. ***An alternative: Introduce quoted material with a complete sentence.***

   In the samples above, the writer has to decide whether the wording of the signal phrase calls for a comma or not, but another possibility is to use an entire sentence as a signal to introduce a quotation. In this case, the correct punctuation is a colon. Study this original quoted material, which appears in Razdan's article, in which she summarizes the opinions of Robert Epstein, editor of *Psychology Today* and a former director of the Cambridge Center for Behavioral Studies.

Original Material

Epstein holds a decidedly unromantic view of courtship and love. Indeed, he argues that it is our myths of "love at first sight" and "a knight in a shining Porsche" that get so many of us into trouble. When the heat of passion wears off—and it always does, he says—you can be left with virtually nothing "except lawyer's bills" (396).

When a quotation follows a complete introductory sentence, here is what it looks like:

- In examining why so many Western marriages fail, Razdan cites the opinion of Robert Epstein, editor of *Psychology Today* and formerly a director of the Cambridge Center for Behavioral Studies: "It is our myths of 'love at first sight' and 'a knight in a shining Porsche' that get so many of us into trouble. When the heat of passion wears off—and it always does, he says—you can be left with virtually nothing 'except lawyer's bills.' " Razdan characterizes his views about "courtship and love" as being "decidedly unromantic" (396).

The colon is the only grammatically correct way to punctuate this sentence. Using a period after your introduction would result in a dropped quotation, which you want to avoid at all costs, and using a comma would result in another error—a comma splice. (See Part 9 for help with comma splices.)

7. ***A second alternative: Use short selected phrases from the quoted material and integrate them into your sentences.***

For example, a student might combine paraphrase and quoted material in a supporting paragraph. Study this original material.

Original Material

My mom and dad barely knew each other on their wedding day—and they certainly hadn't fallen in love. Yet both were confident that their shared values, beliefs, and family background would form a strong bond that, over time, would develop into love (Razdan 395).

Here is the way one writer integrates some phrases from the original material into her sentence.

- In describing her parents' arranged marriage, Razdan explains that, even though her parents had spent little time together before their wedding day, they also trusted that their "shared values, beliefs, and family background" would be a good foundation for a marriage, one that might eventually "develop into love" (395).

8. ***Use correct punctuation with quotation marks.***

Look at the above samples again to see how these rules are illustrated:

- At the end of the quotation, the period goes *inside* the quotation marks. The general rule is that commas and periods go inside quotation marks, while semicolons and colons go outside quotation marks.
- In the original material, the phrases "love at first sight" and "a knight in a shining Porsche" were both printed with double quotation marks. Remember that, as noted before in rule 4 above, you need to use single quotation marks to distinguish between your quotation and quoted material within that quotation.

9. ***When possible, identify the source in a brief appositive phrase the first time he or she is cited.***

   Identifying the person's qualifications establishes your source's authority—his or her knowledge of and experience with the subject. If you just drop the person's name into your sentence, your reader may have no idea who he or she is. The most efficient way to do this is to use an appositive phrase, or a renaming noun phrase. For example, study this sentence:

   (Noun) (Appositive phrase—renaming noun)

   Tiger Woods, the championship golf player, has won the Masters' Tournament four times.

   As you see in this example, one should generally enclose an appositive phrase with commas. In previous samples, the writer used the appositive phrase, "herself the product of an arranged marriage," to describe Anjula Razdan, and Robert Epstein was identified as editor of *Psychology Today* and formerly a director of the Cambridge Center for Behavioral Studies. For more help with appositive phrases, see page 580 in Part 9.

   After the first reference, you may omit the identifying phrase. Also follow these conventions: The first time you cite a source, use the person's full name; after that, use the last name only. Although it may seem rude to refer to a well-known writer by his or her last name only, that is the rule for academic prose. So if you are writing a paper about Judith Ortiz Cofer, whose essay, "More Room," is reprinted in this text, the first time you use her name, write her full name; thereafter, just write "Cofer," *not* "Ms. Cofer" or "Miss Cofer," and certainly not "Judith." You don't know her!

10. ***Use brackets to indicate material you add to quoted material or changes you make for grammatical clarity.***

    Brackets are square parentheses. In the following example, it is not clear whom "their" refers to. Adding "my parents" in brackets clarifies the word for the reader. In this case, the writer was not sure if his reader would know what samosas are, so he clarified that word as well.

- To show how an arranged marriage contrasts with Western-style dating, Razdan writes, "Their [my parents'] relationship was set up over tea and samosas [fried turnovers] by their grandfathers, and they were already engaged when they went on their first date, a chaperoned trip to the movies" (395).

But do not overuse brackets, because they can be distracting for the reader.

11. ***Use an ellipsis to indicate material omitted from a quotation.***

It is permissible to edit quoted material to eliminate wordiness, inessential information, or even information that you paraphrase in another part of the sentence. To do this, use three dots with a space between each (. . .). Do not use an ellipsis to indicate a separation between quoted material on one page and other quoted material one or two pages later. The material omitted should be in close proximity, preferably within the same sentence or paragraph. Study this original passage from Razdan's essay.

Original Material

"People don't really know how to choose a long-term partner," offers Dr. Alvin Cooper, the director of the San Jose Marital Services and Sexuality Center and a staff psychologist at Stanford University. "The major reasons that people find and get involved with somebody else are proximity and physical attraction. And both of these factors are terrible predictors of long-term happiness in a relationship" (Razdan 396).

One student decided to describe Dr. Cooper's qualifications in his own words. The end result looked like this:

- Dr. Alvin Cooper, a staff psychologist at Stanford University and director of the San Jose Marital Services and Sexuality Center, warns the reader about the hazards associated with choosing a marriage partner: "People don't really know how to choose a long-term partner [. . .] The major reasons that people find and get involved with somebody else are proximity and physical attraction. And both of these factors are terrible predictors of long-term happiness in a relationship" (Razdan 396).

The ellipsis shows that the writer omitted several words. MLA recommends that you put brackets around the ellipsis to show that you made this change (since the original material might contain an ellipsis that the writer used), although some instructors think this requirement is overly fussy.

Finally, do not use an ellipsis to show words or phrases you omitted from the beginning or from the end of a quotation. Too many ellipses create an annoying polka dot appearance. Also, it is obvious to the reader that something came before and after quoted material.

12. ***Set up long quotations correctly, but use them sparingly.***

Material over three lines long (three lines of your typing, not the lines in the original source) is treated differently. The easiest way to format a long quotation is to set a temporary left margin on your ruler indented ten spaces or one inch and leave the right margin as it is. Double-space the text and remove the quotation marks. The indented form tells the reader that it is quoted material. Do not forget to use a signal phrase to introduce the quotation. Study this model.

> Initially, Razdan rebelled against her parents' attempts to arrange a marriage for her, following traditional Indian custom. As she grows older, however, she concedes that the Western custom of marrying for love has flaws:
>
> > But for many people, a quiet voice from within wonders: Are we really better off? Who hasn't at some point in their life—at the end of an ill-fated relationship or mid-way through dinner with the third "date-from-hell" this month—longed for a matchmaker to find the right partner? No hassles. No effort. No personal ads or blind dates. (395)

Notice that the end punctuation is different with set-off quotations: The quotation ends with a period followed by the page number in parentheses.

13. ***Be sure to integrate your quotations smoothly and grammatically into your paragraph.***

    Not integrating quoted material into sentences properly is the single biggest error students make in writing papers. Study this material.

> **Original Material**
>
> The major reasons that people find and get involved with somebody else are proximity and physical attraction. And both of these factors are terrible predictors of long-term happiness in a relationship (396).

Study this incorrect example:

- Anjula Razdan cites the testimony of Dr. Alvin Cooper, an expert on marriage and a psychologist at Stanford University. Cooper says that because for many young couples "the major reasons that people find and get involved with somebody else are proximity and physical attraction. And both of these factors are terrible predictors of long-term happiness in a relationship" (396).

Adding the phrase "because for many young couples" in the lead-in phrase makes the sentence both ungrammatical and difficult to read. Deleting the word *because* eliminates this confusion.

14. *Punctuate titles correctly.*

Titles are treated differently depending on what they refer to. Follow these general rules:

- Underline or italicize the titles of books, magazines, and newspapers.

  Examples: Fast Food Nation, Newsweek, The New York Times

  Long Walk to Freedom, Time, St. Louis Post-Dispatch

- Use quotation marks around the titles of essays, articles, poems, short stories, and other short pieces.

  Examples: "Easter's End," "Facing Up to the Ultimate Taboo: Failure," "Stopping by Woods on a Snowy Evening," "Hills Like White Elephants"

The Modern Language Association website no longer provides detailed information about correct MLA format, though you can find answers to some basic questions at www.mla.org/style. Click on FAQs. Also, you can consult any up-to-date standard grammar and usage handbook for more examples and information about rules for using quotations that are not covered in this section.

How to Format Your Essay

If your instructor asks you to follow MLA format, use this sample as a model for the first page of your essay.

Hernandez 1

Luisa Hernandez

English 101

Instructor Ramirez

6 October 2006

Lying and Cheating as a Way of Life

I have been following some of the corporate scandals of the 1990s and thinking about their effect on American culture. For several months, the dominant story in the business media has been the financial mismanagement and accounting fraud of corporate executives at companies like Enron, Tyco, HealthSouth, Adelphia Communications, and WorldCom. In each instance, executives falsified their financial statements to keep their companies' stock prices high, while systematically looting the company's assets for their own personal profit. These criminal actions ruined lives, damaged reputations, and endangered their employees' livelihoods.

As the number of these sordid stories multiplied, it occurred to me that these scandals were just an extension of a trend that has been gaining strength over the past decade: Deception and cheating are acceptable ways to get ahead in life. While it might seem like an exaggeration to

How to Prepare the Works Cited Page

If you take information from a source or if you use quotations from a selection, you must indicate the source of the material. To do this, you must attach a separate Works Cited page at the end of your essay. To prepare his synthesis essay on contemporary attitudes toward work, Pete Glanting used four sources from this text, including paraphrased and quoted material. (A portion of Pete's essay is printed in Part 5.) Study the model below carefully and the explanations that follow it.

Glanting 6

Works Cited

Ehrenreich, Barbara, "Nickel and Dimed: On (Not) Getting by in America." Rpt. in In Tandem. New York: McGraw-Hill, 2008. 314–325.

Guilbault, Rose Castillo, "The Conveyor Belt Ladies." Rpt. in In Tandem. New York: McGraw-Hill, 2008. 63–65.

Nazario, Sonia. "Benefit and Burden," Enrique's Journey. Rpt. in In Tandem. New York: McGraw-Hill, 2008. 535–539.

Schlosser, Eric, "Fast Food Nation: Behind the Counter." Rpt. in In Tandem. New York: McGraw-Hill, 2008. 263–268.

EXPLANATION OF THE WORKS CITED PAGE

Note that this information covers only the most basic requirements for citations. For information on how to format newspaper or magazine articles, books, and websites using MLA style, consult any current English handbook.

- "Works Cited" is centered. If there is only one work, use the singular title "Work Cited." Do not use outdated terms like "Bibliography" or "List of Sources." Do not boldface the title or put it in quotation marks.
- Double-space each citation.
- The author's last name comes first, then the first name, followed by a comma and the name of the article correctly punctuated. Use quotation marks to indicate the title of the essay; underline book titles.
- If all the material you use in your paper comes from a single source, as you see in the above example, from this textbook, you may omit the "Rpt. in" part (which stands for "reprinted in"). If you use material from other print sources or from the World Wide Web, however, you will have to indicate that it is a reprint piece. Ask your instructor if you are in doubt.
- Indent the second and all subsequent lines. The easiest way to do this is to create a hanging indent. On Microsoft Word's ruler line, drag the hourglass-shaped left margin triangles over five spaces. Then drag only the *top* one back to the left margin. The second and subsequent lines of your entry will automatically be indented the correct number of spaces. Be sure to hit "return" after each entry.
- After the title, type the primary city where the publisher is located, followed by a colon. Then type the name of the publishing company, followed by a period.
- Finally, indicate the inclusive page numbers in the book where the selection appears, *not* the page numbers that you used in your citations.
- If there are multiple authors, alphabetize by last name. To do this easily, type your list in any order, being sure to hit "return" after each entry. Then pull down to "Sort" under "Tools," and your list will automatically be alphabetized.

Above all, do not invent your own form! Just follow the model, which will make everything easier on yourself and also make your instructor happy.

PART TWO

Part 2 begins with instruction in reading and writing college-level prose. The first section introduces you to the most fundamental of reading skills: how to determine the writer's main idea and purpose in writing. Learning these skills will help you focus on a main point and on a specific purpose when you write your own essays.

Next are four short selections (as well as a supplementary reading on the text website) to represent exemplary models of personal experience writing. These readings illustrate the broad range available to the autobiographical writer. The practice essay by Kristie Helms recounts spending the lazy days of summer along the banks of the Tennessee River without much parental supervision. Frank Huyla, an emergency room physician, confronts prejudice while working to save a little girl's life. Rose Castillo Guilbault learns a lesson in humility from her summer working in the vegetable sheds in the Salinas valley. K. Oanh Ha examines her experience as a Vietnamese refugee who struggled with her family to survive in Southeast Asian refugee camps. Finally Val Plumwood writes a harrowing tale of being attacked by a crocodile in Australia.

These readings serve as a model for preparing your own essay, and the last section of Part 2 gives practical advice on how to write a personal experience essay. The emphasis in this section is on employing an appropriate level of specific detail, a skill that will serve you well when you encounter more difficult types of writing assignments later in the book.

Finding the Main Idea and Writer's Purpose

The introductions to the next seven parts of the book discuss a particular skill or set of skills that will make you a better reader and help you understand the essays in each section. They are organized by degree of difficulty and by order of importance. The introduction to Part 2 covers these topics and includes a short sample essay for practice:

- Recognizing the difference between fiction and nonfiction prose
- Distinguishing between essays and articles
- Finding the main idea in paragraphs
- Locating thesis statements in longer readings
- Identifying the writer's purpose

THE DIFFERENCE BETWEEN FICTION AND NONFICTION

Writing comes in three types: prose, poetry, and drama. This book is concerned with *prose*—ordinary writing that consists of words grouped into sentences and sentences grouped into paragraphs—just like the print that you are reading on this page. Prose is further divided into two types: nonfiction and fiction.

Your college textbooks, articles in the daily newspaper, magazine essays and articles, as well as all of the readings in this book are nonfiction. Nonfiction deals with real people with real problems and real events in their lives, real issues and ways to resolve them, real events in the world and their aftermath. The novel or the book of short stories that you read at the beach is fiction because it is invented. Simply put, *nonfiction* writing is real, whereas *fiction* writing is imaginative.

THE DIFFERENCE BETWEEN ARTICLES AND ESSAYS

Two important types of nonfiction are essays and articles. In this book—as well as in many of your other classes—you will read both. The difference between an article and an essay is a little tricky, and the distinction is not always clear, especially because magazines may publish both essays and articles. Probably the easiest way to distinguish between them is to think of an article as being more contemporary because it deals with *immediate* or *current* issues and problems. An essay, on the other hand, tends to be more *universal* in scope, meaning that it offers the writer's perceptions about age-old problems that all human beings have faced since time began. An essay is also more literary, more open in its form, and more enduring.

Journalism was once defined as "literature in a hurry." News articles should be well written, but their purpose is to inform readers of the day's events and therefore are not intended to last for decades. Essays, however, are apt to be more timeless. The story you read in the morning paper about a warehouse fire at the waterfront that did $1 million in damage will most likely be forgotten in a month or a year, except of course by the owners and nearby residents. But the essay by Jared Diamond in Part 4 of this book, for example, "Easter's End," about the destruction of Easter Island's natural environment, has significance far beyond the boundaries of that island off the coast of Chile. Diamond's concern is universal: We are ruining the environment.

But these distinctions may not be worth making, and I urge you not to dwell on whether a particular piece of prose is an essay or an article. What *is* important to remember is that essays and articles should be called "essays" and "articles," *not* "stories," which refer only to fiction.

IDENTIFYING THE MAIN IDEA IN PARAGRAPHS

With those important definitions out of the way, we now turn to the comprehension skill that is at the heart of everything in your college career: how to locate the main idea of what you are reading. Let's say that you have just watched *Mr. and Mrs. Smith*, the 2005 action thriller starring Brad Pitt and Angelina Jolie. The next day your friend asks you what the movie was about and whether she should rent it next weekend. You might say something like this:

"Brad Pitt and Angelina Jolie play a couple whose marriage is in trouble. Each work as secret agents for two different shadowy spy agencies. Each thinks that the other has an ordinary job. They also don't know that each has been hired by their agencies as assassins to kill each other."

What have you just done? In these four sentences you have stated the main point of a 2-hour movie—in other words, what it is about. In short, you have summarized the movie's plot and conveyed its main idea.

In your college reading, finding the main idea, of course, can be a little more difficult. There is no trailer to show you the movie's highlights; there are no annotations in the margins to help you and no way of asking the writer what he or she meant. All you have are print and paper, so it is up to you to work through the words and sentences and make sense of it all. Step-by-step, this book—its readings and exercises—will help you make sense of each reading and help you perfect your comprehension skills.

Your understanding of the main idea of the essay starts with your understanding of the paragraphs that make up the essay. As you saw in the introductory section, the paragraph is the main building block of the essay. Further, that point—whether in an essay or a paragraph—has to be supported, developed, and backed up.

If I say, for example, that all college students should be required to take a foreign language, you do not have to accept the statement just because I say so. No idea is so good on its own that it can stand undefended. I might support my claim by saying that learning a foreign language advances one's understanding of how languages work, that it allows one to travel to that country where the language is spoken and get around more easily, that one can order from a menu in that language, or that it makes one less isolated, less insulated.

These reasons are called the *support* or *supporting details*. Since it is easier to find the main idea in paragraphs, we will practice that skill first. But we will move on to finding the main idea in longer passages—in essays—before long.

You may have been taught in your writing classes that every paragraph should have a *topic sentence* (or a main idea sentence) and that the topic sentence should be the paragraph's first sentence. Unfortunately, professional writers often do not abide by this advice. A writer is under no obligation to make your reading experience easy, and few professional writers structure their paragraphs according to a formula. (Although as college students trying to master the craft of writing as college students, you should probably adhere to the advice about structuring your paragraphs around a central thesis, as discussed before.) Still, the every-paragraph-begins-with-a-topic-sentence formula may get you into trouble when you read adult prose. A better way to get at the main idea is to ask yourself these questions:

- What's the point of what I'm reading?
- What is the single most important idea that the writer wants me to understand?

If you can formulate a single sentence—certainly no more than two—that answers these questions, then you will make significant gains in your reading.

If there is a main idea sentence, where should you look for it? It may indeed be the first sentence, but just as often, it might be the sentence *after* the first couple of sentences, or it might be in the middle of the paragraph. It might even be the final sentence. And in some instances, there may be no directly stated main idea sentence at all. We call this last type an *implied main idea*, meaning that the supporting details *suggest* the main point without saying it directly.

Whether it is stated or not, the writer's point must be supported with details, examples, stories, anecdotes (little stories), definitions of unfamiliar terms, explanations, analysis—whatever way the writer can best back up his or her point. The trick is to separate the main point from these supporting ideas.

Let us practice first locating the main idea by reading two paragraphs taken from two popular magazines, *Harper's* and *Discover*, and a third paragraph from Eric Schlosser's book *Fast Food Nation*, an excerpt from which is printed in Part 5 of this text. The first two are annotated for you; that is, I have made brief notes about the content in the left margin. Read each paragraph carefully.

Main idea: The way fish are caught for aquariums needs to be changed.

Reason: Methods of collecting fish are brutal.

Examples: Poisons destroy ecosystems.

- Corals and other fish are killed.
- Only a few stunned fish on the edge are captured.

> The worldwide trade in aquarium fish—currently worth $200 million per year and fueled mostly by demand among home aquarists in the United States, Europe, and Japan—is badly in need of transformation. The collection methods are brutal. Using poisons, primarily sodium cyanide, poor people destroy entire ecosystems in order to capture the few stunned fish surviving on the perimeters. The sodium cyanide begins to kill corals and fish within thirty seconds of contact. A handful of fish at the outermost edge of the destruction, disabled but not dead, are then collected by hand.
>
> With each purchase of a lionfish or butterflyfish, the home aquarist, obliviously or uncaringly, funds this devastation.
>
> Julia Whitty, "Shoals of Time," *Harper's*

Which of these do you think *best* states the main idea of the paragraph?

A. Cruel methods are used to collect fish for home aquariums.

B. The way fish are collected for the world's aquariums needs to be changed.

C. People use sodium cyanide to collect fish for aquariums.

D. There is great demand for aquarium fish in the United States, Europe, and Japan.

Did you choose B? If so, you are correct. Notice that the main idea is indeed represented in the first sentence: "The worldwide trade in aquarium fish . . . is badly in need of transformation." Although answer A—"collection methods are brutal"—might look like the main idea, it is actually the main *supporting statement:* It tells us *why* the way fish are caught needs to be changed. The other two answer choices are minor details; they are there merely to add extra information and evidence for the main point.

Here's another way to think about the main idea: Which of these would be the best title for the paragraph you just read?

A. "Aquarium Fish"

B. "How Fish Are Captured"

C. "Why Fish Collecting Should Be Prohibited"

D. "Collecting Aquarium Fish: The Need to Find a Better Way"

Did you choose D? If so, you chose the right answer. Notice that A is too broad and does not give the writer's point of view. B suggests a process, but again, not the point of view. And C is way off the mark. The writer never says that collecting fish for aquariums should be stopped. Because it includes the essential elements from the paragraph, D is the best answer. The paragraph, then, follows a pattern: The main idea—methods of collecting aquarium fish—is followed by five statements supporting it.

In this first sample paragraph, the main idea was stated. In the sample paragraph below, the main idea is suggested, or implied. Try to figure out what the writer's main point is. Again, the paragraph has been annotated for you.

Asbestos has long been used for fireproofing and insulation.

Asbestos is a dangerous mineral.

It causes asbestosis, a serious disease.

Asbestos is being removed from buildings

This process costs a lot and is dangerous.

Because asbestos material is hazardous, it must be disposed of properly.

> The ancient Greeks were the first to discover the fireproofing and insulating properties of asbestos, but they knew nothing of the mineral's dangers. When asbestos is inhaled, the fibers can cause asbestosis, a stiffening of lung tissue that contributes to heart disease and lung cancer. Because of this risk, asbestos is being removed from schools, hospitals, and thousands of other buildings around the country. It's a costly, time-consuming, and dangerous process, as workers in protective gear use their hands to scrape out the substance, which must then be disposed of as a hazardous material. To prevent asbestos fibers from escaping in the air, areas being cleaned must be sealed in pressurized tents.
>
> "Attacking Asbestos," *Discover*

Consider the six sets of marginal notes. Underline the one that most likely states the main idea. Then within that note, circle the word that seems to be the most important to describe the *subject* of asbestos. You should have underlined the second one and circled "dangerous." Notice that the writer repeats the idea of asbestos being "dangerous" at the end of the paragraph with the synonym "hazardous," which is a good indication that it is the writer's point regarding the subject.

Which of the following represents the best title for this paragraph?

A. "Asbestos Then and Now"

B. "The Hazards of Asbestos"

C. "How to Remove Asbestos"

D. "Asbestos: The Cause of Asbestosis"

The most appropriate title is stated in B. Here is what the ideas in this paragraph look like when they are outlined:

> Background information: Ancient Greeks knew asbestos could be used to fireproof and to insulate.
>
> ***They didn't know that asbestos is a dangerous mineral.*** (implied main idea)
>
> Why? It causes asbestosis, a serious illness.
>
> Solution: Remove asbestos from buildings and dispose of it properly.

Now look at this passage. This time, write your own notes in the space provided.

At Burger King restaurants, frozen hamburger patties are placed on a conveyer belt and emerge from a broiler ninety seconds later fully cooked. The ovens at Pizza Hut and at Domino's also use conveyer belts to ensure standardized cooking times. The ovens at McDonald's look like commercial laundry presses, with big steel hoods that swing down and grill hamburgers on both sides at once. The burgers, chicken, french fries, and buns are all frozen when they arrive at a McDonald's. The shakes and sodas begin as syrup. At Taco Bell restaurants the food is "assembled," not prepared. The guacamole isn't made by workers in the kitchen; it's made at a factory in Michoacán, Mexico, then frozen and shipped north. The chain's taco meat arrives frozen and precooked in vacuum-sealed plastic bags. The beans are dehydrated and look like brownish corn flakes. The cooking process is simple. "Everything's add water," a Taco Bell employee told me. "Just add hot water."

—Eric Schlosser, *Fast Food Nation*

The main idea of this paragraph, as Schlosser wrote it, is *implied* so that you have to figure it out for yourself. To do this, ask yourself what all of these details about fast food being frozen, packaged, precooked, and "prepared" by just adding hot water add up to. The answer to this question will be the main idea. Write your answer here:

____

____

Here is one possibility. Your sentence, of course, may be worded differently, but it should contain the same elements as this one:

> The food served in fast food restaurants is frozen, and it is assembled and cooked with hardly any human intervention.

As Schlosser writes later in the selection: "This food is assembled, not prepared or cooked, just as any other factory product is. Bicycles are assembled, computers are assembled, and Big Macs and Whoppers are assembled, too."

Which of the following would be the best title for the paragraph?

A. "How Fast Food Is Really Prepared"

B. "Why Fast Food Is 'Fast' "

C. "Fast Food Restaurants—Changing the Way America Eats"

D. "New Innovations in Restaurants"

Did you choose A? If so, you are correct.

LOCATING THE THESIS STATEMENT IN LONGER READINGS

Now let's consider articles and essays. You will recall that an essay is composed of individual paragraphs linked together to produce a sustained piece of writing. Whatever the length—whether two pages or twenty—the writer has in mind a focus or a point, which, like the main idea of a paragraph, may be either explicitly stated or implied. This main idea is called the *thesis* or *thesis statement*. After all, the essay that you read and the essay that you write have to be about something.* A writer may place the thesis near the beginning of the essay, in the middle, or at the end, but usually it comes somewhere near the beginning, often after an introductory section that might comprise anywhere from one to three or four paragraphs. In addition, a thesis might be conveyed in two sentences, though rarely more than that.

*In the movie *Wonder Boys*, Michael Douglas plays a writer who had some success with his first book, but since then, his second literary endeavor—well over 700 pages long and seven years in the making—has been going nowhere. Near the end of the movie, there is a wonderful scene where Douglas drops the manuscript, and all the pages blow away. A cab driver waiting nearby asks Douglas what the novel was about. He replies, "I don't really know."

PRACTICE ESSAY

Girls of Summer: Lazy Days from a Gen X Childhood

Kristie Helms

To practice locating the thesis in a longer selection, read this short article by Kristie Helms. Helms grew up in the South, where she earned a degree in journalism from Murray State University in Kentucky. She works as a community host for the Utne Café, the online version of *Utne*, a magazine that reprints articles from the nation's best alternative publications as well as publishing original articles on a wide variety of environmental and economic issues. The article was originally posted on Café Utne's GenX Form and later published in *Utne*.

Girls of Summer: Lazy Days from a Gen X Childhood

Kristie Helms

Connecting Grammar to Writing

Note that the first and last sentences of paragraph 1 represent a compound sentence—two independent clauses joined by the coordinating conjunction *and.*

1 We lived on the banks of the Tennessee River, and we owned the summers when we were girls. We ran wild through humid summer days that never ended but only melted one into the other. We floated down rivers of weekdays with no school, no rules, no parents, and no constructs other than our fantasies. We were good girls, my sister and I. We had nothing to rebel against. This was just life as we knew it, and we knew the summers to be long and to be ours.

2 The road that ran past our house was a one-lane rural route. Every morning, after our parents had gone to work, I'd wait for the mail lady to pull up to our box. Some days I would put enough change for a few stamps into a mason jar lid and leave it in the mailbox. I hated bothering the mail lady with this transaction, which made her job take longer. But I liked that she knew that someone in our house sent letters into the outside world.

3 I liked walking to the mailbox in my bare feet and leaving footprints on the dewy grass. I imagined that feeling the wetness on the bottom of my feet made me a poet. I had never read poetry, outside of some Emily Dickinson. But I imagined that people who knew of such things would walk to their mailboxes through the morning dew in their bare feet.

4 We planned our weddings with the help of Barbie dolls and the tiny purple wildflowers growing in our side yard. We became scientists and tested concoctions of milk, orange juice, and mouthwash. We ate handfuls of bittersweet chocolate chips and licked peanut butter off spoons. When we ran out of sweets to eat, we snitched sugary Flintstones vitamins out of the medicine cabinet. We became masters of the Kraft macaroni and cheese lunch, and we dutifully called our mother at work three times a day to give her updates on our adventures. But

don't call too often or speak too loudly or whine too much, we told ourselves, or else they'll get annoyed and she'll get fired and the summers will end.

5 We shaped our days the way we chose, far from the prying eyes of adults. We found our dad's *Playboys* and charged the neighborhood boys money to look at them. We made crank calls around the county, telling people they had won a new car. "What kind?" they'd ask. "Red" we'd always say. We put on our mom's old prom dresses, complete with gloves and hats, and sang backup to the C. W. McCall song "Convoy," which we'd found on our dad's turntable.

6 We went on hikes into the woods behind our house, crawling under barbed wire fences and through tangled undergrowth. Heat and humidity found their way through the leaves to our flushed faces. We waded in streams that we were always surprised to come across. We walked past cars and auto parts that had been abandoned in the woods, far from any road. We'd reach the tree line and come out unexpectedly into a cow pasture. We'd perch on the gate or stretch out on the large flat limestone outcrop that marked the end of the Woods Behind Our House.

7 One day a thunderstorm blew up along the Tennessee River. It was one of those storms that make the day go dark and the humidity disappear. First it was still and quiet. There was electricity in the air and then the sharp crispness of a summer day being blown wide open as the winds rushed in. We threw open all the doors and windows. We found the classical radio station from two towns away and turned up the bass and cranked up the speakers. We let the wind blow in and churn our summer day around. We let the music we were only vaguely familiar with roar through the house. And we twirled.

8 We twirled in the living room in the wind and in the music. We twirled and we imagined that we were poets and dancers and scientists and spring brides. We twirled and imagined that if we could let everything—the thunder, the storm, the wind, the world—into that house on the banks of the Tennessee River, we could live in our summer dreams forever. When we were girls.

Each selection in the text will begin with an exercise asking you to identify the main idea. Reprinted here are four sentences from Helms's article. Let's begin by asking you to choose the one sentence that *best* represents the thesis.

A. We twirled and imagined that if we could let everything—the thunder, the storm, the wind, the world—into that house on the banks of the Tennessee River, we could live in our summer dreams forever. When we were girls. [paragraph 8]

B. We lived on the banks of the Tennessee River, and we owned the summers when we were girls. [paragraph 1]

C. We had nothing to rebel against. This was just life as we knew it, and we knew the summers to be long and to be ours. [paragraph 1]

D. We shaped our days the way we chose, far from the prying eyes of adults. [paragraph 5]

Three of these choices are possible candidates for the thesis. Although both B and C are good choices, D stands out from the others because it clearly characterizes and encompasses all of the details and key elements of the summers as she describes them: The girls did what they wanted, away from any parental restrictions. The first answer choice, A, represents the conclusion—a bittersweet retrospective awareness that our summer dreams fade.

Some teachers use the term *funnel pattern* to describe the structure of Helms's introductory section. If you picture an upside down funnel, you can see what this image means. Paragraphs 1–4 establish a mood and an atmosphere, invite the reader into her world, and whet our appetite to continue reading. Then the thesis statement at the beginning of paragraph 5 points the way to the remainder of the essay.

Identifying the Writer's Purpose

Although he or she may not be consciously aware of it when opening a new document on the computer screen, every writer has in mind some *purpose*, the intention or the reason he or she is going to the trouble of writing. The ancient Greeks taught that literature had three aims: to please, to instruct, and to persuade. What exactly did they mean?

The Writer's Purpose in Classical Terms

▪ To please	To delight, tell a story, entertain, amuse, give pleasure to, describe, paint a picture in words
▪ To instruct	To teach, show, inform, examine, expose, analyze, criticize
▪ To persuade	To convince, change one's mind, influence, argue, recommend, give advice to

Further, some instructors describe various types of nonfiction prose writing by identifying a piece of writing as representing one of the four *modes of discourse:*

- *Narrative:* A piece of writing that tells a story about a real event or relates personal experience
- *Descriptive:* A piece of writing that shows what something looks like or feels like

- *Exposition:* A piece of writing that informs, instructs, examines a subject
- *Argumentation or persuasion:* A piece of writing that attempts to convince the reader to accept an opinion or examines one side of a controversial issue

Referring to the earlier classical purposes, we might say that narrative and descriptive prose is writing that *pleases*, expository prose is writing that *instructs*, and obviously, persuasive prose *persuades*.

Sometimes it is hard to see an exact distinction between "instructing" and "persuading" since the very act of instructing us about something that needs to be changed might also convince us of the need for that change. For example, in the little passage about collecting aquarium fish, Julia Whitty informs the reader of the brutal methods used to catch them, but she also implies a persuasive argument—that these methods should be abandoned.

In Kristie Helms's essay, which of the following best identifies her purpose?

A. To inform the reader of what it was like to grow up as a member of Generation X

B. To describe a Tennessee summer

C. To argue for closer parental control over children's summer activities

D. To relate and describe her childhood summers in Tennessee

Let us examine these choices one by one. A is off the mark, because, aside from the subtitle, Helms never refers to Generation X in the essay. B is too broad and misinterprets the content. Also Helms is describing a sequence of summers where she and her sister roamed free, not one specific summer. C is inaccurate, since Helms and her sister were quite content to be outside their parents' control. That leaves D, which correctly states her purpose to tell the reader a story about what her childhood summers were like.

When you write essays of your own, try to ascertain your exact purpose in writing—that is, beyond the fact that your instructor gave the assignment for which you will receive a grade. To help you master this important skill, each exercise following the readings in this book will contain one question on writer's purpose.

To complete this introductory practice essay, here are a few of the exercises—in abbreviated form—that you will be asked to complete following each reading selection. For this first set, the answers are provided after each exercise. Ask your instructor for help if you do not understand an answer choice.

EXERCISES

A. Comprehending Main Ideas

Choose the correct answer.

1. Helms writes that their summers were characterized by long days with
   a. nothing to eat in the house.
   b. no summer school.
   c. no rules or parents.
   d. no friends in the neighborhood to play with.

2. Helms writes that she felt like a poet when she
   a. wrote poems in her special journal.
   b. walked to the mailbox in bare feet over the wet grass.
   c. entered a poetry contest in a national magazine.
   d. read Emily Dickinson's poems and tried to imitate her style.

3. Helms emphasizes that, above all, their carefree summers allowed them to
   a. practice independence and self-reliance.
   b. learn how to be deceptive and sneaky about their misbehaviors.
   c. develop an intellectual curiosity about nature and the world around them.
   d. indulge in their limitless imaginations about what they could be and do.

ANSWERS: 1. c 2. b 3. d

B. Sequencing

The sentences in this excerpt from the selection have been scrambled. Read the sentences and choose the sequence that puts them back into logical order. Do not refer to the original selection.

1. Some days I would put enough change for a few stamps into a mason jar lid and leave it in the mailbox. **2.** But I liked that she knew that someone in our house sent letters into the real world. **3.** The road that ran past our house was a one-lane rural route. **4.** I hated bothering the mail lady with this transaction, which made her job take longer. **5.** Every morning, after our parents had gone to work, I'd wait for the mail lady to pull up to our box.

a. 5, 3, 1, 4, 2
b. 3, 5, 1, 4, 2
c. 5, 1, 3, 4, 2
d. Correct as written.

ANSWER: b

C. Distinguishing Between Main Ideas and Supporting Details

The following sentences come from paragraph 5. Label them as follows: MI if the sentence represents a *main idea* and SD if the sentence represents a *supporting detail.*

1. We shaped our days the way we chose, far from the prying eyes of adults.
2. We found our dad's *Playboy*s and charged the neighborhood boys money to look at them.
3. We made crank calls around the county, telling people they had a won a new car.
4. "What kind?" they'd ask.
5. "Red" we'd always say.
6. We put on our mom's old prom dresses, complete with gloves and hats, and sank backup to the C. W. McCall song "Convoy," which we'd found on our dad's turntable.

ANSWERS: 1. MI 2.–6. SD

D. Understanding Vocabulary

Look through the paragraphs listed below and find a word that matches each definition. Refer to a dictionary if necessary. An example has been done for you.

EXAMPLE: clear images or ideas, arrangements [paragraphs 1–2] constructs

1. pertaining to the countryside [1–2] ____________
2. mixtures, blends [4–5] ____________
3. filched, took without permission [4–5] ____________
4. watching closely, interfering, meddling [5–6] ____________
5. stir up, mix up, agitate [7–8] ____________

ANSWERS: 1. rural 2. concoctions 3. snitched 4. prying 5. churn

DISCUSSION QUESTIONS

1. How would you characterize a typical summer day as Helms describes it?
2. In what specific ways does Helms's experience contrast with the way children are raised today, at least based on your firsthand observation of children in your community or neighborhood?

EXPLORE THE WEB

- The Café, *Utne*'s award-winning community forum, features discussions on more than eighty topics, arranged in the following categories: culture, community and society, spirit, body, play, media, local/regional, men and women. These forums can be accessed at this address: http://cafeutne.org/cafe.
- For a complete list of America's generations from the founding of the nation as well as full explanations of the characteristics of Generation X and Generation Y, see these two Wikipedia sites:

  http://en.wikipedia.org/wiki/Generation_X

  http://en.wikipedia.org/wiki/Generation_Y

Reading Selections

The four narrative readings in Part 2 cover a wide range of personal experience and reflect diverse styles of writing. Exercises following each reading will measure your comprehension as well as other related reading skills.

Sugar

Frank Huyler

Frank Huyler works as an emergency room physician in Albuquerque, New Mexico. The book from which this selection comes, *The Blood of Strangers: Stories from Emergency Medicine* (1999), portrays seemingly small but poignant incidents from his experience working in the ER. Huyler has also published poetry in several journals, as well as a novel, *The Laws of Invisible Things* (2004). Note that this essay is the basis for a writing assignment using analysis at the end of Part 5.

VOCABULARY ANALYSIS

Note: Each selection begins with a brief explanation of how to break vocabulary words into prefix, root, and suffix, using one or two words that you will encounter in the selection. Learning these word parts will help you greatly in the future when you come across other words with the same word elements.

The Prefix *intra-*

When a patient is fed *intravenously* (paragraph 35), fluids are given "inside the veins." The prefix *intra-* means "within" or "inside of." Do not confuse *intra-* with the similar-sounding prefix *inter-*, which means "between" or "among." A pair of words using these prefixes is often heard in American schools and colleges, whose students may play both *intermural* and *intramural* sports. *Intermural* sports refers to those played between two different schools, while *intramural* sports refer to those played *within* the same school. *Intramural* means literally "between the walls."

The Prefix *hypo-*

Hypoglycemia refers to an abnormally low level of glucose (sugar) in the blood. The prefix *hypo-* comes from the Greek and means "low." Other terms beginning with this prefix are *hypodermic* (a kind of needle used to give injections under the skin) and *hypothermia* (abnormally low body temperature). The prefix *hyper-* meaning "excessive," as in the word *hyperactive,* is the opposite of *hypo-*.

Another Word You Need to Know

triage [paragraph 2]
The word *triage,* from the French verb *trier* ("to sort"), refers to the process of sorting injured people based on their need for medical treatment or based on the likelihood that they will benefit from it.

Sugar

Frank Huyler

1 The little girl was running around the room, screeching happily, and when she saw me she hid under the bed. I could see her peering at me from between the legs of the gurney as I stood with her chart in my hand. Her father shook his head, grinned, and looked at his wife. "I told you there's nothing wrong with her."

2 I looked down at the chart. On it the triage nurse had written, in bold black letters, "Two-year-old acting weird."

3 "I'm Dr. Huyler," I said. "What can I do for you?"

4 "Nothing," the man said, and his wife hushed him.

5 "She's not acting right," she said. She wore an African print dress, and I found myself staring at the intricate pattern of swirling reds and browns. Her hair was cornrowed, a bead at the end of each strand.

6 "They're Medicaid," the triage nurse had whispered pointedly in my ear. The implication was clear: they wanted something for free. Tylenol, a work excuse. But it was ten o'clock on a Friday night.

7 "What has she been doing?"

8 "It's kind of hard to explain. She just isn't acting herself. I noticed it right away. But she's been fine ever since we got here."

9 "Can you be more specific?" I could feel myself getting impatient. There were half a dozen patients waiting, the ER was full. I wondered why they hadn't called their regular pediatrician.

10 "Well," she said, thinking. "You know how people look when they're staring into a mirror? Kind of blank?" I nodded. "She's like that. Only there isn't a mirror. There's nothing there."

11 The child's vital signs were completely normal. Her mother coaxed her out from under the bed and held her wriggling in her arms as I listened to her heart and lungs, looked into her ears.

Connecting Grammar to Writing

Note the mix of short and long sentences in paragraph 12. The short sentences express main points, while the two longer ones add variety, making for a pleasing style.

12 I'm uneasy with children. I must have been a cold, white form to her, large, bending down with my stethoscope and light. I could see nothing wrong with her. She looked impeccably cared for, without any sign of the abuse I had been vaguely and secretly considering. I always do. It's been drummed into us.

13 "Does she have any medical problems at all?"

14 "No," the father said, anticipating my questions. "She's always been healthy. She's had all her shots. She's growing like she should, and she can talk a little, only now she won't 'cause she's shy." He wagged a finger, and she giggled, hiding her face with the bottle her mother had given her.

15 "Has she had any recent stress, something that might have upset her?" They looked at each other.

16 "I don't think so."

17 "Is there any history of seizures in the family?"

18 Her mother thought for a while. "I think my brother might have seizures," she said finally, "but I haven't seen him in a long time."

19 "And right now she's acting normally?"

20 "She's fine," her father said to his wife. "Come on, let's go. If she does it again we'll come back. It's past her bedtime."

21 I considered what I'd heard. A vague history of blank spells; it could mean anything, from a rare type of seizure to the vagaries of the two-year-old mind. She could see her pediatrician on Monday, I thought. She was a completely normal child.

22 On my way out the door, though, I turned around. "Is there any chance she might have gotten into someone's medications? Does anyone in the family take medications regularly?"

23 "Well, she stays with my mother when we're at work. She takes medicines."

24 "What kind of medicine does she take?"

25 "I'm not sure. Something for her blood pressure and a sugar pill."

26 Oral hypoglycemics—sugar pills—are among the most dangerous of overdoses. They can drop blood sugar profoundly, cause brain damage, seizures, coma. Designed for adult diabetics, they are long-lasting, and one pill could kill a small child, even many hours later.

27 "Let's check her blood sugar," I said, "just to be sure. And please call your mother, find out exactly what she takes."

28 From the doctor's station I could hear the child shrieking as the nurse drew her blood. Her mother spoke into the phone a few feet away.

29 "My mother takes glipizide," she said, handing me a piece of paper where she'd written it down. "She ran out of her blood pressure medicine two weeks ago."

30 A sugar pill.

31 The nurse came out of the room with a syringe full of blood. The child's mother and I watched as she eased a single drop from the tip of the needle onto

the portable blood-sugar machine she held in her hand. It digested the blood for a few seconds, then displayed the number on the screen. Forty-two.

32 "It that low?" her mother asked.

33 "It's about half of what it should be," I replied, stunned. "She must have taken one of your mother's sugar pills."

34 "My mother is legally blind. She probably dropped one and didn't notice."

35 "We need to keep her in the hospital for at least a day and give her sugar intravenously." I said it quietly, half to myself.

36 "Will she be all right?" She was afraid, staring at me.

37 "She'll be fine." And suddenly I began to shake. "But I'm very glad you brought her in. You may have saved her life."

38 "My husband wanted to put her to bed," she said softly, looking off down the hall.

39 It was suddenly clear. Sometime that afternoon the girl had taken the pill, and by the time her parents came home she was showing the effects of low blood sugar: the staring spells, the blank look.

40 "What did you do when you saw she was acting weird?"

41 "We gave her a bottle," the father said, standing with us now. "And then we gave her a sucker."

42 They had given her sugar. When she arrived in the ER her blood sugar had risen enough for her to look and act herself, but it wouldn't have lasted long. Later that night, when the whole family was asleep, it would have fallen again, and she might never have woken up.

43 As I watched the girl skip and jump around us, the pain of the needle forgotten already, I felt sick, cold and damp, terrified by what I had almost missed. One question, an afterthought. That was all it had been.

44 From time to time I think about her. I imagine her playing in parks, jumping on the couch, shrieking in the bathtub. I imagine her head teeming with small thoughts, and the motion of her hands, her eyes, alive in the world, going out into it, entering it, decade after decade ahead.

EXERCISES

A. Determining the Main Idea and Writer's Purpose

Choose the best answer.

1. The main idea of the selection is that
   a. emergency room physicians must make life-and-death decisions that affect both patient and family.
   b. emergency room physician grow weary and impatient from hearing their patients' complaints.

c. emergency room personnel are trained to be observant and watchful for signs of abuse in the children they treat.
d. the author's single question, asked almost as an afterthought, prevented a near tragedy from occurring.

2. With respect to the main idea, the writer's purpose is to
   a. present information.
   b. relate a story.
   c. present an argument.
   d. offer helpful advice.

B. Comprehending Main Ideas

Choose the correct answer.

1. When the parents arrived in the emergency room with their little girl, she was
   a. acting perfectly normal.
   b. suffering from a high temperature.
   c. acting strangely.
   d. abnormally quiet.

2. When Huyler began to examine the child, he discovered that
   a. she was unusually cold.
   b. she seemed vacant or blank.
   c. her vital signs were normal.
   d. she had been abused.

3. Oral hypoglycemics are sugar pills that, when taken by an adult,
   a. cause the blood sugar to rise.
   b. cause the blood sugar to drop.
   c. regulate the amount of sugar in the blood.
   d. diminish one's craving for food.

4. One would take hypoglycemics to control
   a. diabetes.
   b. high blood pressure.
   c. seizures.
   d. blank spells.

5. The child's life was saved because
   a. the parents realized that she wasn't acting right and took her to the ER.
   b. the doctor persisted in trying to find out what was wrong with the child.
   c. the grandmother reported that the child had taken one of her sugar pills.
   d. a, b, and c.
   e. only a and b.

C. Sequencing

The sentences in this paragraph from the selection have been scrambled. Read the sentences and choose the sequence that puts them back into logical order, in this case chronological or time order. Do not refer to the original selection.

1. When she arrived in the ER her blood sugar had risen enough for her to look and act herself, but it wouldn't have lasted long. **2.** Later that night, when the whole family was asleep, it would have fallen again, and she might never have woken up. **3.** They had given her sugar.

a. 3, 1, 2
b. 1, 3, 2
c. 2, 1, 3
d. Correct as written

D. Locating Supporting Details

For each main idea stated here, find details that support it.

1. The parents hadn't agreed on whether they should take the child to the ER.
   a. ______________________________
   ____
   b. ______________________________
2. The little girl had undoubtedly taken one of her grandmother's sugar pills because she exhibited two symptoms:
   a. ______________________________
   b. ______________________________

E. Interpreting Meaning

Write your answers for these questions in your own words.

1. Look again at paragraphs 5 and 6. Medicaid is government-sponsored health insurance for low-income people. Why was the nurse's whispered comment in the doctor's ear incorrect—that the parents wanted something for free?
   ____
   ____

2. Read paragraph 43 again. What lesson does Huyler's experience suggest for ER personnel?

____

____

____

F. Understanding Vocabulary

Look through the paragraphs listed below and find a word that matches each definition. Refer to a dictionary if necessary. An example has been done for you.

EXAMPLE: complex, having many interrelated parts [paragraphs 1–5] intricate

1. inference, insinuation, suggestion [6–9] ____________
2. essential or necessary for life [10–14] ____________
3. flawlessly, immaculately [11–14] ____________
4. unpredictable ideas, whimsical or unusual notions [16–21] ____________
5. swarming, abounding, spilling over [41–44] ____________

DISCUSSION QUESTIONS

1. Comment of Huyler's personality traits and medical skills, based on this incident and on his reactions to the child and her parents.
2. What emotions does Huyler experience as he recounts the narrative? Ultimately, what lesson does his encounter with this little girl's medical condition reinforce?
3. Huyler alludes to two problems with the state of contemporary medicine in the beginning of the narrative—the problem of Medicaid and the necessity of personnel being on the lookout for possible child abuse. What do Huyler's and the nurse's initial response tell the reader about the kinds of problems ER personnel encounter every day and the emotional effects constant exposure to such encounters have on them?
4. What role, if any, does race play in this selection?

Essay topics pertaining to this selection begin at the end of Part 2 on page 90.

EXPLORE THE WEB

The incidence of adult-onset (Type 2) diabetes has increased enormously in the past decade. In addition, children are increasingly being diagnosed with Type-2 diabetes. Do some research, using Google or your favorite search engine, to learn about the symptoms and causes of this serious disease. Start with these three sites:

http://diabetes.niddk.nih.gov/dm/pubs/overview

www.webmd.com

www.diabetes.org/type-2-diabetes.jsp

Find answers to these questions:

1. How much have diabetes rates increased in the United States in the last decade?
2. What are the causes of Type 2 diabetes?
3. What are some typical health problems that diabetes sufferers experience?

The Conveyor Belt Ladies

Rose Castillo Guilbault

Rose Castillo Guilbault was born in Nogales, Mexico, and later immigrated with her family to the United States, where they settled near King City, a small farming town in California's Salinas Valley, known as the "lettuce capital of the world." Guilbault graduated from San Jose State University with a degree in broadcast journalism; she also has advanced degrees from Pepperdine University and from the University of San Francisco. In her varied journalistic career, she has written articles for the *San Francisco Chronicle,* produced documentaries and public affairs programs for KCBS in San Francisco, and served as a producer of local programming at KGO-TV in San Francisco. Currently, Guilbault is Vice President of Corporate Communications and Public Affairs for the California State Automobile Association.

This excerpt is from her recent book, *Farmworker's Daughter: Growing Up Mexican in America* (2005), which recounts her memories of growing up in Nogales and King City from a bicultural perspective. In this selection, Guilbault describes her summer experiences before college working with Mexican American women who migrated each year to King City for seasonal work in the packing sheds.

VOCABULARY ANALYSIS

Monotonous [paragraph 6]

Sorting tomatoes was *monotonous* work for Guilbault and her fellow conveyor-belt workers. The Greek prefix *mono-* ("one" or "single") precedes many common words in English. *Monotonous,* ("having one tone," "repetitiously dull") can be broken down like this: *mono-* ("single") + *tonos* ("tone"). Other words with this prefix are *monologue* ("a long speech made by one person") and *monopoly,* ("economic control by one group"). What do these three words mean?

monotheism ______________________________

monochrome ______________________________

monopoly ______________________________

____

The Conveyor Belt Ladies

Rose Castillo Guilbault

1 The conveyor belt ladies were migrant women, mostly from Texas. I worked with them during the summers of my teenage years. I call them conveyor belt ladies because I got to know them while sorting tomatoes on a conveyor belt.

2 The women and their families arrived in May for the carrot season, spent the summer in the tomato sheds, and stayed through October for the bean harvest. After that, they emptied from town, some returning to their homes in Texas while others continued on the migrant trail, picking cotton in the San Joaquin Valley or grapefruits and oranges in the Imperial Valley.

3 Most of these women had started in the fields. The vegetable packing sheds were a step up, easier than the backbreaking jobs in the fields. The work in the sheds was often more tedious than strenuous, paid better, and provided fairly steady hours and clean bathrooms. Best of all, you didn't get rained on.

4 I had started sorting tomatoes with my mother in high school. I would have preferred working in a dress shop or babysitting like my friends, but I had a dream that would cost a lot of money—college—and the fact was that sorting tomatoes was the highest-paying work in town. The job consisted of picking out the flawed tomatoes on the conveyor belt before they rolled into the shipping boxes at the end of the line. These boxes were immediately loaded onto delivery trucks, so it was important not to let bad tomatoes through.

5 The work could be slow or intense, depending on the quality of the tomatoes and how many there were. Work increased when the company deliveries got backlogged or after rain delayed picking. During those times, it was not

unusual to work from 7:00 a.m. until midnight. I never heard anyone complain about overtime, though. Overtime meant desperately needed extra money.

6 It would have been difficult not to like the women. They were an entertaining group, easing the long, monotonous hours with bawdy humor and spicy gossip. They poked fun at all the male workers and did hysterical impersonations of the supervisor. Although he didn't speak Spanish (other than "*¡Mujeres, trabajo, trabajo!* Women, work, work!"), he sensed he was being laughed at. He would stamp his foot and forbid us from talking until break time. But it would have been much easier to tie the women's tongues in knots than to keep them quiet. Eventually the ladies had their way and their fun, and the men learned to ignore them.

7 Pretty Rosa described her romances and her pending wedding to a handsome fieldworker. Berta told me that Rosa's marriage would cause her nothing but headaches because the man was younger and too handsome. María, large and placid, described the births of each of her nine children, warning me about the horrors of labor and delivery.

8 At other moments they could turn melancholic, telling of babies who died because their mothers couldn't afford medical care, the alcoholic husbands who were their "cross to bear," the racism they experienced in Texas, where they were referred to as "dirty Mexicans" or "Mexican dogs" and not allowed in certain restaurants.

9 I was appalled and deeply moved by these confidences, and the injustices they endured enraged me. I could do little but sympathize. My mother, no stranger to suffering, said I was too impressionable when I emotionally relayed to her the women's stories.

10 "If they were in Mexico, life would be even harder. At least there are opportunities here; you can work," she'd say.

11 During that first summer, I learned to respect the conveyor belt ladies.

12 The last summer I worked in the packing shed turned out to be the last I lived at home. I had just finished junior college and was transferring to a university. At this point I was "overeducated" for seasonal work, but if you counted the overtime, it was still the best-paying job. So I went back one last time.

13 The ladies treated me with warmth and respect. I was a college student and they thought I deserved special treatment.

14 Aguedita, the crew chief, moved me to softer and better-paying jobs within the plant. I moved from the conveyor belt to shoving boxes down a chute and finally to weighing boxes of tomatoes on a scale—the highest-paying position for a woman.

15 When the union representative showed up to collect dues, the women hid me in the bathroom. They had determined it was unfair for me to have to pay dues since I worked only during the summer. We played a cat-and-mouse game with him all summer. "You ladies aren't hiding students, are you?" he'd ask suspiciously.

16 "Why does *la unión* charge our poor students anyway?" The ladies would distract him with questions and complaints until he tired of answering them and had to leave for his next location.

17 María, with the nine children, tried to feed me all summer, bringing extra tortillas, which were delicious. I accepted them with some guilt, wondering if I was taking food away from her children. Others brought rental contracts or other documents for me to explain and translate.

18 The last day of work was splendidly beautiful, golden and warm. The conveyor belt's loud humming was turned off, silenced for the season. The women sighed as they removed their aprons. Some of them walked off, calling, "*¡Hasta la próxima!* Until next time!"

19 But most of the conveyor belt ladies came over to me, shook my hand, and gave me a blessing or a big hug.

20 "Don't come back. Make us proud, *hija*."[1]

---

[1]Daughter.

EXERCISES

A. Determining the Main Idea and Writer's Purpose

Choose the best answer.

1. The main idea of the selection is that
   a. summer jobs can offer rewarding experiences for students.
   b. working in the vegetable-packing sheds and sorting vegetables was a difficult, tedious job.
   c. the conveyor belt ladies were accustomed to their daily hardships and injustices.
   d. despite her initial misgivings, the writer learned to respect and admire the lives of the conveyor belt ladies she worked with.
2. With respect to the main idea, the writer's purpose is to
   a. entertain the reader.
   b. describe her experiences and those of her coworkers.
   c. list facts about migrant workers.
   d. argue for better working conditions in the agricultural industry.

B. Comprehending Main Ideas

Choose the correct answer.

1. Guilbault writes that most of the conveyor belt ladies were from
   a. the local Salinas Valley.
   b. Mexico.

c. Texas.
d. all over Central America.

2. At first, Guilbault states that she
   a. was afraid she would be physically unable to do the work.
   b. would have preferred working in a dress shop or babysitting.
   c. would not earn enough money to attend college.
   d. would be ridiculed by the other workers because she was a student.

3. The conveyor belt ladies eased the monotonous hours by
   a. playing jokes on the supervisors.
   b. playing games.
   c. listening to music.
   d. engaging in humor and gossip.

4. The conveyor belt ladies told Guilbault of their personal sufferings, which made her feel
   a. ashamed and embarrassed at her own good fortune.
   b. indifferent and unsympathetic.
   c. appalled yet powerless to do anything.
   d. melancholic and depressed.

5. Because Guilbault was a college student, the conveyor belt ladies
   a. treated her with warmth and respect.
   b. were envious of her.
   c. treated her with hostility.
   d. complained when she was given easier jobs.

C. Identifying Supporting Details

Place an X in the space for each detail that *directly* supports this main idea from the selection: "At other moments they could turn melancholic."

1. _____ Pretty Rosa described her romances and her pending wedding to a handsome fieldworker.

2. _____ María described the births of each of her nine children.

3. _____ They recounted the alcoholic, abusive husbands who were their "cross to bear."

4. _____ They told of babies who had died because their mothers couldn't afford medical care.

5. _____ They recounted the racism they experienced in Texas, where they were branded as "dirty Mexicans" or "Mexican dogs" and not allowed in certain restaurants.

D. Interpreting Meaning

Choose the best answer.

1. Read paragraph 8 again. A good title for this paragraph is
   a. "Problems Migrant Workers Face."
   b. "Lack of Opportunities for Migrants."
   c. "The Effects of Poverty and Racism."
   d. "The Melancholy Lives of Mexican Migrant Workers."
2. From the writing in paragraphs 9–10, the reader can conclude that Guilbault's mother
   a. shared her daughter's unhappiness over hearing the women's stories.
   b. was proud of her daughter for taking up the conveyor belt ladies' cause.
   c. identified with the women's suffering but thought that they were still fortunate to have jobs.
   d. thought her daughter was being foolish to become so involved in her coworkers' troubles.

E. Understanding Vocabulary

Look through the paragraphs listed below and find a word that matches each definition. Refer to a dictionary if necessary. An example has been done for you.

EXAMPLE: seasonal, moving from place to place [paragraphs 1–4] migrant

1. tiresome, boring [3–5] ____________
2. hilarious, extremely funny [6–8] ____________
3. off-color, humorously coarse or lewd [6–8] ____________
4. imitations, impressions [6–8] ____________
5. about to happen, imminent [7–9] ____________
6. calm, undisturbed [7–9] ____________
7. gloomy, sorrowful, despondent [8–11] ____________
8. dismayed, filled with consternation [9–12] ____________

DISCUSSION QUESTIONS

1. Guilbault's mother implies that the conveyor belt ladies were resigned to their hard lives in America. Why might this have been true?

2. Guilbault eventually came to respect the women she worked with. What specific qualities did she admire?

EXPLORE THE WEB

To find a sampling of opinion about Guilbault's book, *Farmworker's Daughter*, from which this selection comes, go to Google and type the following string in the search box:

"Rose Castillo Guilbault" + "Farmworker's Daughter" + criticism

Refugee's Journey

K. Oanh Ha

The War in Indochina, which had been fought unsuccessfully by the French and then by the Americans, finally ended in April 1975, when the communist North Vietnamese army captured the capital of South Vietnam, Saigon, and reclaimed the country. Saigon was immediately renamed Ho Chi Minh City. Before the fall of Saigon, American soldiers had undertaken a massive evacuation, airlifting well-connected Vietnamese, foreign nationals, and diplomats out of the country.

As K. Oanh Ha reports in this newspaper article, first published in the *San Jose Mercury News*, 1.6 million ordinary Vietnamese citizens who wished to escape the new communist regime escaped the country by fleeing in boats. These "boat people" crowded into vessels and made their way to refugee camps in various Southeast Asian countries. K. Oanh Ha received her BA in English from UCLA and is currently a reporter for the *San Jose Mercury News*, covering stories about and from Asia.

VOCABULARY ANALYSIS

Two Useful Prefixes: *re-* and *dis-*

A *prefix* is an affix, a part of a word attached to a base word or root that indicates a particular meaning. *Re-* is one such prefix, which is attached to dozens of words in English to convey the idea of a repeated action or of doing something a second time. In the selection, Ha uses two words beginning with this prefix: *refurbished* [paragraph 2] and *retracing* [paragraph 7]. *Refurbished* is used to describe the riverboat that took them to the refugee camp, meaning that the boat had been *renovated* (literally, "made new again"), while *retracing* means to repeat or to trace one's steps again from a previous journey.

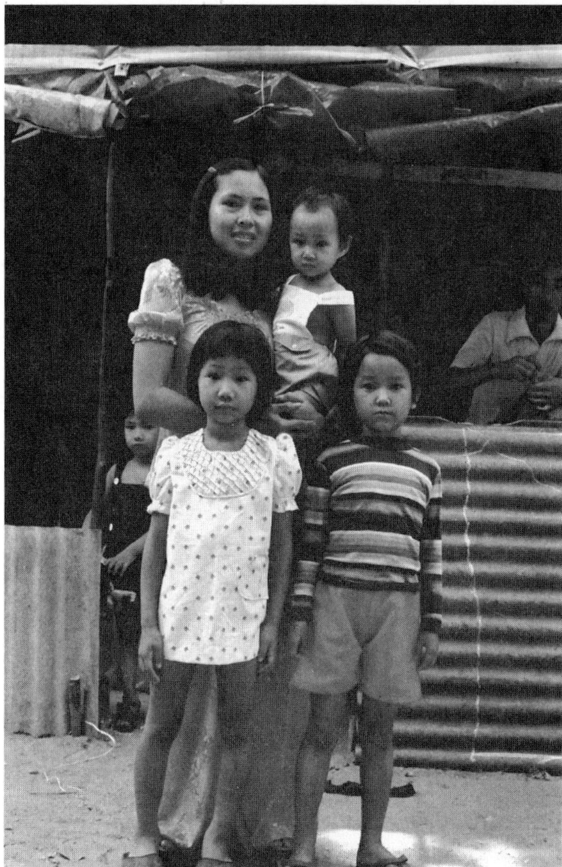

The writer at age 6 or 7 (bottom left in white dress), her little sister (bottom right), and family friends. The photo was taken in 1980 on their last day at the Malaysian refugee camp on Puala Bidong, where they lived for a year before immigrating to Orange County, California.

Another common prefix is *dis-*, which actually can have several meanings. Ha describes the former refugee camp as having been *dismantled* [paragraph 23], meaning "taken apart" or "disassembled." In this case, the prefix *dis-* means "to undo," as you see in the word above, *disassembled,* as well as in words like *disable* or *disentangle.*

Refugee's Journey

K. Oanh Ha

1 The small fishing boat flew over the waves, landing with a thud after each whitecap. A dark mass emerged, then gave way to the scraggly shapes of an island. Puala Bidong.

2 The last time I approached this tiny Malaysian island, I was not yet 6 years old. It was November 1979. My family and 407 other refugees who had escaped

Vietnam were squeezed onto a 125-foot-long refurbished riverboat. We had survived four harrowing pirate attacks and a storm that threw two-story-high waves over the deck of our small boat. Two baby boys had been born on the journey, and my great-uncle, already sick from liver disease, had died.

3 As the island came into view that November day, there was nothing but sound. Shouts of joy, relief and anticipation. Puala Bidong was the site of a refugee camp, our way station to better lives in the West.

4 More than two decades later, I am returning as an American tourist. The only sounds are the roar of the boat and the slap of the water. I am looking for something less certain than the safe haven my parents sought. I am seeking a piece of my personal and family history.

5 Other refugees may understand my search. Unlike some immigrants who voluntarily leave their home countries for better opportunities and never look back, our forced exile is a scar. The scar might lighten, but it never completely disappears. In my family's case, we are not fully who we were before we landed at Bidong. But we are not fully American either.

6 Bidong is the place where our assimilation began, with English classes and vocational training for my parents, as tailors. Now, after a lifetime of embracing my assimilation into American life, I am traveling back in time to find out more about who we were before we were changed.

7 My family had been among the vast middle class in Vietnam. My father was a carpenter. We weren't wealthy or connected enough to leave with the Americans in 1975 when the war ended. Then in 1979, the communist government took away the businesses and personal assets of Chinese families and began expelling them. My paternal grandfather and his family were ethnic Chinese.

8 My extended family decided to flee; there were nearly 30 of us. We were among the 1.6 million Vietnamese who journeyed across the South China Sea between the late 1970s and the late 1980s to reach refugee camps in Southeast Asian countries.

9 We arrived at Bidong at the height of the boat exodus and shared the island—not quite a square mile—with 43,000 other refugees. Once lush, the island had been stripped of much of its vegetation, which was used to build shelters. When it rained, black, smelly mud oozed everywhere. Our outhouse was the rocky cliffs overlooking the sea, making most of the beach below, with its crystal-clear waters and white sand, unusable.

10 The Malaysian Red Cross, along with the U.N. High Commissioner for Refugees, built a school, clinic and library. The United Nations supplied us with basic food rations and medical care, but everything else had to be purchased. My parents worked as tailors to support us in the micro-economy that sprang up; they returned before curfew every night. I took care of my brother and sister. In my few memories of the island, my baby sister, Dung, is riding on my hip.

Selling Jewelry to Buy Shelter

11 My parents don't talk much about Bidong because it was a place of such hardship. It was here that my mother sold her gold wedding necklace. She had saved it once; days earlier, she had skillfully hidden it in my bowl of rice porridge as pirates boarded our boat. At Bidong she had to sell it to buy the wood-and-tarp shack that sheltered our family of five. What moves me most is to realize that my mom was 25 and my dad 27—a few years younger than I am now—when they arrived on the island with three children under the age of 6.

12 We lived there for nearly a year before my family received permission to go to America, sponsored by an uncle who had already resettled in California. We joined him in Orange County in the fall of 1980. We were no longer refugees, and my scattered young memories of that life were replaced by happier ones.

13 The Puala Bidong refugee camp was officially shut down in 1991. The only people who visit it now are former refugees and recreational divers attracted by the coral and sunken boats surrounding the island.

14 My visit this spring was a pilgrimage of sorts. I sometimes feel as if my past is quickly receding from me, overtaken by my hyphenated, Americanized life. Though Vietnamese is my first language, I call upon my Spanish-speaking skills more often. I'm married to a white American and am pregnant with our second child.

15 When I was growing up, all I ever wanted to be was American. I was proud that I had no accent when I spoke English. At school, my friends and I distanced ourselves from the newly arrived Vietnamese we called FOBs—a put-down meaning "fresh off the boat." I rolled my eyes when my parents scolded me for being "too American." My mother taunted me: "You'll always be Vietnamese, with your black hair and brown skin."

16 Perhaps she was right; perhaps that was what I was running away from. When I turned 18, I became a U.S. citizen and legally changed my name to Kyrstin. My parents couldn't pronounce it.

Connecting Grammar to Writing

In paragraph 16, note the use of parallel structure in these two independent clauses connected with a semicolon: "Perhaps she was right; perhaps that was what I was running away from." Repeating the word *perhaps* creates balance, which is also reinforced by the punctuation.

Vietnam Filled Identity Gaps

17 At 20, I revisited Vietnam for the first time since our escape and felt an instant connection. It was partly because my relatives there were so welcoming. It was there that I started my journey back to that part of me that will always be Vietnamese. Over the next few years, I slowly began to recognize the gaps in my identity.

18 The truth is, as Americanized as I am, I don't feel fully American. I'm too Americanized to be Vietnamese. Yet I feel I need to reclaim that part of my heritage, so I can be as comfortable with it as I am with my American self. At 26, I changed my name back to the one my parents gave me: Oanh.

19 Reconnecting with my past took on even more import when I became a mother two years ago. I speak Vietnamese daily now—more than I ever have in

my adult life—because I want my son, Luke, to be able to speak it. Luke and his sister will undoubtedly go through their own identity issues, and I want to be able to hold up my end. How can I explain to them what being Vietnamese is all about if I'm uncertain myself?

20 One piece of that puzzle is on Bidong. I sought the Jefferson reporting fellowship this year from the East-West Center at the University of Hawaii partly because I knew Malaysia was on the travel itinerary.

21 Now, I was here. Puala Bidong.

22 The day was gray, overcast. Once the island came into view, it was apparent it would be nothing like my memories. Nature had reclaimed it, covering the terrain with a dense, green tropical forest. The jetty where my family and thousands of other refugees had first set foot on the island had mostly collapsed. All that remained were concrete blocks and wood pilings jutting from the shallow waters.

23 Most of the settlement had been dismantled and razed when the camp closed. I found the larger buildings, including the clinic and school, still standing, though barely. Roofs had collapsed, but signs advertising tailor shops, hair salons and other businesses were still in place.

24 Inside the Catholic church my family attended, the cross was gone, the light green paint was peeling and faint, and the rows of wooden pews were rotting. Although I seldom attend church anymore, I felt compelled to cross myself.

25 Just outside the church was a reminder of how dangerous our journey had been. On top of a cliff overlooking the sea was a plaque that read: "In memory of 38 refugees who drowned within sight of freedom." They lost their lives on Jan. 3, 1987.

26 I gave up the idea of hiking around the island after just an hour. Frankly, there wasn't a whole lot left to see. I had hoped to witness more physical evidence of the daily life and hardships we encountered on Bidong. It seems that the island had moved on.

27 Still, I'm glad I went back. What was important was the physical journey itself, the retracing of my family's steps. I went back so I could move forward.

28 I didn't tell my parents about my trip to the island until I got back from my fellowship. They were bemused that I had made a special trip to see it. They wanted to look at the photos of my visit there, but didn't reminisce about life in the camp as much as I had hoped. I guess they've moved on with their lives, too.

Straddling Two Cultures

29 At their home, my parents proudly hang a lacquered clock in the shape of Vietnam. And our family altar, with photos of our ancestors, is prominently displayed in the living room. But after years of futilely trying to get us children to speak only Vietnamese at home, my parents now speak to us in a mix of

Vietnamese and English. They love to listen to songs by Lionel Ritchie and Joe Cocker. My mother, Hanh, now often calls herself by a modified, American version of her name: Hannah.

30 There's a single flag propped among my mother's carefully tended garden—Old Glory, flown as a show of support for the troops in Iraq. We feel more like an American family now than we ever did. My brother, Vu, now 26, is a Marine in Iraq, a reservist who was called to active duty at the beginning of the war. He's part of a unit working with refugees who are internally displaced within Iraq.

31 Before I left for my trip, Vu and I exchanged e-mail about what we remembered of our life on Bidong. We remembered that going to the beach was a luxury; my parents were too busy working. The few times we went swimming, Vu and I remembered, we were more focused on the people squatting on the rocks and on trying to avoid what they were sending our way.

32 Now as I headed back toward the boat, I said goodbye to the island for the second, and probably the last time. Then I went snorkeling.

EXERCISES

A. Determining the Main Idea and Writer's Purpose

Choose the best answer.

1. Here are four excerpts from the selection. Which *best* represents the central idea of the selection as a whole?
   a. Other refugees may understand my search. Unlike some immigrants who voluntarily leave their home countries for better opportunities and never look back, our forced exile is a scar. [paragraph 5]
   b. Now, after a lifetime of embracing my assimilation into American life, I am traveling back in time to find out more about who we were before we were changed. [paragraph 6]
   c. My parents don't talk much about Bidong because it was a place of such hardship. [paragraph 11]
   d. Reconnecting with my past took on even more import when I became a mother two years ago. [paragraph 19]
2. With respect to the main idea, the writer's purpose is to
   a. show the hardships Vietnamese immigrants and boat people endured while living in refugee camps and their subsequent emotional scars.
   b. describe the journey immigrants from war-torn countries made to reach freedom.

c. persuade the reader that immigrants should try to reconstruct their families' history by returning to their old countries.

d. retrace her family's history before they became assimilated by revisiting the refugee camp, their way station between Vietnam and the United States.

B. Comprehending Main Ideas

Choose the correct answer.

1. Ha states that her family's immigration experience was different from that of other immigrant families because her family

   a. were wealthy and therefore given special treatment in the refugee camp.

   b. had left their country voluntarily and had no regrets about leaving.

   c. were forced to leave, making their exile more difficult to accept.

   d. found the refugee camp a place of safe haven rather than of turmoil.

2. Ha's family was forced to leave Vietnam because

   a. the communist government confiscated the assets of Vietnamese of Chinese descent and then expelled them.

   b. the American soldiers ordered them to leave the country for their own safety.

   c. they refused to live under a repressive communist regime.

   d. moderately wealthy Vietnamese were considered middle class and therefore were not allowed to share in the workers' paradise.

3. In the refugee camp at Puala Bidong, Ha's mother was forced to sell her gold wedding necklace in order to obtain

   a. sufficient food for her family.

   b. shelter.

   c. passage to the United States.

   d. English lessons for her children.

4. When the writer was growing up, she experienced a "hyphenated American life," meaning that she

   a. was neither Vietnamese nor American.

   b. decided to reject her Vietnamese heritage.

   c. embraced both Vietnamese and American customs.

   d. looked Vietnamese but was really Americanized.

5. When Ha returned to the Malaysian island and the site of the refugee camp, she found
   a. that nature had reclaimed it and that little of the camp was left.
   b. the Malaysian government had carefully restored and preserved the camp.
   c. she recognized every landmark from the year she lived there.
   d. she realized how lucky she was to have escaped her past life.

C. Locating Supporting Details

For each main idea stated here, find details that support it.

1. When K. Oanh Ha was growing up, all she ever wanted to be was American.
   a. ______________________________
   b. ______________________________
   ____

2. Ha's parents straddle two cultures.
   a. ______________________________
   ____
   b. ______________________________
   ____

D. Analyzing Structure and Meaning

Choose the best answer.

1. Read paragraph 5 again. In your own words, write a main idea sentence for this paragraph.

   ____

   ____

2. Which of the following *best* explains why the writer returned to Puala Bidong?
   a. Her parents had told her many stories about their life in the refugee camp, and she wanted to see it for herself.
   b. She went there to write a story for the *Mercury News*.
   c. She wanted to fill in the gaps in her identity by seeing the camp again.
   d. She received a Jefferson scholarship, which included a stay in Malaysia.

3. Look again at paragraphs 22–25, which is an example of writing that
   a. tells a narrative or story.
   b. seeks to convince the reader.
   c. explains or discusses the topic.
   d. uses lots of descriptive details.

E. Understanding Vocabulary

Write the dictionary definition for each underlined word in the phrases below.

1. the scraggly shapes [paragraph 1] ______________________________
2. four harrowing pirate attacks [2]: ______________________________
3. our forced exile is a scar [5] ______________________________
4. our assimilation began [6] ______________________________

   ____
5. began expelling them [7] ______________________________
6. the boat exodus [9] ______________________________
7. a pilgrimage of sorts [14] ______________________________
8. my past is receding [14] ______________________________
9. my mother taunted me [15] ______________________________
10. after years of futilely trying [29] ______________________________

DISCUSSION QUESTIONS

1. Why do you suppose that Ha did not tell her parents in advance that she was taking a trip to the site of the refugee camp at Puala Bidong?
2. In what specific ways did her return to the camp allow her to move on with her life?

EXPLORE THE WEB

K. Oanh Ha has written a series of seven stories about the Vuongs, a Vietnamese family and their experiences living through the fall of Saigon and their subsequent life in the United States. You can access the series at the following address. You will have to register, but the content is free.

www.mercurynews.com/mld/mercurynews/news/special_packages/fall_of_saigon

Being Prey: Surviving a Crocodile Attack

Val Plumwood

Activist, academic writer, and scholar, Val Plumwood is currently Australian Research Council Fellow at the Australian National University. She enjoys a worldwide reputation as a pioneer in environmental philosophy. The incident she describes in this narrative excerpt occurred in February 1985 near the city of Darwin in Kakadu National Park located on the northern coast of Australia. The article was originally published in a different form in *Travelers' Tales* (1999); it was also selected for inclusion in *The Best Science and Nature Writing 2001.*

VOCABULARY ANALYSIS

-ity (Noun Suffix)

Five words in this selection illustrate this common noun suffix. (A *prefix*, you will remember, is a word part that comes at the beginning of a word that often indicates meaning. A *suffix* is a word part added to the end of a root, which makes the root into another part of speech. In other words, suffixes commonly indicate grammatical parts of speech rather than convey meaning.) The noun suffix *–ity* is added to adjectives to form abstract nouns that express a state or condition. In paragraph 10, then, *subjectivity* means "the condition of being subjective," and *timidity* in paragraph 3 means "the state of being timid." The selection also contains the words *integrity*, *eternity*, and *capacities* (the latter is the plural spelling).

Being Prey: Surviving a Crocodile Attack

Val Plumwood

1 In the early wet season, Kakadu's paperbark wetlands are especially stunning, as the water lilies weave white, pink, and blue patterns of dreamlike beauty over the shining thunderclouds reflected in their still waters. Yesterday, the water lilies and the wonderful bird life had enticed me into a joyous afternoon's idyll as I ventured onto the East Alligator Lagoon for the first time in a canoe lent by the

park service. "You can play about on the backwaters," the ranger had said, "but don't go onto the main river channel. The current's too swift, and if you get into trouble, there are the crocodiles. Lots of them along the river!" I followed his advice and glutted myself on the magical beauty and bird life of the lily lagoons, untroubled by crocodiles.

2 Today, I wanted to repeat that experience despite the drizzle beginning to fall as I neared the canoe launch site. I set off on a day trip in search of an Aboriginal rock art site across the lagoon and up a side channel. The drizzle turned to a warm rain within a few hours, and the magic was lost. The birds were invisible, the water lilies were sparser, and the lagoon seemed even a little menacing. I noticed now how low the 14-foot canoe sat in the water, just a few inches of fiberglass between me and the great saurians,[1] close relatives of the ancient dinosaurs. Not long ago, saltwater crocodiles were considered endangered, as virtually all mature animals in Australia's north were shot by commercial hunters. But after a decade and more of protection, they are now the most plentiful of the large animals of Kakadu National Park. I was actively involved in preserving such places, and for me, the crocodile was a symbol of the power and integrity of this place and the incredible richness of its aquatic habitats.

Connecting Grammar to Writing

In paragraph 3, note that each sentence begins with a dependent clause or phrase, each punctuated with a comma. Sentence 1 contains a lengthy prepositional phrase; sentence 2, a dependent adverb clause; sentence 3, a participial phrase.

3 After hours of searching the maze of shallow channels in the swamp, I had not found the clear channel leading to the rock art site, as shown on the ranger's sketch map. When I pulled my canoe over in driving rain to a rock outcrop for a hasty, sodden lunch, I experienced the unfamiliar sensation of being watched. Having never been one for timidity, in philosophy or in life, I decided, rather than return defeated to my sticky trailer, to explore a clear, deep channel closer to the river I had traveled along the previous day.

4 The rain and wind grew more severe, and several times I pulled over to tip water from the canoe. The channel soon developed steep mud banks and snags. Farther on, the channel opened up and was eventually blocked by a large sandy bar. I pushed the canoe toward the bank, looking around carefully before getting out in the shallows and pulling the canoe up. I would be safe from crocodiles in the canoe—I had been told—but swimming and standing or wading at the water's edge were dangerous. Edges are one of the crocodile's favorite food-capturing places. I saw nothing, but the feeling of unease that had been with me all day intensified.

5 The rain eased temporarily, and I crossed a sandbar to see more of this puzzling place. As I crested a gentle dune, I was shocked to glimpse the muddy waters of the East Alligator River gliding silently only 100 yards away. The channel had led me back to the main river. Nothing stirred along the riverbank, but a great tumble of escarpment cliffs up on the other side caught my attention. One especially striking rock formation—a single large rock balanced precariously on a much smaller one—held my gaze. As I looked, my whispering sense of unease turned into a shout of danger. The strange formation put me sharply in mind of two things: of the indigenous Gagadgu owners of Kakadu, whose advice about coming here I had not sought, and of the precariousness of my own life,

of human lives. As a solitary specimen of a major prey species of the saltwater crocodile, I was standing in one of the most dangerous places on earth.

6 I turned back with a feeling of relief. I had not found the rock paintings, I rationalized, but it was too late to look for them. The strange rock formation presented itself instead as a telos[2] of the day, and now I could go, home to trailer comfort.

7 As I pulled the canoe out into the main current, the rain and wind started up again. I had not gone more than five or ten minutes down the channel when, rounding a bend, I saw in midstream what looked like a floating stick—one I did not recall passing on my way up. As the current moved me toward it, the stick developed eyes. A crocodile! It did not look like a large one. I was close to it now but was not especially afraid; an encounter would add interest to the day.

8 Although I was paddling to miss the crocodile, our paths were strangely convergent. I knew it would be close, but I was totally unprepared for the great blow when it struck the canoe. Again it struck, again and again, now from behind, shuddering the flimsy craft. As I paddled furiously, the blows continued. The unheard of was happening; the canoe was under attack! For the first time, it came to me fully that I was prey. I realized I had to get out of the canoe or risk being capsized.

9 The bank now presented a high, steep face of slippery mud. The only obvious avenue of escape was a paperbark tree near the muddy bank wall. I made the split-second decision to leap into its lower branches and climb to safety. I steered to the tree and stood up to jump. At the same instant, the crocodile rushed up alongside the canoe, and its beautiful, flecked golden eyes looked straight into mine. Perhaps I could bluff it, drive it away, as I had read of British tiger hunters doing. I waved my arms and shouted, "Go away!" (We're British here.) The golden eyes glinted with interest. I tensed for the jump and leapt. Before my foot even tripped the first branch, I had a blurred, incredulous vision of great toothed jaws bursting from the water. Then I was seized between the legs in a red-hot pincer grip and whirled into the suffocating wet darkness.

10 Our final thoughts during near-death experiences can tell us much about our frameworks of subjectivity. A framework capable of sustaining action and purpose must, I think, view the world "from the inside," structured to sustain the concept of a continuing, narrative self; we remake the world in that way as our own, investing it with meaning, reconceiving it as sane, survivable, amenable to hope and resolution. The lack of fit between this subject-centered version and reality comes into play in extreme moments. In its final, frantic attempts to protect itself from the knowledge that threatens the narrative framework, the mind can instantaneously fabricate terminal doubt of extravagant proportions: *This is not really happening. This is a nightmare from which I will soon awake.* This desperate delusion split apart as I hit the water. In that flash, I glimpsed the world for the first time "from the outside," as a world no longer my own, an unrecognizable bleak landscape composed of raw necessity, indifferent to my life or death.

11 Few of those who have experienced the crocodile's death roll have lived to describe it. It is, essentially, an experience beyond words of total terror. The crocodile's breathing and heart metabolism are not suited to prolonged struggle, so the roll is an intense burst of power designed to overcome the victim's resistance quickly. The crocodile then holds the feebly struggling prey underwater until it drowns. The roll was a centrifuge of boiling blackness that lasted for an eternity, beyond endurance, but when I seemed all but finished, the rolling suddenly stopped. My feet touched bottom, my head broke the surface, and coughing, I sucked at air, amazed to be alive. The crocodile still had me in its pincer grip between the legs. I had just begun to weep for the prospects of my mangled body when the crocodile pitched me suddenly into a second death roll.

12 When the whirling terror stopped again I surfaced again, still in the crocodile's grip next to a stout branch of a large sandpaper fig growing in the water. I grabbed the branch, vowing to let the crocodile tear me apart rather than throw me again into that spinning, suffocating hell. For the first time I realized that the crocodile was growling, as if angry. I braced myself for another roll, but then its jaws simply relaxed; I was free. I gripped the branch and pulled away, dodging around the back of the fig tree to avoid the forbidding mud bank, and tried once more to climb into the paperbark tree.

13 As in the repetition of a nightmare, the horror of my first escape attempt was repeated. As I leapt into the same branch, the crocodile seized me again, this time around the upper left thigh, and pulled me under. Like the others, the third death roll stopped, and we came up next to the sandpaper fig branch again. I was growing weaker, but I could see the crocodile taking a long time to kill me this way. I prayed for a quick finish and decided to provoke it by attacking it with my hands. Feeling back behind me along the head, I encountered two lumps. Thinking I had the eye sockets, I jabbed my thumbs into them with all my might. They slid into warm, unresisting holes (which may have been the ears, or perhaps the nostrils), and the crocodile did not so much as flinch. In despair, I grabbed the branch again. And once again, after a time, I felt the crocodile jaws relax, and I pulled free.

14 I knew I had to break the pattern; up the slippery mud bank was the only way. I scrabbled for a grip, then slid back toward the waiting jaws. The second time I almost made it before again sliding back, braking my slide by grabbing a tuft of grass. I hung there, exhausted. *I can't make it*, I thought. *It'll just have to come and get me*. The grass tuft began to give away. Flailing to keep from sliding farther, I jammed my fingers into the mud. This was the clue I needed to survive. I used this method and the last of my strength to climb up the bank and reach the top. I was alive!

15 Escaping the crocodile was not the end of my struggle to survive. I was alone, severely injured, and many miles from help. During the attack, the pain from the injuries had not fully registered. As I took my first urgent steps, I knew

something was wrong with my leg. I did not wait to inspect the damage but took off away from the crocodile toward the ranger station.

16 After putting more distance between me and the crocodile, I stopped and realized for the first time how serious my wounds were. I did not remove my clothing to see the damage to the groin area inflicted by the first hold. What I could see was bad enough. The left thigh hung open, with bits of fat, tendon, and muscle showing, and a sick, numb feeling suffused my entire body. I tore up some clothing to bind the wounds and made a tourniquet for my bleeding thigh, then staggered on, still elated from my escape. I went some distance before realizing with a sinking heart that I had crossed the swamp above the ranger station in the canoe and could not get back without it.

17 I would have to hope for a search party, but I could maximize my chances by moving downstream toward the swamp edge, almost two miles away. I struggled on, through driving rain, shouting for mercy from the sky, apologizing to the angry crocodile, repenting to this place for my intrusion. I came to a flooded tributary and made a long upstream detour looking for a safe place to cross.

18 My considerable bush[3] experience served me well, keeping me on course (navigating was second nature). After several hours, I began to black out and had to crawl the final distance to the swamp's edge. I lay there in the gathering dusk to await what would come. I did not expect a search party until the following day, and I doubted I could last the night.

19 The rain and wind stopped with the onset of darkness, and it grew perfectly still. Dingoes[4] howled, and clouds of mosquitoes whined around my body. I hoped to pass out soon, but consciousness persisted. There were loud swirling noises in the water, and I knew I was easy meat for another crocodile. After what seemed like a long time, I heard the distant sound of a motor and saw a light moving on the swamp's far side. Thinking it was a boat, I rose up on my elbow and called for help. I thought I heard a faint reply, but then the motor grew fainter and the lights went away. I was as devastated as any castaway who signals desperately to a passing ship and is not seen.

20 The lights had not come from a boat. Passing my trailer, the ranger noticed there was no light inside it. He had driven to the canoe launch site on a motorized trike and realized I had not returned. He had heard my faint call for help, and after some time, a rescue craft appeared. As I began my 13-hour journey to Darwin Hospital, my rescuers discussed going upriver the next day to shoot a crocodile. I spoke strongly against this plan: I was the intruder, and no good purpose could be served by random revenge. The water around the spot where I had been lying was full of crocodiles. That spot was under six feet of water the next morning, flooded by the rains signaling the start of the wet season.

21 In the end I was found in time and survived against many odds. A similar combination of good fortune and human care enabled me to overcome a leg infection that threatened amputation or worse. I probably have Paddy Pallin's

incredibly tough walking shorts to thank for the fact that the groin injuries were not as severe as the leg injuries. I am very lucky that I can still walk well and have lost few of my previous capacities. The wonder of being alive after being held—quite literally—in the jaws of death has never entirely left me. For the first year, the experience of existence as an unexpected blessing cast a golden glow over my life, despite the injuries and the pain. The glow has slowly faded, but some of that new gratitude for life endures, even if I remain unsure whom I should thank. The gift of gratitude came from the searing flash of near-death knowledge, a glimpse "from the outside" of the alien, incomprehensible world in which the narrative of self has ended.

22 . . . [T]he story of the crocodile encounter now has, for me, a significance quite the opposite of that conveyed in the master/monster narrative. It is a humbling and cautionary tale about our relationship with the earth, about the need to acknowledge our own animality and ecological vulnerability. I learned many lessons from the event, one of which is to know better when to turn back and to be more open to the sorts of warnings I had ignored that day. As on the day itself, so even more to me now, the telos of these events lies in the strange rock formation, which symbolized so well the lessons about the vulnerability of humankind I had to learn, lessons largely lost to the technological culture that now dominates the earth. In my work as a philosopher, I see more and more reason to stress our failure to perceive this vulnerability, to realize how misguided we are to view ourselves as masters of a tamed and malleable nature. . . .

---

[1]*Saurians* refers to Sauria, the suborder of reptiles including lizards, crocodiles, and alligators. The Greek root is *sauros* or "lizard." (Ed.)

[2]*Telos* is a word of Greek origin meaning "the end result of a goal-oriented process." The word also appears above.

[3]"Bush" here refers to the Australian bush, the vast area of the country that is not settled. (Ed.)

[4]Dingoes are wild dogs native to Australia. (Ed.)

EXERCISES

A. Determining the Main Idea and Writer's Purpose

Choose the best answer.

1. The main idea of the selection is that
   a. surviving a near-death crocodile attack gave the writer a glimpse into an incomprehensible part of nature and of human life.
   b. crocodiles are fiercely dangerous creatures that prey on humans if they venture into their waters.

c. the writer's experience in the Australian bush was useful when she encountered a crocodile.
d. in confronting her crocodile attacker, Plumwood learned that human endurance and the will to triumph can conquer every peril in nature.

2. With respect to the main idea, the writer's purpose is to
   a. describe an exotic location in a faraway place.
   b. tell a frightening story that gave the writer a new perspective on life.
   c. present an account of the writer's experience as a naturalist.
   d. observe and describe a powerful creature in its own environment.

B. Comprehending Main Ideas

Choose the correct answer.

1. Before she set off in a canoe to explore, the park ranger at Kakadu National Park told the writer not to
   a. venture into the main river channel.
   b. stay out in the water too long.
   c. climb onto the channel's muddy banks.
   d. be afraid of the park's crocodiles.
2. While the writer crossed the sandbar to see the place from a closer view, she initially felt both
   a. wonder and delight.
   b. unease and fear of danger.
   c. anxiety and panic.
   d. curiosity and a desire to see more.
3. Plumwood writes that, when faced with danger, it is human nature to
   a. alter reality by doubting that the danger is real.
   b. feel terrified by the reality of the situation.
   c. feel intimately connected to the reality of the situation.
   d. adopt a purely objective point of view
4. After the crocodile attacked the first two times, the writer was able to escape the crocodile's grasp by
   a. scrambling back into her canoe and paddling furiously.
   b. leaping into the branches of a nearby tree growing in the water.
   c. hitting the crocodile on the head with her canoe paddle.
   d. climbing to safety on the muddy bank away from the water.

5. As a result of her near-death experience, Plumwood
   a. decided to investigate potential dangers before setting off on such an adventure again.
   b. promised to seek the advice of experts before starting off on a dangerous journey.
   c. felt gratitude for the gift of life.
   d. sustained lifelong crippling serious injuries to her leg.

C. Sequencing

The sentences in this paragraph from the selection have been scrambled. Read the sentences and choose the sequence that puts them back into logical order. Do not refer to the original selection.

1. I knew I had to break the pattern; up the slippery mud bank was the only way. **2.** I scrabbled for a grip, then slid back toward the waiting jaws. **3.** The second time I almost made it before sliding back, breaking my slide by grabbing a tuft of grass. **4.** I hung there, exhausted. **5.** *I can't make it, I thought.*

a. 2, 1, 3, 5, 4
b. 1, 2, 4, 5, 3
c. 3, 1, 4, 5, 2
d. Correct as written.

D. Identifying Supporting Details

Place an **X** in the space for each sentence from the selection that *directly* supports this main idea: "Few of those who have experienced the crocodile's death roll have lived to describe it."

1. _____ It is, essentially, an experience beyond words of total terror.
2. _____ The crocodile's breathing and heart metabolism aren't suited to prolonged struggle.
3. _____ The roll is an intense burst of power designed to overcome the victim's resistance quickly.
4. _____ The crocodile then holds the feebly struggling prey underwater until it drowns.
5. _____ I prayed for a quick finish and decided to provoke it by attacking it with my hands.
6. _____ After putting more distance between me and the crocodile, I stopped and realized for the first time how serious my wounds were.

READING

E. Interpreting Meaning

Choose the best answer or write your answers to these questions in your own words.

1. The first part of the essay establishes a mood that strongly contrasts with the mood after the attack. What contrasts in emotion are suggested?

   wonder and optimism and fear and unease

2. Paragraph 10 is quite difficult. Study it carefully and also read the last sentence of the selection, which repeats the same idea. To help you, first, what do the words *inside* and *outside* refer to in the phrases "from the inside" and "from the outside"?

   "From the inside" refers to inside the human mind; "from the outside" refers to anything outside the human mind, in this case, a creature from a place so unfamiliar to humans as to be both alien and incomprehensible.

   Then write a sentence summarizing Plumwood's main point in the paragraph.

   When a human being has a near-death experience, the natural tendency is to "remake" the situation into something rational and solvable; in other words, we deny reality and pretend that the terrible thing isn't really happening.

a 3. A good title for paragraph 11 would be
   a. "Experiencing Total Terror."
   b. "Why Crocodiles Kill."
   c. "An Unbelievable Experience."
   d. "Crocodile Behavior."

4. Look through paragraph 11 and 12 again. List three phrases that convey the intense violence of the crocodile's attack.

   "an experience beyond words of total terror"; "the roll is an intense burst of power"; "holds the feebly struggling prey underwater until it drowns"; "the roll was a centrifuge of boiling blackness"; "the whirling terror" (Any 3)

5. What action probably saved Plumwood from dying?

   sticking her fingers into the mud

F. Understanding Vocabulary

Look through the paragraphs listed below and find a word that matches each definition. Refer to a dictionary if necessary. An example has been done for you.

EXAMPLE: threatening, frightening [paragraph 2] menacing

1. the state of being whole and unimpaired [2] ____________
2. natural environments, surroundings [2] ____________
3. an intricate network, a labyrinth [3] ____________
4. soggy, damp [3] ____________
5. referring to native inhabitants [5] ____________
6. not inclined to believe [9] ____________
7. agreeable, open to [10] ____________
8. make up, invent [10] ____________
9. gloomy, offering little hope [10] ____________
10. overwhelmed, nearly destroyed [19] ____________

DISCUSSION QUESTIONS

1. What are some of the devices that the writer uses to maintain interest and to create suspense and terror in the reader?
2. How do you respond to Plumwood as a person? Do you consider her a heroine, a foolish risk taker, or what? Support your opinion by making specific references to her behavior.

EXPLORE THE WEB

Photographs of Kakadu National Park, along with information about the park, are available at these three sites:

www.deh.gov.au/parks/kakadu

en.wikipedia.org/wiki/Kakadu_National_Park

gorp.away.com/gorp/location/australi/park/no_kakad.html

About Personal Experience

This section explains how to write two types of papers based on personal experience. The first type is a narrative essay in which you relate an experience of your own; the second type is an expository essay in which you respond to, analyze, and evaluate an experience described by one of the writers in the preceding readings.

ACADEMIC WRITING

Although writing about personal experience, your own or that of others, may seem to be a skill useful mainly for your English courses, in fact composing and evaluating narratives (stories) about personal experience may be part of academic assignments as well as of professional writing tasks.

Typical Academic Assignments Requiring Writing about Personal Experience

- Writing a journal or log detailing your experiences during an internship or service learning project
- Writing an evaluation of a collaborative project
- Writing an application for an internship
- Writing a review or response to a biography or autobiography of a noted person in your field of study

WRITING ABOUT A PERSONAL EXPERIENCE OF YOUR OWN

At the start of a composition course, many instructors ask their students to write a personal experience essay. This assignment allows students to become familiar with writing college papers, and the subject matter—oneself—is available to everyone. Most people like to talk about themselves and have their experiences validated by a thoughtful reader. Writing about a personal experience gives you the opportunity to record a significant event in your life and to fix it permanently on paper in a coherent fashion, just as a photograph indelibly recalls and fixes a memory in our minds. This permanent fixing—whether in an essay or in a photograph—produces a more coherent version than the random impressions that characterize the typically scattered workings of the human mind.

Further, writing a paper about a past experience affords you the luxury of retrospection—the ability to assess the event with the benefit of time and distance. Often it takes many years for us to realize the full impact of something on our lives. Since our perspective may change as we mature, we see reality more clearly—or at least differently—in hindsight than we do while we are in the thick of things.

To prepare a personal experience essay, you will first need to choose an event or experience that had particular significance for you or that had a major impact on you—whether positive or negative. If you draw a blank during the invention step of the writing process, look through the readings in Part 2 for inspiration.

For example, in "The Conveyor Belt Ladies," Rose Castillo Guilbault describes her first experience in the world of work, sorting tomatoes with Mexican immigrants. Initially resentful at not doing more dignified work, like working in a clothing store or babysitting, Guilbault ends up getting an education about life, endurance, hardship, and sacrifice from the uneducated women she works with. Education is not just book learning; it can come from unexpected sources. Perhaps you had a similar experience with your first job, learning something about the world in a place where you least expected it.

DEVELOPING THE ESSAY WITH DETAILS: SHOW, DON'T TELL

Once you have chosen your topic, you can begin to take notes and to brainstorm. Although a personal experience does not always need a formal thesis statement, your essay must have a central idea around which the details are organized. Recall that Kristie Helms's essay about her Tennessee childhood summers stated the thesis explicitly: "We shaped our days the way we chose, far from the prying eyes of adults." On the other hand, David Sedaris's essay, "Our Perfect Summer," which you will read in Part 3, only hints at the thesis—the family's initial excitement about the prospect of buying a beach cottage ends when Sedaris and his siblings realize that his father's reneging was just another of many failed and empty promises.

To make a narrative essay interesting for your reader, you will need lots of specific details to flesh out your central point. An old axiom about writing is worth repeating: *Show, don't tell.* This means that the writer must select details to reinforce the point and to show the reader exactly what the writer means. Not providing details or leaving vague or general statements undeveloped means that readers are forced to invent their own details. This omission is the mark of a lazy writer. To illustrate, Kristie Helms embeds small but telling details in "Girls of Summer." Instead of writing, "We made easy things for lunch," she writes, "We became masters of the Kraft macaroni and cheese lunch." This detail adds only a couple of words but also gives the reader a specific visual image of the familiar blue box.

Here is what happens when a writer does not supply specific details. For example, what if David Sedaris had written this sentence in "Our Perfect Summer"?

> Having a beach house would change the way I behaved at school.

A sentence like this would not give the reader any particular idea of what owning a beach cottage meant or how it changed his life. Instead, he incorporates details relevant to his life and thereby makes this passage much more incisive and revealing.

> A waitress passed the table and, without saying please, I demanded another Coke. She went to fetch it and I settled back in my chair, drunk with the power of a second home. When school began my classmates would court me, hoping I might invite them for a weekend, and I would make a game of pitting them against one another. This was what a person did when people liked him for all the wrong reasons, and I would grow to be very good at it.

Look at how much Sedaris suggests here: His parents are so wrapped up in their dream of buying a beach cottage that Sedaris is allowed to get away with demanding a second Coke, nor is he reprimanded for forgetting to say "please." His admission that he would pit one friend against another, courting favor among rivals who hoped to finagle an invitation to spend a weekend, rings true for a 12-year-old boy unsure of his social standing. The main idea of the passage—being "drunk with power"—establishes the dominant impression that having a beach house will change him and everything about him. All of these details make the passage much more appealing to read, and your essays will be similarly appealing if you incorporate them into your own writing.

ANALYZING PERSONAL EXPERIENCE IN A READING

If your instructor assigns you to write an essay analyzing one of the personal experience essays you have read, you will need to choose *what is to you* the single most important aspect of that selection and then comment on it and evaluate it. If you wish to use quotations to support your ideas (or if your instructor requires them), refer to the section "Using Quotations" in Part 1. Also you might want to look ahead to the introduction to Part 5 and read the section "Writing an Analysis and a Synthesis Essay." During your brainstorming, you can draw upon these questions for inspiration:

- What experience is described?
- How does the writer describe it? What are some important details?
- What is the effect of the experience on the writer?
- Of what larger significance is the experience?

TOPICS FOR WRITING A PERSONAL EXPERIENCE ESSAY

1. Consider again Kristie Helms's essay, "Girls of Summer," in which she describes her summers free from parental supervision. Write a short essay in which you describe a typical summer during your childhood or adolescence, using pertinent, specific details.
2. Does a child whom you know today—perhaps a niece, a nephew, or a sibling—spend summers in the same ways you did? How are they similar? How are they different? Write about your observations of a child, or perhaps of several children that you know, and the way they use their leisure time in comparison to your own experience.
3. Frank Huyler's article, "Sugar," describes a near-tragedy that he was able to ward off at the last minute by asking a lucky question. Describe a near-tragedy that you experienced or witnessed that was narrowly averted. Explain the situation, using specific details; then explain how an inspired decision stopped something terrible from occurring.
4. Describe an experience where you learned something about the world from an unexpected source, or write a narrative essay in which you show how a firsthand experience taught you something about the world and changed your thinking.
5. K. Oanh Ha's journey to Puala Bidong, the refugee camp where she lived before immigrating to the United States, allowed her to fill in the gaps in her identity. Have you made a similar journey into your past? Write a short essay describing the trip, its purpose, and your findings.
6. If your family emigrated from another country, interview a family member about his or her experiences. Focus in particular on the difficulties the person encountered adjusting to the country, having to straddle two cultures as a hyphenated American.
7. Thomas Wolfe, the American novelist, wrote a famous book called *You Can't Go Home Again*. Does the concept suggested in this title ring true for you, or not? Have you ever returned to a favorite locale, one that

figured importantly in your life? Write a short essay describing such a trip. Include details that contrast the nostalgic memory of the past with the reality of the present.

8. Val Plumwood faced a thoroughly terrifying enemy in the crocodile she encountered. Write a short narrative in which you describe an experience where you felt, as Plumwood did, "total terror." It does not have to be an incident as harrowing as a crocodile attack, but everyone has felt intense fear at one time or another—perhaps from a playground bully, a sadistic teacher, or a malicious neighbor.

TOPICS RELATED TO THE READINGS

1. Choose one of the selections in Part 2 that particularly appeals to you. Using the questions listed before the topics as a guide, discuss the experience described in the context in which it occurred and examine its impact on the writer's life.
2. Kristie Helms describes herself as a member of Generation X. Do some research on the World Wide Web about Generation X—who they are, how they are characterized, and so forth. Then write a short essay in which you present your findings. How do the experiences Helms describes relate to your findings?
3. What qualities and characteristics make Frank Huyler an effective emergency room physician? Write a short essay in response, using details from the situation he describes to support your points.
4. Examine the relationship between Rose Castillo Guilbault and her conveyor belt coworkers. What did these women represent for her? What did she represent for them? Were there mutual benefits in their relationship, or was the benefit only one-sided? And if so, for which side?
5. If your family immigrated from another culture, contrast your family's experience with that of K. Oanh Ha in "Refugee's Journey." Before undertaking this assignment, you should read the section on writing comparison and contrast essays in Part 6.
6. Conflict is at the core of K. Oanh Ha's essay. Read the essay again carefully, making a note of the various examples of cultural and personal conflict. Then write a short essay summarizing your findings.
7. In a good unabridged dictionary, look up the word *hubris*, a word from Greek. To what extent do Val Plumwood's actions in "Being Prey" suggest hubris? Write a short essay examining her behavior in light of this concept.

PART THREE

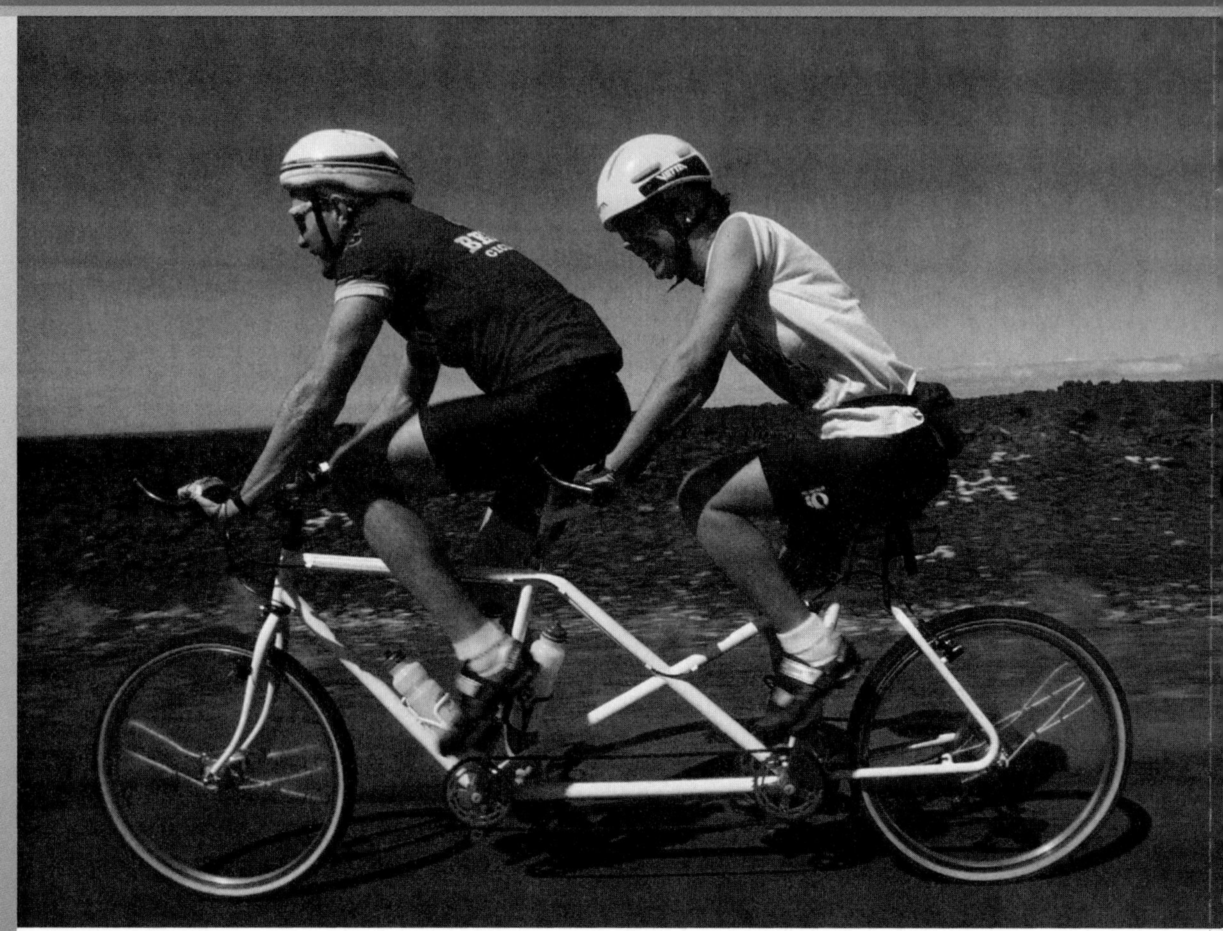

READING

WRITING

3

In Part 3 we turn to improving your vocabulary. Not only will an improved vocabulary enhance your comprehension and enjoyment of your reading assignments, but you can also begin to incorporate new words in your own essays, thereby ensuring a more mature writing style. The first section presents some useful techniques for acquiring new words, as well as suggestions for using context clues to determine the meanings of new words and for using print and online dictionaries.

One primary goal of *In Tandem* is to help college students learn how to write analytical essays, but instead of beginning with the complexities involved with this type of essay, we begin with a more accessible type of analysis—the profile. Accordingly, the first several readings in Part 3 represent profiles that show individuals enmeshed in a particular set of circumstances: While on an airplane trip, Lori Hope sees a man of Middle Eastern descent acting suspiciously and agonizes about what course she should take. Susan Orlean profiles 10-year-old Colin Duffy, revealing his quirky individuality. David Sedaris writes with both humor and poignancy about his family's improbable plan to buy a summer cottage; his profile reveals much about the dysfunctional dynamics of his family. A profile can also have a place as its subject. In the last selection, Curtis Wilkie writes a profile of his adopted city, New Orleans. Also in this section are three photographs reprinted for you to analyze. Included with the exercise material following each reading is a dictionary exercise giving you practice and reinforcement in the skills discussed in the introductory section.

The third section of Part 3 shows you how to write your own profile. The suggested topics will give you opportunity to analyze a person's personal attributes or perhaps the attributes of a particular community that you are familiar with, as Wilkie does with New Orleans.

Acquiring New Vocabulary

When students in my reading and composition classes complain that they often have difficulty concentrating when they read, we discuss the problem at length. While poor concentration may be the result of many factors—trying to balance classes and work, personal problems, lack of sleep, financial worries—the problem may also lie with lack of vocabulary. Reading is tedious if there are too many unfamiliar words on the page, making the reader lose focus and become discouraged. Because a deficient vocabulary is a major obstacle to good reading comprehension, learning more vocabulary words is a crucial step to helping you become a better reader. After all, if you do not know what key words on the page mean, you may not understand very well what a writer is saying.

As you embark on this most necessary of skills, keep in mind that acquiring a solid reading vocabulary is a lifelong proposition. One goal you should have in this course is to acquire as many college-level vocabulary words as you can as you read each selection. Another goal after the course ends is to continue to acquire words from your reading assignments and from your everyday reading.

The best way to improve your vocabulary is to read a lot. Unfortunately, there is no shortcut or substitute for this method. The idea is simple: The more you read, the more new words you are exposed to. Memorizing long lists of words in isolation or working through vocabulary self-improvement books may fool you into thinking you are learning new words, but their meanings won't stick, and such activities deprive you of encountering words in real writing.

This textbook will help you embark on a systematic vocabulary acquisition program. To this end, as you have already seen in Part 2, each selection begins with a brief section called "Vocabulary Analysis," where you will learn common prefixes, suffixes, and roots—the component parts of many words, especially those derived from Latin and Greek—and where you will learn how to break words down into their meaningful parts. Further, each selection ends with one vocabulary exercise to test your mastery of significant words from the reading. Lastly, this introductory section explores some helpful techniques for you to implement that will give you immediate and long-term results, including these topics:

- Six Techniques for Acquiring Words
- Using Context Clues
- Using the Dictionary Effectively

■ SIX TECHNIQUES FOR ACQUIRING WORDS

1. ***Use vocabulary note cards.***

   Writing new vocabulary words on 3″ × 5″ index cards is an excellent way to help you remember them. The cards' compact size makes them portable, and they are easy to stow in a backpack, pocket, or purse. You can quickly review new words while you are waiting at the bus stop or for class to begin. To prepare your cards, follow these steps: On one side, write the word (underline it for emphasis), the context in which it occurred (meaning of the original sentence), the part of speech, and if necessary, its pronunciation. On the other side, write the definition and perhaps the etymology. Study this example from the Practice Essay by Lori Hope, "Did I Save Lives or Engage in Racial Profiling?"

Front side of card—word in original context, part of speech, and pronunciation

> *I may have gotten an innocent man jettisoned from the plane*
>
> *jĕt´ĭ-sən, jĕt´ĭ-zən*   *verb*

Reverse side of card—the major definitions, language word derived from, and its meaning

> *(1) To cast overboard or off;*
>
> *(2) (Informal.) To discard (something) as unwanted or burdensome (to jettison a plan)*
>
> *Latin, from iectare, to throw*

Notice that on the reverse side of the card I included both dictionary definitions and underlined the appropriate one according to the way the word was used in the original sentence. (This is called the word's context.) If your time is limited, then just record the word on one side (but be sure to include the context) and the pertinent definition on the reverse.

Which words should you write down? You should not overwhelm yourself with dozens of unfamiliar words, so I suggest at first that you note those words that you have seen before in your reading but that you cannot readily define. They are not completely unfamiliar, and they are probably common enough in adult prose to make them a worthwhile addition to your vocabulary. As your stock of new vocabulary words grows, you can then turn to recording unfamiliar words. Keep in mind, too, that even the best reader often encounters a word he or she doesn't know and has to look it up.

2. ***Use the three-dot method.***

   Another technique to help you learn words is the *three-dot method.* It works like this: When you look up a word in the dictionary, make a small dot in pencil next to the entry word. The second time you look it up, make another dot. The third time you look the word up, add a third dot, and this time, learn it! Any word that crops up three times in your reading is an important word that belongs in your active reading vocabulary.

3. ***Develop an interest in etymology.***

   Etymology refers to the study of word origins, their meanings and the languages from which they derive. There are often interesting stories behind the origins of words, and paying attention to these origins can help you remember new words. The etymology of words can be found in any good unabridged dictionary, usually at the end of all the definitions enclosed in brackets. Here are three examples of words with unusual etymologies from two reading selections in Part 3:

   - In the essay by Susan Orlean, "The American Man, Age Ten," she describes the way her 10-year-old subject, Colin Duffy walks: "a new way of walking that has a little macho hitch and swagger." The adjective *macho* derives from the Spanish noun *machismo,* which describes a strong or exaggerated sense of masculinity. The original Spanish word in turn derives from the Latin word for male, *masculus.*[1]
   - In describing the way he and his mother imitated a woman's remark that they had overheard in a store, David Sedaris writes that their voices sounded "pinched and snobbish." This word, like its variant forms—*snob, snobbery,* and *snobbishness*—derives from early British slang. In England, the word *snob* used to refer to a shoemaker or cobbler, and since a shoemaker was considered to be a member of the working class, the word eventually was used to describe a lower-class person who strives to appear more refined or higher class than he or she really is. In a strange linguistic twist, today the word *snob* refers to a person who thinks he or she is superior to others.
   - One last example. In Curtis Wilkie's profile of his hometown, New Orleans, he describes the relative lack of racial discrimination in New Orleans, saying that one comes upon it [discrimination] in "the unlikeliest of places, by penetrating the depths of the Bible Belt, running the gantlet of Klan territory…" Also spelled *gauntlet,* this

[1]All etymologies referred to here are from *The American Heritage Dictionary of the English Language,* 4th ed.

word, of Swedish origin, derives from a form of medieval torture or punishment in which a person was forced to run between two lines of people armed with sticks or other weapons who beat him as he passed through. In this context, Wilkie is alluding to the danger to African Americans that the Ku Klux Klan posed.

4. ***Learn key Latin and Greek word parts.***

   Something like 60 percent of English words come from Latin and French and another 15 percent derive from Greek, often through Latin, as well. The readings in Part 3 contain several words from Latin, among them these two:

   - David Sedaris in an amusing but sad profile of his family, "Our Perfect Summer," writes of the "rejuvenating power of real estate." This word derived from Latin can be broken down like this:
     - re- [again] + juvenate [young].

     Re- is a common prefix attached to dozens of English words (*refurbish, reinvent, recapture,* and *revamp,* to cite a few). The Latin root *iuvenus* ("young") is seen in the related word *juvenile.*
   - In paragraph 52 Sedaris describes the role his father plays like this: "an actor auditioning for the role of a benevolent millionaire." This word combines the Latin prefix *bene-*, meaning "well," and *volens*, the Latin root meaning "to wish." A *benevolent* person, then, is kindly and generous. You can see the prefix in these words: *benefactor* (one who helps another); *benediction* (a blessing, or literally "good sayings"); and *benefit* (an advantage or something that promotes well-being).

   An extensive list of important Latin and Greek prefixes, roots, and suffixes is available on the website that accompanies this text. Go to www.mhhe.com/spearstandem1, and click on the cover of this book. From there, click on "Student Center" and then on "Word Parts." Learning one or two of these word parts every day will serve you well in your vocabulary acquisition program.

5. ***Consider word families.***

   Thinking of a word as part of a cluster of related words will help expand your word recognition when you read. For example, consider the word *potential* as Lori Hope uses it in the Practice Essay. In paragraph 7 she refers to her son's *potential* as she weighs the decision of whether or not to report a suspicious passenger on their flight. *Potential* means having the capability of doing something that is not yet realized. It derives from the Latin root *potens*, meaning "power." This same root is at the heart of several related words, among them *potency* (the quality of being powerful); *potentate* (a monarch or other powerful person); *potentiate* (to make powerful); and *impotent* (lacking physical strength or the ability to perform sexually).

6. ***Subscribe to a word-of-the-day website.***

   Word-of-the-day websites offer a painless way to learn new words. Most of them offer the same features: a vocabulary word followed by pronunciation symbols, a definition, a sentence or two using the word, and usually the word's etymology. You can visit a site each day for free, or more conveniently, some offer subscriptions so that you can receive the word of the day via e-mail. Here are three word-of-the-day sites to check out, including some recent sample words so that you can see which might be most appropriate for your level. (Note that by the time you read this text, one or more of these sites may have moved or expired. If you are unable to locate a particular site, do a search on your favorite search engine to get updated addresses.)

Word-of-the-Day Websites

Dictionary.com Word of the Day (subscription is $3 per month)

dictionary.reference.com/wordoftheday

vicissitudes, garrulous, acumen, introspection

Yahoo! Education (no subscription available)

education.yahoo.com/college/wotd

abbreviate, nurture, derivative, collaborate

Merriam-Webster's Word of the Day (free subscription)

www.m-w.com

harbinger, laissez-faire, reprobate, microburst

USING CONTEXT CLUES

The word *context* refers to the circumstances or setting, more specifically, to the words and phrases that surround a particular word and that *may* help you figure out its meaning. Although the method is not perfect or foolproof, context clues can yield a meaning acceptable enough so that you do not have to look up every unfamiliar word in the dictionary. Consider all the words you have learned since you were a baby. While growing up, you came across new words all the time, and eventually—even without turning to the dictionary—you figured out their meanings because of the several contexts in which you have encountered them. You learned words by absorption, by osmosis. No one is born with a vocabulary!

This practice of absorbing new words by exposure and by reading, however, has one major drawback: It takes years to accomplish. And since time is of the essence, you need to develop some shortcuts. When you encounter a new word, first try to break it down into its component parts, as techniques 4 and 5 illustrated above. Then look for *context clues*, which are explained here in some detail. Of course, if structural analysis or context clues don't produce an adequate definition and if you think that an accurate definition is crucial to your understanding of the passage, you'll have to look it up.

To get familiar with the way these clues work, here are three types of clues illustrated with short excerpts from some of the readings in Part 3. Study these excerpts carefully. The context clue for each italicized word is highlighted.

Synonyms

A *synonym* is a word that is close in meaning to the word in question. This is the easiest type of context clue to recognize. For example, Susan Orlean's profile of 10-year-old Colin Duffy includes a paragraph about his awareness of racial differences:

> In his opinion, the most popular boy in his class is Christian, who happens to be black, and Colin's favorite television character is Steve Urkel on *Family Matters*, who is black, too, but otherwise he seems uninterested in or *oblivious* to race.

Although "uninterested in" is not an exact synonym for *oblivious*, ("unaware of" or "unmindful of"), the meanings are similar enough to give you an accurate understanding without turning to the dictionary. You will notice that the conjunction "or" in the above example indicates a synonym.

Examples or a Series of Details

Another type of context clue is an *example*—a particular instance of something more general—or perhaps a cluster of details in a sentence or paragraph that may reveal the meaning of an unfamiliar word. In the article, "Did I Save Lives or Engage in Racial Profiling?" Lori Hope describes an incident when she saw a young man of Middle Eastern descent acting suspiciously on a flight she and her teenage son were on. She faces a terrible dilemma: Should she report him to the crew or not? She writes,

> And I wondered, "What if he goes to the bathroom to light his bomb?" Then I looked at my son—I thought of his *potential*, his brilliance as a musician and mathematician.

Since her son is only 16 years old, he couldn't be a professional musician or a renowned mathematician, but he did have the promise to become one or the other. As noted earlier, the meaning of *potential* is revealed by the two examples that follow it, suggesting "promise" or "capability that is not yet realized."

Situation

The *situation* or the circumstances in which a word is used may give you a hint as to its meaning. Here are the last two sentences of a paragraph in which Curtis Wilkie describes the way people in New Orleans speak:

> The people of the white working class are affectionately known as "Yats," as in the expression, "Where y'at?" And the black citizens, who constitute the city's majority, speak in a *patois* that would be unrecognizable upriver in Mississippi.

There is no need to turn to the dictionary, even if you have never encountered the word *patois*. It clearly refers to a manner of speaking, in this case a regional dialect.

Consider one final example. Susan Orlean's profile of Colin Duffy includes a discussion of the jobs he and his classmates are assigned in their classroom; among them are feeding the birds, putting the chairs on the tables, washing the chalkboard, and recycling. For some reason, recycling was the most popular job, but, as Orlean writes:

> Colin ended up with the job of taking down the chairs each morning. He accepted the task with a sort of *resignation*—this was going to be just a job rather than a mission.

Colin is clearly disappointed, but he accepts the assignment as just another job. *Resignation*, then, means accepting the necessity of doing what one cannot escape.

USING THE DICTIONARY EFFECTIVELY

When context clues and your knowledge of word parts are not enough to give you a sufficient definition, you will need to turn to the dictionary. This section introduces you to specific features of standard college dictionaries. You should study this material closely and refer to it often until you have mastered it. These suggestions show you how best to use this wonderful resource for good results.

First, it is imperative that you have a good, up-to-date dictionary—not some tattered edition you bought at a garage sale or your father's hand-me-down *Webster's* from the 1970s. If you can afford to, invest in your academic future and buy two dictionaries: an unabridged and an abridged version. The word *abridged* means "reduced or condensed." Therefore, an *abridged* dictionary, usually published in an inexpensive paperback format, contains fewer words than an *unabridged* dictionary. The eleventh edition of the *Merriam-Webster Collegiate Dictionary* contains more than 225,000 words. In contrast, the paperback *Merriam-Webster Dictionary* states that it has around 95,000 entries. Unabridged dictionaries also offer many features that the paperback editions do not—for example, maps, photographs, drawings, usage notes, extended explanations of etymologies, notes on regional expressions, and so forth.

Aside from the number of entries, each kind of dictionary has its own advantages. The lighter paperback dictionary is portable. An unabridged dictionary is heavy to carry around and therefore is better kept at home. Ask your instructor to recommend one, or choose one of these three widely used dictionaries. Each comes in both an abridged and an unabridged version. In alphabetical order:

American Heritage College Dictionary
Merriam-Webster's Collegiate Dictionary
Random House College Dictionary

The Features of a Dictionary

No matter which dictionary you choose, all contain the same features. Here is a brief overview of the important ones.

Guide Words

Guide words are printed in boldface in the top margin of each page; they indicate the first and last words and help you locate words quickly.

Entry

The word *entry* refers simply to the word that you are looking up. It is printed in boldface type in the left margin; dots separate the syllables.

Pronunciation Symbols

Pronunciation symbols are printed in parentheses and follow the entry. English has a complicated pronunciation system: The language has approximately seventy-five different sounds but only twenty-six letters to represent them. A single vowel letter like *a*, for example, can be pronounced seven ways, as in these words: *cat* (ă); *lake* (ā); *bar* (är); *bare* (âr); *part* (är); *law;* (ô); and *father* (ä). The pronunciation symbols follow a standardized system so that you know how each letter or combination of letters should be pronounced in an unfamiliar word. Ask your instructor for help if you do not know how to pronounce these symbols. In the college edition of the *American Heritage Dictionary*, these symbols are printed in the lower-right corner of each *right-hand* page. Some dictionaries print them across the bottom of both pages.

Stress Marks

Stress or *accent* marks are as important as pronunciation symbols for pronouncing words correctly. Referring to the relative degree of loudness of each syllable, stress marks are printed *after* the syllable to be stressed, as you can see in this word: *solid* (sol´ĭd). In this case, the first syllable, *sol*, receives primary stress or emphasis.

English has three kinds of stress. Primary or heavy stress is shown by a heavy boldface mark, like this: '. Secondary, or weak, stress is shown by the same mark printed in lighter type, like this: '. And unstressed syllables, such as those containing a neutral vowel sound—symbolized by a pronunciation symbol called a "schwa," which is written like an upside down "e" (ə)—are unmarked. For example, the word *magnification* contains all three types of stress: măg´nə fĭ kā´ shən. The first syllable takes the secondary stress, the third syllable takes the primary stress, and the second and fourth syllables are unstressed.

Parts of Speech and Inflected Forms

Following the dictionary pronunciation symbols is an abbreviation indicating the entry word's part of speech. For example, *n.* = noun; *v.* = verb, *adj.* = adjective, *adv.* = adverb, and so forth. *Inflected forms*—the forms of the word that take word endings, or *inflections*—are also included.

Thus, you can look up the proper way to spell the present participle and past tense of a word like *magnify:* In *magnifying* (the present tense form), the *y* changes to *i*, and the ending signifying the past tense (*-ed*) is added. In *magnifying* (the present participle), the ending *–ing* is added; and in *magnifies*, the present tense for the third person singular (that is, the form used with "he," "she," or "it") changes to *i*, and the ending *–es* is added. Similarly, the dictionary indicates the plural form of *ox* as *oxen*.

Order of Definitions

The one significant difference in dictionaries is in the order of definitions if a word has more than one meaning. The *American Heritage*, *Merriam-Webster Collegiate*, and *Random House* college editions follow this system: If a word has multiple senses (two or more meanings, in other words), the central and often the most commonly sought meaning is listed first. Less common, older forms, and obsolete senses are listed next. *However*, this does not mean that you should choose the first meaning listed and look no further. The context is crucial in determining which sense best fits a particular word's meaning. This concept will be illustrated in a little more detail at the end of this section.

Note that, unlike the dictionaries listed above, the *Webster's New World Dictionary* organizes its definitions historically, which means that the earliest sense or senses of a word come first, with more modern senses following. If you are unsure about which method your particular dictionary uses, ask your instructor for help or refer to the early pages of the dictionary, called the "front matter," where there will be a description of the "Order of Senses" or something similar.

Variant Forms

If the word has other grammatical forms, the dictionary will list those after the last definition. If you look up *enforce* (verb), for example, the dictionary

READING

Entries

Pronunciation symbols

Variant forms

Parts of speech

Definitions

cys•ti•cer•coid (sĭs′tĭ-sûr′koid) *n.* The larval stage of certain tapeworms, resembling a cysticercus but having the scolex completely filling the enclosing cyst. [CYSTICERC(US) + –OID.]

cys•ti•cer•co•sis (sĭs′tĭ-sər-kō′sĭs) *n.* The condition of being infested with cysticerci. [CYSTICERC(US) + –OSIS.]

cys•ti•cer•cus (sĭs′tĭ-sûr′kəs) *n., pl.* **-ci** (-sī′) The larval stage of many tapeworms, consisting of a single invaginated scolex enclosed in a fluid-filled cyst. [NLat. : Gk. *kustis*, cyst; see CYST + Gk. *kerkos*, tail.]

cystic fibrosis *n.* A hereditary disease of the exocrine glands, affecting mainly the pancreas, respiratory system, and sweat glands and characterized by the production of abnormally viscous mucus, usu. resulting in chronic respiratory infections and impaired pancreatic function.

cys•tine (sĭs′tēn′) *n.* A white crystalline amino acid, $C_6H_{12}N_2O_4S_2$, found in many proteins, esp. keratin. [< its discovery in bladder stones.]

cys•ti•tis (sĭ-stī′tĭs) *n.* Inflammation of the urinary bladder.

cysto– or **cyst–** *pref.* Bladder; cyst; sac: *cystocele.* [< NLat. *cystis*, bladder < Gk. *kustis.*]

cys•to•cele (sĭs′tə-sēl′) *n.* Herniation of the urinary bladder through the wall of the vagina.

cys•toid (sĭs′toid′) *adj.* Formed like or resembling a cyst. ❖ *n.* A cystoid structure.

cys•to•lith (sĭs′tə-lĭth′) *n.* **1.** *Botany* A mineral concretion, usu. of calcium carbonate, occurring in the epidermal cells of certain plants, such as figs. **2.** See **urinary calculus.**

cys•to•scope (sĭs′tə-skōp′) *n.* A tubular instrument used to examine the interior of the urinary bladder and ureter. **—cys′to•scop′ic** (-skŏp′ĭk) *adj.* **—cys•tos′co•py** (sĭ-stŏs′kə-pē) *n.*

cys•tos•to•my (sĭ-stŏs′tə-mē) *n., pl.* **-mies** The surgical formation of an opening into the urinary bladder.

-cyte *suff.* Cell: *leukocyte.* [NLat. *-cyta* < Gk. *kutos*, hollow vessel. See **(s)keu-** in App.]

Cy•the•ra (sĭ-thîr′ə, sĭth′ər-ə) also **Kí•thi•ra** (kē′thē-rä′) An island of S Greece in the Mediterranean Sea S of the Peloponnesus; chief center for the worship of Aphrodite.

Cyth•e•re•a (sĭth′ə-rē′ə) *n. Greek Mythology* See **Aphrodite.**

cy•ti•dine (sī′tĭ-dēn′) *n.* A nucleoside, $C_9H_{13}N_3O_5$, composed of cytosine and ribose. [CYT(O)– + –ID(E) + –INE².]

cyto– or **cyt–** *pref.* Cell: *cytoplasm.* [< Gk. *kutos*, hollow vessel. See **(s)keu-** in App.]

cy•to•chem•is•try (sī′tō-kĕm′ĭ-strē) *n.* The branch of biochemistry that studies the chemical composition and activity of cells. **—cy′to•chem′i•cal** (-kĕm′ĭ-kəl) *adj.*

cy•to•chrome (sī′tə-krōm′) *n.* Any of a class of iron-containing proteins important in cell respiration as catalysts of oxidation-reduction reactions.

cy•to•gen•e•sis (sī′tō-jĕn′ĭ-sĭs) *n.* The formation, development, and variation of cells.

cy•to•ge•net•ics (sī′tō-jə-nĕt′ĭks) *n.* (*used with a sing. verb*) The branch of biology that deals with heredity and the cellular components associated with heredity. **—cy′to•ge•net′ic, cy′to•ge•net′i•cal** *adj.* **—cy′to•ge•net′i•cal•ly** *adv.* **—cy′to•ge•net′i•cist** (-sĭst) *n.*

cy•tog•e•ny (sī-tŏj′ə-nē) *n.* See **cytogenesis.**

cy•to•kine (sī′tə-kīn′) *n.* Any of several proteins, such as the interleukins and lymphokines, that act as intercellular mediators in an immune response. [CYTO– + Gk. *kinein*, to move; see KININ.]

cy•to•ki•ne•sis (sī′tō-kə-nē′sĭs, -kī-) *n.* The division of the cytoplasm of a cell following the division of the nucleus. **—cy′to•ki•net′ic** (-nĕt′ĭk) *adj.*

cy•to•ki•nin (sī′tə-kī′nĭn) *n.* Any of a class of plant hormones that promote cell division and growth and delay the senescence of leaves.

cy•tol•o•gy (sī-tŏl′ə-jē) *n.* The branch of biology that deals with cell formation, structure, and function. **—cy′to•log′ic** (-tə-lŏj′ĭk), **cy′to•log′i•cal** *adj.* **—cy•tol′o•gist** *n.*

cy•tol•y•sin (sī-tŏl′ĭ-sĭn) *n.* A substance, such as an antibody, capable of dissolving or destroying cells. [CYTOLYS(IS) + –IN.]

cy•tol•y•sis (sī-tŏl′ĭ-sĭs) *n.* The dissolution or destruction of a cell. **—cy′to•lyt′ic** (sī′tə-lĭt′ĭk) *adj.*

cy•to•me•gal•ic (sī′tō-mĭ-găl′ĭk) *adj.* Of, relating to, or characterized by greatly enlarged cells.

cy•to•meg•a•lo•vi•rus (sī′tə-mĕg′ə-lō-vī′rəs) *n.* Any of a group of herpes viruses that attack and enlarge epithelial cells.

cy•to•mem•brane (sī′tə-mĕm′brān) *n.* See **cell membrane.**

cy•to•path•ic (sī′tə-păth′ĭk) *adj.* Of or relating to degeneration or disease of cells.

cy•to•path•o•gen•ic (sī′tə-păth′ə-jĕn′ĭk) *adj.* Of, relating to, or producing pathological changes in cells. **—cy′to•path′o•ge•nic′i•ty** (-jə-nĭs′ĭ-tē) *n.*

cy•to•phil•ic (sī′tə-fĭl′ĭk) *adj.* Having an affinity for cells.

cy•to•pho•tom•e•ter (sī′tō-fō-tŏm′ĭ-tər) *n.* An instrument used to identify and locate the chemical compounds within a cell by measuring the intensity of light passing through stained sections of the cytoplasm. **—cy′to•pho′to•met′ric** (-tə-mĕt′rĭk) *adj.* **—cy′to•pho•tom′e•try** *n.*

cy•to•plasm (sī′tə-plăz′əm) *n.* The protoplasm outside the nucleus of a cell. **—cy′to•plas′mic** (-plăz′mĭk) *adj.* **—cy′to•plas′mi•cal•ly** *adv.*

cy•to•plast (sī′tə-plăst′) *n.* The intact cytoplasm of a single cell. **—cy′to•plas′tic** (-plăs′tĭk) *adj.*

cy•to•sine (sī′tə-sēn′) *n.* A pyrimidine base, $C_4H_5N_3O$, that is the constituent of DNA and RNA involved in base-pairing with guanine. [CYT(O)– + (RIB)OS(E) + –INE².]

cy•to•skel•e•ton (sī′tə-skĕl′ĭ-tn) *n.* The internal framework of a cell, composed largely of actin filaments and microtubules.

cy•to•sol (sī′tə-sôl′, -sŏl′) *n.* The fluid component of cytoplasm, excluding organelles and the insoluble, usu. suspended cytoplasmic components. [CYTO– + SOL(UTION).]

cy•to•sta•sis (sī′tə-stā′sĭs, -stăs′ĭs) *n.* Arrest of cellular growth and multiplication.

cy•to•stat•ic (sī′tə-stăt′ĭk) *adj.* Inhibiting or suppressing cellular growth and multiplication. ❖ *n.* A cytostatic agent. **—cy′to•stat′i•cal•ly** *adv.*

cy•to•tax•on•o•my (sī′tō-tăk-sŏn′ə-mē) *n.* The classification of organisms based on cellular structure and function, esp. on the structure and number of chromosomes. **—cy′to•tax′o•nom′ic** (-tăk′sə-nŏm′ĭk) *adj.* **—cy′to•tax•on′o•mist** *n.*

cy•to•tech•nol•o•gist (sī′tə-tĕk-nŏl′ə-jĭst) *n.* A technician trained in medical examination and identification of cellular abnormalities. **—cy′to•tech•nol′o•gy** *n.*

cy•to•tox•ic (sī′tə-tŏk′sĭk) *adj.* Of, relating to, or producing a toxic effect on cells. **—cy′to•tox•ic′i•ty** (-tŏk-sĭs′ĭ-tē) *n.*

cytotoxic T cell *n.* See **killer cell.**

cy•to•tox•in (sī′tə-tŏk′sĭn) *n.* A substance having a specific toxic effect on certain cells.

CZ *abbr.* Canal Zone

czar (zär, tsär) *n.* **1.** also **tsar** or **tzar** (zär, tsär) A male monarch or emperor, esp. one of the emperors who ruled Russia before the revolution of 1917. **2.** A person having great power; an autocrat. **3.** *Informal* An appointed official having special powers to regulate or supervise an activity. [Russ. *tsar′* < ORuss. *tsĭsarĭ*, emperor, king < O Church Slavonic *tsěsarĭ* < Goth. *kaisar* < Gk. < Lat. *Caesar*, emperor. See CAESAR.] **—czar′dom** *n.*

USAGE NOTE The word *czar* can also be spelled *tsar. Czar* is the most common form in American usage and virtually the only one employed in the extended senses "any tyrant" or, informally, "one in authority." But *tsar* more accurately transliterates the Russian and appears more often in scholarly writing with reference to one of the Russian emperors.

czar•das (chär′däsh′) *n.* **1.** An intricate Hungarian dance characterized by variations in tempo. **2.** Music for this dance. [Hung. *csárdás* < *csárda*, wayside tavern < Serbo-Croatian *čardak*, watchtower < Turk. *çardak*, hut, trellis < Pers. *chār ṭāq* < *chahār ṭāq*, four-cornered vault : *chahār*, four (< OIran. *cathwārō*; see **kʷetwer-** in App.) + *ṭāq*, vault (< Ar., arch).]

czar•e•vitch (zär′ə-vĭch′, tsär′-) *n.* The eldest son of a Russian czar. [Russ. *tsarevich* : *tsar′*, czar; see CZAR + *-evich*, masc. patronymic suff.]

cza•rev•na (zä-rĕv′nə, tsä-) *n.* **1.** The daughter of a Russian czar. **2.** The wife of a czarevitch. [Russ. *tsarevna* : *tsar′*, czar; see CZAR + *-evna*, fem. patronymic suff.]

cza•ri•na (zä-rē′nə, tsä-) *n.* The wife of a Russian czar. [Alteration (perh. influenced by Lat. *rēgīna*, queen) of Russ. *tsaritsa*; see CZARITZA.]

czar•ism (zär′ĭz′əm, tsär′-) *n.* The system of government in Russia under the czars. **—czar′ist** *adj. & n.*

cza•rit•za (zä-rĭt′sə, tsä-rēt′-) *n.* An empress of Russia. [Russ. *tsaritsa* : *tsar′*, czar; see CZAR + *-itsa*, fem. suff.]

Czech (chĕk) *n.* **1a.** A native or inhabitant of the Czech Republic. **b.** A native or inhabitant of Bohemia. **c.** A person of Czech descent. **2.** The Slavic language of the Czechs. [Pol. < Czech *Čech.*] **—Czech** *adj.*

Czech•o•slo•va•ki•a (chĕk′ə-slə-vä′kē-ə, -slō-) A former country of central Europe; formed in 1918 and divided in 1993 into the Czech Republic and Slovakia. **—Czech′o•slo′vak, Czech′o•slo•va′ki•an** *adj. & n.*

Czech Republic A country of central Europe; part of Czechoslovakia from 1918–93. Cap. Prague. Pop. 10,333,000.

Czer•ny (chĕr′nē), **Karl** 1791–1857. Austrian pianist and composer whose works include *School of the Left Hand.*

Czę•sto•cho•wa (chĕn′stə-kō′və, chĕN′stô-hô′vä) A city of S Poland N of Katowice. Pop. 258,266.

Cyprus

Czech Republic

ă	pat	oi	boy
ā	pay	ou	out
âr	care	ŏŏ	took
ä	father	ōō	boot
ĕ	pet	ŭ	cut
ē	be	ûr	urge
ĭ	pit	th	thin
ī	pie	*th*	this
îr	pier	hw	which
ŏ	pot	zh	vision
ō	toe	ə	about,
ô	paw		item

Stress marks:
′ (primary);
′ (secondary), as in
lexicon (lĕk′sĭ-kŏn′)

cussed. **2.** Open to dispute. **—de•bat′a•bly** *adv.*

de•bate (dĭ-bāt′) *v.* **-bat•ed, -bat•ing, -bates** —*intr.* **1.** To consider something; deliberate. **2.** To engage in argument by discussing opposing points. **3.** To engage in a formal discussion or argument. **4.** *Obsolete* To fight or quarrel. —*tr.* **1.** To deliberate on; consider. **2.** To dispute or argue about. **3.** To discuss or argue (a question, for example) formally. **4.** *Obsolete* To fight or argue for or over. ❖ *n.* **1.** A discussion involving opposing points; an argument. **2.** Deliberation; consideration: *passed the motion with little debate.* **3.** A formal contest of argumentation in which two opposing teams defend and attack a given proposition. **4.** *Obsolete* Conflict; strife. [ME *debaten* < OFr. *debatre* : *de-*, de- + *battre*, to beat; see BATTER[1].] **—de•bate′ment** *n.* **—de•bat′er** *n.*

de•bauch (dĭ-bôch′) *v.* **-bauched, -bauch•ing, -bauch•es** —*tr.* **1a.** To corrupt morally. **b.** To lead away from excellence or virtue. **2.** To reduce the value or quality of; debase. **3.** *Archaic* To cause to forsake allegiance. —*intr.* To indulge in dissipation. ❖ *n.* **1.** The act or a period of debauchery. **2.** An orgy. [Fr. *débaucher* < OFr. *desbauchier*, to lead astray, rough-hew timber : *des-*, de- + *bauch*, beam, of Gmc. orig.] **—de•bauch′ed•ly** (-bô′chĭd-lē) *adv.* **—de•bauch′er** *n.*

de•bauch•ee (dĭ-bô′chē′, dĕb′ə-shē′, -shā′) *n.* A person who habitually indulges in debauchery or dissipation; a libertine.

de•bauch•er•y (dĭ-bô′chə-rē) *n., pl.* **-ies 1a.** Extreme indulgence in sensual pleasures; dissipation. **b. debaucheries** Orgies. **2.** *Archaic* Seduction from morality, allegiance, or duty.

de•ben•ture (dĭ-bĕn′chər) *n.* **1.** A certificate or voucher acknowledging a debt. **2.** An unsecured bond issued by a corporation or governmental agency and backed only by the credit standing of the issuer. **3.** A customhouse certificate providing for the payment of a drawback. [ME *debentur* < Lat. *dēbentur*, they are due, third pers. pl. pr. passive of *dēbēre*, to owe. See **ghabh-** in App.]

de•bil•i•tate (dĭ-bĭl′ĭ-tāt′) *tr.v.* **-tat•ed, -tat•ing, -tates** To sap the strength or energy of; enervate. [Lat. *dēbilitāre*, *dēbilitāt-* < *dēbilis*, weak. See **bel-** in App.] **—de•bil′i•ta′tion** *n.* **—de•bil′i•ta′tive** *adj.*

de•bil•i•tat•ed (dĭ-bĭl′ĭ-tā′tĭd) *adj.* Showing impairment of energy or strength; enfeebled.

de•bil•i•ty (dĭ-bĭl′ĭ-tē) *n., pl.* **-ties** The state of being weak or feeble; infirmity. [ME *debilite* < OFr. < Lat. *dēbilitās* < *dēbilis*, weak. See **bel-** in App.]

deb•it (dĕb′ĭt) *n.* **1a.** An item of debt as recorded in an account. **b.** An entry of a sum in the debit or left-hand side of an account. **c.** The sum of such entries. **d.** The left-hand side of an account where bookkeeping entries are made. **2.** A drawback; a detriment. ❖ *tr.v.* **-it•ed, -it•ing, -its 1.** To enter (a sum) on the left-hand side of an account. **2.** To charge with a debit. [ME *debite* < Lat. *dēbitum*, debt. See DEBT.]

debit card *n.* A bankcard used to make an electronic withdrawal from funds on deposit in a bank, as in purchasing goods or obtaining cash advances.

deb•o•nair also **deb•o•naire** (dĕb′ə-nâr′) *adj.* **1.** Suave; urbane. **2.** Affable; genial. **3.** Carefree and gay; jaunty. [ME *debonaire*, gracious, kindly < OFr. < *de bon aire*, of good lineage or disposition : *de*, of (< Lat. *dē*; see DE-) + *bon*, *bonne*, good (< Lat. *bonus*; see **deu-**[2] in App.) + *aire*, nest, family; see AERIE.] **—deb′o•nair′ly** *adv.* **—deb′o•nair′ness** *n.*

de•bone (dē-bōn′) *tr.v.* **-boned, -bon•ing, -bones** To remove the bones from: *debone a chicken breast.*

Deb•o•rah (dĕb′ər-ə, dĕb′rə) In the Bible, a judge who aided the Israelites in their victory over the Canaanites. [Heb. *dəbôrâ*, bee.]

de•bouch (dĭ-bouch′, -bo͞osh′) *v.* **-bouched, -bouch•ing, -bouch•es** —*intr.* **1.** To march from a narrow or confined area into the open. **2.** To emerge; issue. —*tr.* To cause to emerge or issue. [Fr. *déboucher* : *dé-*, out of (< OFr. *des-*; see DE-) + *bouche*, mouth (< Lat. *bucca*).]

de•bouch•ment (dĭ-bouch′mənt, -bo͞osh′-) *n.* **1.** The act or an instance of marching from a narrow confined area into the open. **2.** A debouchure.

de•bou•chure (dĭ-bo͞o′sho͝or′) *n.* An opening or mouth, as of a river or stream.

De•bre•cen (dĕb′rĭt-sĕn′, -rĕ-tsĕn′) A city of E Hungary near the Romanian border E of Budapest. Pop. 217,497.

de•bride•ment (dā-brēd-mäN′, dĭ-brēd′mənt) *n.* Surgical removal of dead or contaminated tissue and foreign matter from a wound. [Fr. *débridement* < *débrider*, to unbridle, debride (< the likening of constricting bands of tissue to bridles) < OFr. *desbrider* : *des-*, de- + *bride*, bridle (prob. < MHGer. *bridel*, rein).] **—de•bride′** *v.*

de•brief (dē-brēf′) *tr.v.* **-briefed, -brief•ing, -briefs 1.** To question to obtain knowledge or intelligence gathered esp. on a military mission. **2.** To instruct not to reveal classified information after leaving employment.

de•bris also **dé•bris** (də-brē′, dā-, dā′brē′) *n.* **1a.** The scattered remains of something broken or destroyed; rubble or wreckage. **b.** Carelessly discarded refuse; litter. **2.** *Geology* An accumulation of relatively large rock fragments: *glacial debris.* [Fr. *débris* < OFr. *debrisier*, to break to pieces : *de-*, intensive pref.; see DE- + *brisier*, to break (< VLat. **brisāre*, to press grapes, prob. of Celt. orig.).]

Debs (dĕbz), **Eugene Victor** 1855–1926. Amer. labor organizer and socialist leader who ran unsuccessfully for President five times between 1900 and 1920.

debt (dĕt) *n.* **1.** Something owed, such as money, goods, or services. **2a.** An obligation or liability to pay or render something to someone else. **b.** The condition of owing. **3.** An offense requiring forgiveness or reparation; a trespass. [ME *dette* < OFr. < VLat. **dēbita*, pl. of Lat. *dēbitum*, debt, neut. p. part. of *dēbēre*, to owe. See **ghabh-** in App.] **—debt′less** *adj.*

debt•or (dĕt′ər) *n.* **1.** One that owes something to another. **2.** One who is guilty of a trespass or sin. [ME *dettour* < OFr. *dettor* < Lat. *dēbitor* < *dēbitus*, p. part. of *dēbēre*, to owe. See DEBT.]

de•bug (dē-bŭg′) *tr.v.* **-bugged, -bug•ging, -bugs 1.** To remove a hidden electronic device, such as a microphone, from. **2.** To search for and correct malfunctioning elements or errors in: *debug a computer program.* **3.** To remove insects from, as with a pesticide. **—de•bug′ger** *n.*

de•bunk (dē-bŭngk′) *tr.v.* **-bunked, -bunk•ing, -bunks** To expose or ridicule the falseness or exaggerated claims of: *debunk a supposed miracle drug.* **—de•bunk′er** *n.*

De•bus•sy (də-byo͞o′sē, dĕb′yo͞o-sē′, də-bü-sē′), **Claude Achille** 1862–1918. French composer considered the first exponent of musical impressionism.

de•but also **dé•but** (dā-byo͞o′, də-, dā′byo͞o′) *n.* **1.** A first public appearance, as of a performer. **2.** The formal presentation of a young woman to society. **3.** The beginning of a course of action. ❖ *tr. & intr.v.* **-buted** (-byo͞od′), **-but•ing** (-byo͞o′ĭng), **-buts** (-byo͞oz′) *Usage Problem* To present in or make a debut. [Fr. *début* < *débuter*, to give the first stroke in a game, begin : *dé-*, from, away (< OFr. *de-*; see DE-) + *but*, goal, target (< OFr. *butte*; see BUTT[3]).]

USAGE NOTE *Debut* is widely used as a verb, both intransitively (*Her new series will debut next March on network television*) and transitively (*The network will debut her new series next March*). These usages are well established in connection with entertainment and the performing arts but are not entirely acceptable when used of other sorts of introductions, as of products or publications.

deb•u•tante (dĕb′yo͞o-tänt′, dā′byo͞o-) *n.* A young woman making a formal debut into society. [Fr. *débutante*, fem. pr. part. of *débuter*, to begin. See DEBUT.]

De•bye (də-bī′), **Peter Joseph Wilhelm** 1884–1966. Dutch-born Amer. physicist who won a 1936 Nobel Prize.

dec. *abbr.* **1.** deceased **2.** declension **3.** declination **4.** decorated **5.** decrescendo

Dec. *abbr.* December

deca– or **dec–** also **deka–** or **dek–** *pref.* Ten: *decane.* [Gk. *deka-* < *deka*, ten. See **dekm̥** in App.]

dec•ade (dĕk′ād′, dĕ-kād′) *n.* **1.** A period of ten years. **2.** A group or series of ten. [ME, a group of ten < OFr. < LLat. *decas*, *decad-* < Gk. *dekas* < *deka*, ten. See **dekm̥** in App.]

dec•a•dence (dĕk′ə-dəns, dĭ-kād′ns) *n.* **1.** A process, condition, or period of deterioration or decline, as in morals or art; decay. **2.** often **Decadence** A literary movement esp. of late 19th-century France and England characterized by refined aestheticism, artifice, and the quest for new sensations. [Fr. *décadence* < OFr. *decadence* < Med.Lat. *dēcadentia*, a decaying, declining < VLat. **dēcadere*, to decay. See DECAY.]

dec•a•den•cy (dĕk′ə-dən-sē, dĭ-kād′n-) *n.* Decadence.

dec•a•dent (dĕk′ə-dənt, dĭ-kād′nt) *adj.* **1.** Being in a state of decline or decay. **2.** Marked by or providing unrestrained gratification; self-indulgent. **3.** often **Decadent** Of or relating to literary Decadence. ❖ *n.* **1.** A person in a condition or process of mental or moral decay. **2.** often **Decadent** A member of the Decadence movement. [Fr. *décadent*, back-formation < *décadence*, decadence. See DECADENCE.] **—dec′a•dent•ly** *adv.*

de•caf (dē′kăf′) *n. Informal* Decaffeinated coffee. **—de′caf′** *adj.*

de•caf•fein•at•ed (dē-kăf′ə-nā′tĭd, -kăf′ē-ə-) *adj.* Having the caffeine removed: *decaffeinated coffee.* **—de•caf′fein•ate′** *v.* **—de•caf′fein•a′tion** *n.*

dec•a•gon (dĕk′ə-gŏn′) *n.* A polygon with ten angles and ten sides. [Med.Lat. *decagonum* < Gk. *dekagōnon* < neut. of *dekagōnos*, having ten angles : *deka*, ten; see **dekm̥** in App. + *-gōnos*, angled; see -GON.] **—de•cag′o•nal** (dĭ-kăg′ə-nəl) *adj.* **—de•cag′o•nal•ly** *adv.*

dec•a•he•dron (dĕk′ə-hē′drən) *n., pl.* **-drons** or **-dra** (-drə) A polyhedron with ten faces. **—dec′a•he′dral** *adj.*

de•cal (dē′kăl′, dĭ-kăl′) *n.* **1.** A picture or design transferred by decalcomania. **2.** A decorative sticker. [Short for DECALCOMANIA.]

de•cal•ci•fy (dē-kăl′sə-fī′) *v.* **-fied, -fy•ing, -fies** —*tr.* To remove calcium or calcium compounds from (bones or teeth, for example). —*intr.* To lose calcium or calcium compounds. **—de•cal′ci•fi•ca′tion** (-fĭ-kā′shən) *n.* **—de•cal′ci•fi′er** *n.*

de•cal•co•ma•ni•a (dē-kăl′kə-mā′nē-ə, -măn′yə) *n.* **1.** The process of transferring pictures or designs printed on specially prepared paper to materials such as glass or metal. **2.** A decal. [Fr. *décalcomanie* : *décalquer*, to transfer a tracing (*dé-*, from < Lat. *dē-*; see DE- + *calquer*, to trace; see CALQUE) + *manie*, craze, from its popularity in the 19th cent. (< Lat. *mania*, madness; see MANIA).]

de•ca•les•cence (dē′kə-lĕs′əns) *n.* A sudden slowing in the rate

365

debate ← Guide words

decalescence

Usage note

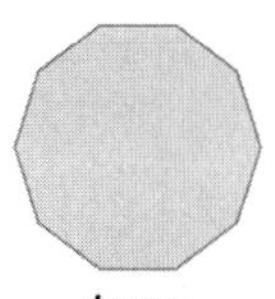

decagon

Etymology

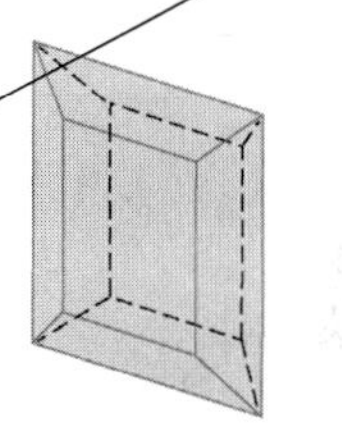

decahedron

ă pat	oi boy	← Pronunciation key	
ā pay	ou out		
âr care	o͝o took		
ä father	o͞o boot		
ĕ pet	ŭ cut		
ē be	ûr urge		
ĭ pit	th thin		
ī pie	*th* this		
îr pier	hw which		
ŏ pot	zh vision		
ō toe	ə about, item		
ô paw			

Stress marks: ← Stress marks
′ (primary);
′ (secondary), as in
lexicon (lĕk′sĭ-kŏn′)

lists as variants *enforceability* (noun); *enforceable* (adjective); *enforcement* (noun); and *enforcer* (noun).

Etymology

You have already seen some examples of etymology, which refers to the linguistic origin of a word, that is, the language(s) from which it came into English. Etymology also refers to the word's history. It is printed in brackets, [ ], either before or after the definitions, depending on your dictionary. When you look up a word in the dictionary to see where it came from, the originating language will be abbreviated. For example, *OF* indicates Old French, *ME* indicates Middle English, *L* or *Lat* refers to Latin, *Gk* means Greek, and so forth. A complete list of those abbreviations can be found in the front matter of your dictionary.

Other Features

Some dictionaries include useful drawings in the margins. The *American Heritage* dictionaries (both the college edition and the unabridged edition) are particularly generous in this regard, allowing you to see, for example, the location of El Salvador on a small map of Central America, what a French chateau or castle looks like, and a photograph of Olympic running champion Carl Lewis, just to cite three random examples from my dictionary. Thus the dictionary goes far beyond being merely a resource for looking up words: It is also a mini-atlas, a biographical index, and a provider of all kinds of useful information from the world around you.

Sample Dictionary Column

Now that you are familiar with some of the more important dictionary terminology, reprinted here is one column from the *American Heritage College Dictionary*. Study the arrows that identify the features discussed above.

Choosing the Right Definition

Students often justly complain that they are confused when looking up words in the dictionary because they are often confronted with so many definitions from which to choose. This is indeed the tricky part, but your task will be made easier if you carefully consider the context around an unfamiliar word and then scan through all of the definitions until you find the one that seems to fit best. To illustrate this problem and its resolution, study these two examples. Paragraph 5 of Curtis Wilkie's profile of New Orleans opens with this sentence:

> It was a city sustained more by spirit by *corporeal* commodities; by a determination to enjoy life in spite of adversity.

The dictionary lists two meanings for the adjective *corporeal:*

> **1.** Of, relating to, or characteristic of the body. See synonyms at **bodily**.
> **2.** Of a material nature, tangible.

If you know that a commodity, which *corporeal* describes here, is an article used in trade or in commerce, then you can determine that the second definition is only one that makes sense.

Here is a second example: In Susan Orlean's profile of 10-year-old Colin Duffy, she describes his dream of moving to Wyoming like this:

> When he dreams, he dreams about moving to Wyoming, which he has visited with his family. His plan is to buy land there, and have some sort of ranch that would definitely include horses. Sometimes when he talks about this, it sounds as ordinary and hard-boiled as a real estate appraisal; other times it can sound fantastical and wifty and achingly naïve, informed by the last inklings of childhood—the musings of a *balmy* real estate appraiser assaying a wonderful and magical landscape that erodes from memory a little bit every day.

Although there are some other difficult words here, I am particularly interested in the word *balmy* because its three dictionary definitions are so distinctly different. Of these three, which one fits best?

> **1.** Having the quality or fragrance of balm; soothing. **2.** Mild and pleasant: *a balmy breeze.* **3.** Eccentric in behavior.

The most appropriate is the third definition. Both of these examples illustrate the importance of scanning through all definitions rather than just assuming that the first one is the one you want.

Online Dictionaries

Online dictionaries have the advantage of being free, and if you have ready access to a computer, there is a certain convenience to simply typing in a word to determine its meaning. If you have a fast broadband connection (cable modem or DSL), it is probably just as fast to look up the meaning of a word online as it is to flip through the dictionary's pages. Here are the two best-known online dictionaries:

- www.bartleby.com/61 sponsored by Houghton Mifflin, which publishes the *American Heritage Dictionary of the English Language*
- www.m-w.com is sponsored by Merriam-Webster, which publishes *Merriam-Webster's Collegiate Dictionary*

Going to either site and typing in a word will give you the same basic information—definitions, pronunciation, and variant forms—that the print editions offer. But there *are* differences between the print and online versions. For example, I tested the two online sites listed above and compared them with the print versions by typing in "Easter Island," the subject of Jared Diamond's "Easter's End" in Part 4.

In the unabridged print version of the *American Heritage Dictionary*, the entry for "Easter Island" is accompanied by an extensive definition and a color photo of two statues of the colossal heads found on Rapa Nui. (See page 108 for photos.) Typing in the phrase "Easter Island" into the search box at www.bartleby.com/61 leads you to a choice of three links. Clicking on the first one yields the same definition as in the print dictionary, but no photograph. Clicking on the menu option "Illustrations" provides an alphabetical list of available illustrations. I clicked on the choice where the photograph of the Easter Island statues would be found ("diesel engine" to "eccentric"), scrolled down to a page containing lots of little photographs, and found—no photograph! Typing in "Easter Island" in the search box at www.m-w.com gave only one sentence with geographic information but did offer a link to www.brittanica.com where more information, along with photographs, is available. If you simply need a definition without supplemental pictures and links, then a print dictionary is certainly more efficient.

On the other hand, an online dictionary may give you a definition when the print version fails. You might remember, for example, this sentence from Susan Orlean's essay, used earlier as an illustration of how to choose the best definition according to the context:

> Sometimes when he talks about this, it sounds as ordinary and hard-boiled as a real estate appraisal; other times it can sound fantastical and *wifty* and achingly naïve, informed by the last inklings of childhood.

None of my print dictionaries had an entry for *wifty*, but I was finally able to track down its meaning on the www.m-w.com website. *Wifty* means "ditsy," a slang word meaning "stupid," "silly," or "scatterbrained." In this context, "silly" is probably the meaning Orlean has in mind. The etymology of the word is listed as unknown.

From this admittedly limited experience with online dictionaries, there is no doubt that they have their uses, but to rely on one for all one's college work seems cumbersome. The portability and inexpensive price of a good paperback dictionary and the comprehensiveness of a good unabridged dictionary seem to far outweigh the use of a computer in this regard.

To conclude this introduction, the course will have been successful if you find yourself unwilling to be content with a haphazard guess as to a new word's meaning and if you find that with each passing year you find fewer and fewer words to look up. Nothing builds confidence as much as a good reading vocabulary. The thrill of recognition does wonders for one's morale: "I saw that word in David Sedaris's essay, and even better, I remember what it means!"

Did I Save Lives or Engage in Racial Profiling?

Lori Hope

Lori Hope wrote this article for *Newsweek* magazine's weekly column called "My Turn." The incident she describes occurred in December 2001, a few days after the so-called shoe bomber, Richard Reid, was arrested for trying to ignite a shoe containing an explosive device aboard a Paris-to-Miami flight. In the aftermath of the September 11, 2001, World Trade Center terrorist attacks, airlines have struggled to ensure their passengers' safety without violating civil liberties. In this context, *racial profiling* refers to singling out male passengers of Middle Eastern descent as being potential terrorists. Hope explores her own dilemma with regard to this civil rights issue.

VOCABULARY ANALYSIS

-ism (Noun Suffix)

The suffix *-ism* is frequently attached to nouns to indicate a doctrine, practice, theory, or principle. Hope's article concerns racial profiling to prevent acts of *terrorism,* the use or threatened use of random violence against people either to intimidate or to coerce them in some way. Recent acts of terrorism have been committed for political, ideological, or religious reasons. English has numerous words ending in *-ism,* among them, *realism, romanticism, barbarism, Catholicism, socialism, sexism,* to cite just a few.

Did I Save Lives or Engage in Profiling?

Lori Hope

Connecting Grammar to Writing

In the first sentence of paragraph 2, Hope uses dashes to separate the appositive phrase "an avowed liberal" from the rest of the sentence. She could have used commas, but the effect would not be so emphatic.

1 Half a lifetime ago, I read a magazine essay that took deep root within me, and still sprouts whenever I find myself tempted to react to someone based on skin color. The author, an African-American, described what it was like to see people cross the street when he walked toward them on a sidewalk.

2 When racial profiling became an issue in the war against terrorism, I—an avowed liberal—found myself wondering what I would do if I saw someone who appeared to be of Middle Eastern descent behaving in a way that could be considered "suspicious." A few months ago I stopped wondering.

3 A plane my 16-year-old son and I were scheduled to board was swapped with another because of mechanical problems. Although I was relieved to know we were boarding an aircraft that checked out, I still felt uneasy about flying

because of the "shoe bomber" incident three days earlier. I hadn't noticed security checking anyone's shoes.

4 Once settled into the aisle seat, with my son next to the window, I learned there could be another delay because of weather. Before opening my novel I noticed a man in the exit row two seats ahead, looking toward the rear of the plane. He was olive-skinned, black-haired and clean-shaven, with a blanket covering his legs and feet. I thought that was strange, because I felt so warm. No one else was using a blanket.

5 Nine-C, as I called him, sat motionless for 10 minutes, except for glancing nervously down the aisle every few minutes. Then his leg started to shake, and he seemed to be reaching for something under his blanket. He bent over. Adrenaline coursed through my body. I sensed something horrible. The plane was still on the ground, but I felt airsick.

6 "You're being ridiculous," I told myself. "Nine-C just wants to get home. He's cold; he has to use the bathroom. Just relax and keep your water bottle handy, in case he lights a match."

7 But he was very big, and the people sitting near him were not. And I wondered, "What if he goes to the bathroom to light his bomb?" Then I looked at my son—I thought of his potential, his brilliance as a musician and mathematician. How could I tell if 9-C was a terrorist? I couldn't.

8 I forced myself to walk to the rear of the plane. "What should a passenger do if she sees someone behaving in a way she considers odd?" I asked the flight attendant.

9 "Tell me about it."

10 "I'm probably just being paranoid," I started, and described what I'd seen. When I got back to my seat, I tried to forget my suspicions, having turned them over to an expert. A few minutes later, a flight attendant asked the passengers in row nine how they were doing. Another attendant came down the aisle, looking carefully at both sides.

11 "We need to de-ice the wings," announced the captain, apologizing for yet another delay. He emerged from the cockpit, walked back to 9-C's row and looked out to examine the wings. The other pilot did the same.

12 Soon afterward, we learned we were returning to the gate because of "another minor mechanical problem." Absorbed in my book, I hardly paid attention. When I looked up a chapter later, I saw that 9-C was gone. Was he in the bathroom?

13 We took off, and once at cruising altitude, I walked to the rear to see if he'd changed seats. But he was nowhere. I asked the flight attendant where he was. "We don't know what happens once security gets them. After the shoe-bomber, we're glad to get rid of anyone suspicious."

14 I felt awful. I didn't mean for 9-C to be taken away. I had probably ruined an innocent traveler's day, not to mention delaying an already late flight. And I hadn't even noticed he'd gone. I vowed not to scare my son; I'd keep the story to myself.

15 But I couldn't. The head flight attendant asked me to come to the front of the plane. My heart pounded and my cheeks burned; I felt ashamed and afraid.

"Thank you for alerting us to that man," he said, smiling. "We all observed him, including our pilots. He seemed depressed, but also very nervous. Security did a background check and decided to question him. If he's OK, we'll compensate him. You did the right thing. Once we're in the air, it's too late."

16 We were moved to first class, and I wrote an incident report. Later, while waiting for our luggage, I reeled with questions: Had other passengers wondered about 9-C? Where was he now? Would I ever know whether he was a danger? Most important, had I become a racial profiler, bulldozing the roots of that powerful essay that had shaped me in my youth?

17 Perhaps I had. But I'm not sure I regret it. I can live with the guilt, grief and anger. Even though I lost a part of myself and may have gotten an innocent man jettisoned from the plane, it's not the same world it was half a lifetime ago.

EXERCISES

A. Determining the Main Idea and Writer's Purpose

Choose the best answer.

1. The main idea of the selection is that the author
   a. was convinced that the passenger in seat 9-C was a terrorist.
   b. experienced mixed feelings after she alerted a flight attendant about a suspicious passenger.
   c. was tense and nervous about flying in the aftermath of the 2001 terrorist attacks.
   d. believes that racial profiling is an unfair and dangerous practice that violates civil liberties.

2. The writer's purpose in relating the experience on her flight is to
   a. describe a moral dilemma she confronted.
   b. examine the reasons that incidents of racial profiling have increased.
   c. present her opinion on a controversial issue.
   d. defend her behavior to potential critics.

B. Comprehending Main Ideas

Choose the correct answer.

1. Hope recalls a magazine essay written by an African American writer who described what it was like when people

a. denied him a job for which he was qualified.
b. crossed to the other side of the street when he walked toward them.
c. looked at him suspiciously wherever he went.
d. refused to sit next to him on a bus or streetcar.

2. The man in seat 9-C aroused the author's suspicion more because of
   a. his appearance rather than his behavior.
   b. his behavior rather than his appearance.
   c. both his appearance and his behavior.
   d. a vague, undefined, and unexpressed sense that something was wrong.

3. What specifically prompted the author to alert the flight attendant to the strange behavior of the man in seat 9-C was
   a. the thought of her son's future.
   b. her fear about flying.
   c. the thought of everything she had to lose in life.
   d. her paranoia.

4. The author's suspicions about the passenger were confirmed by
   a. her son.
   b. her fellow passengers.
   c. the flight crew.
   d. a later news account about the man's identity.

5. Ultimately, the author concludes that she
   a. made the wrong decision by unfairly targeting an innocent man.
   b. disrupted the lives of her fellow passengers for nothing.
   c. will have to live with the guilt and anger over the situation she was placed in.
   d. made the right decision, given the world we now live in.

C. Vocabulary and Dictionary Exercise

Using a college edition of an unabridged dictionary, answer the following questions on these vocabulary words in the selection.

1. From paragraph 2: an *avowed* liberal
   a. Write the definition of *avowed* that fits the context.

   ____

b. How is the "a" in *avow* pronounced?

____

c. Is the stress mark on the first or the second syllable?

____

2. From paragraph 7: I thought of his *potential*

   a. What part of speech is *potential* as it is used in this sentence?

   ____

   b. In the etymological section, what language is listed as the original or first language where the word originated?

   ____

   c. What word did it come from, and what was its meaning in that original language?

   ____

3. From paragraph 10: I'm probably just being *paranoid*

   a. Look up the noun form of this word—*paranoia*. What language does this word derive from, and what was its original meaning?

   ____

   b. Write the dictionary definition for *paranoid* in this context.

   ____

   c. Write the other noun form for *paranoia*, referring to a person suffering from this illness.

   ____

4. From paragraph 11: "We need to *de-ice* the wings," announced the captain.

   a. Which of these definitions fits the meaning of the prefix *de-* in this word? **1.** Do or make the opposite of; reverse. **2.** Remove or remove from. **3.** Out of. **4.** Reduce; degrade. **5.** Derived from.

   ____

   b. What part of speech is *de-ice*?

   ____

5. From paragraph 15: "We'll *compensate* him."

   a. What guide words appear on the dictionary page where *compensate* appears?

   ____

b. In the word's three syllables, which vowel is pronounced like a schwa (ə)?

____

c. Which of the three syllables is stressed?

____

d. Which of these definitions fits the meaning of the word in this context? **1.** To offset; counterbalance. **2.** To make satisfactory payment or reparation to; recompense or reimburse. **3.** To stabilize the purchasing power of a monetary unit.

____

6. From paragraph 16: I *reeled* with questions

a. What part of speech is *reeled* as it is used in this sentence?

____

b. After consulting your dictionary, write the best definition for this word according to the context.

____

7. From paragraph 17: an innocent man *jettisoned* from the plane

a. Look up the etymology of *jettison* and write the original meaning of the word in Middle English.

____

b. Is the meaning of the word in the context in which Hope uses it more specific or more general than this original meaning?

____

c. What does it mean?

____

EXPLORE THE WEB

The following three websites provide different perspectives about the practice of racial profiling as it affects civil liberties.

www.pbs.org/newshour/bb/terrorism/july-dec01/racial_profile.html

www.scu.edu/SCU/Centers/Ethics/publications/ethicalperspectives/profiling.html

http://writ.news.findlaw.com/colb/20011010.html

Reading Selections

The American Man, Age Ten

Susan Orlean

Susan Orlean has been a staff writer for the *New Yorker* since 1992. In addition, she has written for *Rolling Stone, Outside, Vogue,* and *Esquire.* She studied history and literature at the University of Michigan at Ann Arbor, after which she moved to Portland, Oregon, where she began writing small journalistic pieces. She is the author of the best-selling book *The Orchid Thief,* which was the basis of a Spike Jonze movie, *Adaptation.* Her specialty might be called "soft" journalism—stories about ordinary people and ordinary places. Her most recent book is *My Kind of Place: Travel Stories from a Woman Who's Been Everywhere* (2005), a collection of stories that she describes as being about "places and situations," though they are not travel stories in the traditional sense of the word. She also served as guest editor for *Best American Essays 2005.* The selection reprinted here was first published in *Esquire* magazine in 1992; it is reprinted as well in her collection of essays, *The Bullfighter Checks Her Makeup* (2001).

VOCABULARY ANALYSIS

The Prefix *pre-* [paragraph 70]

You can see the prefix *pre-* both in the word *prefix* and in *presage,* used in paragraph 70 to mean "to warn in advance" or "to portend." The verb can be pronounced either "pri saj'," with the accent on the second syllable, or "pres' ig," with the accent on the first syllable. The prefix *pre-,* from Latin meaning "before," begins dozens of English words, in addition to those cited above, for example, *preamble* (a preliminary statement); *precursor* (something that comes before); *premonition* (a forewarning); *prefabricate* (to manufacture before); *prenuptial* (before a wedding); and *prepubescent* (occurring before puberty).

The American Man, Age Ten

Susan Orlean

1 If Colin Duffy and I were to get married, we would have matching superhero notebooks. We would wear shorts, big sneakers, and long, baggy T-shirts depicting famous athletes every single day, even in the winter. We would sleep in our clothes. We would both be good at Nintendo Street Fighter II, but Colin would be better than me. We would have some homework, but it would never be too hard and we would always have just finished it. We would eat pizza and candy for all of our meals. We wouldn't have sex, but we would have crushes on each other and, magically, babies would appear in our home. We would win the lottery and then buy land in Wyoming, where we would have one of every kind of cute animal. All the while, Colin would be working in law enforcement—probably the FBI. Our favorite movie star, Morgan Freeman, would visit us occasionally. We would listen to the same Eurythmics song ("Here Comes the Rain Again") over and over again and watch two hours of television every Friday night. We would both be good at football, have best friends, and know how to drive; we would cure AIDS and the garbage problem and everything that hurts animals. We would hang out a lot with Colin's dad. For fun, we would load a slingshot with dog food and shoot it at my butt. We would have a very good life.

2 Here are the particulars about Colin Duffy: He is ten years old, on the nose. He is four feet eight inches high, weighs seventy-five pounds, and appears to be mostly leg and shoulder blade. He is a handsome kid. He has a broad forehead, dark eyes with dense lashes, and a sharp, dimply smile. I have rarely seen him without a baseball cap. He owns several, but favors a University of Michigan Wolverines model, on account of its pleasing colors. The hat styles his hair into wild disarray. If you ever managed to get the hat off his head, you would see a boy with a nimbus of golden-brown hair, dented in the back, where the hat hits him.

3 Colin lives with his mother, Elaine; his father, Jim; his older sister, Megan; and his little brother, Chris, in a pretty pale blue Victorian house on a bosky street in Glen Ridge, New Jersey. Glen Ridge is a serene and civilized old town twenty miles west of New York City. It does not have much of a commercial district, but it is a town of amazing lawns. Most of the houses were built around the turn of the century and are set back a gracious, green distance from the street. The rest of the town seems to consist of parks and playing fields and sidewalks and backyards—in other words, it is a far cry from South-Central Los Angeles and from Bedford-Stuyvesant and other, grimmer parts of the country where a very different ten-year-old American man is growing up today.

4 There is a fine school system in Glen Ridge, but Elaine and Jim, who are both schoolteachers, choose to send their children to a parents' cooperative elementary school in Montclair, a neighboring suburb. Currently, Colin is in fifth

grade. He is a good student. He plans to go to college, to a place he says is called Oklahoma City State College University. OCSCU satisfies his desire to live out west, to attend a small college, and to study law enforcement, which OCSCU apparently offers as a major. After four years at Oklahoma City State College University, he plans to work for the FBI. He says that getting to be a police officer involves tons of hard work, but working for the FBI will be a cinch, because all you have to do is fill out one form, which he has already gotten from the head FBI office. Colin is quiet in class but loud on the playground. He has a great throwing arm, significant foot speed, and a lot of physical confidence. He is also brave. Huge wild cats with rabies and gross stuff dripping from their teeth, which he says run rampant throughout his neighborhood, do not scare him. Otherwise, he is slightly bashful. This combination of athletic grace and valor and personal reserve accounts for considerable popularity. He has a fluid relationship to many social groups, including the superbright nerds, the ultra-jocks, the flashy kids who will someday become extremely popular and socially successful juvenile delinquents, and the kids who will be elected president of the student body. In his opinion, the most popular boy in his class is Christian, who happens to be black, and Colin's favorite television character is Steve Urkel on *Family Matters*, who is black, too, but otherwise he seems uninterested in or oblivious to race. Until this year, he was a Boy Scout. Now he is planning to begin karate lessons. His favorite schoolyard game is football, followed closely by prison dodgeball, blob tag, and bombardo. He's crazy about athletes, although sometimes it isn't clear if he is absolutely sure of the difference between human athletes and Marvel Comics action figures. His current athletic hero is Dave Meggett. His current best friend is named Japeth. He used to have another best friend named Ozzie. According to Colin, Ozzie was found on a doorstep, then changed his name to Michael and moved to Massachusetts, and then Colin never saw him or heard from him again.

5 He has had other losses in his life. He is old enough to know people who have died and to know things about the world that are worrisome. When he dreams, he dreams about moving to Wyoming, which he has visited with his family. His plan is to buy land there and have some sort of ranch that would definitely include horses. Sometimes when he talks about this, it sounds as ordinary and hard-boiled as a real estate appraisal; other times it can sound fantastical and wifty and achingly naive, informed by the last inklings of childhood—the musings of a balmy real estate appraiser assaying a wonderful and magical landscape that erodes from memory a little bit every day. The collision in his mind of what he understands, what he hears, what he figures out, what popular culture pours into him, what he knows, what he pretends to know, and what he imagines makes an interesting mess. The mess often has the form of what he will probably think like when he is a grown man, but the content of what he is like as a little boy.

Connecting Grammar to Writing

In paragraph 5, sentence 5, Orlean uses two pronouns—*this* and *it* (twice). What do these pronouns refer to? (Hint: Look at the preceding sentence and find the noun that serves as their antecedent.) Be sure when you use pronouns like this that there is a clear antecedent so that the reader does not get confused.

6 He is old enough to begin imagining that he will someday get married, but at ten he is still convinced that the best thing about being married will be that he will be allowed to sleep in his clothes. His father once observed that living with Colin was like living with a Martian who had done some reading on American culture. As it happens, Colin is not especially sad or worried about the prospect of growing up, although he sometimes frets over whether he should be called a kid or a grown-up; he has settled on the word *kid-up*. Once, I asked him what the biggest advantage to adulthood will be, and he said, "The best thing is that grown-ups can go wherever they want." I asked him what he meant, exactly, and he said, "Well, if you're grown up, you'd have a car, and whenever you felt like it, you could get into your car and drive somewhere and get candy."

7 Colin loves recycling. He loves it even more than, say, playing with little birds. That ten-year-olds feel the weight of the world and consider it their mission to shoulder it came as a surprise to me. I had gone with Colin one Monday to his classroom at Montclair Cooperative School. The Co-op is in a steep, old, sharp-angled brick building that had served for many years as a public school until a group of parents in the area took it over and made it into a private, progressive elementary school. The fifth-grade classroom is on the top floor, under the dormers, which gives the room the eccentric shape and closeness of an attic. It is a rather informal environment. There are computers lined up in an adjoining room and instructions spelled out on the chalkboard—BRING IN: (1) A CUBBY WITH YOUR NAME ON IT, (2) A TRAPPER WITH A 5-POCKET ENVELOPE LABELED SCIENCE, SOCIAL STUDIES, READING/LANGUAGE ARTS, MATH, MATH LAB/COMPUTER; WHITE LINED PAPER; A PLASTIC PENCIL BAG; A SMALL HOMEWORK PAD, (3) LARGE BROWN GROCERY BAGS—but there is also a couch in the center of the classroom, which the kids take turns occupying, a rocking chair, and three canaries in cages near the door.

8 It happened to be Colin's first day in fifth grade. Before class began, there was a lot of horsing around, but there were also a lot of conversations about whether Magic Johnson had AIDS or just HIV and whether someone falling in a pool of blood from a cut of his would get the disease. These jolts of sobriety in the midst of rank goofiness are a ten-year-old's specialty. Each one comes as a fresh, hard surprise, like finding a razor blade in a candy apple. One day, Colin and I had been discussing horses or dogs or something, and out of the blue he said, "What do you think is better, to dump garbage in the ocean, to dump it on land, or to burn it?" Another time, he asked me if I planned to have children. I had just spent an evening with him and his friend Japeth, during which they put every small, movable object in the house into Japeth's slingshot and fired it at me, so I told him that I wanted children but that I hoped they would all be girls, and he said, "Will you have an abortion if you find out you have a boy?"

9 At school, after discussing summer vacation, the kids began choosing the jobs they would do to help out around the classroom. Most of the jobs are humdrum—putting the chairs up on the tables, washing the chalkboard, turning

the computers off or on. Five of the most humdrum tasks are recycling chores—for example, taking bottles or stacks of paper down to the basement, where they would be sorted and prepared for pickup. Two children would be assigned to feed the birds and cover their cages at the end of the day.

10 I expected the bird jobs to be the first to go. Everyone loved the birds; they'd spent an hour that morning voting on names for them (Tweetie, Montgomery, and Rose narrowly beating out Axl Rose, Bugs, Ol' Yeller, Fido, Slim, Lucy, and Chirpie). Instead, they all wanted to recycle. The recycling jobs were claimed by the first five kids called by Suzanne Nakamura, the fifth-grade teacher; each kid called after that responded by groaning, "Suzanne, aren't there any more recycling jobs?" Colin ended up with the job of taking down the chairs each morning. He accepted the task with a sort of resignation—this was going to be just a job rather than a mission.

11 On the way home that day, I was quizzing Colin about his worldviews.

12 "Who's the coolest person in the world?"

13 "Morgan Freeman."

14 "What's the best sport?"

15 "Football."

16 "Who's the coolest woman?"

17 "None. I don't know."

18 "What's the most important thing in the world?"

19 "Game Boy." Pause. "No, the world. The world is the most important thing in the world."

20 Danny's Pizzeria is a dark little shop next door to the Montclair Cooperative School. It is not much to look at. Outside, the brick facing is painted muddy brown. Inside, there are some saggy counters, a splintered bench, and enough room for either six teenagers or about a dozen ten-year-olds who happen to be getting along well. The light is low. The air is oily. At Danny's, you will find pizza, candy, Nintendo, and very few girls. To a ten-year-old boy, it is the most beautiful place in the world.

21 One afternoon, after class was dismissed, we went to Danny's with Colin's friend Japeth to play Nintendo. Danny's has only one game, Street Fighter II Champion Edition. Some teenage boys from a nearby middle school had gotten there first and were standing in a tall, impenetrable thicket around the machine.

22 "Next game," Colin said. The teenagers ignored him.

23 "Hey, we get next game," Japeth said. He is smaller than Colin, scrappy, and, as he explained to me once, famous for wearing his hat backward all the time and having a huge wristwatch and a huge bedroom. He stamped his foot and announced again, "Hey, we get next game."

24 One of the teenagers turned around and said, "Fuck you, *next game*," and then turned back to the machine.

25 "Whoa," Japeth said.

26 He and Colin went outside, where they felt bigger.

27 "Which street fighter are you going to be?" Colin asked Japeth.

28 "Blanka," Japeth said. "I know how to do his head-butt."

29 "I hate that! I hate the head-butt," Colin said. He dropped his voice a little and growled, "I'm going to be Ken, and I will kill you with my dragon punch."

30 "Yeah, right, and monkeys will fly out of my butt," Japeth said.

31 Street Fighter II is a video game in which two characters have an explosive brawl in a scenic international setting. It is currently the most popular video arcade game in America. This is not an insignificant amount of popularity. Most arcade versions of video games, which end up in pizza parlors, malls, and arcades, sell about two thousand units. So far, some fifty thousand Street Fighter II and Street Fighter II Championship Edition arcade games have been sold. Not since Pac-Man, which was released the year before Colin was born, has there been a video game as popular as Street Fighter. The home version of Street Fighter is the most popular home video game in the country, and that, too, is not an insignificant thing. Thirty-two million Nintendo home systems have been sold since 1986, when it was introduced in this country. There is a Nintendo system in seven of every ten homes in America in which a child between the ages of eight and twelve resides. By the time a boy in America turns ten, he will almost certainly have been exposed to Nintendo home games, Nintendo arcade games, and Game Boy, the handheld version. He will probably own a system and dozens of games. By ten, according to Nintendo studies, teachers, and psychologists, game prowess becomes a fundamental, essential male social marker and a schoolyard boast.

32 The Street Fighter characters are Dhalsim, Ken, Guile, Blanka, E. Honda, Ryu, Zangief, and Chun Li. Each represents a different country, and they each have their own special weapon. Chun Li, for instance, is from China and possesses a devastating whirlwind kick that is triggered if you push the control pad down for two seconds and then up for two seconds, and then you hit the kick button. Chun Li's kick is money in the bank, because most of the other fighters do not have a good defense against it. By the way, Chun Li happens to be a girl—the only female Street Fighter character.

33 I asked Colin if he was interested in being Chun Li. There was a long pause. "I would rather be Ken," he said.

34 The girls in Colin's class at school are named Cortnerd, Terror, Spacey, Lizard, Maggot, and Diarrhea. "They do have other names, but that's what we call them," Colin told me. "The girls aren't very popular."

35 "They are about as popular as a piece of dirt," Japeth said. "Or, you know that couch in the classroom? That couch is more popular than any girl. A thousand times more." They talked for a minute about one of the girls in their class, a tall blonde with cheerleader genetic material, who they allowed was not quite as gross as some of the other girls. Japeth said that a chubby, awkward boy in their class was boasting that this girl liked him.

36 "No way," Colin said. "She would never like him. I mean, not that he's so... I don't know. I don't hate him because he's fat, anyway. I hate him because he's nasty."

37 "Well, she doesn't like him," Japeth said. "She's been really mean to me lately, so I'm pretty sure she likes me."

38 "Girls are different," Colin said. He hopped up and down on the balls of his feet, wrinkling his nose. "Girls are stupid and weird."

39 "I have a lot of girlfriends, about six or so," Japeth said, turning contemplative. "I don't exactly remember their names, though."

40 The teenagers came crashing out of Danny's and jostled past us, so we went inside. The man who runs Danny's, whose name is Tom, was leaning across the counter on his elbows, looking exhausted. Two little boys, holding Slush Puppies, shuffled toward the Nintendo, but Colin and Japeth elbowed them aside and slammed their quarters down on the machine. The little boys shuffled back toward the counter and stood gawking at them, sucking on their drinks.

41 "You want to know how to tell if a girl likes you?" Japeth said. "She'll act really mean to you. That's a sure sign. I don't know why they do it, but it's always a sure sign. It gets your attention. You know how I show a girl I like her? I steal something from her and then run away. I do it to get their attention, and it works."

42 They played four quarters' worth of games. During the last one, a teenager with a quilted leather jacket and a fade haircut came in, pushed his arm between them, and put a quarter down on the deck of the machine.

43 Japeth said, "Hey, what's that?"

44 The teenager said, "I get next game. I've marked it now. Everyone knows this secret sign for next game. It's a universal thing."

45 "So now we know," Japeth said. "Colin, let's get out of here and go bother Maggie. I mean Maggot. Okay?" They picked up their backpacks and headed out the door.

46 Psychologists identify ten as roughly the age at which many boys experience the gender-linked normative developmental trauma that leaves them, as adult men, at risk for specific psychological sequelae often manifest as deficits in the arenas of intimacy, empathy, and struggles with commitment in relationships. In other words, this is around the age when guys get screwed up about girls. Elaine and Jim Duffy, and probably most of the parents who send their kids to Montclair Cooperative School, have done a lot of stuff to try to avoid this. They gave Colin dolls as well as guns. (He preferred guns.) Japeth's father has three motorcycles and two dirt bikes but does most of the cooking and cleaning in their home. Suzanne, Colin's teacher, is careful to avoid sexist references in her presentations. After school, the yard at Montclair Cooperative is filled with as many fathers as mothers—fathers who hug their kids when they come prancing out of the building and are dismayed when their sons clamor for Supersoaker water guns and war toys or take pleasure in beating up girls.

47 In a study of adolescents conducted by the Gesell Institute of Human Development, nearly half the ten-year-old boys questioned said they thought they had

adequate information about sex. Nevertheless, most ten-year-old boys across the country are subjected to a few months of sex education in school. Colin and his class will get their dose next spring. It is yet another installment in a plan to make them into new, improved men with reconstructed notions of sex and male-female relationships. One afternoon I asked Philip, a schoolmate of Colin's, whether he was looking forward to sex education, and he said, "No, because I think it'll probably make me really, really hyper. I have a feeling it's going to be just like what it was like when some television reporters came to school last year and filmed us in class and I got really hyper. They stood around with all these cameras and asked us questions. I think that's what sex education is probably like."

48 At a class meeting earlier in the day:

49 Colin's teacher, SUZANNE: Today was our first day of swimming class, and I have one observation to make. The girls went into their locker room, got dressed without a lot of fuss, and came into the pool area. The boys, on the other hand, the *boys* had some sort of problem doing that rather simple task. Can someone tell me what exactly went on in the locker room?

50 KEITH: There was a lot of shouting.

51 SUZANNE: Okay, I hear you saying that people were being noisy and shouting. Anything else?

52 CHRISTIAN: Some people were screaming so much that my ears were killing me. It gave me, like, a huge headache. Also, some of boys were taking their towels, I mean, after they had taken their clothes off, they had their towels around their waists and then they would drop them really fast and then pull them back up, really fast.

53 SUZANNE: Okay, you're saying some people were being silly about their bodies.

54 CHRISTIAN: Well, yeah, but it was more like they were being silly about their pants.

55 Colin's bedroom is decorated simply. He has a cage with his pet parakeet, Dude, on his dresser, a lot of recently worn clothing piled haphazardly on the floor, and a husky brown teddy bear sitting upright in a chair near the foot of his bed. The walls are mostly bare, except for a Spiderman poster and a few ads torn out of magazines he has thumbtacked up. One of the ads is for a cologne, illustrated with several small photographs of cowboy hats; another, a feverish portrait of a woman on a horse, is an ad for blue jeans. These inspire him sometimes when he lies in bed and makes plans for the move to Wyoming. Also, he happens to like ads. He also likes television commercials. Generally speaking, he likes consumer products and popular culture. He partakes avidly but not indiscriminately. In fact, during the time we spent together, he provided a running commentary on merchandise, media, and entertainment:

56 "The only shoes anyone will wear are Reebok Pumps. Big T-shirts are cool, not the kind that are sticky and close to you, but big and baggy and long, not the kind that stop at your stomach."

57 "The best food is Chicken McNuggets and Life cereal and Frosted Flakes."

58 "Don't go to Blimpie's. They have the worst service."

59 "I'm not into Teenage Mutant Ninja Turtles anymore. I grew out of that. I like Donatello, but I'm not a fan. I don't buy the figures anymore."

60 "The best television shows are on Friday night on ABC. It's called TGIF, and it's *Family Matters, Step by Step, Dinosaurs,* and *Perfect Strangers*, where the guy has a funny accent."

61 "The best candy is Skittles and Symphony bars and Crybabies and Warheads. Crybabies are great because if you eat a lot of them at once you feel so sour."

62 "Hyundais are Korean cars. It's the only Korean car. They're not that good because Koreans don't have a lot of experience building cars."

63 "The best movie is *City Slickers*, and the best part was when he saved his little cow in the river."

64 "The Giants really need to get rid of Ray Handley. They have to get somebody who has real coaching experience. He's just no good."

65 "My dog, Sally, costs seventy-two dollars. That sounds like a lot of money but it's a really good price because you get a flea bath with your dog."

66 "The best magazines are *Nintendo Power*, because they tell you how to do the secret moves in the video games, and also *Mad* magazines and *Money Guide*—I really like that one."

67 "The best artist in the world in Jim Davis."

68 "The most beautiful woman in the world is not Madonna! Only Wayne and Garth think that! She looks like maybe a... a... slut or something. Cindy Crawford looks like she would look good, but if you see her on an awards program on TV she doesn't look that good. I think the most beautiful woman in the world probably is my mom."

69 Colin thinks a lot about money. This started when he was about nine and a half, which is when a lot of other things started—a new way of walking that has a little macho hitch and swagger, a decision about the Teenage Mutant Ninja Turtles (con) and Eurythmics (pro), and a persistent curiosity about a certain girl whose name he will not reveal. He knows the price of everything he encounters. He knows how much college costs and what someone might earn performing different jobs. Once, he asked me what my husband did; when I answered that he was a lawyer, he snapped, "You must be a rich family. Lawyers make $400,000 a year." His preoccupation with money baffles his family. They are not struggling, so this is not the anxiety of deprivation; they are not rich, so he is not responding to an elegant, advantaged world. His allowance is five dollars a week. It seems sufficient for his needs, which consist chiefly of quarters for Nintendo and candy money. The remainder is put into his Wyoming fund. His fascination is not just specific to needing money or having plans for money: It is as if money itself, and the way it makes the world work, and the realization that almost everything in the world can be assigned a price, has possessed him. "I just pay attention to things like that," Colin says. "It's really very interesting."

70 He is looking for a windfall. He tells me his mother has been notified that she is in the fourth and final round of the Publisher's Clearinghouse Sweepstakes. This is not an ironic observation. He plays the New Jersey lottery every Thursday night. He knows the weekly jackpot; he knows the number to call to find out if he has won. I do not think this presages a future for Colin as a high-stakes gambler; I think it says more about the powerful grasp that money has on imagination and what a large percentage of a ten-year-old's mind is made up of imaginings. One Friday, we were at school together, and one of his friends was asking him about the lottery, and he said, "This week it was $4 million. That would be I forget how much every year for the rest of your life. It's a lot, I think. You should play. All it takes is a dollar and a dream."

71 Until the lottery comes through and he starts putting together the Wyoming land deal, Colin can be found most of the time in the backyard. Often, he will have friends come over. Regularly, children from the neighborhood will gravitate to the backyard, too. As a technical matter of real-property law, title to the house and yard belongs to Jim and Elaine Duffy, but Colin adversely possesses the backyard, at least from 4:00 each afternoon until it gets dark. As yet, the fixtures of teenage life—malls, video arcades, friends' basements, automobiles—either hold little interest for him or are not his to have.

72 He is, at the moment, very content with his backyard. For most intents and purposes, it is as big as Wyoming. One day, certainly, he will grow and it will shrink, and it will become simply a suburban backyard and it won't be big enough for him anymore. This will happen so fast that one night he will be in the backyard, believing it a perfect place, and by the next night he will have changed and the yard as he imagined it will be gone, and this era of his life will be behind him forever.

73 Most days, he spends his hours in the backyard building an Evil Spider-Web Trap. This entails running a spool of Jim's fishing line from every surface in the yard until it forms a huge web. Once a garbageman picking up the Duffys' trash got caught in the trap. Otherwise, the Evil Spider-Web Trap mostly has a deterrent effect, because the kids in the neighborhood who might roam over know that Colin builds it back there. "I do it all the time," he says. "First I plan who I'd like to catch in it, and then we get started. Trespassers have to beware."

74 One afternoon when I came over, after a few rounds of Street Fighter at Danny's, Colin started building a trap. He selected a victim for inspiration—a boy in his class who had been pestering him—and began wrapping. He was entirely absorbed. He moved from tree to tree, wrapping; he laced fishing line through the railing of the deck and then back to the shed; he circled an old jungle gym, something he'd outgrown and abandoned a few years ago, and then crossed over to a bush at the back of the yard. Briefly, he contemplated making his dog, Sally, part of the web. Dusk fell. He kept wrapping, paying out fishing line an inch at a time. We

could hear mothers up and down the block hooting for their kids; two tiny children from next door stood transfixed at the edge of the yard, uncertain whether they would end up inside or outside the web. After a while, the spool spun around in Colin's hands one more time and then stopped; he was out of line.

It was almost too dark to see much of anything, although now and again the light from the deck would glance off a length of line, and it would glint and sparkle. "That's the point," he said. "You could do it with thread, but the fishing line is invisible. Now I have this perfect thing and the only one who knows about it is me." With that, he dropped the spool, skipped up the stairs of the deck, threw open the screen door, and then bounded into the house, leaving me and Sally the dog trapped in his web.

EXERCISES

A. Determining the Main Idea and Writer's Purpose

Choose the best answer.

1. Here are four excerpts from the selection. Which *best* captures Colin Duffy's character and spirit?
   a. Colin loves recycling. He loves it even more than, say, playing with little birds. That ten-year-olds feel the weight of the world and consider it their mission to shoulder it came as a surprise to me.
   b. . . . he happens to like ads. He also likes television commercials. Generally speaking, he likes consumer products and popular culture. He partakes avidly but not indiscriminately.
   c. The collision in his mind of what he understands, what he hears, what he figures out, what popular culture pours into him, what he knows, what he pretends to know, and what he imagines makes him an interesting mess. The mess often has the form of what he will probably think like when he is a grown man, but the content of what he is like as a little boy.
   d. . . . there were also lots of conversations about whether Magic Johnson had AIDS or just HIV and whether someone falling in a pool of blood from a cut of his would get the disease. These jolts of sobriety in the midst of rank goofiness are a ten-year-old's specialty. Each one comes as a fresh, hard surprise.

2. With respect to the main idea, the writer's purpose is to
   a. depict the unique characteristics, activities, hopes, and dreams of a ten-year-old American boy.
   b. examine the cultural influences that shape American children today.

c. explore the pervasive attraction of video games, sports, and advertisements for American boys today.

d. show how one model family is raising a well-adapted child.

B. Comprehending Main Ideas

Choose the correct answer.

1. Orlean describes the town of Glen Ridge, New Jersey, where Colin Duffy lives with his family as being
   a. serene and civilized.
   b. grim and depressing.
   c. affluent and racially segregated.
   d. culturally isolated from nearby New York City.

2. Colin plans to attend Oklahoma City State College University where he hopes to study
   a. sports psychology.
   b. environmental science.
   c. law enforcement.
   d. landscape architecture.

3. In terms of his social standing at school, Orlean describes Colin as
   a. being in the superbright group of nerds.
   b. being in the group known as superjocks.
   c. striving to be in the flashy and socially successful group.
   d. enjoying a fluid relationship with all groups.

4. Colin and his friends hang out at Danny's Pizzeria after school in order to
   a. annoy the teenage boys who hang out there.
   b. play Nintendo.
   c. eat candy and pizza.
   d. flirt with girls.

5. In his backyard, Colin Duffy is building
   a. a Superior Super Nintendo game system.
   b. a Radical Recycling Mechanism.
   c. an Evil Spider-Web Trap.
   d. a revolutionary doghouse for his dog, Sally.

READING

C. Interpreting Meaning (or Analyzing Structure and Meaning)

Answer these questions in your own words.

1. Colin Duffy is a 10-year-old boy, not a 10-year-old man. What's the significance of the title, and how does the title reflect her purpose in writing? Where is this purpose best revealed in the essay?

____

____

____

____

2. What do the collection of details in paragraph 1 reveal about the writer and about her relationship with Colin? What side of the writer do these details show?

____

____

____

3. Read paragraph 3 again. What contrast is Orlean making in this paragraph?

____

____

4. In paragraph 6, Orlean quotes Colin's father as saying this about his son: "[L]iving with Colin was like living with a Martian who had done some reading on American culture." What does he mean?

____

____

____

5. Read paragraph 31 again. A good title for this paragraph would be
   a. "The Popularity of Nintendo."
   b. "Popular Arcade Games."
   c. "Video Games' Educational Value."
   d. "Nintendo as a Male Social Marker."

D. Understanding Vocabulary

Look through the paragraphs listed below and find a word that matches each definition. Refer to a dictionary if necessary. An example has been done for you.

EXAMPLE: state of disorder [paragraphs 1–2] disarray

1. moving without restraint, unchecked [4] ____________
2. courage, bravery [4] ____________
3. unaware, unconscious [4] ____________
4. lacking world experience and understanding [5–6] ____________
5. thoughts, contemplations, reflections [5–6] ____________
6. clear-headedness, gravity, soberness [7–8] ____________
7. routine, boring, unexciting [8–9] ____________
8. unresisting acceptance, submission [9–10] ____________
9. tightly packed, impossible to enter [20–30] ____________
10. noisy fight, quarrel, clash [31–32] ____________
11. haphazardly, unselectively [55] ____________
12. describing a strong or exaggerated masculinity [69–70] ____________
13. be attracted by, be drawn to [71–72] ____________
14. preventive, discouraging [73–74] ____________
15. remained motionless with amazement, fascination [74–75] ____________

E. Vocabulary and Dictionary Exercise

Answer these questions. You may need to consult a dictionary for this exercise.

1. In paragraph 2, Orlean describes Colin Duffy as having "a *nimbus* of golden-brown hair." What language does *nimbus* derive from, and what did it mean in that language?

   ____

READING

2. The adjective *bosky* (see paragraph 3) derives from three languages. In chronological order, from the newest to the original, list them here. Then write the meaning of the word.

____

3. The comparative form of the adjective *grim* is *grimmer*, used in the last sentence of paragraph 3. What are the noun and adverb forms of *grim*?

____

4. In paragraph 5, Orlean writes that Colin's dream of moving to Wyoming sounds like "the musings of a balmy real estate appraiser *assaying* a wonderful and magical landscape." The *American Heritage* lists these definitions for the verb *assay*. Write the definition that is the most appropriate for the verb *assay* according to the context.

   1. To subject to chemical analysis. **2.** To examine by trial or experiment; put to a test. **3.** To evaluate, assess. **4.** To attempt; try.

____

5. Here is the word *contemplative* from paragraph 39 written in dictionary pronunciation symbols. Which syllable receives primary stress? Put a heavy stress mark (') after the stressed syllable.
   kən tem plə tĭv

____

   Now do the same for the verb and noun forms: kŏn təm plāt (verb)

____

   kŏn təm plā shən (noun)

____

6. What does the suffix *-ist*, as in *psychologist* (paragraph 46) mean?

____

7. Orlean uses the word *empathy* in paragraph 46. What does this word mean, and how does it differ from the related word, *sympathy?* Which one is stronger in meaning?

____

____

____

____

DISCUSSION QUESTIONS

1. Consider again the title of the essay. How does the deliberate choice of "man" rather than "boy" suit her purpose in writing?
2. This essay was first published as a magazine article in 1992. What changes in a child's life might the intervening fifteen or more years have brought?
3. Colin Duffy's family is evidently financially comfortable. How is this level of affluence specifically borne out in Colin's life?
4. Where in the essay does Orlean concede that Colin is not a representative American 10-year-old boy, and why is this concession necessary and/or effective?
5. Colin is clearly a boy in transition, still a child but also on his way to becoming a man. What does Orlean's essay suggest about how a boy-becoming-a-man learns gender roles? What seem to be the most significant influences in Colin's life?

EXPLORE THE WEB

Susan Orlean sponsors a comprehensive and amusing website with lots of information about her background, her interests, and her writings. Her recent *New Yorker* articles are included there, as well as a schedule of her various appearances and book-signings around the country. You can also read about her Welsh Springer Spaniel Cooper and see pictures of him. The address is

www.susanorlean.com.

Our Perfect Summer

David Sedaris

Humorist David Sedaris is acclaimed for his two best-selling books, *Me Talk Pretty One Day* (2001) and *Dress Your Family in Corduroy and Denim* (2004). The targets of Sedaris's humor, which some might describe as warped, are often himself and his family, including his six siblings. He frequently collaborates with his sister, Amy Sedaris, under the pseudonym "The Talent Family." The selection reprinted here from the *New Yorker* exemplifies how a humorist can find something at once funny and poignant in a past event, in this case, his family's dream of owning a beach cottage in North Carolina. For the past few years, Sedaris has lived in Paris, because as he explains it, he smokes and most Parisians smoke.

VOCABULARY ANALYSIS

misfortune [paragraph 19]

The word *misfortune* begins with the common prefix *mis*-. However, *mis*- has two quite different meanings, and you have to be careful to distinguish between them. In the word misfortune, the prefix *mis*- means "bad." So misfortune means bad luck. But *mis*- can also be attached to words to form *misspell, mispronounce,* and *mislead,* in which case the prefix means "wrong" or "improper."

In these two words, does *mis*- mean "wrong" or "bad"?

misunderstand ____________________

mismanage ____________________

Our Perfect Summer

David Sedaris

1 My mother and I were at the dry cleaner's, standing behind a woman we had never seen. "A nice-looking woman," my mother would later say. "Well put together. Classy." The woman was dressed for the season in a light cotton shift patterned with oversize daisies. Her shoes matched the petals and her purse, which was black-and-yellow striped, hung over her shoulder, buzzing the flowers like a lazy bumblebee. She handed in her claim check, accepted her garments, and then expressed gratitude for what she considered to be fast and efficient service. "You know," she said, "people talk about Raleigh but it isn't really true, is it?"

2 The Korean man nodded, the way you do when you're a foreigner and understand that someone has finished a sentence. He wasn't the owner, just a helper who'd stepped in from the back, and it was clear he had no idea what she was saying.

3 "My sister and I are visiting from out of town," the woman said, a little louder now, and again the man nodded. "I'd love to stay awhile longer and explore, but my home, well, *one* of my homes is on the garden tour, so I've got to get back to Williamsburg."

4 I was eleven years old, yet still the statement seemed strange to me. If she'd hoped to impress the Korean, the woman had obviously wasted her breath, so who was this information for?

5 "My home, well, *one* of my homes"; by the end of the day my mother and I had repeated this line no less than fifty times. The garden tour was unimportant, but the first part of her sentence brought us great pleasure. There was, as indicated by the comma, a pause between the words "home" and "well," a brief moment in which she'd decided, *Oh, why not?* The following word—"one"—had

blown from her mouth as if propelled by a gentle breeze, and this was the difficult part. You had to get it just right or else the sentence lost its power. Falling somewhere between a self-conscious laugh and a sigh of happy confusion, the "one" afforded her statement a double meaning. To her peers it meant, "Look at me, I catch myself coming and going!" and to the less fortunate it was a way of saying, "Don't kid yourself, it's a lot of work having more than one house."

6 The first dozen times we tried it our voices sounded pinched and snobbish, but by midafternoon they had softened. We wanted what this woman had. Mocking her made it seem hopelessly unobtainable, and so we reverted to our natural selves.

7 "My home, well, one of my homes…" My mother said it in a rush, as if she were under pressure to be more specific. It was the same way she said, "My daughter, well, one of my daughters," but a second home was more prestigious than a second daughter, and so it didn't really work. I went in the opposite direction, exaggerating the word "one" in a way that was guaranteed to alienate my listener.

8 "Say it like that and people are going to be jealous," my mother said.

9 "Well, isn't that what we want?"

10 "Sort of," she said. "But mainly we want them to be happy for us."

11 "But why should you be happy for someone who has more than you do?"

12 "I guess it all depends on the person," she said. "Anyway, I suppose it doesn't matter. We'll get it right eventually. When the day arrives I'm sure it'll just come to us."

13 And so we waited.

14 At some point in the mid- to late nineteen-sixties, North Carolina began referring to itself as "Variety Vacationland." The words were stamped onto license plates, and a series of television commercials reminded us that, unlike certain of our neighbors, we had both the beach *and* the mountains. There were those who bounced back and forth between one and the other, but most people tended to choose a landscape and stick to it. We ourselves were Beach People, Emerald Isle People, but that was mainly my mother's doing. I don't think our father would have cared whether he took a vacation or not. Being away from home left him anxious and crabby, but our mother loved the ocean. She couldn't swim, but enjoyed standing at the water's edge with a pole in her hand. It wasn't exactly what you'd call fishing, as she caught nothing and expressed neither hope nor disappointment in regard to her efforts. What she thought about while looking at the waves was a complete mystery, yet you could tell that these thoughts pleased her, and that she liked herself better while thinking them.

15 One year our father waited too late to make our reservations, and we were forced to take something on the sound. It wasn't a cottage but a run-down house, the sort of place where poor people lived. The yard was enclosed by a chain-link fence and the air was thick with the flies and mosquitoes normally

blown away by the ocean breezes. Midway through the vacation a hideous wooly caterpillar fell from a tree and bit my sister Amy on the cheek. Her face swelled and discolored, and within an hour, were it not for her arms and legs, it would have been difficult to recognize her as a human. My mother drove her to the hospital, and when they returned she employed my sister as Exhibit A, pointing as if this were not her daughter but some ugly stranger forced to share our quarters. "*This* is what you get for waiting until the last minute," she said to our father. "No dunes, no waves, just *this*."

Connecting Grammar to Writing

Study Sedaris's punctuation in paragraph 16, particularly his use of commas. Note that the frequent commas used to separate and enclose make the sentences easy to read.

16 From that year on, our mother handled the reservations. We went to Emerald Isle for a week every September and were always oceanfront, a word that suggested a certain degree of entitlement. The oceanfront cottages were on stilts, which made them appear if not large, then at least imposing. Some were painted, some were sided, "Cape Cod style," with wooden shingles, and all of them had names, the cleverest being "Loafer's Paradise." The owners had cut their sign in the shape of two moccasins resting side by side. The shoes were realistically painted and the letters were bloated and listless, loitering like drunks against the soft faux leather.

17 "Now *that's* a sign," our father would say, and we would agree. There was The Skinny Dipper, Pelican's Perch, Lazy Daze, The Scotch Bonnet, Loony Dunes, the name of each house followed by the name and home town of the owner. "The Duncan Clan—Charlotte," "The Graftons—Rocky Mount," "Hal and Jean Starling of Pinehurst": signs that essentially said, "My home, well, *one* of my homes."

18 While at the beach, we sensed more than ever that our lives were governed by luck. When we had it—when it was sunny—my sisters and I felt as if we were somehow personally responsible. We were a fortunate family, and therefore everyone around us was allowed to swim and dig in the sand. When it rained, we were unlucky, and stayed indoors to search our souls. "It'll clear after lunch," our mother would say, and we would eat carefully, using the placemats that had brought us luck in the past. When that failed, we would move on to Plan B. "Oh, Mother, you work too hard," we'd say. "Let us do the dishes. Let us sweep sand off the floor." We spoke like children in a fairy tale, hoping our goodness might lure the sun from its hiding place. "You and Father have been so kind to us. Here, let us massage your shoulders."

19 If by late afternoon it still hadn't cleared, my sisters and I would drop the act and turn on one another, searching for the spoiler who had brought us this misfortune. Which of us seemed the least dissatisfied? Who had curled up on a mildewed bed with a book and a glass of chocolate milk, behaving as though the rain were not such a bad thing after all? We would find this person, most often my sister Gretchen, and then we would beat her.

20 The summer I was twelve, a tropical storm moved up the coast, leaving a sky the same mottled pewter as Gretchen's subsequent bruises, but the following year we started with luck. My father found a golf course that suited him, and for the

first time in memory even he seemed to enjoy himself. Relaxing on the deck with a gin-and-tonic, surrounded by his toast-colored wife and children, he admitted that this really wasn't so bad. "I've been thinking, to hell with these rental cottages," he said. "What do you say we skip the middle-man and just buy a place?"

21 He spoke in the same tone he used when promising ice cream. "Who's up for something sweet?" he'd ask, and we'd pile into the car, passing the Tastee-Freez and driving to the grocery store, where he'd buy a block of pus-colored ice milk reduced for quick sale. Experience had taught us not to trust him, but we wanted a beach house so badly it was impossible not to get caught up in the excitement. Even our mother fell for it.

22 "Do you really mean this?" she asked.

23 "Absolutely," he said.

24 The next day, they made an appointment with a real-estate agent in Morehead City. "We'll just be discussing the possibility," my mother said. "It's just a meeting, nothing more." We wanted to join them but they took only Paul, who was two years old and unfit to be left in our company. The morning meeting led to half a dozen viewings, and when they returned my mother's face was so impassive it seemed almost paralyzed. "It-was-fine," she said. "The-real-estate-agent-was-very-nice." We got the idea that she was under oath to keep something to herself, and the effort was causing her actual physical pain.

25 "It's all right," my father said. "You can tell them."

26 "Well, we saw this one place in particular," she told us. "Now, it's nothing to get worked up about, but…"

27 "But it's perfect," my father said. "A real beauty, just like your mother here." He came from behind and pinched her on the bottom. She laughed and swatted him with a towel and we witnessed what we would later come to recognize as the rejuvenating power of real estate. It's what fortunate couples turn to when their sex life has faded and they're too pious for affairs. A second car might bring people together for a week or two, but a second home can revitalize a marriage for up to nine months after the closing.

28 "Oh, Lou," my mother said. "What am I going to do with you?"

29 "Whatever you want, Baby," he said. "Whatever you want."

30 It was queer when people repeated their sentences, but we were willing to overlook it in exchange for a beach house. My mother was too excited to cook that night, and so we ate dinner at the Sanitary Fish Market, in Morehead City. On taking our seats I expected my father to mention inadequate insulation or corroded pipes, the dark undersides of home ownership, but instead he discussed only the positive aspects. "I don't see why we couldn't spend our Thanksgivings here. Hell, we could even come for Christmas. Hang a few lights, get some ornaments, what do you think?"

31 A waitress passed the table and, without saying please, I demanded another Coke. She went to fetch it and I settled back in my chair, drunk with the power

of a second home. When school began my classmates would court me, hoping I might invite them for a weekend, and I would make a game of pitting them against one another. This was what a person did when people liked him for all the wrong reasons, and I would grow to be very good at it.

32 "What do you think, David?" my father asked. I hadn't heard the question but said that it sounded good to me. "I like it," I said. "I like it."

33 The following afternoon our parents took us to see the house. "Now, I don't want you to get your hopes up too high," my mother said, but it was too late for that. It was a fifteen-minute drive from one end of the island to the other, and along the way we proposed names for what we had come to think of as our cottage. I'd already given it a good deal of thought but waited a few minutes before offering my suggestion. "Are you ready?" I said. "Our sign will be the silhouette of a ship."

34 Nobody said anything.

35 "Get it?" I said. "The shape of a ship. Our house will be called The Ship Shape."

36 "Well, you'd have to write that on the sign," my father said. "Otherwise nobody will get it."

37 "But if you write out the words you'll ruin the joke."

38 "What about The Nut Hut?" Amy said.

39 "Hey," my father said. "Now, there's an idea." He laughed, not realizing, I guess, that there already was a Nut Hut. We'd passed it a thousand times.

40 "How about something with the word 'sandpiper' in it?" my mother said. "Everybody likes sandpipers, right?"

41 Normally I would have hated them for not recognizing my suggestion as the best, but this was clearly a special time and I didn't want to ruin it with brooding. Each of us wanted to be the one who came up with the name, and inspiration could be hiding anywhere. When the interior of the car had been exhausted of ideas, we looked out the windows and searched the passing landscape.

42 Two thin girls braced themselves before crossing the busy road, hopping from foot to foot on the scalding pavement. "The Tar Heel," Lisa called out. "No, The Wait 'n' Sea. Get it? S-E-A."

43 A car trailing a motorboat pulled up to a gas pump. "The Shell Station!" Gretchen shouted.

44 Everything we saw was offered as a possible name, and the resulting list of nominees confirmed that, once you left the shoreline, Emerald Isle was sorely lacking in natural beauty. "The TV Antenna," my sister Tiffany said. "The Telephone Pole," "The Toothless Black Man Selling Shrimp from the Back of His Van."

45 "The Cement Mixer." "The Overturned Grocery Cart." "Gulls on a Garbage Can." My mother inspired "The Cigarette Butt Thrown Out the Window" and suggested we look for ideas on the beach rather than on the highway. "I mean, my God, how depressing can you get?" She acted annoyed, but we could tell she was really enjoying it. "Give me something that suits us," she said. "Give me something that will last."

46 What would ultimately last were these fifteen minutes on the coastal highway, but we didn't know that then. When older, even the crankiest of us would accept them as proof that we were once a happy family: our mother young and healthy, our father the man who could snap his fingers and give us everything we wanted, the whole lot of us competing to name our good fortune.

47 The house was, as our parents had promised, perfect. This was an older cottage with pine-panelled walls that gave each room the thoughtful quality of a den. Light fell in strips from the louvred shutters and the furniture, which was included in the sale, reflected the tastes of a distinguished sea captain. Once we'd claimed bedrooms and laid awake all night, mentally rearranging the furniture, it would be our father who'd say, "Now hold on a minute, it's not ours yet." By the next afternoon, he had decided that the golf course wasn't so great after all. Then it rained for two straight days, and he announced that it might be wiser to buy some land, wait a few years, and think about building a place of our own. "I mean, let's be practical." Our mother put on her raincoat. She tied a plastic bag over her head and stood at the water's edge, and for the first time in our lives we knew exactly what she was thinking.

48 By our final day of vacation our father had decided that instead of building a place on Emerald Isle we should improve the home we already had. "Maybe add a pool," he said. "What do you kids think about that?" Nobody answered.

49 By the time he finished wheedling it down, the house at the beach had become a bar in the basement. It looked just like a real bar, with tall stools and nooks for wine. There was a sink for washing glasses and an assortment of cartoon napkins illustrating the lighter side of alcoholism. For a week or two my sisters and I tottered at the counter, pretending to be drunks, but then the novelty wore off and we forgot all about it.

50 On subsequent vacations, both with and without our parents, we would drive by the cottage we had once thought of as our own. Each of us referred to it by a different name, and over time qualifiers became necessary. ("You know, *our* house.") The summer after we didn't buy it, the new owners, or "those people," as we liked to call them, painted The Ship Shape yellow. In the late seventies, Amy noted that The Nut Hut had extended the carport and paved the driveway. Lisa was relieved when the Wait 'n' Sea returned to its original color and Tiffany was incensed when The Toothless Black Man Selling Shrimp from the Back of His Van sported a sign endorsing Jesse Helms in the 1984 senatorial campaign. Five years later my mother called to report that The Sandpiper had been badly damaged by Hurricane Hugo. "It's still there," she said, "but barely." Shortly thereafter, according to Gretchen, The Shell Station was torn down and sold as a vacant lot.

51 I know that such a story does not quite work to inspire sympathy. ("My home, well, *one* of my homes fell through.") We had no legitimate claim to self-pity, were ineligible even to hold a grudge, but that didn't stop us from complaining.

52 In the coming years, our father would continue to promise what he couldn't deliver, and in time we grew to think of him as an actor auditioning for the role

of a benevolent millionaire. He'd never get the part but liked the way that the words felt in his mouth. "What do you say to a new car?" he'd ask. "Who's up for a cruise to the Greek isles?" In response he expected us to play the part of an enthusiastic family, but we were unwilling to resume our old roles. As if carried by a tide, our mother drifted further and further away, first to twin beds and then down the hall to a room decorated with seascapes and baskets of sun-bleached sand dollars. It would have been nice, a place at the beach, but we already had a home. A home with a bar. Besides, had things worked out you wouldn't have been happy for us. We're not that kind of people.

EXERCISES

A. Main Idea and Writer's Purpose

Choose the best answer.

1. Which of these four sentences *best* represents the central idea?
   a. While at the beach, we sensed more than ever that our lives were governed by luck. [paragraph 18]
   b. In the coming years, our father would continue to promise what he couldn't deliver and in time we grew to think of him as an actor... [paragraph 52]
   c. When older, even the crankiest of us would accept them [those minutes] as proof that we were once a happy family. [paragraph 46]
   d. By the time he finished wheedling it down, the house at the beach had become a bar in the basement. [paragraph 49]

2. With respect to the main idea, the writer's purpose is to
   a. describe a typical summer at the beach with his family.
   b. explain why summer vacations are important for a family to bond.
   c. contrast the various roles he, his siblings, and his parents played.
   d. write a narrative about a turning point in his family's relationships.

B. Comprehending Main Ideas

Choose the correct answer.

1. The woman's sentence, "well, *one* of my homes is on the garden tour," brought Sedaris and his mother great pleasure because
   a. they thought that the woman was bragging.
   b. they felt sorry for all the extra work she would have to do to manage more than one home.

c. deep down, they were envious of her wealth.
d. a, b, and c.
e. only a and c.

2. For family vacations, Sedaris and his family
   a. chose either the beach or the mountains, depending on their mood.
   b. always chose the beach.
   c. always chose the mountains.
   d. argued among themselves over the best place to go.

3. The beach cottage that Sedaris's family looked at
   a. was impractically small for a family of their size.
   b. needed a lot of work to make it habitable.
   c. was overpriced and came unfurnished.
   d. was perfect in every way for them.

4. The family decided not to buy the beach cottage because
   a. they couldn't afford it.
   b. the father backed out of his promise by chipping away at the original plan.
   c. they couldn't agree on a sign or a name to describe it.
   d. their father decided that he hated playing golf.

5. That summer marked *two* changes in Sedaris's family, namely,
   a. an unwillingness for the mother and children to play their old roles.
   b. the inevitability of their parents divorcing.
   c. the knowledge that they had been living beyond their means.
   d. a growing sense of self-pity.
   e. the realization that their father was full of empty promises that he could never fulfill.

C. Sequencing

The sentences in this paragraph from the selection have been scrambled. Read the sentences and choose the sequence that puts them back into logical order. Do not refer to the original selection.

1. It wasn't a cottage but a run-down house, the sort of place where poor people lived. **2.** Midway through the vacation a hideous woolly caterpillar fell from a tree and bit Amy on the cheek. **3.** The yard was enclosed by a chain-link fence and the air was thick with the flies and mosquitoes normally blown away by the ocean breezes. **4.** One year my father waited too late to make our reservations, and we were forced to take something on the sound.

Which of the following represents the correct sequence for these sentences?

a. 1, 3, 2, 4
b. 3, 2, 1, 4
c. 4, 1, 3, 2
d. Correct as written.

D. Interpreting Meaning

Write your answers for these questions in your own words.

1. Read paragraphs 16 and 17 carefully again. In describing the cottages' various signs, what is Sedaris suggesting?

____

____

2. Look through the essay again and find some other examples of the father's grandiose but empty promises.

____

____

E. Understanding Vocabulary

Look through the paragraphs listed below and find a word that matches each definition. Refer to a dictionary if necessary. An example has been done for you.

EXAMPLE: went back to the old ways [paragraphs 5–6] reverted

1. impressive, high status [7–13] ______
2. cause to become unfriendly, estrange [6–13] ______
3. privilege, right, power [15–17] ______
4. impressive, striking in appearance [15–17] ______
5. blotchy, spotted [19–23] ______
6. unemotional, unexpressive [24–27] ______
7. revitalizing, reinvigorating [24–30] ______
8. moping, feeling sorry for oneself [39–44] ______

9. unable, not qualified [50–52] ____________________
10. kindly, generous [50–52] ____________________

DISCUSSION QUESTIONS

1. In what ways did the summer that is the subject of this essay change Sedaris and his family?
2. How would you characterize the dynamics operating in Sedaris's family? In particular consider the father's role as it unfolds throughout the narrative.
3. Reading between the lines and drawing conclusions from what Sedaris suggests but does not say directly, you might see a problem that his family did not openly acknowledge. What is it?

Essay topics pertaining to this selection are on page 157.

EXPLORE THE WEB

A collection of David Sedaris's commentaries on NPR can be found at

www.npr.org/programs/specials/lists/sedaris.

The New Orleans That Was

Curtis Wilkie

On August 29, 2005, Hurricane Katrina slammed into the Gulf Coast states of Florida, Alabama, Mississippi, and Louisiana. The resulting storm surge of 28 feet was the highest ever recorded in the United States, and the waves and wind destroyed entire towns in the region covering some 90,000 square miles, or roughly the size of Great Britain. Initially, the city of New Orleans, at the mouth of the Mississippi River, seemed to have been spared a direct hit, but the next day two levees protecting the city from the Mississippi River and from Lake Pontchartrain broke, and 80 percent of the city was completely inundated. In some areas, water was 20 feet deep.

The resulting human tragedy was broadcast on television, and the world watched in horror as the people who stayed behind, primarily poor African Americans, faced increasingly desperate circumstances. Those too poor to leave town faced rising flood waters; many drowned or died of exhaustion, hunger, and lack of medical attention. Thousands of more fortunate refugees eventually made their way to safe havens in other states. The migration has been called the biggest single dispersion of people since the Dust Bowl migrations. The final number of people who died will never be known, but estimates have ranged from 1,600 to more than 1,800; the estimate for rebuilding the Gulf Coast is $200 billion.

The writer of this piece, Curtis Wilkie, is a professor of journalism at the University of Mississippi in Oxford, as well as a resident of the French Quarter of New Orleans. He is also the author of *Dixie: A Personal Odyssey Through Events That Shaped the Modern South*. He wrote this profile for the *San Jose Mercury News*, six days after Hurricane Katrina struck his adopted city.

VOCABULARY ANALYSIS

The Suffix *-ize*

The suffix *-ize* is one of the most common word endings in English. Its most common meaning is "to cause to be" or "to make into" based on the meaning of the root noun or adjective to which it is attached. For example, *popularized* [paragraph 4] means "made popular" and *metastasized* [paragraph 2] means "to be changed or transformed," always in a negative sense. One says, for example, that a cancer may *metastasize*, meaning that it migrates from a primary site to another site or sites. To determine the meaning of verbs ending in *-ize*, first locate the root, determine its meaning, and then add the verb ending. For example, to *jeopardize* means "to put into jeopardy" and *maximize* means "to make as large or as great as possible."

The New Orleans That Was

Curtis Wilkie

1 We knew we lived in a danger zone, poised below sea level between three watery giants. It fit with the city's devil-may-care reputation, and the presence of water was part of New Orleans' allure.

2 In the years after World War II, when landlocked Sun Belt cities such as Atlanta and Nashville and Houston metastasized into soulless, sprawling metropolises barely distinguishable from Indianapolis, New Orleans retained its exotic character. Not so much an outpost of the Old South as an odd, seafaring city that often staggered like the proverbial drunken sailor. With its Creole cuisine, voodoo queens and the background beat of timpani, New Orleans more closely resembled a Third World capital in the Caribbean.

3 (Writing about my adopted home now, I find I am using past tense. That feels so sad and wrong because New Orleans exuded *joie de vivre*.)[1]

4 Living in New Orleans was quite different. A bad 1987 movie popularized the term "The Big Easy." The people of New Orleans never called their city that.

Connecting Grammar to Writing

In keeping with journalistic practice, Wilkie does not use a comma to separate the final two elements in the series at the end of paragraph 4. In your papers, however, it is better to use a comma between each element in a series to avoid confusion.

Nothing was particularly easy in New Orleans, with its tropical heat, poverty, endemic public corruption, appalling murder rate and racial divides.

5 It was a city sustained more by spirit than corporeal commodities; by a determination to enjoy life in spite of adversity. The real slogan for New Orleans was a rallying cry: *Laissez les bons temps rouler*—let the good times roll. And the official nickname was "The Crescent City" for the way the Mississippi River curls around New Orleans like a scimitar. It was so disorienting to wake in the morning and see the sun rising over the "west" side of the river that New Orleanians did not use normal directional guides. Instead, south, north, east and west were called, respectively, uptown, downtown, riverside and lakeside.

Strength from Water

6 New Orleans drew its strength from the water. Its commerce, its food, its music were all directly related to the water. Even its accent. Native New Orleanians do not speak with a drawl or say "you all." Their tongues carry the unpolished sounds of distant ports in New York, and their pronunciations are said to have been imported by mariners. The people of the white working class are affectionately known as "Yats," as in the expression, "Where y'at?" And the black citizens, who constitute the city's majority, speak in a patois that would be unrecognizable upriver in Mississippi.

7 One might not think of the city in the same league as Hong Kong or the Netherlands' Rotterdam, but New Orleans was one of the largest ports in the world. In my student days, the wildest joint in town was a bar on Decatur Street, across from an old wharf, with Latin music, gorgeous women and merchant seamen from around the globe. The place was called La Casa de los Marinos, and it reflected the risky, gamy lifestyle of the city.

8 Along the Mississippi River, miles of wharves and docks served the heavy barge and container ship traffic. Toward Baton Rouge, the channel led into an infernal corridor of refineries and chemical plants, infesting the land along the levees like so many cancer cells. At nights, the surroundings blazed like one of Dante's circles from hell.

9 Though some old plantation homes survive along River Road, this was never the land of Tara. The faux river steamboats that set out from downtown two or three times a day were strictly for tourist consumption. New Orleans worked the river like a beast of burden. But we always knew, walking in the French Quarter with the ships moving high over our heads on the other side of the levee, that the beast could spring out of control.

Seemingly Placid

10 While the river was at our front door, Lake Pontchartrain lay behind us. Twenty-six miles across, it made the biblical Sea of Galilee look like a puddle. Though the lake lurked out there, as far as the eye could see, there was little ominous about it. Pontchartrain represented a recreational resource.

11 For the tony, there were yacht clubs and marinas. For the more common folk, there were fishing camps and once an amusement park called Pontchartrain Beach. Those of us who grew up in the radio age have never been able to purge from our minds the silly jingle that advertised the spot:

"At the beach! At the beach!
"At Pontchartrain Beach!
"You'll have fun! You'll have fun!
"Every day of the week!"

12 The park closed years ago, and the lake was so poisoned by toxic runoff that fish died and swimming was discouraged. But in recent years, the waters were being restored. There was even talk that the roller coasters and carousels might be revived.

13 Out of sight, though only a few miles away, the Gulf of Mexico was the third arm that held New Orleans in a watery embrace. During boom times, the gulf furnished the lifeblood for the city's economy through the oil and gas industry. The petroleum market crashed in the region a quarter-century ago, and downtown towers that were built to accommodate the executive suites of the oil companies were emptied. Yet hundreds of hardy Louisiana men still worked the offshore rigs.

14 The gulf was also the source of vast seafood supplies so essential to New Orleans' restaurants. The central ingredients for the pompano amandine or the shrimp remoulade that one ate for lunch at Galatoire's were usually only hours out of the gulf.

15 So from the beginning, New Orleans harbored a water culture and a freewheeling environment foreign to the rest of the South. There was a hypnotic appeal to the place. Even in the face of earlier floods and hurricanes, and modern thunderstorms that boiled out of the gulf almost every afternoon in the summer, most people who were born there stayed there, and countless others came to live there. Perhaps we were drawn by some dangerous mystique, just as Californians defiantly live along geological fault lines. Or New Englanders endure the prison of winter. Or beach lovers rebuild again and again after storms wash away their own homes.

16 Over the years, New Orleans became home for tens of thousands of Mississippians escaping the stern dictates of the fundamentalist Southern Baptist Church. With its round-the-clock bars and jazz halls and striptease artists, it was an El Dorado for those of us who suffered under Prohibition and Sunday blue laws imposed by Baptist leaders. New Orleans existed, to use another old slogan, as "the city that care forgot." It was a hedonistic empire, built along the water, long before Las Vegas was built on the sand.

17 Water was conductive to good times. Strangely enough, so was Roman Catholicism. The denomination ruled the city with a tolerance for drinking and dancing and song. The church also discouraged racial discrimination. As a result, New Orleans had less racial conflict than other cities in the region.

18 Walker Percy, the philosophical novelist, Catholic convert and son of the Mississippi Delta, moved to New Orleans early in his life and wrote lovingly of the city in an essay:

19 "One comes upon it," he wrote, "in the unlikeliest of places, by penetrating the depths of the Bible Belt, running the gantlet of Klan[2] territory, the pine barrens of south Mississippi, Bogalusa, and the Florida parishes of Louisiana. Out and over a watery waste and there it is, a proper enough American city, and yet within the next few hours the tourist is apt to see more nuns and naked women than he ever saw before."

Another Disaster

20 Many Mississippians of Percy's generation came to New Orleans bearing the mythology of the great flood of 1927, when the Mississippi River breached the levee system and swept over dozens of towns and thousands of acres of cotton land in the Delta.

21 The disaster was vividly described by John M. Barry in "Rising Tide: The Great Mississippi Flood of 1927 and How It Changed America." The book, published in 1997, has haunting passages as Barry recounts how members of Percy's own family and other planters kept black farmworkers effectively trapped on the top of a levee to ensure that they would not flee the Delta forever. The incident has an avatar in the Superdome.[3]

22 In the same flood, nearly 80 years ago, self-styled aristocrats downriver in New Orleans relieved pressure on their city from the rampaging river by dynamiting the levee and flooding the less-prosperous parishes of St. Bernard and Plaquemines. Those two parishes are underwater again today.

23 The late Aaron Henry, who grew up in the Delta, attended Xavier University in New Orleans and went on to become a civil rights leader, was philosophical about the river's power. He once wrote in a personal journal:

24 "That old Mississippi River has never had one ounce of racial prejudice. It will drown or wash away a white man just as quick as a Negro and never think twice about it. When it comes busting over those levees, it doesn't stop to ask where the colored section is, it just takes it all."

25 This time, water is taking New Orleans, irrespective of the complexion of the neighborhoods. Affluent sections along the lakeshore are inundated just as surely as the poorer shotgun houses near the industrial canal. While white and black share misfortune, much of the misery is on the backs of those too poor to get out of town. The scenes out of New Orleans are the stuff of nightmares. Bewildered and terrified people, sleeping on elevated highways or roaming flooded streets in uncivilized packs.

26 If New Orleans served as America's Venice—and the approach to New Orleans over swamp and water was reminiscent of arriving in Venice by train—the city is becoming America's Babylon. The pious would say that New Orleans has always

been a bit like Babylon, a wicked city. But New Orleans was a great and glorious city, too. And, like Babylon, it seems to be slipping into ruin.

[1]Hearty or carefree joy of life. From the French for "joy of living."
[2]The Klan refers to the Ku Klux Klan, a secret group of white supremacists operating in the South who engage in acts of terror against blacks—burning crosses in their front yards or lynching them. The Klan's strength diminished after the 1960s.
[3]The Superdome in New Orleans, home stadium for the New Orleans Saints football team, was used as a shelter during Hurricane Katrina. It soon filled with more than 25,000 people, who lived in unsanitary conditions and without sufficient food and water for four days until they were finally evacuated.

EXERCISES

A. Determining the Main Idea and Writer's Purpose

Choose the best answer.

1. The main idea of the selection is that New Orleans
   a. was doomed to be destroyed because of its unusual geographic features and precarious location.
   b. exerts an exotic and hypnotic appeal that made it a unique place, one unlike any other Southern city.
   c. is a more racially tolerant and harmonious city than other cities of its size.
   d. developed a water culture that tragically and ironically became the force that destroyed it.

2. The writer's purpose is to
   a. write a retrospective look at New Orleans, showing its cultural influences, distinctive characteristics, and unique appeal.
   b. write a history of New Orleans, emphasizing its contributions to American culture.
   c. criticize state and federal officials for allowing New Orleans to be destroyed.
   d. explain the reasons why natives and tourists alike enjoy New Orleans.

B. Comprehending Main Ideas

Choose the correct answer.

1. Wilkie states that the city's uniqueness—its history and culture—derives from
   a. its wonderful restaurants.
   b. its tradition of jazz music.

c. its racial mix.
d. the presence of water.

2. New Orleans is unlike other Southern cities, which he characterizes as
   a. cities that cling to their glory days before the Civil War.
   b. soulless and sprawling metropolises.
   c. monuments to modern consumerism.
   d. cities with substantial racial strife.

3. According to Wilkie, the spirit of New Orleans residents is represented by their
   a. determination to enjoy life in spite of adversity.
   b. stubborn refusal to give up in the face of disaster.
   c. willingness to live with the danger and threat of floods and hurricanes.
   d. racial harmony, which should be a model for other urban areas.

4. Which of the following was *not* referred to in the essay as a slogan for New Orleans?
   a. "The City That Care Forgot"
   b. "The Crescent City"
   c. "Sin City"
   d. "The Big Easy"

5. Wilkie writes that New Orleans has had less racial conflict than other Southern cities largely because of
   a. the influence of the fundamentalist Southern Baptist Church.
   b. immigrants from Caribbean nations who brought with them a tradition of racial harmony.
   c. its status as a port city with a mix of people of many cultures and races.
   d. the influence of the Roman Catholic Church.

C. Locating Supporting Details

For the main idea stated here, find three details from the selection that support it. "The presence of water was part of New Orleans' allure."

____

____

____

D. Understanding Allusions

An *allusion* is a reference to something outside the selection that reinforces or sheds new light on the writer's ideas. The reference may be from any area, but usually allusions come from history, literature, mythology, or religious texts like the Bible or the Koran. Wilkie uses four allusions in this selection. Using either an unabridged dictionary or a web-based information site like http://en.wikipedia.org/wiki, www.msn.com, or www.ask.com, identify these allusions and explain their connection to the ideas they refer to.

1. "Though some old plantation homes survive along River Road, this was never the land of *Tara*." [paragraph 9]

2. "While the river was at our front door, Lake Pontchartrain lay behind us. Twenty-six miles across, it made the biblical *Sea of Galilee* look like a puddle." [paragraph 10]

3. "It was an *El Dorado* for those of us who suffered under Prohibition and Sunday blue laws by Baptist leaders." [paragraph 16]

4. "If New Orleans served as America's Venice—and the approach to New Orleans over swamp and water was reminiscent of arriving in Venice by train—the city is becoming America's *Babylon*... and like Babylon, it seems to be slipping into ruin." [paragraph 26]

____

____

____

E. Understanding Vocabulary

Write the dictionary definition for each underlined word in the phrases below.

1. poised below sea level [paragraph 1] ____________________
2. the city's devil-may-care reputation [1] ____________________
3. New Orleans retained its exotic character [2] ____________________
4. endemic public corruption [4] ____________________
5. corporeal commodities [5] ____________________
6. in spite of adversity [5] ____________________
7. it was so disorienting [5] ____________________
8. there was little ominous about it [10] ____________________
9. for the tony, there were yacht clubs and marinas [11] ____________________
10. we were drawn by some dangerous mystique [15] ____________________
11. Californians defiantly live along fault lines [15] ____________________
12. water was conducive to good times [17] ____________________

F. Vocabulary and Dictionary Exercise

Answer these questions. You may need to consult a dictionary for this exercise.

1. Paragraphs 6 and 9 contain two words derived from French: *patois* and *faux*. Write the dictionary pronunciation for each word in the spaces below.

   patois ________________ *faux* ________________

2. In the first sentence of paragraph 15, Wilkie writes, "New Orleans *harbored* a water culture." What part of speech is *harbored*?

   ____

   What does it mean in this context?

   ____

3. In paragraph 16 Wilkie writes that New Orleans was "a *hedonistic* empire." The adjective *hedonistic* derives from the classical Greek philosophy *hedonism*. What does a hedonist believe in?

   ____

4. The word *gantlet* (see paragraph 19) has a variant spelling. What is it?

   ____

   What does the phrase "to run the gauntlet" mean?

   ____

   ____

5. Look again at the last sentence of paragraph 21, where Wilkie writes, "The incident has an *avatar* in the Superdome." What language does the word *avatar* derive from?

   ____

   What does it mean in this context?

   ____

6. The adjective *pious* has two different noun forms (see paragraph 26). Write them in these spaces. (Hint: For one, look in the section of the dictionary for words beginning with *pie-*.)

   ____

   As Wilkie uses it, does the word *pious* have more of a positive or a negative connotation or emotional association?

   ____

DISCUSSION QUESTIONS

1. What are the major cultural influences that make New Orleans such an unusual city, different from other American cities and, more particularly, from other Southern cities?
2. In paragraph 4, Wilkie alludes to New Orleans' "racial divides," and later in paragraph 17, he writes, "New Orleans had less racial conflict than other cities in the region." Do these two references to race relations contradict each other? How might they be reconciled?
3. Explain in your own words the draw that dangerous places have on residents. (See paragraph 15.) What impulses govern people who deliberately choose to live in environments prone to natural disasters?

EXPLORE THE WEB

- If you enjoy cooking, you can try some of the delicious recipes from the Culinary Institute of New Orleans. The address of the home page is www.ci-no.com. Once there, click on "Cooking with Class" and follow the directions to locate recipes for dozens of New Orleans' specialties.
- See photographs of what New Orleans looked like before Hurricane Katrina damaged it. A series of photographs and links sponsored by the Association of American Geographers, including photos of Lake Pontchartrain, the city's famous cemeteries, the French Quarter, and other areas can be found at www.placesonline.org/sitelists/nam/usa/louisiana/neworleans.asp.

Three Photographs for Analysis

Hurricane Katrina: Houston

This photograph, dated September 2005, was taken by Steve Ueckert of the *Houston Chronicle* a week after Hurricane Katrina slammed into the Gulf Coast states of Mississippi, Alabama, and Louisiana. Thousands of storm victims, particularly from New Orleans, were taken to various Texas cities—in particular Houston, Dallas, and San Antonio—where they spent several days in shelters trying to rebuild their lives. The federal government announced a plan to hand out debit cards of $2,000 for each family displaced by the storm.

As you examine this picture, you will see that the people are photographed in profile and in silhouette. In our grandparents' days, silhouettes were a popular form of photography. The subject was photographed in black from the side or profile angle, usually on a white background, which has

Long lines of people wait both outside and inside the Reliant Arena in Houston for representatives of the Federal Emergency Management Agency to issue debit cards.

the effect of revealing a general outline but without particular or individual details. The silhouette form, thus, works well for Ueckert's photograph because it allows the viewer to read into the subjects' feelings and emotions. To analyze this photograph, consider these questions:

- What specifically does the photograph depict? What are the subjects doing?
- What time of day was the photograph taken?
- What else besides its human subjects does the photograph show?
- Look at both the foreground (the figures in front) and the background. What do you see?
- Now imagine what these subjects are feeling and thinking. How would you describe their feelings? What qualities do they exhibit?
- Do these people appear to be behaving in the same way that people who must stand in lines everywhere (for example, at a movie theater or at the bank) behave, or do they somehow seem different?

BILOXI, MISS.: Christallie Ewing, 5, waits on her grandmother's lap for a children's program at the Salvation Army shelter Thursday.

Hurricane Katrina: Biloxi, Mississippi

Biloxi, Mississippi, a lovely town on the Gulf of Mexico, famous for its antebellum (pre-Civil War) houses and offshore gambling casinos, was almost completely destroyed by Hurricane Katrina. Biloxi residents were evacuated to inland shelters as well as to neighboring states. This photograph, also dated September 2005, a few days after Hurricane Katrina destroyed much of the Gulf Coast, was taken by Rob Carr of the Associated Press.

Unlike Ueckert's photograph shot in black and white and with the subjects in silhouette, this style of photograph is called a headshot. Study the photograph carefully and then consider these questions:

- What does the photograph reveal about Christallie?
- How would you describe what she is thinking and feeling?
- What does the photograph reveal about her reactions to her situation?

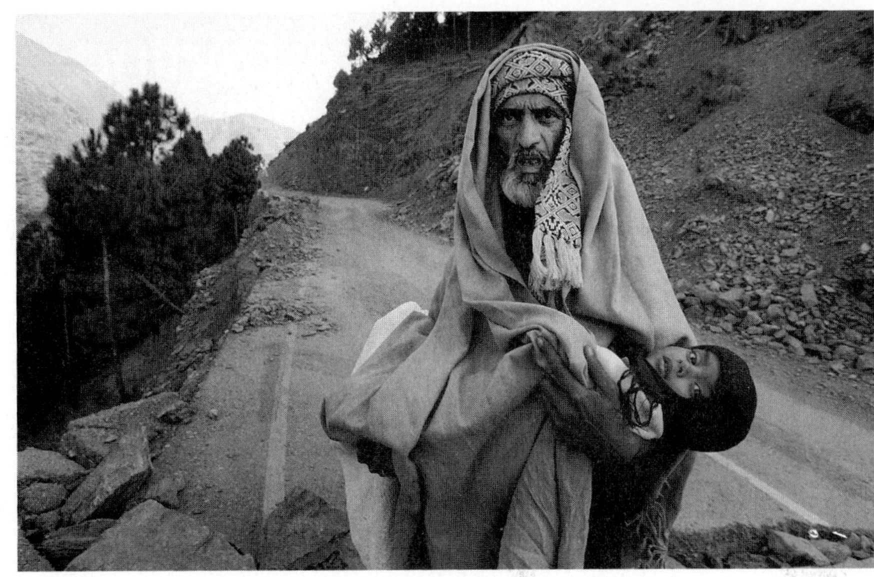

Quake survivor Sher Afzal, 42, carries his son, Mohammad Zaid, 3, for medical treatment down a road in Budho on the outskirts of Balakot, Pakistan, on Wednesday.

Earthquake: Northern Pakistan

On October 8, 2005, a devastating earthquake registering 7.6 on the Richter scale hit northern Pakistan. Because of the area's isolated location in mountainous terrain, relief was slow to arrive. It was estimated that around 74,000 people died and another 69,000 were injured. This photograph shows a survivor carrying his little boy for medical treatment. It was taken by Richard Vogel for the Associated Press. Study the photograph and then answer these questions.

- What kind of environment is depicted?
- How would you describe what the father and his son are feeling?
- Why do you think the photographer took this particular shot to illustrate the aftermath of the quake?

WRITING

Writing a Profile: Examining Personal Attributes

THE PROFILE—A DEFINITION

The readings in Part 3 all describe the subject at a specific time or observed in a particular set of circumstances. The short form of the profile forces each writer to select pertinent and illuminating details. The three photographs on the preceding pages portray the subject visually. In each instance—whether described in words or in a picture—the subject is revealed within the context of a specific environment. What all these pieces have in common goes beyond a mere assemblage of biographical or autobiographical or historical facts. As profiles, each treats some specific aspect of the subject but does not attempt to offer a complete portrayal.

In the readings, we see the subject against the backdrop of an event that has special significance. For example, Lori Hope faces a dilemma when she observes a man of Middle Eastern descent acting suspiciously just before her flight takes off, David Sedaris reveals serious cracks in his family's happy façade during their futile discussions about buying a beach cottage, and in the website reading, "A Shirt Full of Bees," Bill McKibben has a life-altering experience when he is stung by dozens of yellow jackets. A profile does not have to have only a human subject; it can have as its subject a city: Curtis Wilkie describes the allure of his home town, New Orleans, with affection and with candor, before the terrible destruction wrought by Hurricane Katrina.

In these readings the concept of time is fluid. Lori Hope's decision to alert the aircraft crew to a suspicious passenger occurred in a split second. David Sedaris relates sad truths about his family that began one summer but that continued into an indefinite future. The most complete profile is by Susan Orlean, who clearly spent a great deal of time with Colin Duffy, observing him and his interactions with his friends. This careful observation stems from her purpose—to portray the life of a representative 10-year-old American boy.

ACADEMIC WRITING

Understanding how to identify and write about key aspects of a person or a place can be useful in many college courses as well as in your professional life.

Typical Academic Assignments Requiring Writing a Profile

- Defining a personality type for a psychology paper
- Describing the attributes of a typical member of a particular culture for a sociology or anthropology paper
- Analyzing a character in a play or novel for a literature course by examining his or her qualities

HOW TO WRITE A PROFILE

Writing a profile offers you an opportunity to write an analytical essay on an accessible subject. A *profile* is an essay whose subject is a person or a place; the purpose of the profile is to provide an analysis and appraisal of that person or place. A profile requires you not merely to recount the actions or behavior described in the article but also to assess and to evaluate those actions according to some criteria. Further, a profile might ask you to make broader inferences about your own experiences or about other people caught in similar circumstances. How might you react, for example, if you observed an airplane passenger acting suspiciously? Did a family vacation from your past provide a revelation and a deeper understanding of your parents' strengths and weaknesses? What does it mean to be "an American man"? How could you capture your community's essence so that an outsider could understand it?

Just as the profile writers represented here carefully selected relevant details, so must you as you prepare your profile. I suggest that you follow these prewriting steps: First, as always, annotate the essay you choose to write about. (See the beginning of Part 4 for specific instructions in annotating.) Then on a piece of paper write what strikes you as the most significant aspect of the person you read about. Use two or three adjectives (descriptive words) that best explain and characterize the person. (Some examples of descriptive words might be *energetic, stubborn, naïve, dignified,* and *introspective.*) Whatever words you choose may eventually be included in your thesis. Next, return to the essay, and this time, list all of the details that seem to support your characterization.

Before you start to write your rough draft, ask yourself these questions. Answers to these questions may be the basis of the body paragraphs. Of necessity, the questions are somewhat generic, so that not all of them will be pertinent to your subject.

- Where does the essay take place? Is the setting of any particular significance?
- When does the essay take place? Is the time of any particular significance?

- What is the subject doing? What activity is he or she engaged in? Why? If possible, can you assess the reason or motive behind the activity?
- Are there any particular or unusual circumstances underlying the action?
- How would you describe the subject's attributes in terms of personality, interests, motivation, or behavior? What makes your subject "tick"?
- Is there a particular incident that provokes the subject to action? If so, what is it and how does the person react?
- How did you react to the subject and to his or her behavior? What is your overall assessment?
- Can you extend your exploration and comment on the larger significance of what you read?

TOPICS FOR WRITING A PROFILE OF YOUR OWN

1. Choose a person who has played an important part in your life. Write a profile of your subject, taking care to choose pertinent details that both describe him or her and reveal the person's identity.
2. Susan Orlean's affectionate portrayal of Colin Duffy might serve as an inspiration for an essay. If you know a particular child well—your own child, a sibling, a niece or nephew—carefully observe the child's behavior, usual activities, interests, and relationships with friends, and write a profile of your subject. Another possibility is to choose a girl and, using Orlean's essay as a model, write your own profile titled "The American Woman, Age Ten" (or whatever age your subject is).
3. Write a short narrative in which you describe a situation where an older person—a relative, a teacher, a mentor, a friend—taught you something important about what it means to become an adult.
4. Write a profile of a person you are well acquainted with who is caught in particularly difficult circumstances or who is facing a particularly distressing situation. Using Lori Hope's article or Bill McKibben's essay (see the website accompanying this text) as a model, show how this person resolved the situation and any ambiguities it entailed.
5. David Sedaris and his siblings eventually realized that their father's golden promises were hollow and not to be trusted. Whom did you learn early on in your life not to trust? Write a profile of a person whom you judge to be untrustworthy.
6. Following the example of Curtis Wilkie's profile of New Orleans, write a profile of a town or city or geographic location that you are intimately familiar with. Choose pertinent and illuminating details that show your subject's allure.

7. In Part 4, Mark Edmundson in "The Teacher Who Opened My Mind" presents a profile of Frank Lears, a new teacher at the writer's high school. If you have had a teacher who opened your mind the way Lears opened Edmundson's, write a profile of that person, including both a physical description and the specific techniques that made the subject so unforgettable in helping you see the world through new eyes.

■ TOPICS RELATED TO THE READINGS

1. Did Lori Hope do the right thing when she alerted the airline staff to the oddly behaving passenger? What were her stated reasons for doing this? Discuss the problems and benefits associated with her decision and come to a conclusion of your own about what she did. If you have ever been in a similar situation—observing a person who has the potential to inflict great harm—include a paragraph describing the situation you were in, how you reacted, and why you reacted in this way.
2. Consider again Lori Hope's concluding words: "it's not the same world it was half a lifetime ago." Write a short essay in which you explore the many changes that the 2001 terrorist attacks brought about, either in you personally or in the nation itself.
3. Is Colin Duffy representative of American 10-year-olds? Write a short essay comparing and contrasting Duffy with a child whom you know who is around the same age.
4. What, to you, is the central quality or trait that characterizes David Sedaris's family? Write an essay in which you examine the relationships between, first, the children and their parents, and then between the parents themselves.
5. Look again at the three photographs at the end of the reading selections. The first shows a group of hurricane survivors waiting in line, the second shows a little girl waiting, and the third shows a Pakistani father seeking medical treatment for his son after a terrible earthquake. Study them carefully, and use the questions accompanying each one as a starting point. Choose one of these three pictures as the subject of a short essay in which you show what the photograph reveals about the subject(s) and the feelings and emotions that it reveals. How does the photograph help the viewer to understand the situation that the subject(s) are in?

PART FOUR

The emphasis in Part 4 is on three interrelated skills—annotating, paraphrasing, and summarizing—that together lay the groundwork for the reading and writing assignments in the remainder of the text. The first section presents an overview of annotating skills, including an explanation of the process, sample annotations for you to study, and exercises pertaining to a hypothetical writing assignment. The readings include five selections. In addition to Richard Wolkomir's essay, in which he describes how Ken Adams, an illiterate Vermont farmer, learned to read, similarly Barbara Kingsolver and Mark Edmundson's essays are linked by a common theme: the impact that reading made on two disparate people—a rebellious teenage girl headed for trouble (Kingsolver) and an unmotivated, lackluster student (Edmundson), who had never read a book in his life that wasn't about football. The readings end with two more academic selections: an excerpt by Bill Bryson about human cells and Jared Diamond's cautionary account of the ruined environment of Easter Island.

The final section presents a comprehensive discussion of how to write paraphrases and summaries. Included here are instruction in the two processes, sample paraphrases and summaries of excerpts from the readings in Part 4, and practice topics that also pertain to the readings. This is a crucial section, and these three skills need to be mastered before you undertake the more complex writing assignments in the second half of the book.

Learning to Annotate

As you will recall from the introduction to the text, the underlying principle of this book is that good reading promotes good writing. Reading and writing well are twin undertakings; they work in tandem, each reinforcing the other. In Part 4 of the text, you will see more clearly how this interconnectedness works with more difficult assignments. In this part we take up three complementary skills—annotating, paraphrasing, and summarizing. All three are extraordinarily useful for college students, or for that matter for anyone who must understand, absorb, remember, and condense information from the printed page. This introductory section explains and demonstrates how to annotate. Following the reading selections, the writing section explains and illustrates some simple rules for writing paraphrases and summaries.

Because students sometimes confuse these terms, assuming incorrectly that they are all synonyms for the same activity, let us first define them so we can see how they differ from one another.

- ***Annotating*** A study and comprehension skill, which includes writing notes in the margin of a text, circling words you don't know, noting questions, and otherwise interacting with the text.
- ***Paraphrasing*** A comprehension and writing skill, which includes putting a writer's words into your own words without leaving anything out, similar to translating.
- ***Summarizing*** A comprehension and writing skill, which includes condensing a writer's words by identifying only the main points and omitting unimportant supporting details.

How are these three skills connected? Annotating is the first step to writing successful paraphrases and summaries. Paraphrasing is a necessary component of summaries. All three—annotating, paraphrasing, and summarizing—show how well you have understood what you read. All three will be required when you do assignments for Parts 5–7—writing comparison and contrast, cause-and-effect, analysis, and synthesis essays.

THE PURPOSE OF ANNOTATING

My students often complain that they have a "bad memory" because they say they do not remember a lot of what they read. They also complain that when they read they have trouble focusing and staying on track. A student may say that her mind drifts, that other things intrude, blocking out the words on the page. We have all had the experience of reading a whole page, only to reach the bottom and think, "What did I just read?" Actually, I think that the source of these problems in concentration and focus may partially lie elsewhere. The culprit is *passive reading*. Rather than being actively involved with the print on the page, passive readers read the material once and unwisely assume that they can get the full meaning without doing the hard work that good comprehension requires.

It is almost impossible for a reader—even very experienced readers—to comprehend college-level reading material well and to remember what is important without annotating. (Note the specific emphasis here on college reading assignments, where good comprehension is required. This observation does not pertain to the casual reading you do in popular magazines to pass the time, to the novel you read for fun, or to the daily paper.) Besides helping you concentrate, annotating also allows you to interact with the text, to identify the important points, and most important to provide a focus for your reading. When you write analytical and synthesis essays, where you are asked to incorporate ideas from a reading selection in support of a thesis, good annotation skills will help you identify visually relevant ideas for your paper, either as material you directly quote or as material you paraphrase. Careful annotating, then, allows you to concentrate; you read *actively* and pull out appropriate ideas that support your thesis.

READING WITH A PENCIL IN YOUR HAND: HOW TO ANNOTATE

As noted before, to annotate means that you make notes in the margins and mark up the text itself.[1] You already have seen the annotation process demonstrated in Part 2, where marginal annotations identified main and supporting ideas in short paragraphs. The next section explains this process in more detail. Throughout the text, you will have many opportunities to practice annotating.

First, we need to establish from the beginning that annotating does *not* mean highlighting your text with a neon yellow, green, or pink pen. Many students use these pens as a study aid (actually, more as a crutch); most

[1]If you are uncomfortable marking up a textbook or if you want to resell the book at the end of the course, make a photocopy of the selection, and you can mark the text to your heart's content.

reading instructors, however, discourage this practice because such marks only delay learning. Highlighting your text tells you only that the material is important to learn—some day! And students often are uncertain if they are doing it properly and so end up highlighting too much. Seen in this light, highlighting is a passive activity. Also it is impossible to use highlighters to write legible notes because the nibs are too thick. Study these suggestions for good annotating:

Techniques for Annotating

■ Main ideas	Jot down phrases restating the main idea using your own words as much as possible.
■ Phrases or sentences you don't understand	Place a question mark in the margin.
■ Unfamiliar vocabulary words	Circle them in the text.
■ Questions to ask in class	Write in the margin and mark with a clear symbol, perhaps with double question marks.
■ Ideas that you disagree with	Place a star or some other symbol in the margin.

To illustrate this process, consider the opening paragraphs from Part 4's Practice Essay by Richard Wolkomir, "Making Up for Lost Time: The Rewards of Reading at Last." This article by Richard Wolkomir takes up the problem of adult illiteracy, focusing on a 64-year-old Vermont resident named Ken Adams, whom the writer tutored. It seems that in elementary school Ken Adams was passed along from grade to grade without ever being able to read. First, read the passage; then study how one experienced college student annotated it.

The paragraphs are numbered for you.

Ken says he was a slow learner who was passed along; his parents didn't encourage him.

1. I decide simply to blurt it out. "Ken?" I ask. "Why didn't you learn to read?" Through the Marshfield community center's window, I see snowy fields and the Vermont village's clapboard houses. Beyond, mountains bulge. "I was a slow learner," Ken says. "In school they just passed me along, and my folks told me I wasn't worth anything and wouldn't amount to anything."

??What's "Vermontese"??

2. Ken Adams is 64, his hair white. He speaks Vermontese, turning "I" into "Oy," and "ice" into "oyce." His green Buckeye Feeds cap is blackened with engine grease from fixing his truck's transmission, and pitch from chain-sawing pine logs. It is 2 degrees below zero outside on this

December afternoon; he wears a green flannel shirt over a purple flannel shirt. He is unshaven, weather reddened. He is not a tall man, but a lifetime of hoisting hay bales has thickened his shoulders.

Ken learns to read from children's picture books.

3. Through bifocals, Ken frowns at a children's picture book, *Pole Dog*. He is studying a drawing: an old dog waits patiently by a telephone pole, where its owners abandoned it. He glares at the next pictures. Cars whizzing by. Cruel people tormenting the dog. "Looks like they're shootin' at him, to me!" he announces. "Nobody wants an old dog," he says.
4. Ken turns the page. "He's still by the pole," he says. "But there's that red car that went by with those kids, ain't it?" He turns the page again. The red car has stopped to take the old dog in, to take him home. "*Somebody* wants an old dog!" Ken says. "Look at that."

Why Wolkomir volunteered.

5. This is my first meeting with Ken. It is also my first meeting with an adult who cannot read.

Illiterates are fairly common, but they hide their inability to read, so they're not obvious to others.

6. I decided to volunteer as a tutor after a librarian told me that every day, on the sidewalks of our (prim) little Vermont town, I walk by illiterate men and women. We are unaware of them because they can be clever at hiding their inability to read. At a post office counter, for instance, when given forms to fill out, they say, "Could you help me with this? I left my glasses home."

Nearly 50% of American adults don't read well or even at all, according to '93 Dept. of Ed. stats.

??Why are there so many adults who can't read??

7. Ken Adams is not alone in his (plight). A 1993 U.S. Department of Education report on illiteracy said 21–23 percent of U.S. adults—about 40 million—read minimally, enough to decipher an uncomplicated meeting announcement. Another 25–28 percent read and write only slightly better. For instance, they can fill out a simple form. That means about *half* of all U.S. adults read haltingly. Millions, like Ken Adams, hardly read at all.

■ COMMENTS ON SAMPLE ANNOTATIONS

Studying this student's annotations of the opening paragraphs of Wolkomir's article reveals the following characteristics:

- The notes are brief and for the most part use the reader's own words.
- Annotations for descriptive details are omitted (for example, the minor details in paragraphs 2, 3, and 4). It is perfectly all right to leave some paragraphs annotation-free. Keep your annotations sparse and as free from clutter as possible. Keep your purpose in mind.
- Two vocabulary words that she needs to look up are circled.
- The main point of this introductory section is identified with asterisks.
- The reader asked two questions (see the material marked by double question marks). She was able to figure out the first one from the context; the

other, however, anticipates a main idea that the writer will get to in the body of the article, and more interestingly, also anticipates part of the writing assignment her instructor devised for this selection. (See below.)

To get some practical experience in annotating, here is a short exercise that pertains to the Practice Essay. For illustration purposes, we will refer only to Wolkomir's essay; a more authentic assignment would most likely ask you to use information from other material, as well. Here is the topic.

> How serious is the problem of adult illiteracy in the United States? In an essay of approximately 750 words, discuss the causes of adult illiteracy in America and explain some of the problems that adult illiterates face in their daily lives as the result of their inability to read well or even to read at all. Use Richard Wolkomir's article (as well as other assigned material) in support of your thesis.

Printed here again are the sample annotations. Which ones from this initial section of the article would be pertinent to this topic? Remember that the focus of the assignment is on two issues: (1) the causes of adult illiteracy and (2) problems adult illiterates face. In the space, label each annotation as follows: **P** for pertinent and **NP** for not pertinent.

1. Ken says he was a slow learner who was passed along; his parents didn't encourage him.
2. What's "Vermontese"?
3. Learning to read from children's picture books.
4. Why writer volunteered.
5. Illiterates are fairly common, but they hide their inability to read, so they're not obvious to others.
6. Nearly 50% of American adults don't read well or even at all, according to '93 Dept. of Ed. stats.
7. Why are there so many adults who can't read?

Now check your answers. The first annotation addresses two causes of adult illiteracy, and number 6 shows the seriousness of the problem. The rest are irrelevant to this topic. Notice that when you annotate an essay or article from which you will take information, your marginal notes should address only the particular dimensions of the topic. Not only does this step save time as you read, but it also allows you to focus on only applicable ideas.

Now read the entire essay by Richard Wolkomir. While reading, keep your focus on the topic above and annotate the selection *only* for material relevant to the assignment above.

PRACTICE ESSAY

Making Up for Lost Time: The Rewards of Reading at Last

Richard Wolkomir

Richard Wolkomir graduated in 1964 from Syracuse University with a bachelor's degree in American studies with a minor in journalism. After working as a writer-editor for the McGraw-Hill Publishing Company in New York City, he moved to Vermont where he currently lives. A winner of many awards for his writing, Wolkomir has written extensively for *Reader's Digest* and *National Geographic*, although now he writes mainly for the *Smithsonian* magazine, where this selection was first published in 1996. In it he recounts his experience helping Ken Adams, a 64-year-old Vermont farmer and a most unusual man: He was an illiterate who wanted to learn to read.

VOCABULARY ANALYSIS

Animal Adjectives: The Suffix *-ine*

Wolkomir recounts a book he loved as a child about a mouse, Peter Churchmouse, who has a *feline* friend, the rectory cat. The English adjective suffix *-ine* is added to a countless number of Latin roots referring to animals. They can either describe an animal or behavior associated with a particular animal. *Feline* (Latin root *felis*, "cat"), then, refers either to the animal itself or to behavior that is "catlike." Some other words with this suffix are *canine* (referring to a dog, from the Latin word for dog, *canis*); *lupine* (describing a wolf, from Latin, *lupus*); and *serpentine* (serpentlike), obviously from *serpent*, a word that comes to us, ultimately, from Sanskrit, an ancient language. What animal do these adjectives refer to? Check a dictionary if you are unsure.

leonine ____________ **piscine** ____________

bovine ____________ **equine** ____________

porcine ____________ **ursine** ____________

MAKING UP FOR LOST TIME: THE REWARDS OF READING AT LAST

Richard Wolkomir

1 I decide simply to blurt it out. "Ken?" I ask. "Why didn't you learn to read?" Through the Marshfield community center's window, I see snowy fields and the Vermont village's clapboard houses. Beyond, mountains bulge. "I was a slow

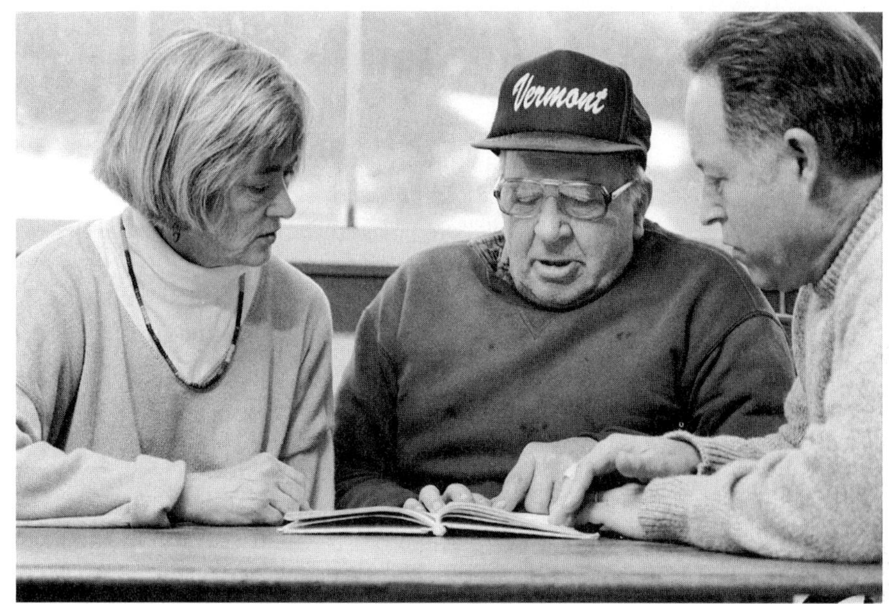

Richard Wolkomir (right) helps Ken Adams. Source: © 1999 Sue Owrutsky

learner," Ken says. "In school they just passed me along, and my folks told me I wasn't worth anything and wouldn't amount to anything."

2 Ken Adams is 64, his hair white. He speaks Vermontese, turning "I" into "Oy," and "ice" into "oyce." His green Buckeye Feeds cap is blackened with engine grease from fixing his truck's transmission, and pitch from chain-sawing pine logs. It is 2 degrees below zero outside on this December afternoon; he wears a green flannel shirt over a purple flannel shirt. He is unshaven, weather reddened. He is not a tall man, but a lifetime of hoisting hay bales has thickened his shoulders.

3 Through bifocals, Ken frowns at a children's picture book, *Pole Dog.* He is studying a drawing: an old dog waits patiently by a telephone pole, where its owners abandoned it. He glares at the next pictures. Cars whizzing by. Cruel people tormenting the dog. "Looks like they're shootin' at him, to me!" he announces. "Nobody wants an old dog," he says.

4 Ken turns the page. "He's still by the pole," he says. "But there's that red car that went by with those kids, ain't it?" He turns the page again. The red car has stopped to take the old dog in, to take him home. "*Somebody* wants an old dog!" Ken says. "Look at that!"

5 This is my first meeting with Ken. It is also my first meeting with an adult who cannot read.

6 I decided to volunteer as a tutor after a librarian told me that every day, on the sidewalks of our prim little Vermont town, I walk by illiterate men and women. We are unaware of them because they can be clever at hiding their

inability to read. At a post office counter, for instance, when given forms to fill out, they say, "Could you help me with this? I left my glasses home."

7 Ken Adams is not alone in his plight. A 1993 U.S. Department of Education report on illiteracy said 21–23 percent of U.S. adults—about 40 million—read minimally, enough to decipher an uncomplicated meeting announcement. Another 25–28 percent read and write only slightly better. For instance, they can fill out a simple form. That means about *half* of all U.S. adults read haltingly. Millions, like Ken Adams, hardly read at all.

8 I wanted to meet nonreaders because I could not imagine being unable to decipher a street sign, or words printed on supermarket jars, or stories in a book. In fact, my own earliest memory is about reading. In this memory, in our little Hudson River town, my father is home for the evening from the wartime lifeboat factory where he is a foreman. And he has opened a book.

9 "Do you want to hear about Peter Churchmouse?" my father asks. Of course! It is my favorite, from the little library down the street. My father reads me stories about children lost in forests. Cabbage-stealing hares. A fisherman who catches a talking perch. But my favorite is Peter Churchmouse, a small but plucky cheese addict who befriends the rectory cat. Peter is also a poet, given to reciting original verse to his feline friend during their escapades. I cannot hear it enough.

10 My father begins to read. I settle back. I am taking a first step toward becoming literate—I am being read to. And although I am only 2, I know that words can be woven into tales.

11 Now, helping Ken Adams learn to read, I am re-entering that child's land of chatty dogs and spats-wearing frogs. Children's books—simply worded, the sentences short—are perfect primers, even for 60-year-olds who turn the pages with labor-thickened fingers and who never had such books read to them when they were children.

12 "Do you remember what happened from last time?" asks Sherry Olson, of Central Vermont Adult Basic Education, who tutors Ken an hour and a half each week.

13 I have volunteered as Sherry's aide. My work requires too much travel for me to be a full-fledged tutor. But I am actually relieved, not having sole responsibility for teaching an adult to read. That is because—when I think about it—I don't know how I read myself. I scan a printed page; the letters magically reveal meaning. It is effortless. I don't know how I do it. As for teaching a man to read from scratch, how would I even begin?

14 Sherry, a former third-grade teacher, gives me hints, like helping Ken to learn words by sight so that he doesn't have to sound out each letter. Also, we read stories so Ken can pick out words in context. Ken reads Dr. Seuss rhyming books and tales about young hippopotamuses helping on the family farm. At the moment, we are reading a picture book about Central American farmers who experience disaster when a volcano erupts.

15 "The people had to move out, and put handkerchiefs over their noses!" Ken says, staring at the pages. He starts to read: "They … prayed? … for the …

fire? . . ." "Yes, that's right, fire," Sherry says. "They prayed for the fire to . . . go out?" "That word is 'stop,'" Sherry says.

16 I listen carefully. A few sessions ahead, it will be my turn to try teaching. "They prayed for the fire to *stop*," Ken says, placing a thick forefinger under each word. "They watched from the s . . ." "Remember we talked about those?" Sherry says. "When a word ends in a silent *e*, what does that silent *e* do to the vowel?" "It makes it say itself," Ken says. "So what's the vowel in *s-i-d-e*?" she asks. "It's *i*, and it would say its own name,'" Ken says, pronouncing it "oy." "So that would be 'side.'" "Good," Sherry says.

17 Ken reads the sentence: "They watched from the side of the hill!" He sounds quietly triumphant. "They-uh," he says, in backcountry Vermontese. "That's done it."

18 After the session, I stand a few minutes with Ken in the frozen driveway. He has one foot on the running board of his ancient truck, which he somehow keeps going. He tells me he was born in 1931 into a family eking out an existence on a hardscrabble farm. His trouble in school with reading is puzzling, because Ken is intelligent.

19 For instance, he says he was late today because he had to fix his truck. And now he launches into a detailed analysis of the transmission mechanisms of various species of trucks. Also, during the tutoring session, we played a game that required strewing word cards upside down on a table and remembering their locations. Ken easily outscored both Sherry and me in this exercise.

20 Ken described himself as a "slow learner," but clearly he is not slow. Sherry has told me he probably suffers from a learning disability. People with these perceptual disorders experience difficulties such as seeing letters reversed. Although their intelligence may actually be above average, learning to read is difficult for them. They need individual tutoring.

21 "It was a one-room school, with eight grades, so I didn't get much attention there," Ken tells me. "It was just the same as the folks at home were doing when they kicked me along through the grades, and when you got to be 16, that's when they kicked you out."

22 After he left school, he left home. "Then you knock around, one farm to another," he says. "I'd get $15 a week, and room and board." Besides farming, he worked in bobbin mills and sawmills and granite quarries. "Then I was at a veneer mill in Bradford," he says. "After that I was caretaker at a farm for six years until I had to give it up because I had heart attacks."

23 Now he subsists on a $400-a-month Social Security disability pension plus $90 a month in food stamps. He lives alone in a farmhouse he built himself more than 25 years ago, five miles up a mountain dirt road. He earns money for his medicines by cutting firewood, haying, digging postholes with his tractor, snowplowing and cutting brush. "I'm doing odds-and-ends jobs where you can take your time, because the doctor told me I have to stop whenever I feel I need to rest," he says.

24 He cannot afford electricity from the power company, but he gets what current he needs, mostly for lights, by—ingeniously—drawing it from car batteries.

To recharge the batteries, he hooks them up in his truck for a day. He also can charge them with a diesel generator. He waits until prices dip to buy fuel for his generator and tractor. "I've got a few maples around my house," he tells me. "I'll find a rusted-out evaporator, fix it up and make syrup—there's always a few things I can do, I guess."

25 I ask how he's managed all these years, not reading. He says his bosses did the reading for him. And now a Marshfield couple, lifelong friends, help him read his mail and bills and notices. But they are entering their 80s. "Now I've got to learn to read myself, as a backup," Ken says.

26 To find out more about what illiteracy does to people like Ken, I telephoned the U.S. Department of Education and spoke with the Deputy Secretary, Madeleine Kunin. She told me that only 3–5 percent of adult Americans cannot read at all. "But literacy is a moving target," she said. "We figure the 40 million who do read, but at the lowest proficiency levels, have difficulty handling some of the tasks they need to hold a job today." Kunin, a former Vermont governor, cited that state's snowplow drivers: "Now they have computers attached, and they need a high school degree just to drive a snowplow."

27 Ken arrives for his next session in a dark mood. It turns out his tape recorder, used for vocabulary practice, is broken. "I can't fix it because the money's all gone for this month," he says. "I had to go to the doctor, and that's $30, and it was $80 for the pills, and they keep going up." He says one of his prescriptions jumped from $6.99 to $13 in two months. "I don't know if I'll keep taking them," he says. Illiteracy has condemned Ken to a lifetime of minimum-wage poverty.

28 He brightens reading a story. It is about a dog, John Brown, who deeply resents his mistress's new cat. Ken stumbles over a word. "Milk?" Sherry and I nod. "Go and give her some milk," Ken reads, then pauses to give us a dispatch from the literacy front: "I was trying to figure that out, and then I see it has an *i*," he says.

29 My own first attempt at solo tutoring finally comes, and I am edgy. Sherry has wryly admonished Ken, "You help Richard out." I show him file cards, each imprinted with a word for Ken to learn by sight. He is supposed to decipher each word, then incorporate it in a sentence. I write his sentence on the card to help him when he reviews at home. Ken peers at the first word. "All," he says, getting it easily. He makes up a sentence: "We all went away."

30 "That's right," I say. Maybe this won't be so hard after all. I write Ken's sentence on the card for him. Then I flip another card. Ken peers at it, his face working as he struggles with the sounds. "As," he says.

31 During our last session, he confused "as" and "at." Now he has it right. So he has been doing his homework.

32 "As we went down the road, we saw a moose," Ken says, composing a sentence. That reminds him that the state recently allowed moose hunting, game officials arguing that moose have become so plentiful they cause highway accidents. "Yesterday, I come around a turn and there was *ten* moose, a big male and females

and young ones," Ken says. "They shouldn't be shooting those moose—they ain't hurting anyone, and it ain't the moose's fault if people don't use their brakes."

33 I flip another card. "At!" Ken says, triumphing over another of our last session's troublemakers. "We are at the school." But the next word stumps him. It is "be." I put my finger under the first letter. "What's that sound?" I ask. When he stares in consternation, I make the sound "buh." But Ken is blocked. He can't sound out the next letter, even though he has often done it before. "Eeeee," I say, trying to help. "Now put the two sounds together."

34 Ken stares helplessly at the word. I am beginning to understand the deep patience needed to tutor a man like Ken, who began these sessions a year before, knowing the alphabet but able to sound out only a few words. "Buh ... eeee," I say, enunciating as carefully as I can. "Buh ... eeee," Ken repeats. Abruptly, his forehead unfurrows. "Oh, that's 'be,'" he says. "Be—We should be splitting wood!"

35 "Was that what you were doing before the tutoring session?" I ask, to give us both a break. "Nope, plowing snow with my tractor for my friend who broke off his ankle," Ken says.

36 That is arresting information. When I ask what happened, Ken says his octogenarian friend was chain-sawing cherry trees when a bent-back branch lashed out, smashing his lower leg. Ken, haying a field, saw his friend ease his tractor down from the mountainside woodlot, grimacing in agony, working the tractor's pedals with his one good foot.

37 Ken himself once lost his grip on a hay bale he was hoisting. A twig poking from the bale blinded his right eye. Now learning to read is doubly difficult because his remaining eye often tires and blurs. These grim country stories of Ken's make my worries—delayed flights, missed appointments—seem trivial. I flip another card: "But." "Bat," Ken says cautiously. "Buh ... uh ... tuh," I prompt. "But," he finally says. "I would do it, but I have to go somewhere else."

38 I write Ken's sentence on the card and he reads it back. But he stumbles over his own words, unable to sound out "would." I push down rising impatience by remembering the old man in the woods, crawling toward his tractor, dragging that smashed leg.

39 Finally, I put away the cards, glad to be done with them. Tutoring can be frustrating. Why are even easy words sometimes so hard to get? Now we look at a puzzle. On one side it has pictures of various automobile parts. On the other side are printed the parts' names. The idea is to match the pictures and the names. Before I can start asking Ken to try sounding out big terms like "connecting rod," he points to one of the drawings. It looks to me like deer antlers. "Carburetor?" I guess. "Exhaust manifold," Ken says.

40 "What's this one?" I inquire. For all I know, it might be something Han Solo is piloting through hyperspace. "Starter," Ken says. It seems to me he is gloating a little. He points again. "Camshaft?" I ask. Ken corrects me. "Crankshaft," he says, dryly.

41 It is a standoff. I know the printed words. Ken knows the actual objects to which the words refer. "When I was a kid," he tells me, "I bought an old '35 truck. Sometimes it had brakes and sometimes it didn't. I was probably 17. It made lots of smoke, so mosquitoes never bothered me. But one day I got sick of it. I put it under a pine tree and I hoisted the engine up into the tree to look at it. The pressure plate weren't no good. And the fellow showed me how to fix it."

42 That reminds Ken of a later episode. "One time we had to get the hay in, but the baler was jammed. We had the guys from the tractor place, but they could not fix it. Finally I asked the old guy for some wrenches and I adjusted it, and I kept on adjusting, and after that it worked perfectly. I just kept adjusting it a hair until I had it. And then we were baling hay!" No wonder Ken's bosses were happy to do his reading for him. Even so, in our late 20th-century wordscape, illiteracy stymies people like him. And working with Ken has me puzzled: Why do so many people fail to learn to read?

43 I telephoned an expert, Bob Caswell, head of Laubach Literacy International, a nonprofit organization that trains tutors worldwide. He told me many nonreaders, like Ken Adams, suffer from perceptual reading disorders. But there are other reasons for illiteracy, and it is by no means confined to any one part of the population.

44 "People think adult nonreaders are mainly poor, urban minorities, but 41 percent are English-speaking whites," Caswell said, adding that 22 percent are English-speaking blacks, 22 percent are Spanish-speaking, and 15 percent are other non-English speakers. More than half of nonreading adults live in small towns and suburbs. Caswell cited U.S. Department of Labor figures that put illiteracy's annual national cost at $225 billion in workplace accidents, lost productivity, unrealized tax revenues, welfare and crime. One big reason for this whopping problem is *parents* who read poorly.

45 Well over a third of all kids now entering public schools have parents who read inadequately, he said. "Everywhere we find parents who *want* to read to their kids, but can't," he added. "And a child with functionally illiterate parents is twice as likely to grow up to be functionally illiterate."

46 But as I met some of Ken Adams' fellow students, I discovered all sorts of causes for being unable to decipher an English sentence. For instance, I met a woman who had escaped from Laos to Connecticut knowing only Laotian. She learned enough English watching *Sesame Street* ("Big Bird and all that," she told me), and later from being tutored, to become a citizen.

47 I also met a man in his 30s who worked on a newspaper's printing press. He could not spell the simplest words. He said it was because, at age 10, he had begun bringing alcohol to school in peanut-butter jars. After his son was born, he turned to Alcoholics Anonymous and mustered the courage to seek tutoring.

48 I met another man who had dropped out of school in frustration. Not until he tried to enlist in the military did he discover he was nearly deaf. The operator of a

creamery's cheese-cutting machine told me he never learned to read because his family had been in a perpetual uproar, his mother leaving his father seven times in one year. And I met a farm wife, 59, who rarely left her mountaintop. But now, with tutoring she was finally learning to read, devouring novels—"enjoyment books," she called them.

49 In central Vermont, these struggling readers receive free tutoring from nonprofit Adult Basic Education offices, each employing a few professionals, like Sherry Olson, but relying heavily on armies of volunteers, like me. Other states have their own systems. Usually, the funding is a combination of federal and state money, sometimes augmented with donations. Mostly, budgets are bare bones.

50 Many states also rely on nonprofit national organizations, like Laubach Literacy Action (Laubach International's U.S. division) and Literacy Volunteers of America, both headquartered in Syracuse, New York, to train volunteers. Laubach's Bob Caswell told me that, nationwide, literacy services reach only 10 percent of adult nonreaders. "Any effort is a help," he said.

51 Help has come late for Ken Adams. Reviewing his portfolio, I found the goals he set for himself when he began: "To read and write better. And to get out and meet people and develop more trust." Asked by Sherry to cite things that he does well, he had mentioned "fixing equipment, going to school and learning to read, trying new things, telling stories, farming." He remembered being in a Christmas play in second grade and feeling good about that. And he remembered playing football in school: "They would pass it to me and I'd run across the goal to make a score." He mentioned no fond family memories. But he had some good moments. "I remember the first time I learned to drive a tractor," he had said. "We were working in the cornfields. I was proud of that." And a later notation, after he had several months of tutoring, made me think of Ken living alone in his hand-built farmhouse on ten acres atop the mountain. "I like to use recipes," he said. "I use them more as I learn to read and write better. I made Jell-O with fruit, and I make bean salad. I feel good I can do that."

52 In our tutoring sessions, between bouts with the vocabulary cards, Ken tells me he was the oldest of four children. When he was small, his father forced him to come along to roadside bars, and then made Ken sit alone in the car for hours. Ken remembers shivering on subzero nights. "He always said I'd never amount to nothing," Ken says.

53 I ask Ken, one day, if his inability to read has made life difficult. He tells me, "My father said I'd never get a driver's license, and he said nobody would ever help me." Ken had to walk five miles down his mountain and then miles along highways to get to work. "And," he recalls, "I was five years in the quarries in Graniteville—that was a long way." Sometimes he paid neighbors to drive him down the mountain. "They said the same as my father, that I'd never get a license," he says. "They wanted the money."

54 It was not until he was 40 years old that he applied for a license. He had memorized sign shapes and driving rules, and he passed easily. "After I got my license I'd give people a ride down myself," he says. "And they'd ask, 'How much? And I'd always say, 'Nothing, not a danged thing!'"

55 To review the words he has learned, Ken maintains a notebook. On each page, in large block letters, he writes the new word, along with a sentence using the word. He also tapes to each page a picture illustrating the sentence, as a memory aid. To keep him supplied with pictures to snip, I bring him my old magazines. He is partial to animals. He points to one photograph, a black bear cub standing upright and looking back winsomely over its shoulder. "That one there's my favorite," Ken says. And then he tells me, glowering, that he has seen drivers swerve to intentionally hit animals crossing the road. "That rabbit or raccoon ain't hurting anyone," he says.

56 We start a new book, *The Strawberry Dog*. Ken picks out the word "dog" in the title. "That dog must eat strawberries," he says. "I used to have a dog like that. I was picking blackberries. Hey, where were those berries going? Into my dog!"

57 We read these books to help Ken learn words by sight and context. But it seems odd, a white-haired man mesmerized by stories about talkative beavers and foppish toads. Yet, I find myself mesmerized, too. The sessions are reteaching me the exhilaration I found in a narrative as a child, listening to my father read about Peter Churchmouse. Our classes glide by, a succession of vocabulary words—"house," "would," "see"—interwoven with stories about agrarian hippopotamuses and lost dogs befriended.

58 One afternoon it is my last session with Ken. We have wrestled with words through a Christmas and a March sugaring, a midsummer haying, an October when Ken's flannel shirts were specked with sawdust from chain-sawing stove logs. Now the fields outside are snowy; it is Christmas again.

59 My wife and I give Ken a present that she picked out. It is bottles of jam and honey and watermelon pickles, nicely wrapped. Ken quickly slides the package into his canvas tote bag with his homework. "Aren't you going to open it?" Sherry asks. "I'll open it Christmas day," Ken says. "It's the only present I'll get." "No, it isn't," she says, and she hands him a present she has brought.

60 And so we begin our last session with Ken looking pleased. I start with a vocabulary review. "Ignition coil," Ken says, getting the first card right off. He gets "oil filter," too. He peers at the next card. "Have," he says. And he reads the review sentence: "Have you gone away?"

61 He is cruising today. When I flip the next card, he says "There's that 'for.'" It is a word that used to stump him. I turn another card. He gets it instantly. "But." He gets "at," then another old nemesis, "are." I ask him to read the card's review sentence. "Are we going down ... street?" he says. He catches himself. "Nope. That's down*town*!"

62 I am amazed at Ken's proficiency. A while ago, I had complained to my wife that Ken's progress seemed slow. She did some math: one and half hours of tutoring a week, with time off for vacations and snowstorms and truck breakdowns, comes to about 70 hours a year. "That's like sending a first grader to school for only 12 days a year," she said. And so I am doubly amazed at how well Ken is reading today. Besides, Sherry Olson has told me that he now sounds out—or just knows—words that he never could have deciphered when he began. And this reticent man has recently read his own poems to a group of fellow tutees—his new friends—and their neighbors at a library get-together.

63 But now we try something new, a real-world test: reading the supermarket advertising inserts from a local newspaper. Each insert is a hodgepodge of food pictures, product names and prices. I point to a word and Ken ponders. "C" he says finally. "And it's got those two *e's*—so that would be 'coffee'!" I point again. He gets "Pepsi." Silently, he sounds out the letters on a can's label. "So that's 'corn,'" he announces. He picks out "brownies." This is great. And then, even better, he successfully sounds out the modifier: "Fudge," he says. "They-uh!"

64 We're on a roll. But now I point to the page's most tortuous word. Ken starts in the middle again, "ta?" I point my finger at the first letters. "Po," he says, unsure. As always when he reads, Ken seems like a beginning swimmer. He goes a few strokes. Flounders.

65 "Po-ta ...," Ken says. He's swum another stroke. "To," he says, sounding out the last syllable. "Po-ta-to, po-ta-to—Hey, that's potato!" He's crossed the pond. "Ken!" I say. "Terrific!" He sticks out his chin. He almost smiles. "Well, I done better this time," he says. "Yup, I did good."

EXERCISES

A. Determining the Main Idea and Writer's Purpose

Choose the best answer.

1. The main idea of the selection is that
   a. illiteracy is the most difficult problem American educators face today.
   b. learning to read as an adult is a tedious but rewarding activity.
   c. teaching an illiterate adult is a frustrating process that requires time, profound patience, and understanding.
   d. adult illiterates can never master reading skills they should have learned as children.

2. With respect to the main idea, the writer's purpose is to
   a. urge teachers to do a better job of teaching children to read.
   b. criticize the nation's teachers for passing students along, thereby dooming them to illiteracy and underemployment.
   c. explain the difficulties and triumphs one adult illiterate experienced as he learned to read.
   d. promote adult literacy programs and encourage the reader to volunteer in these programs.

B. Comprehending Main Ideas

Choose the correct answer.

1. According to a U.S. Department of Education report on illiteracy and another report cited in the selection, only 3 to 5 percent of adult Americans are completely illiterate; however, the number of adult Americans who read haltingly or minimally is around
   a. 10 percent.
   b. 25 percent.
   c. 40 percent.
   d. 50 percent.
2. Wolkomir finds that the most appropriate materials for teaching an adult learner like Ken Adams are
   a. the daily newspaper and supermarket ads.
   b. children's books.
   c. books on subjects that the student is interested in.
   d. comic books.
3. According to Sherry Olson, the primary reading tutor, Ken Adams's difficulty with learning to read as a child was probably the result of
   a. brain damage at birth.
   b. his own unwillingness to do his schoolwork.
   c. his elementary teachers' incompetence.
   d. an undiagnosed perceptual reading disorder.
4. Bob Caswell of Laubach Literacy International reports that adult non-readers are
   a. not confined to any one segment of the population.
   b. generally urban minorities.
   c. unwilling to take the necessary steps to learn to read.
   d. live on farms where reading is not a necessary skill.

5. One particular problem for more than a third of children now entering public schools is that they may fall behind because
   a. their school districts have cut budgets drastically.
   b. their parents are themselves functionally illiterate and cannot help them much.
   c. their classrooms are understaffed.
   d. their instructors cannot agree on the best method to teach reading.

C. Locating Supporting Details

For each main idea stated here, find details that support it.

1. Sherry, Ken Adams's primary tutor, gives the writer tips on how to go about helping Ken learn to read. [paragraph 14]

   a. ______________________________

   ____

   b. ______________________________

2. Ken Adams describes himself as a "slow learner," but clearly he is not slow. [20]

   a. ______________________________

   b. ______________________________

D. Interpreting Meaning

1. From paragraph 13, what are the two important points Wolkomir makes about learning to read, at least for most people? He finds the process both

   ____

2. What is the purpose of the statistics cited in paragraphs 7 and 26?

   ____

3. Read paragraph 26 again. A good title for this paragraph would be
   a. "Literacy: A Moving Target."
   b. "Adult Literacy Statistics."
   c. "Why a High School Education Is No Longer Enough."
   d. "How Illiteracy Affects Its Victims."

4. Look again at paragraphs 36 and 37 in which the writer cites "grim country stories." Why are these stories significant?

____

____

5. Look again at paragraphs 46–48 and write the sentence that states the main idea for this section.

____

____

E. Understanding Vocabulary

Look through the paragraphs listed below and find a word that matches each definition. Refer to a dictionary if necessary. An example has been done for you.

EXAMPLE: neat, tidy, orderly [paragraphs 6–7] prim

1. a bad or unfortunate situation [7–8] ______________
2. getting only with great effort or strain [phrase—18–19] ______________
3. resourcefully, inventively, cleverly [23–24] ______________
4. dryly, ironically, humorously [28–29] ______________
5. gently cautioned, reminded [28–29] ______________
6. state of dismay or anxiety [32–33] ______________
7. pronouncing precisely and slowly [33–34] ______________
8. increased, amplified, added to [49–50] ______________
9. enthralled, captivated, spellbound [55–57] ______________
10. state of being stimulated, feeling of elation [55–57] ______________
11. source of harm, a difficult opponent to conquer [61–62] ______________
12. restrained, reserved, inclined to keep one's thoughts to oneself [61–62] ______________

DISCUSSION QUESTIONS

1. How does Wolkomir account for his own fond memories about reading as a child and his love of reading?
2. What apparently are some of the reasons that in elementary school Ken Adams's teachers didn't recognize his difficulty and help him?
3. Based on Ken Adams's experience, what are some specific problems in the workforce that illiterate adults or poor readers might encounter?
4. For the writer, what did tutoring Ken Adams teach him about reading? What other lessons did these sessions teach him?
5. What are some of the benefits that Ken Adams has derived from learning to read?

EXPLORE THE WEB

An updated report with many links on the state of literacy in the United States is available at this site sponsored by the National Institute for Literacy:

www.nifl.gov

Reading Selections

How Mr. Dewey Decimal Saved My Life

Barbara Kingsolver

Barbara Kingsolver, an American writer of both fiction and nonfiction, was raised in eastern Kentucky, an area of the state that lies between the coal-mining region of the east and the wealthy horse farms of the west. After receiving a degree from DePauw University, she did graduate work in biology at the University of Arizona. After leaving school, Kingsolver worked during the day as a freelance journalist, and at night she wrote fiction. Her books have been well received by both critics and the reading public. She is best known for two novels, *The Bean Trees* (1988) and *The Poisonwood Bible* (1998). This selection is taken from her 1995 collection of essays, *High Tide in Tucson.*

VOCABULARY ANALYSIS

The Prefix *inter-*

The word *interlude* [paragraph 5] means an interruption, a break—an episode that comes in the middle of something. The word derives from Latin and can be broken down like this: *inter-* ("between") + *ludus* ("play"). Indeed, another meaning of *interlude* comes from drama—a short entertainment between the acts of a play. English has dozens of words that begin with the prefix *inter-*, among them, *interrupt, interchange, interfere, intergalactic, intermarry, international, intersperse*, and *intervene*.

The Suffix *-cide*

Homicides [paragraph 17] refer to the killings of human beings, from the Latin root *homo-* ("man") and the Latin suffix *-cide* ("killing"). Here are four more words ending with this suffix:

suicide killing oneself

genocide killing an entire race of people

matricide killing one's mother

pesticide an agent that kills insects

What do these three words mean? Consult a dictionary if you are unsure.

patricide ______________________________

infanticide ______________________________

herbicide ______________________________

How Mr. Dewey Decimal Saved My Life

Barbara Kingsolver

1 A librarian named Miss Truman Richey snatched me from the jaws of ruin, and it's too late now to thank her. I'm not the first person to notice that we rarely get around to thanking those who've helped us most. Salvation is such a heady thing the temptation is to dance gasping on the shore, shouting that we are alive, till our forgotten savior has long since gone under. Or else sit quietly, sideswiped and embarrassed, mumbling that we really did know pretty much how to swim. But now that I see the wreck that could have been, without Miss Richey, I'm of a fearsome mind to throw my arms around every living librarian who crosses my path, on behalf of the souls they never knew they saved.

2 I reached high school at the close of the sixties, in the Commonwealth of Kentucky, whose ranking on educational spending was I think around fifty-first, after Mississippi and whatever was below Mississippi. Recently Kentucky has drastically changed the way money is spent on its schools, but back then, the wealth of the county decreed the wealth of the school, and few coins fell far from the money trees that grew in Lexington. Our county, out where the bluegrass begins to turn brown, was just scraping by. Many a dedicated teacher served out earnest missions in our halls, but it was hard to spin silk purses out of a sow's ear budget. We didn't get anything fancy like Latin or Calculus. Apart from English, the only two courses of study that ran for four consecutive years, each one building upon the last, were segregated: Home Ec for girls and Shop for boys. And so I stand today, a woman who knows how to upholster, color-coordinate a table setting, and plan a traditional wedding—valuable skills I'm still waiting to put to good use in my life.

3 As far as I could see from the lofty vantage point of age sixteen, there was nothing required of me at Nicholas County High that was going to keep me off the streets; unfortunately we had no streets, either. We had lanes, roads, and rural free delivery routes, six in number, I think. We had two stoplights, which

were set to burn green in all directions after 6 P.M., so as not, should the event of traffic arise, to slow anybody up.

4 What we *didn't* have included almost anything respectable teenagers might do in the way of entertainment. In fact, there was one thing for teenagers to do to entertain themselves, and it was done in the backs of Fords and Chevrolets. It wasn't upholstering skills that were brought to bear on those backseats, either. Though the wedding-planning skills did follow.

5 I found myself beginning a third year of high school in a state of unrest, certain I already knew what there was to know, academically speaking—all wised up and no place to go. Some of my peers used the strategy of rationing out the Science and Math classes between periods of suspension or childbirth, stretching their schooling over the allotted four years, and I envied their broader vision. I had gone right ahead and used the classes up, like a reckless hiker gobbling up all the rations on day one of a long march. Now I faced years of Study Hall, with brief interludes of Home Ec III and IV as the bright spots. I was developing a lean and hungry outlook.

6 We did have a school library, and a librarian who was surely paid inadequately to do the work she did. Yet there she was, every afternoon, presiding over the study hall, and she noticed me. For reasons I can't fathom, she discerned potential. I expect she saw my future, or at least the one I craved so hard it must have materialized in the air above me, connected to my head by little cartoon bubbles. If that's the future she saw, it was riding down the road on the back of a motorcycle, wearing a black leather jacket with "Violators" (that was the name of our county's motorcycle gang, and I'm not kidding) stitched in a solemn arc across the back.

7 There is no way on earth I really would have ended up a Violator Girlfriend—I could only dream of such a thrilling fate. But I was set hard upon wrecking my reputation in the limited ways available to skinny, unsought-after girls. They consisted mainly of cutting up in class, pretending to be surly, and making up shocking, entirely untrue stories about my home life. I wonder now that my parents continued to feed me. I clawed like a cat in a gunnysack against the doom I feared: staying home to reupholster my mother's couch one hundred thousand weekends in a row, until some tolerant myopic farm boy came along to rescue me from sewing-machine slavery.

8 Miss Richey had something else in mind. She took me by the arm in study hall one day and said, "Barbara, I'm going to teach you Dewey Decimal."

9 One more valuable skill in my life.

10 She launched me on the project of cataloging and shelving every one of the, probably, thousand books in the Nicholas County High School library. And since it beat Home Ec III by a mile, I spent my study-hall hours this way without audible complaint, so long as I could look plenty surly while I did it. Though it was hard to see the real point of organizing books nobody ever looked at. And since it was my God-given duty in those days to be frank as a plank, I said as much to Miss Richey.

11 She just smiled. She with her hidden agenda. And gradually, in the process of handling every book in the room, I made some discoveries. I found *Gone With the Wind*, which I suspected my mother felt was kind of trashy, and I found Edgar Allan Poe, who scared me witless. I found that the call number for books about snakes in 666. I found William Saroyan's *Human Comedy*, down there on the shelf between Human Anatomy and Human Physiology, where probably no one had touched it since 1943. But I read it, and it spoke to me. In spite of myself I imagined the life of an immigrant son who believed human kindness was a tangible and glorious thing. I began to think about words like *tangible* and *glorious*. I read on. After I'd read all the good ones, I went back and read Human Anatomy and Human Physiology and found that I liked those pretty well too.

12 It came to pass in two short years that the walls of my high school dropped down, and I caught the scent of a world. I started to dream up intoxicating lives for myself that I could not have conceived without the books. So I didn't end up on a motorcycle. I ended up roaring hell-for-leather down the backroads of transcendent, reeling sentences. A writer. Imagine that.

13 The most important thing about the books I read in my rebellion is that they were not what I expected. I can't say I had no previous experience with literature; I grew up in a house full of books. Also, I'd known my way around the town's small library since I was tall enough to reach the shelves (though the town librarian disliked children and censored us fiercely) and looked forward to the Bookmobile as hungrily as more urbane children listened for the ice cream truck. So dearly did my parents want their children to love books they made reading aloud the center of our family life, and when the TV broke they took about two decades to get around to fixing it.

14 It's well known, though, that when humans reach a certain age, they identify precisely what it is their parents want for them and bolt in the opposite direction like lemmings for the cliff. I had already explained to my classmates, in an effort to get dates, that I was raised by wolves, and I really had to move on from there. If I was going to find a path to adult reading, I had to do it my own way. I had to read things I imagined my parents didn't want me looking into. Trash, like *Gone With the Wind*. (I think, now, that my mother had no real problem with *Gone With the Wind*, but wisely didn't let on.)

15 Now that I am a parent myself, I'm sympathetic to the longing for some control over what children read, or watch, or do. Our protectiveness is a deeply loving and deeply misguided effort to keep our kids inside the bounds of what we know is safe and right. Sure, I want to train my child to goodness. But unless I can invoke amnesia to blot out my own past, I have to see it's impossible to keep her inside the world I came up in. That world rolls on, and you can't step in the same river twice. The things that prepared me for life are not the same things that will move my own child into adulthood.

Connecting Grammar to Writing

Paragraph 16 opens with this clause: "What snapped me out of my surly adolescence and moved me on . . . ." Is this a noun clause, adjective clause, or adverb clause?
What is the verb of the sentence?

16 What snapped me out of my surly adolescence and moved me on were books that let me live other people's lives. I got to visit the Dust Bowl and London and the Civil War and Rhodesia. The fact that Rhett Butler said "damn" was a snoozer to me—I hardly noticed the words that mothers worried about. I noticed words like *colour bar*, spelled "colour" the way Doris Lessing wrote it, and eventually I figured out it meant racism. It was the thing that had forced some of the kids in my county to go to a separate school—which wasn't even a school but a one-room CME church—and grow up without plumbing or the hope of owning a farm. When I picked up *Martha Quest*, a novel set in southern Africa, it jarred open a door that was right in front of me. I found I couldn't close it.

17 If there is danger in a book like *Martha Quest*, and the works of all other authors who've been banned at one time or another, the danger is generally that they will broaden our experience and blend us more deeply with our fellow humans. Sometimes this makes waves. It made some at my house. We had a few rocky years while I sorted out new information about the human comedy, the human tragedy, and the ways some people are held to the ground unfairly. I informed my parents that I had invented a new notion called justice. Eventually, I learned to tone down my act a little. Miraculously, there were no homicides in the meantime.

18 Now, with my adolescence behind me and my daughter's still ahead, I am nearly speechless with gratitude for the endurance and goodwill of librarians in an era that discourages reading in almost incomprehensible ways. We've created for ourselves a culture that undervalues education (compared with the rest of the industrialized world, to say the least), undervalues breadth of experience (compared with our potential), downright discourages critical thinking (judging from what the majority of us watch and read), and distrusts foreign ideas. "Un-American," from what I hear, is meant to be an insult.

19 Most alarming, to my mind, is that we the people tolerate censorship in school libraries for the most bizarre and frivolous of reasons. Art books that contain (horrors!) nude human beings, and *The Wizard of Oz* because it has witches in it. Not always, everywhere, but everywhere, always something. And censorship of certain ideas in some quarters is enough to sway curriculums at the national level. Sometimes profoundly. Find a publishing house that's brave enough to include a thorough discussion of the principles of evolution in a high school text. Good luck. And yet, just about all working botanists, zoologists, and ecologists will tell you that evolution is to their field what germ theory is to medicine. We expect our kids to salvage a damaged earth, but in deference to the religious beliefs of a handful, we allow an entire generation of future scientists to germinate and grow in a vacuum.

20 The parents who believe in Special Creation have every right to tell their children how the world was made all at once, of a piece, in the year 4,004 B.C. Heaven knows, I tell my daughter things about economic justice that are just

about as far outside the mainstream of American dogma. But I don't expect her school to forgo teaching Western history or capitalist economics on my account. Likewise, it should be the job of Special Creationist parents to make their story convincing to their children, set against the school's bright scenery of dinosaur fossils and genetic puzzle-solving, the crystal clarity of Darwinian logic, the whole glorious science of an evolving world that tells its own creation story. It cannot be any teacher's duty to tiptoe around religion, hiding objects that might raise questions at home. Faith, by definition, is impervious to fact. A belief that can be changed by new information was probably a scientific one, not a religious one, and science derives its value from its openness to revision.

21 If there is a fatal notion on this earth, it's the notion that wider horizons will be fatal. Difficult, troublesome, scary—yes, all that. But the wounds, for a sturdy child, will not be mortal. When I read Doris Lessing at seventeen, I was shocked to wake up from my placid color-blind coma into the racially segregated town I called my home. I saw I had been a fatuous participant in a horrible thing. I bit my nails to the quick, cast nets of rage over all I loved for a time, and quaked to think of all I had—still have—to learn. But if I hadn't made that reckoning, I would have lived a smaller, meaner life.

22 The crossing is worth the storm. Ask my parents. Twenty years ago I expect they'd have said, "Here, take this child, we will trade her to you for a sack of limas." But now they have a special shelf in their house for books that bear the family name on their spines. Slim rewards for a parent's thick volumes of patience, to be sure, but at least there are no motorcycles rusting in the carport.

23 My thanks to Doris Lessing and William Saroyan and Miss Truman Richey. And every other wise teacher who may ever save a surly soul like mine.

EXERCISES

A. Determining the Main Idea and Writer's Purpose

Choose the best answer.

1. The main idea of the selection is that
   a. contemporary American culture undervalues education and experience and discourages critical thinking.
   b. censorship—whether over books in the library or over teaching concepts like evolution—should not be tolerated.
   c. shelving and cataloguing books in the high school library was a waste of time since hardly anyone ever read them.
   d. the writer made some discoveries about herself and about the outside world when she began reading books from her high school library.

2. Which of the following excerpts from the selection best identifies the writer's purpose?
   a. "A librarian named Miss Truman Richey snatched me from the jaws of ruin, and it's too late now to thank her."
   b. "It came to pass in those two short years that the walls of my high school dropped down, and I caught the scent of a world."
   c. "Now, with my adolescence behind me and my daughter's still ahead, I am nearly speechless with gratitude for the endurance and goodwill of librarians in an era that discourages reading in almost incomprehensible ways."
   d. "Most alarming, to my mind, is that we the people tolerate censorship in school libraries for the most bizarre and frivolous of reasons."

B. Comprehending Main Ideas

Choose the correct answer.

1. Kingsolver writes that the school she attended, Nicholas County High School, at the end of the 60s was
   a. poorly funded.
   b. well funded.
   c. segregated.
   d. well respected academically.

2. According to the writer, the most important thing that teenagers in her town lacked was
   a. sex education.
   b. a community center.
   c. high-level academic courses like calculus and Latin.
   d. entertainment.

3. Which of the following does Kingsolver not mention as a way she compensated for her status as a "skinny, unsought-after" girl?
   a. She became pregnant.
   b. She acted out and cut up in class.
   c. She made up shocking and untrue stories about her family.
   d. She adopted a surly attitude.

4. The books Kingsolver enjoyed reading most and learned from most were those that
   a. were about other troubled teenagers.
   b. were about the adventures of heroes like Dewey Decimal.

c. let her live other people's lives.

d. would have been censored in most school libraries.

5. For Kingsolver, censorship in this country—both in school libraries and in the scientific curriculum—is the result of deference to

a. those who criticize foreign ideas as "un-American."

b. the religious beliefs of a relatively small minority.

c. cowardly and timid school boards that promote only the blandest of curricula.

d. uneducated and ignorant people who impose their ideas on others.

C. Sequencing

The sentences in this excerpt from the selection have been scrambled. Read the sentences and choose the sequence that puts them back into logical order. Do not refer to the original selection.

1. It wasn't upholstering skills that were brought to bear on those backseats, either. **2.** What we *didn't* have included almost anything respectable teenagers might do in the way of entertainment. **3.** Though the wedding-planning skills did follow. **4.** In fact, there was one thing for teenagers to do to entertain themselves, and it was done in the backs of Fords and Chevrolets.

a. 1, 2, 4, 3

b. 2, 4, 1, 3

c. 4, 1, 3, 2

d. Correct as written.

D. Interpreting Meaning

Where appropriate, write your answers to these questions in your own words.

1. Consider this sentence from paragraph 1: "Salvation is such a heady thing the temptation is to dance gasping on the shore, shouting that we are still alive, till our forgotten savior has long since gone under." What metaphorical comparison is suggested in the last part of this quotation? What has happened to the forgotten savior?

____

What kind of salvation is she literally referring to?

____

2. Why does Kingsolver include a description of the "Violators" and "Violator Girlfriends" in paragraphs 6 and 7?

____

____

____

3. What was Miss Richey's, the librarian, "hidden agenda" in asking Kingsolver to shelve and catalogue books?

____

____

4. As suggested in paragraph 12, aside from giving her "the scent of a world" and removing her from the prospect of riding a motorcycle as a Violator Girlfriend, what was another consequence of Kingsolver's reading books?

____

5. From the details she provides in paragraph 17, what can the reader conclude about the connection between Kingsolver's reading and her relationship with her parents?

____

____

____

6. Which of the following best expresses Kingsolver's tone, or emotional attitude, toward the practice of censoring library books and the teaching of evolution in science classes?

   a. skeptical b. scornful
   c. sympathetic d. ambivalent

E. Understanding Vocabulary

Look through the paragraphs listed below and find a word that matches each definition. Refer to a dictionary if necessary. An example has been done for you.

EXAMPLE: intoxicating, exhilarating [paragraphs 1–2] heady

1. ordered authoritatively [1–2] _______________
2. high, elevated [3–4] _______________
3. perceived, detected [6–7] _______________
4. that which can be heard [10–11] _______________
5. that which can be touched, concrete [10–11] _______________
6. supreme, preeminent, surpassing others [11–12] _______________

7. system of beliefs, creed, doctrine [20–21] ____________

8. incapable of being affected by, not influenced by [20–21] ____________

9. undisturbed by disorder, calm [20–21] ____________

10. vacuously and unconsciously foolish [21–22] ____________

F. Vocabulary And Dictionary Exercise

Answer these questions. You may need to consult a dictionary for this exercise.

1. In paragraph 6, Kingsolver writes, "For reasons I can't *fathom*, she [Miss Richey] discerned potential." Choose the dictionary definition that is most appropriate for this word in this context and the part of speech.
   a. *n.* A unit of length equal to 6 feet, used to measure marine depths.
   b. *tr. v.* To penetrate to the meaning or nature of, to comprehend.
   c. *v.* To determine the depth of, sound.

2. The adjective *surly* is used four times in the selection, in paragraphs 7, 10, 16, and 23. Judging from these four contexts, what does the word mean?

   ____

3. The adjective *myopic* [paragraph 7] can be pronounced two ways. Write the pronunciation symbols for this word in the spaces provided.

   ____

   Write the noun form of this adjective along with its meaning.

   ____

4. In paragraph 12, Kingsolver writes, "I started to dream up *intoxicating* lives for myself that I could not have conceived without the books." Here are three definitions for the verb *intoxicate*. Which is the most appropriate one for the adjective in this context?
   a. **1.** To stupefy or excite by the action of a chemical substance such as alcohol.
   b. **2.** To stimulate or excite.
   c. **3.** To poison.

5. Does the word *urbane* [paragraph 13] have anything to do with *urban*? Consult the dictionary to see the etymology of both words.

   ____

   ____

6. Here are two definitions for the adjective *frivolous* (paragraph 19). Which is the better choice of meaning for this context?

   a. **1.** Unworthy of serious attention, trivial: *a frivolous novel.*

   b. **2.** Inappropriately silly: *a frivolous purchase.*

   This adjective has three variant forms. Write the required forms in the spaces provided:

   two nouns ____________________ adverb ____________________

DISCUSSION QUESTIONS

1. To what extent was Kingsolver's high school experience similar to yours? To what extent was it different?
2. From the details that she provides, what can you infer about the Kentucky town where Kingsolver was raised? For example, what were its values? What opportunities were there for young people?
3. In what specific ways did Kingsolver's reading change her?
4. What exactly does Demey Decimal refer to? Why does Kingsolver refer to it as if he was a real person?

EXPLORE THE WEB

- Barbara Kingsolver's home page, which offers FAQs, a bibliography, and excerpts from her books, can be accessed at this address:

  www.kingsolver.com/home/index.asp.

The Teacher Who Opened My Mind
Mark Edmundson

Mark Edmundson was an underachieving student at Medford High School in Massachusetts. He had never read a book in his life that wasn't about football, and he had no idea what he wanted to do with his life. Frank Lears, a new teacher, arrived at Medford High and started an introductory course in philosophy. Although initially hostile and indifferent, Edmundson soon found himself being drawn in and eventually undergoing a life change. Frank Lears was the catalyst for this change, as Edmundson explains in this selection, which is adapted from his 2002 book *Teacher: The One Who Made the Difference.*

After high school, Edmundson studied at the University of Massachusetts at Amherst and graduated from Bennington College in 1974. Following graduation, he moved to Manhattan where he drove a cab, wrote for the *Village Voice*, and worked as a stagehand and as a security agent at rock shows. He completed his doctorate in English from Yale University; he has taught English at the University of Virginia for over twenty years.

VOCABULARY ANALYSIS

The Prefix *a-*

Frank Lears, Edmundson's teacher, amazingly enough, once danced in the classroom. Edmundson says that he was a terrible dancer, "stiff and arrhythmic." The prefix *a-* derives from Greek. When it is attached to a root word, it means "without," or "a complete absence of." In other words, Lears's dancing was completely without rhythm. English has several words that begin with this prefix, among them *apolitical* (having no interest in politics); *amoral* (having no sense of morality); *apathy* (having no feeling); *atheist* (one who does not believe in God); and *anarchy* (a complete absence of order or rule).

Word Root: *phil-*

The Greek root *phil-* (or *–phile*) meaning "love of" is a component of a few English words. The word *philosopher* is composed of these two word parts: *phil-* ("one who loves") + *sophos* ("wisdom"). Here are some other words containing this root:

philanthropist
one who loves mankind and seeks its betterment, often by making charitable donations, from *phil-* + *anthropos* ("man" or "mankind")

philanderer
one who carries on sexual affairs, especially extramarital affairs, from *phil-* + *ander* ("man")

philodendron
a tree-climbing plant, literally, "fond of trees," from *phil-* + *dendros* ("trees")

Philadelphia
the largest city in Pennsylvania, "the city of brotherly love"

Anglophile, Francophile, cinephile
one who loves or has a strong affinity for things, respectively, one who loves things English, one who loves things French, and one who loves the cinema

The Teacher Who Opened My Mind

Mark Edmundson

1 Frank Lears came to Medford High School with big plans for his philosophy course. Together with a group of self-selected seniors, he was going to ponder the eternal questions: beauty, truth, free will, fate, that sort of thing. The class would start out reading *The Story of Philosophy* by Will Durant, then go on to Plato's dialogues, some Aristotle, Leibniz (a particular favorite of Lears'), maybe just a little bit of Kant, then into a discussion of Bertrand Russell's effort to clear the whole thing up with an injection of clean scientific logic. Lears had just graduated from Harvard. All of his intellectual aspirations were intact.

2 On the first day of class, we saw a short, slight man, with olive skin—we thought he might be Mexican—wearing a skinny tie and a moth-eaten suit with a paper clip fastened to the left lapel. He had hunched shoulders and a droopy black mustache. Even when he strove for some dynamism, as he did that first day, explaining his plans for the course, he still had a melancholy presence. Having outlined the course, he turned away from us and began writing on the blackboard, in a script neater than any we would see from him again. It was a quotation from Nietzsche. He told us to get out our papers and pens and spend a couple of pages interpreting the quote "as a limbering-up exercise." I had never heard of Nietzsche. I had never read all the way through a book that was written for adults and that was not concerned exclusively with football.

3 The day before, I'd sat in the office of Mrs. Olmstead, the senior guidance counselor, and been informed that I ranked 270th in a class of nearly 700. My prospects were not bright. We talked about Massachusetts Bay Community College, Salem State Teachers College; we discussed my working for the city of Medford—perhaps I'd start by collecting barrels, then graduate in time to a desk job (my father had some modest connections); I mentioned joining the Marines (I might have made it in time for the Cambodia invasions). Nothing was resolved.

4 As I was mumbling my way out the door, Mrs. Olmstead began talking about a new teacher who was coming to the school, "someone we're especially proud to have." He was scheduled to teach philosophy. I didn't know what philosophy was, but I associated it with airy speculation, empty nothing; it seemed an agreeable enough way of wasting time.

5 So there I was in a well-lit room, wearing, no doubt, some sharp back-to-school ensemble, pegged pants and sporty dice-in-the-back-alley shoes, mildly aching from two or three football-inflicted wounds, and pondering the Nietzsche quotation, which I could barely understand. I felt dumb as a rock, a sentiment with which I, at 17, had no little prior experience. But by putting the quotation on the board, Lears showed me that, in at least one department, his powers of comprehension were a few notches lower than mine. He had misunderstood Medford High School entirely.

6 The appearances had taken him in. No doubt he'd strolled through the building on the day before students arrived; he'd seen desks, chalkboards, supply closets stocked full of paper and books, all the paraphernalia of education. He had seen these things and he'd believed that he was in a school, a place where people quested, by fits and starts, for the truth.

7 But I had acquired a few facts that Lears would not have been primed to receive at Harvard, or at prep school, or at any of the other places where he had filled his hours. Medford High School, whatever its appearances, was not a school. It was a place where you learned to do—or were punished for failing in—a variety of exercises. The content of these exercises mattered not at all. What mattered was form, repetition, and form. You filled in the blanks, conjugated, declined, diagrammed, defined, outlined, summarized, recapitulated, positioned, graphed. It did not matter what: English, geometry, biology, history, all were the same. The process treated your mind as though it were a body part capable of learning a number of protocols, then repeating, repeating. If you'd done what you should have at Medford High, the transition into a factory, into an office, into the Marines would be something you'd barely notice; it would be painless.

Connecting Grammar to Writing

In paragraph 8 and throughout the entire essay, notice that book titles are italicized. In your own writing you can either italicize them or underline them. Either way is correct. But use quotation marks for titles of articles or essays.

8 Before Lears arrived, I never rebelled against the place, at least not openly. I didn't in part because I believed that Medford High was the only game there was. The factories where my father and uncles worked were extensions of the high school; the TV shows we watched were manufactured to fit the tastes for escape that such places form; the books we were assigned to read in class, *Ivanhoe, Silas Marner, The Good Earth*, of which I ingested about 50 pages each, could, as I saw it then, have been written by the English teachers, with their bland, babbling goodness and suppressed hysterias (I've never had the wherewithal to check back into them). Small bursts of light came through in the Beethoven symphonies my father occasionally played at volume on our ancient stereo (the music sounded like it was coming in over a walkie-talkie) and the Motown tunes I heard on Boston's black radio station, WILD, but these sounds were not connected to any place or human possibility I knew about. So I checked out. I went low to the ground, despondent, suspicious, asleep in the outer self, barely conscious within.

9 This condition Frank Lears changed. That now, however imperfectly, I can say what's on my mind, and that I know what kind of life I hope for, I owe not to him alone, of course, but to many. Frank Lears pushed open the door to those others, though, other worlds, other minds.

10 For three months, Lears did his best with Will Durant and *The Story of Philosophy*. We barely gave him an inch. Dubby O'Day (Donald O'Day on his report cards and disciplinary citations) made enormous daisy chains out of the rubber bands he used to bind the advertising circulars he delivered on Saturday mornings or sat, his body tight with concentrated energy, inking in all of the *o*'s in the textbook. Tom Vincents pried tufts of grass off the soles of his soccer

cleats; Michael de Leo and Tom Cappalano, wide receiver and quarterback for the Medford Mustangs (I blocked for them, sporadically), contemplated pass plays and the oncoming game with Newton, or Somerville, or Everett. Nora Balakanian was high school beautiful. Sandra Steinman, the school's only hippie—she wore wire-rim glasses and work boots and was, by her own choice, of no social consequence at all—conversed with Lears on subjects no one else cared about.

11 Lears thought well of himself. And we all wondered, if unspokenly, where this guy might have gotten his considerable lode of self-esteem. Teachers, as we could have told him, were losers out-and-out. And this one in particular wasn't strong or tough or worldly. He wore ridiculous clothes, old formal suits, and that weird paper clip in his lapel; he talked like a dictionary; his accent was overcultivated, queer, absurd. Yet he thought highly of himself. And not much at all, it wasn't difficult to see, of us. He mocked us, and not always so genially, for never doing the reading, never knowing the answer, never having a thought in our heads. We were minor fools, his tone implied, for ignoring this chance to learn a little something before being fed live to what was waiting. For our part, we sat back, and waited to see what would turn up.

12 One day in mid-December or so, Lears walked in and told us to pass back our copies of *The Story of Philosophy*. Then he told us that he had some other books for us to read but that we'd have to pay for them ourselves. Lears, it turned out, had asked no one's permission to do this; it just struck him as a good idea to try to get people who never picked up a book to do some reading by giving them work that might speak to their experience. At Medford High, this qualified as major educational innovation, real breakthrough thinking. And, of course, there were plenty of rules against using books that hadn't been approved by the school board. The books that Lears picked were on a theme, though I had no idea of that at the time. *The Stranger, One Flew Over the Cuckoo's Nest*, Freud's *Group Psychology and the Analysis of the Ego, Siddhartha:* The first three were about the oppressions of conformity (among other things), the last about the Buddha's serene, fierce rebellion against it. For the first few weeks, since virtually no one but Sandra would read a book at home, we simply sat in a circle and read the pages aloud in turn. Periodically, Lears would ask a question, and usually, in the beginning, it was he who would answer it or decide finally to let it drop. One day, when we were reading *The Stranger*, Lears asked us about solitude. What does it mean to be alone? Is it possible? What would it mean to be genuinely by oneself? Sandra Steinman raised her hand, no doubt ready to treat us to a description of Zen meditation and its capacity to melt the ego beyond solitude into pure nothingness. But Lears must have seen something ripple across Nora Balakanian's beautiful face. He gestured in her direction, though she hadn't volunteered.

13 Nora was a high school princess, whose autobiography, I'd have guessed back then, would have translated into a graph peaking from prom to prom, with

soft valleys of preparation in between. But what Nora did, in her teasing nasal voice, was to run through a litany of defenses against being alone. She mentioned listening to the radio and talking on the phone, then playing the songs and conversations over in her mind, and a myriad of other strategies, ending, perceptively enough, with our habit of blocking out the present by waiting for things to happen in the future. But Nora did not express herself with detachment. She said "I." "This is how I keep from being alone." "And why," asked Lears, "is it hard to be alone?" "Because," Nora answered, "I might start to think about things."

14 Nora had been, up until that point, one of the Elect, predestined for all happiness; suddenly she had gone over to the terminally Lost. One of the great sources of grief for those who suffer inwardly is their belief that others exist who are perpetually and truly happy. From the ranks of the local happy few, Nora had just checked out, leaving some effective hints about those she'd left behind.

15 The book that mattered to me wasn't *The Stranger*, which had gotten Nora going, or Freud's book on the herd instinct (when I was writing my dissertation, a literary critical reading of Freud, my working text of *Group Psychology* was, somehow, the one that had belonged to Dubby O'Day, with the *o*'s colored in to about page 20), but Kesey's *One Flew Over the Cuckoo's Nest*. It's a hard book for me to read now, with its pumped-up, cartoon hero, Randall Patrick McMurphy. But at the time it was all in all. I read it in a lather, running through it in about 10 hours straight, then starting in again almost immediately.

16 But that didn't happen right off. It was probably on the fifth day of reading the book out loud in class that a chance remark Lears made caught my attention, or what there was of it then to catch. He said that prisons, hospitals, and schools were on a continuum, controlling institutions with many of the same protocols and objectives, and that Kesey, with his bitter portrait of the mental hospital, might be seen as commenting on all these places.

17 This idea, elementary as it was, smacked me with the force of revelation. Here was a writer who was not on the side of the teachers, who in fact detested them and their whole virtuous apparatus. That the book was in part crude and ugly I knew even at that time: Blacks in it are twisted sadists, the women castrators or sweet whores. But it was the anti-authoritarian part that swept me in; here was someone who found words—gorgeous, graffiti-sized, and apocalyptic—for what in me had been mere inchoate impulses.

18 Soon Lears started bringing things into class. Every Friday we got some music: I remember hearing Billie Holiday, Mozart, the Velvet Underground. He also showed us art books, read a poem from time to time, and brought in friends of his to explain themselves. A panel from Students for a Democratic Society[1] appeared one day to discuss the Vietnam War with us. (Most of us were in favor.)

19 One February day, a group of black students burst into the room and announced that this was the anniversary of Malcolm X's death. Lears looked up

mildly from his place in the circle and asked the foremost of them, "And when was he born, Malcolm Little?" The young man gave a date. Lears nodded and invited them to sit down. It was the first time I'd had an extended conversation about politics with blacks. More discussions followed and, though they didn't stop the ongoing racial guerrilla war at Medford High, they were something.

20 When the weather warmed up, the class occasionally went outside to sit on the grass and hold discussions there. This sometimes resulted in one or two of us nodding off, but Lears didn't much care; he had most of us most of the time now. He sat cross-legged, and laughed, and we answered the questions he asked, because what he thought mattered. It was a first, this outdoors business; no one at Medford High would have imagined doing it. One Thursday afternoon, just as we were wrapping up a discussion of Thoreau, Lears gave us a solemn, mischievous look, the sort of expression shrewd old rabbis are supposed to be expert in delivering, and said, "There's been some doubt expressed about our going outside." Then he told a story. Jingles McDermott, the feared school disciplinarian, had approached Lears in the faculty cafeteria as other teachers milled around. What would happen, McDermott asked Lears, if everyone held class outside?

21 Now this was familiar stuff to us all. McDermott's question came out of that grand conceptual bag that also contained lines like "Did you bring gum for everyone?" and "Would you like to share that note with the whole class?" McDermott was trying to treat Lears like a student, like one of us—and in front of his colleagues.

22 McDermott did not know that Lears, however diminutive, thought himself something of a big deal and so would not have been prepared when Lears drew an easy breath and did what every high school kid would like to do when confronted with this sort of bullying. He didn't fight it, didn't stand on his dignity. He simply ran with it.

23 What if everyone held class outside on sunny days? Suppose that happened? And from there, Lears went on to draw a picture of life at Medford High School that had people outside on the vast lawn talking away about books and ideas and one thing and another, hanging out, being lazy, being absorbed, thinking hard from time to time, and reveling in the spring. It was Woodstock and Socrates' agora[2] fused, and Lears spun it out for us, just as he had for McDermott. What if that happened, he asked us? How tragic would it be?

24 We went outside whenever we chose to after that. It was very odd: I had been at Medford High for three years and I had never seen McDermott lose a round. After class was over that day, Tom Cappalano, the quarterback, said, "You know, Lears can really be an asshole when he wants to be." In Medford, there were 50 intonations you could apply to the word "asshole." Spun right, the word constituted high praise.

25 That year of teaching was the last for Frank Lears. He got married, went to law school, and, I heard, eventually moved to Maine, where he could pursue a life a little akin to the one Thoreau, his longtime idol, managed to lead during his stay at Walden. I haven't seen Lears in about 25 years. But I do carry around with me the strong

sense that the party, the outdoor extravaganza, he invited us to, me and Nora and Dubby and even Jingles McDermott, is still a live possibility. I had great teachers after Frank Lears, some of the world's most famous in fact, but I never met his equal. What I liked most about him, I suppose, was that for all the minor miracle of what he accomplished with us, he was no missionary: He served us but also himself. His goodness had some edge to it. He got what he wanted out of Medford High, which was a chance to affront his spiritual enemies, though with some generosity, and to make younger people care about the sorts of things he cared about, to pull them out of their parents' orbit and into his. All good teaching entails some kidnapping.

26 As well as some sorrow: Good teachers have many motivations, but I suspect that loneliness is often one of them. You need a small group, a coterie, to talk to; unable to find it in the larger world, you try to create it in the smaller sphere of a classroom. Lears, who seemed at times a little lost in his life, a brilliant orphan, did something like that with us.

27 What Lears taught—or at least what I gleaned from him—is that anything that's been successfully institutionalized, however rebellious it may seem or however virtuous, is stifling. What's called subversion only lasts for an instant in a school or a hospital or a home; it's quickly swept up to become part of the protocol, an element in "the way we do things around here." At the time, Kesey and Camus collided well enough with the dead protocols of Medford High, but now, for all I know, they fit in fine—alienation has become standard issue.

28 One pays for the kind of mental exhilaration that Lears initiated in his students. One pays in self-doubt and isolation, in the suspicion that what seems to be true resistance is merely a perverse substitute for genuine talent, a cheap way of having something to say. Lears' path, so appealing in its first steps, separated me from my family, cut me loose from religion and popular faith, sent me adrift beyond the world bordered by TV and piety and common sense. One step down that road followed another, and now, at 50, I probably could not turn around if I wished to.

29 Still, the image I most often hit on when I think about Lears glows brightly. It's late spring, a gloomy dead day. He's standing beside the beat-up phonograph at the back of the room with a record he's brought in by the Incredible String Band. I dislike the record and open my book, the *Autobiography of Malcolm X*, which has not been assigned in any class, and disappear into it. He cranks the music just a little louder. I keep reading. But then, curious, I raise my head. The racket of the String Band floods in. And there in the back of the room, Lears is dancing away. He's a terrible dancer, stiff and arrhythmic. Not until I saw Bob Dylan in concert did I ever see anyone dance so self-consciously. It struck me that this was probably the first time anyone had ever danced in this classroom. But here was Lears, bringing it off. It was like some strokes of light rendered by a painter for the first time, though with an unsteady enough hand. Lears had scored a benevolent victory over Medford High School. (You could say that he'd

beaten them at their game, but really he'd shown them a new one.) He had a right to a little celebration.

[1]A left-leaning activist student group from the 1960s that championed civil rights and an end to America's participation in the Vietnam War.
[2]In ancient Greece, a place to congregate, particularly the marketplace, often where ideas were exchanged.

EXERCISES

A. Determining the Main Idea and Writer's Purpose

Choose the best answer.

1. The main idea of the selection is that for the writer
   a. high school meant nothing more than a chance to slack off, a transition on the way to working in a factory or an office or to joining the Marines.
   b. high school was a bastion of conformity and mindless repetition, and therefore was an institution that he rebelled against openly.
   c. Frank Lears's teaching and assigned reading showed him the true nature of institutions and the importance of anti-authoritarianism.
   d. Frank Lears was a natural teacher who changed the lives of his students with his mocking yet gentle persuasion.

2. With respect to the main idea, the writer's purpose is to
   a. analyze the reasons that so many high school students are turned off to education.
   b. explore the influence of some significant books in his life.
   c. show the advantages of dissent and rebellion as a way to reform American education.
   d. demonstrate how the presence of one teacher can foster a lifelong, far-reaching change in attitude and outlook.

B. Comprehending Main Ideas

Choose the correct answer.

1. Edmundson writes that when he heard about the philosophy course that the new teacher, Frank Lears, would be teaching, he
   a. had no idea what philosophy was and thought it was probably just empty speculation.
   b. signed up for the course with great anticipation and enthusiasm.

c. thought that the course would be just another opportunity to waste time.

d. was impressed that Lears, a Harvard graduate, would be interested in teaching such a high-level course at Medford High.

2. Edmundson characterizes Medford High School as
   a. simply a place where most of the students marked time and socialized.
   b. more interested in emphasizing mind-numbing repetition and form, not really a school at all.
   c. a place where the Marines and other branches of the armed services could recruit new members.
   d. a place to prepare students for good jobs at the local factories.

3. In addition to his odd manner of dress and accent, Frank Lears exhibited two unusual traits, specifically, he
   a. thought highly of himself, and he mocked his students for being fools.
   b. was arrogant and had no interest in trying to engage his students.
   c. hated popular culture and popular activities like playing football.
   d. deliberately rebelled against the administration's rules and fostered rebellion in his students.

4. Three books that Lears assigned his students to read—*The Stranger, One Flew Over the Cuckoo's Nest*, and *Group Psychology and the Analysis of the Ego*—had a common, theme, namely,
   a. the importance of philosophy in one's daily life.
   b. the conflict between the reason and emotion.
   c. the oppressions of conformity.
   d. the pleasures of solitude.

5. Edmundson says that he never met a teacher who was the equal of Frank Lears. What made him especially effective was his
   a. penchant for expressing scorn and resentment against Medford High's silly rules and stultifying way of teaching.
   b. way of drawing students into his orbit and making them care about what he cared about.
   c. way of making difficult philosophical concepts clear and understandable.
   d. refusal to abandon his hope that he would eventually get through to his students, despite their obvious lack of interest in learning.

C. Interpreting Meaning

Where appropriate, write your answers to these questions in your own words.

1. Read paragraph 1 again. In the last sentence after describing Lears's background, he ends the paragraph by saying, "All of his intellectual aspirations were intact." What does he mean?

____

____

____

2. What evidence does Edmundson provide to support his contention that "Medford High was not a school" [paragraph 7]?

____

____

____

3. Choose the choice that would be the best title for paragraph 8.
   a. "Mass Culture for the Masses"
   b. "Trapped in an Unthinking Life"
   c. "Bright Lights in the Dark"
   d. "The Factory as an Extension of High School"

4. In your own words, explain the meaning of these two quotations. In paragraph 25, "All good teaching entails some kidnapping":

____

____

____

In paragraph 26, Edmundson describes Lears as "a brilliant orphan." What does he mean?

____

____

D. Understanding Vocabulary

Write the dictionary definition for each underlined word in the phrases below.

1. he still had a <u>melancholy</u> presence [paragraph 2] _______________

2. outlined, summarized, <u>recapitulated</u> [7] ____________

3. learning a number of <u>protocols</u> [7, also 16 & 27] ____________

4. the <u>wherewithal</u> to check back into them [8] ____________

5. I went low to the ground, <u>despondent</u> [8] ____________

6. his considerable <u>lode</u> of self-esteem [11] ____________

7. a <u>litany</u> of defenses against being alone [13] ____________

8. a <u>myriad</u> of other strategies [13] ____________

9. schools were on a <u>continuum</u> [16] ____________

10. Lears, however <u>diminutive</u> [22] ____________

11. <u>reveling</u> in the spring [23] ____________

12. a life <u>akin</u> to the one Thoreau managed to lead [25] ____________

13. a chance to <u>affront</u> his spiritual enemies [25] ____________

14. what I <u>gleaned</u> from him [27] ____________

15. the world bordered by TV and <u>piety</u> [28] ____________

E. Vocabulary and Dictionary Exercise

Answer these questions. You may need to consult a dictionary for this exercise.

1. The word *paraphernalia* [paragraph 6] comes from the Greek. What was the original meaning of the word? What does it mean today?

____

____

____

2. The noun *oppressions* [paragraph 12] has some variant forms. Write the required forms in the spaces provided:

   two other nouns ______________________

   verb ______________________

   adjective ______________________

   adverb ______________________

3. In paragraph 17, Edmundson writes that Lears found words "gorgeous, graffiti-sized, and *apocalyptic*." Which dictionary definition fits the meaning of *apocalyptic* in this context?
   a. involving or portending widespread destruction or ultimate doom
   b. characterized by usually exaggerated predictions of or allusions to a disastrous outcome
   c. of a revelatory or prophetic nature

4. The word *inchoate* [also paragraph 17] is not pronounced the way it looks: ĭn chōt'.

   Write the correct pronunciation in the space. Be sure to include the correct stress mark.

   ____

   Choose the dictionary definition that fits the meaning of the word in this context.
   a. in an initial or early stage
   b. Imperfectly formed or developed

5. What context clue in paragraph 26 tells you the meaning of the word *coterie*?

   ____

   What language does this word derive from?

   ____

DISCUSSION QUESTIONS

1. The etymology of the word *educate* from Latin is *e-* ("out of") + *ducere* (to lead out). In what way might Edmundson's selection reinforce the idea that education can be dangerous? Dangerous to whom and to what?
2. Edmundson's view of American high schools, at least of the one he attended, is clearly negative in its anti-authoritarianism. How did he

come to adopt this attitude? What was Frank Lears's specific contribution to developing this attitude? What is the primary revelation he experienced about its true nature of the high school as an institution?

3. In paragraph 11, Edmundson writes:

   > Lears thought well of himself. And we all wondered, if unspokenly, where this guy might have gotten his considerable lode of self-esteem. Teachers, as we could have told him, were losers out-and-out.

   How prevalent is the opinion expressed here that teachers are "losers"? Examine this statement honestly, and if you believe it to be a widespread opinion, try to identify the reasons behind it. And in more general terms, would you say that Americans hold teachers in high esteem, in the same way that, to cite just two examples, they are held in France and China? If not, why not? If they are highly regarded, why is teaching a relatively low-paying profession in the United States?

4. It seems like a paradox when Edmundson writes that "Good teachers have many motivations, but I suspect that loneliness is often one of them." How can you reconcile this paradox?

5. Which paragraph to you *best* sums up the importance of Frank Lears on Edmundson's life?

EXPLORE THE WEB

- The radical 1960s organization, Students for a Democratic Society (SDS), mentioned in paragraph 18, began as a social protest group popular in American universities but gradually evolved into a mechanism for organizing massive protests against America's involvement in the Vietnam War. You can learn more about this group by going to Google or your favorite search engine and typing in "Students for a Democratic Society" + history.
- The year 1969 saw the Summer of Love and the Woodstock Festival, both of which were pivotal events in modern American culture. The Woodstock generation took its name from the enormous rock concert in August 1969 at Max Yasgur's farm in Bethel, New York. Go to Google or to your favorite search engine and type in "Woodstock Festival" + history. Of particular note is this site: www.yasgurrorad.com/history.html.

Cells

Bill Bryson

Bill Bryson is the author of several nonfiction books, best distinguished, perhaps, by his characteristic self-deprecating humor and wry perspective on human folly and frailty. Bryson's first best-selling book, *Mother Tongue* (1991), focused on the quirks of the English language. More recently, he published two very readable travel memoirs, the first about a long trek along the Appalachian Trail in *A Walk in the Woods* (1998) and the second about Australia in his travel memoir, *In a Sunburned Country* (2000). His most recent book, *The Life and Times of the Thunderbolt Kid* (2006), chronicles his early life in Des Moines, Iowa. He lived in England for twenty years, where he wrote for many major British and American publications. He currently lives in New Hampshire. This selection represents a portion of a chapter titled "Cells" from his 2003 book, *A Short History of Nearly Everything*.

VOCABULARY ANALYSIS

Word Root—Pathogens

Pathogens [paragraph 7] are disease-causing agents. The word is composed of two Greek elements: *pathos* ("suffering," also "passion") + *genes* ("born"). In current English, the word *pathos* refers to a quality, from either an experience or from a work of art, that arouses pity or sympathy. Other words containing the root *pathos* are as follows:

pathetic describing something that arouses pity

sympathy the act of sharing another's feelings

empathy identification with and understanding of another's feelings

pathology the study of the nature and causes of diseases

You were introduced to the Greek prefix *a-* in the Edmundson selection. What does the word *apathy* mean?

____

Cells

Bill Bryson

1 It starts with a single cell. The first cell splits to become two and the two become four and so on. After just forty-seven doublings, you have ten thousand trillion

(10,000,000,000,000,000) cells in your body and are ready to spring forth as a human being.[1] And every one of those cells knows exactly what to do to preserve and nurture you from the moment of conception to your last breath.

2 You have no secrets from your cells. They know far more about you than you do. Each one carries a copy of the complete genetic code—the instruction manual for your body—so it knows not only how to do its job but every other job in the body. Never in your life will you have to remind a cell to keep an eye on its adenosine triphosphate levels or to find a place for the extra squirt of folic acid that's just unexpectedly turned up. It will do that for you, and millions more things besides.

3 Every cell in nature is a thing of wonder. Even the simplest are far beyond the limits of human ingenuity. To build the most basic yeast cell, for example, you would have to miniaturize about the same number of components as are found in a Boeing 777 jetliner and fit them into a sphere just five microns across; then somehow you would have to persuade that sphere to reproduce.

4 But yeast cells are as nothing compared with human cells, which are not just more varied and complicated, but vastly more fascinating because of their complex interactions.

5 Your cells are a country of ten thousand trillion citizens, each devoted in some intensively specific way to your overall well-being. There isn't a thing they don't do for you. They let you feel pleasure and form thoughts. They enable you to stand and stretch and caper. When you eat, they extract the nutrients, distribute the energy, and carry off the wastes—all those things you learned about in junior high school biology—but they also remember to make you hungry in the first place and reward you with a feeling of well-being afterward so that you won't forget to eat again. They keep your hair growing, your ears waxed, your brain quietly purring. They manage every corner of your being. They will jump to your defense the instant you are threatened. They will unhesitatingly die for you—billions of them do so daily. And not once in all your years have you thanked even one of them. So let us take a moment now to regard them with the wonder and appreciation they deserve.

Connecting Grammar to Writing

The last sentence of paragraph 6 is called a parenthetical sentence, not just because it is enclosed in parentheses, but also because it represents an idea that is not necessary to the discussion. It presents extra information. Bryson could have diminished the importance of this idea by putting it in a footnote.

6 We understand a little of how cells do the things they do—how they lay down fat or manufacture insulin or engage in many of the other acts necessary to maintain a complicated entity like yourself—but only a little. You have at least 200,000 different types of protein laboring away inside you, and so far we understand what no more than about 2 percent of them do. (Others put the figure at more like 50 percent; it depends, apparently, on what you mean by "understand.")

7 Surprises at the cellular level turn up all the time. In nature, nitric oxide is a formidable toxin and a common component of air pollution. So scientists were naturally a little surprised when, in the mid-1980s, they found it being produced in a curiously devoted manner in human cells. Its purpose was at first a mystery,

but then scientists began to find it all over the place—controlling the flow of blood and the energy levels of cells, attacking cancers and other pathogens, regulating the sense of smell, even assisting in penile erections. It also explained why nitroglycerine, the well-known explosive, soothes the heart pain known as angina. (It is converted into nitric oxide in the bloodstream, relaxing the muscle linings of vessels, allowing blood to flow more freely.) In barely the space of a decade this one gassy substance went from extraneous toxin to ubiquitous elixir.

8 You possess "some few hundred" different types of cells, according to the Belgian biochemist Christian de Duve, and they vary enormously in size and shape, from nerve cells whose filaments can stretch to several feet to tiny, disc-shaped red blood cells to the rod-shaped photocells that help to give us vision. They also come in a sumptuously wide range of sizes—nowhere more strikingly than at the moment of conception, when a single beating sperm confronts an egg eighty-five thousand times bigger than it (which rather puts the notion of male conquest into perspective). On average, however, a human cell is about twenty microns wide—that is about two hundredths of a millimeter—which is too small to be seen but roomy enough to hold thousands of complicated structures like mitochondria, and millions upon millions of molecules. In the most literal way, cells also vary in liveliness. Your skin cells are all dead. It's a somewhat galling notion to reflect that every inch of your surface is deceased. If you are an average-sized adult you are lugging around about five pounds of dead skin, of which several billion tiny fragments are sloughed off each day. Run a finger along a dusty shelf and you are drawing a pattern very largely in old skin.

9 Most living cells seldom last more than a month or so, but there are some notable exceptions. Liver cells can survive for years, though the components within them may be renewed every few days. Brain cells last as long as you do. You are issued a hundred billion or so at birth, and that is all you are ever going to get. It has been estimated that you lose five hundred of them an hour, so if you have any serious thinking to do there really isn't a moment to waste. The good news is that the individual components of your brain cells are constantly renewed so that, as with the liver cells, no part of them is actually likely to be more than about a month old. Indeed, it has been suggested that there isn't a single bit of any of us—not so much as a stray molecule—that was part of us nine years ago. It may not feel like it, but at the cellular level we are all youngsters.

---

[1]Actually, quite a lot of cells are lost in the process of development, so the number you emerge with is really just a guess. Depending on which source you consult the number can vary by several orders of magnitude. The figure of ten thousand trillion (or quadrillion) is from Margulis and Sagan, 1986.

READING

■ EXERCISES

A. Determining the Main Idea and Writer's Purpose

Choose the best answer.

1. Here are four excerpts from the selection. Which *best* represents the thesis of the article?
   a. Every cell in nature is a thing of wonder. Even the simplest are far beyond the limits of human ingenuity.
   b. After just forty-seven doublings, you have ten thousand trillion cells in your body and are ready to spring forth as a human being. And every one of those cells knows exactly what to do to preserve and nurture ...
   c. We understand a little of how cells do the things they do ... but only a little.
   d. ... it has been suggested that there isn't a single bit of any of us—not so much as a stray molecule—that was part of us nine years ago. It may not feel like it, but at the cellular level we are all youngsters.

2. With respect to the main idea, the writer's purpose is to
   a. describe the physical appearance of human cells
   b. explain various theories about the way human cells work.
   c. show the relationship between cell structure and human behavior.
   d. explain how cells serve as the instruction manual for the human body to function.

B. Comprehending Main Ideas

Choose the correct answer.

1. According to Bryson, a human being begins with
   a. a single cell.
   b. ten thousand trillion cells.
   c. forty-seven chromosomes.
   d. an instruction manual.

2. Each human cell carries with it
   a. a prescribed amount of adenosine triphosphate
   b. a complete copy of the genetic code.
   c. nutrients necessary to survive.
   d. the ability to reproduce itself.

3. Human cells are different from yeast cells because they
   a. contain proteins, fats, and insulin.
   b. distribute energy throughout the body.
   c. are simpler in structure and capability.
   d. are much more varied and capable of complex interactions.

4. Bryson writes that the size and shape of human cells
   a. depend on the function of the organ they are associated with.
   b. are pretty much the same throughout the human body.
   c. vary widely throughout the body.
   d. cannot be studied because they are too small to observe.

5. According to Bryson, skin cells
   a. vary somewhat in size and shape according to their location on the body's surface.
   b. are all dead and are constantly being sloughed off.
   c. are capable of being renewed.
   d. are incapable of being renewed.

C. Sequencing

The sentences in this excerpt from the selection have been scrambled. Read the sentences and choose the sequence that puts them back into logical order. Do not refer to the original selection.

1. You have no secrets from your cells. **2.** They know far more about you than you do. **3.** Each one carries a copy of the complete genetic code—the instruction manual for your body—so it knows not only how to do its job but every other job in the body. **4.** Never in your life will you have to remind a cell to keep an eye on its adenosine triphosphate levels or to find a place for the extra squirt of folic acid that's just unexpectedly turned up. **5.** It will do that for you, and millions more things besides.

a. 3, 2, 1, 5, 4 c. 1, 3, 5, 2, 4
b. 4, 2, 3, 1, 5 d. Correct as written.

D. Identifying Supporting Details

Place an **X** in the space for each detail that *directly* supports this main idea from the selection: "Your cells are a country of ten thousand trillion citizens, each devoted in some intensively specific way to your overall well-being."

1. _____ Cells let you feel pleasure and form thoughts.

2. _____ Cells extract nutrients from what you eat, distribute the energy, and carry off the wastes.

3. _____ We don't understand very well how cells do the things they do, for example, manufacturing insulin.

4. _____ Cells are also full of some surprises, like the role of nitric oxide in controlling blood flow and energy level.

5. _____ Cells manage every facet of your being and will jump to your defense if you are threatened.

E. Interpreting Meaning

Choose the best answer.

1. Read paragraph 3 again, in which Bryson uses an analogy—an imaginative comparison—between a yeast cell and a Boeing 777 jetliner. The purpose of this analogy is to
   a. show what a yeast cell looks like.
   b. prove that yeast cells are simple in structure.
   c. prove that yeast cells are an important means of transporting vital substances in the human body.
   d. show the incredible complexity embodied in even the simplest type of cell.

2. A good title for paragraph 5 would be
   a. "The Wondrous Workings of Cells."
   b. "Why Cells Are Underappreciated."
   c. "Cells and the Functioning of the Human Body."
   d. "Cells as Citizens of a Country."

3. Which of the following best characterizes Bryson's tone, or emotional attitude, toward his subject, especially in paragraphs 1–6?
   a. objective, impartial, neutral
   b. informative, instructive
   c. honest, candid, sincere
   d. awestruck, full of wonder

4. Who is the likely audience for *A Short History of Nearly Everything*, from which this selection is taken?
   a. The general reading public, educated but not necessarily possessing scientific knowledge.
   b. A specialized audience of scientists, particularly cell biologists.

c. High school and college science teachers.

d. There is no way to tell who the audience is.

F. Understanding Vocabulary

Look through the paragraphs listed below and find a word that matches each definition. Refer to a dictionary if necessary. An example has been done for you.

EXAMPLE: nourish, help to grow and develop [paragraphs 1–2] nurture

1. cleverness, inventive skill and imagination [3–4] ________
2. frisk about, frolic, leap [5] ________
3. take out, remove [5] ________
4. being, individual, person [6–7] ________
5. arousing fear or dread [6–7] ________
6. an element of a system [7; also used in the plural in 9] ________
7. inessential, not related to the subject [7] ________
8. existing everywhere, omnipresent [7] ________
9. a substance believed necessary to maintain life [7] ________
10. lavishly, splendidly [8] ________
11. causing irritation or vexation [8] ________
12. shed or cast off [8—phrase] ________

DISCUSSION QUESTIONS

1. What are some of the devices Bryson uses to engage the reader, especially one without a strong background in science?
2. What seems to be Bryson's central idea about human cells? Does he seem more interested in their structure, in their function, or in something else altogether?
3. Although Bryson doesn't reveal any personal details in this selection, nonetheless, can you form an opinion about the sort of person he is?

EXPLORE THE WEB

You can search for photographs of human cells by going to Google and typing in "human cells" in the Images box. Or try these sites for some fascinating and hauntingly beautiful pictures of various types of human cells:

www.cellsalive.com

people.eku.edu/ritchisong/301notes1.htm

en.wikipedia.org/wiki/Red_blood_cell

www.tiscali.co.uk/reference/encyclopaedia/hutchinson/m0024929.html

The Online Biology Book, sponsored by Estrella Mountain Community College in Arizona, offers a compendium of information and review of basic biology. Of particular note for students who want more information about basic cell structure, including visual images, click on 4. Cells 1: Origins and 5. Cells 2: Cellular Organization.

www.estrellamountain.edu/faculty/farabee/biobk/biobooktoc.html

Finally, a treasure trove of information, interactive games, and Ten Cool Science Sites, is sponsored by the San Francisco Exploratorium. There is something for everyone—children as well as adults—on this site, for example, "Information on Endangered Mammals," "Worm Watch," "Putting DNA to Work," and "Race: The Power of Illusion."

www.exploratorium.edu/learning_studio/cool/life.html

Easter's End

Jared Diamond

Jared Diamond is currently a professor of geography at UCLA. He began his academic career in physiology, but later expanded his area of interest into evolutionary biology and biogeography, in the course of which he made several trips to New Guinea and the Solomon Islands. His book, *Guns, Germs, and Steel: The Fates of Human Societies* (1997), which investigates the role of geography on human societies and their evolution, was awarded the Pulitzer Prize in 1998 in the category of general nonfiction.

"Easter's End," first published in *Discover*, is a thought-provoking look at the civilization that flourished on Easter Island (an island that belongs to Chile) in Polynesia. In it, Diamond describes what the civilization was like when it reached its peak between A.D. 1200 to 1500, marked in particular by the hundreds of mysterious and huge stone statues along the coast, called *moai*. But the civilization—including both human and plant life—eventually declined.

Diamond offers some hypotheses to explain why, and in telling Easter Island's story, he finds a grim parallel for modern human civilization. An expanded version of this material is included in Diamond's most recent book, *Collapse: How Societies Choose to Fail or Succeed* (2005).

VOCABULARY ANALYSIS

The Prefix *extra-*

In English, many compound words are formed with the prefix *extra-*, meaning "outside" or "beyond." The word *extraterrestrial* [see paragraph 13] describes an inhabitant of another world, combining the prefix with *terra*, the Latin root for "earth." Other words beginning with this prefix are *extraordinary*, *extramarital*, *extracurricular*, and *extrasensory*.

Easter's End

Jared Diamond

1 Among the most riveting mysteries of human history are those posed by vanished civilizations. Everyone who has seen the abandoned buildings of the Khmer, the Maya, or the Anasazi is immediately moved to ask the same question: Why did the societies that erected those structures disappear?

2 Their vanishing touches us as the disappearance of other animals, even the dinosaurs, never can. No matter how exotic those lost civilizations seem, their framers were humans like us. Who is to say we won't succumb to the same fate? Perhaps someday New York's skyscrapers will stand derelict and overgrown with vegetation, like the temples at Angkor Wat and Tikal.

3 Among all such vanished civilizations, that of the former Polynesian society on Easter Island remains unsurpassed in mystery and isolation. The mystery stems especially from the island's gigantic stone statues and its impoverished landscape, but it is enhanced by our associations with the specific people involved: Polynesians represent for us the ultimate in exotic romance, the background for many a child's and an adult's vision of paradise. My own interest in Easter was kindled over 30 years ago when I read Thor Heyerdahl's fabulous accounts of his *Kon-Tiki* voyage.

4 But my interest has been revived recently by a much more exciting account, one not of heroic voyages but of painstaking research and analysis. My friend David Steadman, a paleontologist, has been working with a number of other researchers who are carrying out the first systematic excavations on Easter intended to identify the animals and plants that once lived there. Their work is contributing to a new interpretation of the island's history that makes it a tale not only of wonder but of warning as well.

5 Easter Island, with an area of only 64 square miles, is the world's most isolated scrap of habitable land. It lies in the Pacific Ocean more than 2,000 miles west of the nearest continent (South America), 1,400 miles from even the nearest habitable island (Pitcairn). Its subtropical location and latitude—at 27 degrees south, it is approximately as far below the equator as Houston is north of it—help give it a rather mild climate, while its volcanic origins make its soil fertile. In theory, this combination of blessings should have made Easter a miniature paradise, remote from problems that beset the rest of the world.

6 The island derives its name from its "discovery" by the Dutch explorer Jacob Roggeveen, on Easter (April 5) in 1722. Roggeveen's first impression was not of a paradise but of a wasteland: "We originally, from a further distance, have considered the said Easter Island as sandy; the reason for that is this, that we counted as sand the withered grass, hay, or other scorched and burnt vegetation, because its wasted appearance could give no other impression than of a singular poverty and barrenness."

7 The island Roggeveen saw was a grassland without a single tree or bush over ten feet high. Modern botanists have identified only 47 species of higher plants native to Easter, most of them grasses, sedges, and ferns. The list includes just two species of small trees and two of woody shrubs. With such flora,[1] the islanders Roggeveen encountered had no source of real firewood to warm themselves during Easter's cool, wet, windy winters. Their native animals included nothing larger than insects, not even a single species of native bat, land bird, land snail, or lizard. For domestic animals, they had only chickens.

8 European visitors throughout the eighteenth and early nineteenth centuries estimated Easter's human population at about 2,000, a modest number considering the island's fertility. As Captain James Cook recognized during his brief visit in 1774, the islanders were Polynesians (a Tahitian man accompanying Cook was able to converse with them). Yet despite the Polynesians' well-deserved fame as a great seafaring people, the Easter Islanders who came out to Roggeveen's and Cook's ships did so by swimming or paddling canoes that Roggeveen described as "bad and frail." Their craft, he wrote, were "put together with manifold small planks and light inner timbers, which they cleverly stitched together with very fine twisted threads. ... But as they lack the knowledge and particularly the materials for caulking and making tight the great number of seams of the canoes, these are accordingly very leaky, for which reason they are compelled to spend half the time in bailing." The canoes, only ten feet long, held at most two people, and only three or four canoes were observed on the entire island.

9 With such flimsy craft, Polynesians could never have colonized Easter from even the nearest island, nor could they have traveled far offshore to fish. The islanders Roggeveen met were totally isolated, unaware that other people existed. Investigators in all the years since his visit have discovered no trace of the islanders' having any outside contacts: not a single Easter Island rock or product has turned up elsewhere, nor has anything been found on the island that could

have been brought by anyone other than the original settlers or the Europeans. Yet the people living on Easter claimed memories of visiting the uninhabited Sala y Gomez reef 260 miles away, far beyond the range of the leaky canoes seen by Roggeveen. How did the islanders' ancestors reach that reef from Easter, or reach Easter from anywhere else?

10 Easter Island's most famous feature is its huge stone statues, more than 200 of which once stood on massive stone platforms lining the coast. At least 700 more, in all stages of completion, were abandoned in quarries or on ancient roads between the quarries and the coast, as if the carvers and moving crews had thrown down their tools and walked off the job. Most of the erected statues were carved in a single quarry and then somehow transported as far as six miles—despite heights as great as 33 feet and weights up to 82 tons. The abandoned statues, meanwhile, were as much as 65 feet tall and weighed up to 270 tons. The stone platforms were equally gigantic: up to 500 feet long and 10 feet high, with facing slabs weighing up to 10 tons.

11 Roggeveen himself quickly recognized the problem the statues posed: "The stone images at first caused us to be struck with astonishment," he wrote, "because we could not comprehend how it was possible that these people, who are devoid of heavy thick timber for making any machines, as well as strong ropes, nevertheless had been able to erect such images." Roggeveen might have added that the islanders had no wheels, no draft animals, and no source of power except their own muscles. How did they transport the giant statues for miles, even before erecting them? To deepen the mystery, the statues were still standing in 1770, but by 1864 all of them had been pulled down, by the islanders themselves. Why then did they carve them in the first place? And why did they stop?

12 The statues imply a society very different from the one Roggeveen saw in 1722. Their sheer number and size suggest a population much larger than 2,000 people. What became of everyone? Furthermore, that society must have been highly organized. Easter's resources were scattered across the island: the best stone for the statues was quarried at Rano Raraku near Easter's northeast end; red stone, used for large crowns adorning some of the statues, was quarried at Puna Pau, inland in the southwest; stone carving tools came mostly from Aroi in the northwest. Meanwhile, the best farmland lay in the south and east, and the best fishing grounds on the north and west coasts. Extracting and redistributing all those goods required complex political organization. What happened to that organization, and how could it ever have arisen in such a barren landscape?

13 Easter Island's mysteries have spawned volumes of speculation for more than two and a half centuries. Many Europeans were incredulous that Polynesians—commonly characterized as "mere savages"—could have created the statues or the beautifully constructed stone platforms. In the 1950s, Heyerdahl argued that Polynesia must have been settled by advanced societies of American Indians, who in turn must have received civilization across the Atlantic from more advanced

societies of the Old World. Heyerdahl's raft voyages aimed to prove the feasibility of such prehistoric transoceanic contacts. In the 1960s the Swiss writer Erich von Däniken, an ardent believer in Earth visits by extraterrestrial astronauts, went further, claiming that Easter's statues were the work of intelligent beings who owned ultramodern tools, became stranded on Easter, and were finally rescued.

14 Heyerdahl and Von Däniken both brushed aside overwhelming evidence that the Easter Islanders were typical Polynesians derived from Asia rather than from the Americas and that their culture (including their statues) grew out of Polynesian culture. Their language was Polynesian, as Cook had already concluded. Specifically, they spoke an eastern Polynesian dialect related to Hawaiian and Marquesan, a dialect isolated since about A.D. 400, as estimated from slight differences in vocabulary. Their fishhooks and stone adzes resembled early Marquesan models. Last year DNA extracted from 12 Easter Island skeletons was also shown to be Polynesian. The islanders grew bananas, taro, sweet potatoes, sugarcane, and paper mulberry—typical Polynesian crops, mostly of Southeast Asian origin. Their sole domestic animal, the chicken, was also typically Polynesian and ultimately Asian, as were the rats that arrived as stowaways in the canoes of the first settlers.

15 What happened to those settlers? The fanciful theories of the past must give way to evidence gathered by hardworking practitioners in three fields: archeology, pollen analysis, and paleontology.

16 Modern archeological excavations on Easter have continued since Heyerdahl's 1955 expedition. The earliest radiocarbon dates associated with human activities are around A.D. 400 to 700, in reasonable agreement with the approximate settlement date of 400 estimated by linguists. The period of statue construction peaked around 1200 to 1500, with few if any statues erected thereafter. Densities of archeological sites suggest a large population; an estimate of 7,000 people is widely quoted by archeologists, but other estimates range up to 20,000, which does not seem implausible for an island of Easter's area and fertility.

17 Archeologists have also enlisted surviving islanders in experiments aimed at figuring out how the statues might have been carved and erected. Twenty people, using only stone chisels, could have carved even the largest completed statue within a year. Given enough timber and fiber for making ropes, teams of at most a few hundred people could have loaded the statues onto wooden sleds, dragged them over lubricated wooden tracks or rollers, and used logs as levers to maneuver them into a standing position. Rope could have been made from the fiber of a small native tree, related to the linden, called the hauhau. However, that tree is now extremely scarce on Easter, and hauling one statue would have required hundreds of yards of rope. Did Easter's now barren landscape once support the necessary trees?

18 That question can be answered by the technique of pollen analysis, which involves boring out a column of sediment from a swamp or pond, with the most

recent deposits at the top and relatively more ancient deposits at the bottom. The absolute age of each layer can be dated by radiocarbon methods. Then begins the hard work: examining tens of thousands of pollen grains under a microscope, counting them, and identifying the plant species that produced each one by comparing the grains with modern pollen from known plant species. For Easter Island, the bleary-eyed scientists who performed that task were John Flenley, now at Massey University in New Zealand, and Sarah King of the University of Hull in England.

19 Flenley and King's heroic efforts were rewarded by the striking new picture that emerged of Easter's prehistoric landscape. For at least 30,000 years before human arrival and during the early years of Polynesian settlement, Easter was not a wasteland at all. Instead, a subtropical forest of trees and woody bushes towered over a ground layer of shrubs, herbs, ferns, and grasses. In the forest grew tree daisies, the rope-yielding hauhau tree, and the toromiro tree, which furnishes a dense, mesquite-like firewood. The most common tree in the forest was a species of palm now absent of Easter but formerly so abundant that the bottom strata of the sediment column were packed with its pollen. The Easter Island palm was closely related to the still-surviving Chilean wine palm, which grows up to 82 feet tall and 6 feet in diameter. The tall, unbranched trunks of the Easter Island palm would have been ideal for transporting and erecting statues and constructing large canoes. The palm would also have been a valuable food source, since its Chilean relative yields edible nuts as well as sap from which Chileans make sugar, syrup, honey, and wine.

20 What did the first settlers of Easter Island eat when they were not glutting themselves on the local equivalent of maple syrup? Recent excavations by David Steadman, of the New York State Museum at Albany, have yielded a picture of Easter's original animal world as surprising as Flenley and King's picture of its plant world. Steadman's expectations for Easter were conditioned by his experiences elsewhere in Polynesia, where fish are overwhelmingly the main food at archeological sites, typically accounting for more than 90 percent of the bones in ancient Polynesian garbage heaps. Easter, though, is too cool for the coral reefs beloved by fish, and its cliff-girded coastline permits shallow-water fishing in only a few places. Less than a quarter of the bones in its early garbage heaps (from the period 900 to 1300) belonged to fish; instead, nearly one-third of all bones came from porpoises.

21 Nowhere else in Polynesia do porpoises account for even 1 percent of discarded food bones. But most other Polynesian islands offered animal food in the form of birds and mammals, such as New Zealand's now extinct giant moas and Hawaii's now extinct flightless geese. Most other islanders also had domestic pigs and dogs. On Easter, porpoises would have been the largest animal available—other than humans. The porpoise species identified at Easter, the common dolphin, weighs up to 165 pounds. It generally lives out at sea, so it could not have

been hunted by line fishing or spearfishing from shore. Instead, it must have been harpooned far offshore, in big seaworthy canoes built from the extinct palm tree.

22 In addition to porpoise meat, Steadman found, the early Polynesian settlers were feasting on seabirds. For those birds, Easter's remoteness and lack of predators made it an ideal haven as a breeding site, at least until humans arrived. Among the prodigious numbers of seabirds that bred on Easter were albatross, boobies, frigate birds, fulmars, petrels, prions, shearwaters, storm petrels, terns, and tropic birds. With at least 25 nesting species, Easter was the richest seabird breeding site in Polynesia and probably in the whole Pacific.

23 Land birds as well went into early Easter Island cooking pots. Steadman identified bones of at least six species, including barn owls, herons, parrots, and rail. Bird stew would have been seasoned with meat from large numbers of rats, which the Polynesian colonists inadvertently brought with them; Easter Island is the sole known Polynesian island where rat bones outnumber fish bones at archeological sites. (In case you're squeamish and consider rats inedible, I still recall recipes for creamed laboratory rat that my British biologist friends used to supplement their diet during their years of wartime food rationing.)

24 Porpoises, seabirds, land birds, and rats did not complete the list of meat sources formerly available on Easter. A few bones hint at the possibility of breeding seal colonies as well. All these delicacies were cooked in ovens fired by wood from the island's forests.

25 Such evidence lets us imagine the island onto which Easter's first Polynesian colonists stepped ashore some 1,600 years ago, after a long canoe voyage from eastern Polynesia. They found themselves in a pristine paradise. What then happened to it? The pollen grains and the bones yield a grim answer.

26 Pollen records show that destruction of Easter's forests was well under way by the year 800, just a few centuries after the start of human settlement. Then charcoal from wood fires came to fill the sediment cores, while pollen of palms and other trees and woody shrubs decreased or disappeared, and pollen of the grasses that replaced the forest became more abundant. Not long after 1400 the palm finally became extinct, not only as a result of being chopped down but also because the now ubiquitous rats prevented its regeneration: of the dozens of preserved palm nuts discovered in caves on Easter, all had been chewed by rats and could no longer germinate. While the hauhau tree did not become extinct in Polynesian times, its numbers declined drastically until there weren't enough left to make ropes from. By the time Heyerdahl visited Easter, only a single, nearly dead toromiro tree remained on the island, and even that lone survivor has now disappeared. (Fortunately, the toromiro still grows in botanical gardens elsewhere.)

27 The fifteenth century marked the end not only for Easter's palm but for the forest itself. Its doom had been approaching as people cleared land to plant gardens; as they felled trees to build canoes, to transport and erect statues, and

Connecting Grammar to Writing

Paragraph 27 ends with a particularly effective example of a sentence using a colon to introduce an appositive. The colon tells us that the writer will complete the thought and further explain the phrase *the most extreme examples of forest destruction anywhere in the world.*

to burn; as rats devoured seeds; and probably as the native birds died out that had pollinated the trees' flowers and dispersed their fruit. The overall picture is among the most extreme examples of forest destruction anywhere in the world: the whole forest gone, and most of its tree species extinct.

28 The destruction of the island's animals was as extreme as that of the forest: without exception, every species of native land bird became extinct. Even shellfish were overexploited, until people had to settle for small sea snails instead of larger cowries. Porpoise bones disappeared abruptly from garbage heaps around 1500; no one could harpoon porpoises anymore, since the trees used for constructing the big seagoing canoes no longer existed. The colonies of more than half of the seabird species breeding on Easter or on its offshore islets were wiped out.

29 In place of these meat supplies, the Easter Islanders intensified their production of chickens, which had been only an occasional food item. They also turned to the largest remaining meat source available: humans, whose bones became common in late Easter Island garbage heaps. Oral traditions of the islanders are rife with cannibalism; the most inflammatory taunt that could be snarled at an enemy was "The flesh of your mother sticks between my teeth." With no wood available to cook these new goodies, the islanders resorted to sugarcane scraps, grass, and sedges to fuel their fires.

30 All these strands of evidence can be wound into a coherent narrative of a society's decline and fall. The first Polynesian colonists found themselves on an island with fertile soil, abundant food, bountiful building materials, ample lebensraum,[2] and all the prerequisites for comfortable living. They prospered and multiplied.

31 After a few centuries, they began erecting stone statues on platforms, like the ones their Polynesian forebears had carved. With passing years, the statues and platforms became larger and larger, and the statues began sporting ten-ton red crowns—probably in an escalating spiral of one-upmanship, as rival clans tried to surpass each other with shows of wealth and power. (In the same way, successive Egyptian pharaohs built ever-larger pyramids. Today Hollywood movie moguls near my home in Los Angeles are displaying their wealth and power by building ever more ostentatious mansions. Tycoon Marvin Davis topped previous moguls with plans for a 50,000-square-foot house, so now Aaron Spelling has topped Davis with a 56,000-square-foot house. All that those buildings lack to make the message explicit are ten-ton red crowns.) On Easter, as in modern America, society was held together by a complex political system to redistribute locally available resources and to integrate the economies of different areas.

32 Eventually Easter's growing population was cutting the forest more rapidly than the forest was regenerating. The people used the land for gardens and the wood for fuel, canoes, and houses—and, of course, for lugging statues. As forest disappeared, the islanders ran out of timber and rope to transport and erect their statues. Life became more uncomfortable—springs and streams dried up, and wood was no longer available for fires.

33 People also found it harder to fill their stomachs, as land birds, large sea snails, and many seabirds disappeared. Because timber for building seagoing canoes vanished, fish catches declined and porpoises disappeared from the table. Crop yields also declined, since deforestation allowed the soil to be eroded by rain and wind, dried by the sun, and its nutrients to be leeched from it. Intensified chicken production and cannibalism replaced only part of all those lost foods. Preserved statuettes with sunken cheeks and visible ribs suggest that people were starving.

34 With the disappearance of food surpluses, Easter Island could no longer feed the chiefs, bureaucrats, and priests who had kept a complex society running. Surviving islanders described to early European visitors how local chaos replaced centralized government and a warrior class took over from the hereditary chiefs. The stone points of spears and daggers, made by the warriors during their heyday in the 1600s and 1700s, still litter the ground of Easter today. By around 1700, the population began to crash toward between one-quarter and one-tenth of its former number. People took to living in caves for protection against their enemies. Around 1770 rival clans started to topple each other's statues, breaking the heads off. By 1864 the last statue had been thrown down and desecrated.

35 As we try to imagine the decline of Easter's civilization, we ask ourselves, "Why didn't they look around, realize what they were doing, and stop before it was too late? What were they thinking when they cut down the last palm tree?"

36 I suspect, though, that the disaster happened not with a bang but with a whimper. After all, there are those hundreds of abandoned statues to consider. The forest the islanders depended on for rollers and rope didn't simply disappear one day—it vanished slowly, over decades. Perhaps war interrupted the moving teams; perhaps by the time the carvers had finished their work, the last rope snapped. In the meantime, any islander who tried to warn about the dangers of progressive deforestation would have been overridden by vested interests of carvers, bureaucrats, and chiefs, whose jobs depended on continued deforestation. Our Pacific Northwest loggers are only the latest in a long line of loggers to cry, "Jobs over trees!" The changes in forest cover from year to year would have been hard to detect: yes, this year we cleared those woods over there, but trees are starting to grow back again on this abandoned garden site here. Only older people, recollecting their childhoods decades earlier, could have recognized a difference. Their children could no more have comprehended their parents' tales than my eight-year-old sons today can comprehend my wife's and my tales of what Los Angeles was like 30 years ago.

37 Gradually trees became fewer, smaller, and less important. By the time the last fruit-bearing adult palm tree was cut, palms had long since ceased to be of economic significance. That left only smaller and smaller palm saplings to clear each year, along with other bushes and treelets. No one would have noticed the felling of the last small palm.

38 By now the meaning of Easter Island for us should be chillingly obvious. Easter Island is Earth writ small. Today, again, a rising population confronts shrinking resources. We too have no emigration valve, because all human societies are linked by international transport, and we can no more escape into space than the Easter Islanders could flee into the ocean. If we continue to follow our present course, we shall have exhausted the world's major fisheries, tropical rain forests, fossil fuels, and much of our soil by the time my sons reach my current age.

39 Every day newspapers report details of famished countries—Afghanistan, Liberia, Rwanda, Sierra Leone, Somalia, the former Yugoslavia, Zaire—where soldiers have appropriated the wealth or where central government is yielding to local gangs of thugs. With the risk of nuclear war receding, the threat of our ending with a bang no longer has a chance of galvanizing us to halt our course. Our risk now is of winding down, slowly, in a whimper. Corrective action is blocked by vested interests, by well-intentioned political and business leaders, and by their electorates, all of whom are perfectly correct in not noticing big changes from year to year. Instead, each year there are just somewhat more people, and somewhat fewer resources, on Earth.

40 It would be easy to close our eyes or to give up in despair. If mere thousands of Easter Islanders with only stone tools and their own muscle power sufficed to destroy their society, how can billions of people with metal tools and machine power fail to do worse? But there is one crucial difference. The Easter Islanders had no books and no histories of other doomed societies. Unlike the Easter Islanders, we have histories of the past—information that can save us. My main hope for my sons' generation is that we may now choose to learn from the fates of societies like Easter's.

---

[1]Plants as a group; often used with *fauna,* or animals as a group. (Ed.)
[2]German word meaning "living space." (Ed.)

EXERCISES

A. Determining the Main Idea and Writer's Purpose

Choose the best answer.

1. The main idea of the selection is that, among all vanished civilizations, the former Polynesian society on Easter Island remains unsurpassed in mystery and isolation, *and*
   a. sparks our imagination and interest in other remote and vanished civilizations.
   b. offers paleontologists a place to conduct research to identify the plants and animals that once flourished there.

c. is the world's most isolated scrap of habitable land.

d. offers us a new interpretation of the island's history and presents a parallel to the dangers confronting modern civilization.

2. With respect to the main idea, the author's purpose is to

a. warn us that the disaster that befell Easter Island could also happen to us.

b. trace the history of human civilization on Easter Island.

c. describe the statues on Easter Island and explain how they were built and erected.

d. show the painstaking work and important scientific contribution that paleontologists add to the world's store of knowledge.

B. Comprehending Main Ideas

Choose the correct answer.

1. Which geographic characteristics of Easter Island should have made it a "miniature paradise, remote from problems that beset the rest of the world"?

a. its fertile soil and ample water supply

b. its remoteness, fertile soil, and mild climate

c. its industrious population and position as a regional trading center

d. its bountiful food supply and convenient location for nearby islands

2. Until recently, the biggest mystery surrounding the huge stone statues lining Easter Island's coast was

a. why islanders had carved them in the first place.

b. where islanders had found the stone to carve them.

c. how the islanders had been able to transport them and erect them.

d. why the islanders pulled them down.

3. Researchers in archeology, pollen analysis, and paleontology excavating Easter Island have found that it had, in fact,

a. been barren for years, thus deepening the mystery.

b. at one time been extensively forested with various kinds of trees.

c. been colonized by advanced societies of American Indians.

d. contained plants and animals never identified or associated with any other Polynesian island.

4. The Easter Islanders that explorers encountered in the 1700s paddled frail, rickety canoes rather than large, sturdy seagoing canoes other Polynesian islanders constructed. These canoes were of poor quality because

a. all the island's palm trees had been cut down and had become extinct.
b. the island's self-sufficiency made it unnecessary for them to build strong canoes to travel elsewhere.
c. the older generations who knew how to build strong canoes had failed to pass their skills down to succeeding generations.
d. the islanders became apathetic and lazy and didn't care about shoddy handiwork.

5. Diamond speculates that Easter's civilization declined
   a. so slowly that the residents didn't realize from generation to generation what was really happening.
   b. very quickly, wiped out by a combination of unfortunate and cataclysmic events.
   c. despite the residents' best efforts to regenerate it.
   d. in the same fashion and for the same reasons that all the other civilizations in Polynesia declined.

C. Distinguishing Between Main Ideas and Supporting Details

The following sentences come from paragraphs 27 and 28. Label them as follows: **MI** if the sentence represents a *main idea* and **SD** if the sentence represents a *supporting detail.*

1. _____ The fifteenth century marked the end not only for Easter's palm but for the forest itself.
2. _____ Its doom had been approaching as people cleared land to plant gardens; as they felled trees to build canoes, to transport and erect statues, and to burn; as rats devoured seeds; and probably as the native birds died out that had pollinated the trees' flowers and dispersed their fruit.
3. _____ The overall picture is among the most extreme examples of forest destruction anywhere in the world: the whole forest gone, and most of its tree species extinct.
4. _____ The destruction of the island's animals was as extreme as that of the forest: without exception, every species of native land bird became extinct.
5. _____ Even shellfish were overexploited, until people had to settle for small sea snails instead of larger cowries.
6. _____ Porpoise bones disappeared abruptly from garbage heaps around 1500; no one could harpoon porpoises any more, since the trees used for constructing the big seagoing canoes no longer existed.

D. Drawing Conclusions

Mark an **X** before any of these statements that represent reasonable conclusions you can draw from this selection.

1. _____ The most serious threat to our survival lies in overpopulation.
2. _____ Reconstructing the civilization on Easter Island and the reasons for its decline would not have been possible without the research done by paleontologists and biologists.
3. _____ Those Easter Islanders who tried to warn the younger generation about their harmful practices were dismissed as eccentrics or doomsayers.
4. _____ The people who inhabit Easter Island today are making every attempt to capture its past glory.
5. _____ It is not within our power to change the course of civilization; cultures are born, flourish, and die, just as all life on earth does, and human intervention in a society's evolution is futile.
6. _____ Written records—the mark of literate societies—are a better way of preserving descriptions of an area's landscape than are oral tales handed down from generation to generation.
7. _____ Despite the technological advancements that our civilization has produced, it is likely that earth in the future—with its billions of people and dwindling resources—could succumb to the same fate as befell that of the Easter Islanders.

E. Interpreting Meaning

Where appropriate, write your answers for these questions in your own words.

1. Which of the following would be a good title for paragraph 3?
   a. "The Mysterious Stone Statues of Easter Island"
   b. "Easter Island: A Place of Exotic Romance"
   c. "Easter Island: A Vanished Civilization of Mystery and Isolation"
   d. "Polynesian Paradise"

2. Look through the section from paragraphs 31 to 36 and find two parallels Diamond makes between the Easter Islanders and issues and/or behavior in our civilization today.

   ____

   ____

3. In paragraph 36, what words and phrases show us that Diamond's ideas are hypothetical rather than factual?

____

____

4. Find the quotation and identify the number of the paragraph that represents the *single* most important reason Diamond cites for Easter Island's demise?

____

5. Look again at almost any body paragraphs in the article and determine what they have in common structurally.

____

6. Which of the following best describes Diamond's *tone*, or emotional attitude, in this piece?
   a. neutral, informative, objective
   b. somber, concerned, and admonishing
   c. philosophical, reflective, and pensive
   d. provocative, shrill, inflammatory

F. Understanding Vocabulary

Look through the paragraphs listed below and find a word that matches each definition. Refer to a dictionary if necessary. An example has been done for you.

EXAMPLE: suitable for living [paragraphs 4–5] habitable

1. many and varied [8–9] ______________
2. completely lacking, without [10–11—phrase] ______________
3. skeptical, disbelieving [12–13] ______________
4. practicability, likelihood [12–13] ______________
5. passionate, enthusiastic [12–13] ______________
6. difficult to believe [16–17] ______________
7. horizontal layers, bands, or beds [18–19] ______________
8. easily sickened or disgusted [22–23] ______________
9. place of refuge, sanctuary [22–23] ______________
10. immense, huge [22–23] ______________

11. untouched, unspoiled [25–26] ____________

12 insult, verbal abuse [28–29] ____________

13. rich and powerful people, business magnates [30–31] ____________

14. grandiose, pretentiously showy [30–31] ____________

15. were capable of, were equal to a specified task [39–40] ____________

G. Paraphrasing and Summarizing

1. Write a paraphrase of this excerpt from paragraph 38: "By now the meaning of Easter Island for us should be chillingly obvious. Easter Island is Earth writ small. Today, again, a rising population confronts shrinking resources."

____

____

____

____

2. Write a summary of paragraph 36.

____

____

____

DISCUSSION QUESTIONS

1. Describe the kinds of evidence that Diamond uses to reinforce his theory that Easter Island, at one time, was a fertile, productive island, capable of sustaining life.
2. What evidence in the article makes Diamond's hypothesis irrefutable?
3. In the last two paragraphs, what is the fundamental irony that Diamond implies?
4. Do some research and report on what life is like on Easter Island now.

READING

EXPLORE THE WEB

- Information about Easter Island is available at these three sites. The first is Easter Island's home page, which includes several links about the history, culture, and art of the area: www.netaxs.com/~trance/rapanui.html
- "Easter Island in Three Dimensions" features photographs of the island in both two and three dimensions: www.3dphoto.net/stereo/world/latin_america/chile/easter/easter.html.
- Finally, this site provides a virtual photographic tour of the Easter Islands along with links pertaining to the islands' resources and the controversies surrounding the moai: www.mysteriousplaces.com/Easter_Island.

Writing Paraphrases and Summaries

Now that you have read the selections for Part 4 and practiced annotating, we can turn to the writing portion and examine the related skills of paraphrasing and summarizing. Both skills will help you in your college courses for writing analytical and synthesis essays in English and other courses, as well as for writing research papers. But these skills also can extend into the real world. For example, a boss might ask an employee to prepare a summary of the discussion from a lengthy meeting for distribution to other employees, and a secretary who records and distributes the minutes of an official conference, convention, or other gathering is essentially summarizing.

WRITING A SUMMARY: ACADEMIC AND PROFESSIONAL WRITING

Knowing how to identify the most important points in articles, books, or other material that you read, as well as in speeches or lectures you hear, is an essential skill for success in college as well as in the professional world.

Typical Academic Assignments Requiring Writing a Summary

- Summarize a chapter of a complex textbook in order to understand it more fully.
- Summarize an article in a scholarly journal as the introduction to an evaluation or analysis of the article.
- Summarize the main points of a speaker at an on-campus event your professor asks you to attend.

Typical Professional Writing Tasks Requiring Writing a Summary

- Summarize the findings of a committee on which you have been serving.

- Summarize the achievements of the department you chair for your company's annual progress report.
- Summarize your reasons for requesting funding for a project as the final paragraph of a grant proposal.

HOW TO PARAPHRASE

Paraphrasing is one way to test for accurate reading. As you will recall from the introduction to Part 4, *paraphrasing* means restating the writer's words in your own words. Your instructor may assign a paraphrasing exercise or two as a measure of your understanding, or you might want to paraphrase a problematic passage yourself to clarify its meaning. For whatever purpose, the process requires you *to go through one sentence at a time*, rewriting and changing the words into your own words as much as possible, *without changing the meaning of the original*. That's the hard part. Your paraphrase must retain accurately the ideas in the passage and also preserve its flavor and tone. Keep in mind, too, that a paraphrase might occasionally be longer than the original passage. You will see this disparity in length in the sample that follows.

To write a successful paraphrase, consider the suggestions below:

Techniques for Paraphrasing

- Substitute a synonym for key words in the original.
- An exception to the above: Don't strain to find a synonym for major words. If the passage refers to an elephant, for example, use the word *elephant*, not a *pachyderm with wrinkly gray skin*.
- Change the order of ideas within sentences.
- Omit unimportant ideas if your instructor allows.
- Reorder ideas but check to be sure that they flow logically.
- Combine ideas when possible.
- Maintain the flavor and level of formality of the original.

Reprinted here is paragraph 8 of Bill Bryson's excerpt, "Cells," from his intriguing book, *A Short History of Nearly Everything*. You might want to annotate the original passage before proceeding. Then study the paraphrase to the right and compare it with the original. See if you can identify each technique used. Note that the paraphrase is slightly longer than the original passage.

SAMPLE PARAPHRASES

Original Passage

You possess "some few hundred" different types of cells, according to the Belgian biochemist Christian de Duve, and they vary enormously in size and shape, from nerve cells whose filaments can stretch to several feet to tiny, disc-shaped red blood cells to the rod-shaped photocells that help to give us vision. They also come in a superbly wide range of sizes—nowhere more strikingly than at the moment of conception, when a single beating sperm confronts an egg eighty-five thousand times bigger than it is (which rather puts the notion of male conquest into perspective). On average, however, a human cell is about twenty microns wide—that is about two hundredths of a millimeter—which is too small to be seen but roomy enough to hold thousands of complicated structures like mitochondria, and millions upon millions of molecules. In the most literal way, cells also vary in liveliness. Your

Paraphrase

The Belgian biochemist Christian de Duve has stated that the human body has a few hundred different types of cells. These cells differ greatly both in size and in shape. Nerve cells, for example, can be several feet long, blood cells are disc-shaped, and the photo cells that allow us to see are shaped like rods. The size of these cells can also differ rather remarkably in size. The most notable example of this variance in size, perhaps, is the tiny single sperm cell, which at conception unites with the female egg, which is something like 85,000 times bigger. The width of most human cells, though, is about two hundredths of a millimeter—or twenty microns. This makes most human cells too small to be seen by the naked eye, yet they are still big enough to contain the complex substances of mitochondria and millions of little molecules. Finally, cells are different in terms of their "liveliness." For example, it may be a bit troubling skin cells are all dead. It's a somewhat galling notion to reflect that every inch of your surface is deceased. If you are an average-sized adult you are lugging around five pounds of dead skin, of which several billion tiny fragments are sloughed off each day. Run a finger along a dusty shelf and you are drawing a pattern very largely in old skin. (213 words)

to learn that the entire surface of your body is dead and that the total weight of your dead skin cells (at least for an adult of average size) is around five pounds. In addition, every day the average human beings sheds many billion cells of dead skin, just like running your finger along a dusty shelf, which is essentially the same as drawing a pattern in dead skin. (234 words)

Now you try it. Here is the next paragraph from Bill Bryson's selection. Study the original passage carefully, annotate it, and then write your paraphrase in the lines provided in the right column.

Original Passage	**Paraphrase**
Most living cells seldom last more	____________________
than a month or so, but there are	____________________
some notable exceptions. Liver cells	____________________
can survive for years, though the	____________________
components within them may be	____________________
renewed every few days. Brain cells	____________________
last as long as you do. You are issued	____________________
a hundred billion or so at birth, and	____________________
that is all you are ever going to get.	____________________
It has been estimated that you lose	____________________
five hundred of them an hour, so if	____________________
you have any serious thinking to do	____________________
there really isn't a moment to waste.	____________________

The good news is that the individual components of your brain cells are constantly renewed so that, as with the liver cells, no part of them is actually likely to be more than about a month old. Indeed, it has been suggested that there isn't a single bit of any of us—not so much as a stray molecule—that was part of us nine years ago. It may not feel like it, but at the cellular level we are all youngsters. (173 words)

HOW TO SUMMARIZE

Summarizing—the last skill—is the culmination of the other two skills. Before you can write a summary, you must first annotate the text, and you must know how to paraphrase important points. You will recall this definition of a summary from the introduction to Part 4: A summary condenses a writer's words by identifying only the main points and omitting unimportant supporting details. Therefore, the purpose of writing a summary is to *convey only the most important information,* so you have to develop a feel for what to save and what to leave out. This process sounds harder than it really is. When one paints a room, one has to spend more time preparing the surface than actually painting it. Writing a summary is the same; you just have to prepare well and then practice it.

First, study the chart that lists the techniques for summarizing. You may use them all, or you may decide that some work better than others. While you are preparing your summary, I suggest making a photocopy of the assigned selection so that you can mark it up easily.

Techniques for Writing a Summary

- Read the selection and circle unfamiliar words.
- Read the selection again, annotate it, and look up circled words.

- Underline important phrases and sentences and cross out unimportant material.
- Copy the notes from your margins onto a piece of paper, or type them up on a computer.
- Review your notes. Add or delete information as needed.
- Rewrite the selection, condensing where you can. Substitute your own words for the author's, and add transitions to show the relationship between ideas.
- Read through your summary for accuracy and to make sure you haven't introduced your own ideas or opinions.
- Your summary should duplicate the order of ideas and also should reflect the same proportional length for each main idea as the original selection does.
- Unless your instructor gives you different instructions, your summary should be between 10 and 25 percent of the original length.
- It is a good idea to get into the habit of introducing your summary with the writer's name and the title of the selection.

SAMPLE SUMMARIES

Here reproduced again are the two paragraphs from Bill Bryson's selection, "Cells," that you used to practice paraphrasing. Since you are already familiar with the material, this will be a good choice with which to demonstrate the summary writing process. Pay particular attention to the crossed out words and phrases, which represent relatively unimportant details that I thought I could safely omit. The total word count for the two paragraphs is 386 words, so the summary should be no more than about 100 words long.

Original Passage

You possess "some few hundred" different types of cells, according to the Belgian biochemist Christian de Duve, and they vary enormously in size and shape, ~~from~~ nerve cells ~~whose~~ filaments can stretch to several feet ~~to tiny,~~ disc-shaped red blood cells ~~to~~ the rod-shaped photocells ~~that help to give us~~ vision. They also come in a superbly wide range of sizes—nowhere more strikingly than at the moment of conception, ~~when a single beating~~ sperm confronts an egg eighty-five thousand times bigger ~~than it is (which rather puts the notion of male conquest into perspective).~~ On average, however, a human cell is about twenty microns wide~~—that is about two hundredths of a millimeter—which is too small to be seen but roomy enough to hold thousands of complicated structures like mitochondria, and millions upon millions of molecules. In the most literal way~~, cells also vary in liveliness. Your skin cells are all dead. ~~It's a somewhat galling notion to reflect that every inch of your surface is deceased. If you are an average-sized adult you are lugging around five pounds of dead skin, of which~~ several billion tiny fragments are sloughed off each day. ~~Run a finger along a dusty shelf and you are drawing a pattern very largely in old skin.~~

Most living cells seldom last more than a month or so, but there are some notable exceptions. Liver cells can survive for years, though the components within them may be renewed every few days. Brain cells last as long as you do. ~~You are issued a hundred billion or so at birth, and that is all you are ever going to get.~~ It has been estimated that you lose five hundred of them an hour, ~~so if you have any serious thinking to do there really isn't a moment to waste. The good news is that~~ the individual components of your brain cells are constantly renewed so that, as with the liver cells, no part of them is actually likely to be more than about a month old. ~~Indeed, it has been suggested that~~ there isn't a single bit of any of us~~—not so much as a stray molecule~~—that was part of us nine years ago. ~~It may not feel like it, but~~ at the cellular level we are all youngsters.

Sample Summary—First Draft

In "Cells," Bill Bryson writes that, according to Belgian biochemist Christian de Duve, human beings have many different types of cells that vary widely in shape. For example, nerve cells look like long filaments, red blood cells are disc-shaped, and photocells in the eyes are rod-shaped. They also vary widely in size. Most striking is the difference in size at conception between the tiny sperm and the relatively huge egg. But most cells are only about 20 microns wide. Some cells are even dead, for example, human skin. Although most cells die within a month and are therefore renewable, liver cells last a long time, as do brain cells, which are not renewable during a person's lifetime. But the components of liver and brain cells do regenerate themselves. At least at the level of our cells, the human body is actually quite young. (143 words)

Since this first attempt at writing a summary of the two paragraphs turned out to more than 40 words over my self-imposed limit of 25 percent, or 100 words, I had some serious cutting to do. I decided to cut out most of the examples and just to retain Bryson's main points. Here's what the final version looked like:

Sample Summary—Final Draft

According to Bill Bryson in "Cells," human beings have many different types of cells varying widely in shape—for example, nerve cells resemble long filaments, red blood cells look like discs, and the photocells in our eyes look like rods. They also vary widely in size: For example, at conception the tiny sperm and the relatively huge egg are a striking contrast. But most cells are only about 20 microns wide. Skin cells are actually dead, and most other cells die within a month, except for liver and brain cells, which last a long time. On a cellular level, we are actually quite young. (104 words)

■ COMMENT ON THE FINAL DRAFT

Crossing out unnecessary words and phrases, as demonstrated above, allows you more easily to see the difference between main ideas and supporting details. This summary omits some points that at first I wanted to include, for instance, Bryson's statements that "the individual components within them [liver cells] may be renewed every few days" and that "the individual components of your brain cells are constantly renewed." But ultimately I realized that these were relatively minor details, the omission of which would not distort the meaning. To reiterate: A summary, by definition, must necessarily omit some details, and the writer must simply accept that fact.

As a further test, I wrote a *one-sentence* summary of my summary. Stripped down to its main point, Bryson's two paragraphs reinforce a single idea:

Human cells vary widely in size, shape, and activity.

You should recognize by now the interrelatedness of reading well, and annotating while you read, and writing a summary. Being able to pull out the main points is a crucial skill both for accurate and efficient comprehension and for writing essays where you are required to incorporate ideas from reading selections.

Finally, forcing yourself to limit a summary to an arbitrary number of words is an intellectually rigorous and challenging exercise.[1] If you are unsure about how long a summary should be, ask your instructor. I generally recommend the 10–25 percent rule-of-thumb, but some instructors often assign a summary of a single typed page. Whichever length your instructor assigns, being forced to write within a particular word limit requires that you think carefully about what to save and what to drop, how to preserve the meaning of the original using the fewest possible words, and above all, how to capture the essence of the passage.

Here is a passage for you to use to practice summary writing. Following the models above, write a summary of a passage from Barbara Kingsolver's essay, "How Mr. Dewey Decimal Saved My Life," in which she explains the importance of the library for her. The original length is 243 words, so try to keep your summary to around 60 words.

[1]To arrive at a word count, in Microsoft Word, highlight your text and then scroll down from "Tools" to "Word Count."

Original Passage

Now, with my adolescence behind me and my daughter's still ahead, I am nearly speechless with gratitude for the endurance and goodwill of librarians in an era that discourages reading in almost incomprehensible ways. We've created for ourselves a culture that undervalues education (compared with the rest of the industrialized world, to say the least), undervalues breadth of experience (compared with our potential), downright discourages critical thinking (judging from what the majority of us watch and read), and distrusts foreign ideas. "Un-American," from what I hear, is meant to be an insult.

Most alarming, to my mind, is that we the people tolerate censorship in school libraries for the most bizarre and frivolous of reasons. Art books that contain (horrors!) nude human beings, and *The Wizard of Oz* because it has witches in it. Not always, everywhere, but everywhere, always something. And censorship of certain ideas in some quarters is enough to sway curriculums at the national level. Sometimes profoundly. Find a publishing house that's brave enough to include a thorough discussion of the principles of evolution in a high school text. Good luck. And yet, just about all working botanists, zoologists, and ecologists will tell you that evolution is to their field what germ theory is to medicine. We expect our kids to salvage a damaged earth, but in deference to the religious beliefs of a handful, we allow an entire generation of future scientists to germinate and grow in a vacuum.

■ FURTHER ASSIGNMENTS FOR ANNOTATING

For any of these exercises that your instructor assigns, annotate the selection while keeping in mind a particular essay topic based on the reading selection that follows this introduction.

1. Annotate Richard Wolkomir's article, focusing on this question: Using Ken Adams as the primary example, what are some of the effects—both visible and invisible—on adults who are unable to read well?
2. Annotate Mark Edmundson's selection, focusing on this question: What are the qualities that distinguish a great teacher from an ordinary one?

3. Barbara Kingsolver writes, "What snapped me out of my surly adolescence and moved me on were books that let me live other people's lives." Annotate her selection, focusing on this question: In what particular ways did books change her attitude?
4. Annotate Jared Diamond's selection, focusing on this question: What evidence in the article makes Diamond's hypothesis irrefutable?

FURTHER ASSIGNMENTS FOR PARAPHRASING

1. Paraphrase paragraph 7 from Barbara Kingsolver's selection.
2. Paraphrase either paragraph 7 or paragraphs 16 and 17 from Mark Edmundson's selection.
3. Paraphrase paragraph 3 from Bill Bryson's selection.
4. Paraphrase paragraph 38 from Jared Diamond's selection.

FURTHER ASSIGNMENTS FOR WRITING SUMMARIES

Write a summary of about 10 percent of any of the selections in Part 4. Here are the total numbers of words for each selection and the recommended word length for your summary:

Richard Wolkomir	4,100 total words, a summary of around 400 words
Mark Edmundson	2,475 total words, a summary of around 250 words
Barbara Kingsolver	2,625 total words, a summary of around 250 words
Bill Bryson	3,925 total words, a summary of around 400 words
Jared Diamond	4,600 words, a summary of around 450 words

TOPICS RELATED TO THE READINGS

1. Wolkomir shows the impact of learning to read on his pupil, Ken Adams. Edmundson and Kingsolver discuss the importance of reading in their lives and how being introduced to reading changed them forever. Find the common ground in these people's experience. Write an essay in which you compare and contrast Ken Adams, Mark Edmundson, and Barbara Kingsolver, first by finding points of similarity in their attitudes and then in the ways their lives changed

from their exposure to reading. You might want to look ahead to the writing section of Part 6—writing comparison and contrast essays on page 423—before undertaking this assignment.

2. A sidebar newspaper article (*San Francisco Chronicle*, December 16, 2005) was titled, "5% of Adults in U.S. Illiterate in English." Here is the article in its entirety:

   Washington—About 1 in 20 adults in the United States is not literate in English, meaning 11 million people lack the skills to handle many everyday tasks, a federal study shows.

   From 1992 to 2003, adults made no progress in their ability to read sentences and paragraphs or understand other printed material such a bus schedules or prescription labels.

   The adult population did make gains in handling tasks that involve math, such as calculating numbers on tax forms or bank statements. But even in that area, the typical adult showed only enough skills to perform simple daily activities.

   Perhaps most sobering was that adult literacy dropped or was flat across every level of education, from people with graduate degrees to those who dropped out of high school. So even as more people get a formal education, the literacy rate is not rising.

What might be some reasons to account for flattening or declining literacy rates? Write an essay in which you explore some theories or observations that might account for it. You might want to consider your own reading experiences and those of people whom you know as support.

3. Has a teacher ever "turned you around"? What teacher—or perhaps another person—opened your mind? Following Mark Edmundson's method, write a profile of a memorable teacher.
4. In paragraph 27, Edmundson writes: "anything that's been successfully institutionalized, however rebellious it may seem or however virtuous, is stifling. What's called subversion only lasts for an instant in a school or a hospital or a home; it's quickly swept up to become part of the protocol, an element in 'the way we do things around here.'" What is the relationship between high school, at least the Medford High that Edmundson describes, and other conforming institutions? What is Edmundson saying about the nature of institutions, the reason they exist in the form that they do, and the reason that they are so dangerous?
5. Bill Bryson's essay is a model analytical essay examining some features of human cells, their complex structure and function. In the same way, choose a subject that you know well—perhaps a camera, a computer motherboard, a kayak, a restaurant kitchen, or other subject of your choosing—and write an essay analyzing its structure and function.

6. The decline in Easter Island's environment and civilization was so slow and gradual that its residents may not even have been aware of its decline. Here are the last four lines of T. S. Eliot's 1925 poem, "The Hollow Men":

   This is the way the world ends
   This is the way the world ends
   This is the way the world ends
   Not with a bang but a whimper.

   Diamond borrows the last line in paragraph 36 when he writes, "I suspect, though, that the disaster happened not with a bang but with a whimper." What environmental change—especially one that has been a long time in the making—have you observed in a neighborhood, town, city, or even a place in nature that you know well? Write an essay in which you discuss the change, the reasons for the change, and its impact on the environment. You might want to preview the writing section in Part 7—"Writing Cause-Effect Essays" on page 501—before beginning this assignment.
7. What are the chief characteristics of the scientific method of inquiry as Diamond explains it? Why does Diamond describe in such detail the work of Fienley, King, and Steadman (see paragraphs 18–24 in particular). Write an essay showing the corrections between scientific research and the real world.
8. Using both print sources in the library and websites, do some research and report on what the environment and culture of Easter Island are like now.

PART FIVE

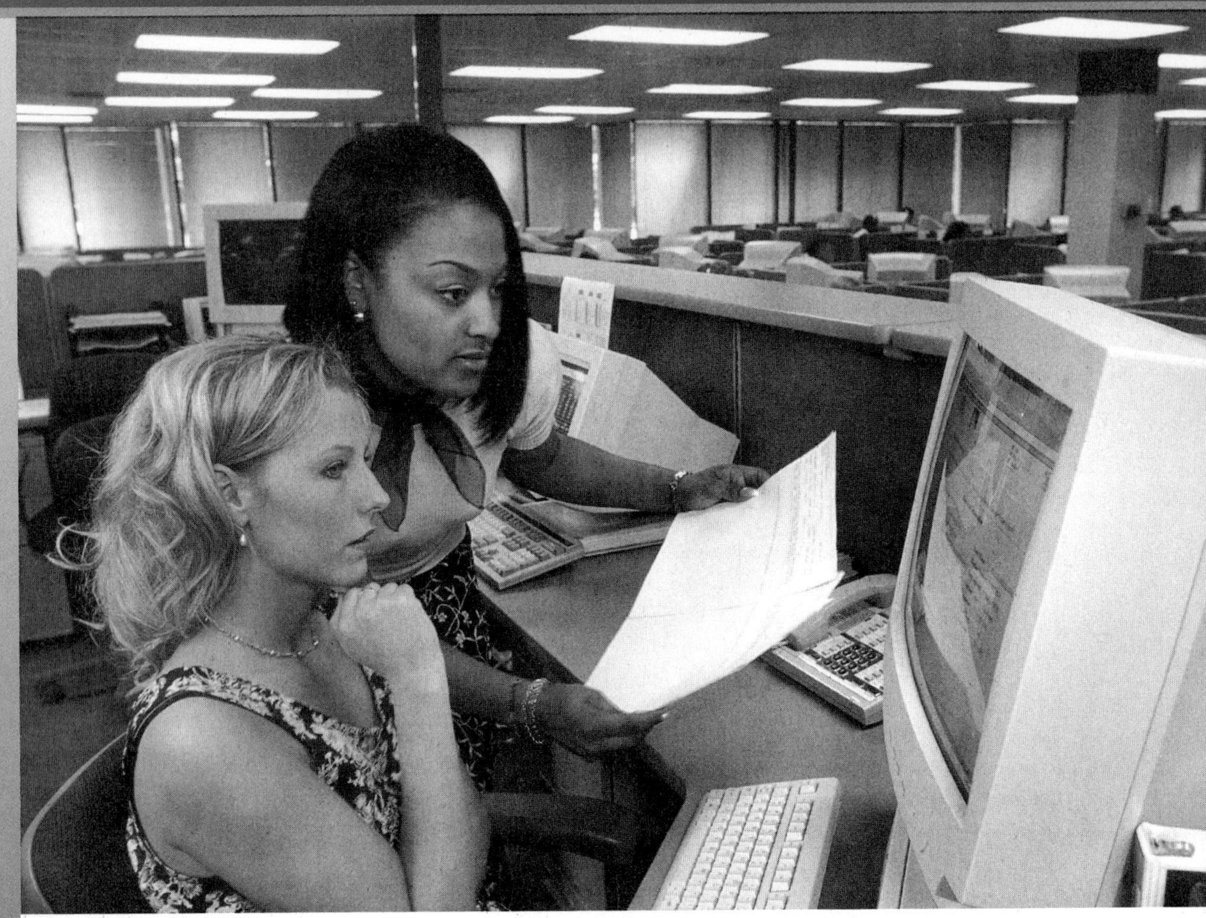

READING

WRITING

5

Part 5 represents the pivotal portion of the text, pivotal because everything you have learned about writing thus far—correctly integrating quoted material, including relevant specific detail, paraphrasing, and summarizing—is necessary and fundamental to writing analytical essays, which ends this part. The first section opens with a discussion of the inference-making process in reading, which results in improved comprehension beyond a mere superficial understanding of the text.

The number of readings in the next section is more extensive than in earlier parts of the text, and their content is more complex, as we move away from reading about personal experience to reading more analytical selections. The first group deals with food and the fast food industry; the next group takes up three facets of the American ethos: work, success, and failure. The exercises for these readings require you to make inferences to help you master this crucial skill. The website includes an additional reading on food—the popularity of American fast food in Paris—and two articles on the experiences of American soldiers in Iraq. These three themes, reflected in the readings, would make suitable topics for an analysis or a synthesis essay.

The final section of Part 5 explains in some detail the process of writing an analysis and a synthesis essay, the fundamental writing assignment that will be required in all of your college courses that require writing. This section shows you the writing process from start to finish, focusing on a most useful technique called the *tell-show-share method*. To illustrate this method, we reprint the work of two former students, Kim Tran and Pete Glanting. Both students had to wrestle with separate assignments to analyze one or more readings and to integrate information and ideas from the reading into a coherent whole. Sample notes, thesis statements, as well as introductory and body paragraphs show you how both students effectively fulfilled their respective assignments. (Note, too, that an earlier draft of Pete's two body paragraphs appears in Part 9 as a proofreading exercise.) Several topics for writing analysis and synthesis essays (some based on the readings and some independent of the readings) end the section.

Making Inferences and Seeing Connections

INFERENCES—A DEFINITION

To make an *inference* means to read between the lines of a text and to draw meaning from what the writer does not directly say but surely intends to suggest. Therefore, making inferences means going beyond and underneath the surface meaning to extract a deeper level of understanding. The inference process thus reinforces the thinking process, allowing you to gain insights into the subject and to extend your understanding of that subject.

Two other kinds of inference require us to connect facts to make sense of them when no explanation is offered or to draw a logical conclusion about a future course of action based on the evidence presented. Our conclusion might extend to another similar situation. Thus, the inference-making process is more demanding than mere simple comprehension.

Many of my students find the inference questions to be among the most challenging type of reading exercise. But this skill is eminently worthwhile to develop if you want to become a more proficient reader. You will have ample opportunity to practice making inferences in many of the readings in Parts 5, 6, and 7 of this text.

INFERENCES IN THE REAL WORLD

Let's see how inferences work in the real world: It is a cloudy winter day, and you are driving north on a narrow mountain road. Suddenly, you notice that all of the cars coming toward you have their headlights on, and you wonder why. One possibility is that the cars are part of a funeral procession. Another is that they were just driving in an area in which headlights are required during the day (such as on narrow or windy two-lane roads or in daylight test zones) and that all the drivers forgot to turn off the lights at the end. A third is that they have just emerged from dense fog. Any one of them could be true, but one is *probably* more likely than the other two.

The funeral cortege inference is probably unlikely. Usually the cars in a funeral procession have identifying stickers or signs on their windshields.

Also it would be unlikely that every single driver forgot to turn off the lights at the end of a daylight test section. The most likely possibility is that a patch of dense fog lies ahead. And, of course, if you reach the patch of dense fog as you proceed north, your inference is confirmed.

Here is another situation requiring you to make an inference. Suppose you live next door to a family named Sullivan. One morning you observe that the Sullivan's newspapers are piling up at their front door. From this fact, you might infer three things: (1) They are away on vacation; (2) they forgot to cancel their newspaper delivery; and (3) they forgot to ask someone to pick the papers up so as not to attract burglars.

These conclusions are *logical*; that is, they derive from common experience of seeing newspapers piled up in front of a house. However, they may not actually be *true*. The Sullivans may have been called away on a family emergency and simply were too distraught to remember that the newspapers would pile up. Perhaps the family has been stricken with the flu and has been unable to get out. A more far-fetched inference might be that they have all been murdered, and no one has detected the crime. In the absence of any other information, however, the first three inferences stated earlier are more likely to be accurate. This is the important point about inferences: They are statements more of *probability* than of fact.

FURTHER CONSIDERATIONS ABOUT INFERENCES

To sum up this introduction, when you make an inference—in reading or in life—you draw a logical conclusion, not from something you know with certainty, but rather from what you know to be true from past experience. In reading, we draw a logical conclusion from what the writer surely means to suggest but does not state. That is the reason that making inferences is often called "reading between the lines." We know from experience that, even in daylight, sensible drivers often turn on their lights when driving through dense fog, and we know from our own experience that it is easy to forget to notify the newspaper carrier of our vacation plans.

Just as we should not leap to conclusions about neighbors being murdered from seeing a pile of unclaimed newspapers, so too should we not read into the author's words *beyond what the words suggest or imply*. And this is the fundamental paradox underlying the inference process. In the real world we must rely on past experience to make appropriate inferences. But the situation is a little different when we read: Because our own experiences are necessarily limited, relying on them may lead us astray from the writer's real intentions with the result that we may misread or misinterpret. Thus, in this textbook, it is safer to restrict your answers only to what the writer suggests, not to something you have experienced or something you have read outside the text.

MARKING INFERENCE ANSWERS

In some of the inference sections in Parts 5, 6, and 7, you will be asked to write a sentence or two in your own words stating an appropriate inference that you can draw from a particular passage. For other selections, you will be asked to label statements from the text using this key: Y (yes), N (no), or CT (can't tell). A "yes" answer means that the inference is *probably accurate*. It states something that the writer's words actually imply or suggest. A "no" answer means that the inference is *probably inaccurate*, either because it shows a misreading or a distortion of the writer's words. Or perhaps one part of the inference statement is accurate but another part is not, making the whole statement inaccurate. A "can't tell" answer means that *you can't be sure one way or the other* whether the inference is logical or accurate. This might be the case when the writer either does not mention anything that would allow you to draw such a conclusion, or the conclusion depends on something else you have read or have other knowledge of. In other words, you can't tell from *this* particular passage.

Before we look at some sample inference questions, let's examine the difference between a "no" and a "can't tell" answer in more detail. Think about this statement:

> Blue is a color, and north is a quality.

Is this an accurate statement? The first part makes sense, but north is a direction, not a quality. In the same way, if a complicated inference contains two ideas—one accurate and other inaccurate—mark it N. CT, on the other hand, means just that—you simply can't tell. To return to our earlier headlight example, if only one car coming toward you has its headlights on, you wouldn't have enough information to make an inference one way or another.

The first type of inferences that you will practice with are sometimes called *local inferences* because they refer specifically and only to the material at hand. Later in this introduction, you will practice drawing conclusions, which are sometimes called *global inferences*.

How to Make Accurate Inferences

Keep in mind these suggestions when working through the sample exercises below and the exercises following each reading selection.

- Look up the meanings of any unfamiliar words and consider the definitions in context.
- Think about the possibilities of interpretation based on the writer's words and phrases.

- Look carefully at the way the statement is worded. Then return to the passage and locate the pertinent passage. Test the statement for accuracy.
- Remember that inferences are *statements of probability*, not facts. They proceed from facts, but they are not facts themselves.
- When in doubt about an answer, ask your instructor for help or for further clarification.
- Remember that good readers may disagree over inference answers. Inferences are not always black and white, which is what makes them fun—but challenging.

To illustrate the process of making inferences, here are four short excerpts from selected readings in Parts 2–4, which you may already have been assigned to read. We will begin with some easy ones and work up to more difficult questions.

Practice Exercise 1: K. Oanh Ha, "Refugee's Journey"

> My family had been among the vast middle class in Vietnam. My father was a carpenter. We weren't wealthy or connected enough to leave with the Americans in 1975 when the war ended. Then in 1979, the communist government took away the businesses and personal assets of Chinese families and began expelling them. My paternal grandfather and his family were ethnic Chinese.

Label these inferences **Y** (yes), **N** (no), or **CT** (can't tell).

1. _____ A carpenter would have been considered a member of the middle class in Vietnam in 1975.
2. _____ K. Oanh Ha's family would not have left Vietnam in 1975 even if they had been wealthy or had connections with the Americans.
3. _____ The middle class in Vietnam was larger in 1975 than it is today.

Now check your answers against these suggestions:

1. Y 2. N 3. CT

Inference 1 should be marked "yes," since sentences 1 and 2 make that logical connection between the occupation of carpenter and middle-class status. Inference 2, on the other hand, should be marked "no." Ha is clearly implying (suggesting without saying) that the family would have left with other Vietnamese if they had had the means. And finally inference 3 cannot be answered one way or another because the author provides no information about it.

Practice Exercise 2: Curtis Wilkie, "The New Orleans That Was"

> Living in New Orleans was quite different. A bad 1987 movie popularized the term "the Big Easy." The people of New Orleans never called their city that. Nothing was particularly easy in New Orleans, with its tropical heat, poverty, endemic public corruption, appalling murder rate and racial divides.

Label these inferences **Y**, **N**, or **CT**.

1. _____ "The Big Easy" is a tourist nickname for New Orleans.
2. _____ The nickname "the Big Easy" was used for the first time in a 1987 movie.
3. _____ Life was often difficult for New Orleans residents.

Now check your answers against these suggested answers:

1. CT   2. N   3. Y

The first inference should be marked "can't tell" because the source of this nickname is not mentioned; similarly, the second inference should be marked "no" because of the word *popularized* in the first sentence, which suggests that the nickname already existed before the movie was made. The third inference involves a logical conclusion that one can make from the examples of difficult conditions New Orleanians have had to contend with.

Practice Exercise 3: Barbara Kingsolver, "How Mr. Dewey Decimal Saved My Life"

> As far as I could see from the lofty vantage point of age sixteen, there was nothing required of me at Nicholas County High that was going to keep me off the streets; unfortunately, we had no streets, either. We had lanes, roads, and rural free delivery routes, six in number, I think. We had two stoplights, which were set to burn green in all directions after 6 p.m., so as not, should the event of traffic arise, to slow anybody up.
>
> What we *didn't* have included almost anything respectable teenagers might do in the way of entertainment. In fact, there was one thing for teenagers to do to entertain themselves, and it was done in the backs of Fords and Chevrolets. It wasn't upholstering skills that were brought to bear on those backseats, either. Though the wedding-planning skills did follow.

Label these inferences **Y**, **N**, or **CT**.

1. _____ The town where Kingsolver grew up was most likely small and rural.
2. _____ Kingsolver was challenged academically at Nicholas County High.
3. _____ Many teenaged girls in Kingsolver's town got pregnant and had to get married.
4. _____ At the end of the 60s, when Kingsolver attended high school in Kentucky, teenage girls did not have access to birth control methods.
5. _____ The town was too small and poor to afford entertainment facilities for its teenagers.

Now compare your answers with these:

1. Y 2. N 3. Y 4. CT 5. CT

Here is an explanation of the answers: Inference 1 can be answered "yes" because these facts add up to this conclusion—the unpaved streets, the rural free delivery routes for the mail, and two stoplights both of which burned green at night. Inference 2 warrants a "no" because it misinterprets the first sentence, which suggests that Kingsolver was headed for trouble. If she had been academically challenged, the streets would not have held allure for her. Inference 3 should be answered "yes" because of her not-so-subtle humorous reference to teenagers having sex in the backseats of cars in lieu of other sources of entertainment available to them.

However, inference 4 is problematic. By the late 60s, birth control pills were widely available, as were other methods of contraception. But Kingsolver does not mention these, so it is difficult to tell exactly why girls got pregnant out of wedlock—perhaps from ignorance, perhaps from embarrassment, perhaps from the stigma of using birth control in a conservative rural community, perhaps from an "it-will-never-happen-to-me" mentality. (Also, no birth control method is completely foolproof.) Whatever the reason, Kingsolver offers no clue, making CT the safe answer here. Similarly inference 5 cannot be made one way or the other, as there is no hint as to why the possibilities for entertainment were unavailable. In the absence of any clue in the passage, again, CT is the best answer. Also the town was small, but she says nothing about its being poor.

DRAWING DEFENSIBLE CONCLUSIONS

The questions you have just completed involved *local inferences:* They pertain only to the specifics of the text and do not extend outside it. Another type of inference, however, is the *global inference,* in which you draw conclusions from a writer's words and apply them to other situations. A variation of this type of inference/conclusion allows the reader to predict a course of action from what he or she reads concerning another similar situation. For example, as you will see in the practice exercise below, in "Easter's End," Jared Diamond clearly intends the reader to apply the lessons learned from the destruction of Easter Island's environment to our own reckless disregard of our environment. Easter Island, therefore, represents a precedent that we should take careful notice of lest we suffer the same fate.

Study these three excerpts. Then mark the inferences as before. Each represents a conclusion that one might make from the reading. Decide if the conclusion is logical and therefore defensible, or not logical and therefore not defensible.

Practice Selection 1: Mark Edmundson, "The Teacher Who Opened My Mind"

Edmundson is describing the life-changing effects that his high school philosophy teacher, Frank Lears, had on him.

> One pays for the kind of mental exhilaration that Lears initiated in his students. One pays in self-doubt and isolation, in the suspicion that what seems to be true resistance is merely a perverse substitute for genuine talent, a cheap way of having something to say. Lears's path, so appealing in its first steps, separated me from my family, cut me loose from religion and popular faith, sent me adrift beyond the world bordered by TV and piety and common sense. One step down that road followed another, and now, at 50, I probably could not turn around if I wished to.

1. _____ Sometimes education has unintended consequences that go far beyond book learning.
2. _____ Lears's influence on Edmundson was essentially to turn him into a skeptic.
3. _____ One cannot be said to be truly educated unless one abandons family values, religious upbringing, and popular culture.

Compare your answers with these:

1. Y   2. Y   3. N

The first two inferences can be safely made from the passage. The third inference, however, is not warranted because to accept it would be to base the assumption on only one person's educational experience.

Practice Selection 2: Bill Bryson, "Cells"

> Surprises at the cellular level turn up all the time. In nature, nitric oxide is a formidable toxin and a common component of air pollution. So scientists were naturally a little surprised when, in the mid-1980s, they found it being produced in a curiously devoted manner in human cells. Its purpose

was at first a mystery, but then scientists began to find it all over the place—controlling the flow of blood and the energy levels of cells, attacking cancers and other pathogens, regulating the sense of smell, even assisting in penile erections. It also explained why nitroglycerine, the well-known explosive, soothes the heart pain known as angina.

Mark an **X** before each logical conclusion that you can reasonably and justifiably draw from this paragraph.

1. _____ Nitric oxide is always a dangerous chemical wherever it is found.
2. _____ Before the 1980s, scientists had not investigated the role of nitric oxide in the human body.
3. _____ Air pollution causes elevated amounts of nitric oxide in the human body.
4. _____ If one is experiencing chest pain associated with angina, nitroglycerine is often prescribed.

You should have put an **X** before only numbers 2 and 4.

Practice Selection 3: Jared Diamond, "Easter's End"

By now the meaning of Easter Island for us should be chillingly obvious. Easter Island is Earth writ small. Today, again, a rising population confronts shrinking resources. We too have no emigration valve, because all human societies are linked by international transport, and we can no more escape into space than the Easter Islanders could flee into the ocean. If we continue to follow our present course, we shall have exhausted the world's major fisheries, tropical rain forests, fossil fuels, and much of our soil by the time my sons reach my current age....

It would be easy to close our eyes or to give up in despair. If mere thousands of Easter Islanders with only stone tools and their own muscle power sufficed to destroy their society, how can billions of people with metal tools and machine power fail to do worse? But there is one crucial difference. The Easter Islanders had no books and no histories of other doomed societies. Unlike the Easter Islanders, we have histories of the past—information that can save us. My main hope for my sons' generation is that we may now choose to learn from the fates of societies like Easter's.

Mark an **X** before each logical conclusion that you can reasonably and justifiably draw from Diamond's concluding remarks.

1. _____ The most serious threat to our survival lies in overpopulation.

2. _____ Those Easter Islanders who tried to warn the younger generation about their harmful practices were dismissed as eccentrics or doomsayers.

3. _____ The people who inhabit Easter Island today are making every attempt to capture its past glory.

4. _____ It is not within our power to change the course of civilization; cultures are born, flourish, and die, just as all life on earth does, and human intervention in a society's evolution is futile.

5. _____ Written records—the mark of literate societies—are a better way of preserving descriptions of an area's landscape than are oral tales handed down from generation to generation.

6. _____ Despite the technological advancements that our civilization has produced, it is likely that earth in the future—with its billions of people and dwindling resources—could succumb to the same fate as befell that of the Easter Islanders.

Did you mark an **X** before 1, 5, and 6? If so, you are correct.

At the end of the Practice Essay that follows, you will be given an opportunity to write the answers to inference questions in your own words. The Practice Essay by Bobbie Ann Mason provides a retrospective look at the way her small-farm Kentucky family's daily life revolved around the growing, cultivating, and preparing of food.

PRACTICE ESSAY

The Burden of the Feast

Bobbie Ann Mason

One of the new young writers to emerge from the American South, Bobbie Ann Mason is the author of many works of fiction, most of them set in rural Tennessee and Kentucky and detailing the lives of working-class people. Born in 1940 in Mayfield, Kentucky, where her father was a dairy farmer, Mason graduated from the University of Kentucky in 1962 and worked in publishing and magazines in New York. She received a master's from SUNY-Binghamton in 1966, and a doctorate in English from the University of Connecticut in 1972. Her best-known short story collection is *Shiloh and Other Stories* (1982), which received the Ernest Hemingway Award; her most widely known novel *In Country* (1988) explores the hardships encountered by a Vietnam veteran returning to the South after his tour of duty. Although Mason lives in rural Pennsylvania, much of her writing is set in her native state, as is this selection, first published in *The New Yorker* and included in a different form in her 1999 book, *Clear Springs: A Memoir.*

VOCABULARY ANALYSIS

The Word Root *curr*

Writing about her childhood, Mason says, "I had a *recurrent* food dream." The root of this word *recurrent* comes from the Latin verb *currere*, meaning "to run." Therefore, a *recurrent* dream comes from the related verb *recur*, literally "to run again," in this case, in her dreams. Other words in the family of English words derived from this Latin verb are *current, occur, curriculum* (a list of courses offered by an academic institution), and *currency*, a word that refers to money in circulation. Two other related nouns are *course* (literally, instruction that "runs" for a particular length of time) and *courier*, a person who serves as a messenger, perhaps because they must literally run from place to place in their line of work.

The Burden of the Feast

Bobbie Ann Mason

Connecting Grammar to Writing

Mason uses dashes effectively and judiciously to interrupt the thought, to indicate a parenthetical remark, or to set off an appositive in paragraphs 1, 7, 9, and 10. Study her uses of the dash carefully and note the effect they create in each instance.

1 This Christmas, my two sisters and my brother and I, along with our families, will head toward home, our real home, which is where our seventy-eight-year-old mother, Christy, lives, in western Kentucky. She'll be ready for us with the usual Christmas feast, and what I'm looking forward to most is the green beans and sweet potatoes and creamed corn, the farm fare that once seemed so oppressively ordinary to me. When I was growing up on our fifty-three-acre dairy farm, we were obsessed with food. Food was the center of our lives. Everything we did, every day, revolved around it. We planted it, grew it, harvested it, peeled it, cooked it, served it, consumed it—endlessly, day after day, season after season. This was life on a farm, I can appreciate the value of a country upbringing now, but when I was a girl all that toil drove me crazy.

2 One day my mother and my grandmother were shelling beans and talking about the proper method of drying apples. I was eleven and entirely absorbed with the March girls in "Little Women." Drying apples was not in my dreams, Beth's death was weighing darkly on me at that moment, and I threw a little tantrum—what Mama called a hissy fit.

3 "Can't y'all talk about anything but food?" I screamed.

4 There was a shocked silence. "Well, what else is there?" Granny asked.

5 Granny didn't question her duties, but I did. I didn't want to be hulling beans in a hot kitchen when I was fifty years old. I wanted to be somebody, maybe an airline stewardess. Also, I had been listening to the radio. I had notions.

6 Life for our family was haunted by the fear of crop failure. We ate as if we didn't know where our next meal might come from. All my life, I have had a recurrent food dream: I face a buffet or cafeteria line, laden with beautiful foods. I spend the entire dream choosing the foods I want. The anticipation of eating

them is deliciously agonizing. I always wake up just as I've made my selections but before I get to eat.

7 Working with food was fraught with anxiety and desperation when I was a girl. Like all farmers, we were at the mercy of the weather, and it wasn't to be trusted. My mother watched the skies at evening for any portent of the morrow. A cloud that went over and then turned around and came back was an especially bad sign. Our livelihood—even our lives—depended on forces outside our control.

8 I think this dependence on nature was at the core of my rebellion. I hated the constant sense of helplessness before vast forces, the continuous threat of failure. Farmers didn't take the initiative, I began to see; they reacted to whatever presented itself. More than that, though, I disliked women's part in that dependence.

9 My mother had been raised in a large farm family—kinfolks who had taken her in when she was orphaned—but they had little time for her. One Christmas the only present she got was an orange, while her cousins got dolls. Her life had been hard, and so she allowed me to get spoiled. She never even tried to teach me to cook. "You didn't want to learn," she says now. "You were always busy doing something. You had your nose in a book."

10 From the front yard, where I sat reading under a maple tree, I could see my mother stooped over in the garden and my father on his tractor, far back in the field. No wonder I believed that progress meant freedom from the field and the range. That meant moving to town, I thought. Because we lived only a mile outside the town of Mayfield, I was acutely conscious of being country. I felt inferior to people in town because we had to grow our food and make our clothes; we couldn't just go buy things, the way they did. Although we were self-sufficient and resourceful and held clear title to our land, we farm people lived in a state of psychological poverty. We felt that the fine life in town—celebrated in magazines, on radio, in movies—was denied us. Of course, we weren't poor at all—I knew that. Poor people had too many kids, and they weren't landowners; they rented decrepit little houses with plank floors and trash in the yard. "Poor people are wormy and eat wild onions," Mama said. We weren't poor, but we were country.

11 We had three wardrobes—everyday clothes, school clothes, and Sunday clothes. We didn't wear our school clothes at home, but we could wear them to town. When we got home from church, we had to change back into everyday before we ate Mama's big Sunday dinner. "Don't eat in your good clothes!" Mama always cried. "You'll spill something on them."

12 The truth was, Mama was a natural cook. At harvest time, after she'd got in from the garden and put out a wash, she would whip up a noontime dinner for the men in the field—my father and grandfather and maybe some neighbors and a couple of hired hands: fried chicken with milk gravy, ham, mashed potatoes, lima beans, field peas, corn, slaw, sliced tomatoes, fried apples, biscuits, and peach pie. This was not considered a banquet, only plain hearty food, fuel

for work. All the ingredients except the flour, sugar, and salt came from the farm—the chickens, the hogs, the milk and butter, the potatoes from the potato patch, the beans, peas, corn, cabbage, apples, peaches. Nothing was processed, except by her. She was always butchering and plucking and planting and hoeing and shredding and slicing and creaming (scraping cobs for the creamed corn), and pressure-cooking and canning and freezing and thawing and mixing and shaping and baking and frying.

13 We were known to eat our pie right on the same plate as our turnip greens so as not to mess up another dish. It didn't matter if the peach cobbler oozed all over the turnip-green juice and the pork grease. "It all goes to the same place," Mama said. We never used napkins, and our table manners were boarding-house reach—no "Pass the peas, please." Conversation detracted from the sensuous pleasure of filling yourself. Every meal required meat and vegetables and dessert. We drank milk and iced tea ("ice-tea"). Our salads were fruit Jell-O and slaw. We also ate "poke salet" and wilted lettuce. Mama picked tender young pokeweed in the woods in the spring, before it turned poison, and cooked it a long time to get the bitterness out. We liked it with vinegar and minced boiled eggs. Wilted lettuce was tender new lettuce, shredded, with sliced radishes and green onions, and blasted with hot bacon grease to blanch the rawness. "Too many fresh vegetables in the summer gives people the scours," Daddy said.

14 July was blackberry-picking time. Mama would come back from the fields, where patches of "tame" berries had spread along the fencerows and creek banks, and exclaim, "There are worlds of berries down there!" She always "engaged" the berries to customers. By June, she would say, "I've already got forty gallons of berries engaged."

15 We strode out at dawn, in the dew, and picked until the midmorning sun bore down on our heads. To protect her hands from the thorns, Mama made gloves from old bluejeans, with the fingertips cut out. Following the berries down onto the creek bank, we perched on ledges and tiptoed on unsure footing through thickets. We tunnelled. When Mama saw an especially large berry just out of reach, she would lean her body against the bush and let it support her while she plucked the prize. We picked in quart baskets, then poured the berries into red-and-white Krey lard buckets. The berries settled quickly, and Mama picked an extra quart to top off the buckets. By nine o'clock, the sun was high, and I struggled to the house with my four gallons of blackberries, eager to wash the chiggers off and eat some cereal.

16 From the blackberries, I learned about money. I wouldn't eat the berries, even on my cereal: I wanted the money from selling them. Granny said everything was food, but I was hungry for something else—a kind of food that didn't grow in the ground. Yet I couldn't deny that we were always feasting. We ate sumptuous meals, never missing dessert. At Christmas, we slurped gallons of

boiled custard. Once in a while, Daddy brought home exotic treats—fried oysters in little goldfish cartons and hot tamales wrapped in corn shucks.

17 Food was better in town, we thought. It wasn't plain and ordinary and everyday. The main pleasures were there, too—the barbecue places, the movie shows, all the places to buy things. Woolworth's, with the pneumatic tubes overhead rushing money along a metallic mole tunnel up to a balcony. Lochridge & Ridgway, with an engraved sign on the third-story cornice: "Stoves, Appliances, Plows." On the mezzanine at that store, I bought my first phonograph records, brittle 78s of big-band music—Woody Herman and Glenn Miller, and Glen Gray and his Casa Loma Orchestra playing "No Name Jive." A circuit of the square took you past the grand furniture stores, the two dime stores, the shoe stores, the men's stores, the ladies' stores, the banks, the drugstores. You'd walk past the poolroom and an exhaust fan would blow the intoxicating smell of hamburgers in your face. Before she bought a freezer, Mama kept our meat in a rented food locker in town, near the ice company. She stored the butchered calf there, and she fetched hunks each week to fry. But hamburgers in town were better. They were greasier, and they came in waxed-paper packages.

18 At the corner drugstore, on the courthouse square, Mama and my younger sister Janice and I sat at filigreed wrought-iron tables on a black-and-white mosaic tile floor, eating peppermint ice cream. It was cold in there, under the ceiling fans. The ice cream was served elegantly, in paper cones sunk into black plastic holders. We were uptown.

19 In the summer of 1954, when I was about to enter high school, my mother got a chance to run a restaurant not far from our house, up on Highway 45. My parents knew the owner, and one day he stopped by and asked Mama if she'd like to manage it. She jumped at the opportunity to earn some money. "Why, anybody could cook hamburgers and French fries for the public," Mama said confidently. "That would be easy."

20 She was eager for a chance to buy us things. After the war, she had wanted Daddy to get out of dairy farming and run a small business of some kind, something that would bring in more cash, but he had refused to leave his parents' farm. He was an only child, and my grandparents depended on him to carry on. Mama had swallowed her disappointment. She was resilient and optimistic—when Janice and I were growing up, we always saw her sparkling like morning dew—and she always wanted more for her children.

21 She went to inspect the Mayfield Restaurant—a square cinder-block building with a picture-window view of the highway. There were no trees around, just a gravelled parking area. It was an informal sort of place, with a simple kitchen in back, a few pots and pans, a deep fryer, and a grill. There were five or six tables and a counter with stools. Mama saw potential. "Catfish platters," she said, with her face alight. "Fish and hush puppies. Slaw. French fries."

22 I was so excited I couldn't sleep. Running our own little restaurant could mean we wouldn't have to work in the garden. I wanted nothing more to do with okra and beans. I longed for deliverance and an endless supply of Co'-Colas.

23 A restaurant would hold no fears for her. "It's a chance to make big money," she told me. She told the owner she would try it for two weeks. If she liked the work, the deal was, she would be permitted to rent the business, for a hundred dollars a month.

24 "If it works out, maybe I could make a hundred dollars a *week*," she said.

25 I tagged along. I felt important waiting on customers—strangers driving along the highway and stopping right where I was for a bite to eat. I wanted to meet somebody from New York. When I drew glasses of Coca-Cola from the fountain, the Coke fizzed over crushed ice. I made grilled-cheese sandwiches in the grilled-cheese machine. I experimented with milkshakes. I was flying.

26 Most of all, I loved the jukebox. The first week Mama was there, the jukebox man came by to change records and insert new red-rimmed paper strips of titles: Doris Day and Johnnie Ray duets, "Teardrops from My Eyes," by Ruth Brown, and "P.S. I Love You," by a Kentucky vocal group called the Hilltoppers. I listened avidly to everything. I was fourteen and deeply concerned about my suntan, and I was saving pocket money to buy records.

27 The restaurant also had a television set, which sat in a corner with a "television light" on top—a prism of soft colors which supposedly kept people from ruining their eyes on TV waves. I had no experience with television, and I was captivated by Donald O'Connor's variety show and "I Love Lucy." When the evening crowd came in, Mama was kept busy as she trotted back and forth from the kitchen with her hamburger platters and catfish platters, but she would stop and laugh at something Lucy and Ethel were doing on the screen.

28 Two days before the trial period was up, Mama stopped going to the restaurant. She didn't give up the job voluntarily. My grandfather had stepped in and told her she couldn't go on. "We need you here at home," he said. "Running a hamburger joint out on the highway ain't fitten work."

29 Daddy—who had his own part-time job, delivering milk for a dairy—didn't stand up for her. "How would you make any money, anyway?" he demanded. "By the time you pay out that hundred dollars a month rent and all the expenses, you won't have nothing left. First thing you know, you'll get behind and then you'll be owing *him*."

30 Granny said, "And who's going to do your cooking here at home?"

31 Mama didn't mention the restaurant again, but I thought I saw a little fire go out of her. My own flame was burning brighter. I had had a glimpse of life outside the farm, and I wanted it. I can still see Mama emerging from that restaurant kitchen, carrying two hamburger platters and gabbing with her customers as if

they were old friends who had dropped in to visit and sit a spell. In the glass of the picture window, reflections from the television set flicker like Christmas candles.

EXERCISES

A. Determining the Main Idea and Writer's Purpose

Choose the best answer.

1. The main idea of the selection is that
   a. life for farm families was difficult.
   b. for women, farm life with its endless preoccupation with food and toil, overwhelmed any chance for independence.
   c. a woman's work is never done.
   d. farm life fosters resourcefulness, independence, and a feeling of being one with the land.

2. The writer's purpose in the selection is to
   a. explain the difficulties and limited opportunities in the lives of small farm owners.
   b. mourn an easier, lost way of life in rural communities.
   c. argue for more government support for farm families.
   d. examine the motivations for rebellion among young people raised on farms.

B. Comprehending Main Ideas

Choose the correct answer.

1. Daily life on the Mason's family farm for the women almost exclusively centered around
   a. caring for the dairy cows.
   b. growing and preparing food.
   c. the unpredictable weather.
   d. doing repairs around the farm.

2. Rather than cooking or helping around the farm, Mason preferred to spend her time
   a. daydreaming about her future as a stewardess.
   b. hanging out with her friends in town.

c. earning money by babysitting and selling blackberries.
d. reading.

3. Mason describes a sort of psychological poverty, the result of
   a. being denied the good life offered in the nearby town.
   b. never having enough food to eat.
   c. being considered inferior by the local townspeople.
   d. having an annual income well below the government's poverty level.

4. Mason's mother wanted to cook at the Mayfield Restaurant because
   a. she was tired of working so hard on the farm.
   b. she wanted to earn money to buy her family things that they didn't have.
   c. her husband was not making enough money for the family to survive.
   d. she intended to buy the business after a few months.

5. Which of the following was *not* mentioned as a reason that Mason's mother quit working at the restaurant?
   a. Her father-in-law told her that running a hamburger place wasn't fit work.
   b. Her husband didn't think she would make enough money after paying rent and expenses.
   c. She was needed at home to cook for her family.
   d. She found the work too tiring with all the other duties she had to perform at home.

C. Sequencing

The sentences in this excerpt from the selection may have been scrambled. Read the sentences and choose the sequence that puts them back into logical order. Do not refer to the original selection.

1. I think this dependence on nature was at the core of my rebellion. **2.** Farmers didn't take the initiative, I began to see; they reacted to whatever presented itself. **3.** More than that, though, I disliked women's part in that dependence. **4.** I hated the constant sense of helplessness before vast forces, the continuous threat of failure.

a. 3, 1, 2, 4
b. 1, 3, 2, 4
c. 2, 4, 3, 1
d. 1, 4, 2, 3
e. Correct as written.

D. Locating Supporting Details

For each main idea stated here, find details that support it.

1. Working with food was fraught with anxiety and desperation when I was a girl. [paragraph 7]

   a. ______________________________

   b. ______________________________

2. Both Mason and her mother saw great potential in the Mayfield Restaurant. [paragraphs 21–24]

   a. ______________________________

   ____

   b. ______________________________

   ____

E. Making Inferences

Write your answers to these inference questions in your own words.

1. From what Mason implies in paragraph 2, what might be the value of a "country upbringing"?

   ____

   ____

   ____

2. What can you infer about her family's economic situation from what Mason says in paragraphs 6 and 7?

   ____

   ____

   ____

3. Mason ends paragraph 18, in which she describes eating hamburgers and ice cream at the restaurant and the corner drugstore, by saying "we were uptown." What exactly does she mean in this phrase?

   ____

   ____

   ____

4. What is the connection between the point made in paragraph 8 about not taking initiative and Mason's mother being forced to quit the restaurant?

____

____

____

F. Understanding Vocabulary

Write the dictionary definition for each underlined word in the phrases below.

1. obsessed with food [paragraph 1] _______________
2. the toil drove me crazy [1] _______________
3. a recurrent food dream [6] _______________
4. laden with beautiful foods [6] _______________
5. working with food was fraught with anxiety [7] _______________
6. any portent of the morrow [7] _______________
7. I was acutely conscious [10] _______________
8. only plain hearty food [12] _______________
9. conversation detracted from [13] _______________
10. the sensuous pleasure [13] _______________
11. we ate sumptuous meals [16] _______________
12. on the mezzanine at that store [17] _______________
13. the intoxicating smell of hamburgers [17] _______________
14. she was resilient and optimistic [20] _______________
15. I listened avidly to everything [26] _______________

DISCUSSION QUESTIONS

1. What aspect of farm life as it affects women does Mason seem to be most concerned with? How can you tell?
2. The word *ambivalence* means "of two minds" or "having mixed feelings." Explain Mason's ambivalence as it is revealed in the essay.
3. As Mason describes it, the Mayfield Restaurant was basically a hamburger joint, yet it sounds very different from today's McDonald's, Burger King, or Wendy's. What are some differences between this small town restaurant and the typical fast-food outlet as you have experienced it?

EXPLORE THE WEB

For anyone interested in food, here are two well-known websites that contain a wealth of information about cooking and other culinary topics.

www.epicurious.com

www.joyofbaking.com

READING

Readings on Food and the Fast Food Industry

The first group of readings continue the theme of food production, preparation, and consumption. We begin with a selection from Eric Schlosser's best-selling exposé of the American fast food industry, *Fast Food Nation*, which looks at how McDonald's and other large fast food chains have changed the American landscape and the American workforce. Shannon Brownlee's report from *The Washington Post* explains the economics of pricing in fast food restaurants, focusing on the ubiquitous bag of French fries all such establishments serve. Finally, on the accompanying website, Calvin Trillin writes an amusing account of trying to find the perfect American hamburger in Paris, while also explaining why the French are so fond of American fast food.

Fast Food Nation: Behind the Counter

Eric Schlosser

When it was published in 2001, Eric Schlosser's best-selling book, *Fast Food Nation: The Dark Side of the All-American Meal*, became a contemporary classic. Schlosser, a correspondent for the *Atlantic Monthly*, investigated McDonald's, Burger King, Taco Bell, Kentucky Fried Chicken, and other fast food chains in the tradition of an old-fashioned muckraker. (A *muckraker* is a journalist who thoroughly investigates and exposes misconduct, usually in a particular industry.) In looking at the "dark side" of the fast food industry, Schlosser shows how the fast food industry has permanently changed potato production in Idaho and beef production in Iowa; meanwhile, the fast food industry is at least partly responsible for urban sprawl throughout the country and for the obesity epidemic. In this selection, Schlosser uses the city of Colorado Springs as the backdrop for a behind-the-scenes look at how a typical McDonald's operates.

VOCABULARY ANALYSIS

The Greek Prefix *auto-*

The word *automated* refers to machinery or equipment that runs by itself, without human intervention or control. (Schlosser alludes to automated site selection software programs and robotic drink machines.) The word *automatic* combines the Greek prefix *auto-*, meaning "self" with the Greek root *-matos*, meaning "willing." Many other words in English begin with *auto-*, among them *automobile* ("self-moving") and *autopsy* ("a medical examination of a corpse to determine the cause of death") from *auto-* + *opsis* ["sight", or literally, "a seeing for oneself"]. What do these words mean? Consult a dictionary if you are unsure.

automaton ______________________________

autocracy ______________________________

autonomy ______________________________

autograph ______________________________

Fast Food Nation: Behind the Counter

Eric Schlosser

Connecting Grammar to Writing

The first sentence of paragraphs 1 and 3 begin with a phrase expressing concession (*despite* and *regardless*), which is often a more interesting way of expressing contrast than the more common conjunctions *but* or *yet*.

1 Despite all the talk in Colorado about aerospace, biotech, computer software, telecommunications, and other industries of the future, the largest private employer in the state today is the restaurant industry. In Colorado Springs, the restaurant industry has grown much faster than the population. Over the last three decades the number of restaurants has increased fivefold. The number of chain restaurants has increased tenfold. In 1967, Colorado Springs had a total of twenty chain restaurants. Now it has twenty-one McDonald's.

2 The fast food chains feed off the sprawl of Colorado Springs, accelerate it, and help set its visual tone. They build large signs to attract motorists and look at cars the way predators view herds of prey. The chains thrive on traffic, lots of it, and put new restaurants at intersections where traffic is likely to increase, where development is heading but real estate prices are still low. Fast food restaurants often serve as the shock troops of sprawl, landing early and pointing the way. Some chains prefer to play follow the leader: when a new McDonald's opens, other fast food restaurants soon open nearby on the assumption that it must be a good location.

3 Regardless of the billions spent on marketing and promotion, all the ads on radio and TV, all the efforts to create brand loyalty, the major chains must live with the unsettling fact that more than 70 percent of fast food visits are "impulsive." The decision to stop for fast food is made on the spur of the moment, without much thought. The vast majority of customers do not set out to eat at a Burger King, a Wendy's, or a McDonald's. Often, they're not even planning to stop for food—until they see a sign, a familiar building, a set of golden arches. Fast food, like the tabloids at a supermarket checkout, is an impulse buy. In order to succeed, fast food restaurants must be seen.

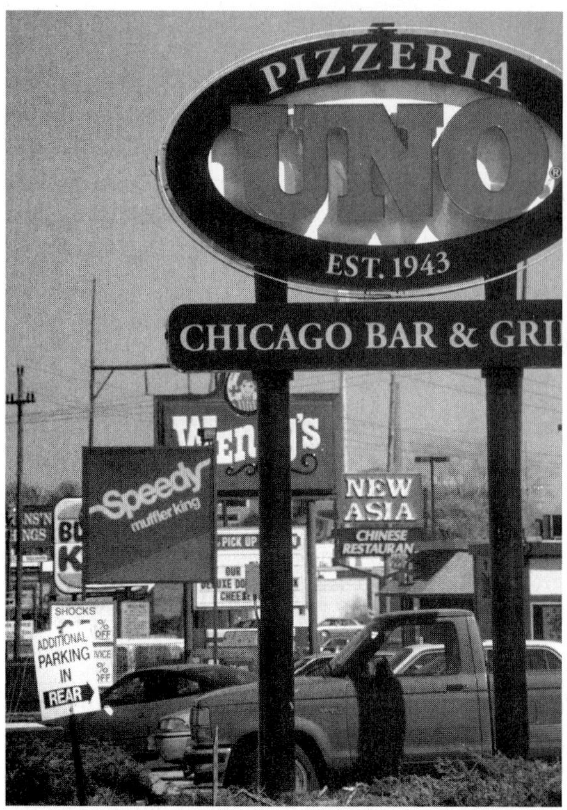

4 The McDonald's Corporation has perfected the art of restaurant site selection. In the early days Ray Kroc flew in a Cessna to find schools, aiming to put new restaurants nearby. McDonald's later used helicopters to assess regional growth patterns, looking for cheap land along highways and roads that would lie at the heart of future suburbs. In the 1980s, the chain became one of the world's leading purchasers of commercial satellite photography, using it to predict sprawl from outer space. McDonald's later developed a computer software program called Quintillion that automated its site-selection process, combining satellite imagery with detailed maps, demographic information, CAD drawings, and sales information from existing stores. "Geographic information systems" like Quintillion are now routinely used as site-selection tools by fast food chains and other retailers. As one marketing publication observed, the software developed by McDonald's permits businessmen to "spy on their customers with the same equipment once used to fight the cold war."

5 The McDonald's Corporation has used Colorado Springs as a test site for other types of restaurant technology, for software and machines designed to cut labor costs and serve fast food even faster. Steve Bigari, who owns five local McDonald's, showed me the new contraptions at his place on Constitution Avenue. It was a rounded, postmodern McDonald's on the eastern edge of the city. The drive-through lanes had automatic sensors buried in the asphalt to monitor the traffic. Robotic drink machines selected the proper cups, filled them with ice, and then filled them with soda. Dispensers powered by compressed carbon dioxide shot out uniform spurts of ketchup and mustard. An elaborate unit emptied frozen french fries from a white plastic bin into wire-mesh baskets for frying, lowered the baskets into hot oil, lifted them a few minutes later and gave them a brief shake, put them back into the oil until the fries were perfectly cooked, and then dumped the fries

underneath heat lamps, crisp and ready to be served. Television monitors in the kitchen instantly displayed the customer's order. And advanced computer software essentially ran the kitchen, assigning tasks to various workers for maximum efficiency, predicting future orders on the basis of ongoing customer flow.

6 Bigari was cordial, good-natured, passionate about his work, proud of the new devices. He told me the new software brought the "just in time" production philosophy of Japanese automobile plants to the fast food business, a philosophy that McDonald's has renamed Made for You. As he demonstrated one contraption after another—including a wireless hand-held menu that uses radio waves to transmit orders—a group of construction workers across the street put the finishing touches on a new subdivision called Constitution Hills. The streets had patriotic names, and the cattle ranch down the road was for sale.

Throughput

7 Every Saturday Elisa Zamot gets up at 5:15 in the morning. It's a struggle, and her head feels groggy as she steps into the shower. Her little sisters, Cookie and Sabrina, are fast asleep in their beds. By 5:30, Elisa's showered, done her hair, and put on her McDonald's uniform. She's sixteen, bright-eyed and olive-skinned, pretty and petite, ready for another day of work. Elisa's mother usually drives her the half-mile or so to the restaurant, but sometimes Elisa walks, leaving home before the sun rises. Her family's modest townhouse sits beside a busy highway on the south side of Colorado Springs, in a largely poor and working-class neighborhood. Throughout the day, sounds of traffic fill the house, the steady whoosh of passing cars. But when Elisa heads for work, the streets are quiet, the sky's still dark, and the lights are out in the small houses and rental apartments along the road.

8 When Elisa arrives at McDonald's, the manager unlocks the door and lets her in. Sometimes the husband-and-wife cleaning crew are just finishing up. More often, it's just Elisa and the manager in the restaurant, surrounded by an empty parking lot. For the next hour or so, the two of them get everything ready. They turn on the ovens and grills. They go downstairs into the basement and get food and supplies for the morning shift. They get the paper cups, wrappers, cardboard containers, and packets of condiments. They step into the big freezer and get the frozen bacon, the frozen pancakes, and the frozen cinnamon rolls. They get the frozen hash browns, the frozen biscuits, the frozen McMuffins. They get the cartons of scrambled egg mix and orange juice mix. They bring the food upstairs and start preparing it before any customers appear, thawing some things in the microwave and cooking other things on the grill. They put the cooked food in special cabinets to keep it warm.

9 The restaurant opens for business at seven o'clock, and for the next hour or so, Elisa and the manager hold down the fort, handling all the orders. As the place starts to get busy, other employees arrive. Elisa works behind the counter. She takes orders and hands food to customers from breakfast through lunch.

When she finally walks home, after seven hours of standing at a cash register, her feet hurt. She's wiped out. She comes through the front door, flops onto the living room couch, and turns on the TV. And the next morning she gets up at 5:15 again and starts the same routine.

10 Up and down Academy Boulevard, along South Nevada, Circle Drive, and Woodman Road, teenagers like Elisa run the fast food restaurants of Colorado Springs. Fast food kitchens often seem like a scene from *Bugsy Malone*, a film in which all the actors are children pretending to be adults. No other industry in the United States has a workforce so dominated by adolescents. About two-thirds of the nation's fast food workers are under the age of twenty. Teenagers open the fast food outlets in the morning, close them at night, and keep them going at all hours in between. Even the managers and assistant managers are sometimes in their late teens. Unlike Olympic gymnastics—an activity in which teenagers consistently perform at a higher level than adults—there's nothing about the work in a fast food kitchen that requires young employees. Instead of relying upon a small, stable, well-paid, and well-trained workforce, the fast food industry seeks out part-time, unskilled workers who are willing to accept low pay. Teenagers have been the perfect candidates for these jobs, not only because they are less expensive to hire than adults, but also because their youthful inexperience makes them easier to control.

11 The labor practices of the fast food industry have their origins in the assembly line systems adopted by American manufacturers in the early twentieth century. Business historian Alfred D. Chandler has argued that a high rate of "throughput" was the most important aspect of these mass production systems. A factory's throughput is the speed and volume of its flow—a much more crucial measurement, according to Chandler, than the number of workers it employs or the value of its machinery. With innovative technology and the proper organization, a small number of workers can produce an enormous amount of goods cheaply. Throughput is all about increasing the speed of assembly, about doing things faster in order to make more.

12 Although the McDonald brothers had never encountered the term "throughput" or studied "scientific management," they instinctively grasped the underlying principles and applied them in the Speedee Service System. The restaurant operating scheme they developed has been widely adopted and refined over the past half century. The ethos of the assembly line remains at its core. The fast food industry's obsession with throughput has altered the way millions of Americans work, turned commercial kitchens into small factories, and changed familiar foods into commodities that are manufactured.

13 At Burger King restaurants, frozen hamburger patties are placed on a conveyor belt and emerge from a broiler ninety seconds later fully cooked. The ovens at Pizza Hut and at Domino's also use conveyor belts to ensure standardized cooking times. The ovens at McDonald's look like commercial laundry presses, with big steel hoods that swing down and grill hamburgers on both sides at once. The burgers, chicken, french fries, and buns are all frozen when they arrive at a McDonald's. The

shakes and sodas begin as syrup. At Taco Bell restaurants the food is "assembled," not prepared. The guacamole isn't made by workers in the kitchen; it's made at a factory in Michoacán, Mexico, then frozen and shipped north. The chain's taco meat arrives frozen and precooked in vacuum-sealed plastic bags. The beans are dehydrated and look like brownish corn flakes. The cooking process is fairly simple. "Everything's add water," a Taco Bell employee told me. "Just add hot water."

14 Although Richard and Mac McDonald introduced the division of labor to the restaurant business, it was a McDonald's executive named Fred Turner who created a production system of unusual thoroughness and attention to detail. In 1958, Turner put together an operations and training manual for the company that was seventy-five pages long, specifying how almost everything should be done. Hamburgers were always to be placed on the grill in six neat rows; french fries had to be exactly 0.28 inches thick. The McDonald's operations manual today has ten times the number of pages and weighs about four pounds. Known within the company as "the Bible," it contains precise instructions on how various appliances should be used, how each item on the menu should look, and how employees should greet customers. Operators who disobey these rules can lose their franchises. Cooking instructions are not only printed in the manual, they are often designed into the machines. A McDonald's kitchen is full of buzzers and flashing lights that tell employees what to do.

15 At the front counter, computerized cash registers issue their own commands. Once an order has been placed, buttons light up and suggest other menu items that can be added. Workers at the counter are told to increase the size of an order by recommending special promotions, pushing dessert, pointing out the financial logic behind the purchase of a larger drink. While doing so, they are instructed to be upbeat and friendly. "Smile with a greeting and make a positive first impression," a Burger King training manual suggests. "Show them you are GLAD TO SEE THEM. Include eye contact with the cheerful greeting."

16 The strict regimentation at fast food restaurants creates standardized products. It increases the throughput. And it gives fast food companies an enormous amount of power over their employees. "When management determines exactly how every task is to be done ... and can impose its own rules about pace, output, quality, and technique," the sociologist Robin Leidner has noted, " [it] makes workers increasingly interchangeable." The management no longer depends upon the talents or skills of its workers—those things are built into the operating system and machines. Jobs that have been "de-skilled" can be filled cheaply. The need to retain any individual worker is greatly reduced by the ease with which he or she can be replaced.

17 Teenagers have long provided the fast food industry with the bulk of its work force. The industry's rapid growth coincided with the baby-boom expansion of that age group. Teenagers were in many ways the ideal candidates for these low-paying jobs. Since most teenagers still lived at home, they could afford to work for wages too low to support an adult, and until recently, their limited skills attracted few other

employers. A job at a fast food restaurant became an American rite of passage, a first job soon left behind for better things. The flexible terms of employment in the fast food industry also attracted housewives who needed extra income. As the number of baby-boom teenagers declined, the fast food chains began to hire other marginalized workers: recent immigrants, the elderly, and the handicapped.

18 English is now the second language of at least one-sixth of the nation's restaurant workers, and about one-third of that group speaks no English at all. The proportion of fast food workers who cannot speak English is even higher. Many know only the names of the items on the menu; they speak "McDonald's English."

19 The fast food industry now employs some of the most disadvantaged members of American society. It often teaches basic job skills—such as getting to work on time—to people who can barely read, whose lives have been chaotic or shut off from the mainstream. Many individual franchisees are genuinely concerned about the well-being of their workers. But the stance of the fast food industry on issues involving employee training, the minimum wage, labor unions, and overtime pay strongly suggests that its motives in hiring the young, the poor, and the handicapped are hardly altruistic.

EXERCISES

A. Determining the Main Idea and Writer's Purpose

Choose the best answer.

1. The main idea of the selection is that
   a. the restaurant industry is the largest private employer in Colorado.
   b. Colorado Springs is McDonald's test site for designing restaurant technology, for software, and for machines used to cut labor costs.
   c. McDonald's is particularly successful because of its regimented approach to hiring and training workers and its standardized menu.
   d. McDonald's Corporation has perfected the process of selecting sites and standardizing every aspect of its restaurant operations.

2. The writer's purpose in the selection is to
   a. argue that the reader should not patronize McDonald's and other fast food restaurants.
   b. criticize fast food restaurants for putting independent restaurants out of business.
   c. examine some common business practices McDonald's employs that the average person might not be aware of.
   d. investigate the hiring, training, and salary practices McDonald's uses with its largely teenage workforce.

B. Comprehending Main Ideas

Choose the correct answer.

1. McDonald's and other fast food chains prefer to situate new restaurants
   a. in established neighborhoods with a high population density.
   b. near areas of high traffic where land is still cheap and where future suburbs will develop.
   c. in inner-city neighborhoods where labor is cheap.
   d. along heavily traveled interstates and other major highways.

2. Despite all the money fast food companies spend on marketing, promotion, and advertising, Schlosser states that most customers eat at such restaurants because
   a. the food is served quickly and is cheap and filling.
   b. fast food restaurants are everywhere and are therefore easy to patronize.
   c. they see a sign or a familiar building and stop in on impulse.
   d. they know that the food served is standardized and therefore safe.

3. To select new restaurant sites, McDonald's currently
   a. employs satellite photography and a computer software program.
   b. follows the lead of other fast food restaurants and locates stores near other existing establishments.
   c. takes customer surveys to find out where diners would like new restaurants to be built.
   d. chooses areas close to schools to achieve a ready-made customer base.

4. As used in the fast food industry, the term *throughput* refers to
   a. the number of customers who order their food at a fast food restaurant's drive-through window.
   b. increasing the speed of assembly and doing every step faster to produce more in a given time.
   c. shortening the amount of time customers eat their meals inside the restaurant, thus ensuring faster customer turnover and higher profits.
   d. shortening the number of items on a restaurant's menu so that fewer employees are needed to assemble the food.

5. Throughout the selection, Schlosser emphasizes two chief characteristics of fast food restaurants and their operations, namely
   a. efficiency and high quality.
   b. good opportunities for employee advancement and fringe benefits.
   c. genuine friendliness and a desire to serve.
   d. standardization and regimentation.

C. Identifying Supporting Details

Place an **X** in the space for each sentence from the selection that *directly* supports this main idea: "Teenagers have long provided the fast food industry with the bulk of its workforce."

1. _____ [Workers] are instructed to be upbeat and friendly.
2. _____ A McDonald's kitchen is full of buzzers and flashing lights that tell employees what to do.
3. _____ Instead of relying upon a small, stable, well-paid, and well-trained workforce, the fast food industry seeks out part-time, unskilled workers who are willing to accept low pay.
4. _____ Teenagers have been the perfect candidates for these jobs, not only because they are less expensive to hire than adults, but also because their youthful inexperience makes them easier to control.
5. _____ The industry's rapid growth coincided with the baby-boom expansion of that age group [teenagers].
6. _____ Since most teenagers still lived at home, they could afford to work for wages too low to support an adult, and until recently, their limited skills attracted few other employers.
7. _____ A job at a fast food restaurant became an American rite of passage, a first job soon left behind for better things.
8. _____ As the number of baby-boom teenagers declined, the fast food chains began to hire other marginalized workers: recent immigrants, the elderly, and the handicapped.
9. _____ English is now the second language of at least one-sixth of the nation's restaurant workers, and about one-third of that group speaks no English at all.

D. Making Inferences

For each of these statements write **Y** (yes) if the inference is an accurate one, **N** (no) if the inference is an inaccurate one, and **CT** (can't tell) if the writer does not give you enough information to make an inference one way or another.

1. _____ Since most customers stop at a fast food restaurant on impulse, it is important that its signs be conspicuous from the street. [paragraph 2]
2. _____ McDonald's is not the only fast food business to use geographic information systems; most of the other chains employ the same technology. [paragraph 2]

3. ____ Foreign countries welcome McDonald's outlets in their countries as symbols of American culture and progress. [essay as a whole]

4. ____ McDonald's adopted the production philosophy, "just in time," from the Japanese automobile industry which improved the speed with which food is made and served to customers. [paragraph 6]

5. ____ "Throughput" means that fast food outlets can save money by reducing labor costs. [paragraphs 11–12]

6. ____ Fast food chains prefer to hire teenagers to staff their restaurants because they are more energetic and more enthusiastic about work than are older workers. [paragraph 17]

E. Interpreting Meaning

Where appropriate, write your answers for these questions in your own words.

1. Read paragraph 2 again. What purpose is served by Schlosser's use of these words: *predators*, *prey*, and *shock troops*?

   ____

   ____

   What do these phrases suggest about his point of view?

   ____

2. Read paragraph 4 again. A good title for this paragraph would be
   a. "How McDonald's Selects New Sites."
   b. "Restaurant Locations."
   c. "Uses for Commercial Satellite Photography."
   d. "Site Selection Tools."

3. In your own words, state the main point of paragraph 5.

   ____

   ____

   Now list three important supporting details for that point.

   ____

   ____

   ____

4. In paragraph 8 Schlosser uses the word *frozen* six times. Why?

   ____

5. Paragraph 13 consists only of several examples but no stated main idea. Based on the many details in the paragraph, what is Schlosser's point?

____

____

F. Understanding Vocabulary

Look through the paragraphs listed below and find a word that matches each definition. Refer to a dictionary if necessary. An example has been done for you.

EXAMPLE: evaluate, calculate [paragraph 4] ______assess______

1. pertaining to human population [4] ________________
2. a complicated piece of equipment [both 5 and 6] ________________
3. warm and sincere, friendly [5–6] ________________
4. plain, not showy [7–8] ________________
5. critical, very important [10–11] ________________
6. inventive, newly introduced [10–11] ________________
7. fundamental value, character [11–12] ________________
8. uniformity, rigid order [16–17] ________________
9. confined to the outer limits or edges, describing social standing [18–19] ________________
10. unselfish, selfless [18–19] ________________

G. Annotating Exercise

In the left margin, annotate the relevant sections of the selection in preparation to write an essay on the particular ways the jobs at McDonald's have been "deskilled."

DISCUSSION QUESTIONS

1. In relation to the selection as a whole, how effective is the description of Elisa Zamot's typical workday at McDonald's?
2. Do you eat at fast food restaurants regularly? If so, what are their attractions? If not, why not?

3. On balance, what is Schlosser's opinion of McDonald's hiring practices? In describing some McDonald's workers as "marginalized" (see paragraph 17), is Schlosser perhaps being too harsh? What's so wrong with giving teenagers recent immigrants, the elderly, or the handicapped jobs? What, ultimately, is his concern with the company's employment practices?

EXPLORE THE WEB

Compare these websites for the four major fast food chain restaurants. Which gives the most complete nutritional information about the food served at their establishments? Which site provides the easiest access to this information?

McDonald's: www.mcdonalds.com

Burger King: www.burgerking.com

In-N-Out Burger: www.inandout.com

Jack in the Box: www.jackinthebox.com

In December 2006 the prestigious research group, the Institute of Medicine, released a report titled "Food Marketing to Children and Youth: Threat or Opportunity?" which targets the advertising of junk food on television as a major cause of child and adolescent obesity. You can read the report and check out other helpful links pertaining to this issue at this address:

www.iom.edu/report.asp?id=31330

Pricing French Fries: A Lesson in Economics

Shannon Brownlee

Shannon Brownlee is currently a Schwartz Senior Fellow at the New America Foundation; she specializes in writing about scientific subjects. She has a degree from the University of California at Santa Cruz, where she has done research on the behavior and sounds of wild dolphins. Her stories and essays about medicine, health care, and biotechnology have appeared in a wide variety of publications such as the *Atlantic Monthly, Business Week, Discover, The New York Times Magazine, Salon, The New Republic,* and *Time*. Her writing has won numerous awards. This article was first published in the *Washington Post National Weekly Edition*.

VOCABULARY ANALYSIS

The Suffixes *-ist, -or,* and *-eur*

Brownlee's article contains three words ending in suffixes used to describe a person who does something. The most common is *-ist*, which refers broadly to one who one who specializes in a field. A *nutritionist* [paragraph 15], therefore, specializes in nutrition, and a *linguist* specializes in languages. This suffix can also describe a supporter or follower; for example, a *feminist* supports women's rights, and a *pacifist* is one who promotes world peace and opposes war.

The suffix *-or* is attached to a noun, usually describing a person or thing that performs a specified action. A *purveyor* [paragraph 17] is a seller of goods; an *editor* edits; a *janitor* performs maintenance; the *accelerator* determines the car's rate of acceleration or speed. It is a variation of the more common suffix *-er*, as in *teacher* or *woodworker.*

The suffix *-eur* is the least common: It almost always attaches to words derived from French. A *restaurateur* [paragraph 14—*not* restauranteur!] manages or owns a restaurant; an *entrepreneur* establishes a business; an *auteur* is a film director—from the French word *autor* ("author"). The feminine version of this ending is *-euse* as in *chanteuse*, a female singer.

Which of the three suffixes listed above is the appropriate one for these nouns? Check a dictionary if you are unsure.

one who exhibits himself for sexual pleasure ____________

a person who commits sabotage ____________

a person who is in debt ____________

a physician who specializes in orthopedics ____________

one who commits treason or betrays his country ____________

Pricing French Fries: A Lesson in Economics

Shannon Brownlee

1 It was probably inevitable that one day people would start suing McDonald's for making them fat. That day came last summer when New York lawyer Samuel Hirsch, filed several lawsuits against McDonald's, as well as four other fast-food companies, on the grounds that they had failed to adequately disclose the bad health effects of their menus. One of the suits involves a Bronx teenager who tips the scale at 400 pounds and whose mother, in papers filed in U.S. District Court in Manhattan, said, "I always believed McDonald's food was healthy for my son."

2 Uh-huh. And the tooth fairy really put that dollar under his pillow. But once you've stopped sniggering at our litigious society, remember that it once seemed

equally ludicrous that smokers could successfully sue tobacco companies for their addiction to cigarettes. And while nobody is claiming that Big Macs are addictive—at least not yet—the restaurant industry and food packagers have clearly helped give many Americans the roly-poly shape they have today. This is not to say that the folks in the food industry want us to be fat. But make no mistake: When they do well economically, we gain weight.

3 It wasn't always thus. Readers of a certain age can remember a time when a trip to McDonald's seemed like a treat and when a small bag of French fries, a plain burger and a 12-ounce Coke seemed like a full meal. Fast food wasn't any healthier back then; we simply ate a lot less of it.

4 How did today's oversized appetites become the norm? It didn't happen by accident or some inevitable evolutionary process. It was to a large degree the result of consumer manipulation. Fast food's marketing strategies, which make perfect sense from a business perspective, succeed only when they induce a substantial number of us to overeat. To see how this all came about, let's go back to 1983, when John Martin became CEO of the ailing Taco Bell franchise and met a young marketing whiz named Elliott Bloom.

5 Using so-called "smart research," a then-new kind of in-depth consumer survey, Bloom had figured out that fast-food franchises were sustained largely by a core group of "heavy users," mostly young, single males, who ate at such restaurants as often as 20 times a month. In fact, 30 percent of Taco Bell's customers accounted for 70 percent of its sales. Through his surveys, Bloom learned what might seem obvious now but wasn't at all clear 20 years ago—these guys ate at fast-food joints because they had absolutely no interest in cooking for themselves and didn't give a rip about the nutritional quality of the food. They didn't even care much about the taste. All that mattered was that it was fast and cheap. Martin figured Taco Bell could capture a bigger share of these hard-core customers by streamlining the food production and pricing main menu items at 49, 59 and 69 cents—well below its competitors.

6 It worked. Taco Bell saw a dramatic increase in patrons, with no drop in revenue per customer. As Martin told Greg Critser, author of "Fat Land: How Americans Became the Fattest People in the World," when Taco Bell ran a test of its new pricing in Texas, "within seven days of initiating the test, the average check was right back to where it was before—it was just four instead of three items." In other words, cheap food induced people to eat more. Taco Bell's rising sales figures—up 14 percent by 1989 and 12 percent more the next year—forced other fast-food franchises to wake up and smell the burritos. By the late '80s, everybody from Burger King to Wendy's was cutting prices and seeing an increase in customers—including bargain-seeking Americans who weren't part of that original hardcore group.

7 If the marketing strategy had stopped there, we might not be the nation of fatties that we are today. But the imperatives of the marketplace are growth and

rising profits, and once everybody had slashed prices to the bone, the franchises had to look for a new way to satisfy investors.

8 And what they found was ... super-sizing.

9 Portion sizes had already been creeping upward. As early as 1972, for example, McDonald's introduced its large-size fries (large being a relative term, since at 3.5 ounces the '72 "large" was smaller than a medium serving today). But McDonald's increased portions only reluctantly, because the company's founder, Ray Kroc, didn't like the image of lowbrow, cheap food. If people wanted more French fries, he would say, "they can buy two bags." But price competition had grown so fierce that the only way to keep profits up was to offer bigger and bigger portions. By 1988, McDonald's had introduced a 32-ounce "super size" soda and "super size" fries.

10 The deal with all these enhanced portions is that the customer gets a lot more food for a relatively small increase in price. So just how does that translate into bigger profits? Because the actual food in a fast-food meal is incredibly cheap. For every dollar a quick-service franchiser spends to produce a food item, only 20 cents, on average, goes toward food. The rest is eaten up by expenses such as salaries, packaging, electric bills, insurance and, of course, the ubiquitous advertising that got you in the door or to the drive-through lane in the first place.

11 Here's how it works. Let's say a $1.25 bag of French fries costs $1 to produce. The potatoes, oil and salt account for only 20 cents of the cost. The other 80 cents goes toward all the other expenses. If you add half again as many French fries to the bag and sell it for $1.50, the non-food expenses stay pretty much constant, while the extra food costs the franchise only 10 more pennies. The fast-food joint makes an extra 15 cents in pure profit, and the customer thinks he's getting a good deal. And he would be, if he actually needed the extra food, which he doesn't because the nation is awash in excess calories.

12 That 20 percent rule, by the way, applies to all food products, whether it's a bag of potato chips, the 2,178-calorie mountain of fried seafood at Red Lobster or the 710-calorie slab of dessert at the Cheesecake Factory. Some foods are even less expensive to make. The flakes of your kid's breakfast cereal, for example, account for only 5 percent of the total amount Nabisco or General Mills spent to make and sell them. Soda costs less to produce than any drink except tap water (which nobody seems to drink anymore), thanks to a 1970s invention that cut the expense of making high-fructose corn syrup. There used to be real sugar in Coke; when Coca-Cola and other bottlers switched to high-fructose corn syrup in 1984, they slashed sweetener costs by 20 percent. That's why 7-Eleven can sell the 64-ounce Double Gulp—half a gallon of soda and nearly 600 calories—for only 37 cents more than the 16-ounce, 89-cent regular Gulp. You'd feel ripped off if you bought the smaller size. Who wouldn't?

13 The final step in the fattening of America was the "upsell," a stroke of genius whose origins are buried somewhere in the annals of marketing. You're already

at the counter, you've ordered a cheeseburger value meal for $3.74, and your server says, "Would you like to super-size that for only $4.47?" Such a deal. The chain extracts an extra 73 cents from the customer, and the customer gets an extra 400 calories—bringing the total calorie count to 1,550, more than half the recommended intake for an adult man for an entire day.

14 When confronted with their contribution to America's expanding waistline, restaurateurs and food packagers reply that eating less is a matter of individual responsibility. But that's not how the human stomach works. If you put more food in front of people, they eat more, as studies have consistently shown over the last decade. My personal favorite: The researcher gave moviegoers either a half-gallon or a gallon bucket of popcorn before the show (it was "Payback," with Mel Gibson) and then measured how much they ate when they returned what was left in the containers afterward. Nobody could polish off the entire thing, but subjects ate 44 percent more when given the bigger bucket.

Connecting Grammar to Writing

Underline the transitional words and phrases in the first four sentences of paragraph 15 and identify the type of logical connection they establish in their respective sentences. Note, too, the way they are set off in the sentence with commas.

15 The downside, of course, is that 20 years of Big Food has trained us to think that oceanic drinks and gargantuan portions are normal. Indeed, once fast food discovered that big meals meant big profits, everybody from Heineken to Olive Garden to Frito Lay followed suit. Today, says Lisa Young, a nutritionist at New York University, super-sizing has pervaded every segment of the food industry. For her PhD, Young documented the changes in portion sizes for dozens of foods over the past several decades. M&M/Mars, for example, has increased the size of candy bars such as Milky Way and Snickers four times since 1970. Starbucks introduced the 20-ounce "venti" size in 1999 and discontinued its "short" 8-ounce cup. When 22-ounce Heinekens were introduced, Young reported, the company sold 24 million of them the first year, and attributed the sales to the "big-bottle gimmick." Even Lean Cuisine and Weight Watchers now advertise "Hearty Portions" of their diet meals. Everything from plates and muffin tins to restaurant chairs and the cut of our Levi's has expanded to match our growing appetites, and the wonder of it all is not that 60 percent of Americans are overweight or obese, but rather that 40 percent of us are not.

16 Where does it end? Marketers and restaurateurs may scoff at lawsuits like the ones brought this summer against fast-food companies, and they have a point: Adults are ultimately responsible for what they put in their own mouths. But maybe there's hope for us yet, because it looks as if fast-food companies have marketed themselves into a corner. "Omnipresence"—the McDonald's strategy of beating out competitors by opening new stores, sometimes as many as 1,000 a year—"has proved costly and self-cannibalizing," says author Critser. With 13,000 McDonald's units alone, most of America is so saturated with fast food there's practically no place left to put a drive-through lane. Now, fast-food companies are killing each other in a new price war they can't possibly sustain, and McDonald's just suffered its first quarterly loss since the company went public 47 years ago.

17 The obvious direction to go is down, toward what nutritional policymakers are calling "smart-sizing." Or at least it should be obvious, if food purveyors cared as much about helping Americans slim down as they would have us believe. Instead of urging Americans to "Get Active, Stay Active"—Pepsi Cola's new criticism-deflecting slogan—how about bringing back the 6.5-ounce sodas of the '40s and '50s? Or, imagine, as Critser does, the day when McDonald's advertises Le Petit Mac, made with high-grade beef, a delicious whole-grain bun and hawked by, say, Serena Williams. One way or another, as Americans wake up to the fact that obesity is killing nearly as many citizens as cigarettes are, jumbo burgers and super-size fries will seem like less of a bargain.

EXERCISES

A. Determining the Main Idea and Writer's Purpose

Choose the best answer.

1. The main idea of the selection is that
   a. streamlining food production, lower prices, and larger portions are major causes of increased obesity rates.
   b. American consumers have demanded ever-increasing portion sizes, resulting in increased obesity rates.
   c. the proliferation of fast food outlets in the United States has led to more people eating most of their meals away from home.
   d. super-sizing has crept into nearly every aspect of American life, from the food we eat, to the cars we drive, to the houses we live in.

2. The writer's purpose in the selection is to
   a. convince people to boycott fast food outlets and super-sized meals.
   b. examine American eating habits in light of increased obesity rates.
   c. examine pricing strategies and profits in the fast food industry.
   d. argue for government regulation of the fast food industry.

B. Comprehending Main Ideas

Choose the correct answer.

1. In describing Americans' weight gain over the past twenty years or so, Brownlee says that it occurred largely
   a. by accident.
   b. as part of an inevitable evolutionary process.
   c. because Americans have become addicted to fast food.
   d. as the result of deliberate manipulation of consumers.

2. Using "smart research," Taco Bell determined that the so-called heavy users eat at fast food restaurants as often as twenty times a month. These heavy users are typically
   a. young children who insist that their parents take them out for fast food.
   b. harried parents too busy with their jobs and other responsibilities to cook.
   c. young single males who don't cook and who want fast, cheap food.
   d. teenagers who enjoy hanging out at fast food restaurants because there is no place else to go.

3. By the late 1980s, other fast food chains were imitating Taco Bell and also seeing an increase in customers, chiefly by
   a. changing from a menu of hamburgers and French fries to burritos and tacos.
   b. cutting prices.
   c. doing more mass media advertising.
   d. redesigning their restaurants to make them more attractive.

4. In a typical $1.25 bag of French fries, the total cost of the actual potatoes, oil, and salt is about
   a. a dollar.
   b. 75 cents.
   c. 50 cents.
   d. 20 cents.

5. Brownlee concludes that fast food outlets are in trouble because they have
   a. opened so many stores that the market has become saturated.
   b. been the target of lawsuits from customers who blame super-sizing for their obesity and other health problems.
   c. encouraged people to be irresponsible in their eating habits.
   d. seen a loss of market share, meaning fewer profits and lower stock prices.

C. Sequencing

The sentences in this excerpt from the selection may have been scrambled. Read the sentences and choose the sequence that puts them back into logical order. Do not refer to the original selection.

1. The deal with all these enhanced portions is that the customer gets a lot more food for a relatively small increase in price. **2.** So just how does that translate into bigger profits? **3.** Because the actual food in a fast-food meal is incredibly cheap. **4.** For every dollar a quick-service franchiser spends to produce a food item, only 20 cents, on average, goes toward food. **5.** The rest is eaten up by expenses such as salaries, packaging, electric bills, insurance and, of course, the ubiquitous advertising that got you in the door or to the drive-through in the first place.

a. 1, 3, 4, 2, 5
b. 2, 5, 4, 1, 3
c. 4, 5, 3, 1, 2
d. Correct as written.

D. Interpreting Meaning

Where appropriate, write your answers to these questions in your own words.

1. Which of these sentences from the article best states the writer's thesis?
   a. It was probably inevitable that one day people would start suing McDonald's for making them fat.
   b. And while nobody is claiming that Big Macs are addictive—at least not yet—the restaurant industry and food packagers have clearly helped give many Americans the roly-poly shape they have today.
   c. The deal with all these enhanced portions is that the customer gets a lot more food for a relatively small increase in price.
   d. The final step in the fattening of America was the "upsell," a stroke of genius whose origins are buried somewhere in the annals of marketing.

2. What type of evidence does Brownlee rely on most to support her points throughout the article as a whole?
   a. the testimony of authorities and experts in the food industry
   b. the personal experiences of veteran fast food patrons who are now obese
   c. her own subjective opinion and observations
   d. facts, statistics, and examples from both marketing studies and scientific research studies

3. In paragraph 1 Brownlee cites a lawsuit filed by a 400-pound Bronx teenager against McDonald's. The boy's mother is quoted as saying, "I always believed McDonald's food was healthy for my son." Brownlee then goes on to say in paragraph 2, "Uh-huh. And the tooth fairy really put that dollar under his pillow." Which of the following most accurately characterizes Brownlee's tone, or emotional feeling, regarding the lawsuit and the mother's statement?

a. hostility, anger
b. sincerity, honesty
c. skepticism, sarcasm
d. humor, amusement

4. From the information presented in paragraph 5, it appears that Taco Bell's "smart research"—an in-depth customer survey—was intended to uncover
   a. the specific demographic group that was the most frequent patron of fast food establishments.
   b. the type of Mexican food that was most appealing to its customers.
   c. how prices could be cut to compete effectively with other fast food outlets.
   d. how the food could be made more appealing to customers' taste and yet could still be prepared fast and taste good.

5. Which of the following would be the best title for paragraph 11?
   a. "How to Price French Fries"
   b. "Food Economics 101"
   c. "How Restaurants Profit from Larger Sizes"
   d. "The Cost of Producing French Fries"

6. We can deduce from the first sentence of paragraph 13 that the word *upsell* means
   a. "to intake."
   b. "to increase the price of."
   c. "to super-size an order."
   d. "to market innovatively."

7. What specifically does Brownlee mean when she writes in paragraph 14 "that's not how the human stomach works"?

   ____

   ____

8. Which of these is the most accurate statement regarding Brownlee's opinion about the origin of the current obesity epidemic?
   a. The fast food restaurants and their super-sizing strategies—the related increase in portion size—are the primary culprits.
   b. Individuals are responsible for monitoring their own intake of calories, and blaming the fast food industry for trying to stay profitable is unfair.

c. Individuals have the responsibility to monitor their own eating habits, but the fast food industry deserves at least some of the blame for increasing portion size.

d. Fast food outlets have proliferated so rapidly across the country that people have little choice but to eat at these establishments.

E. Understanding Vocabulary

Look through the paragraphs listed below and find a word that matches each definition. Refer to a dictionary if necessary. An example has been done for you.

EXAMPLE: laughing, snickering [paragraphs 1–2] ___sniggering___

1. tending to engage in lawsuits [1–2] ____________
2. a standard, model, or pattern regarded as typical [3–4] ____________
3. in poor health, economically troubled [3–4] ____________
4. encouraged, stimulated, persuaded [6–7] ____________
5. requirements, rules, principles [6–7] ____________
6. seeming to exist everywhere at once [9–10] ____________
7. saturated, overflowing with [10–11] ____________
8. chronological records of events, history [12–13] ____________
9. exceptionally large, gigantic [15] ____________
10. penetrated or spread throughout [15] ____________
11. mock, laugh at with derision [16–17] ____________
12. the concept of being everywhere at once [16–17] ____________
13. causing to turn aside, ward off [16–17] ____________
14. peddled or sold goods aggressively [16–17] ____________

DISCUSSION QUESTIONS

1. What is your opinion about the lawsuit filed against McDonald's and four other fast food companies by the Bronx teenager who weighs 400 pounds? His claim is that the companies "had failed to adequately disclose the bad health effects of their menus," thus contributing to his obesity. Should obese people have the right to sue restaurants, claiming that eating their food made them obese? Or is it their responsibility to acquire nutritional information and to eat more sensibly?
2. Brownlee mentions in paragraph 3 that "readers of a certain age" remember that eating at, say, McDonald's or Burger King used to be considered a treat, meaning that it was something done only occasionally. What are some of the forces at work that have changed this pattern of eating? It has been estimated that for many middle-class Americans, 25 percent of their monthly food bill is spent on eating out. If people are not cooking at home as much today, what factors have contributed to this trend?
3. To what extent is advertising in the mass media and marketing among fast food companies to blame for the increase in American obesity rates and the related health problems that obesity engenders, like heart disease and diabetes?

EXPLORE THE WEB

The Slow Food Movement was founded by Carlo Petrini in 1986 as a protest against the opening of a McDonald's outlet near Rome's historic Spanish Steps. Since then, the movement has expanded worldwide. Explore the philosophy behind this movement and the various activities it sponsors. You can start by looking at the website for Slow Food USA at this address:

www.slowfoodusa.org/

The address of the International Slow Food Movement is

www.slowfood.com

For a very funny parody of the plight of a fast food employee, listen to the song "Ding Fries Are Done," sung by Skipper to the tune of the Christmas song, "Carol of the Bells." Here is the web address:

http://load.pquinn.com/binaries/fries

READING

Readings on Work, Success, and Failure

From the country's inception, the American Dream has been characterized by hard work and a success ethic. However, persistent cultural forces and changing economic times—among them the corporate accounting scandals of the late 1990s, the increasing gap between haves and have-nots, and ethical lapses and moral leniency—have resulted in a somewhat tattered version of that American Dream. The winning-is-everything philosophy has filtered down even to elementary schools and children's sports. In the summer of 2006 Congress once again rejected a proposal to raise the minimum wage, making the working-class poor fall even further behind and contributing to the increasing disparity between rich and poor.

The readings in this group examine these many social changes from four very different perspectives. William Ecenbarger explains why winner worship is dangerous and why sometimes failure may even be ennobling. Kirk O. Hanson examines the recent wave of cheating scandals in sports and in corporate America and cautions us about its insidious effects. Former sportswriter C. W. Nevius shows how far some parents will go (they are sometimes humorously referred to as "helicopter parents")—even condoning their children's cheating and threatening lawsuits—all in the name of getting ahead. Finally, an excerpt from Barbara Ehrenreich's contemporary classic, *Nickel and Dimed*, relates her experience working as a waitress for minimum wage in Key West, Florida, and the mean economies such a life requires.

Facing Up to the Ultimate Taboo—Failure

William Ecenbarger

This article first appeared in the opinion section of Connecticut's leading newspaper, the *Hartford Courant*. William Ecenbarger won a Pulitzer Prize as part of the team from the *Philadelphia Inquirer* that covered the 1979 Three Mile Island nuclear accident. He wrote for several news bureaus for UPI from 1961 to 1970, and since then he has been primarily writing travel articles while traveling to over forty countries. His most recent book is *Walkin' the Line: A Journey from Past to Present along the Mason-Dixon* (2000).

VOCABULARY ANALYSIS

The English Suffix *-hood*

You are undoubtedly familiar with the suffix *-hood* in these English words: *childhood, adulthood, sainthood, manhood, sisterhood,* and *brotherhood.* The suffix *-hood* can be attached to nouns to convey the idea of a condition, a state, or a quality. Therefore, *childhood* is the state of being a child, and so forth. Ecenbarger makes up a new word (a *neologism*) when he refers to *wimphood* in paragraph 9, referring to the state of being a wimp, in other words, a coward.

Facing Up to the Ultimate Taboo—Failure

William Ecenbarger

1 It was a numbingly familiar Super Bowl postgame show: seemingly endless coverage of the victorious New England Patriots afire with testosterone-fueled, fist-in-the-air, back-thumping jubilation; and a fleeting, almost subliminal shot of an Eagles player, slumped under a yoke of grief, biting his lips to fight back the tears. The TV director must have thought better of it, for he quickly switched back to the Patriots and their 300-watt, gargoyle smiles. We saw no more of the losers.

2 But how fascinating it would have been to stay with them—any fool can win; it's losing that's the challenge. Moreover, there's a lot to be said for failure. It is so much more interesting than success. Success goes to the head, but losing goes to the heart.

3 After all, who among us has never lost—in a job, in a relationship, on the tennis court? Losing is part of the price of life. It is the human condition. All of us born to sorrow. Born losers.

4 It begins early. Little League, science fairs, spelling bees. Later there are pink slips, unrequited love and, finally, death. Losing is a necessary part of competing. For every winner, there is at least one loser, and usually many more than one. Losing is one of life's constant companions, ever unwelcome, ever there. The Rolling Stones had it right—you can't always get what you want.

5 Nevertheless, losing is a taboo in our society. The ultimate put-down is "loser," and failure is the ultimate f-word. Hundreds of books have been written on how to win; there are scarcely any on how to lose.

6 We forget that losers changed the world. Columbus missed his target by thousands of miles. Thomas Edison had most of his inventing triumphs before the age of 40, and in his later years he rolled up an ever-increasing number of failures. Mozart died impoverished and was buried in the pauper's section of the cemetery. Most of the first edition of "Walden" was remaindered into Thoreau's personal library. Churchill distracted himself from defeat with painting, writing, gardening and breeding butterflies.

7 Winner worship is embedded early. Children returning from games are asked whether they won or lost, when they should be asked whether they had fun, or asked nothing at all. Parents often play games with their children and allow them to win, ill-preparing them for the game of life. Some educators feel that flunking a class is so detrimental to self-esteem that they move children along to the next grade and to bigger failures to come.

Connecting Grammar to Writing

The first sentence of paragraph 8 is somewhat unusual because it contains a sentence within a sentence. Note that Ecenbarger punctuates it correctly by separating it from the sentence it interrupts with parentheses. Which is the only other correct way to punctuate this unusual construction—commas or dashes?

8 Nowhere is winner worship and loser-loathing more evident than in sports (Vince Lombardi, Leo Durocher and Billy Martin all had bad things to say about losers) or in that other great arena: politics. Few losers suffer more acutely than defeated candidates. Jimmy Carter was stunned by his landslide 1980 loss to Ronald Reagan, and for about five years he all but vanished from the national political scene. He took no part in the 1984 presidential campaign—even though his former vice president, Walter Mondale, was running against Reagan. Several years after he, too, was swamped by Reagan, Mondale was asked how long it took to recover. "I'll let you know when the grieving ends," Mondale said.

9 We could pay a terrible price for our loser-loathing. We are a country founded by people who faced down death to start anew, but we could be reduced to wimphood. What better way to avoid losing than to never enter the fray? Americans still revere the image of the lone cowboy, riding off into the sunset in search of his destiny. But how many of us are timid couch potatoes, spectators at the game of life, content to see the spotlight on the winning team, to forget about the other side of every zero-sum transaction?

10 Americans need to confront their losers and their losses. Something as universal as failure deserves our attention. It has its positive side. For one thing, you're among friends. Winning isn't always worth its weight in blue ribbons, and losing can be positive and ennobling if it compels us to examine why we lost. After all, it is the way we learn and the way we live.

EXERCISES

A. Determining the Main Idea and Writer's Purpose

Choose the best answer.

1. The main idea of the selection is that
   a. we pay a terrible price in this country for our loathing of losers and of failure.
   b. learning to be a good loser is an important part of becoming an adult.
   c. winner worship began with sports but has now affected the entire culture.
   d. losing is part of the human condition, but today it is a cultural taboo.

2. The writer's purpose in the selection is to
   a. criticize the media and the sports industries for glorifying winners.
   b. explore the reasons that our fear of losing is both wrong and damaging.
   c. show people how to accept their losses and failures more gracefully.
   d. examine the harm parents do to their children by pushing them to succeed.

B. Comprehending Main Ideas

Choose the correct answer.

1. Ecenbarger thinks that the Super Bowl TV coverage should have prolonged the shot of the losing Philadelphia Eagles players because
   a. viewers could have learned something about losing and about how to lose.
   b. television should cover both the victorious and the losing teams equally.
   c. the players exhibited the worst aspects of losing and poor sportsmanship.
   d. viewers would learn to be more empathetic toward losers.

2. The writer demonstrates that for everyone, losing is
   a. merely a sign of personal failure and of our shortcomings.
   b. closely identified with risk-taking.
   c. an unavoidable part of the human condition that begins early and continues throughout our lives.
   d. associated with moral weakness and lack of resolve, both of which can nevertheless be overcome.

3. Ecenbarger believes that failure is much more interesting than
   a. losing.
   b. success.
   c. competition.
   d. a challenge.

4. The two areas where winner worship and loser loathing are most evident are sports and
   a. the movie industry.
   b. business.
   c. academics.
   d. politics.

5. In the conclusion, Ecenbarger writes that confronting our failures is both positive and ennobling because we
   a. are compelled to examine why we lost.
   b. learn to appreciate and to savor our less frequent victories more.
   c. learn to take more risks and not to fear failing so much.
   d. serve as good examples for our children.

C. Sequencing

The sentences in this excerpt from the selection may have been scrambled. Read the sentences and choose the sequence that puts them back into logical order. Do not refer to the original selection.

1. The TV director must have thought better of it, for he quickly switched back to the Patriots and their 300-watt, gargoyle smiles. **2.** It was a numbingly familiar Super Bowl postgame show: seemingly endless coverage of the victorious New England Patriots afire with testosterone-fueled, fist-in-the-air, back-thumping jubilation; and a fleeting, almost subliminal shot of an Eagles player, slumped under a yoke of grief, biting his lips to fight back the tears. **3.** We saw no more of the losers.

a. 2, 1, 3
b. 2, 3, 1
c. 1, 3, 2
d. Correct as written.

D. Distinguishing Between Main Ideas and Supporting Details

The following sentences come from paragraph 4. Label them as follows: **MI** if the sentence represents a *main idea* and **SD** if the sentence represents a *supporting detail.*

1. _____ It [losing] begins early.
2. _____ Little League, science fairs, spelling bees.
3. _____ Later there are pink slips, unrequited love and, finally, death.
4. _____ Losing is a necessary part of competing.
5. _____ For every winner, there is at least one loser, and usually more than one.
6. _____ Losing is one of life's constant companions, ever unwelcome, ever there.
7. _____ The Rolling Stones had it right—you can't always get what you want.

E. Interpreting Meaning

Where appropriate, write your answers to these questions in your own words.

1. Explain what Ecenbarger means when he writes in paragraph 2, "Any fool can win; it's losing that's the challenge."

   ____

   ____

2. Read paragraph 4 again. A good title for this paragraph is
   a. "You Can't Always Get What You Want."
   b. "Losing Begins Early in Life."
   c. "Losing: The Ever-Present Companion."
   d. "Some Examples of Life's Early Losses."

3. Look again at paragraph 6. First, write the sentence that expresses the main idea.

   ____

   What type of evidence does Ecenbarger present to support the main idea?

   ____

4. Based on the information Ecenbarger presents in paragraph 7, which of the following statements would he be most likely to agree with?
   a. Parents need to be good role models for their children and show them how to cope with personal losses.
   b. Parents should encourage their children to participate in competitive sports.
   c. Flunking a class is detrimental to a child's self-esteem.
   d. Sometimes it is better for a student to flunk a class than to be passed along.

5. Read the end of paragraph 8 again, where Ecenbarger describes Walter Mondale's reaction after he lost the presidency to Ronald Reagan. Which of the following is the most accurate interpretation of Mondale's remark, "I'll let you know when the grieving ends."
   a. Mondale was secretly relieved that he had lost.
   b. Mondale quickly recovered from his loss.

c. Mondale carried a grudge against Reagan for years.

d. Mondale never recovered from his loss.

6. A rhetorical question is one asked for effect and for which the writer does not expect an answer. Write an accurate paraphrase of this rhetorical question from paragraph 9: "What better way to avoid losing than to never enter the fray?"

____

____

How would you characterize his tone or emotional attitude in this rhetorical question? Is he serious or not?

____

F. Understanding Vocabulary

For each word in the left-hand column, find the phrase that best defines it from the right-hand column.

1. _____ jubilation [paragraph 1]	a. conflict, battle, skirmish
2. _____ subliminal [1]	b. causing damage or harm
3. _____ gargoyle [1]	c. not reciprocated or returned in kind
4. _____ unrequited [4]	d. great dislike, abhorrence
5. _____ pauper [6]	e. triumph, joy, rejoicing
6. _____ embedded [7]	f. sharply, intensely
7. _____ detrimental [7]	g. below conscious perception
8. _____ loathing [8 and 9]	h. interaction, exchange
9. _____ acutely [8]	i. an extremely poor person
10. _____ fray [9]	j. bizarre or grotesque in appearance
11. _____ transaction [9]	k. elevating or improving one's character
12. _____ ennobling [10]	l. fixed, caused to be an integral part

DISCUSSION QUESTIONS

1. What are some other areas in American culture, besides sports and politics, where winner worship and loser loathing are evident?
2. How convincing is Ecenbarger's argument? If America is, as he says, a culture that worships winners and loathes losers, how can that observation be reconciled with the oft-observed notion that Americans like to root for the underdog, the little guy?
3. Has Ecenbarger sufficiently supported his contention that Americans are so afraid of losing that they are unwilling to take risks? Does he provide any examples to back up this assertion? Do you detect any contradictions in his argument?

EXPLORE THE WEB

William Ecenbarger's published articles include travel pieces, opinion articles, and articles of a general nature. All of them can be found on his website, along with his autobiography at this address:

www.ecenbarger.com/bio.html

Culture Suggests Cheaters Do Prosper

Kirk O. Hanson

Beginning in 2002, a wave of corporate scandals became public. Companies like Adelphia Communications, Enron, WorldCom, Tyco, and AIG were charged with falsifying their accounting, inflating profits, and hiding losses. Many corporate executives treated their companies like personal piggy banks that they could dip into for their own living expenses. The scandals created a climate of corruption and distrust among the American people. Many executives have been prosecuted in several high-profile trials.

Other cheating scandals emerged as well, sullying Major League Baseball, as several superstars—among them Rafael Palmeiro of the Baltimore Orioles, Mark McGwire, formerly of the St. Louis Cardinals, Jose Canseco of the Oakland Athletics, and Barry Bonds of the San Francisco Giants—were accused of taking illegal performance-enhancing drugs. Several players were called to testify before Congress, and in the case of Palmeiro and McGwire, their testimony tarnished their careers.

In this article, first published in the *San Jose Mercury News*, Kirk O. Hanson examines the phenomenon of cheating in all segments of American society, our growing tolerance for cheating, and its many repercussions. Hanson is university professor and executive director of the Markkula Center for Applied Ethics at Santa Clara University.

VOCABULARY ANALYSIS

Two Related Latin Prefixes—*extra-* and *super-*

In English, many compound words are formed with the prefix *extra-*, meaning "outside" or "beyond." Thus, an *extraordinary* accomplishment or finding [paragraph 5] means one that goes beyond the merely ordinary. Other related words that begin with *extra-* are *extraterrestrial*, an inhabitant of another world (from *terra*, the Latin root for "earth"); *extramarital* (an affair outside marriage), *extracurricular* (describing activities outside the classroom).

Super- is another closely related Latin prefix, suggesting either "above" or "over," "superior," or "excessive." Therefore, a *superstar* [paragraph 7] is a celebrity who is superior to an ordinary star. There are numerous words in English beginning with this prefix, for example, *superabundant*, *supercharge*, *supercool*, *superimpose*, and *superhuman*.

Culture Suggests Cheaters Do Prosper

Kirk O. Hanson

1 It is time to face up to a dirty little secret. Players who use steroids in professional baseball, college coaches who have others take exams for their star athletes, high school students who cheat on the SATs, scientists who fake the results of their research and CEOs who cook the books in American corporations all may be acting rationally.

2 With the opening of baseball season only a few weeks away, much attention will be focused on whether Barry Bonds and other baseball stars may have knowingly taken illegal steroids. If they did, there could be a simple reason why: It was worth it.

3 How can this be? The answer is that today there is so much to be gained by being just a little better than others—by hitting a few more home runs than any other professional baseball player, by getting to and staying at the very top of the modern American corporation, or by being the absolute best in any other field.

4 Salaries and rewards for those who come out on top have gone crazy. The highest-paid baseball player earned $2.3 million in the 1988 season, $6.3 million in 1994 and more than $20 million last year. CEOs got 40 times what the average employee in their company earned in 1980, and 400 times by 2000. The Olympic gold-medal winner who won a nation's praise and an endorsement or two in

the 1970s became an endorsement bonanza by 2000. Who would settle for less when they are bombarded by ads like Nike's during the 1996 Atlanta Olympics: "You don't win silver. You lose gold"?

5 The winner-take-all culture exists in almost every area of American life. Science Magazine, the most prestigious in its field, has reported that in bio-science, what economists call a "tournament market" exists: The first to make an extraordinary finding reaps a hugely disproportionate share of the fame and future grants.

Ahead of the Pack

6 Tempted by these rewards, some people climbing the ladder may do almost anything to get to the top, and some who already have made it there will do almost anything to stay. Athletes turn to performance enhancers to remain superstars as they age; corporate executives falsify the books to retain their regal perks and immense pay. Former WorldCom CFO Scott Sullivan testified recently, for example, that executives at his company fraudulently adjusted the books to please Wall Street, which presumably would help keep the executives secure in their jobs.

7 The superstar culture has seeped even into our middle and high schools. Michael Dillingham, the 49ers team physician and a crusader against drug use by athletes, says parents of high school athletes are sometimes the most eager to try any drug that will give their child an edge.

8 Some children and their parents have convinced themselves that they have to be superstars, and go to Harvard, Stanford or Brown to have a worthwhile life. This attitude leads to cheating by the most qualified, not the least qualified, students in some schools.

9 Adding to the temptation, athletes, high school students and scientists may convince themselves that anyone who is on top has cheated to get there, and therefore they rationalize it for themselves.

10 So, we have become a society captivated by "the winner." We have made the one who dominates the box office, comes out on top in sports or rises to the peak in business a new kind of royalty. It is no wonder people cheat.

11 Cheating has always been with us. But is it worse now? Unfortunately, there are no reliable measures of the level of cheating. There were baseball and business scandals a century ago, and card cheaters were a fixture of the Old West.

12 What seems new to me is that cheating has gone mainstream. It shows up in almost every corner of American life—from professional athletics and Wall Street businesses to high school SATs. And it is tolerated more. There is less outrage and a more forgiving attitude when a baseball player is found with a corked bat or a student is caught cheating on an exam. Have we accepted at some level that cheating is reasonable? I hope not.

13 We would have to delve deeply into the national psyche to determine why we need heroes and celebrities so badly. I suspect it has to do with a spiritual crisis

in American society—a search for what has real meaning. Worshiping heroes and celebrities can be a substitute for finding fulfillment in our own relationships and service.

14 On a more practical level, I blame both the media and our brand of competitive capitalism. Olympics coverage focuses on events where an American may win a gold medal, ignoring those where a great effort produced a silver or bronze. And the media dedicate a disproportionate number of column inches or broadcast time to one member of a nine-member baseball team. Driven by the media attention, fans flock to the ballpark where the superstar is playing, and the superstar demands a huge salary based on the tickets he or she sells.

15 Competitive markets, so effective in the allocation of resources in the U.S. economy, have also led to a frantic bidding war for certain types of top talent. Companies bid excessively for graduates of prestigious MBA programs. CEOs have enough market power to negotiate contracts that enable them to walk away with millions of dollars even if they fail.

Role of Media

16 The media have cooperated fully in creating this "great leader" or rock-star model. Scanning the covers of business magazines, you might think General Electric employed only its former CEO Jack Welch or Hewlett-Packard only Carly Fiorina.[1]

17 Ironically, the media even love the celebrity who is caught cheating, making Martha Stewart a strange kind of icon for her noble prison behavior.

18 The emergence of a "superstar society"—and the "cheating society" that has resulted from it—is bad for all of us. Of course, cheaters make a competition unfair for everyone else.

19 Beyond that, if everybody is tempted to cheat—and if a significant number of people do—it weakens our trust in everyone around us. How can you build friendships with other parents when they are helping their kids cheat in Little League baseball? How can a company build a culture of trust when employees suspect others are trying to cheat to get ahead of them?

20 Cheating also costs more. Every society depends on a mix of enforcement and voluntary compliance to make its businesses, its tax system and its communities work. If we have to use constant surveillance, drug tests and threats of severe penalties to restrain cheaters, it will be costly.

21 There are long-term effects, too. For one thing, if deceit were widespread, it would be the people who are the most proficient cheaters who get ahead—not something we want to reward. More serious, though, is that if people don't trust the system, if they believe everyone else is cheating and they cannot get a fair shake, they will refuse to play. Entrepreneurs will start fewer companies; fewer kids will try out for competitive athletics. A few years ago, the World Bank developed quantitative proof that cheating and corruption in business was holding back the economic development of emerging economies.

22 Must we accept that America has become a winner-take-all society and that cheating works? I don't think so.

23 The answer is not just more enforcement and tougher penalties, though they are necessary. In the long run, only a commitment to different values and to raising our kids in a different way will contain the power of cheating in American life.

24 We have to value "doing your best," not just winning. Only a few high school basketball players will make it to the NBA. We can't have the vast majority believing they are losers. Only a few business people will be CEOs. The rest are not failures.

New Value System

25 Encouraging "doing your best" will require all of us to compliment and celebrate the efforts by those we know and love. The spouse who works hard but doesn't get the promotion deserves a dinner out. The child who studies diligently but gets a C grade should be praised.

26 Above all, we need to raise our children to resist the temptation to cheat. There is no way to make a rational case for honesty when getting that extra edge may help you come out on the top of the heap. My colleague and character education expert Steve Johnson says honesty must be instilled as a habit from an early age.

27 We should demonstrate to our kids that we adults abhor cheating. We should refuse to honor those who cheat—perhaps by boycotting certain baseball games or the stock of an errant company. Let's tell our kids cheaters are jerks. We should support the efforts our schools, sports leagues and courts take to punish cheating.

28 And, of course, our children must never, never see us cheat.

---

[1]Jack Welch retired as CEO of General Electric in 2001; Carly Fiorina, CEO of Hewlett-Packard and one of the most powerful women in American business, was forced out of office by the board of directors in 2005.

EXERCISES

A. Determining the Main Idea and Writer's Purpose

Choose the best answer.

1. The main idea of the selection is that
   a. the increase in cheating that now pervades every corner of American life is the result of our winner-take-all philosophy and the lure of big financial rewards.
   b. it is not surprising that American students are engaging in more deceitful behavior when they see cheating as a way of life in business and athletics.

c. our superstar culture that makes celebrities of business leaders and athletes cheapens our society and contributes to its increasing shallowness.

d. the mass media are responsible for the spiritual crisis in America and the climate of mistrust.

2. The writer's purpose in the selection is to

a. explain why people cheat and warn the reader of the consequences of cheating.

b. examine the ethical dilemmas that surround the problem of cheating.

c. provide a guide for parents who want to raise honest children.

d. explore the phenomenon of widespread cheating in America and the long-term damage it causes.

B. Comprehending Main Ideas

Choose the correct answer.

1. Hanson cites several examples of areas where cheating has taken place—professional baseball, college athletics, scientific research, corporate accounting; he says that people in these areas cheat because

a. they are so clever that they can get away with it.

b. there is much to be gained financially by cheating.

c. there is not sufficient surveillance to prevent cheating from occurring.

d. even if they are caught, the punishments are always light.

2. *Science* magazine reported that in the field of bioscience a "tournament market" exists, which means that

a. the first researcher to make an extraordinary finding gets a huge share of fame and future grants.

b. scientific research has become a battleground to see which research project is most worthy of being funded.

c. researchers work in teams that compete against each other in various projects.

d. scientific innovators are rewarded if their discoveries are found to save lives.

3. Hanson writes that high school students and scientists alike rationalize the prevalence of cheating by assuming that

a. cheating is acceptable only if one does not get caught.

b. if people in high corporate and government positions cheat, it must be acceptable.

c. everyone else who has made it to the top has cheated, so it must be acceptable.

d. the financial rewards that result from cheating are so tantalizing that cheaters lose any sense of right and wrong.

4. Hanson believes that the reason Americans need heroes and celebrities so badly is that we are undergoing a spiritual crisis, which he says is the result of

a. false values of consumerism and materialism.

b. our need to find a substitute for real meaning and fulfillment in our lives.

c. the breakdown of the family unit.

d. a decline in church attendance and religious belief.

5. Hanson mentions several long-term effects of cheating. Which one of the following was *not* mentioned?

a. Cheating weakens our trust in everyone around us.

b. Cheating results in higher costs for surveillance, drug tests, and penalties.

c. Cheating makes people believe that they cannot get a fair deal if everyone else is cheating.

d. Cheating leads to incompetent people doing jobs that they are not qualified for, since they cheated to get where they are in the first place.

e. Cheating, which leads to corruption in business, hinders economic development in emerging economies.

f. Cheating makes competition unfair for those who do not cheat.

C. Sequencing

The sentences in this excerpt from the selection may have been scrambled. Read the sentences and choose the sequence that puts them back into logical order. Do not refer to the original selection.

1. Cheating also costs more. **2.** Every society depends on a mix of enforcement and voluntary compliance to make its businesses, its tax system and its communities work. **3.** If we have to use constant surveillance, drug tests and threats of severe penalties to restrain cheaters, it will be costly.

a. 3, 1, 2

b. 2, 1, 3

c. 1, 3, 2

d. Correct as written.

D. Making Inferences

Write your answers to these questions in your own words.

1. In paragraph 1, what does the phrase "cook the books" most likely mean?

 ____

 ____

2. From what Hanson suggests in paragraph 4, why would an Olympic athlete be disappointed in winning a silver medal instead of a gold medal?

 ____

3. What information in paragraph 6 suggests a reason that executives who committed fraud were allowed to stay in their jobs?

 ____

 ____

 ____

4. What change does Hanson note has occurred toward the problem of cheating?

 ____

 ____

5. What specifically is the role of the media in fostering a culture of cheating?

 ____

 ____

 ____

E. Interpreting Meaning

Where appropriate, write your answers to these questions in your own words.

1. Look again at paragraph 4. First, write the sentence that expresses the main idea.

 ____

 What type of evidence does Hanson present to support the main idea?

 ____

2. Throughout the article, Hanson provides a number of areas of American life where cheating is rampant. List four of them.

____

____

____

3. Irony is a type of expression where the writer suggests a deliberate contrast or incongruity between what one expects and what actually occurs. Look again at paragraph 8 and find an example of irony.

____

____

4. In paragraph 14, Hanson describes a vicious spiral—the relationship between the media's focusing on superstars and high salaries. Explain this connection in your own words.

____

____

5. Explain the cause-effect relationship evident in what Hanson says in paragraph 18. Indicate clearly which is the cause and which is the effect.

____

6. List three of Hanson's recommendations that parents can implement to turn around the situation he describes.

____

____

____

F. Vocabulary in Context

Here are a few vocabulary words from the selection and their definitions. Study these definitions carefully. Then write the appropriate word in each space provided according to the context.

bonanza — a source of great wealth or prosperity

disproportionate — out of proportion in size or shape

bombarded — shower, flood, inundate, assail

reaped — obtained as a result of effort

1. It's no wonder that athletes turn to performance-enhancing drugs to give themselves an edge over the competition. The ______ to be ______ from endorsing products make the temptation too great to resist. For their part, consumers are ________ with advertisements using superstars who earn ____________ salaries in addition to their endorsement fees.

falsify to misrepresent, to state untruthfully

surveillance close observation of a person, especially one under suspicion of wrongdoing

rationalize to devise self-satisfying but incorrect reasons to justify one's behavior

captivate to attract and hold one's attention by charm or excellence

allocation setting apart for a special purpose

2. Whether they are athletes or corporate executives, superstars _______ the public with their dazzling feats on the athletic field and in stock prices. For their part, executives _____ their companies' accounting and _______ their actions by pointing to high stock prices. As Hanson points out, however, the increase in _______ for things like drug testing and ________ to detect wrongdoing end up costing everyone more in the end.

proficient marked by an advanced degree of competence

ironically describing the opposite of what is apparent or intended

abhor to detest, to regard with loathing

errant straying from proper ethical standards

boycott abstain from using or patronizing as an expression of protest

3. _______, Hanson states that today cheaters in high schools tend to be _______ students, in contrast to what we might expect. Hanson recommends that parents must begin teaching their children honesty from the very outset and teach them by example to _____ cheating; for example, parents could ______ companies that engage in _____ accounting practices.

DISCUSSION QUESTIONS

1. In what ways are the examples Hanson chooses to include about people who cheat (athletes, corporate executives, students aiming to win admission to top universities) appropriate for his thesis? Why doesn't he discuss more common types of cheating, for example, like taxpayers who fudge their income tax returns or clerks who short-change customers?

2. In the past—at least in the educational system—it seemed as if students cheated because they were lazy and unwilling to do the hard work required to excel. This article suggests a very different motivation—huge financial rewards, in other words, greed. To what extent do you agree with this assertion? Has Hanson sufficiently proved his thesis?

EXPLORE THE WEB

As noted earlier, Kirk O. Hanson is the executive director of the Markkula Center for Applied Ethics at Santa Clara University. The center's website offers a great deal of information and numerous links for a variety of issues involving ethics in government, business, and international affairs, among others.

www.scu.edu/ethics/about/people/directors/executive/hanson

A Slippery Slope

C.W. Nevius

C. W. Nevius has been a columnist at the *San Francisco Chronicle* since 1984. He covered sports for twenty years and then became a general news columnist. After graduating from the University of Colorado, he taught English for four years in high school and middle school. His book, *Crouching Toddler, Hidden Father: A Zen Guide for New Dads*, was published in 2006. This magazine piece, originally published in the Sunday *San Francisco Chronicle Magazine*, takes up the subject of parental ethics and the shift in attitudes among parents toward cheating.

VOCABULARY ANALYSIS

The Latin Prefix *circum-*

The useful Latin prefix *circum-* means "around" or "on all sides," from the Latin root *circus* meaning "circle." The word *circumvent* [paragraph 4] can be analyzed by looking at its two component parts: *circum-* + *venire* ("to go"). In English, *circumvent* has three meanings: to surround (for example, an enemy); to go around or bypass (for example, a city); or as Nevius uses it, to avoid or get around by artful maneuvering.

Here are a few other words with this prefix:

circumlocution a roundabout expression; indirect language

circumnavigate to sail completely around

circumscribe to draw a line around; to limit or restrict

circumspect paying attention to circumstances or consequences; prudent

A Slippery Slope

C. W. Nevius

1 In 1973, a 14-year-old boy named James Gronen was caught cheating at the All American Soap Box Derby in Akron, Ohio. This was not a case of accidentally putting the wrong kind of wing nuts on the steering wheel.

2 The Boulder, Colo., teen installed a powerful electromagnet in the front of his car. When the heavy metal starting plate was dropped, the magnetic pull gave the car a helpful yank down the hill.

3 The magnet was discovered (partly because officials became suspicious when Gronen's times began to get slower as his battery ran out of juice) and an investigation followed. When it was learned that Gronen's uncle had designed the car, a Boulder County court charged the uncle with "contributing to the delinquency of a minor."

4 And wasn't that what it was? An adult, a role model, encouraged, aided and abetted a child in breaking the rules to get ahead. The uncle was not only cheating, he was sending a powerful and influential life message to his nephew that accepted models of behavior could be bent, ignored or circumvented in order to get what you want.

5 Of course, that was 30 years ago. Things are a lot different today. Not the cheating part—the response to it.

6 What would you call it now when parents attempt to get their student diagnosed with a learning disability to get more time on SAT tests? Or when they do homework and science projects for their kids? Or browbeat the teacher in an attempt to force a better grade? Or file a lawsuit because their little athlete doesn't get enough playing time on the team?

7 In the frenzied new world of pre-college ethics, we call it typical.

8 "I think it is a relatively recent phenomenon,"says Dr. David Anderegg, a professor of psychology at Bennington College in Lenox, Mass., and author of "Worried All the Time: Overparenting in an Age of Anxiety and How to Stop It." "The perception that the world is a terribly competitive place makes parents frantic. Working for your child is perceived as being a good parent and some slip over the line and cheat on the children's behalf."

9 That's not how the parents see it, of course. They aren't cheating, they're "helping." Parents are convinced the stakes are so high that they can justify doing almost anything to give their child an advantage.

10 How bad has it gotten? Well, the Iowa State Fair has begun drug testing for the livestock of teenage 4-H contestants. Animal growth stimulants were turning up in the hand-raised lambs, pigs and calves. Anything to win.

11 Eric Hartwig is the principal at Menlo-Atherton High School on the Peninsula. As Hartwig says, in many ways Menlo-Atherton is "the state of California shrunk down to 2,100 kids." It is ethnically diverse, demographically split, and students range from the offspring of CEOs in pricey Atherton to the mean streets of East Palo Alto. But the parents of almost all of the students have the same vision.

12 "Parents see the school (college) as the key to success in life, and they aren't shy about expressing themselves," he says. "What we want to avoid is the perfect storm between the parents' expectations, and the student trying to live up to them."

13 Often those expectations mean inflated grades. Advanced placement, or honors, classes mean a student can have a grade point average above 4.0. There are high school students who will tell you they'd love to take a high school journalism class, for example, but because there is no advanced placement credit for the school newspaper, their parents say they can't afford the negative hit on their GPA. A simple A isn't good enough anymore.

14 "Academic achievement has become quite precious as early as kindergarten," says Dr. John Walkup, associate professor of child psychology at Johns Hopkins School of Medicine. "And that means every jump after that is more intense."

15 When those expectations and that intensity come together it's not a pretty sight. "Alice" (not her real name) was a young, popular, enthusiastic, energetic teacher at a Bay Area public elementary school. Under onslaught from the new breed of hyper-parent she lasted two years before resigning.

16 "It got to the point where it affected my health," Alice says. "I got into kind of a state of depression. It felt like my soul was being attacked."

17 Alice's experience is apparently typical of teachers all over the country. Grades are often the first battleground. When research for this story began, one parent said she'd heard of a mother who marched into the principal's office with a computer spreadsheet to prove that her son deserved an A. It sounded apocryphal, but apparently it was not.

18 "I've seen that," says Hartwig at Menlo-Atherton. "They come in with spreadsheets. They don't want a B. They want their son or daughter to get into X, Y, Z college, and a B won't make it."

19 It doesn't just happen to high school. It starts when the kids are still carrying Spider-Man lunch boxes. Teachers joke that PTA actually stands for "power trip association." Walkup says some psychologists have begun to talk about "parents who care too much."

20 "Anything that made the student uncomfortable," says Alice when asked what would trigger the parental reflex. "If they got something wrong on a test, the parents would say, 'I can see why they said that. They need to get that right.' They would say, 'Oh no, my child can't get a C. My child is not a C student.'"

21 Homework? Well, that's just a suggestion isn't it? Alice had parents stop by to tell her that their kids were just too busy with after-school activities to turn in assignments that week.

22 Unless, of course, it was a major project. If it was a key grade, Mom and Dad would step in and draw up the charts and build the models themselves.

23 "I would have parents call me on Monday and say I had ruined their weekend. And I knew exactly what they meant—that they'd done the work," Alice says. "We had kids with winning science projects who would go to the district science fair. When they got there they would have to talk about their project, and they didn't know the first thing about it."

24 "It sends a message," Walkup says. "You can't handle the situation, so I'll handle it for you."

25 "Some parents," says San Francisco-based educational psychologist Jane McClure of the firm McClure, Mallory and Baron, "don't seem to recognize the ethics of it. It is so important to them that they justify any means."

26 McClure has been on the front lines of a recent battle. Students with a diagnosed learning disability, such as dyslexia, are by law given more time on tests. Suddenly, beginning around 1997, the number of students with learning disabilities took an unexpected jump. Even more surprising, a large percentage of the increase came from affluent, upper-crust public and private schools.

27 According to the College Board, which creates and administrates SAT I, SAT II and the PSAT (preliminary, or practice SAT), in 1993 only 12,259 students were granted "accommodations" for the SAT tests. Last year there were 32,654.

28 The reason is simple. Parents realized that if they could get a learning disability designation, their kids could take an extra hour or more on the test. When some of them came to psychologists such as McClure, they already knew the diagnosis they wanted to hear. They just wanted her to confirm it. You'd think a parent would be delighted to hear that a child did not have a learning disability. Not always true.

29 "I've had them say, 'Are you sure?'" McClure says. "I tell them the numbers either show it or they don't. I've had people call me back and say they went to another psychologist and the child tested for a learning disability. And of course there are a couple of psychologists who will always find learning disabilities."

30 McClure says her firm has gone to a policy of demanding payment before the testing. Too many parents didn't bother to pay the bill if they didn't get the right results. As savvy modern parents know, the magic words are "Section 504 of the Rehabilitation Act." Once a student gets his "504," he gets, among other accommodations, extra time on every test as long as he is in school.

31 "I didn't even know what a 504 was," says Menlo-Atherton's Pam Wemberly, a high school coach since 1968 and the school's athletic director. "All of a sudden all these papers started coming across my desk. I'd say it has been in the last two or three years."

32 Expect this problem to only get worse. Although some of the loopholes have been closed, making it tougher to get the learning-disability designation, this year, for the first time, students who got extra time on their SAT test will not have the results "flagged" or marked to show that they had an accommodation. That's better for those who were embarrassed by the stigma of having problems with reading, of course, but for the kids who are only working the system, it is a free pass. They get more time even though they don't really need it, and there's no down side for their test scores.

33 "What concerns me is that I see some parents who begin to think of this as a way of living," Walkup says. "I tell them, (extra time) is good news now, but it is short term. At some time the gap has to close. No one is going to give a surgeon an extra two hours to complete the surgery."

34 After all this rule-bending, it isn't hard to imagine the next step. The Internet, with its Web sites that sell term papers and plenty of chances to cut and paste information, makes cheating easy. Unfortunately for students, teachers are using programs to catch them. But often that isn't the end of the story.

35 "I hear parents saying that high school is the means to get into college," says Mike Riera, a former high school counselor, co-author of the book "Right From Wrong: Instilling a Sense of Integrity in Your Child," and host of the radio show "Family Talk" (KNEW). So parents think, "OK then, cheating makes perfect sense. It is a means to an end."

36 "I have had families tell me that if a student cheats and gets caught at school," says McClure, "the first reaction is not to sit down with the child and ask why he was doing that. It is to attack the teacher. This isn't fair. Or the teacher is overly rigid."

37 That was the basis of a case that captured the headlines a year ago, when Christine Pelton, a biology teacher at a high school in Piper, Kan., caught one-fifth of her 118 students plagiarizing work on the biggest assignment of the year. As she warned them in a "contract" they were asked to sign at the start of the year, school policy was clearly laid out.

38 "The punishment for first-offense cheating is no credit for the assignment," the contract read. That meant 28 students took a zero on a project that accounted for 50 percent of their grade. They flunked.

39 But the parents sent up a howl and went to the school board to complain. The school board caved in, decreasing the value of the assignment to 30 percent and giving the students partial credit. Pelton, a second-year teacher, resigned.

40 "I went to my class and tried to teach the kids," she said at the time, "but they hollered and said, 'We don't have to listen to you anymore.' They knew if they didn't like anything in my classroom, from here on out they could just go to the school board and complain."

41 Piper, Kan., ended up getting far more media attention that it ever wanted, and all the members of the school board were either recalled or replaced, but

someone like Professor Anderegg says it may be typical to weaken the rules to diminish the penalties, but it isn't helping anyone.

42 "I teach in a college," he says, "and the penalties for plagiarism are severe. You get an F in the class and it goes on your permanent record. To get them off the hook is not really a favor."

43 Hartwig, Menlo-Atherton's principal, sees parents attempting to get their kids out of punishments every year. Even when they admit that the student committed the violation.

44 "We had a very tough one a couple of years ago," says Hartwig. "The student was not only suspended from the team; he had to give up his role as team captain. He thought that was going to be a key piece to getting into a prestigious college. I told him since he was a junior he could come back and do it next year. The response from the parents was, by then it will be too late.

45 "I've had that kind of thing every year. A student will break a major rule, and parents will try everything to appeal that. But there's a larger issue here. A rule against drinking or drugs, that's serious. You have to stand by rules or they don't mean anything."

46 Brave words, but what about the reality? Riera says he has worked with schools with some ironclad rules. Break one, and the student is expelled.

47 "But what they'd do is expel the student and then let them back in a week later," Riera says. "Their theory was who said an expulsion has to be permanent? It was just like a suspension."

48 But what about breaking the rule in the first place? Wasn't that the real problem? Parents don't have time to worry about that. There's a college career to consider.

49 Last year at a Bay Area school a top athlete was caught holding a marijuana cigarette in his hand on school grounds. He was suspended, but not for long. His parents got a lawyer who argued that someone handed the student the burning joint and he had no idea what it was.

50 The student was reinstated in school within a week and he was back on the team in time for the big event of the year.

51 "Things have changed," says Hartwig. "Stakes are higher. We have a continually evolving history in our courts in litigation and parents are increasingly skilled at using that. I've had a few parents who were lawyers themselves. They've brought that to the table."

52 The latest trend is what are called "disappointment" lawsuits. These are generally seen in sports when a parent is upset with his or her child's coach. In April of last year, for example, parents of players on an Omaha high school soccer team threatened a lawsuit because the coach wasn't doling out equal playing time. To prove it, they began to bring stopwatches to games to document how long each player was on the field. The coach resigned.

53 If you think that's an isolated case, think again. John Emme, a baseball coach at Corona del Mar High School in Southern California, has already fought off two

lawsuits by the father of a pitcher on the team. Emme finally turned around and filed a suit against the father, adding to the long list of sports-related legal action for young athletes.

54 Or consider Lynn Rubin of Union City. Rubin sounds like a pretty reasonable fellow when you talk to him. He admits that it is "a long shot . . . way out in zoom-zoom land" to think that his son, Jawaan Rubin, will ever play in the NBA.

55 At least that's what he says now.

56 Two years ago Jawaan and Rubin shocked high school sports. When he was a sophomore, Jawaan was asked to try out for the James Logan varsity team. After the tryout, head coach Blake Chong, citing a policy that sophomores were limited to junior varsity, told Jawaan he would not be on the varsity team.

57 Rubin, who said the family had already rearranged their schedules for varsity team practices, filed a $1.5 million lawsuit, basing the amount on Jawaan's projected earnings from a professional basketball career.

58 "We were all talking about that as coaches because that really concerned us," says Wemberly, who has coached the women's basketball team at Menlo-Atherton for more than 30 years. "I think what you are seeing is parents who really think that their child has exceptional abilities, and they have spent X-thousands of dollars grooming Johnny. We're not looking at the real world here."

59 As an example, Wemberly says, of some 600 athletes in the Menlo-Atherton sports programs last year exactly one got a college scholarship.

60 Rubin has dropped the suit, saying he realized the school district, financially strapped, didn't have the funds to mount a costly legal battle. Jawaan, now a senior, will transfer to San Leandro for the basketball season after sitting out all of last year.

61 Lynn says he expects Jawaan to "be in a good college program, probably Oregon," after the April 15 signing date. But in Oregon, a member of the basketball office says flatly, "We are not actively recruiting him."

62 Is it possible Jawaan will end up starring for the basketball team at Oregon? Sure. But what seems more likely is that he will be yet another of the kids who found that dreams and reality don't always coincide.

63 Wemberly has never forgotten a girl whose father drove her incessantly on the basketball court in order to get a college scholarship. She got one, but only lasted a year at the school. She'd had it.

64 But the lesson is larger than sports. It should also resonate with parents who pushed and prodded teachers to get those grades up so their son or daughter could get into the "right" school. It may only get their student into a school where he or she is clinging to academic life by his or her fingernails.

65 "It is like saying a high school basketball player has a 30-point scoring average when actually he has a 20-point average," Riera says. "He gets into a big program, rides the bench, has a stressful experience and feels like a failure. Where somebody else goes to a Division II school, has a great experience and maybe is team captain. It is all about the match, not the school."

Connecting Grammar to Writing

Writing instructors usually caution students against writing one-sentence paragraphs, but an exception is the sentence used as a transition between an essay's parts. See paragraphs 66 and 68 for an example of this technique.

66 In many ways the academic experience is no different.

67 "It is madness to get kids into a 'good' college and then they flounder," says Anderegg. "I hear it all the time. Kids go to these colleges after years of grade inflation and fall flat on their faces. Kids come back and they say, 'I thought I wanted to go to an Ivy League school, but I couldn't believe they were so mean!' What they mean is when you take a test and earn a 70, guess what? They give you a 70."

68 Or consider the effort to get a learning disability designation for the SAT test.

69 According to testing funded by the College Board, students who actually have a disability can increase their scores as much as 32 points on verbal and 26 on math with extended time. But the gain for students who do not have a disability is essentially zero.

70 "Studies have shown that giving them extra time doesn't help," says McClure, the educational psychologist. "If you don't know it, you don't know it."

71 Besides, suppose a student didn't get into a college of first choice? Why is that such a horrible thing?

72 "You talk to parents about the salutary effects of failure and they look at you like you are crazy," says Anderegg. "Because they know that if their children experience any failure they are going to immediately start to take drugs and go to prison."

73 The idea, the experts say, is to step back and give the student a little space. Let them try to work out their grades, their college, their life.

74 "Listen," says Walkup, "if you don't have constant challenges your kid will never grow strong. And if you under-prepare your kid for the challenges for life they will resent it for the rest of your life."

EXERCISES

A. Determining the Main Idea and Writer's Purpose

Choose the best answer.

1. The main idea of the selection is that
   a. cheating has become a way of life in nearly every area of American life.
   b. many parents want to do what is best for their children, which sometimes means cheating on their behalf to get an extra edge over the competition.
   c. parents who engage in unethical behavior on behalf of their children are sending them the wrong message and not preparing them for the reality of life's challenges.
   d. the increasing competitiveness of life in America makes it almost impossible for children to get ahead without resorting to some sort of cheating.

2. The writer's purpose in the selection is to
   a. examine the changes over the past few years in pre-college ethics and parents' role in condoning cheating on their children's behalf.
   b. warn teachers and athletic coaches not to cave in to unrealistic parental demands and threats.
   c. advise students on how to cope with the stresses and pressures of academic life.
   d. explain how parents can raise children with high ethical standards.

B. Comprehending Main Ideas

Choose the correct answer.

1. At the beginning of the article Nevius describes the actions of the uncle of a soap box derby entrant who designed a soap box car with an illegal mechanism. Nevius says that it was right that the uncle was charged with contributing to the delinquency of a minor because
   a. the boy could have won on his own, without the illegal tampering with the car.
   b. the boy had an unfair advantage over other competitors because his uncle was an engineer.
   c. the soap box derby rules clearly prohibited the electromagnetic device he had installed.
   d. the uncle was sending the boy a message that it is acceptable to cheat to get what you want.

2. According to Dr. David Anderegg, a Bennington College psychologist, instances of parental cheating have increased primarily because parents
   a. have become increasingly frantic about excessive competition in our society.
   b. think that their children are overburdened with too much work.
   c. are unable to resist their children's whining and pleading for help.
   d. feel guilty over the number of hours they work outside the home and therefore endorse cheating on their behalf as a way to compensate.

3. In American high schools today, one area of intense competition surrounds the matter of grades, specifically the problem of
   a. plus and minus grades given rather than letter grades.
   b. grades given for effort, not for actual work completed.
   c. grade inflation—grades that aren't worth as much as they used to be.
   d. teachers who grade inconsistently or unfairly.

4. Parents who do their children's science projects or other homework assignments for them are teaching their children that
   a. most teachers cannot tell the difference between a project done by a student and one done by a parent.
   b. the end (a good grade) justifies the means (cheating) to achieve it.
   c. the grade is the only thing that matters, not the effort that goes into the project.
   d. science projects are a waste of time for nonscientifically inclined students.

5. The realities of grade inflation, getting disability accommodations for taking the SAT, and lawsuits over enforcement of rules can have nasty consequences for students, especially when they
   a. get into a good college and then flounder academically.
   b. get caught for cheating or plagiarizing in college.
   c. are living away from home and do not have access to parents to complete assignments for them.
   d. have to plagiarize by downloading papers from the Internet.

C. Locating Supporting Details

For each main idea stated here, find two details that support it.

1. Cheating has always been a fact of life, but 30 years after the Soap Box Derby cheating incident, it's parents' responses to cheating that have changed. [paragraphs 6–8]

   ____

   ____

   ____

   ____

   ____

2. Parents who help their children with their science fair project are one example of crossing an ethical line, with unfortunate consequences. [paragraphs 23–24]

   a. ______________________________

   ____

   b. ______________________________

   ____

D. Making Inferences

For each of these statements write **Y** (yes) if the inference is an accurate one, **N** (no) if the inference is an inaccurate one, or **CT** (can't tell) if the writer does not give enough information to make an inference one way or another.

1. _____ In the incident of the All American Soap Box Derby and the boy who installed an illegal device, the boy confessed to his uncle's having designed the car. [paragraph 3]

2. _____ According to Dr. David Anderegg, the Bennington College professor of psychology, being a good parent most likely means *not* helping children with school projects or browbeating a teacher into changing a grade. [8–9]

3. _____ Parents justify cheating on behalf of their children because they realize that everyone else is cheating, so they really have no choice. [9]

4. _____ The need to maintain a high grade point average, even one beyond a 4.0, results in students not being able to take extracurricular classes that they are interested in. [13]

5. _____ For many parents, the path to getting their child accepted into a good college starts with getting him or her into the "right" kindergarten. [19]

6. _____ The increase in the number of students requesting accommodations for learning disabilities while they take the SAT is the result of better detection and diagnosis of learning disabilities. [26–28]

7. _____ In the long run, it is damaging to the student to allow extra time for tests when there is no justification for it; in the real world, there are no such accommodations for disabilities. [33]

8. _____ The effect of the Piper, Kansas, plagiarism case resulted in more, not less, respect for the high school teachers for sticking to the rules. [39–40]

9. _____ The Omaha, Nebraska, soccer coach didn't give his players equal time on the field because using the best players would assure the team's victory. [52]

10. _____ Parents need to have more realistic expectations for their children, both in academics and in athletics, and even let them fail once in a while. [article as a whole]

E. Understanding Vocabulary

Look through the paragraphs listed below and find a word that matches each definition. Refer to a dictionary if necessary. An example has been done for you.

EXAMPLE: supported, incited, urged on [paragraphs 3–4] abetted

1. agitated, frantic [6–8] ______
2. describing human populations and their characteristics [11] ______
3. attack, assault, outpouring [14–15] ______
4. a common reading disorder [25–27] ______
5. well-informed, perceptive, shrewd [29–30] ______
6. a mark of disgrace or abnormality [32–33] ______
7. adherence to a strict moral or ethical code [34–35] ______
8. rigid, fixed [46–47] ______
9. legal proceedings, legal action [49–51] ______
10. distributing, giving out, dispensing [52–53—phrase] ______
11. prepare or provide for [60–61] ______
12. correspond, be identical [61–63] ______
13. evoke a feeling of shared emotion or belief [64–66] ______
14. struggle, act clumsily or in confusion [65–67] ______
15. favorable to one's personality, beneficial [70–72] ______

DISCUSSION QUESTIONS

1. What is the significance of the title of Nevius's article, "A Slippery Slope"? A good dictionary should offer the definition of this phrase if you are unsure of its meaning.
2. How would you characterize the evidence that Nevius uses throughout the article to support his thesis that the new parental ethics are damaging children today? Does his evidence seem sufficient? Does the testimony of the experts he cites seem balanced? Are all geographic areas of the country represented?
3. Nevius cites only one example of a parent, Lynn Rubin of Union City, California, who initially filed a lawsuit against the school district

protesting a policy of not allowing sophomores to play on the school's varsity basketball team. Mr. Rubin does not come off very well in this discussion [see paragraphs 54–62]. Why doesn't Nevius use the testimony of more parents? Is this a weakness in the article, or does the omission serve his larger purpose?

EXPLORE THE WEB

What is the policy at your college or university with regard to plagiarism? Go to your school's home page, locate the policy and the penalties, if they are listed, and evaluate them according to whether they seem too strict, too lenient, or reasonable and fair. To locate the information, try looking at such subjects as "Student Policies," "Academic Discipline," or "Student Conduct."

You can find several articles online concerning the 2002 Piper, Kansas, plagiarism case. Do a search of your own, or start with these two:

www.njsbf.com/njsbf/student/eagle/winter03-2.cfm

http://archives.cnn.com/2002/fyi/teachers.ednews/03/19/plagiarism.dispute.ap

Nickel and Dimed: On (Not) Getting By in America

Barbara Ehrenreich

Barbara Ehrenreich is a contributing editor of *Harper's* magazine and investigative writer on a variety of social issues. In January 1999, *Harper's* published a long essay, a portion of which is reprinted here. That piece later led to a full-length book of the same title. Ehrenreich's mission was to find out how working-class people survive on minimum wage, but instead of engaging in a more traditional research study, she decided to join the low-wage workforce. She found low-paying jobs in different regions of the country, working as a Wal-Mart clerk in Michigan, as a cleaning woman for Merry Maids in Portland, Maine, and as a waitress in Key West, Florida, the subject of this particular excerpt. Ehrenreich's most recent book is *Dancing in the Streets: A History of Collective Joy (2007).*

VOCABULARY ANALYSIS

The Greek Suffix *-logy*

Some might call Ehrenreich a student of *social anthropology*—the study of human societies. This word combines the Greek elements *anthropo-* ("human")

and the Greek suffix *-logy* ("study of" or "science"). Here are some other words ending in this useful suffix:

archeology the study of antiquity, of man's past culture

biology the study of animal and plant life

etymology the study of word origins

pathology the scientific study of the nature of disease

theology the study of God and of divine truths

Nickel and Dimed: On (Not) Getting By in America

Barbara Ehrenreich

1 At the beginning of June 1998 I leave behind everything that normally soothes the ego and sustains the body—home, career, companion, reputation, ATM card—for a plunge into the low-wage workforce. There, I become another, occupationally much diminished "Barbara Ehrenreich"—depicted on job-application forms as a divorced homemaker whose sole work experience consists of housekeeping in a few private homes. I am terrified, at the beginning, of being unmasked for what I am: a middle-class journalist setting out to explore the world that welfare mothers are entering, at the rate of approximately 50,000 a month, as welfare reform kicks in. Happily, though, my fears turn out to be entirely unwarranted: during a month of poverty and toil, my name goes unnoticed and for the most part unuttered. In this parallel universe where my father never got out of the mines and I never got through college, I am "baby," "honey," "blondie," and, most commonly, "girl."

2 My first task is to find a place to live. I figure that if I can earn $7 an hour—which, from the want ads, seems doable—I can afford to spend $500 on rent, or maybe, with severe economies, $600. In the Key West area, where I live, this pretty much confines me to flophouses and trailer homes—like the one, a pleasing fifteen-minute drive from town, that has no air-conditioning, no screens, no fans, no television, and, by way of diversion, only the challenge of evading the landlord's Doberman pinscher. The big problem with this place, though, is the rent, which at $675 a month is well beyond my reach. All right, Key West is expensive. But so is New York City, or the Bay Area, or Jackson Hole, or Telluride, or Boston, or any other place where tourists and the wealthy compete for living space with the people who clean their toilets and fry their hash browns.[1] Still, it is a shock to realize that "trailer trash" has become, for me, a demographic category to aspire to.

3 So I decide to make the common trade-off between affordability and convenience, and go for a $500-a-month efficiency thirty miles up a two-lane highway from the employment opportunities of Key West, meaning forty-five minutes if there's no road construction and I don't get caught behind some sun-dazed Canadian tourists. I hate the drive, along a roadside studded with white crosses commemorating the more effective head-on collisions, but it's a sweet little place—a cabin, more or less, set in the swampy back yard of the converted mobile home where my landlord, an affable TV repairman, lives with his bartender girlfriend. Anthropologically speaking, a bustling trailer park would be preferable, but here I have a gleaming white floor and a firm mattress, and the few resident bugs are easily vanquished.

4 Besides, I am not doing this for the anthropology. My aim is nothing so mistily subjective as to "experience poverty" or find out how it "really feels" to be a long-term low-wage worker. I've had enough unchosen encounters with poverty and the world of low-wage work to know it's not a place you want to visit for touristic purposes; it just smells too much like fear. And with all my real-life assets—bank account, IRA, health insurance, multiroom home—waiting indulgently in the background, I am, of course, thoroughly insulated from the terrors that afflict the genuinely poor.

5 No, this is a purely objective, scientific sort of mission. The humanitarian rationale for welfare reform—as opposed to the more punitive and stingy impulses that may actually have motivated it—is that work will lift poor women out of poverty while simultaneously inflating their self-esteem and hence their future value in the labor market. Thus, whatever the hassles involved in finding child care, transportation, etc., the transition from welfare to work will end happily, in greater prosperity for all. Now there are many problems with this comforting prediction, such as the fact that the economy will inevitably undergo a downturn, eliminating many jobs. Even without a downturn, the influx of a million former welfare recipients into the low-wage labor market could depress wages by as much as 11.9 percent, according to the Economic Policy Institute (EPI) in Washington, D.C.

6 But is it really possible to make a living on the kinds of jobs currently available to unskilled people? Mathematically, the answer is no, as can be shown by taking $6 to $7 an hour, perhaps subtracting a dollar or two an hour for child care, multiplying by 160 hours a month, and comparing the result to the prevailing rents. According to the National Coalition for the Homeless, for example, in 1998 it took, on average nationwide, an hourly wage of $8.89 to afford a one-bedroom apartment, and the Preamble Center for Public Policy estimates that the odds against a typical welfare recipient's landing a job at such a "living wage" are about 97 to 1. If these numbers are right, low-wage work is not a solution to poverty and possibly not even to homelessness.

7 It may seem excessive to put this proposition to an experimental test. As certain family members keep unhelpfully reminding me, the viability of low-wage work could be tested, after a fashion, without ever leaving my study. I could just

pay myself $7 an hour for eight hours a day, charge myself for room and board, and total up the numbers after a month. Why leave the people and work that I love? But I am an experimental scientist by training. In that business, you don't just sit at a desk and theorize; you plunge into the everyday chaos of nature, where surprises lurk in the most mundane measurements. Maybe, when I got into it, I would discover some hidden economies in the world of the low-wage worker. After all, if 30 percent of the workforce toils for less than $8 an hour, according, to the EPI, they may have found some tricks as yet unknown to me. Maybe—who knows?—I would even be able to detect in myself the bracing psychological effects of getting out of the house, as promised by the welfare wonks at places like the Heritage Foundation. Or, on the other hand, maybe there would be unexpected costs—physical, mental, or financial—to throw off all my calculations. Ideally, I should do this with two small children in tow, that being the welfare average, but mine are grown and no one is willing to lend me theirs for a month-long vacation in penury. So this is not the perfect experiment, just a test of the best possible case: an unencumbered woman, smart and even strong, attempting to live more or less off the land.

8 On the morning of my first full day of job searching, I take a red pen to the want ads, which are auspiciously numerous. Everyone in Key West's booming "hospitality industry" seems to be looking for someone like me—trainable, flexible, and with suitably humble expectations as to pay. I know I possess certain traits that might be advantageous—I'm white and, I like to think, well-spoken and poised—but I decide on two rules: One, I cannot use any skills derived from my education or usual work—not that there are a lot of want ads for satirical essayists anyway. Two, I have to take the best-paid job that is offered me and of course do my best to hold it; no Marxist rants or sneaking off to read novels in the ladies' room. In addition, I rule out various occupations for one reason or another: Hotel front-desk clerk, for example, which to my surprise is regarded as unskilled and pays around $7 an hour, gets eliminated because it involves standing in one spot for eight hours a day. Waitressing is similarly something I'd like to avoid, because I remember it leaving me bone tired when I was eighteen, and I'm decades of varicosities and back pain beyond that now. Telemarketing, one of the first refuges of the suddenly indigent, can be dismissed on grounds of personality. This leaves certain supermarket jobs, such as deli clerk, or housekeeping in Key West's thousands of hotel and guest rooms. Housekeeping is especially appealing, for reasons both atavistic and practical: it's what my mother did before I came along, and it can't be too different from what I've been doing part-time, in my own home, all my life.

9 So I put on what I take to be a respectful-looking outfit of ironed Bermuda shorts and scooped-neck T-shirt and set out for a tour of the local hotels and supermarkets. Best Western, Econo Lodge, and HoJo's all let me fill out application

forms, and these are, to my relief, interested in little more than whether I am a legal resident of the United States and have committed any felonies. My next stop is Winn-Dixie, the supermarket, which turns out to have a particularly onerous application process, featuring a fifteen-minute "interview" by computer since, apparently, no human on the premises is deemed capable of representing the corporate point of view. I am conducted to a large room decorated with posters illustrating how to look "professional" (it helps to be white and, if female, permed) and warning of the slick promises that union organizers might try to tempt me with. The interview is multiple choice: Do I have anything, such as child-care problems, that might make it hard for me to get to work on time? Do I think safety on the job is the responsibility of management? Then, popping up cunningly out of the blue: How many dollars' worth of stolen goods have I purchased in the last year? Would I turn in a fellow employee if I caught him stealing? Finally, "Are you an honest person?"

10 Apparently, I ace the interview, because I am told that all I have to do now is show up in some doctor's office tomorrow for a urine test. This seems to be a fairly general rule: if you want to stack Cheerio boxes or vacuum hotel rooms in chemically fascist America, you have to be willing to squat down and pee in front of some health worker (who has no doubt had to do the same thing herself). The wages Winn-Dixie is offering—$6 and a couple of dimes to start with—are not enough, I decide, to compensate for this indignity.[2]

Connecting Grammar to Writing

In paragraph 11, Ehrenreich puts "cheese sauce" in quotation marks, not because she is quoting an item on the menu, but because the sauce is not made from real cheese. Quotations here cast doubt on the sauce's authenticity.

11 I lunch at Wendy's, where $4.99 gets you unlimited refills at the Mexican part of the Superbar, a comforting surfeit of refried beans and "cheese sauce." A teenage employee, seeing me studying the want ads, kindly offers me an application form, which I fill out, though here, too, the pay is just $6 and change an hour. Then it's off for a round of the locally owned inns and guesthouses. At "The Palms," let's call it, a bouncy manager actually takes me around to see the rooms and meet the existing housekeepers, who, I note with satisfaction, look pretty much like me—faded ex-hippie types in shorts with long hair pulled back in braids. Mostly, though, no one speaks to me or even looks at me except to proffer an application form. At my last stop, a palatial B&B, I wait twenty minutes to meet "Max," only to be told that there are no jobs now but there should be one soon, since "nobody lasts more than a couple weeks." (Because none of the people I talked to knew I was a reporter, I have changed their names to protect their privacy and, in some cases perhaps, their jobs.)

12 Three days go by like this, and, to my chagrin, no one out of the approximately twenty places I've applied calls me for an interview. I had been vain enough to worry about coming across as too educated for the jobs I sought, but no one even seems interested in finding out how overqualified I am. Only later will I realize that the want ads are not a reliable measure of the actual jobs available at any particular time. They are, as I should have guessed from Max's comment, the employers' insurance policy against the relentless turnover of the

low-wage workforce. Most of the big hotels run ads almost continually, just to build a supply of applicants to replace the current workers as they drift away or are fired, so finding a job is just a matter of being at the right place at the right time and flexible enough to take whatever is being offered that day. This finally happens to me at one of the big discount hotel chains, where I go, as usual, for housekeeping and am sent, instead, to try out as a waitress at the attached "family restaurant," a dismal spot with a counter and about thirty tables that looks out on a parking garage and features such tempting fare as "Pollish [sic] sausage and BBQ sauce" on 95-degree days. Phillip, the dapper young West Indian who introduces himself as the manager, interviews me with about as much enthusiasm as if he were a clerk processing me for Medicare, the principal questions being what shifts can I work and when can I start. I mutter something about being woefully out of practice as a waitress, but he's already on to the uniform: I'm to show up tomorrow wearing black slacks and black shoes; he'll provide the rust-colored polo shirt with HEARTHSIDE embroidered on it, though I might want to wear my own shirt to get to work, ha ha. At the word "tomorrow," something between fear and indignation rises in my chest. I want to say, "Thank you for your time, sir, but this is just an experiment, you know, not my actual life."

13 So begins my career at the Hearthside, I shall call it, one small profit center within a global discount hotel chain, where for two weeks I work from 2:00 till 10:00 P.M. for $2.43 an hour plus tips.[3] In some futile bid for gentility, the management has barred employees from using the front door, so my first day I enter through the kitchen, where a red-faced man with shoulder-length blond hair is throwing frozen steaks against the wall and yelling, "Fuck this shit!" "That's just Jack," explains Gail, the wiry middle-aged waitress who is assigned to train me. "He's on the rag again"—a condition occasioned, in this instance, by the fact that the cook on the morning shift had forgotten to thaw out the steaks. For the next eight hours, I run after the agile Gail, absorbing bits of instruction along with fragments of personal tragedy. All food must be trayed, and the reason she's so tired today is that she woke up in a cold sweat thinking of her boyfriend, who killed himself recently in an upstate prison. No refills on lemonade. And the reason he was in prison is that a few DUIs caught up with him, that's all, could have happened to anyone. Carry the creamers to the table in a monkey bowl, never in your hand. And after he was gone she spent several months living in her truck, peeing in a plastic pee bottle and reading by candlelight at night, but you can't live in a truck in the summer, since you need to have the windows down, which means anything can get in, from mosquitoes on up.

14 At least Gail puts to rest any fears I had of appearing overqualified. From the first day on, I find that of all the things I have left behind, such as home and identity, what I miss the most is competence. Not that I have ever felt utterly competent in the writing business, in which one day's success augurs nothing at all

for the next. But in my writing life, I at least have some notion of procedure: do the research, make the outline, rough out a draft, etc. As a server, though, I am beset by requests like bees: more iced tea here, ketchup over there, a to-go box for table fourteen, and where are the high chairs, anyway? Of the twenty-seven tables, up to six are usually mine at any time, though on slow afternoons or if Gail is off, I sometimes have the whole place to myself. There is the touch-screen computer-ordering system to master, which is, I suppose, meant to minimize server-cook contact, but in practice requires constant verbal fine-tuning: "That's gravy on the mashed, okay? None on the meatloaf," and so forth—while the cook scowls as if I were inventing these refinements just to torment him. Plus, something I had forgotten in the years since I was eighteen: about a third of a server's job is "side work" that's invisible to customers—sweeping, scrubbing, slicing, refilling, and restocking. If it isn't all done, every little bit of it, you're going to face the 6:00 P.M. dinner rush defenseless and probably go down in flames. I screw up dozens of times at the beginning, sustained in my shame entirely by Gail's support—"It's okay, baby, everyone does that sometime"—because, to my total surprise and despite the scientific detachment I am doing my best to maintain, I care.

15 The whole thing would be a lot easier if I could just skate through it as Lily Tomlin in one of her waitress skits, but I was raised by the absurd Booker T. Washingtonian precept that says: If you're going to do something, do it well. In fact, "well" isn't good enough by half. Do it better than anyone has ever done it before. Or so said my father, who must have known what he was talking about because he managed to pull himself, and us with him, up from the mile-deep copper mines of Butte to the leafy suburbs of the Northeast, ascending from boilermakers to martinis before booze beat out ambition. As in most endeavors I have encountered in my life, doing it "better than anyone" is not a reasonable goal. Still, when I wake up at 4:00 A.M. in my own cold sweat, I am not thinking about the writing deadlines I'm neglecting; I'm thinking about the table whose order I screwed up so that one of the boys didn't get his kiddie meal until the rest of the family had moved on to their Key Lime pies. That's the other powerful motivation I hadn't expected—the customers, or "patients," as I can't help thinking of them on account of the mysterious vulnerability that seems to have left them temporarily unable to feed themselves. After a few days at the Hearthside, I feel the service ethic kick in like a shot of oxytocin, the nurturance hormone. The plurality of my customers are hard-working locals—truck drivers, construction workers, even housekeepers from the attached hotel—and I want them to have the closest to a "fine dining" experience that the grubby circumstances will allow. No "you guys" for me; everyone over twelve is "sir" or "ma'am." I ply them with iced tea and coffee refills; I return, mid-meal, to inquire how everything is; I doll up their salads with chopped raw mushrooms, summer squash slices, or whatever bits of produce I can find that have survived their sojourn in the cold-storage room mold-free.

16 There is Benny, for example, a short, tight-muscled sewer repairman, who cannot even think of eating until he has absorbed a half hour of air-conditioning and ice water. We chat about hyperthermia and electrolytes until he is ready to order some finicky combination like soup of the day, garden salad, and a side of grits. There are the German tourists who are so touched by my pidgin "Willkommen" and "Ist alles gut?" that they actually tip. (Europeans, spoiled by their trade-union-ridden, high-wage welfare states, generally do not know that they are supposed to tip. Some restaurants, the Hearthside included, allow servers to "grat" their foreign customers, or add a tip to the bill. Since this amount is added before the customers have a chance to tip or not tip, the practice amounts to an automatic penalty for imperfect English.) There are the two dirt-smudged lesbians, just off their construction shift, who are impressed enough by my suave handling of the fly in the piña colada that they take the time to praise me to Stu, the assistant manager. There's Sam, the kindly retired cop, who has to plug up his tracheotomy hole with one finger in order to force the cigarette smoke into his lungs.

17 Sometimes I play with the fantasy that I am a princess who, in penance for some tiny transgression, has undertaken to feed each of her subjects by hand. But the non-princesses working with me are just as indulgent, even when this means flouting management rules—concerning, for example, the number of croutons that can go on a salad (six). "Put on all you want," Gail whispers, "as long as Stu isn't looking." She dips into her own tip money to buy biscuits and gravy for an out-of-work mechanic who's used up all his money on dental surgery, inspiring me to pick up the tab for his milk and pie. Maybe the same high levels of agape can be found throughout the "hospitality industry." I remember the poster decorating one of the apartments I looked at, which said "If you seek happiness for yourself you will never find it. Only when you seek happiness for others will it come to you," or words to that effect—an odd sentiment, it seemed to me at the time, to find in the dank one-room basement apartment of a bellhop at the Best Western. At the Hearthside, we utilize whatever bits of autonomy we have to ply our customers with the illicit calories that signal our love. It is our job as servers to assemble the salads and desserts, pouring the dressings and squirting the whipped cream. We also control the number of butter patties our customers get and the amount of sour cream on their baked potatoes. So if you wonder why Americans are so obese, consider the fact that waitresses both express their humanity and earn their tips through the covert distribution of fats.

18 Ten days into it, this is beginning to look like a livable lifestyle. I like Gail, who is "looking at fifty" but moves so fast she can alight in one place and then another without apparently being anywhere between them. I clown around with Lionel, the teenage Haitian busboy, and catch a few fragments of conversation with Joan, the svelte fortyish hostess and militant feminist who is the only one of us who dares to tell Jack to shut the fuck up. I even warm up to Jack when, on a slow night and to make up for a particularly unwarranted attack on my abilities,

or so I imagine, he tells me about his glory days as a young man at "coronary school"—or do you say "culinary"?—in Brooklyn, where he dated a knockout Puerto Rican chick and learned everything there is to know about food. I finish up at 10:00 or 10:30, depending on how much side work I've been able to get done during the shift, and cruise home to the tapes I snatched up at random when I left my real home—Marianne Faithfull, Tracy Chapman, Enigma, King Sunny Ade, the Violent Femmes—just drained enough for the music to set my cranium resonating but hardly dead. Midnight snack is Wheat Thins and Monterey Jack, accompanied by cheap white wine on ice and whatever AMC has to offer. To bed by 1:30 or 2:00, up at 9:00 or 10:00, read for an hour while my uniform whirls around in the landlord's washing machine, and then it's another eight hours spent following Mao's central instruction, as laid out in the Little Red Book, which was: Serve the people.

19 I could drift along like this, in some dreamy proletarian idyll, except for two things. One is management. If I have kept this subject on the margins thus far it is because I still flinch to think that I spent all those weeks under the surveillance of men (and later women) whose job it was to monitor my behavior for signs of sloth, theft, drug abuse, or worse. Not that managers and especially "assistant managers" in low-wage settings like this are exactly the class enemy. In the restaurant business, they are mostly former cooks or servers, still capable of pinch-hitting in the kitchen or on the floor, just as in hotels they are likely to be former clerks, and paid a salary of only about $400 a week. But everyone knows they have crossed over to the other side, which is, crudely put, corporate as opposed to human. Cooks want to prepare tasty meals; servers want to serve them graciously; but managers are there for only one reason—to make sure that money is made for some theoretical entity that exists far away in Chicago or New York, if a corporation can be said to have a physical existence at all. Reflecting on her career, Gail tells me ruefully that she had sworn, years ago, never to work for a corporation again. "They don't cut you no slack. You give and you give, and they take."

20 Managers can sit—for hours at a time if they want—but it's their job to see that no one else ever does, even when there's nothing to do, and this is why, for servers, slow times can be as exhausting as rushes. You start dragging out each little chore, because if the manager on duty catches you in an idle moment, he will give you something far nastier to do. So I wipe, I clean, I consolidate ketchup bottles and recheck the cheesecake supply, even tour the tables to make sure the customer evaluation forms are all standing perkily in their places—wondering all the time how many calories I burn in these strictly theatrical exercises. When, on a particular dead afternoon, Stu finds me glancing at a *USA Today* a customer has left behind, he assigns me to vacuum the entire floor with the broken vacuum cleaner that has a handle only two feet long, and the only way to do that without incurring orthopedic damage is to proceed from spot to spot on your knees.

21 On my first Friday at the Hearthside there is a "mandatory meeting for all restaurant employees," which I attend, eager for insight into our overall marketing strategy and the niche (your basic Ohio cuisine with a tropical twist?) we aim to inhabit. But there is no "we" at this meeting. Phillip, our top manager except for an occasional "consultant" sent out by corporate headquarters, opens it with a sneer: "The break room—it's disgusting. Butts in the ashtrays, newspapers lying around, crumbs." This windowless little room, which also houses the time clock for the entire hotel, is where we stash our bags and civilian clothes and take our half-hour meal breaks. But a break room is not a right, he tells us. It can be taken away. We should also know that the lockers in the break room and whatever is in them can be searched at any time. Then comes gossip; there has been gossip; gossip (which seems to mean employees talking among themselves) must stop. Off-duty employees are henceforth barred from eating at the restaurant, because "other servers gather around them and gossip." When Phillip has exhausted his agenda of rebukes, Joan complains about the condition of the ladies' room and I throw in my two bits about the vacuum cleaner. But I don't see any backup coming from my fellow servers, each of whom has subsided into her own personal funk; Gail, my role model, stares sorrowfully at a point six inches from her nose. The meeting ends when Andy, one of the cooks, gets up, muttering about breaking up his day off for this almighty bullshit.

22 Just four days later we are suddenly summoned into the kitchen at 3:30 P.M. even though there are live tables on the floor. We all—about ten of us—stand around Phillip, who announces grimly that there has been a report of some "drug activity" on the night shift and that, as a result, we are now to be a "drug-free" workplace, meaning that all new hires will be tested, as will possibly current employees on a random basis. I am glad that this part of the kitchen is so dark, because I find myself blushing as hard as if I had been caught toking up in the ladies' room myself: I haven't been treated this way—lined up in the corridor, threatened with locker searches, peppered with carelessly aimed accusations—since junior high school. Back on the floor, Joan cracks, "Next they'll be telling us we can't have sex on the job." When I ask Stu what happened to inspire the crackdown, he just mutters about "management decisions" and takes the opportunity to upbraid Gail and me for being too generous with the rolls. From now on there's to be only one per customer, and it goes out with the dinner, not with the salad. He's also been riding the cooks, prompting Andy to come out of the kitchen and observe—with the serenity of a man whose customary implement is a butcher knife—that "Stu has a death wish today."

23 Later in the evening, the gossip crystallizes around the theory that Stu is himself the drug culprit, that he uses the restaurant phone to order up marijuana and sends one of the late servers out to fetch it for him. The server was caught, and she may have ratted Stu out or at least said enough to cast some suspicion on him, thus accounting for his pissy behavior. Who knows? Lionel, the busboy,

entertains us for the rest of the shift by standing just behind Stu's back and sucking deliriously on an imaginary joint.

24 The other problem, in addition to the less-than-nurturing management style, is that this job shows no sign of being financially viable. You might imagine, from a comfortable distance, that people who live, year in and year out, on $6 to $10 an hour have discovered some survival stratagems unknown to the middle class. But no. It's not hard to get my co-workers to talk about their living situations, because housing, in almost every case, is the principal source of disruption in their lives, the first thing they fill you in on when they arrive for their shifts. After a week, I have compiled the following survey:

- Gail is sharing a room in a well-known downtown flophouse for which she and a roommate pay about $250 a week. Her roommate, a male friend, has been hitting on her, driving her nuts, but the rent would be impossible alone.
- Claude, the Haitian cook, is desperate to get out of the two-room apartment he shares with his girlfriend and two other, unrelated, people. As far as I can determine, the other Haitian men (most of whom only speak Creole) live in similarly crowded situations.
- Annette, a twenty-year-old server who is six months pregnant and has been abandoned by her boyfriend, lives with her mother, a postal clerk.
- Marianne and her boyfriend are paying $170 a week for a one-person trailer.
- Jack, who is, at $10 an hour, the wealthiest of us, lives in the trailer he owns, paying only the $400-a-month lot fee.
- The other white cook, Andy, lives on his dry-docked boat, which, as far as I can tell from his loving descriptions, can't be more than twenty feet long. He offers to take me out on it, once it's repaired, but the offer comes with inquiries as to my marital status, so I do not follow up on it.
- Tina and her husband are paying $60 a night for a double room in a Days Inn. This is because they have no car and the Days Inn is within walking distance of the Hearthside. When Marianne, one of the breakfast servers, is tossed out of her trailer for subletting (which is against the trailer-park rules), she leaves her boyfriend and moves in with Tina and her husband.
- Joan, who had fooled me with her numerous and tasteful outfits (hostesses wear their own clothes), lives in a van she parks behind a shopping center at night and showers in Tina's motel room. The clothes are from thrift shops.[4]

25 It strikes me, in my middle-class solipsism, that there is gross improvidence in some of these arrangements. When Gail and I are wrapping silverware in napkins—the only task for which we are permitted to sit—she tells me she is

thinking of escaping from her roommate by moving into the Days Inn herself. I am astounded: How can she even think of paying between $40 and $60 a day? But if I was afraid of sounding like a social worker, I come out just sounding like a fool. She squints at me in disbelief, "And where am I supposed to get a month's rent and a month's deposit for an apartment?" I'd been feeling pretty smug about my $500 efficiency, but of course it was made possible only by the $1,300 I had allotted myself for start-up costs when I began my low-wage life: $1,000 for the first month's rent and deposit, $100 for initial groceries and cash in my pocket, $200 stuffed away for emergencies. In poverty, as in certain propositions in physics, starting conditions are everything.

26 There are no secret economies that nourish the poor; on the contrary, there are a host of special costs. If you can't put up the two months' rent you need to secure an apartment, you end up paying through the nose for a room by the week. If you have only a room, with a hot plate at best, you can't save by cooking up huge lentil stews that can be frozen for the week ahead. You eat fast food, or the hot dogs and styrofoam cups of soup that can be microwaved in a convenience store. If you have no money for health insurance—and the Hearthside's niggardly plan kicks in only after three months—you go without routine care or prescription drugs and end up paying the price. Gail, for example, was fine until she ran out of money for estrogen pills. She is supposed to be on the company plan by now, but they claim to have lost her application form and need to begin the paperwork all over again. So she spends $9 per migraine pill to control the headaches she wouldn't have, she insists, if her estrogen supplements were covered. Similarly, Marianne's boyfriend lost his job as a roofer because he missed so much time after getting a cut on his foot for which he couldn't afford the prescribed antibiotic.

27 My own situation, when I sit down to assess it after two weeks of work, would not be much better if this were my actual life. The seductive thing about waitressing is that you don't have to wait for payday to feel a few bills in your pocket, and my tips usually cover meals and gas, plus something left over to stuff into the kitchen drawer I use as a bank. But as the tourist business slows in the summer heat, I sometimes leave work with only $20 in tips (the gross is higher, but servers share about 15 percent of their tips with the busboys and bartenders). With wages included, this amounts to about the minimum wage of $5.15 an hour. Although the sum in the drawer is piling up, at the present rate of accumulation it will be more than a hundred dollars short of my rent when the end of the month comes around. Nor can I see any expenses to cut. True, I haven't gone the lentil-stew route yet, but that's because I don't have a large cooking pot, pot holders, or a ladle to stir with (which cost about $30 at Kmart, less at thrift stores), not to mention onions, carrots, and the indispensable bay leaf. I do make my lunch almost every day—usually some slow-burning, high-protein combo like frozen chicken patties with melted cheese on top and canned pinto beans on the side. Dinner is at the Hearthside, which offers its employees a choice of BLT, fish sandwich,

or hamburger for only $2. The burger lasts longest, especially if it's heaped with gut-puckering jalapeños, but by midnight my stomach is growling again.

28 So unless I want to start using my car as a residence, I have to find a second, or alternative, job. I call all the hotels where I filled out housekeeping applications weeks ago—the Hyatt, Holiday Inn, Econo Lodge, HoJo's, Best Western, plus a half dozen or so locally run guesthouses. Nothing. Then I start making the rounds again, wasting whole mornings waiting for some assistant manager to show up, even dipping into places so creepy that the front-desk clerk greets you from behind bulletproof glass and sells pints of liquor over the counter. But either someone has exposed my real-life housekeeping habits—which are, shall we say, mellow—or I am at the wrong end of some infallible ethnic equation: most, but by no means all, of the working housekeepers I see on my job searches are African Americans, Spanish-speaking, or immigrants from the Central European post-Communist world, whereas servers are almost invariably white and monolingually English-speaking. When I finally get a positive response, I have been identified once again as server material. Jerry's, which is part of a well-known national family restaurant chain and physically attached here to another budget hotel chain, is ready to use me at once. The prospect is both exciting and terrifying, because, with about the same number of tables and counter seats, Jerry's attracts three or four times the volume of customers as the gloomy old Hearthside.

---

[1]According to the Department of Housing and Urban Development, the "fair-market rent" for an efficiency is $551 here in Monroe County, Florida. A comparable rent in the five boroughs of New York City is $704; in San Francisco, $713; and in the heart of Silicon Valley, $808. The fair-market rent for an area is defined as the amount that would be needed to pay rent plus utilities for "privately owned, decent, safe, and sanitary rental housing of a modest (non-luxury) nature with suitable amenities." [Ehrenreich's note. The "fair market rent" would be higher today—much higher in New York City or San Francisco. (Editor)]

[2]According to the *Monthly Labor Review* (November 1996), 28 percent of work sites surveyed in the service industry conduct drug tests (corporate workplaces have much higher rates), and the incidence of testing has risen markedly since the 1980s. The rate of testing is highest in the South (56 percent of work sites polled), with the Midwest in second place (50 percent). The drug most likely to be detected—marijuana, which can be detected in urine for weeks—is also the most innocuous, while heroin and cocaine are generally undetectable three days after use. Prospective employees sometimes try to cheat the tests by consuming excessive amounts of liquids and taking diuretics and even masking substances available through the Internet. [Editor's note]

[3]According to the Fair Labor Standards Act, employers are not required to pay "tipped employees," such as restaurant servers, more than $2.13 an hour in direct wages. However, if the sum of tips plus $2.13 an hour falls below the minimum wage, or $5.15 an hour, the employer is required to make up the difference. This fact was not mentioned by managers or otherwise publicized at either of the restaurants where I worked. [Ehrenreich's note]

[4]I could find no statistics on the number of employed people living in cars or vans, but according to the National Coalition for the Homeless's 1997 report "Myths and Facts About Homelessness," nearly one in five homeless people (in twenty-nine cities across the nation) is employed in a full- or part-time job. [Ehrenreich's note]

Postscript: Ehrenreich took a waitress job at Jerry's, working the morning and lunch shift at the Hearthside and then working the 2:00–10:00 P.M. at Jerry's. When she arrived at Jerry's on her second day, one of her fellow waitresses greeted her with surprise, saying, "Well, it's good to see you again. Hardly anyone comes back after the first day."

EXERCISES

A. Determining the Main Idea and Writer's Purpose

Choose the best answer.

1. The main idea of the selection is that low-wage earners in America
   a. benefit both economically and socially from the reforms in the welfare system.
   b. find it possible to survive on minimum wage, but it takes luck, sacrifice, and generosity from their family and friends.
   c. suffer the most in a recession because they tend to be unskilled and undereducated.
   d. find it nearly impossible to survive on minimum wage because their wages cannot cover rent and other necessities of life.

2. The writer's purpose in the selection is to
   a. demonstrate through personal experience the truth of her claim.
   b. convince the reader of the need for further welfare reform.
   c. complain about how hard the life of a waitress is.
   d. examine some common workplace practices that alienate low-wage workers.

B. Comprehending Main Ideas

Choose the correct answer.

1. When Ehrenreich first conceived of her plan, she was initially terrified that she
   a. would not have enough experience to do the jobs she applied for.
   b. would be recognized and exposed as a journalist.
   c. would not earn enough money to live on.
   d. would abandon the project early if she became too discouraged.

2. Ehrenreich believed that reform of the welfare system
   a. was long overdue and much-needed policy that would lift women out of poverty and give them self-esteem.
   b. was simply a political tactic to win over conservative voters.

c. offered too rosy a view of its benefits and may contribute to a worsening economy and depressed wages.

d. did not go far enough because there weren't enough job-training programs to help low-skilled workers get jobs.

3. After searching newspaper ads for housekeeping jobs at various motels and hotels, Ehrenreich concluded that

a. she was overqualified for these jobs.

b. no one would hire her because she was white.

c. the posting continual ads was merely the employers' way of ensuring a steady supply of workers to replace those who quit.

d. the poor economy had caused a downturn in tourism, which affected the hospitality industry's low-wage employees.

4. At low-wage establishments, Ehrenreich complained that managers

a. were more concerned with squeezing every nickel out for the corporation than with serving customers well or treating employees nicely.

b. deliberately flouted employment laws because they knew that their employees needed the work and would not complain.

c. ignored obvious violations of their stated no-drug policy.

d. violated labor laws and paid less than minimum wage.

5. As Ehrenreich got to know her coworkers, she discovered that, for almost all of them, the one constant source of disruption in their lives was

a. problems with personal relationships.

b. the inability to get ahead because of their lack of skills and education.

c. The difficulty in finding housing.

d. substance abuse problems.

C. Sequencing

The sentences in this excerpt from the selection may have been scrambled. Read the sentences and choose the sequence that puts them back into logical order. Do not refer to the original selection.

1. This seems to be a fairly general rule: if you want to stack Cheerio boxes or vacuum hotel rooms in chemically fascist America, you have to be willing to squat down and pee in front of some health worker (who has no doubt had to do the same thing herself). **2.** The wages Winn-Dixie is offering—$6 and a couple of dimes to start with—are not enough, I decide to compensate for this indignity. **3.** Apparently, I ace the interview, because I am told that all I have to do now is show up in some doctor's office tomorrow for a urine test.

a. 3, 1, 2
b. 3, 2, 1
c. 1, 3, 2
d. Correct as written.

D. Identifying Supporting Details

Place an **X** in the space for each sentence from the selection that *directly* supports this main idea: "There are no secret economies that nourish the poor; on the contrary, there are a host of special costs."

1. _____ I'd been feeling pretty smug about my $500 efficiency, but of course it was made possible only by the $1,300 I had allotted myself for start-up costs when I began my low-wage life.
2. _____ If you can't put up the two months' rent you need to secure an apartment, you end up paying through the nose for a room by the week.
3. _____ If you have only a room, with a hot plate at best, you can't save by cooking up huge lentil stews that can be frozen for the week ahead.
4. _____ You eat fast food, or the hot dogs and styrofoam cups of soup that can be microwaved in a convenience store.
5. _____ The seductive thing about waitressing is that you don't have to wait for payday to feel a few bills in your pocket, and my tips usually cover meals and gas, plus something left over to stuff into the kitchen drawer I use as a bank.

E. Making Inferences

Write your answers for these questions in your own words.

1. What can you infer might be the "humanitarian rationale for welfare" that Ehrenreich alludes to in paragraph 5?

   ____

2. Read the end of paragraph 9 again. What can you infer about Winn-Dixie from the computer interview questions the writer must answer? What seem to be the company's main concerns about its employees?

   ____

   ____

3. From the end of paragraph 12, what can you infer was the reason that Phillip hired Ehrenreich so quickly for a waitress job?

   ____

4. Read paragraphs 15–17 again. How does the writer treat her dining patrons?

5. In paragraph 28, Ehrenreich describes her own housekeeping habits as "mellow." What does she mean?

6. What is the general impression of managers in terms of the way they treat their employees, as Ehrenreich describes them?

F. Interpreting Meaning

Where appropriate, write your answers for these questions in your own words.

1. In paragraph 3, what does Ehrenreich mean when she writes, "anthropologically speaking, a bustling trailer park would be preferable"?

2. Which of the following is the best title for paragraph 5?
   a. "A Scientific Mission"
   b. "A Defense of Welfare Reform"
   c. "Welfare Reform: Rosy Theory vs. Hard Facts"
   d. "The Humanitarian Rationale for Welfare Reform"

3. Where in the essay does Ehrenreich anticipate objections to her plan or the fact that she is a middle-class white woman who has never known poverty, making the experiment unrealistic?

4. Read paragraph 10 again. Explain Ehrenreich's reaction to Winn-Dixie's interview process.

5. In paragraph 10, what does Ehrenreich think about low-wage employees having to submit to a urine test to detect the presence of drugs?

____

What phrase reveals her attitude?

____

6. What does Ehrenreich mean at the end of paragraph 17 when she talks about how waitresses measure out pats of butter and sour cream?

____

____

G. Understanding Vocabulary

Look through the paragraphs listed below and find a word that matches each definition. Refer to a dictionary if necessary. An example has been done for you.

EXAMPLE: needless, having no justification, groundless [paragraph 1] unwarranted

1. avoiding, escaping [2] _______________
2. defeated, conquered [3] _______________
3. intending to inflict punishment [5] _______________
4. a flowing in, mass arrival [5] _______________
5. ordinary, commonplace [7] _______________
6. extreme poverty, destitution [7] _______________
7. suggesting favorable circumstances [8] _______________
8. poor, impoverished [8] _______________
9. troublesome, oppressive [9] _______________
10. steady, persistent, unremitting [12] _______________
11. nimble, moving lightly and quickly [13] _______________
12. violation of the law, breaking a rule [17] _______________
13. secret, not practiced openly [17] _______________
14. criticisms, harsh reprimands [21] _______________
15. incapable of being wrong [28] _______________

H. Summarizing Exercise

Summarize paragraph 5.

____

____

____

____

____

DISCUSSION QUESTIONS

1. Why did Ehrenreich decide to live in the world of the low-wage worker instead of just pretending that she was working and adding up the figures?
2. Look again at paragraphs 5–7. In terms of the selection as a whole, what is the function of this section? If it were omitted, would her observations carry as much weight, or not?
3. What is your reaction to Ehrenreich's experiment? Does her method seem like the best way to assess the problems low-wage earners face every day of their lives, or does it carry limitations? Did her approach impress you, or do you object to her method?

EXPLORE THE WEB

Ehrenreich's book received a large amount of coverage in the press, with mixed reviews over her methods and findings. Go to your favorite search engine (Google, Netscape, Yahoo, or another), do a search by typing in the title of the book, and see what the critics had to say about this work. To get started, in the search box, type in the following string:

Ehrenreich + Nickel and Dimed + Reviews

Writing an Analysis and a Synthesis Essay

We now come to a more difficult writing challenge, one that will serve you well throughout your college career. If you could write papers based only on your personal experience, you would soon find the exercise to be quite limiting. Looking at the world through only your own lens would produce a myopic view of reality. Also, it would be the very antithesis of an education. You may recall that the word *educate* derives from the Latin prefix *e-* ("out of") and *ducare* ("to lead"). It is hard to undergo this *leading-out* process, then, if one examines only his or her own experience.

For this reason, college composition instructors ask their students to read nonfiction prose as well as fiction, representing a wide variety of topics, opinions, structures, and styles, and to write about what they have read. And as we have emphasized throughout this text, writing and reading skills connect; they work together in tandem. As the readings become more difficult, so do the writing challenges. And writing analysis and synthesis essays—the core of many if not most college writing assignments—pose the biggest challenge. We have all had the experience of our mind's going blank in the face of a writing assignment. To counteract that feeling of confusion and perplexity, this section will show you, step by step, how to prepare for, organize, and develop topics requiring analysis and synthesis.

WRITING ANALYSIS AND SYNTHESIS: ACADEMIC AND PROFESSIONAL WRITING

Writing and thinking analytically allow you to solve problems, to evaluate circumstances, and to explain your views on these topics to others, whether in the classroom or in the world of work.

Typical Academic Assignments Requiring Writing an Analysis or Synthesis

- Analyze the economic causes of the American Civil War for a history course.
- Analyze the causes of a chemical reaction for a chemistry course.

- Analyze the elements of water color painting for an evaluation you are writing of a particular artist's work for an art course.

Typical Professional Writing Tasks Requiring Writing an Analysis or Synthesis

- Analyze the evidence that led to the arrest and conviction of an individual.
- Analyze the reasons for a decline in the number of applicants for a particular type of work.
- Analyze the possible causes of an increase in industrial accidents during a particular period of time.

DEFINITION OF AN ANALYTICAL ESSAY

"To analyze" means to explore a subject by breaking it down into its component parts, first to examine the implications and workings of each component and then to determine how each component works to make the whole function. For example, we can analyze a bicycle wheel by breaking it down into its component parts—outer rim, spokes, and hub. Then we can describe how each of these parts makes the wheel function.

Although writing an analytical essay, unhappily, is not as easy as this illustration suggests, the same principle operates—you look at individual elements first to see how they connect, and you show how they connect to an unifying principle, the *thesis*. The thesis makes the connections among the parts clear. Stated another way, analysis asks you to identify a particular idea in a reading, show its importance in relation to the essay as a whole, and comment on its significance. In the next section you will learn to apply a useful analytical tool called the tell-share-show method.

A CASE IN POINT: ANALYZING "SUGAR" BY FRANK HUYLER

Let's demonstrate the analytical method by looking at one of the early essays in this book, "Sugar" by Frank Huyler (pages 56–58). I have chosen this essay because it is short, accessible, and open to interpretation. Be sure to read this essay, either as a review or for the first time, before continuing with this section.

Huyler is an emergency room physician in Albuquerque, New Mexico. One night two African American parents brought their daughter into the ER because they thought she was acting "weird" and because she was "not looking right." Huyler examined the girl, who by then was acting normally. Later, he discovered—through persistent questioning—that the girl had taken one of her grandmother's medications, causing her blood sugar level to drop. Without Huyler's intervention and persistence, the child might have died.

That is what the essay is about, but the preceding is only a summary; there is no essay there, and certainly no analysis. A summary provides the facts, but no insight. No insight, no essay.

To begin an analysis of Huyler's essay, you first have to isolate what you think the most significant elements are. One student, Kim Tran, identified three elements in this essay: First, the brief exchange between the triage nurse and Huyler, then the conversation between Huyler and the parents and their report on their daughter's symptoms, and last, Huyler's attempts to diagnose the child's condition. (Of course, there is also the little girl, but Kim realized immediately that her analysis wouldn't go anywhere if she wrote only about the little girl, as she plays only a secondary role to Huyler's larger purpose.)

After Kim read the essay for perhaps the third or fourth time, she realized that the triage nurse's early remark to Huyler had great significance in light of what might have happened if the doctor had responded to her remark, and it shaped her interpretation of Huyler's subsequent behavior. Here is the quotation that she marked in her text:

> "They're Medicaid," the triage nurse had whispered pointedly in my ear. The implication was clear; they wanted something for free. Tylenol. A work excuse. But it was ten o'clock on a Friday night. (56)

In the nurse's whispered remark, Kim discovered an idea that might work as a starting point for her essay. For Kim, this insight emerged from her close reading of the material and her thinking about the material and her interpretation of it. Whatever it is, this insight into an idea or experience has to have special significance *for you*. It will not descend like a thunderbolt from the heavens, and no one can make this discovery for you. Other students might read the same essay and discover something entirely different.

Even more important, whatever significant element you choose to focus on, *your observation must be grounded in the text.* I cannot emphasize this principle enough. Your observations must be connected to evidence in the reading, evidence that substantiates your point of view. Without this connection, the interpretation will not work. If you pull opinions out of the air that are not grounded in the text, your essay will be only empty speculation. In the next section, we will see how Kim expanded her initial interpretation during the brainstorming and how her notes led her to a thesis.

BRAINSTORMING FOR AN ANALYTICAL ESSAY—SAMPLE NOTES

So when Kim returned to the quotation from Huyler's essay, what implications did she see in this brief exchange? With the quotation as her starting point, Kim opened a blank file on her computer and began typing ideas as they came to her. In this brainstorming session, she did not worry about logical order or sentence structure or spelling. She asked questions and gave some tentative answers. But each writer has to find his or her own way. Here are the notes that Kim wrote and turned in before she began to write the essay itself:

The nurse seems to write the parents off as being not only poor because they have Medicaid insurance, but also she thinks that they fit a stereotype, they're people with public health insurance want something for nothing. She suspects that they may be slackers who may be making up the story about their daughter's not acting right. Huyler doesn't directly say that the little girl's parents are African American but the details about the mother's appearance, her dress and the beaded cornrows, say to me that they are. Why else would he include those details? The nurse's remark marginalizes them. She accuses them of something based on past prejudice without knowing all the facts.

Does the triage nurse show bias? I think so. But if she hadn't whispered what she had in Huyler's ear, I couldn't say this. Why does the doctor react as he does? Why does he mention that it's 10 P.M. on a Friday night? I think he's saying that something may really be wrong with the child, even though she seems to be acting normally now. If they just wanted "something for free," wouldn't they have picked a more convenient time?

Why does Huyler persist in questioning the parents? What is his role? To listen to a prejudiced nurse or to save lives? Doesn't this show that he resists the nurse's opinion, especially when that opinion is not helpful in finding out what is wrong with the child? But then he becomes "impatient" himself. He feels tension in the ER. He sees that other patients are waiting to be seen, and these parents' explanation of their daughter's symptoms isn't going as fast as he would like. Other people need his help, too.

What are his options? He could ignore the parents' concerns, but it seems as if he has to take their observations seriously. A trained physician knows that parents are the best people to judge their child's condition because they are with the child more than any one else and therefore know what is normal behavior and what's not. Even if their explanation is vague and the child seems to be OK, he isn't willing to assume that she will recover on her own or that she can wait to see her own doctor after the weekend. He works like a detective, probing and prodding until finally he hits on something—perhaps the child got into someone's medication. After that, the mystery of the child's condition is solved.

So what does all of this add up to? The doctor rises above stereotyped thinking. His persistence saves the child's life. By the end of his examination, he realizes what would have happened to the little girl if he had sent her home.

WRITING THE THESIS STATEMENT

Even though Kim's notes are sprawling and unedited, they do lead to a focal point, an organizing principle for an essay—the thesis statement that will guide the essay from start to finish. Notice how she asked questions in her notes, allowing her to explore the many ramifications of this situation and the doctor's position with regard to both the nurse and the child's parents. After this brainstorming process, Kim felt ready to write some trial thesis statements, and in the next class she discussed them with the other students in a peer group assignment:

1. Emergency room personnel are supposed to show diligence and care and put prejudicial feelings aside. In Frank Huyler's essay, "Sugar," the tension between the triage nurse, the parents of a sick child, and Huyler, an ER physician, eventually shows the day-to-day stresses that both personnel and patients experience.
2. Huyler describes an incident when some parents brought their child into the ER with mysterious symptoms. This incident shows how racial bias displayed by one hospital staff member in the ER might have had catastrophic results if not for the doctor's persistence.
3. As a trained emergency room physician, Frank Huyler demonstrates a steadfast commitment to getting at the truth about a patient's condition.

Of these three thesis statements, Kim finally decided during peer review that the second one was the best, the one she could most easily defend. She then tightened and revised the thesis by combining the two sentences into one. Here is her thesis, this time with the key words circled:

> In describing an incident when parents brought their child into the ER with mysterious symptoms, Huyler, a trained emergency-room physician, shows how racial bias displayed by an ER nurse might have had catastrophic results if not for his persistence.

Note that the thesis restricts the direction and scope of the paper, and the key words will help her both organize the discussion to follow and keep it on track. These key words make it impossible for the essay to be developed effectively only by summary.

Once a student reaches this point in the essay-writing process, it is time for a well-deserved break. Kim put the notes and thesis statements away and let her ideas bounce around in her head for a day or two before she started to write her first draft. Then comes the harder part—actually putting words on paper in some sort of organized form. However, Kim's early preparation up to this point meant that the actual writing of the paper would not be so burdensome. She would not experience the "terror of the blank screen," because by the time she sat down to write, she had a pretty good idea of the direction in which she wanted her essay to go.

WRITING THE INTRODUCTORY PARAGRAPH

There is no ironclad rule for writing the introduction. But a few guidelines might help you get past this difficult step. The introduction usually contains the thesis statement, but not in the first sentence, which would make the opening too abrupt. You want to give the reader something to look forward to, and if you present the thesis right away, you give away your main point without seducing the reader into wanting to continue. Further, the introductory paragraph should set the scene; it should include the writer's name and the title of the selection, and it should give the reader an overview of the essay you are analyzing. *Then* comes the thesis. Therefore, most composition instructors prefer the thesis statement to come at the end of the introductory paragraph or paragraphs. (Remember that it is permissible to write a two- or even a three-paragraph introduction if the subject is complex.) You can also add a paragraph or two after the thesis briefly summarizing what the essay is about before you begin your analysis. Whatever method you use, length and structure of the introduction should be appropriate for the scope and content of your essay.

After writing three or four drafts of the introductory paragraph for her analysis of "Sugar," Kim came up with this:

Introduction—

Orientation to the subject—the atmosphere in the ER on typical TV dramas

Inclusion of essay title and author's name.

Tension in the ER

Most of us are familiar with the conventional scenes in big city emergency rooms from TV programs like "Chicago Hope," "ER," and "Grey's Anatomy." The typical hospital drama depicts a seemingly unlimited number of crises and a frenzied atmosphere as personnel struggle to save one life after another. Frank Huyler's short essay, "Sugar," presents a rather different picture of ER life at the Albuquerque hospital where

Thesis statement—last sentence; key words are circled

> he works—one that is less frenzied, but nonetheless still full of tension. In describing an incident when parents brought their child into the ER with mysterious symptoms, Huyler, a trained emergency room physician, shows how racial bias displayed by an ER nurse might have had catastrophic results if not for his persistence.

One final note on writing introductions: At all costs avoid the direct announcement opening, of which there are two typical versions: "In this essay I intend to show how an emergency room physician exercised diligence and concern for a patient. …" or "The purpose of my paper is to show how. …" This announcement opening is not only dull and trite; it also violates the conventions of college academic writing. The key words in Kim's thesis statement make it sufficiently obvious to the reader what she is going to talk about, making the direct announcement approach unnecessary.

Polish your thesis until you are satisfied with its scope. You can always go back and revise it later, either broadening it or narrowing it as your discussion takes shape.

WRITING THE ANALYSIS—THE TELL-SHOW-SHARE METHOD

Many of my colleagues and I have found one method that has worked well to teach students how to write an analytical essay. It is called the *tell-show-share method*, devised by Jeff Rackham and Olivia Bertagnolli and published in a fine textbook, *Windows* (HarperCollins, 1994). Unfortunately, this book is no longer in print, but Rackham's and Bertagnolli's explanation is so clear, practical, and relatively easy to implement that I would like to reprint it in their own words. This method can be used to analyze any type of writing—an essay, an article, a speech, a poem, or a short story. First, Rackham and Bertagnolli describe basic essay structure, focusing on the purpose of the introduction and the body:

> **The Body of the Essay** We've often wished the traditional term for the major portion of an essay was something other than "body." It sounds so dead, lying there naked and headless. But the central core of an essay can't be dead, or

deadening, any more than an introduction can. If we compare an introduction to a camcorder taking a panoramic survey of the whole scene, the body of an essay can be thought of as a zoom lens focusing on various specific details—on a key passage or on special terms, events, examples, actions, or arguments. Each detail must be seen clearly by the reader. Each must be discussed, analyzed, or compared to another element. And before the camera moves away to focus on something else, the significance of each detail must be made perfectly clear or the importance suggested in such a way that the reader knows further observations and insights will be forthcoming. Again, the organization of all this may flow naturally, organically, out of your deep investment in the subject. But certain conventions continue to be expected of you. The most traditional organization has three components, and these stages apply not only to the paper as a whole, but to each subpoint within the body.

Then they describe the tell-show-share method:

- ***Tell the reader something.*** Make an observation. What's the point? What have you noticed or become aware of? What context does the point occur in? That is, where does it occur in the essay or story or poem? Remember that giving the context not only clarifies for the reader, it affects the way we understand the point itself.
- ***Show it (or demonstrate it).*** What evidence do you have to support your observation? Summarize specific examples, events, actions, statements. Integrate key quotations from the text.
- ***Share your thoughts and feelings.*** Why is this point significant? What do we learn by having focused in on it? If you're writing about an essay or factual work, can you analyze the specific idea you're considering for its logic? How sound is the evidence the author provides? How does the author's argument here relate to other arguments later? If you're writing about fiction, poetry, or drama, how does the incident or language or whatever reveal some insight into character? How does the event build toward a particular emotional response? What does it all suggest?[1]

WRITING THE ANALYSIS—TWO SAMPLE BODY PARAGRAPHS

Here are two body paragraphs Kim wrote to develop her thesis. You can see the origin of her final interpretation in her brainstorming notes. Key words from the thesis are circled. These words and phrases create thematic unity and keep the discussion on track.

[1]Jeff Rackham and Olivia Bertagnolli, *Windows: Exploring Personal Values through Reading and Writing* (HarperCollins 1994), 64–66.

FIRST BODY ¶

Tell (make an observation and establish the context). Emphasize the key words, racial tension

At the beginning of "Sugar," the tension in the ER is apparent not just in the anxious parents' justifiable concern for their daughter's condition, but also in subtle racial tension. The triage nurse who takes down the parents' information responds to them negatively. The parents, who are most likely African American judging from the details Huyler provides about the wife's bright African print dress and cornrows, are on Medicaid, a government-sponsored health insurance program. But the nurse does not keep her opinions to herself. Huyler writes,

> "They're Medicaid," the triage nurse had whispered pointedly in my ear. The implication was clear; they wanted something for free. Tylenol. A work excuse. But it was ten o'clock on a Friday night. (56)

Show (use a pertinent, reinforcing quotation). Share (show why the quotation is significant and what it means)

Without knowing all the facts or giving Huyler a chance to examine the girl, the nurse has labeled them as scammers. Her whispered comment to Huyler reveals her annoyance and stereotyped thinking. Her tone is accusatory, and the remark is intended to marginalize them.

SECOND BODY ¶

Tell

Huyler reveals his own tensions, and his dilemma is apparent, too, as his impatience mounts. He notices other patients waiting in the ER; other people need his help. The parents' description of the child's symptoms is vague; he isn't getting anywhere with them. He notes, too, that her parents seem to be taking good care of the child:

> I could see nothing wrong with her. She looked impeccably cared for, without any sign of the abuse I had been vaguely

Show

> and secretly considering. I always do. It's been drummed into us. (57)

Share

Fortunately, Huyler ignores the nurse's pointed comment, just as he realizes that his own suspicion about abuse is unfounded. He reasons that people who are working the system would probably not venture into the ER late on a Friday night and make up a story about a child not acting right. Curbing his impatience, he realizes that he cannot let this child go home without getting to the source of her problem. In his experience as a trained physician, parents are the best people to evaluate their child's condition. So he persists in questioning them.

Rackham and Bertagnolli end their explanation of the tell-show-share analytical pattern with this observation:

> *Tell, Show, Share* could be phrased with more intellectual pomp. *Make a Statement, Provide Supporting Evidence, Discuss or Assess the Meaning.* However you want to phrase it, the final step in this conventional pattern is the crucial element, the point where your personal response and interpretation take over. Yet without the first two components, the reader is usually lost. All three are needed for clarity.

Study Kim's introduction and two sample body paragraphs above in light of these final comments to see how these elements fit together. Note that the "tell" portion includes key words from the thesis, the "show" section uses examples and quotations that reaffirm the thesis, and the "share" section includes your interpretation of the details Kim finds significant. Repeating the key words in the body paragraphs creates thematic unity and continuity so that all the elements work together—the context (the setting or environment where the situation occurs), the situation described, pertinent and reinforcing quotations, and finally the analysis of the quoted material, its significance, and the aftermath.

One final reminder: Summarizing is not a substitute for analysis. However, it is perfectly all right, in fact it is necessary as Kim's body paragraphs show, to refer to events in the essay or article that pertain to the thesis, as long as you do not merely summarize what the writer said.

A SPECIAL KIND OF ANALYSIS—THE SYNTHESIS ESSAY

Throughout this book, you have been exposed to topics that ask you to analyze another writer's observation and that require you to find implications. In this section, we discuss how to prepare another kind of analytical essay using multiple sources. It is called the *synthesis essay*. The verb *synthesize* means "to combine, so as to form a new, complex product."

Polyester is a synthetic fabric; so are nylon, spandex, and Velcro. In each case, several chemical elements are put together to form a completely new fabric. In the same way, a *synthesis* essay requires the writer to select information from two or more essays in support of a thesis. To do this, the writer must read and annotate the material carefully and interact closely with the texts. The writer must make connections and discover relationships between the texts. The Velcro analogy is appropriate to see how synthesis works. The inventor of this miracle fastening tape put together two separate elements—little nylon loops on one strip and nylon pile on another strip. Individually, the loops and the pile would not work as a fastener, but when pushed together, the loops stick to the pile, creating an incredibly strong bond—and an entirely new product. In the same way, a synthesis essay offers the student's insight into the readings, and the thesis statement takes the discussion in a new direction from what the essays say when considered separately.

WRITING A SYNTHESIS ESSAY

The synthesis essay relies on paraphrase and summary, but its purpose is not to paraphrase or to summarize. It also may use comparison and contrast, though those are not its main purposes. Most of all it relies on analysis—selecting various writers' ideas and organizing and interpreting them in a new way—much like a child's kaleidoscope reveals different patterns of the little colored bits of glass with each shake of the cylinder.

Once you establish the thesis—the assertion that explains your particular focus—you then support it with two types of evidence: ideas and observations from the writers' texts (including paraphrase, summary, and quotations) and your own thoughts and reactions to what you have read. The tell-show-share method works well for synthesis papers, as you will see. You might also be asked to bring in your own experience as it relates to what the writers have said. We will look at the various steps involved in this process. A word of warning: Allow yourself plenty of time to prepare a synthesis assignment. Starting the night before will result in a shoddy paper that neither you nor your instructor will be proud of.

Pete Glanting's composition instructor asked the class to read four readings on work and attitudes toward work:

- Rose Castillo Guilbault, "The Conveyor Belt Ladies" (Part 2)
- Eric Schlosser, "Fast Food Nation: Behind the Counter" (Part 5)
- Barbara Ehrenreich, "Nickel and Dimed: On (Not) Getting by in America" (Part 5)
- Sonia Nazario, "Benefit and Burden" (Part 8)

Here is the assignment:

> These four selections discuss various aspects of the world of work, especially the subject of entry-level jobs. Using *three* of these readings, write a synthesis essay of four to five pages in which you defend a thesis of your own devising on the subject of low-skill, low-wage jobs. You might focus on workers' attitudes toward their jobs, the lessons learned from doing such work, or any other relevant aspect of this subject. In addition to material from the readings, evidence for this essay may also come from your own experience or observation.

This kind of broad, open-ended question leaves lots of room for maneuvering and for individual interpretation. It also entails a problem, because the writer has to arrive at a focus, since the instructor has not provided one. Pete's first task (of course, after he carefully read and annotated the material) was to choose which essays to include and to come up with a defensible thesis, one that would carry him through the 1,000–1,250-word limit. Because a thesis did not immediately present itself and because he could not wait for divine inspiration, he had to do some searching.

Ask Questions

The first step is to jot down questions on a piece of paper or on the computer. Don't worry at this stage if some of them do not appear to be immediately relevant. Pete wrote these questions as he thought about the four readings:

- Why does Rose Castillo Guilbault take a summer job sorting vegetables when she really wanted to do something more conventional, like babysitting? What did she learn from this experience?

- Elisa Zamot is a teenager who works at McDonald's in Colorado Springs. What is her typical workday like? How does she feel about her job? What skills is she learning from working there? What does Schlosser suggest is in store for her future?
- Barbara Ehrenreich became a waitress in Key West to see if a worker could survive financially on a minimum-wage salary. What did she learn about the conflict between managers and employees from her experience as a waitress? What did she find out from her fellow employees? Is a minimum-wage job a realistic way for former welfare recipients to become self-sufficient?
- Does Nazario conclude that immigrants have more of a positive or a negative impact on the job market for native-born Americans, especially those with low educational and skill levels? Who benefits and who loses when immigrants take over minimum-wage jobs? What are the larger social implications when companies rely on immigrant labor?

Look for Patterns and Connections

Pete next examined these questions critically. By finding answers to these questions, a pattern finally emerged that led to a defensible thesis. He also saw that there were some extraneous ones that could be discarded. His notes looked like this:

- Guilbault liked the "seasonal sorority"; she learned humility from her Latino coworkers.
- Poor Elisa Zamot. Her 7-hour day at McDonald's doesn't seem to have many advantages, only drudgery and routine. Her life is pathetic. She ends the day dead tired, has energy only to watch TV, and then she has to get up and do it all over again the next day. Also she's only 16, so why isn't she in school? Is she a dropout? Schlosser doesn't say, but can't I infer it?

- Ehrenreich's research is to see if low-paying jobs will "lift poor women out of poverty while simultaneously inflating their self-esteem." She is appalled by her experience working as a waitress. The fact that she has to take on a second waitressing job to make it (is this typical?) shows that you can't survive just on minimum wage. She resents being exploited by management, whom she describes as unfeeling dolts with an eye only on the bottom line.
- Nazario explains how whole industries have shifted from native workers to poorly educated immigrant workers because they can get away with paying them lower wages. She concludes that the short-term effect is "a sea of poor and working-class neighborhoods amid islands of affluence." Native-born Americans suffer when immigrants replace them because they will work for less.

Since at first glance there seems to be little uniformity of opinion evident among these four writers, Pete put his questions and notes aside for a day. But when he looked at his notes again, a pattern emerged concerning the ramifications associated with dead-end jobs. Because Guilbault's experience was positive, Pete decided that hers was the one essay in the group he would mention only briefly. The assignment also required him to include his own experiences with regard to the world of low-paid jobs, and so he introduced that element into the opening paragraph. Here is Pete's opening paragraph:

<u>Introduction</u>—Summary of own experience

I have worked as a courtesy clerk (a euphemism for a bagger) at my local neighborhood market, the Bi-Rite, for 3 years, which helps me pay my college expenses. I have to put up with rude customers, a short-tempered boss, and a job that requires me to be on my feet all day. Still, the market is within walking distance of my house, and my hours are flexible. But beyond these factors, what do minimum-wage jobs really teach us? Some writers we read examine the world of low-skill workers

Gradual narrowing down of subject, leading to a thesis statement

Key words are circled

> and reached very different conclusions. Although Guilbault relates a positive experience her summer job working in the vegetable-sorting sheds, Schlosser and Ehrenreich cite the depressing aspects of low-skilled work, while Nazario explores the serious social and economic consequences associated with companies that rely on cheap immigrant labor.

Let's examine the thesis: Pete realized that the subordinating conjunction *although* (indicating a concession) would work to establish the contrast that emerged in his notes. Also Pete's thesis alludes to all four essays listed in the assignment, but he does not necessarily have to discuss all three in equal detail. He might cover the Guilbault essay somewhat quickly at the beginning and focus the majority of his discussion on Schlosser, Ehrenreich, and Nazario. The structure of the thesis, with the use of the concession clause (*although*) allows for this disproportion in coverage.

In writing your synthesis essay, you must make use of paraphrase, summary, and reinforcing quotations; you can also use the tell-show-share pattern as you develop the thesis. Here are the first two body paragraphs Pete wrote to develop the thesis above synthesizing the writers' experiences to support his thesis. Note that the key words from the thesis, "depressing aspects" and "serious social and economic consequences," guide the discussion in the remainder of the essay. We reprint the first two body paragraphs to illustrate.

FIRST BODY ¶

Tell: Establish context and explain Guilbault's experience. Note key words from thesis are repeated

> While many of us perhaps might take pity on those who have so few options in life that they must labor at low-skill minimum-wage jobs, such jobs are not always as bleak as they might appear; some people deliberately seek out such work and learn a beneficial lesson in the process. For Rose Guilbault, her annual summer job sorting tomatoes in the vegetable sheds of the Salinas Valley paid her more than she could have earned babysitting. She swallowed her pride and took the job so she could save money for college. But she also learned an

WRITING

Show: Use a reinforcing quotation

Share: Explain what it means

unexpected life lesson from her migrant coworkers. In "The Conveyor Belt Ladies," Guilbault describes the confidences her Latino coworkers revealed to her—sad stories of abuse, sickness, and discrimination. She writes, "I was appalled and deeply moved by these confidences, and the injustices they endured enraged me" (64). Working with her coworkers raised her social consciousness. She felt helpless as she listened to their stories about their suffering and hardship. She also learned humility, and eventually she became ashamed of her initial selfishness and feelings of superiority.

SECOND BODY ¶

Tell: Second example—Zamot's experience

Show: Two short reinforcing quotations

Low-wage jobs, however, do not always offer the consolations and compensations as Guilbault's summer job did. In the case of Eliza Zamot, whose typical workday Eric Schlosser describes in "Fast Food Nation: Behind the Counter," there seems to be no future for her despite her obvious diligence in performing her McDonald's job in Colorado Springs. She is 16 years old, yet she is leading an adult life. Every day consists of the same humdrum, mind-numbing routine, and at the end of the day, she barely has enough energy to lie on the couch and lift the TV remote. Schlosser writes that the fast food industry deliberately hires teenage workers, "instead of relying upon a small, stable, well-paid, and well-trained work force" (266). The industry's reasoning is this:

> Teenagers have been the perfect candidates for these jobs, not only because they are less expensive to hire than adults, but also because their youthful inexperience makes them easier to control. (266)

Share: Explain what they mean

> From Schlosser's description, the only entity benefiting from Zamot's hard work is McDonald's. At age 16 she should be in high school, but I surmise that she has dropped out, making her the perfect fast food outlet worker: Without an education or higher skills, her future is limited, while McDonald's benefits from having a worker who knows her place and won't make a lot of unreasonable demands for promotion, better pay, or union representation.

Pete's essay goes on to examine Ehrenreich's experience in another paragraph before turning to Nazario's analysis of the impact of cheap immigrant labor on American social patterns. His final body paragraph examines his own experience working as a courtesy clerk at San Francisco's Bi-Rite Supermarket, where he brings in his own observations as they pertain to the thesis.

These three sample paragraphs should give you a sufficiently complete picture of how the tell-show-share method of analysis and synthesis works. Note that Pete selected relevant quotations and examples from Guilbault's and Schlosser's essays and integrated them smoothly into the two body paragraphs, thus ensuring thematic unity. This means that each paragraph advances and develops some aspect of the thesis. As a reminder, if you need help with writing analyses or synthesis essays, you might want to consult the eminently useful On-Line Writing Lab (OWL) sponsored by Purdue University mentioned earlier in this text. The address is http://owl.English.purdue.edu/. But the first step should be to see your instructor for help.

TOPICS RELATED TO THE READINGS

1. Bobbie Ann Mason paints a portrait of life on a small farm in America in the mid-twentieth century. Write an essay in which you examine the different attitudes toward food procurement, food preparation, and mealtimes expressed in the essay in contrast with the ways your family performs these activities.
2. Write an essay summarizing Eric Schlosser's observations about the effects of fast food chain restaurants on a community. Then write two or three more paragraphs in which you examine the effects a *particular* fast food restaurant has had on your community. You might want to consider traffic patterns, eating habits, employment matters, or esthetics.

3. Write an essay in which you offer your own experiences patronizing fast food restaurants. Do you limit your patronage of, say, McDonald's or Burger King, to a special treat, as Shannon Brownlee suggests was prevalent in the past? Or are you perhaps one of the "heavy users" that Brownlee cites in paragraph 5? Include in your essay the appeal of fast food restaurants and the inducements (advertising, special promotions, and the like) that are used to entice customers.
4. In paragraph 1 of her essay, Shannon Brownlee cites the case of a 400-pound Bronx teenager who is suing McDonald's and four other fast food companies for having "failed to adequately disclose the bad health effects of their menus." Go to three different fast food outlets in your community and take careful notes on the following: the location of nutritional information, the specific content of the information provided, and the presence or absence of any warnings about the nutritional value of the meals served. Then write an essay in which you present your findings and analyze the effectiveness of this information.
5. In "Facing Up to the Ultimate Taboo—Failure," William Ecenbarger expounds on his thesis that failure begins early and continues throughout life. He also chastises Americans for fearing failure so much that we are in danger of being reduced to "wimphood." Write a narrative essay in which you describe an incident in your experience where you confronted failure. What was the situation? How did you feel about failing? What lesson(s) did you learn, if any? As an alternative, write about his second observation and relate a potentially risky activity that you deliberately dodged to avoid failing.
6. Kirk O. Hanson suggests in "Culture Suggests Cheaters Do Prosper" that parents teach their children early that honesty is a virtue. What kind of value system did your parents instill in you? Did they teach by example (that is, by not cheating themselves)? What did they teach you about what to do if you saw cheating going on around you?
7. Write an essay in which you examine the ethical implications of an issue as Hanson does in his article on cheating, "Culture Suggests Cheaters Do Prosper." First, go to this website where Arthur Caplan, another well-known academic ethicist, offers several position papers on a variety of ethical issues: www.washingtonspeakers.com/speakers/speaker.cfm?SpeakerID=3105. Choose an issue of your own, or choose one from this list: cloning, stem cell research, genetic modification of food, genetic testing, assisted suicide, or genetic manipulation to produce designer babies. Use information from the site (be sure to cite the source properly), debate the ethical pros and cons of the issue, and come to a conclusion of your own.
8. If you have worked in a restaurant or other consumer-oriented business, have your experiences matched those of Barbara Ehrenreich, as she describes them in "Nickel and Dimed"? Examine one of your

experiences in the working world and show how it confirms or refutes Ehrenreich's experience.

9. Ehrenreich presents statistics to show the problems unskilled workers face: A minimum-wage worker cannot survive financially. She writes, "If these numbers are right, low-wage work is not a solution to poverty and possibly not even to homelessness." Write a short essay in which you respond to this statement. If she is right, then what *is* the solution?

TOPICS FOR WRITING AN ANALYSIS OR A SYNTHESIS ESSAY

1. Using the two readings on fast food by Schlosser and Brownlee, write a synthesis essay in which you explore the effects of fast food restaurants on one aspect of American life. Some examples might be jobs, nutrition, the environment, or another topic that interests you.
2. Use the assignment given to Pete Glanting's class: The four selections by Guilbault, Schlosser, Ehrenreich, and Nazario discuss various aspects of the world of work, especially the subject of entry-level jobs. Using *three* of these readings, write a synthesis essay of four to five pages in which you defend a thesis of your own devising on the subject of low-skill, low-wage jobs. You might focus on workers' attitudes toward their jobs, the lessons learned from doing such work, or any other relevant aspect of this subject. In addition to material from the readings, evidence for this essay may also come from your own experience or observation.
3. Kirk Hanson and William Ecenbarger both examine the phenomenon of a winner-take-all philosophy that pervades American life. Devise a thesis developing a insight common to both articles and support it both with the writers' observations and your own.
4. Using two or all three of the essays by Ecenbarger, Hanson, and Nevius, write a synthesis essay in which you examine the changes that have occurred in American society regarding the way today's American children are raised. What does each writer have to say about the direction parenting has taken? What are the problems each uncovers? What are the solutions?
5. Annotate the two web-based readings on the American military experience in Iraq: "My Piece of History—The View from Iraq" and "Dispatches from Iraq—Soldiers' Stories." What to you is the most significant aspect of what American soldiers are facing in Iraq? Devise a thesis that summarizes their experience and use evidence from the soldiers' accounts, the short quotations in the *Washington Post* article, and their e-mails to their families at home in support.

PART SIX

READING

WRITING

Part 6 continues the discussion begun in Part 5 on reading and writing analytical essays. The first section opens with a summary of patterns of development; this discussion not only shows how the patterns relate to common thought processes but also shows how to identify them in your reading and how to use them to develop ideas in your writing. These patterns include listing of details, examples, cause-effect, process, and comparison and contrast.

Most of the readings in the next section either represent the comparison and contrast pattern or invite the reader to make significant comparisons. (In Part 7, the readings demonstrate the cause-effect pattern.) Before the selections, we consider Adam Goodheart's account of a popular evening Italian pastime—the *passeggiata*. One writing topic might ask you to contrast this charming and rather anachronistic activity with the way most Americans spend their evenings. Paco Underhill's selection contrasts shopping habits of men and women, and Gautam Naik and Anjula Razdan offer insights into some very different methods of finding suitable marriage partners in Morocco, India, and the United States. On the website reading, Malcolm Gladwell examines the phenomenon of speed dating as it is used in New York City. Finally, in an essay that has become something of a classic, James Fallows explains why boys and girls throw balls differently and presents some theories to account for these differing styles.

The writing section shows you two conventional methods of organizing and developing comparison and contrast essays. This section also instructs you in how to adapt the tell-show-share method first discussed in Part 5 to prepare a comparison and contrast essay based on the readings.

Recognizing Common Patterns of Development

Now that you have become familiar with some of the more basic skills—locating and identifying the main idea, annotating, learning how to acquire new vocabulary words, and making logical inferences—we now turn to a skill that can lead to a more meaningful level of reading comprehension and a skill that will also serve you well when you write essays. *Patterns of development* refer to the various ways writers—both student and professional—expand on the subject at hand. These patterns include listing facts or details, examples, reasons (cause and effect), process (sequential steps), and contrast (showing differences). These patterns of development mirror logical processes in our everyday thinking.

PATTERNS OF DEVELOPMENT AND PATTERNS OF THINKING

Let's say that you are wrestling with a big decision about your future.You know that you are interested in helping people, and you come up with a list of careers in which such an interest would be required for someone to succeed and to be happy. On a sheet of paper you note the following career choices: nurse, doctor, teacher, aid worker, mental health worker, social worker. What you have just done is provide *examples*, specific instances of careers in which you could help others.

Now you have another decision facing you: Should you apply to Augusta State University 200 miles away or study for the first two years at Rockport Community College in your home town and then transfer to Augusta? This time, you write down the positive and negative aspects of both institutions and both choices and note their differences. Now you are *contrasting*.

Finally, when it comes time to apply to Augusta State, you will need to go through a series of steps: get your transcripts in order, fill out the application, perhaps apply for financial aid or look for scholarships, arrange for a tour of the campus. as well as meet with a counselor and review the prerequisites for your major. If you do these steps in a logical, sequential order, you'll be engaging in a *process*.

In each example, you can see the connections between patterns of development and ways in which we use them in our everyday lives. When we refer to patterns of development in writing, we are referring to the internal logic of a passage—the way a writer gets his or her ideas across and expands on them. Which pattern a writer uses depends on the subject. We will illustrate each pattern with some short passages. Studying these patterns will accomplish two things: (1) help you stay on track as you read and follow the writer's thinking process; (2) help you develop your own topics and make your writing more readable.

LISTING FACTS OR DETAILS

The pattern of *listing facts* or *details* is perhaps the simplest one to recognize. Following the main idea, each subsequent sentence presents factual evidence to support the main assertion. Consider this passage from a *New Yorker* article on the grueling Tour de France cycling race held every summer. Before he retired, the American cyclist Lance Armstrong won this race seven times. In this excerpt, Michael Specter supports the main idea—identified in the margin—with a list of facts that prove his point:

> The physical demands on competitive cyclists are immense. One day, they will have to ride two hundred kilometres through the mountains; the next day there might be a long, flat sprint lasting seven hours. Because cyclists have such a low percentage of body fat, they are more susceptible to infections than other people. (At the beginning of the Tour, Armstrong's body fat is around four or five per cent; this season Shaquille O'Neal, the most powerful player in the N.B.A., boasted that his body-fat level was sixteen percent.)
>
> The Tour de France has been described as the equivalent of running twenty marathons in twenty days. During the nineteen-eighties and nineties, Wim H. M. Saris, a professor of nutrition at the University of Maastricht, conducted a study of human endurance by following participants in the Tour. . . .
>
> Looking at a wide range of physical activities, Saris and his colleagues measured the metabolic demands made on people engaged in each of them. "On average, cyclists expend sixty-five hundred calories a day for three weeks, with peak days of ten thousand calories," he said. "If you are sedentary, you are burning perhaps twenty-five hundred calories a day. Active people might burn as many as thirty-five hundred. . . ."
>
> —Michael Specter, "The Long Ride," *The New Yorker*

LISTING FACTS IN VISUAL MATERIAL

Graphs present complicated material in a form that is easy to comprehend and to interpret. Graphic material can be in the form of bar graphs, line graphs, or pie charts. Here is an example of a bar graph accompanying an article on the increasing popularity of digital cameras in comparison to 35 millimeter and other types of cameras. Graphs can be "read" and interpreted just as print material can.

To read a graph like this, first look at the title, "Digital Dominates the Camera Market" and the accompanying summary statement underneath it. Then look at the little box that indicates a shorthand way to display large amounts, in this case, "film" is represented by light gray and "digital" is represented by darker gray. Finally, look at the bottom horizontal line, which lists years covered from 1994 to 2005 and then at the right-hand vertical column, which lists, by fives, sales in millions of units.

After you study the graph, answer these questions:

Digital Dominates the Camera Market.

About 3 of every 4 cameras sold in 2004 were digital, according to estimates by the Photo Marketing Association International.

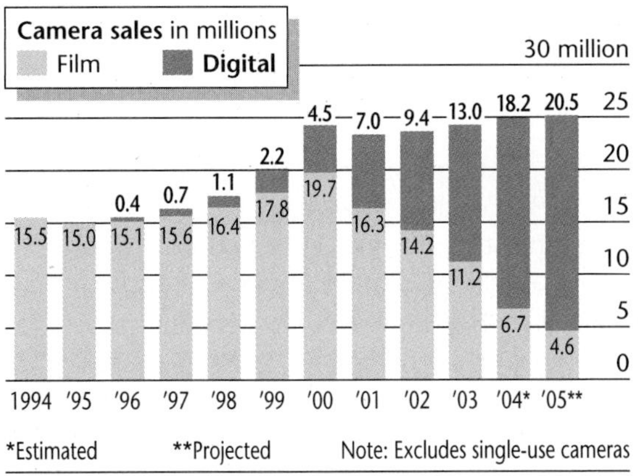

Source: Photo Marketing Association International, Todd Trumbull/*The Chronicle.*

1. In what year did digital cameras make their first appearance?

   ____

2. How many types of both cameras were sold in 1999?

   ____

3. In what year did the sales of digital cameras first exceed that of film cameras?

   ____

4. What was the projected ratio between film cameras and digital cameras sold in 2005?

   ____

5. What kind of cameras are excluded from these statistics?

   ____

6. Where do these statistics come from?

   ____

EXAMPLES

An *example* is a specific instance of something more general. As you saw earlier, nursing and social work are examples of fields where one can help people. Consider this paragraph about the Ohlone Indians who inhabited parts of Northern California hundreds of years ago. The writer Malcolm Margolin begins with a statement that, in comparison to Europeans, the Ohlones seemed lazy. (You can tell that the writer is challenging this observation because he puts the word *laziness* in quotation marks.) Note that the first example is preceded with the helpful transitional phrase, "for example," and the next three little examples follow logically from that connector.

> The episodic character of the harvesting also helps explain another much noted Ohlone characteristic: their so-called "laziness." For them hard work came only in spurts. Deer hunting, for example, was an arduous pursuit that demanded fasting, abstinence, great physical strength, and single-mindedness of purpose. The acorn harvest, the seed harvest, and the salmon harvest also involved considerable work for short periods of time. But when the work was over, there was little else to do. Unlike agricultural people, the Ohlones had no fields to plow, seeds to plant, crops to cultivate, weeds to pull, domestic animals to care for, or irrigation ditches to dig or maintain. So at the end of a harvest they often gave themselves over to "entire indolence," as one visitor described it—a habit that infuriated the Europeans who assumed that laziness was sinful and that hard work was not just a virtue for a God-given condition of human life.
>
> — Malcolm Margolin, *The Ohlone Way*

Let's look at a second passage using examples to develop the main assertion. In 2005, the world celebrated the fiftieth anniversary of Dr. Jonas Salk's scientific breakthrough—the development of a vaccine that could conquer polio, as writer Susan Levine says, "one of the most dreaded diseases of the 20th century." (Ask family members who were children during the late 1940s and 1950s to recount their memories of the polio scare.) In this excerpt from a *Washington Post* article titled "Polio's Enduring Legacy," Levine focuses on the town of Wytheville, in Virginia's Blue Ridge Mountains, which was hard hit by the epidemic. As you read the passage, identify the main idea in the margin and note where the examples begin.

> Wytheville was devastated by its encounter. The toll: 189 cases, nearly two dozen deaths. In one extended family, five of the children fell ill. Incredibly, each survived. A historical account, to be published next month by the town's museums department, recalls the highway signs warning of the outbreak; motorists speeding through with their windows rolled up tight.

The local semi-pro baseball team, the Statesmen, canceled its season because no opponents would come to play. Churches canceled services and broadcast Sunday school lessons over the radio. Everyone feared going out, making contact.

Among the few businesses that stayed busy were the two funeral homes, which turned their hearses into ambulances to transport the sick to Roanoke and Richmond. Some trips had so many patient-passengers that drivers would lay them crosswise in the vehicle. Sometimes the children didn't make it to the hospital. Even casket salesmen kept their distance.

—Susan Levine, "Polio's Enduring Legacy," *Washington Post National Weekly Edition*, April 18–24, 2005

CAUSE AND EFFECT

Every situation has reasons that account for it, and every situation has effects that derive from it. For example, let's suppose that the local school district has just announced that its students showed no improvement in the annual standardized reading tests. That is the situation.

The faculty and administration assess this situation and try to determine why test scores did not improve. Doing so involves ascribing *reasons*—or *causes*—for the lack of improvement. They might cite, for example, that there are many English-language learners in the district, that class sizes are too large to teach reading effectively, that the textbook series emphasizes the whole language approach, which has not proven as useful as a more eclectic approach, that children need to spend more time reading on their own, that parents need to become more involved, and so forth.

Then they examine the likely results—or the *effects*—of the situation: Students with poor reading skills are apt to fall behind as they progress from grade to grade, leading to overall lowered academic performance and decreased academic and job opportunities. Parents might pull their children out of low-performing schools, thus changing the community's demographics, while newcomers with children might decide to look elsewhere to buy or rent. (High test scores in public schools have a strong correlation with property values.) Other effects would likely involve recommendations. Without some drastic changes, the situation may grow worse: Teachers must lobby for a better reading series and must assign more reading homework; parents must spend more time reading to their children and demonstrate to them that reading is fun by reading themselves. Finally, class size must be reduced.

In other words, the causes produce a situation, which, in turn, leads to effects. Let's examine the cause-effect pattern in a short excerpt from an essay called "The Life and Death of a Western Gladiator," in which Charles Finney describes the life cycle of a diamondback rattlesnake. One section in particular centers on the situation faced by a newborn snake. As you read the passage, underline once the words or phrases that show a *cause* and underline twice the *effects*.

> The direct rays of the sun could, in a short time, kill him. If the temperature dropped too low he would freeze. Without food, he would starve. Without moisture he would die of dehydration. If a man or a horse stepped on him he would be crushed.
>
> Thus it was at the hour of his birth. Thus it would be, with modifications, all his life.

In this paragraph from *Collapse: How Societies Choose to Fail or Succeed,* scientist Jared Diamond assesses the impact (the effects) of global warming in Montana. Annotate the passage by writing in the margin the following: "situation," "immediate effect," and "long-term effect."

> The most visible effect of global warming in Montana, and perhaps anywhere in the world, is in Glacier National Park. While glaciers all over the world are in retreat—on Mt. Kilimanjaro, in the Andes and Alps, on the mountains of New Guinea, and around Mt. Everest—the phenomenon has been especially well studied in Montana because its glaciers are so accessible to climatologists and tourists. When the area of Glacier National Park was first visited by naturalists in the late 1800s, it contained over 150 glaciers; now, there are only about 35 left, mostly at just a small fraction of their first-reported size. At present rates of melting, Glacier National Park will have no glaciers at all by the year 2030. Such declines in the mountain snowpack are bad for irrigation systems, whose summer water comes from melting of the snow that remains up in the mountains. It's also bad for well systems tapping the Bitterroot River's aquifer, whose volume has decreased because of drought.

In 2004 and 2005, several destructive hurricanes battered the Caribbean nations of Haiti, the Dominican Republic, Cuba, as well as the Gulf Coast states of Florida, Louisiana, Mississippi, and Texas. Read this excerpt from an article by *San Francisco Chronicle* science writer Keay Davidson, written a few days after Hurricanes Katrina and Rita hit the U.S. coast. After you read it once, read it again, this time annotating the text in the left margin showing the cause-effect pattern.

> Scientists are confident that an era of super-hurricanes is unfolding in the Atlantic, and has been at least since the mid-1990s. It has been particularly evident since last year, when repeated hurricane disasters in Florida set the stage for this year's cataclysm in New Orleans and the recent mayhem along the Texas and Louisiana coasts.
>
> They just can't agree on one thing: *why* it's happening.
>
> Some scientists say the wave of hurricanes is the product of global warming spurred by greenhouse gases from cars and industries. Others say it's the latest wave in a recurrent and completely natural series of cyclonic assaults on the United States' eastern and southeastern states.

Whichever theory is correct—and conceivably—both might be true—one thing seems sure: The expected hurricane assaults of the next decade or so could cost the nation plenty, both in lives and reconstruction costs.

— Keay Davidson, "Many Theories on Root of Strong Hurricanes," *San Francisco Chronicle*, October 3, 2005, p. A4

PROCESS

If you want to make an omelet for your Sunday morning breakfast, you could follow a cookbook recipe or you could follow your instincts. Either way, you would go through a *process*, a series of steps that, if followed in order, would produce something edible. First you would crack three eggs into a bowl and beat them. Then you would melt a little butter in a pan. Next, you would grate some cheese, chop some onions and green pepper, add the eggs and vegetables to the pan, and cook the mixture. In writing, the process pattern works the same way, whereby writers describe sequential steps for two reasons: (1) to show how to do something, for example, how to make an omelet, how to change a flat tire, or how to burn a CD; or (2) to show how something occurred, for example, how glaciers formed during the Ice Age or how Mavericks, one of the world's most challenging and most dangerous surfing areas, claimed the life of a prominent surfer. With the first type, the reader could conceivably duplicate the process described, whereas with the second type, the reader is getting information without any intention of duplicating an impossible series of events.

In this illustrative paragraph, Sophie Petit-Zerman discusses the phenomenon of laughter and answers this question: "Is it true that laughing can make us healthier?" Each step in the process is numbered to help you follow the discussion:

> [Laughter is] undoubtedly the best medicine. For one thing it's exercise. [1] It activates the cardiovascular system, so heart rate and blood pressure increase, [2] then the arteries dilate, causing blood pressure to fall again. [3] Repeated short, strong contractions of the chest muscles, diaphragm, and abdomen increase blood flow into our internal organs, and forced respiration—the *ha! ha!*—makes sure that this blood is well oxygenated. [4] Muscle tension decreases, and indeed [5] we may temporarily lose control of our limbs, as in the expression "weak with laughter."
>
> — Sophie Petit-Zerman, "No Laughing Matter," *Discover*

The following excerpt, also by science writer Keay Davidson, revisits the subject of hurricanes—in this case Hurricane Rita, a 2005 Category 5 storm—and explains how a hurricane is formed, detailing each step in chronological order. He wrote this article as the hurricane was developing off the Gulf Coast. Along the Gulf of Mexico, hurricane season extends from June through November. As you read, number the steps that go into the process in the left margin.

> Just as an oil fire speeds down an oil slick, a hurricane is fueled, partly guided and intensified by masses of warm, moist air that form over currents of warm ocean water.
>
> That's how Hurricane Rita has grown with frightening speed from a puny low-pressure cell and swelled into a massive, potentially city-busting Category 5 monster as it bears down on the Gulf Coast.
>
> The difference between the formation of ordinary clouds and the generation of hurricanes is partly a matter of degree: Both owe their existence to rising bubbles of warm, moist air. For hurricanes, though, an additional factor is the formation of a huge, spinning low-air-pressure cell that continually refuels itself by sucking in more and more warm, moist air.
>
> Being of lower density than cool air, warm air is buoyant and rises like a hot-air balloon. If it's a humid day, the rising warm air hoists large amounts of water vapor into the heavens. As a moist, warm air parcel ascends, the moisture condenses and cools into large water droplets and clouds—e.g., the fluffy, sheep-like little cumulus clouds that meander innocently across the sky.
>
> But on exceptionally warm, humid days, that process goes into overdrive, sometimes with scary results. On such days, the intense heat and humidity *continually* pump parcels of warm, moist air skyward.
>
> As the air parcels rise, they continually release latent heat that propels the rising warm air even higher—as if the warm air were pulling it up by its own bootstraps, as the saying goes.
>
> Exceptionally warm, moist air can rise so high that it forms extremely tall thunderstorms on hurricanes. The taller they are, the more violent they tend to be.
>
> This atmospheric scenario plays out most dramatically in tropical waters. Especially at this time of year, tropical waters are a vast reservoir of heat and moisture waiting to be transformed into hurricane-like energies. As warm air continually rises, it drains enough air from the surface to form large low-pressure cells into which outside warm air and moisture spiral, reinforcing the process.
>
> —Keay Davidson, "Hurricane Fuel: Warm, Moist Air Over Warm Ocean Water," *San Francisco Chronicle*, September 22, 2005

USING PROCESS IN VISUAL MATERIAL

Visual material often accompanies an article, especially one on a scientific subject, to present that subject graphically. The visual material aids and clarifies the reader's understanding, especially when the process is a complicated one. This graphic aid, titled "Hurricane Dynamics," accompanied the above

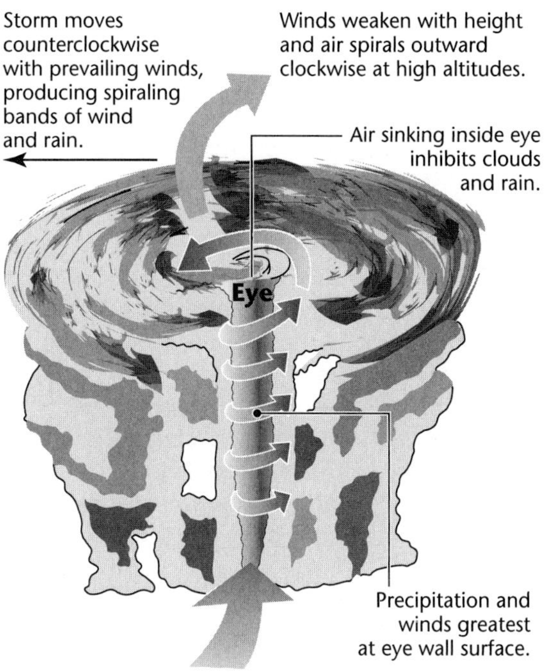
Storm moves counterclockwise with prevailing winds, producing spiraling bands of wind and rain.
Winds weaken with height and air spirals outward clockwise at high altitudes.
Air sinking inside eye inhibits clouds and rain.
Eye
Precipitation and winds greatest at eye wall surface.
Warm, humid air feeds hurricane and spirals in toward eye, gaining speed.

Hurricane Dynamics

JOHN BLANCHARD/*The Chronicle.*

article by Davidson that describes how hurricanes are formed. One difficulty posed by a drawing like this is where one should start "reading" it. After some consideration, I decided that the most logical beginning point is the center (showing the eye of the hurricane); then move to the lower left corner, then clockwise to the upper left corner, then to the right corner, and finally to the lower right corner. In this way, you can visualize the way hurricanes form and gather strength.

COMPARISON AND CONTRAST

To *compare* means to examine similarities between essentially dissimilar subjects, whereas to *contrast* means to examine differences between essentially similar subjects. A writer often uses transitions to keep the reader from becoming confused as he or she shuttles from one subject or subtopic to the other. Both methods are illustrated in three sample passages.

The first is by Bill Bryson, whose essay "Cells" appears in Part 4. In the beginning of this excerpt, Bryson fancifully and briefly compares the human cell to a refinery, and then, more extensively, to a metropolis—a densely crowded and busy city. The verb *compared* in the first sentence is also helpful because it alerts you to the pattern that he has imposed on the material.

> The cell has been compared to many things, from "a complex chemical refinery" (by the physicist James Trefil) to "a vast, teeming metropolis" (the biochemist Guy Brown). A cell is both of those things and neither. It is like a refinery in that it is devoted to chemical activity on a grand scale, and like a metropolis in that it is crowded and busy and filled with interactions that seem confused and random but clearly have some system to them. But it is a much more nightmarish place than any city or factory that you have ever seen. To begin with there is no up or down inside the cell (gravity doesn't meaningfully apply at the cellular scale), and not an atom's width of space is unused. There is activity *everywhere* and a ceaseless thrum of electrical energy. You may not feel terribly electrical, but you are. The food we eat and the oxygen we breathe are combined in the cells into electricity. The reason we don't give each other massive shocks or scorch the sofa when we sit is that it is all happening on a tiny scale: a mere 0.1 volts traveling distances measured in nanometers. However, scale that up and it would translate as a jolt of twenty million volts per meter, about the same as the charge carried by the main body of a thunderstorm.
>
> —Bill Bryson, "Cells," *A Short History of Nearly Everything*

In the next passage, Bill McKibben contrasts two forms of mass media in terms of the way each presents the news—television and newspapers. To help you see how skillfully McKibben moves from subject to subject, in the margin annotate the passage by writing "TV" or "newspaper," at each point where the type of medium is discussed.

> Perhaps the greatest distortion of TV news comes from the very fact of its seeming comprehensiveness. Each day, it fills its allotted hours no matter what, and each day it fills them with a crackling urgency. A newspaper comes out every day, too, but a newspaper has various ways of letting you know whether or not an event is important. The single most useful thing about the *Times* is that the width of the type size of the lead headline each morning lets you know how it compares, in the view of the paper's editors, with all the other lead stories since the *Times* began. It has a way of saying to its readers, "Nothing earthshaking happened today; it's O.K. to read the reviews or the sports." TV has almost no flexibility of this sort.
>
> —Bill McKibben, "Reflections: Television," *The New Yorker*

Here is one final example of a paragraph employing the contrast pattern. Historian Barbara Tuchman distinguishes between the certainty of studying the tides and the uncertainty of gaining reliable lessons from history.

> I know very little (a euphemism for "nothing") about laboratory science, but I have the impression that conclusions are supposed to be logical; that is, from a given set of circumstances a predictable result should follow. The trouble is that in human behavior and history it is impossible to isolate or

> repeat a given set of circumstances. Complex human acts cannot be either reproduced or deliberately initiated—or counted upon like the phenomena of nature. The sun comes up every day. Tides are so obedient to schedule that a timetable for them can be printed like that for trains, though more reliable. In fact, tides and trains sharply illustrate my point: One depends on the moon and is certain; the other depends on man and is uncertain.
>
> —Barbara Tuchman, "Is History a Guide to the Future?" *Practicing History*

COMBINING PATTERNS OF DEVELOPMENT

In complex writing for an adult audience, a writer usually varies the pattern of development according to the requirements of the subject, and in a lengthy essay, he or she may employ several different patterns as the subject is expanded upon in the body. Similarly, a writer may combine two or more methods in a single supporting paragraph. In this last section, we will examine two paragraphs representing multiple patterns. As before, annotate each selection by writing in the left margin the type of pattern each reveals.

The first excerpt is from Mark Edmundson's profile of his high school philosophy teacher, Frank Lears, reprinted in Part 4; it reflects two patterns discussed here.

> But I had acquired a few facts that Lears would not have been primed to receive at Harvard, or at prep school, or at any of the other places where he had filled his hours. Medford High School, whatever its appearances, was not a school. It was a place where you learned to do—or were punished for failing in—a variety of exercises. The content of these exercises mattered not at all. What mattered was form, repetition, and form. You filled in the blanks, conjugated, declined, diagrammed, defined, outlined, summarized, recapitulated, positioned, graphed. It did not matter what: English, geometry, biology, history, all were the same. The process treated your mind as though it were a body part capable of learning a number of protocols, then repeating, repeating. If you'd done what you should have at Medford High, the transition into a factory, into an office, into the Marines would be something you'd barely notice; it would be painless.

Finally, this paragraph from the conclusion of Barbara Kingsolver's essay, "How Mr. Dewey Decimal Saved My Life," also from Part 4, reflects four different patterns. As before, identify each by writing the type of each pattern in the left margin.

> Most alarming, to my mind, is that we the people tolerate censorship in school libraries for the most bizarre and frivolous of reasons. Art books that

contain (horrors!) nude human beings, and *The Wizard of Oz* because it has witches in it. Not always, but everywhere, always something. And censorship of certain ideas in some quarters is enough to sway curriculum at the national level. Sometimes profoundly. Find a publishing house that's brave enough to include a thorough discussion of the principles of evolution in a high school text. Good luck. And yet, just about all working botanists, zoologists, and ecologists will tell you that evolution is to their field what germ theory is to medicine. We expect our kids to salvage a damaged earth, but in deference to the religious beliefs of a handful, we allow an entire generation of future scientists to germinate and grow in a vacuum.

In the exercises accompanying the Practice Essay by Adam Goodheart and the readings that follow it, you will have an opportunity to do further practice in identifying the various patterns of development.

PRACTICE ESSAY

Passing Fancy: The *Passeggiata*

Adam Goodheart

Adam Goodheart is a freelance writer who lives in Washington, D.C. He has traveled widely in Italy and Sicily and other more remote and exotic locales. In addition to publishing articles for *The New York Times*, the *Washington Post, Outside*, and the *Atlantic Monthly*, he also wrote a bimonthly "Time Traveler" column for *Civilization*, the magazine of the Library of Congress, of which he was a founding member. The magazine was published from 1994 to 2000. This article, which describes the *passeggiata* ritual of southern Italy, was first published in *Civilization* and reprinted in *Utne*.

VOCABULARY ANALYSIS

Two Word Roots: *ped-* (Latin) + *pedo-* (Greek)

The *passeggiata* is a social custom in Italian cities and towns where *pedestrians* [paragraph 8] stroll up and down streets. The word *pedestrian* contains the Latin root *ped-* or "foot," and many other English words also contain this root, among them *pedal, pedicure, pedestal* (the base or "foot" of a statue), *peddler* (one who sells goods, originally on foot), and *pedometer* (a device that measures the distance one walks).

A similar-appearing root *pedo-*, from the Greek word *paid* meaning "child," can be seen in these words: *pediatrician, pedagogue* (a teacher of children), *pedophile* (one who is sexually attracted to children), and *pedomorphism* (a condition where juvenile characteristics are retained in adult mammals). When in doubt about the meaning of a word containing one of these two roots, consider the context carefully or consult your dictionary.

Passing Fancy: The *Passeggiata*

Adam Goodheart

1 The dance starts at dusk. Every evening, the natives—men, women, and children—leave their houses and assemble in the square to enact an age-old ritual, an intricate pattern of footsteps that binds together their community, advertises the power of their clans, and perpetuates ancient mating rituals.

2 These particular natives aren't wearing grass skirts or brandishing tribal totems. These particular natives are very much a part of the modern world. They may, in fact, be wearing Armani suits and carrying cell phones. The daily ritual is called the *passeggiata*, and it's a custom nearly as embedded in southern Italian culture as eating pasta. Rarely discussed by natives or described by anthropologists, it is—like many honest, not-for-the-tourist-trade rituals—so deeply rooted as to be almost involuntary, almost unconscious.

3 The *passeggiata* is not a dance in the literal sense. But to call it a "stroll," as the word is usually translated into English, is to ignore everything but the walking. I first discovered the *passeggiata* in Sciacca, a fishing town on the southwestern Sicilian coast. In a stately baroque piazza, with the Mediterranean on one side and the city hall on the other, the townspeople would turn out, dressed to the nines, and walk up and down, up and down.

4 The town square couldn't have been much more than a hundred yards long. And the townspeople, most of them, had been pacing these same worn stones every day of their lives since they were old enough to put one foot in front of the other. Still, they seemed to take undiminished enjoyment in the act—or not enjoyment, perhaps, but rather an emotion somewhere between pleasure and duty. When they reached the end of the piazza, they would turn smartly on their heels and walk straight back to the other side—turn and repeat, dozens of times in an evening. The nightly dance has continued into the age of e-mail and cell phones. And not just in the small towns, either. Perhaps the loveliest *passeggiata* I found was in the ancient center of Naples. Here, the tangled maze of alleys and tunnel-like byways is split right down the middle by a thoroughfare: long, narrow, and perfectly straight. It is as if an upswelling of Vesuvian geology had struck a lateral crack straight through the city.

5 That street, called Spaccanapoli—literally, "split Naples"—has been one of the city's main avenues since Roman times. Walk down it on a winter evening, as I did: The shops are closed, but the street is crowded; human figures loom suddenly in the near-Calcuttan blackness beneath the palazzos that tower on

either side. Often, you hear people before you see them: friends greeting each other, parents calling to their children, the banter of teenagers. It isn't supposed to be this way. In his book *Bowling Alone*, Harvard social scientist Robert D. Putnam examines the decline in group activities and social rituals. Blaming television—and what he vaguely terms "generational change"—Putnam concludes that "social capital has eroded steadily and sometimes dramatically over the past two generations." He even delivers an offhand blow to southern Italy, which he singles out as an even more "uncivic" place than America. "The very concept of citizenship is stunted there," he proclaims.

6 What, then, about the *passeggiata?* Ask a group of strolling Italians, and they will probably just shrug—or even blush a little, as though you'd caught them doing something shameful, something that smacks of laziness and backwardness, the things that separate a place like Naples from such bustling paradises as Milan or Seattle. They even have derogatory nicknames for the *passeggiata:* "sweeping the floor," they'll call it, or "swimming laps." "The only reason we do this," snorted one young man I spoke to in a small town, "is that there's nothing else to do here. If I lived in America, I'd never have to bother." And yet, grudgingly, they also confess a certain appreciation.

7 The *passeggiata* has always been associated with sex. When you walk down Spaccanapoli, for instance, you see young couples, lips locked, inhaling each other across café tables, stone pilings in the piazzas, or the seats of tiny Vespas that become, miraculously, capacious bowers of love. Then they detach suddenly with seeming unconcern, glance briefly at each other with a look of civilized curiosity, and start to stroll again. Young men walk arm in arm, too, but this isn't a sexual thing—just an expression of comradeship. The *passeggiata* is about renewing connections of all kinds.

8 Every ritual has its geographic variations. The *passeggiata* in Rome these days is really just a shopping circuit: down the Via Condotti (Armani, Gucci, Bulgari) to the Via Babuino (Missoni, Kenzo), then up the Corso—the same route taken by the emperors on their triumphal processions. In the ruins of old Pompeii, the carefully constructed street crossings—stepping stones to keep feet from getting muddied—attest to to the ancient Roman concern for pedestrians. As for modern Pompei, the town has long since dropped the second *i* from its name but the *passeggiata* continues, with preteens tossing firecrackers and their older siblings smoking marijuana as their grandparents, strolling past palm trees, lament the lack of rain. I had heard that one of the most famous strolls in Italy was in Naples on a Sunday evening, down the long avenue that curves alongside the bay. Yet I found the strollers there had taken to their cars and Vespas: The bumper-to-bumper traffic was the *passeggiata*, moving through the exhaust fumes at a pace slower than a leisurely stroll.

9 The best *passeggiatas* are the ones in the small towns, where they are slow and stately. Eboli, in the hills south of Naples, is a town made famous by the writer

and painter Carlo Levi, exiled nearby in the 1930s, with his book *Christ Stopped at Eboli*. The title implies that it was a godforsaken outpost of civilization. Eboli has even less going for it today. The town center, bombed in World War II, is now an ugly agglomeration of concrete buildings. When I arrived in Eboli, the main square had been completely fenced off for "restoration," which in Italy means that it has been closed anywhere from four months to 40 years, and will remain so indefinitely.

10 The barista[1] at a little café told me that, yes, of course Eboli has a *passeggiata*. When the restoration started in the square, the *passeggiata* shifted to the nearby Corso Umberto, a street lined with pizzerias and clothing shops (no Missoni here, but lots of maternity clothes), whose main adornment was a newly installed bronze statue of Carlo Levi "in appreciation," its plinth noted sardonically, "of notoriety conferred." Within a few hours, it was full of strolling people.

11 I stood near one end of the route (a nondescript stretch of pavement where the flow doubled back on itself) and watched. After a few laps, I realized that I kept seeing the same people, but in different combinations. Here came a blond woman pushing a stroller. Next lap, she was arm in arm with a younger woman, and the stroller was nowhere to be seen. Later, they'd been joined by an old lady who was pushing the stroller. Next, the three women were surrounded by men, jackets draped over their shoulders, smoking cigarettes.

12 I couldn't manage the dignified saunter they all affected with such grace. I would speed up involuntarily and crawl up the heels of a pair of lovers or overshoot the end of the *passeggiata* course. But when I just stood and watched, I appreciated, as I never had before, that the Italian verb *passeggiare*—to walk—contains the root of the word *passage:* an oceanic journey, a royal progress, the ebb and flow of time.

[1]Italians drink their coffee standing at a coffee bar, which is not like an American bar that serves alcohol. The person who prepares the coffee is a *barista*, literally "one who works at a bar." English has adopted the Italian word to describe the same employee at Starbucks and other coffee purveyors.

EXERCISES

A. Determining the Main Idea and Writer's Purpose

Choose the best answer.

1. The main idea of the selection is that the *passeggiata* is
   a. an outmoded way for a town's residents to communicate with each other in the absence of technological devices.
   b. a relic of ancient traditions in southern Italy, now in danger of dying out.

c. primarily a place for young people to seek romantic partners and to court each other in an open setting.

d. a daily ritual and custom deeply embedded in the culture of southern Italy.

2. The writer's purpose in the selection is to
   a. describe the *passeggiata*, its purpose, cultural role, and expression.
   b. convince the American audience to institute the *passeggiata* custom in their communities.
   c. lament or express sorrow for the passing of traditional rituals in our fast-paced culture.
   d. explain the difficulty of an outsider trying to adapt to the *passeggiata*.

B. Comprehending Main Ideas

Choose the correct answer.

1. Which of the following does Goodheart *not* include in his explanation of the *passeggiata*'s role in southern Italian towns and cities?
   a. It is a way to bind a community together.
   b. It is done to appeal to the tourist trade.
   c. It shows off the power of family and clans.
   d. It serves as the location for an ancient mating ritual.

2. According to Goodheart, the emotions of those engaging in the evening *passeggiata* are a mix of
   a. affection, embarrassment, and boredom.
   b. patriotism, pride, and pleasure.
   c. pleasure, enjoyment, and duty.
   d. family loyalty and community loyalty.

3. Goodheart cites the opinion of Robert D. Putnam, author of the book *Bowling Alone*, who blames the decline in group activities and social rituals on what he calls "generational change" *and*
   a. our materialistic society.
   b. the Internet.
   c. the mobility of modern American life.
   d. television.

4. Of all the *passeggiatas* that he has observed, Goodheart writes that the best ones are those
   a. that take place in small towns like Eboli.

READING

b. that take place in large cities like Naples and Rome.

c. where shoppers stroll and look in store windows.

d. in which people drive automobiles or Vespas rather than walk.

5. The root of the Italian word *passeggiata* is related to the English word *passage*, both of which come from the verb

a. "to show off."

b. "to walk."

c. "to travel."

d. "to explore."

C. Sequencing

The sentences in this excerpt from the selection may have been scrambled. Read the sentences and choose the sequence that puts them back into logical order. Do not refer to the original selection.

1. Rarely discussed by natives or described by anthropologists, it is—like many honest, not-for-the-tourist trade rituals—so deeply rooted as to be almost involuntary, almost unconscious. **2.** The daily ritual is called the *passeggiata*, and it's a custom nearly as embedded in southern Italian culture as eating pasta. **3.** These particular natives aren't wearing grass skirts or brandishing tribal totems. **4.** They may, in fact, be wearing Armani suits and carrying cell phones. **5.** These particular natives are very much a part of the modern world.

a. 5, 3, 4, 1, 2

b. 3, 5, 4, 2, 1

c. 2, 1, 3, 4, 5

d. Correct as written.

D. Interpreting Meaning

Where appropriate, write your answers to these questions in your own words.

1. In paragraph 1, Goodheart refers to the *passeggiata* as a dance because

a. the ritual is performed with music.

b. it requires a lot of energy to perform, just as a dance does.

c. the walkers are graceful and lithe as dancers are.

d. the steps are as formalized and intricate as a dance.

2. A good title for paragraph 7 would be

a. "Sex and the Italian City."

b. "Flirting, Italian Style."

c. "The *Passeggiata* and Sex."
d. "Bowers of Love."

3. Which of these excerpts from the selection *best* states the thesis?
   a. Every evening, the natives—men, women, and children—leave their houses and assemble in the square to enact an age-old ritual, an intricate pattern of footsteps that binds together their community, advertises the power of their clans, and perpetuates ancient mating rituals. [paragraph 1]
   b. Rarely discussed by natives or described by anthropologists, it is—like many honest, not-for-the-tourist-trade rituals—so deeply rooted as to be almost involuntarily, almost unconscious. [paragraph 2]
   c. The *passeggiata* is about renewing connections of all kinds. [paragraph 7]
   d. . . . I appreciated, as I never had before, that the Italian verb *passeggiare*—to walk—contains the root of the word *passage:* an oceanic journey, a royal progress, the ebb and flow of time. [paragraph 12]

E. Making Inferences

Write your answers to these questions in your own words.

1. Read paragraphs 2 and 4 again. What inference can you make about the effect of cell phones and e-mail on the evening *passeggiata* in Italy?

   ____

2. From paragraph 3, why does the English word *stroll* not accurately describe the *passeggiata?*

   ____

   ____

3. From paragraph 5, what inference can you make about Goodheart's opinion of the comment by Robert D. Putnam who, in *Bowling Alone*, said that southern Italy was even more "uncivic" than the United States?

   ____

   ____

4. From the last paragraph, does the *passeggiata* seem to be easy or difficult for an outsider to participate in?

   ____

F. Understanding Vocabulary

Look through the paragraphs listed below and find a word that matches each definition. Refer to a dictionary if necessary. An example has been done for you.

EXAMPLE: causes to continue indefinitely [paragraphs 1–2] perpetuates

1. showing off, displaying ostentatiously [2–3] ____________
2. caused to be an integral part of a whole [2–3] ____________
3. an elaborately ornate style of the seventeenth and eighteenth centuries [3–4] ____________
4. appear suddenly out of the darkness [5–6] ____________
5. arrested, checked, impeded the growth of [5–6] ____________
6. calls or brings to mind, evokes [5–6—phrase] ____________
7. disparaging, critical, belittling [6–7] ____________
8. reluctantly, unwillingly [6–7] ____________
9. roomy, spacious [7–8] ____________
10. complain about, express regret over [8–9] ____________
11. dignified, impressive, majestic [8–9] ____________
12. a confused or jumbled mass [8–9] ____________
13. mockingly, scornfully, sarcastically [10–11] ____________
14. quality of having a bad name [10–11] ____________
15. lacking distinctive qualities [10–11] ____________

DISCUSSION QUESTIONS

1. What is your considered reaction to the *passeggiata* custom of southern Italy? As Goodheart describes it, do you find it charming, bizarre, or outmoded, or perhaps something altogether different? Examine your thinking.
2. In paragraph 5, Goodheart alludes to the well-publicized study of alienation in contemporary American culture done by Robert D. Putnam in *Bowling Alone*. Aside from television and "generational change," what are some other factors that have contributed to the decline in group activities and social rituals in the United States?

3. How do you and your family or your friends spend a typical evening? Do these activities involve others—whether family, friends, or others in the community, or are they done alone? Is the *passeggiata* a characteristic of a healthy society or a static one?

EXPLORE THE WEB

For a different, perhaps less idealistic interpretation of the southern Italian custom of the *passeggiata*, Susan Jacoby's three-part series on the small Adriatic town of Mola (near the industrial port of Bari on Italy's east coast) is a comprehensive look at the townspeople, their customs, and their class and economic status. Part 1, "Walking the Piazza in Mola di Bari" describes the *passeggiata* and its revival after World War II but also the goals and dreams of the town's inhabitants.

Parts 2 and 3, "The Making of a New Immigrant Family," follow some members of the DeLiso and DeCarolis families who immigrated to the United States and explain how they adapted Italian customs to their new life in New York. Although the material was written thirty years ago, the experiences described nicely illuminate the challenges, frustrations, and dreams of these immigrants. Susan Jacoby is a freelance writer who wrote these articles under the auspices of the Alicia Patterson Foundation and the Rockefeller Foundation. Once you access this address, scroll down to find the three parts listed above.

www.aliciapatterson.org/APF001974/Jacoby/Jacoby.html

Reading Selections

Shop Like a Man

Paco Underhill

Paco Underhill and his New York company, Envirosell, established a new area of study: the science of shopping. For over twenty years, Underhill, who describes himself as a retail anthropologist, has advised corporate clients—among them Starbucks, McDonald's, and Blockbuster—on how to improve their customer base. He gathers research by following customers around stores and public spaces and videotaping their behavior. Underhill's most recent book is *The Call of the Mall* (2004), an analysis of consumerism and Americans' love–hate relationship with the mall, the American consumer's Mecca. In *Why We Buy: The Science of Shopping* (1999), from which this selection comes, Underhill explains modern-day consumer behavior, in particular the differences in male and female shopping styles.

VOCABULARY ANALYSIS

The Prefix *proto-*

Underhill's firm conducted a study for "a wireless phone provider that was developing a *prototype* retail store." The Greek prefix *proto-* means "first in time" or "earliest." A *prototype*, then, is the "first type" of something built—in other words, a model—whether it is a store, a computer, or a new automobile. Other words beginning with this prefix are *protohumans* (the first human species), *protohistory*, *proton*, and *protoplasma* (the living matter of plant and animal cells providing essential life functions).

Shop Like a Man

Paco Underhill

1 When they were a client I used to tell Woolworth's, if you would just hold Dad's Day at your stores once a week, you'd bring in a lot more money.

2 They didn't listen. You may have heard.

3 Men and women differ in just about every other way, so why shouldn't they shop differently, too? The conventional wisdom on male shoppers is that they don't especially like to do it, which is why they don't do much of it. It's a struggle just to get them to be patient company for a woman while she shops. As a result, the entire shopping experience—from packaging design to advertising to merchandising to store design and fixturing—is generally geared toward the female shopper.

Connecting Grammar to Writing

In the first sentence of paragraph 4, Underhill uses a series of gerunds to describe the process of shopping. Underline these gerunds. (There are seven.)

4 Women do have a greater affinity for what we think of as shopping—walking at a relaxed pace through stores, examining merchandise, comparing products and values, interacting with sales staff, asking questions, trying things on and ultimately making purchases. Most purchasing traditionally falls to women, and they usually do it willingly—even when shopping for the mundane necessities, even when the experience brings no particular pleasure, women tend to do it in dependable, agreeable fashion. Women take pride in their ability to shop prudently and well. In a study we ran of baby products, women interviewed insisted that they knew the price of products by heart, without even having to look. (Upon further inquiry, we discovered that they were mostly wrong.) As women's roles change, so does their shopping behavior—they're becoming a lot more like men in that regard—but they're still the primary buyer in the American marketplace.

5 In general, men, in comparison, seem like loose cannons. We've timed enough shoppers to know that men always move faster than women through a store's aisles. Men spend less time looking, too. In many settings it's hard to get them to look at anything they hadn't intended to buy. They usually don't like asking where things are, or any other questions, for that matter. (They shop the way they drive.) If a man can't find the section he's looking for, he'll wheel about once or twice, then give up and leave the store without ever asking for help. You can watch men just shut down.

6 You'll see a man impatiently move through a store to the section he wants, pick something up, and then, almost abruptly, he's ready to buy, having taken no apparent joy in the process of finding. You've practically got to get out of his way. When a man takes clothing into a dressing room, the only thing that stops him from buying it is if it doesn't fit. Women, on the other hand, try things on as only part of the consideration process, and garments that fit just fine may still be rejected on other grounds. In one study, we found that 65 percent of male shoppers who tried something on bought it, as opposed to 25 percent of female shoppers. This is a good argument for positioning fitting rooms nearer the men's department than the women's, if they are shared accommodations. If they are not, men's dressing rooms should be very clearly marked, because if he has to search for it, he may just decide it's not worth the trouble.

7 Here's another statistical comparison: Eighty-six percent of women look at price tags when they shop. Only 72 percent of men do. For a man, ignoring the

price tag is almost a measure of his virility. As a result, men are far more easily upgraded than are women shoppers. They are also far more suggestible than women—men seem so anxious to get out of the store that they'll say yes to almost anything.

8 Now, a shopper such as that could be seen as more trouble than he's worth. But he could also be seen as a potential source of profits, especially given his lack of discipline. Either way, men now do more purchasing than ever before. And that will continue to grow. As they stay single longer than ever, they learn to shop for things their fathers never had to buy. And because they marry women who work long and hard too, they will be forced to shoulder more of the burden of shopping. The manufacturers, retailers and display designers who pay attention to male ways, and are willing to adapt the shopping experience to them, will have an edge in the twenty-first century.

9 The great traditional arena for male shopping behavior has always been the supermarket. It's here, with thousands of products all within easy reach, that you can witness the carefree abandon and restless lack of discipline for which the gender is known. In one supermarket study, we counted how many shoppers came armed with lists. Almost all of the women had them. Less than a quarter of the men did. Any wife who's watching the family budget knows better than to send her husband to the supermarket unchaperoned. Giving him a vehicle to commandeer, even if it is just a shopping cart, only emphasizes the potential for guyness in the experience. Throw a couple of kids in with Dad and you've got a lethal combination; he's notoriously bad at saying no when there's grocery acquisitioning to be done. Part of being Daddy is being the provider, after all. It goes to the heart of a man's self-image.

10 I've spent hundreds of hours of my life watching men moving through supermarkets. One of my favorite video moments starred a dad carrying his little daughter on his shoulders. In the snacks aisle, the girl gestures toward the animal crackers display. Dad grabs a box off the shelf, opens it and hands it up—without even a thought to the fact that his head and shoulders are about to be dusted with cookie crumbs. It's hard to imagine Mom in such a wanton scenario. Another great lesson in male shopping came about watching a man and his two small sons pass through the cereal aisle. When the boys plead for their favorite brand, he pulls down a box and instead of carefully opening it along the reclosable tab, he just rips the top, knowing full well that once the boys start in, there won't be any need to reclose it.

11 Supermarkets are places of high impulse buying for both sexes—fully 60 to 70 percent of purchases there were unplanned, grocery industry studies have shown us. But men are particularly suggestible to the entreaties of children as well as eye-catching displays.

12 There's another profligate male behavior that invariably shows itself at supermarkets, something we see over and over on the video we shoot at the registers: The man almost always pays. Especially when a man and woman are shopping

together, he insists on whipping out his wad and forking it over, lest the cashier mistakenly think it's the woman of the house who's bringing home the bacon. No wonder retailers commonly call men wallet carriers. Or why the conventional wisdom is, sell to the woman, close to the man. Because while the man may not love the experience of shopping, he gets a definite thrill from the experience of paying. It allows him to feel in charge even when he isn't. Stores that sell prom gowns depend on this. Generally, when Dad's along, the girl will get a pricier frock than if just Mom was there with her.

13 In some categories, men shoppers put women to shame. We ran a study for a store where 17 percent of the male customers we interviewed said they visited the place more than once a week! Almost one-quarter of the men there said they had left the house that day with no intention of visiting the store—they just found themselves wandering in out of curiosity. The fact that it was a computer store may have had something to do with it, of course. Computer hardware and software have taken the place of cars and stereo equipment as the focus of male love of technology and gadgetry. Clearly, most of the visits to the store were information-gathering forays. On the videotape, we watched the men reading intently the software packaging and any other literature or signage available. The store was where men bought software, but it was also where they did most of their learning about it. This underscores another male shopping trait—just as they hate to ask directions, they like to get their information firsthand, preferably from written materials, instructional videos or computer screens.

14 A few years back we ran a study for a wireless phone provider that was developing a prototype retail store. And we found that men and women used the place in very different ways. Women would invariably walk right up to the sales desk and ask staffers questions about the phones and the various deals being offered. Men, however, went directly to the phone displays and the signs that explained the agreements. They then took brochures and application forms and left the store—all without ever speaking to an employee. When these men returned to the store, it was to sign up. The women, though, on average required a third visit to the store, and more consultation, before they were ready to close.

15 For the most part, men are still the ones who take the lead when shopping for cars (though women have a big say in most new-car purchases), and men and women perform the division of labor you'd expect when buying for the home: She buys anything that goes inside, and he buys everything that goes outside—mower and other gardening and lawn-care equipment, barbecue grill, water hose and so on. This is changing as the percentage of female-headed households rises, but it still holds.

16 Even when men aren't shopping, they figure prominently in the experience. We know that across the board, how much customers buy is a direct result of how much time they spend in a store. And our research has shown over and over

that when a woman is in a store with a man, she'll spend less time there than when she's alone, with another woman or even with children. Here's the actual breakdown of average shopping time from a study we performed at one branch of a national housewares chain:

woman shopping with a female companion: 8 minutes, 15 seconds
woman with children: 7 minutes, 19 seconds
woman alone: 5 minutes, 2 seconds
woman with man: 4 minutes, 41 seconds

17 In each case, what's happening seems clear: When two women shop together, they talk, advise, suggest and consult to their hearts' content, hence the long time in the store; with the kids, she's partly consumed with herding them along and keeping them entertained; alone, she makes efficient use of her time. But with him—well, he makes it plain that he's bored and antsy and likely at any moment to go off and sit in the car and listen to the radio or stand outside and watch girls. So the woman's comfort level plummets when he's by her side; she spends the entire trip feeling anxious and rushed. If he can somehow be occupied, though, she'll be a happier, more relaxed shopper. And she'll spend more time and money. There are two main strategies for coping with the presence of men in places where serious shopping is being done.

18 The first one is passive restraint, which is not to say handcuffs. Stores that sell mainly to women should all be figuring out some way to engage the interest of men. If I owned The Limited or Victoria's Secret, I'd have a place where a woman could check her husband—like a coat. There already exists a traditional space where men have always felt comfortable waiting around. It's called the barbershop. Instead of some ratty old chairs and back issues of *Playboy* and *Boxing Illustrated*, maybe there could be comfortable seats facing a big-screen TV tuned to ESPN or the cable channel that runs the bass-fishing program. Even something that simple would go a long way toward relieving wifely anxiety, but it's possible to imagine more: *Sports Illustrated* in-store programming, for instance—a documentary on the making of the swimsuit issue, perhaps, or highlights of last weekend's NFL action.

19 If I were opening a brand-new store where women could shop comfortably, I'd find a location right next to an emporium devoted to male desire—a computer store, for instance, somewhere he could happily kill half an hour. Likewise, if I were opening a computer software store, I'd put it next to a women's clothing shop and guarantee myself hordes of grateful male browsers.

20 But you could also try to sell to your captive audience. A women's clothing store could prepare a video catalog designed especially for men buying gifts—items like scarves or robes rather than shoes or trousers. Gift certificates would sell easily there; he already knows that she likes the store. Victoria's Secret could really go to town with a video catalog for men. They could even stage a little fashion show.

21 (The only precaution you'd need to take is in where to place such a section. You want customers to be able to find it easily, but you don't want it so near the entrance that the gaze of window shoppers falls on six lumpy guys in wind breakers slumped in BarcaLoungers watching TV.)

22 The second, and ultimately more satisfying, strategy would be to find a way to get the man involved in shopping. Not the easiest thing to do in certain categories, but not impossible either.

23 We were doing a study for Pfaltzgraff, the big stoneware dish manufacturer and retailer. Their typical customer will fall in love with one particular pattern and collect the entire set—many, many pieces, everything from dinner plate and coffee cup to mustard pot, serving platter and napkin ring. It is very time-consuming to shop the store, especially when you figure in how long it takes to ring the items up and wrap them so that they don't break. Just the kind of situation designed to drive most men nuts. A typical sale at Pfaltzgraff outlet stores can run into the hundreds of dollars—all the more reason to find a way to get men involved.

24 As we watched the videotape, we noticed that for some unknown reason men were tending to wander over toward the glassware section of the store. They were steering clear of the gravy boats and the spoon rests and drifting among the tumblers and wineglasses. At one point we saw two guys meander over to the beer glasses, where one of them picked one up and with the other hand grabbed an imaginary beer tap, pulled it and tilted the glass as if to fill it. And I thought, well, of course—when company's over for dinner and the woman's cooking in the kitchen, what does the man do? He makes drinks. That's his socially acceptable role. And so he's interested in all the accoutrements, all the tools of the bartender trade—every different type of glass and what it's for, and the corkscrew and ice tongs and knives and shakers. They're being guys about it.

25 My first thought was that the stores should put in fake beer taps, like props, for men to play with. We ended up advising them to pull together all the glassware into a barware section—to put up on the wall some big graphic, like a photo of a man pulling a beer, or making some martinis in a nice chrome shaker. Something so that men would walk in and see that there was a section meant for them, somewhere they could shop. All the bottle openers in the different patterns, say, would be stocked there, too. And because men prefer to get their information from reading, the store could put up a chart showing what type of glass is used for what—the big balloons and the long stems and the flutes and the rocks glass and steins.

26 And by doing all that you could take the man—who had been seen as a drag on business and an inconvenience to the primary shopper—and turn him into a customer himself. Or at least an interested bystander.

27 We did a study for Thomasville, the furniture maker, and thought that there, too, getting the man more involved would make it easier to sell such big-ticket items.

The solution was simple: Create graphic devices, like displays and posters, showing the steps that go into making the furniture, and use visuals, like cross sections and exploded views, to prove that in addition to looking good, the pieces were well made. Emphasizing construction would do a lot toward overcoming male resistance to the cost of new furniture, but the graphics would also give men something to study while their wives examined upholstery and styling.

28 One product where men consistently outshop women is beer. And that's in every type of setting—supermarket or convenience store, men buy the beer. (They also buy the junk food, the chips and pretzels and nuts and other entertainment food.) So we advised a supermarket client to hold a beer-tasting every Saturday at 3 P.M., right there in the beer aisle. They could feature some microbrew or a new beer from one of the major brewers, it didn't matter. The tastings would probably help sell beer, but even that wasn't the point. It would be worth it just because it would bring more men into the store. And it would help transform the supermarket into a more male-oriented place.

29 That should be the goal of every retailer today. All aspects of business are going to have to anticipate how men's social roles change, and the future is going to belong to whoever gets there first. A good general rule: Take any category where women now predominate, and figure out how to make it appealing to men.

Source: From Paco Underhill, *Why We Buy*. © 1999 by Obat, Inc. Reprinted with permission of Simon & Schuster Adult Publishing Group.

EXERCISES

A. Determining the Main Idea and Writer's Purpose

Choose the best answer.

1. The main idea of the selection is that
   a. men are more suggestible to graphics and physical displays in a retail environment than women are.
   b. men and women behave so differently while shopping that retailers are confused about strategies to increase their sales.
   c. retailers and designers should adapt the shopping experience to involve male shoppers more in the shopping experience.
   d. men are better shoppers than women, especially when buying cars or technological equipment.

2. With respect to the main idea, the writer's purpose is to
   a. illustrate how men and women's shopping behavior differs.
   b. persuade retailers and display artists to redesign their stores.

c. warn consumers about deceptive strategies stores use to entice them to buy.

d. poke fun at men for their peculiar shopping behavior.

B. Comprehending Main Ideas

Choose the correct answer.

1. One primary difference between the way men and women shop concerns
   a. the amount of time they spend and how quickly or slowly they move through a retail space.
   b. the type of merchandise that they shop for.
   c. the different amounts of money they spend for similar items.
   d. their willingness to comparison shop and the influence of advertising slogans on their buying habits.

2. When shopping in a supermarket,
   a. men use a list more than women do.
   b. women use a list more than men do.
   c. men and women use lists about equally.
   d. no reliable statistics exist about which gender uses a list more often.

3. In a computer store, men prefer to get their information about hardware and software
   a. by doing preliminary research at home before going shopping.
   b. by talking to sales clerks.
   c. by watching television advertisements.
   d. by reading the packaging and other available literature in the store.

4. Underhill suggests that retailers might solve the problem of male boredom while their wives or girlfriends shop if they
   a. located their stores near a male-oriented business like a computer store.
   b. had pretty girls model clothing throughout the store.
   c. opened up a barbershop within the store.
   d. installed large-screen televisions advertising the store's merchandise.

5. When Underhill's firm did a study for the furniture maker Thomasville, the researchers found that men would become more involved if
   a. their wives asked their advice about what styles to buy.
   b. the store provided displays and posters showing how the furniture was made.

c. the male shoppers were allowed to use a computer-drawing program to see how the furniture would look in their homes.

d. the sales staff encouraged male shoppers to try out the furniture themselves.

C. Locating Supporting Details

For each main idea stated here, find two details that support it.

1. The great traditional arena for male shopping behavior has always been the supermarket. [paragraph 9]

 a. ______________________________

 b. ______________________________

2. A few years back we ran a study for a wireless phone provider that was developing a prototype retail store. And we found that men and women used the place in very different ways. [paragraph 14]

 a. ______________________________

 b. ______________________________

D. Interpreting Meaning

Where appropriate, write your answers to these questions in your own words.

1. A good title for paragraph 4 would be
 a. "The Science of Shopping."
 b. "Why Women Shop."
 c. "Traditional Gender Roles."
 d. "Characteristics of Women Shoppers."

2. What does Underhill mean in paragraph 5 when he writes that in comparison to women shoppers, men seem like "loose cannons."

 ____

3. In paragraph 12 Underhill states that retailers follow this "conventional wisdom": sell to the woman, close to the man." What does he mean by the word *close*?

 ____

4. Throughout the selection, Underhill relies on two types of evidence to develop his thesis. The first is contrast—showing the differences between how men and women shop—and the second is

a. defining important terms.
b. explaining the steps in a process.
c. citing the results of various scientific studies.
d. using examples and illustrations from his observations.

5. How would you characterize the information in the conclusion, paragraph 29?
   a. It represents a fundamental rule that all retailers should adopt.
   b. It warns of problems ahead if retailers don't change their practices.
   c. It explains why men shop differently than women.
   d. It shows how and why the retail industry is changing.

E. Making Inferences

For each of these statements write **Y** (yes) if the inference is an accurate one, **N** (no) if the inference is an inaccurate one, or **CT** (can't tell) if the writer does not give enough information to make an inference one way or another.

1. _____ Retailers call men "wallet carriers" because most men are the primary breadwinners and thus are responsible for paying for household items.
2. _____ Consider the information presented in paragraphs 16–17. A woman spends the least amount of time shopping with a man because he typically wants to spend more money than she does.
3. _____ Underhill seems to prefer male shoppers because they are more profligate, that is, they are not as cautious about spending money as women are.
4. _____ Men and women's styles also vary considerably when they shop on the Internet.
5. _____ Women are less likely to give in to the demands of children for snack items or favorite brands of cereal than men are.
6. _____ The goal of retailers should be to make the overall shopping experience more appealing and enjoyable for male customers.

F. Understanding Vocabulary

For each word in the left-hand column, find the phrase that best defines it from the right-hand column.

1. conventional [paragraph 3]	a. the first model, the first of its kind
2. affinity [4]	b. marketplace, a large retail store
3. mundane [4]	c. drops quickly and straight down

4. prudently [4]	d. irresponsible, reckless
5. virility [7]	e. natural attraction
6. lethal [9]	f. submitting without resistance
7. wanton [10]	g. carefully, cautiously, practically
8. entreaties [11]	h. expeditions, ventures
9. profligate [12]	i. customary, conforming to practice
10. forays [13]	j. manliness, sense of masculinity
11. prototype [14]	k. pleas, earnest requests
12. plummets [17]	l. accessories, paraphernalia
13. passive [18]	m. common, ordinary, routine
14. emporium [19]	n. deadly, here used humorously
15. accoutrements [24]	o. extravagant, wasteful

DISCUSSION QUESTIONS

1. Do Underhill's observations about the contrasting patterns in male and female shopping behavior ring true from your experience? Perhaps in mixed groups of both sexes, examine and test Underhill's comments for accuracy.
2. Reading between the lines, can you detect any evidence of sexism, any overt bias in Underhill's remarks?
3. Is the "science of shopping" a valid field of study? Are Underhill's recommendations just another example of American consumerism run amok? American consumers are bombarded with excessive and intrusive advertising and so many pitches for separating us from our money that one might argue that these recommendations are counter to what should be the goal of retailers—prudent shopping rather than more reasons to buy. Consider and discuss.

EXPLORE THE WEB

The company that Paco Underhill started, Envirosell, has a website explaining more about the company, how it works, its mission, and more important for your purposes, excerpts from Underhill's two books. Go to the address below, and then click on "Publications."

www.envirosell.com/index.html

Malcolm Gladwell, the author of the website selection "Speed Dating," is a renowned *New Yorker* writer. He wrote a comprehensive and balanced article about Paco Underhill titled "A Reporter at Large: The Science of Shopping."

After accessing the site below, click on "The New Yorker Archive" and then scroll down to November 4, 1996.

www.gladwell.com

Speed Dating, Berber Style

Gautam Naik

Berbers are Caucasian aboriginal people who live in the North African countries of Libya, Algeria, and Morocco. Their language is Amazigh. Although some Berbers, those seeking marriage partners as described in this article, are nomadic, traditionally Berbers have been small farmers. Gautam Naik wrote this article for the *Wall Street Journal,* the leading daily business newspaper in the United States. The paper, however, regularly publishes feature articles and human interest stories on the front page, such as this one.

Gautam Naik grew up in Calcutta, India, and attended graduate school in the United States. After graduation in 1992, he joined the *Wall Street Journal* as a general assignment reporter in New York. Eventually he was reassigned to Europe, where he covered the telecommunications and drug industries, and later science and public health. In 2005 he returned to New York to cover science and health for the *Wall Street Journal*. He writes that "The Berber dating story was among the weirder assignments I have embarked on, and one of the more memorable."

VOCABULARY ANALYSIS

The Root *vert*

Naik briefly summarizes Berber history in paragraphs 6–8, noting that Morocco's King Mohammed VI has paid attention to Berber concerns and therefore has been able to *avert* the kinds of problems Berbers have experienced in neighboring Algeria. To *avert* means "to prevent," literally "to turn away." Here is its derivation from Latin: *ab-* ("away") + *vertere* ("to turn")

Some other English words with the Latin root *vertere* as the root are listed here:

convert to change into another form, to turn around or to transform

divert to turn aside from a course, to distract [from *dis-* ("away") + *vertere*]

pervert to turn away from what is considered morally right, corrupt, literally to turn the wrong way [*per-* ("completely") + *vertere*]

vertigo a sensation of dizziness, a feeling that one is whirling around, from Latin *vertigo* for whirling

What does the word *revert* mean?

Speed Dating, Berber Style

Gautam Naik

1 IMILCHIL, Morocco—As Rakia Al-Mamouni pushed through the throng, she was on the lookout for just one thing: a potential husband.

2 She ignored the man who rushed by carrying a sheep across his shoulders. She didn't seem to care for the hawker selling goats' heads. But she did stop when a young, well-dressed fellow ambled over to her and said: "You have captured my liver."

3 Not the most eloquent pickup line ever. But for the Berbers of the Atlas mountains in Morocco, who consider the liver to be where love resides, it's a lovely sentiment.

4 It got the attention of the heavily made-up Ms. Mamouni, who chatted briefly with the young man. But the 19-year-old wasn't swept away. "We'll see what happens," she said as she moved on, with eyes peeled for other prospects.

5 Each year, hundreds of marriageable Berbers gather for this three-day dating ritual, which has been practiced among nomadic tribes in these arid, windy mountains for centuries. Today, the ritual has developed into a major Berber bazaar and a tourist attraction.

6 The original inhabitants of North Africa, Berbers have lived in the region for about 4,000 years. When the Arabs invaded in the seventh century, some tribes, who fought fiercely, were driven into the Atlas mountains or into the Sahara. In Morocco, Berber resistance helped kick out the next group of occupiers—the French—in 1956, and Berbers now make up 60% of the country's 30 million inhabitants. Berber tribes also live in Algeria, Tunisia, and Libya; most have converted to Islam.

7 The Berbers have found a champion in Morocco's new king, Mohammed VI, who assumed the throne in 1999. His mother is Berber and, local Berbers say, he has paid more attention to their cause so as to avert the kind of Berber unrest common in neighboring Algeria.

8 Morocco recently set up a Royal Institute for Amazigh Culture. This month, Amazigh, the Berber language, will be taught for the first time in Moroccan schools. And to promote tourism, the government has become more involved in the Imilchil dating festival. The treacherous road to Imilchil, which climbs to a height of 9,240 feet, was recently paved.

9 Most of the Berbers who attend the dating festival are nomads from three local tribes who travel for days across great distances and over sheer mountain passes. Though many come to trade goods, others come to seek love.

10 It isn't the most romantic of dating venues. At this year's event, which took place the last three days in August, about 5,000 nomads set up camp in an area the size of three football fields. It turned into a loud, smelly bazaar. Camel and mule owners yelled. Raw meat hung on hooks, and barbecues

threw off thick smoke. The blazing sun at times was obscured by a fierce, dusty wind.

11 Decked out in a poncho-like dress and immaculate silver shoes, 16-year-old Rabha stepped into the singles arena. To show herself to be unmarried, she wore her purple scarf rounded against her head. (Married women wear their scarves in a conical shape.) Men approached her, usually to say something about their livers. Nearby, men were test driving mules and loading indignant, roaring camels into trucks.

12 Rabha ignored the hubbub. And she ended several meetings with a rapidly withdrawn handshake—a signal that the man should move on. Finally she met a man she liked, and they agreed to a longer rendezvous after the evening prayer. "It's not easy for me," said Rabha, who declined to give her last name. "My parents are dead and I need someone willing to take me on, as well as my two brothers."

"Commitment-Shy"

13 Moubarak Louch, a 38-year-old Berber employed by the army, has been coming to the dating festival for years. But things have never gone his way. "I'm commitment-shy," he said. Another explanation could be his style. He walks up to women and loudly proclaims his attraction to them.

14 He turned plenty of heads, but usually not the ones he wanted. "You're not serious. Get out of my way!" shouted one woman, as others looked on, amused. When an especially pretty woman brushed him off, Mr. Louch wailed, "Oh, come back! You've burned my liver."

15 At this year's dating festival, five couples were hitched by a local judge in a large tent. Other nuptials will occur within a month, away from public gaze. Some Berbers already have their eye on someone but come to Imilchil to pop the question.

16 Hussain Ouaali, 46, first attended more than two decades ago. He met several women but fancied one. She quizzed him for two hours on how many sheep he owned and where he usually roamed before agreeing to marry him. Are they happy? "We have eight children. That's proof enough," said Mr. Ouaali, who now goes to Imilchil to buy supplies for the winter.

Roots in Legend

17 The dating festival is said to have its roots in a centuries-old legend. According to the tale, a pair of young lovers from rival tribes wanted to marry, but their parents refused. The pair shed enough tears to form two lakes and then drowned themselves. The tragedy united the tribes. They also decided henceforth to let their children pick their own spouses at a once-a-year meeting, at Imilchil. Most Berber marriages are still arranged with the help of parents or family.

18 The dating festival is increasingly turning into a commercial event. This year, the province's governor showed up in a motorcade. One vendor erected a 20-foot-high inflatable Coke bottle. And several bus tours arrived from distant towns. "Some people may disagree with this, but foreigners bring money to the local population," said Majid Laabab, an official at the tent set up by the tourist department.

Some Still Defiant

19 Some locals remain defiant. "This is my land," declared a hand-lettered sign attached to a nearby Berber tea stall.

20 Some Berbers aren't concerned about the encroachment of modernity, the latest threat to their ancient culture. "There's change everywhere in the world, so why not here?" said Moha Ouai Ben Hadou, a nomad from a nearby valley, who cut a dashing figure despite his grubby robe and dusty beard.

21 But some things don't change. When Mr. Ben Hadou was younger and played drums for a tribal band, he was a hit on the Imilchil dating circuit. "I could speak to 10 women a day," he recalled. He first met his future wife at the dating festival, and they tied the knot the very next day. Though long and happily married, he still has an eye for the ladies. "If I just pick up my drums," said the 50-year-old Mr. Ben Hadou, "I can easily attract them again."

EXERCISES

A. Determining the Main Idea and Writer's Purpose

Choose the best answer.

1. The main idea of the selection is that
   a. Berbers have a long and rich cultural history.
   b. The Berber dating festival has its roots in an ancient legend.
   c. The traditional Berber dating festival has become a popular tourist destination.
   d. The tradition of the Berber dating festival allows nomads from all over to locate suitable marriage partners.

2. With respect to the main idea, the writer's purpose is to
   a. explain where the dating ritual originated and how it works.
   b. relate the experiences of several prospective marriageable Berbers.
   c. mourn the changes that have affected the traditional festival.
   d. urge people in other cultures to adopt the Berber dating festival.

B. Comprehending Main Ideas

Choose the correct answer.

1. According to the article, the Berber dating festival
   a. is held annually more as a tradition than as a serious way for people to find marriage partners.
   b. has become a tourist attraction and a major bazaar.
   c. has been discouraged by the Moroccan government.
   d. is a place where most Berbers locate a marriage partner.

2. In 1956, the Berbers served in the resistance movement against the occupiers of Morocco by helping to kick out
   a. the Arabs.
   b. the British.
   c. the Americans.
   d. the French.

3. King Mohammed VI of Morocco is interested in Berber causes, because
   a. he himself is a Berber.
   b. his father was a Berber.
   c. his mother was a Berber.
   d. he married a Berber woman.

4. The Berbers who attend the dating ritual are mostly people who
   a. have not been successful in finding a marriage partner in the traditional ways.
   b. are nomadic and live in remote mountain areas.
   c. are rebelling against the traditional marriage arranged by parents or family.
   d. are poor and do not have enough money to provide the traditional dowry.

5. The dating ritual has its roots in an ancient legend, which concerned a pair of lovers who
   a. ran away to Imilchil when their parents refused to allow them to marry.
   b. met at a dating ritual in Imilchil, much like the festival held today.
   c. were forced into an unhappy arranged marriage that ended tragically.
   d. drowned themselves after their parents refused to allow them to marry.

C. Sequencing

The sentences in this excerpt from the selection may have been scrambled. Read the sentences and choose the sequence that puts them back into logical order. Do not refer to the original selection.

1. Morocco recently set up a Royal Institute for Amazigh Culture. **2.** And to promote tourism, the government has become more involved in the Imilchil dating festival. **3.** This month, Amazigh, the Berber language, will be taught for the first time in Moroccan schools. **4.** The treacherous road to Imilchil, which climbs to a height of 9,240 feet, was recently paved.

a. 4, 1, 2, 3
b. 1, 3, 2, 4
c. 3, 1, 4, 2
d. Correct as written.

D. Identifying Supporting Details

Place an **X** in the space for each detail that *directly* supports this main idea from the selection: "The dating festival is increasingly turning into a commercial event."

1. _____ One vendor put up a 20-foot-high inflatable Coke bottle.
2. _____ At this year's festival, five couples were married by a judge in a huge tent.
3. _____ Some Berbers, like Mr. Ouaali goes to the dating festival at Imilchil to buy the winter's supplies.
4. _____ Tour buses filled with people from distant towns or with foreigners attend the festival.
5. _____ One hawker sold goats' heads.

E. Making Inferences

Write your answers to these questions in your own words.

1. From paragraphs 3 and 4, what can we infer about the effect of the pickup line, "You have captured my liver," on Ms. Mamouni?

____

____

2. From the first part of the selection, and from paragraph 9 in particular, what can we infer about why the dating festival has been held for centuries in Morocco?

____

____

3. From paragraph 11, why would a Berber man not approach a woman wearing her scarf in a conical shape?

___

4. From paragraphs 13 and 14, what can the reader infer about the kind of technique that works best for a Berber man seeking a mate?

___

___

5. Besides physical attractiveness, what other quality do Berber women look for in a potential mate? See paragraph 16.

___

___

6. From paragraph 17, what can you infer about the reason that the dating festival at Imilchil is held only once a year?

___

___

___

___

F. Vocabulary In Context

Here are a few vocabulary words from the selection and their definitions. Study these definitions carefully. Then write the appropriate word in each space provided according to the context.

nomadic describing those who move from place to place, itinerant

rendezvous a specified meeting place

eloquent well-expressed, moving

prospects potential mates, likely candidates

arid extremely dry

1. For Berbers who inhabit the _____ regions of Morocco and who lead _____ lives, the once-a-year _____ to find a potential mate is an exciting event. Berber men keep watch for attractive _____, and when they find one, they may use the pickup line, "You have captured my liver," which apparently sounds more _____ in Berber culture than it does in ours.

obscured hid from view, made dim or indistinct

hubbub loud confusion, tumult, uproar

venue location, site

treacherous very dangerous, hazardous

2. The Moroccan government has come to the aid of the annual dating festival by building a new highway to pave the ________ mountain road that leads to Imilchil. Once there, the ____ resembles a huge bazaar, with so much smoke from barbeques and dust from the wind that the sun is ______. The whole event is marked by a big _____ that only the most determined are able to ignore.

defiant rebellious, resistant, contemptuous

avert prevent, turn away

encroachment infringement, violation

3. Some Berbers are resentful of the __________ of modern practices on the dating festival. They remain _____ over the influx of tourists and commercial vendors. Still others defend the modernization. Another change in Morocco is that the country's new king, Mohammed VI, has worked hard to ____ the sort of violence and unrest that has been common among Berbers in Algeria.

DISCUSSION QUESTIONS

1. Consider this selection in light of Malcolm Gladwell's selection, "Speed Dating." (See the text website.) From Gladwell's description, how is speed dating similar to the Berber festival? How does it differ?
2. The writer suggests in paragraph 19 that some Moroccans are unhappy about the increasing commercialization of the dating festival. What are some of the modern practices that seem to be encroaching on the Berber dating festival?

EXPLORE THE WEB

National Geographic sponsors a website titled "Among the Berbers," which includes photographs, an overview of Berber history and culture, and many related links concerning these valiant people and their struggle to maintain their traditions.

http://magma.nationalgeographic.com/ngm/0501/feature4

What's Love Got to Do With It?

Anjula Razdan

Anjula Razdan is a senior editor at *Utne* magazine, a magazine devoted to environmental and social issues as well as reprinting articles from the alternative press. As she writes in this article, the concept of arranged marriages is foreign to Westerners, though ironically, the freedom to choose one's marriage partner is a relatively recent phenomenon. Here she examines some of the drawbacks to the ideal of enduring romantic love and shows how Internet dating is closer to the traditional arranged marriage than our current hit-or-miss style.

VOCABULARY ANALYSIS

The Prefix *auto-*

The Greek prefix *auto-* means "self," and the root *nomos* means "ruling." Therefore, putting these two word parts together, *autonomy* means "the right to govern oneself," in other words, self-ruling. Many other words in English begin with this prefix. Here are some of the most common ones:

autograph *from auto- + graphein ("writing"); one's signature*

automobile *from auto- + movere ("to move"); a self-propelled vehicle*

autocracy *from auto- + krates ("ruler"); rule by single person*

What do these words beginning with *auto-* mean? Consult a dictionary if necessary. Be sure to indicate the word root and its meaning.

autobiography ______________________________

____

autodidact ______________________________

autopsy ______________________________

____

The Root *patri-*

Razdan writes that dating websites play the role of *patriarchal* grandfathers, "searching for good matches based on any number of criteria you select." The adjective *patriarchal* derives from the noun form *patriarch*, the ruler of a family, tribe, or clan—usually the senior male member of the group. Derived originally from the Greek root *patria-*, it spread into Latin, then into Old French, and finally into Middle English. Other words with this root are *patriotism* ("love of one's fatherland"); *patriarchy* (a social system in which the father is the head of the family and ruler of the group); and *patricide* (the killing of one's father, from *patri-* + *-cide* ("killing").

What's Love Got to Do With It?

Anjula Razdan

1 One of the greatest pleasures of my teen years was sitting down with a bag of cinnamon Red Hots and a new LaVyrle Spencer romance, immersing myself in another tale of star-crossed lovers drawn together by the heart's mysterious alchemy. My mother didn't get it. "Why are you reading that?" she would ask, her voice tinged with both amusement and horror. Everything in her background told her that romance was a waste of time.

2 Born and raised in Illinois by parents who emigrated from India 35 years ago, I am the product of an arranged marriage, and yet I grew up under the spell of Western romantic love—first comes love, *then* comes marriage—which both puzzled and dismayed my parents. Their relationship was set up over tea and samosas by their grandfathers, and they were already engaged when they went on their first date, a chaperoned trip to the movies. My mom and dad still barely knew each other on their wedding day—and they certainly hadn't fallen in love. Yet both were confident that their shared values, beliefs, and family background would form a strong bond that, over time, would develop into love.

3 "But, what could they possibly know of *real love*?" I would ask myself petulantly after each standoff with my parents over whether or not I could date in high school (I couldn't) and whether I would allow them to arrange my marriage (I wouldn't). The very idea of an arranged marriage offended my ideas of both love and liberty—to me, the act of choosing whom to love represented the very essence of freedom. To take away that choice seemed like an attack not just on my autonomy as a person, but on democracy itself.

4 And, yet, even in the supposedly liberated West, the notion of choosing your mate is a relatively recent one. Until the 19th century, writes historian E. J. Graff in *What Is Marriage For?: The Strange Social History of Our Most Intimate Institution* (Beacon Press, 1999), arranged marriages were quite common in Europe as a way of forging alliances, ensuring inheritances, and stitching together the social, political, and religious needs of a community. Love had nothing to do with it.

5 Fast forward a couple hundred years to 21st-century America, and you see a modern, progressive society where people are free to choose their mates, for the most part, based on love instead of social or economic gain. But for many people, a quiet voice from within wonders: Are we really better off? Who hasn't at some point in their life—at the end of an ill-fated relationship or midway through dinner with the third "date-from-hell" this month—longed for a matchmaker to find the right partner? No hassles. No effort. No personal ads or blind dates.

6 The point of the Western romantic ideal is to live "happily ever after," yet nearly half of all marriages in this country end in divorce, and the number of never-married adults grows each year. Boundless choice notwithstanding, what does it mean when the marital success rate is the statistical equivalent of a coin toss?

Connecting Grammar to Writing

"In paragraphs 7 and 9 the writer uses appositives to identify people. Underline to identify people Underline the appositives in both paragraphs. Notice that in the first case two appositives identify the person's credentials, whereas in the second case the person's name becomes the appositive.

7 "People don't really know how to choose a long-term partner," offers Dr. Alvin Cooper, the director of the San Jose Marital Services and Sexuality Centre and a staff psychologist at Stanford University. "The major reasons that people find and get involved with somebody else are proximity and physical attraction. And both of these factors are terrible predictors of long-term happiness in a relationship."

8 At the moment we pick a mate, Cooper says, we are often blinded by passion and therefore virtually incapable of making a sound decision.

9 *Psychology Today* editor Robert Epstein agrees. "[It's] like getting drunk and marrying someone in Las Vegas," he quips. A former director of the Cambridge Center for Behavioral Studies, Epstein holds a decidedly unromantic view of courtship and love. Indeed, he argues it is our myths of "love at first sight" and "a knight in a shining Porsche" that get so many of us into trouble. When the heat of passion wears off—and it always does, he says—you can be left with virtually nothing "except lawyer's bills."

10 Epstein points out that many arranged marriages result in an enduring love because they promote compatibility and rational deliberation ahead of passionate impulse. Epstein himself is undertaking a bold step to prove his theory that love can be learned. He wrote an editorial in *Psychology Today* last year seeking women to participate in the experiment with him. He proposed to choose one of the "applicants," and together they would attempt to fall in love—consciously and deliberately. After receiving more than 1,000 responses, none of which seemed right, Epstein yielded just a little to impulse, asking Gabriela, an intriguing Venezuelan woman he met on a plane, to join him in the project. After an understandable bout of cold feet, she eventually agreed.

11 In a "love contract" the two signed on Valentine's Day this year to seal the deal, Epstein stipulates that he and Gabriela must undergo intensive counseling to learn how to communicate effectively and participate in a variety of exercises designed to foster mutual love. To help oversee and guide the project, Epstein has even formed an advisory board made up of high-profile relationship experts, most notably Dr. John Gray, who wrote the best-selling *Men Are From Mars, Women Are From Venus*. If the experiment pans out, the two will have learned to love each other within a year's time.

12 It may strike some as anathema to be so premeditated about the process of falling in love, but to hear Epstein tell it, most unions fail exactly because they aren't intentional enough; they're based on a roll of the dice and a determination to stake everything on love. What this means, Epstein says, is that most people lack basic relationship skills, and, as a result, most relationships lack emotional and psychological intimacy.

13 A divorced father of four, Epstein himself married for passion—"just like I was told to do by the fairy tales and by the movies"—but eventually came to regret it. "I had the experience that so many people have now," he says, "which

is basically looking at your partner and going, 'Who are you?'" Although Epstein acknowledges the non-Western tradition of arranged marriage is a complex, somewhat flawed institution, he thinks we can "distill key elements of [it] to help us learn how to create a new, more stable institution in the West."

14 Judging from the phenomenon of reality-TV shows like *Married By America* and *Meet My Folks* and the recent increase in the number of professional matchmakers, the idea of arranging marriages (even if in nontraditional ways) seems to be taking hold in this country—perhaps nowhere more powerfully than in cyberspace. Online dating services attracted some 20 million people last year (roughly one-fifth of all singles—and growing), who used sites like Match.com and Yahoo Personals to hook up with potentially compatible partners. Web sites' search engines play the role of patriarchal grandfathers, searching for good matches based on any number of criteria that you select.

15 Cooper, the Stanford psychologist and author of *Sex and the Internet: A Guidebook for Clinicians* (Brunner-Routledge, 2002)—and an expert in the field of online sexuality—says that because online interaction tends to downplay proximity, physical attraction, and face-to-face interaction, people are more likely to take risks and disclose significant things about themselves. The result is that they attain a higher level of psychological and emotional intimacy than if they dated right away or hopped in the sack. Indeed, online dating represents a return to what University of Chicago Humanities Professor Amy Kass calls the "distanced nearness" of old-style courtship, an intimate and protected (cyber)space that encourages self-revelation while maintaining personal boundaries.

16 And whether looking for a fellow scientist, someone else who's HIV-positive, or a B-movie film buff, an online dater has a much higher likelihood of finding "the one" due to the computer's capacity to sort through thousands of potential mates. "That's what computers are all about—efficiency and sorting," says Cooper, who believes that online dating has the potential to lower the nation's 50 percent divorce rate. There is no magic or "chemistry" involved in love, Cooper insists. "It's specific, operationalizable factors."

17 Love's mystery solved by "operationalizable factors"! Why does that sound a little less than inspiring? Sure, for many people the Internet can efficiently facilitate love and help to nudge fate along. But, for the diehard romantic who trusts in surprise, coincidence, and fate, the cyber-solution to love lacks heart. "To the romantic," observes English writer Blake Morrison in *The Guardian*, "every marriage is an arranged marriage—arranged by fate, that is, which gives us no choice."

18 More than a century ago, Emily Dickinson mocked those who would dissect birds to find the mechanics of song:

Split the Lark—and you'll find the Music—
Bulb after Bulb, in Silver rolled—

Scantily dealt to the Summer Morning
Saved for your Ear when Lutes be old.

Loose the Flood—you shall find it patent—
Gush after Gush, reserved for you—
Scarlet Experiment! Skeptic Thomas!
Now, do you doubt that your Bird was true?

19 In other words, writes Deborah Blum in her book, *Sex on the Brain* (Penguin, 1997), "kill the bird and [you] silence the melody." For some, nurturing the ideal of romantic love may be more important than the goal of love itself. Making a more conscious choice in mating may help partners handle the complex personal ties and obligations of marriage; but romantic love, infused as it is with myth and projection and doomed passion, is a way to live *outside* of life's obligations, outside of time itself—if only for a brief, bright moment. Choosing love by rational means might not be worth it for those souls who'd rather roll the dice and risk the possibility of ending up with nothing but tragic nobility and the bittersweet tang of regret.

20 In the end, who really wants to examine love too closely? I'd rather curl up with a LaVyrle Spencer novel or dream up the French movie version of my life than live in a world where the mechanics of love—and its giddy, mysterious buzz—are laid bare. After all, to actually unravel love's mystery is, perhaps, to miss the point of it all.

EXERCISES

A. Determining the Main Idea and Writer's Purpose

Choose the best answer.

1. The main idea of the selection is that
   a. the arranged marriage is a preferable way to choose a marriage partner over the Western ideal of choosing a partner based on romantic love.
   b. marriage as an institution is doomed to fail if the criteria for choosing a mate are physical attraction and proximity, or physical closeness.
   c. the Western ideal of romantic marriage is so ingrained in our culture that any other system, even seeking a marriage partner on the Internet, will never become widely adopted.
   d. regardless of what system is used to choose a partner—arranged marriage or marriage for romance—analyzing love's mystery and subjecting it to scrutiny misses the point of the experience.

2. The writer's purpose in the selection is to
   a. argue for a return to the traditional patriarchal form of arranged marriage.
   b. argue for the freedom to marry the person of one's own choice.
   c. debate the various benefits and drawbacks of both arranged marriages and marrying for romantic love.
   d. summarize the conclusions of various researchers who have studied marriage as an institution.

B. Comprehending Main Ideas

Choose the correct answer.

1. Razdan writes that her parents, themselves the products of an arranged marriage in India,
   a. insisted on arranging her marriage.
   b. allowed her to date whomever she wanted in the American fashion.
   c. chaperoned all her dates in high school.
   d. were troubled by her acceptance of the Western ideal of romantic love.

2. Until the nineteenth century, arranged marriages were common in Europe. Razdan cites some reasons that this system prevailed. Which of the following reasons was *not* cited?
   a. the need to foster romantic love
   b. the need to forge alliances
   c. the need to bind together a community's various needs
   d. the need to ensure inheritances

3. The main drawback of marrying for romantic love, according to Dr. Alvin Cooper, is that we are
   a. too influenced by the media, especially in movies that portray romantic love as gloriously magical, a feeling that sweeps us off our feet.
   b. blinded by passion and therefore incapable of making a sound decision.
   c. convinced that "love at first sight" is the best way to choose a partner, thereby ensuring that we do not really get to know the person well enough.
   d. too rebellious, insisting on making our own choice in a marriage partner rather than accepting someone our parents consider suitable.

4. According to *Psychology Today* editor Robert Epstein, most relationships fail because they lack
   a. sufficient romantic love, so that when the bloom fades, love fades as well.
   b. emotional and psychological intimacy and lack of sufficient intention.
   c. sexual passion, on which other types of intimacy builds.
   d. self-revelation, the opening up of ourselves to another person.

5. According to Dr. Alvin Cooper, arranging marriages in cyberspace via online dating services works because it
   a. allows people to choose a partner based on shared common interests.
   b. takes away the magic and the chemistry of love.
   c. is efficient at sorting through thousands of potential mates.
   d. encourages self-revelation while maintaining personal boundaries.
   e. all of the above.
   f. only a, c, and d.

C. Distinguishing between Main Ideas and Supporting Details

The following sentences come from paragraph 2. Label them as follows: **MI** if the sentence represents a *main idea* and **SD** if the sentence represents a *supporting detail.*

1. _____ The very idea of an arranged marriage offended the writer's freedom to choose her own mate.
2. _____ Razdan's parents met each other in India when they were introduced by their grandfathers.
3. _____ The rationale for arranged marriages is that the couple shares values, beliefs, and family background; love develops later.
4. _____ The failure rate of marriages in the United States is 50 percent, the result perhaps of believing the Western romantic ideal, to "live happily ever after."
5. _____ Robert Epstein signed a "love contract" with a woman from Venezuela.
6. _____ Robert Epstein argues that love can be learned, as a result of making a decision based on rational deliberation rather than on passionate impulse.

D. Interpreting Meaning

Choose the best answer.

1. From paragraphs 1 and 2, which of the following can we infer about Razdan's parents?
   a. They married for romantic love.
   b. First they fell in love, and then they sought their parents' approval.
   c. First they were introduced; then they married and later fell in love.
   d. They always resented being forced into an arranged marriage.

2. Read paragraph 5 again. A good title for this paragraph would be
   a. "The Freedom to Choose One's Mate."
   b. "A Quiet Voice from Within."
   c. "Some Benefits of using a Matchmaker."
   d. "Dates from Hell."

3. From the information in paragraph 5, what can we infer about the motivation behind arranged marriages? What benefits does this system confer?
   a. social and economic gain
   b. romantic love based on shared interests and intimacy
   c. stronger alliances between families
   d. providing jobs for matchmakers

4. What is the relationship between the two parts of the first sentence from paragraph 6? "The point of the Western romantic ideal is to live 'happily ever after,' yet nearly half of all marriages in this country end in divorce, and the number of never-married adults grows each year."
   a. steps in a process
   b. a general concept and its definition
   c. a general concept and an illustration of it
   d. contrast

5. Razdan writes that "boundless choice notwithstanding," marriage is "the statistical equivalent of a coin toss." Later she cites *Psychology Today* editor Robert Epstein who writes, "[It's] like getting drunk and marrying someone in Las Vegas." What do both statements suggest as being the fundamental problem with marrying for romantic love?
   a. The odds are only 50-50 that a marriage based on romantic love will work out.
   b. People get married for the wrong reasons.

c. People are overly optimistic about their choice of a marriage partner.

d. Marriage is a gamble if one gets married in Las Vegas.

6. Razdan cites the testimony of Dr. Alvin Cooper and Robert Epstein, both of whom criticize the contemporary ideal of marrying for romantic love. What fundamental argument against this romantic ideal do both critics have in common?

   a. An arranged marriage takes the guesswork out of the process and ensures a lifetime commitment based on family alliance.

   b. Physical attraction, proximity, and passion are poor criteria for choosing a marriage partner because the elements of rationality and deliberation are missing.

   c. We need to redefine marriage so that it more closely conforms to the models as practiced in other parts of the world.

   d. Internet dating takes the romance out of the equation, thus ensuring a marriage built on shared interests and emotional compatibility.

7. Read paragraphs 10–12 again. From the way the information is presented, what can you infer about Razdan's opinion of the "love contract" and Epstein's experiment to learn to love someone?

   a. She thinks the experiment has merit.

   b. She thinks the experiment needs to be studied further.

   c. She thinks the experiment is ridiculous.

   d. There is no way to tell one way or the other what she thinks.

8. Based on what Razdan says in the final two paragraphs, which of the following most accurately represents her opinion?

   a. She thinks that romantic love is magical and shouldn't be analyzed, lest the magic be ruined.

   b. She thinks that Westerners should adapt the best aspects of arranged marriages to the Western model.

   c. She thinks that arranged marriages are safer and more enduring than marrying for romantic love.

   d. Her own opinion is not evident.

E. Understanding Vocabulary

Look through the paragraphs listed below and find a word that matches each definition. Refer to a dictionary if necessary. An example has been done for you.

EXAMPLE: a magical process of transforming something ordinary into something unusual [paragraphs 1–2] alchemy

1. troubled, upset, alarmed [2–3] ____________
2. irritably, demonstrating ill-temper [2–3] ____________
3. giving shape to, fashioning, creating [3–4] ____________
4. unlimited, endless [5–7] ____________
5. state of being near or close [7 and 15] ____________
6. makes a clever, witty joke [7–9] ____________
7. short period of time spent in a particular way [9–10] ____________
8. turns out well, is successful [11–12—phrase] ____________
9. something greatly reviled or loathed [11–12] ____________
10. specifies, lays down as a condition [11–12] ____________
11. make easy, smooth the progress of [16–17] ____________
12. push, prod, move a little in one direction [16–17] ____________
13. describing someone who stubbornly resists change [16–17] ____________
14. filled, steeped [19–20] ____________
15. describing the sensation of feeling lightheaded [19–20] ____________

DISCUSSION QUESTIONS

1. Go through the article and identify the statements and clichés associated with romantic love. What are some of the other characteristics of this Western ideal that Razdan does not include?
2. From the end of paragraph 15, Amy Kass refers to the concept of "distanced nearness" that people gain from online interaction, similar to the old-style version of courtship. In what particular way do these forms differ from the way most Westerners choose a marriage partner?
3. On balance, has Razdan presented a fair and accurate appraisal of both styles of choosing marriage partners? What other information might you need before deciding which system has more merit than the other?
4. Is Internet dating as close to the concept of arranged marriage as Razdan seems to think?

EXPLORE THE WEB

Here are two other articles by Anjula Razdan published in *Utne*, both available on the web: "Apparently, Looks Might Kill" examines dangerous chemicals in cosmetics:

www.voiceyourself.com/article.php?section=5&more=1&id=1118

"The Chick Lit Challenge" looks at the literary genre called "chick lit" and debates the controversy over the genre, whose critics argue that the genre is actually an antifeminist phenomenon that smothers true feminist expression:

www.utne.com/pub/2004_122/promo/11091-1.html

Throwing Like a Girl

James Fallows

James Fallows studied American literature and history at Harvard and later economics at Oxford University as a Rhodes scholar. For over twenty years he has worked at the *Atlantic Monthly*, where he is currently the national correspondent. In addition to magazine journalism, Fallows is the author of *Breaking the News: How the Media Undermine American Democracy, Looking at the Sun, More Like Us*, and *National Defense,* which won the American Book Award for nonfiction. He is also a frequent contributor to *Slate* and the *New York Review of Books*.

The impetus for this article, written during the first Clinton administration, was Fallows's observation that Bill and Hillary Clinton threw out the ceremonial ball to mark the opening of the 1994 baseball season in entirely different ways. This led him to wonder why boys' and girls' styles of throwing balls are so markedly dissimilar. Here, Fallows speculates about why girls look so awkward when they throw a ball.

VOCABULARY ANALYSIS

The Prefix *ambi-*

Ambidextrous [paragraph 14] means, literally, "two handed." The word can be analyzed like this: *ambi-* ("on both sides") + *dexter* ("right"). An ambidextrous person can eat or write or throw a ball equally well with either hand. Here are three more words that begin with *ambi-*. What do they mean? Check a dictionary if you are unsure.

ambiguous ______________________________

ambivalence ______________________________

____

ambisexual ______________________________

Throwing Like a Girl

James Fallows

1 Most people remember the 1994 baseball season for the way it ended—with a strike rather than a World Series. I keep thinking about the way it began. On opening day, April 4, Bill Clinton went to Cleveland and, like many Presidents before him, threw out a ceremonial first pitch. That same day Hillary Rodham Clinton went to Chicago and, like no First Lady before her, also threw out a first ball, at a Cubs game in Wrigley Field.

2 The next day photos of the Clintons in action appeared in newspapers around the country. Many papers, including *The New York Times* and *The Washington Post*, chose the same two photos to run. The one of Bill Clinton showed him wearing an Indians cap and warm-up jacket. The President, throwing lefty, had turned his shoulders sideways to the plate in preparation for delivery. He was bringing the ball forward from behind his head in a clean-looking throwing action as the photo was snapped. Hillary Clinton was pictured wearing a dark jacket, a scarf, and an oversized Cubs hat. In preparation for her throw she was standing directly facing the plate. A right-hander, she had the elbow of her throwing arm pointed out in front of her. Her forearm was tilted back, toward her shoulder. The ball rested on her upturned palm. As the picture was taken, she was in the middle of an action that can only be described as throwing like a girl.

3 The phrase "throwing like a girl" has become an embattled and offensive one. Feminists smart at its implication that to do something "like a girl" is to do it the wrong way. Recently, on the heels of the O. J. Simpson case, a book appeared in which the phrase was used to help explain why male athletes, especially football players, were involved in so many assaults against women. Having been trained (like most American boys) to dread the accusation of doing anything "like a girl," athletes were said to grow into the assumption that women were valueless, and natural prey.

4 I grant the justice of such complaints. I am attuned to the hurt caused by similar broad-brush stereotypes when they apply to groups I belong to—"dancing like a white man," for instance, or "speaking foreign languages like an American," or "thinking like a Washingtonian."

5 Still, whatever we want to call it, the difference between the two Clintons in what they were doing that day is real, and it is instantly recognizable. And since

seeing those photos I have been wondering. Why, exactly, do so many women throw "like a girl"? If the motion were easy to change, presumably a woman as motivated and self-possessed as Hillary Clinton would have changed it. (According to her press secretary, Lisa Caputo, Mrs. Clinton spent the weekend before opening day tossing a ball in the Rose Garden with her husband, for practice.) Presumably, too, the answer to the question cannot be anything quite as simple. Because they *are* girls.

6 A surprising number of people think that there is a structural difference between male and female arms or shoulders—in the famous "rotator cuff," perhaps—that dictates different throwing motions. "It's in the shoulder joint," a well-educated woman told me recently. "They're hinged differently." Someday researchers may find evidence to support a biological theory of throwing actions. For now, what you'll hear if you ask an orthopedist, an anatomist, or (especially) the coach of a women's softball team is that there is no structural reason why men and women should throw in different ways. This point will be obvious to any male who grew up around girls who liked to play baseball and became good at it. It should be obvious on a larger scale this summer, in broadcasts of the Olympic Games.[1] This year, for the first time, women's fast-pitch softball teams will compete in the Olympics. Although the pitchers in these games will deliver the ball underhand, viewers will see female shortstops, center fielders, catchers, and so on pegging the ball to one another at speeds few male viewers could match.

7 Even women's tennis is a constant if indirect reminder that men's and women's shoulders are "hinged" the same way. The serving motion in tennis is like a throw—but more difficult, because it must be coordinated with the toss of the tennis ball. The men in professional tennis serve harder than the women, because they are bigger and stronger. But women pros serve harder than most male amateurs have ever done, and the service motion for good players is the same for men and women alike. There is no expectation in college or pro tennis that because of their anatomy female players must "serve like a girl." "I know many women who can throw a lot harder and better than the normal male," says Linda Wells, the coach of the highly successful women's softball team at Arizona State University. "It's not gender that makes the difference in how they throw."

8 So what is it, then? Since Hillary Clinton's ceremonial visit to Wrigley Field, I have asked men and women how they learned to throw, or didn't. Why did I care? My impetus was the knowledge that eventually my sons would be grown and gone. If my wife, in all other ways a talented athlete, could learn how to throw, I would still have someone to play catch with. My research left some women, including my wife, thinking that I am some kind of obsessed lout, but it has led me to the solution to the mystery. First let's be clear about what there is to be explained.

9 At a superficial level it's easy to tick off the traits of an awkward-looking throw. The fundamental mistake is the one Mrs. Clinton appeared to be making

in the photo: trying to throw a ball with your body facing the target, rather than rotating your shoulders and hips ninety degrees away from the target and then swinging them around in order to accelerate the ball. A throw looks bad if your elbow is lower than your shoulder as your arm comes forward (unless you're throwing sidearm). A throw looks really bad if, as the ball leaves your hand, your wrist is "inside your elbow"—that is, your elbow joint is bent in such a way that your forearm angles back toward your body and your wrist is closer to your head than your elbow is. Slow-motion film of big-league pitchers shows that when they release the ball, the throwing arm is fully extended and straight from shoulder to wrist. The combination of these three elements—head-on stance, dropped elbow, and wrist inside the elbow—mechanically dictates a pushing rather than a hurling motion, creating the familiar pattern of "throwing like a girl."

10 It is surprisingly hard to find in the literature of baseball a deeper explanation of the mechanics of good and bad throws. Tom Seaver's pitching for the Mets and the White Sox got him into the Hall of Fame, but his book *The Art of Pitching* is full of bromides that hardly clarify the process of throwing, even if they might mean something to accomplished pitchers. His chapter "The Absolutes of Pitching Mechanics," for instance, lays out these four unhelpful principles: "Keep the Front Leg Flexible!" "Rub Up the Baseball." "Hide the Baseball!" "Get it Out, Get it Up!" (The fourth refers to the need to get the ball out of the glove and into the throwing hand in a quick motion.)

11 A variety of other instructional documents, from *Little League's Official How-to-Play Baseball Book* to *Softball for Girls & Women*, mainly reveal the difficulty of finding words to describe a simple motor activity that everyone can recognize. The challenge, I suppose, is like that of writing a manual on how to ride a bike, or how to kiss. Indeed, the most useful description I've found of the mechanics of throwing comes from a man whose specialty is another sport: Vic Braden made his name as a tennis coach, but he has attempted to analyze the physics of a wide variety of sports so that they all will be easier to teach.

12 Braden says that an effective throw involves connecting a series of links in a "kinetic chain." The kinetic chain, which is Braden's tool for analyzing most sporting activity, operates on a principle like that of crack-the-whip. Momentum builds up in one part of the body. When that part is suddenly stopped, as the end of the "whip" is stopped in crack-the-whip, the momentum is transferred to and concentrated in the next link in the chain. A good throw uses six links of chain, Braden says. The first two links involve the lower body, from feet to waist. The first motion of a throw (after the body has been rotated away from the target) is to rotate the legs and hips back in the direction of the throw, building up momentum as large muscles move body mass. Then those links stop—a pitcher stops turning his hips once they face the plate—and the momentum is transferred to the next link. This is the torso, from waist to shoulders, and since its mass is less than that of the legs, momentum makes it rotate faster than the

hips and legs did. The torso stops when it is facing the plate, and the momentum is transferred to the next link—the upper arm. As the upper arm comes past the head, it stops moving forward, and the momentum goes into the final links—the forearm and wrist, which snap forward at tremendous speed.

13 This may sound arcane and jerkily mechanical, but it makes perfect sense when one sees Braden's slow-mo movies of pitchers in action. And it explains why people do, or don't, learn how to throw. The implication of Braden's analysis is that throwing is a perfectly natural action (millions and millions of people can do it), but not at all innate. A successful throw involves an intricate series of actions coordinated among muscle groups, as each link of the chain is timed to interact with the next. Like bike riding or skating, it can be learned by anyone—male or female. No one starts out knowing how to ride a bike or throw a ball. Everyone has to learn.

14 Readers who are happy with their throwing skills can prove this to themselves in about two seconds. If you are right-handed, pick up a ball with your left hand and throw it. Unless you are ambidextrous or have some other odd advantage, you will throw it "like a girl." The problem is not that your left shoulder is hinged strangely or that you don't know what a good throw looks like. It is that you have not spent time training your leg, hip, shoulder, and arm muscles on that side to work together as required for a throw. The actor John Goodman, who played football seriously and baseball casually when he was in high school, is right-handed. When cast in the 1992 movie *The Babe*, he had to learn to bat and throw left-handed, for realism in the role of Babe Ruth. For weeks before the filming began, he would arrive an hour early at the set of his TV show, *Roseanne*, so that he could practice throwing a tennis ball against a wall left-handed. "I made damn sure no one could see me," Goodman told me recently. "I'm hard enough on myself without the derisive laughter of my so-called friends." When *The Babe* was released, Goodman told a newspaper interviewer, "I'll never say something like 'He throws like a girl' again. It's not easy to learn how to throw."

Connecting Grammar to Writing

Look up noun clauses in part 9 of this text. Then underline the three noun clauses in the first sentence of paragraph 15.

15 What Goodman discovered is what most men have forgotten: That if they know how to throw now, it is because they spent time learning at some point long ago. (Goodman says that he can remember learning to ride a bicycle but not learning to throw with his right hand.) This brings us back to the roots of the "throwing like a girl" phenomenon. The crucial factor is not that males and females are put together differently but that they typically spend their early years in different ways. Little boys often learn how to throw without noticing that they are learning. Little girls are more rarely in environments that encourage them to learn in the same way. A boy who wonders why a girl throws the way she does is like a Frenchman who wonders why so many Americans speak French "with an accent."

16 "For young boys it is culturally acceptable and politically correct to develop these skills," says Linda Wells, of the Arizona State softball team. "They are

mentored and networked. Usually girls are not coached at all, or are coached by Mom—or if it's by Dad, he may not be much of an athlete. Girls are often stuck with the bottom of the male talent pool as examples. I would argue that rather than learning to 'throw like a girl,' they learn to throw like poor male athletes. I say that a bad throw is 'throwing like an old man.' This is not gender, it's acculturation."

17 Almost any motor skill, from doing handstands to dribbling a basketball, is easier to learn if you start young, which is why John Goodman did not realize that learning to throw is difficult until he attempted it as an adult. Many girls reach adulthood having missed the chance to learn to throw when that would have been easiest to do. And as adults they have neither John Goodman's incentive to teach their muscles a new set of skills nor his confidence that the feat is possible. Five years ago Joseph Russo, long a baseball coach at St. John's University, gave athletic-talent tests to actresses who were trying out for roles in *A League of Their Own*, a movie about women's baseball. Most of them were "well coordinated in general, like for dancing," he says. But those who had not happened to play baseball or softball when they were young had a problem: "It sounds silly to say it, but they kept throwing like girls." (The best ball-field talents, by the way, were Madonna, Demi Moore, and the rock singer Joan Jett, who according to Russo "can really hit it hard." Careful viewers of *A League of Their Own* will note that only in a fleeting instant in one scene is the star, Geena Davis, shown actually throwing a ball.)

18 I'm not sure that I buy Linda Wells's theory that most boys are "mentored" or "networked" into developing ball skills. Those who make the baseball team, maybe. But for a far larger number the decisive ingredient seems to be the hundreds of idle hours spent throwing balls, sticks, rocks, and so on in the playground or the back yard. Children on the playground, I think, demonstrate the moment when the kinetic chain begins to work. It is when a little boy tries to throw a rock farther than his friend can, or to throw a stick over a telephone wire thirty feet up. A toddler's first, instinctive throw is a push from the shoulder, showing the essential traits of "throwing like a girl." But when a child is really trying to put some oomph into the throw, his natural instinct is to wind up his body and let fly with the links of the chain. Little girls who do the same thing—compete with each other in distance throwing—learn the same way; but whereas many boys do this, few girls do. Tammy Richards, a woman who was raised on a farm in central California, says that she learned to throw by trying to heave dried cow chips farther than her brother could. It may have helped that her father, Bob Richards, was a former Olympic competitor in the decathlon (and two-time Olympic champion in the pole vault), and that he taught all his sons and daughters to throw not only the ball but also the discus, the shotput, and the javelin.

19 Is there a way to make up for lost time if you failed to invest those long hours on the playground years ago? Of course. Adults may not be able to learn to speak

unaccented French, but they can learn to ride a bike, or skate, or throw. All that is required for developing any of these motor skills is time for practice—and spending that time requires overcoming the sense of embarrassment and futility that adults often have when attempting something new. Here are two tips that may help.

20 One is a surprisingly valuable drill suggested by the Little League's *How-to-Play* handbook. Play catch with a partner who is ten or fifteen feet away—but do so while squatting with the knee of your throwing side touching the ground. When you start out this low, you have to keep the throw high to get the ball to your partner without bouncing it. This encourages a throw with the elbow held well above the shoulder, where it belongs.

21 The other is to play catch with a person who can throw like an athlete but is using his or her off hand. The typical adult woman hates to play catch with the typical adult man. She is well aware that she's not looking graceful, and reacts murderously to the condescending tone in his voice ("That's more like it, honey!"). Forcing a right-handed man to throw left-handed is the great equalizer. He suddenly concentrates his attention on what it takes to get hips, shoulder, and elbow working together. He is suddenly aware of the strength of character needed to ignore the snickers of onlookers while learning new motor skills. He can no longer be condescending. He may even be nervous, wondering what he'll do if his partner makes the breakthrough first and he's the one still throwing like a girl.

---

[1]This article was published just before the 1996 Summer Olympics.
Source: From James Fallows, "Throwing Like a Girl," *Atlantic Monthly*, August 1996. Reprinted by permission of the author.

EXERCISES

A. Determining the Main Idea and Writer's Purpose

Choose the best answer.

1. The main idea of the selection is that
   a. boys throw balls harder and faster than girls do.
   b. boys and girls encounter different experiences as they are growing up.
   c. boys and girls throw balls differently for a variety of reasons.
   d. boys receive more attention from adults as they are developing their athletic skills than girls do.

2. The writer's purpose in the selection is to
   a. warn parents not to treat their male and female children differently.
   b. recommend changing the way boys and girls are trained athletically.

c. observe and explain the reasons that boys and girls have different throwing styles.

d. summarize scientific research on the difference between boys' and girls' anatomies.

B. Comprehending Main Ideas

Choose the correct answer.

1. Concerning the fact that boys and girls have completely different styles of pitching, Fallows says that

   a. there is no anatomical reason to account for the difference.

   b. boys' and girls' shoulder joints are hinged differently.

   c. orthopedists and sports coaches disagree on the reasons.

   d. boys' shoulder joints are larger, thereby making them stronger pitchers.

2. The fundamental mistake girls (and women) make when they throw a ball is

   a. not throwing it hard enough.

   b. standing facing the target head on.

   c. rotating the shoulders and hips ninety degrees before throwing.

   d. forgetting to look at the target they are aiming for.

3. To explain an effective throw, Vic Braden has devised the theory of the "kinetic chain," which describes the effectiveness of building up and transferring, from one link to another,

   a. strength.

   b. momentum.

   c. kinetic energy.

   d. a hurling motion.

4. Throwing a ball well, according to both Fallows and the actor John Goodman,

   a. requires years of practice and expert coaching.

   b. depends on one's natural athleticism.

   c. is impossible to learn as an adult.

   d. is not innate and must be learned.

5. For Fallows, the crucial element in determining whether boys and girls become throwers is

   a. practicing with their parents, even if the adults are not very skilled.

   b. studying materials like the Little League *How-to-Play* handbook.

c. competing with other children in distance throwing.

d. joining a baseball or softball team with a talented coach.

C. Locating Supporting Details

For each main idea stated here, find details that support it.

1. Vic Braden says that an effective throw involves connecting a series of links in a "kinetic chain," which works on the principle like that of crack-the-whip. [paragraph 12]

   a. ______________________________

   b. ______________________________

   ____

   ____

2. Arizona State University softball team coach Linda Wells has a theory about why boys and girls throw differently. [paragraph 16]

   a. ______________________________

   ____

   b. ______________________________

   ____

D. Making Inferences

Write your answers to these questions in your own words.

1. From the article as a whole and specifically from paragraph 9, why didn't Hillary Clinton throw the ceremonial baseball more effectively at the Chicago Cubs opening game, despite practicing for a weekend before the game?

   ____

   ____

2. In paragraph 8, why does Fallows describe himself with the phrase "obsessed lout"? What is he implying in this choice of words?

   ____

   ____

   ____

3. From Fallows's explanations in paragraphs 9, 12, and 13, what are the *two* fundamental problems with the appearance and effectiveness of women's pitches?

____

____

4. In paragraph 10, why does Fallows say that Tom Seavers's principles for pitching are "unhelpful"?

____

5. In paragraph 14, why does Fallows recommend that men pick up and throw a ball with the opposite arm?

____

____

____

E. Interpreting Meaning

Where appropriate, write your answers to these questions in your own words.

1. Why is the theory that women's shoulder joints are "hinged" differently wrong? What two pieces of evidence does Fallows offer to challenge the theory? [See paragraph 6.]

____

____

____

____

2. Explain the main point discussed in paragraph 7.

____

____

3. In paragraph 16, why does Linda Wells, the Arizona State softball coach, prefer to use the phrase "throwing like an old man" to "throwing like a girl"?

____

____

4. Explain the difference that Wells makes at the end of paragraph 16 between the words *gender* and *acculturation*.

____

____

F. Understanding Vocabulary

For each word in the left-hand column, find the phrase that best defines it from the right-hand column.

1. dread [paragraph 3]	a. stimulus, incentive, impulse
2. grant [4]	b. surface, external
3. attuned [4]	c. mysterious, understood only by a few
4. impetus [8]	d. mocking, sarcastic
5. lout [8]	e. vital, most essential or important
6. superficial [9]	f. be worried or anxious about
7. bromides [10]	g. feeling of uselessness, pointlessness
8. arcane [13]	h. displaying a superior attitude, arrogant
9. derisive [14]	i. an unrefined, rude man
10. crucial [15]	j. concede, acknowledge
11. incentive [17]	k. motivation, inducement
12. futility [19]	l. snide laughter
13. condescending [21]	m. commonplace remarks, vague platitudes
14. snickers [21]	n. familiar with, accustomed to

DISCUSSION QUESTIONS

1. Fallows's subject matter in this article is potentially dangerous. How does he manage to avoid offending feminists, if in fact he does succeed in this regard? How does Fallows avoid being politically incorrect? How does he avoid being accused of generalizing or stereotyping?
2. Explain the supposed connection Fallows makes in paragraph 3 between male athletes' involvement in assaults against women and the phrase doing something "like a girl."
3. To what extent are gender traits instilled in children because of parental expectations?
4. One theory about the reason that boys do better in math and science is that they tend to gravitate toward toys requiring spatial skills, for example, Lego's, erector sets, and the like, while girls tend to gravitate toward more ladylike activities like reading, playing with dolls, playing "house," having tea parties, and so forth. Should parents encourage gender-specific interests, or should they try to raise their children with gender-neutral toys?

EXPLORE THE WEB

This website discusses the phenomenon of "throwing like a girl" with accompanying photographs. The title is "The Girl Throw—Throwing Like a Girl":

www.kidzworld.com/site/p371.htm

For a completely different interpretation of the phenomenon Fallows discusses, see this online article published in Pennsylvania State University's Sports Medicine Newsletter, from Penn State's College of Health. The title is "'Throwing Like a Girl' Is a Total Misnomer":

www.psu.edu/ur/NEWS/news/sportsmedoct97.html

ANALYZING CARTOONS

Some cartoons are intended merely to make us laugh about human frailty and foibles; others are intended to make a more serious comment about contemporary events or about political or social situations. Political cartoons that appear on the editorial page of major metropolitan daily newspapers are especially effective at commenting on the news of the day and molding public opinion in a humorous, ironic, or satiric way.

Whatever the type, cartoons usually require the reader to make inferences. It is the nature of cartoons to strip a situation down to only its essential elements. These elements are, of course, the drawing itself, the situation that the drawing exemplifies, and any caption material (the writing under the cartoon), or sometimes dialogue. The careful reader must piece these elements together to make connections, especially if there is no caption, and to infer the central meaning and the cartoonist's intention.

The two cartoons that follow illustrate both types. The first one pokes fun at modern parenting, while the second one makes a political statement. The tone of many cartoons—evident in both cartoons reprinted here—may be ***satirical;*** that is, the cartoonist's intent is to poke fun at a government or social policy with an eye toward effecting change, with getting us to see the folly in our behavior. Cartoons may rely on ***hyperbole*** (exaggeration for effect), as you will see in the political cartoon, which satirizes the Pentagon's penchant for congratulating itself when an Al-Qaida terrorist operative has been captured or killed. Study each cartoon carefully, and then answer the questions that follow.

New Yorker Cartoon

Alex Gregory

"So he got a trophy for good sportsmanship—that doesn't mean he won't go to law school."

1. What situation does the cartoon depict?

 ____

 ____

 ____

2. What type of people are the parents depicted? How can you tell?

 ____

 ____

 ____

3. What does a trophy for "good sportsmanship" suggest? Why might a child receive such a trophy?

 ____

 ____

 ____

4. Why are the parents dismayed at their son's winning this trophy?

 ____

 ____

5. What modern parenting practice is this cartoon poking fun at?

6. Why doesn't the cartoonist depict the boy's face?

7. How would you describe the emotion that this cartoon evokes in the reader?

Atlanta Journal-Constitution Cartoon

Mike Luckovich

This cartoon appeared on the editorial pages of many American newspapers in the fall of 2005, when terrorists in the group called Al-Qaida (sometimes

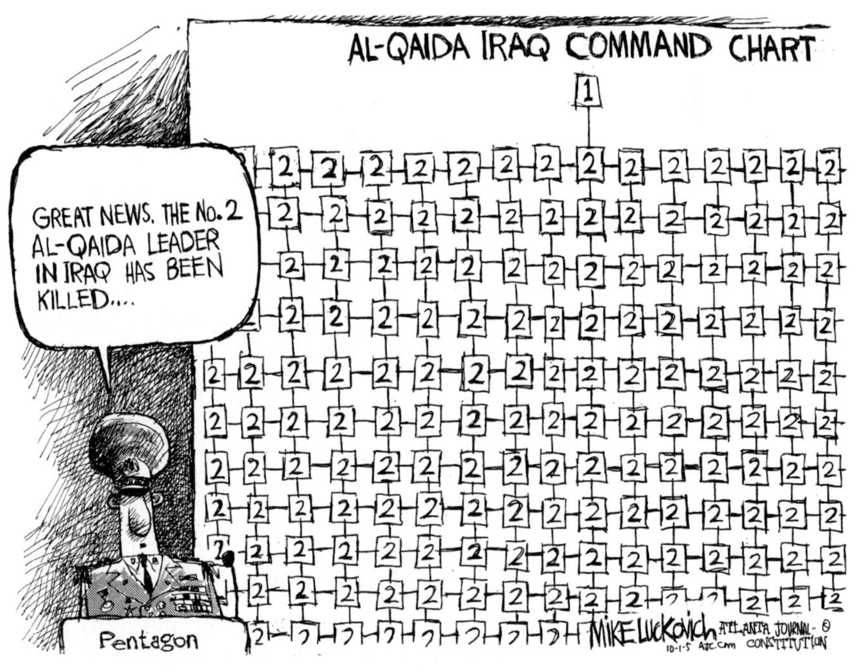

Reprinted by permission of Mike Luckovich and Creators Syndicate, Inc.

spelled Al-Qaeda) were causing havoc around the world with suicide bombings and terrorist attacks.

1. What situation does this cartoon depict?

___

___

___

2. What does the organizational chart behind the Pentagon spokesman indicate?

___

___

3. Is the Pentagon spokesman supposed to be aware of the chart?

___

4. What political reality is this cartoon satirizing?

___

___

___

___

___

___

ANALYZING A PHOTOGRAPH

As the old saying goes, if a picture is worth a thousand words, then one must be able to describe what's going on in a photograph, if not in a thousand words, at least in a few dozen. Photographs capture a moment in time, whether the subject is a landscape, a portrait, or an event. When you look at a photograph of a person, such as the one reprinted here, examine the composition: Who is the person? When was it taken? What is he doing? What does he represent? If there is any background, what is included or depicted? Are there any noticeable or distinguishing characteristics in the subject's appearance? What is the subject's facial expression? What is the subject thinking? What do you think he is feeling? The last two questions will require you to make inferences.

American Soldier Photograph

The information concerning this photograph is a bit sketchy, so you will have to rely on careful observation to interpret it. The photograph was taken

U.S. Army Specialist Norris Tollerson, August 2000, Fort Lewis, Washington.

in August 2000 at Fort Lewis, Washington. The man depicted is U.S. Army Specialist Norris Tollerson. He is holding a rifle during an urban combat training session.

1. What does this photograph depict?

____

____

____

____

____

2. What do you think Tollerson was feeling when this photo was taken?

____

3. What is the overall effect of a photograph like this?

____

____

____

____

____

____

ANALYZING ADVERTISEMENTS

Advertising is ubiquitous in American culture, and this ubiquity makes it especially important that we evaluate ads critically not just for their cleverness but for the message they project and the intent behind them. Most ads—whether on television, in print sources, on billboards or other public places—want us to part with our money. But ads for consumer products are not the only type of advertising distributed through the media. Public service announcements—that is, advertisements sponsored by nonprofit organizations—promote a variety of social causes. Some examples are organizations against drunk or buzzed driving, childhood obesity, domestic violence, emergency preparedness, and so forth.

Two public service print advertisements are printed here for you to analyze. As you study these ads, consider these questions. The first pertain to the advertisement's visual elements:

- What is depicted? Explain the scene and any action, if relevant.
- Examine every detail carefully. What does each visual element contribute to the ad's intended message?
- If the announcement shows people, examine their dress, their behavior, their appearance.

Next, study the text (ad copy), and consider these questions:

- Who sponsors the advertisement? Is the sponsor clearly indicated?
- What does the text in the advertisement say?
- What message does the advertisement convey?
- To whom is the message addressed? Who is the intended audience?

Finally, consider the total effect—the combination of visual elements with text—and consider these questions:

- What is the advertisement's intended message? What does the advertiser want the audience to do or to think?
- Does the advertisement want the viewer to change his or her behavior?
- Is contact information provided so that the viewer can learn more about the sponsoring organization and its work?

Now study and evaluate these two advertisements. At the end of Part 6, there is an essay topic asking you to compare and contrast these public service announcements.

The first advertisement is sponsored by the National Center for Family Literacy.

The Best Way Out

National Center for Family Literacy

FOR RENT
The best way out is by coming in.
The Hernandez family found a way out of poverty – it started by coming in to a family literacy program. No surprise, given that a majority of adults who learn with their kids improve in everything from language skills to getting their GED. Together, they learn "literacy" isn't just about reading and writing, it's about developing skills – skills they use for a better life. Know a family we can help? Or would you like to help? Call **1-877-FAMLIT-1**, or visit us at **www.famlit.org**.
National Center for Family Literacy

And here is the second advertisement, which is part of a national campaign for High School Dropout Prevention.

The Back Pat

High School Dropout Prevention

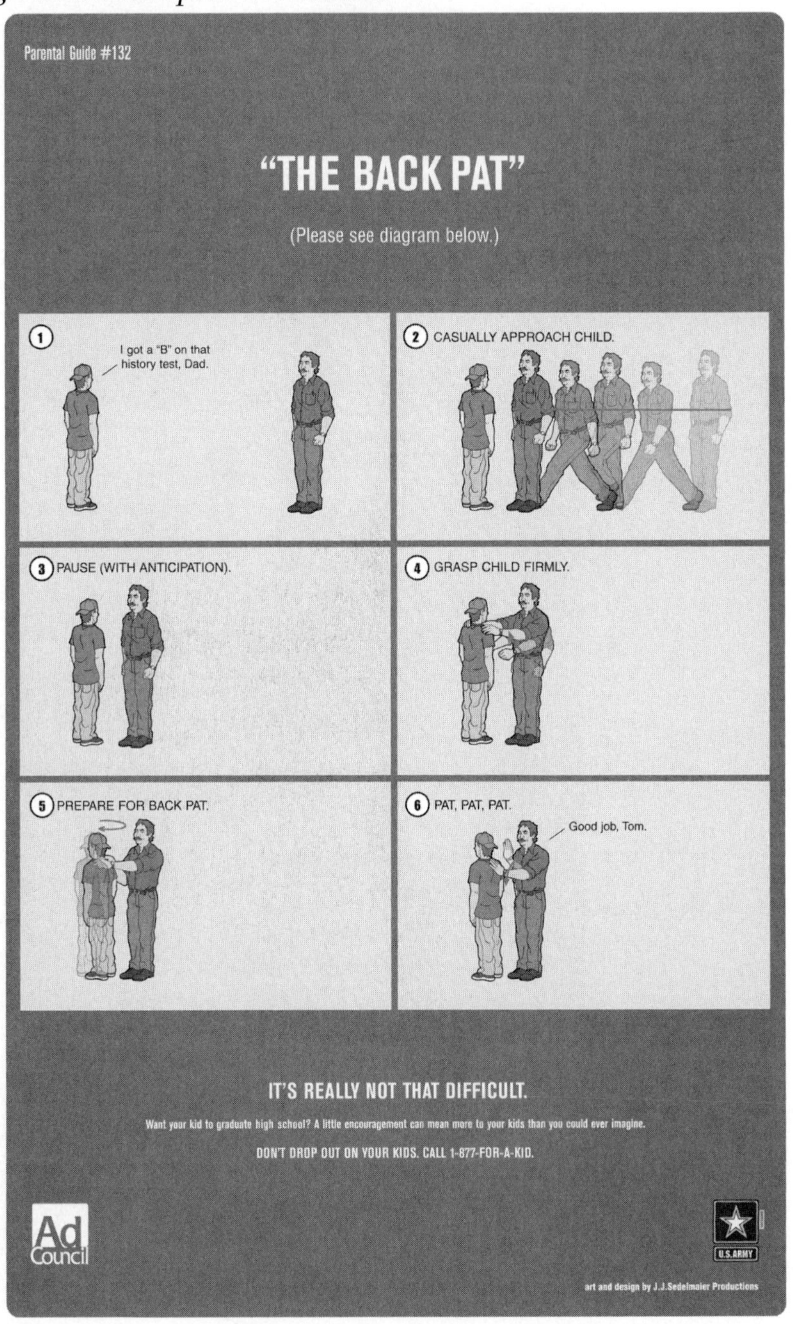

Writing Comparison and Contrast Essays

COMPARING AND CONTRASTING

A comparison-contrast essay is a type of informative or expository essay that represents a common arrangement of ideas. The comparison and contrast method involves putting two subjects side by side to examine their similarities and differences. In the real world, we engage in comparison and contrast all the time: Should I wear jeans or a skirt to the party? Which diet is healthier—vegetarian or vegan? Of all the *Star Wars* movies, which is the best? The process can apply to weightier matters, too. If Samantha Cancino is trying to decide whether to apply to Evergreen State University or Cascade Technical Institute, she might list and then explore a few pertinent features of each institution (for example, geographic location, the size of the student body, the curriculum, the quality of a particular field of study, and tuition fees and availability of financial aid packages) and make an educated decision about which to attend after examining all of these matters.

WRITING TO COMPARE AND CONTRAST: ACADEMIC AND PROFESSIONAL WRITING

The ability to compare and contrast thoughtfully and, more important, to infer significance from the differences and similarities you observe will stand you in good stead, whether in college courses or later in your professional life.

Typical Academic Assignments Requiring Writing to Compare and Contrast

- For a history class, compare and contrast the causes of the French involvement and the American involvement in Vietnam from 1940 to 1975.

- For an art history class, discuss similarities and differences in the early and late works of Picasso.
- For a nursing class, explain the similarities and differences in the treatments of heart disease that have been developed since 1980.

Typical Professional Writing Tasks Requiring Writing to Compare and Contrast

- Compare and contrast the views of several political candidates and evaluate how these differences might relate to concerns of the company for which you work.
- Compare and contrast the results you anticipate if one or the other of two alternative plans are implemented in your workplace.
- Compare and contrast a patient's condition at the beginning and at the end of a particular time period or before and after receiving prescribed medication or treatment.

SOME DEFINITIONS

Although members of the general public often use the words *compare* and *contrast* interchangeably, in fact the words *do* have different meanings. To *compare* means to examine *relevant and significant similarities* between two or more things that we usually consider different. For example, we might compare television viewing and air travel to discover that these two seemingly different activities are really quite similar. Or we might compare the ways in which undergoing a job interview is similar to meeting a new girlfriend's parents.

To *contrast*, however, means to examine *the differences* between two things that most people consider similar. A family in the market for a new car might contemplate whether they should buy Ford Explorer SUV with its roomy interior, four-wheel drive, and off-road capabilities, or a Toyota Prius, with its smaller interior, fuel-saving gasoline-electric hybrid engine, and environmentally friendly benefits. Both vehicles provide a means of transport; both have four wheels, a steering wheel, an engine, and a transmission, but these features are so obvious as to be unworthy of discussion. What the family needs to focus on is the qualities that distinguish a Ford Explorer from a Toyota Prius and thereby to determine which is the better vehicle for them—and perhaps for the environment. Thus, the differences under examination must be both *relevant and significant.* Some examples would be performance, fuel economy, cost of routine maintenance, registration and insurance costs, as well as the impact on the environment.

Which method—comparison or contrast—would be appropriate for Samantha Cancino to use in her appraisal of Evergreen and Cascade Institute?

Like the preceding Explorer–Prius example, both are colleges, but if she were writing a paper on these choices, merely comparing their similarities would not be very useful. The fact that both have dorms, classroom buildings, a library, grass, and cute squirrels running up and down the trees shows no insight and produces nothing particularly meaningful. Contrast is the more appropriate pattern in this case.

Some topics might require you to compare *and* to contrast. In this case, you might want to dispense with the comparisons quickly and focus on the contrasting elements. Whichever method you use, your points of discussion must demonstrate clarity of thinking. For example, when discussing the advantages and disadvantages of the geographic locations of Evergreen and Cascade, Samantha must keep these points together, probably within the same paragraph. If Cascade is located in a large metropolitan area and Evergreen is located in a small rural town, she would discuss these diverse locations together and not introduce irrelevant material like the size of the dormitory rooms.

BRAINSTORMING AND TAKING NOTES FOR A COMPARISON AND CONTRAST ESSAY

As with writing any kind of essay, you first have to prepare and lay the groundwork. This means deciding what subjects to write about and then making a list of relevant points. Consider this topic:

Contrast dating via an online dating service with traditional forms of dating. To do your analysis, choose one of these three online sites:

- http://personals.yahoo.com
- www.eharmony.com/singles/servlet/home
- www.match.com

You are probably quite familiar with traditional dating methods, but if you are unfamiliar with Internet dating sites, you will have to do some research. Spend a little time becoming familiar with the features of two or three representative sites, and choose the one site that most appeals to you. Perhaps talk to friends or relatives who have tried Internet dating to take advantage of their experience.

The first step in the brainstorming process is to take a piece of paper (or divide your computer screen into two columns) and to label one "Yahoo Personals" (or whichever site you have chosen) and the other "Traditional Dating." Now comes the hard part: In each column list some subtopics that logically apply to both types of dating. These subtopics will form the basis for your supporting paragraphs. Once the subtopics are in place, you can then add notes to amplify them. These notes will consist of examples and observations from your experience, perhaps from the experience of friends and relatives and from your research into the chosen Internet dating site.

AN INTERLUDE AND SOME REPEATED ADVICE

Perhaps at this point in the text and in your course, it is worth repeating some advice from Part 1 concerning writing essays:

> *No insight, no essay.* Whether or not a paper successfully communicates to the reader depends wholly on an insight, a perception, a unique observation that belongs solely to the writer. A successful paper does not just rehash the obvious or state what everyone else in the crowd thinks about a subject—a sure recipe for a dull paper that might earn a C but doesn't have much else going for it. The brainstorming process—if done properly—should give you the insight you are looking for, the hook that will entice your reader, carry you through the writing process, and make your essay memorable both for you to write and your audience to read.

This need for insight, perception, and observation is the reason I stress that the comparisons and contrasts you derive from your two subjects should be both relevant and significant. Your writing will improve dramatically if you make the subject come alive for your reader. You can accomplish this—even with a topic that has been discussed by countless other college students—by adding engaging and relevant examples unique to your perspective on the subject. No two writers will bring the same examples and observations to the same subject, and it is your job as a writer to dig deep enough into the subject and to add details and examples that will sustain your reader's interest throughout the essay. Finally, keep in mind that your instructor may well have thirty or more essays to read with each assignment, so it is worth the time and effort to make your essay stand out from the rest of the pack.

ORGANIZING THE ESSAY—TWO APPROACHES

Writing a comparison and contrast essay entails a special problem, because you have two subjects to worry about instead of just one. For the assignment to contrast traditional forms of dating with dating via websites, here are five suggested subtopics that I came up with in a brainstorming session, though you would undoubtedly come up other ideas of your own: (1) the ease and convenience of meeting new and suitable people; (2) becoming acquainted; (3) monetary considerations; (4) risks and liabilities; (5) benefits. Fortunately, there are only two ways to organize a comparison and contrast essay. Both of these organizational methods are described here.

The Subject-by-Subject Method

In the subject-by-subject method, each aspect of the first subject is dealt with fully, point by point. Then each aspect of the second subject is dealt with fully, point by point. Here is what an outline using the subject-by-subject method would look like:

Introduction

I. Traditional dating
   A. Ease and convenience of meeting potential dates
   B. Becoming acquainted
   C. Monetary considerations
   D. Risks and liabilities
   E. Benefits

II. Yahoo and other dating websites
   A. Ease and convenience of meeting potential dates
   B. Becoming acquainted
   C. Monetary considerations
   D. Risks and liabilities
   E. Benefits

Conclusion

This pattern looks simple enough to organize, but it also has some serious limitations. For a complex topic like this—with five separate subtopics to explore—the reader can easily become lost. It is difficult to remember what he read about in the "risks and liabilities" section from the first half when he reaches the discussion of risks and liabilities section in the second half. The elements are just too far apart, making true contrasts difficult to achieve. Another disadvantage is that an essay tends to look more like two separate essays stuck together in the middle with perhaps only a transition like "in contrast" linking them. This method, then, probably is more appropriate if your subject is relatively simple with only a couple of subtopics to be discussed.

The Point-by-Point Method

This method is more useful with a complex topic with three or more points to develop. With the point-by-point method, you discuss each subtopic related to both subjects side by side, either in a single paragraph or in two or more paragraphs to form a section. An outline of a point-by-method organized essay looks like this:

Introduction

I. Ease and convenience of meeting potential dates
   A. Traditional dating
   B. Yahoo and other dating websites

II. Becoming acquainted
   A. Traditional dating
   B. Yahoo and other dating websites

III. Monetary considerations
   A. Traditional dating
   B. Yahoo and other dating websites

IV. Risks and liabilities
   A. Traditional dating
   B. Yahoo and other dating websites

V. Benefits
   A. Traditional dating
   B. Yahoo and other dating websites

Conclusion

No matter which method of organization you use, your introduction should be enticing and should orient your reader to your subject, and your final paragraph should assess the worth of each method and come to a conclusion of which is the preferable method. In addition, after writing your first draft, you might find that you have too many points, making the paper tedious to read. In this case, eliminate one or two, as you see fit.

USING THE TELL-SHOW-SHARE METHOD

In Part 5, you were introduced to a method for developing analysis and synthesis papers called *tell-show-share*. You can easily adapt the tell-show-share method to develop a comparison and contrast essay or, for that matter, to develop any expository essay you are assigned to write in your college courses. For example, if you are asked to write an essay contrasting online dating services with the traditional form of dating practices, you might write a body paragraph explaining how selecting a date from a website contrasts with the traditional methods. You can organize the notes you took during the brainstorming session in the same way you did to write an analysis, with a couple of minor modifications. The "tell" part is the main idea of the paragraph, the "show" part describes and contrasts the two methods, and the "share" part evaluates these methods. So your first body paragraph might look something like this:

Tell (the main idea of the paragraph)

Show (examples of traditional dating & use of websites)

Share (explain why one method is better than another)

> The process of arranging dates has changed markedly with the advent of the Internet. In the old days, a young woman would sit by the telephone waiting for it to ring, or perhaps a friend or relative would fix her up with a suitable match. Not only are blind dates tense and awkward, they also usually don't work out, resulting in wasted time for both parties. In the 1960s, as an aftermath of the sexual revolution and the rise of feminism, a young woman might be more adventuresome and think nothing of asking a guy out. But the Internet has changed much of that. Dating sites like match.com, eharmony.com, and Yahoo personals allow one to scrutinize potential dates according to personal preferences and to screen subjects for appearance, interests, geographic location, religious preferences, or any number of other qualifications. The older generation undoubtedly finds the Internet method mechanical and potentially dangerous. After all, it's very easy for sexual predators to disguise themselves with a false online persona. But for busy singles, especially those who live in large urban areas, finding dating partners online makes a lot of sense. The hit-or-miss aspect of traditional dating is solved by Internet sites because they essentially filter out people who are completely unsuitable for one reason or another.

ACHIEVING COHERENCE

A final consideration is your audience. Your reader will have difficulty staying on track if you move too abruptly from subject to subject or from point to point. *Coherence*—which means that your ideas hold together logically—is most easily accomplished by using transitional words and phrases. Here is a list of some of the more common transitions appropriate for comparing and contrasting:

Transitions Pointing to Similarities	**Transitions Pointing to Differences**
similarly	but *or* yet
in the same way	however
in the same manner	on the contrary
likewise	nevertheless *or* nonetheless
also	on the other hand
likewise	in contrast

USING COMPARISON AND CONTRAST TO WRITE ABOUT A SELECTION

You can use either of the two methods described above for a comparison and contrast essay in which you discuss ideas in two or more reading selections. For example, here is topic 4 from the first group of suggested topics below:

> What do the American version of speed dating as described by Malcolm Gladwell (see website) and the Moroccan version as described by Gautam Naik have in common? How are they different?

To prepare an essay on this topic, begin by making two columns—one for Gladwell and the other for Naik—as suggested above. But this time, your notes will consist of information gleaned from the two readings. You will have to uncover the information yourself—based on your careful annotation and reading from which you can make connections and discern differences. You can start by asking these questions:

- Why do people engage in speed dating in Manhattan, as Gladwell describes it? Why do people engage in the practice in Morocco, as Naik describes it?
- What setting is described in each selection? How do they differ?

- What happens in both venues? How is the speed dating structured?
- What is each writer's purpose in describing the process?

These are only four possibilities. Perhaps you can think of others. Then use the point-by-point method to organize your remarks and the tell-show-share method as explained above to develop the essay.

TOPICS FOR COMPARISON AND CONTRAST ESSAYS

1. It seems clear that the Italian *passeggiata* is a venerable tradition that helps residents maintain their ties (and of course gives younger residents a proper venue for some serious flirting), but it also seems that even residents in the smallest American town would find it nearly impossible to implement this ritual on the local village green. If this observation is valid, what factors in American civic life would make the *passeggiata* an unlikely American custom? What features in American culture operate to foster what Robert D. Putnam calls "uncivic" behavior? Write an essay in which you examine some of these features. Try to go beyond the usual finger pointing at television.
2. In "Passing Fancy" Adam Goodheart cites three benefits of the Italian *passeggiata:* "[It] binds together their community, advertises the power of their clans, and perpetuates ancient mating rituals" [paragraph 1]. Choose *one* of these three benefits and write an essay in which you examine how this benefit is accomplished in American society.
3. Describe your ideal mate. Begin by listing your specific requirements for marrying—the appropriate age to marry; the number of children to have, if any; the importance of shared religious, ethnic, or racial backgrounds; possible careers; goals for the future. Then list the emotional qualities and personal characteristics you hope to find in your partner.
4. What values *and* customs militate against the idea of arranged marriages in the United States? Does the practice of arranged marriage have any appeal for you? Why or why not?
5. Examine the rituals involved in the mating selection process in North America or in another culture with which you are familiar.
6. In paragraph 9 Fallows describes the process of throwing a ball badly. In paragraph 12, Vic Braden describes the process of correctly throwing a ball, based on his theory of a kinetic chain. In the same way, write a short essay of a paragraph or two, in which you analyze either the *wrong* way or the *right* way of performing some physical activity that you know how to do well. Some examples might be serving a ball in tennis, rollerblading, dribbling a basketball, playing a guitar, typing on a computer keyboard, or another similar activity. If you wish, you

might consider writing an essay in which you describe both ways, contrasting them.

7. If you have a sibling or siblings of the opposite sex, write a comparison and contrast essay in which you describe any differences in the way you were raised. Some areas to consider include parental expectations, rules or standards of behavior and discipline, and types of entertainment (toys, dolls, games, sports, and so forth).

MISCELLANEOUS TOPICS

1. Write a comparison and contrast essay on two movies, two science fiction novels you have read, two rock bands.
2. Compare and contrast two different jobs you have held in the past, for example, working in a bank and working in a restaurant, or working in a video store and babysitting.
3. Compare and contrast two teachers you have had in the past, perhaps focusing on one teacher in a high school class and one instructor in a college class.

TOPICS RELATED TO THE READINGS

1. Adam Goodheart's essay, "Passing Fancy," describes an evening ritual common in southern Italian villages, towns, and cities. Write a short essay of approximately 500–600 words in which you contrast the Italian ritual of *passeggiata* with the way residents spend their evenings in your community.
2. A variant on topic 1 above: If you are from a different culture, write a short essay of perhaps 750 words contrasting these three elements: the *passeggiata* of southern Italy, an evening ritual practiced in your native culture, and an evening ritual practiced in your American community. (For a topic that requires you to examine three ideas, simply adapt either organizational method and add a third element.)
3. Write a comparison and contrast essay on one of these two topics derived from Paco Underhill's selection, "Shop Like a Man": (a) Describe your own shopping behavior and contrast it with Underhill's observations, being sure to pay attention to the characteristics he ascribes to the shopping habits of your same sex. (b) Describe and contrast your shopping habits with those of someone of the opposite sex. For either topic, be sure to focus on the characteristics Underhill ascribes to the shopping style of each gender.

4. After reading the selections by Gladwell and Naik, write an essay presenting your reactions to the concept of speed dating. How does the dating festival function for Morocco's Berber population? How does speed dating function for Manhattan's young singles? Write a short essay in which you set forth the advantages and disadvantages of speed dating, citing both the Moroccan and American versions.
5. Both Naik and Razdan present two very different types of dating and mating rituals from what commonly occurs in North America. Write an informative essay in which you examine the Moroccan system of speed dating and the Indian custom of arranged marriages. Then explain the custom of finding a suitable marriage partner as it is practiced in the United States, or perhaps in another culture with which you are familiar. Finally, come to a conclusion of your own about which system offers the most advantages in producing stable marriages.
6. Compare Fallows's article with one published online by David A. Gershaw titled "A Line on Life: Throwing Like a Girl," which is available at www.jiskha.com/social_studies/psychology/throwing_girl.html. Note the citation at the bottom of the online article. Write an essay in which you answer this question: Is the online article an example of plagiarism, and if it is, what is the evidence?
7. Study the public service announcements from the National Center for Family Literacy and from the U.S. Army on preventing high school students from dropping out. Write a comparison and contrast essay in which you examine the advertisements' purpose, audience, message, and method(s) of conveying that message.
8. Choose one of the visual images—one of the cartoons or the photograph at the end of the reading section of Part 6—and write a paragraph or two analyzing it in terms of its effect on the reader.

PART SEVEN

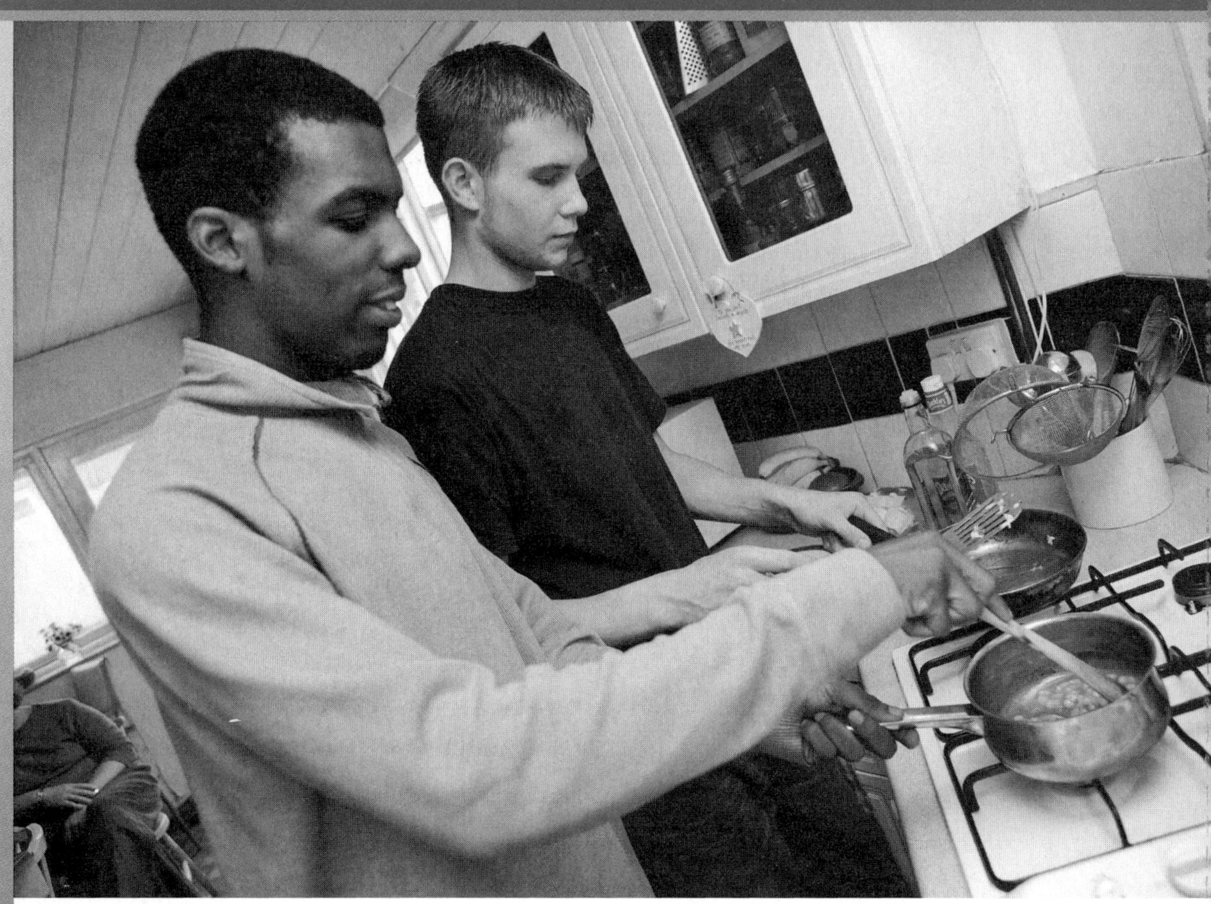

READING

WRITING

Part 7 begins with an explanation of the usefulness of transitional expressions—words, sentences, or sometimes an entire paragraph. These expressions show you the logical connections writers make between ideas and serve as useful markers to keep you on track. In your own writing, you can use them as stylistic devices to ensure that your discussion maintains unity and coherence.

The reading selections all demonstrate the cause-effect method of development and therefore serve as a natural springboard to the cause and effect writing assignments that conclude Part 7. The Practice Essay by Barry Glassner is an excerpt about the media's deliberate exploitation of sensational events, thereby creating unnecessary and irrational fears. Anwar Accawi's reading recounts the impact of the first telephone in his small Lebanese village, and Judith Ortiz Cofer's selection examines the patriarchal nature of her grandparents' marriage, in particular focusing on the problems Puerto Rican women encountered because legal birth control was unavailable. Next, Nelson Mandela relates the circumcision ceremony by which Xhosa boys become men, and Megan Stack analyzes the reasons that, at least in some Middle Eastern countries, Islamic women are required to wear a veil in public and the ramifications of this requirement.

The writing section takes up various considerations in preparing a cause-effect essay, whether the topic relates to one or more of the readings in Part 7 or to a topic of one's own choosing.

Identifying Transitional Elements

■ TRANSITIONAL ELEMENTS IN READING

You will recall that the introduction to Part 4 showed you the advantages of annotating the text and reading with a pencil in your hand. This technique helps the reader maintain focus. Still, even the best reader may become distracted while reading and lose the thread of the writer's ideas, especially when reading academic prose. We have all found ourselves at the bottom of a page but with no idea of what we have just read. This distraction or loss of focus is especially apt to occur when we are tired or anxious about the cares of the day or when the subject matter is difficult or unfamiliar.

In this section we will look at another way to avoid getting lost on the page, and that is to pay attention to some useful devices called transitions. *Transitional elements*, sometimes called *markers*, point to logical relationships between ideas. They "mark" the place where a writer moves to a new idea or indicates a particular logical connection between what comes before and what comes after. In this way, transitions serve as a bridge between ideas, helping us follow the writer's thinking, keeping us on track, and showing us where a shift in thought—sometimes a very subtle shift—occurs.

As you will see, transitions can be either single words or phrases. And sometimes an entire paragraph may be used in this way, pointing back to the preceding paragraph while at the same time pointing ahead to the next idea in the chain of ideas. Some writers use lots of transitions; others use none at all. But when they are present, they are most useful.

Two cautions about transitions: (1) Do not assume that because frequently transitions are little words (*and, but, yet, thus, so*) they do not count; and (2) contrary to what some students have been taught, transitions do not necessarily come at the beginning of sentences. They can appear in the middle of sentences or even at the end. The various positions in sentences of transitional elements will be illustrated later in this section.

By studying a number of examples of passages using transitions, you will quickly become proficient in locating them. I have classified the transitional elements according to the logical relationship they signal. Each category is followed by a list of common transitions and one or more short passages from some of the readings in this text.

Transitions That Indicate Additional Information

These transitions are most commonly used to list facts and details and examples. Note that these transitions usually signal that something of equal importance follows. Here are some examples:

and
next
besides
in the same way
in addition
further
furthermore
moreover
either . . . or
neither . . . nor
next
also
first
second (and so on)

Examples from the Readings

What seems new to me is that cheating has gone mainstream. It shows up in almost every corner of American life—from professional athletics and Wall Street businesses to high school SATs. *And* it is tolerated more.

—Kirk O. Hanson, "Culture Suggests Cheaters Do Prosper"

The other problem, *in addition to* the less-than-nurturing management style, is that this job shows no sign of being financially viable.

—Barbara Ehrenreich, "Nickel and Dimed: On (Not) Getting by in America"

With such flimsy craft, Polynesians could never have colonized Easter [Island] from even the nearest island, *nor* could they have traveled far offshore to fish.

—Jared Diamond, "Easter's End"

The statues imply a society very different from the one Roggeveen saw in 1722. Their sheer number and size suggest a population much larger than 2,000 people. What became of everyone? *Furthermore*, that society must have been highly organized.

—Jared Diamond, "Easter's End"

Transitions That Introduce Examples or Illustrations

These transitions signal that a writer is going to give an example or illustration to reinforce a more general idea. Here are a few:

for example
for instance
to illustrate
as a case in point
consider the following
namely

Examples from the Readings

A 1993 U. S. Department of Education Report on illiteracy says 21–23 percent of U.S. adults—about 40 million—read minimally, enough to decipher an uncomplicated meeting announcement. Another 25–38 percent read and write only slightly better. *For instance,* they can fill out a simple form.

—Richard Wolkomir, "Making Up for Lost Time: The Rewards of Reading at Last"

That 20 percent rule, by the way, applies to all food products, whether it's a bag of potato chips, the 2,178-calorie mountain of fried seafood at Red Lobster or the 710-calorie slab of dessert at the Cheesecake Factory. Some foods are even less expensive to make. The flakes of your kid's breakfast cereal, *for example,* account for only 5 percent of the total amount Nabisco or General Mills spent to make and sell them.

—Shannon Brownlee, "Pricing French Fries: A Lesson in Economics"

Transitions That Show Chronological Order or Time Progression

This group of transitions is particularly evident in the process pattern or in narratives. Writers use them to ensure a logical progression of steps or a logical sequence of events. Look at these examples:

then
meanwhile
later
after
eventually
soon
finally
after a few days

next
last July
in 2007

Examples from the Readings

Each year, hundreds of marriageable Berbers gather for this three-day dating ritual, which has been practiced among nomadic tribes in these arid, windy mountains for centuries. *Today,* the ritual has developed into a major Berber bazaar and tourist attraction.

—Gautam Naik, "Speed Dating, Berber Style"

Finally, the telephone took my family away, too. My father got a call from an old army buddy who told him that an oil company in southern Lebanon was hiring interpreters and instructors. My father applied for a job and got it, and we moved to Sidon, where I went to Presbyterian missionary school and graduated in 1962. *Three years later,* having won a scholarship, I left Lebanon for the United States.

—Anwar F. Accawi, "The Telephone"

Transitions That Show Contrast or Differences

This type of transition helps keep the reader on track when the writer is moving back and forth, showing the differences between two subjects. Consider these examples:

but
yet
still
however
nevertheless
nonetheless
on the other hand
in contrast
instead
whereas
while

Examples from the Readings

The hijab [the scarf Muslim women are required to wear in public] is an expression of personal devotion to Islam, *but* critics decry it as an emblem of patriarchal repression.

—Megan Stack, "The Many Layers of the Veil"

There are Muslim countries where women have no choice but to cover their heads. Religious police in Saudi Arabia and Iran hunt and even beat bareheaded women. *Yet* in Turkey and Tunisia, there is the opposite pressure. The hijab is banned from public schools and offices, and veiled women complain of ridicule and abuse.

—Megan Stack, "The Many Layers of the Veil"

When a man takes clothing into a dressing room, the only thing that stops him from buying it is if it doesn't fit. Women, *on the other hand*, try things on as only part of the consideration process, and garments that fit just fine may still be rejected on other grounds.

—Paco Underhill, "Shop Like a Man"

They [cells] also come in a sumptuously wide range of sizes—nowhere more strikingly than at the moment of conception, when a single beating sperm confronts an egg eighty-five thousand times bigger than it. . . . On average, *however*, a human cell is about twenty microns wide.

—Bill Bryson, "Cells"

Transitions That Show Comparison or Similarity

If you recall that the word *comparison* means to show how two things are similar in some important way, a writer may indicate such a relationship with one of these transitions:

similarly
likewise
in the same way
in comparison

Examples from the Readings

I tell my daughter things about economic justice that are just about as far outside the mainstream dogma. But I don't expect her school to forgo teaching Western history or capitalist economics on my account. *Likewise*, it should be the job of Special Creationist parents to make their story convincing to their children.

—Barbara Kingsolver, "How Mr. Dewey Decimal Saved My Life"

With passing years, the statues and platforms became larger and larger, and the statues began sporting ten-ton red crowns—probably in an escalating spiral of one-upmanship, as rival clans tried to surpass each other with shows of wealth and power. . . . On Easter, *as in modern America*, society was held together by a complex political system to redistribute locally available resources and to integrate the economies of different areas.

—Jared Diamond, "Easter's End"

Transitions That Show Cause-Effect Connections

Although not as common, there are a few transitional elements that announce themselves as indicating a cause-effect relationship, in the way that, say, the transitional phrase *in contrast* points to an obvious contrast. The writer can show cause only by using words like *because* or *for* (which is a coordinating conjunction also meaning "because") or by writing a phrase like *one reason for*, or other similar expressions. However, there are a few transitions that indicate *effect* or *result*. Here are some transition examples:

as a result
consequently
therefore
thus
then
hence
and so

Examples from the Readings

Here's another statistical comparison: Eighty-six percent of women look at price tags when they shop. Only 72 percent of men do. For a man, ignoring the price tag is almost a measure of his virility. *As a result*, men are far more easily upgraded than are women shoppers.

—Paco Underhill, "Shop Like a Man"

[Chief Megliqili is speaking]: "There sit our sons . . . young, healthy, and handsome, the flower of the Xhosa tribe, the pride of our nation. We have just circumcised them in a ritual that promises them manhood, but I am here to tell you that it is an empty, illusory promise, a promise that can never be fulfilled. *For* we Xhosas, and all black South Africans, are a conquered people. We are slaves in our own country."

—Nelson Mandela, "Long Walk to Freedom"

Finally, an anxious Papá approached his wife to tell her that the new room was finished and ready to be occupied. And Mamá, they say, replied: "Good it's for *you*." *And so* it was that Mamá discovered the only means of birth control available to a Catholic woman of her time: sacrifice.

—Judith Ortiz Cofer, "More Room"

Transitions That Show Emphasis

Generally, most good professional writers seldom show emphasis by using gimmicky punctuation like exclamation marks or formatting devices like underlining. Instead, they make their language strong and vivid and occasionally use emphatic transitions such as these:

of course
undoubtedly/without a doubt
certainly
indeed
in fact
truly

Examples from the Readings

What we *didn't* have included almost anything respectable teenagers might do in the way of entertainment. *In fact*, there was one thing for teenagers to do to entertain themselves, and it was done in the backs of Fords and Chevrolets.

—Barbara Kingsolver, "How Mr. Dewey Decimal Saved My Life"

The downside [of supersizing], *of course*, is that 20 years of Big Food has trained us to think that oceanic drinks and gargantuan portions are normal. *Indeed*, once fast food discovered that big meals meant big profits, everybody from Heineken to Olive Garden to Frito Lay followed suit.

—Shannon Brownlee, "Pricing French Fries: A Lesson in Economics"

Transitions That Show Concession

To *concede* means to admit that something is true while at the same time something else is also true. Consider this sentence:

Although Sarah is afraid of water, she has decided to take up sailing.

In making this statement, I concede (make the concession) that Sarah is afraid of water, but I also assert that despite that fear she is going to learn to sail. In this example, "Although Sarah is afraid of water" is called in grammar an adverb clause of concession. Concession clauses and phrases are enormously useful, and good writers use them all the time, much more, I would hazard to guess, than they use the more common conjunctions *but* or *yet*.

A side note: Years ago I remember reading that Bill Robinson, former director of composition at San Francisco State University, performed a computer analysis of nonfiction prose written by a dozen or so American writers considered masters of the written word (George Orwell, E. B. White, Joan Didion, and so forth). His aim was to try to discern if any particular stylistic patterns emerged in their writing that would distinguish them from lesser writers. His conclusion: These writers liberally used appositive phrases and clauses and phrases showing concession.[1] Here are four words and phrases showing concession:

although (always one word)
while even though (always two words)
in spite of
despite

In this list, note that *although, even though,* and *while* introduce concession clauses (a type of adverb clause), and *in spite of* and *despite* introduce concession phrases. An example of the latter occurs in this sentence: In spite of Kevin's hard work and excellent class attendance, he finds organic chemistry to be a most difficult class.

Examples from the Readings

While the hauhau tree did not become extinct in Polynesian times, its numbers declined drastically until there weren't enough left to make ropes from.

—Jared Diamond, "Easter's End"

Despite all the talk in Colorado about aerospace, biotech, computer software, telecommunications, and other industries of the future, the largest private employer in the state today is the restaurant industry.

—Eric Schlosser, "Fast Food Nation: Behind the Counter"

[1]For a further explanation of these stylistic devices, see the discussion of appositives on page 580 in Part 9. Adverb clauses are discussed in Part 9 on pages 583–584. You have to be particularly careful to punctuate concession clauses and phrases properly. They are always dependent and thus should not be punctuated with a period or a semicolon at the end; instead, always join them to an independent clause with a comma.

Regardless of the billions spent on marketing and promotion, all the ads on radio and TV, all the efforts to create brand loyalty, the major chains must live with the unsettling fact that more than 70 percent of fast food visits are "impulsive."

—Eric Schlosser, "Fast Food Nation: Behind the Counter"

Even in the face of earlier floods and hurricanes, and modern thunderstorms that boiled out of the gulf almost every afternoon in the summer, most people who were born there stayed there, and countless others came to live there.

—Curtis Wilkie, "The New Orleans That Was"

The town square couldn't have been much more than a hundred yards long. And the townspeople, most of them, had been pacing these same worn stones every day of their lives since they were old enough to put one foot in front of the other. *Still,* they seemed to take undiminished enjoyment in the act—or not enjoyment, perhaps, but rather an emotion somewhere between pleasure and duty.

—Adam Goodheart, "Passing Fancy: The Passeggiata"

TRANSITIONAL ELEMENTS IN WRITING

As mentioned earlier, some writers use no transitions at all. A writer is under no obligation to use transitional elements to make the reader's job easier. If you look through the readings in this text, you will quickly see that the use of transitions varies widely among the writers represented. In your own writing, use transitions judiciously; that means use them wisely and appropriately, and resist the temptation to use one in every sentence. Study how writers that you enjoy reading link their sentences. The reader ideally should not become aware of transitions. They are there to reinforce relationships and connections—not to serve as decorative enhancements.

The Placement of Transitional Elements in Sentences

What determines the placement of transitional elements in sentences? Most often, their position is simply the function of grammatical expression.[2] For example, the coordinating conjunctions *and, but, for, yet,* and so on usually come either between two independent clauses or, less commonly, at

[2]See the discussion of the various types of conjunctions (words or phrases used to join grammatical elements) on pages 575–576 in Part 9 for a fuller understanding of these grammatical constraints.

the beginning of sentences. Conjunctive adverbs such as *however, moreover, though*, or *therefore*, may join two sentences, or, because they are adverbs that in English can move about in a sentence more freely than other parts of speech, they may be embedded within a sentence.

Some writers, *however*, deliberately move these conjunctive adverbs to other places in the sentence, probably because doing so sounds better to the ear (as I have done in this sentence by moving *however* from the more usual starting position in this sentence). Beginning too many sentences with a transitional word or phrase not only seems formulaic but also imparts a heavy, clunky sound. Note that such elements are considered *parenthetical expressions* because they interrupt the flow of the sentence and could be omitted altogether.[3] Therefore, they should be separated by commas. For example, in the selection "Cells," Bill Bryson writes:

> They [cells] also come in a sumptuously wide range of sizes—nowhere more strikingly than at the moment of conception, when a single beating sperm confronts an egg eighty-five thousand times bigger than it. . . . On average, *however*, a human cell is about twenty microns wide.
>
> —Bill Bryson, "Cells"

The last sentence would more typically be written like this:

> *However*, on average, a human cell is about twenty microns wide.

But he also could have written this, with the parenthetical *however* coming at the end:

> On average, a human cell is about twenty microns wide, *however*.

All three are grammatically correct, but to our ears the original sentence is more pleasing.

Look at this excerpt from Paco Underhill's selection, "Shop Like a Man," in which he writes:

> The conventional wisdom on male shoppers is that they don't especially like to do it, which is why they don't do much of it. It's a struggle just to get them to be patient company for a woman while she shops. *As a result*, the entire shopping experience—from packaging design to advertising to merchandising to store design and fixturing—is generally geared toward the female shopper.

Where else in the last sentence could the transitional phrase *as a result* be placed and still work both grammatically and stylistically? It could conceivably

[3]See page 603 in Part 9 for a fuller explanation on the uses of parenthetical words and phrases and the correct way to punctuate them.

go after the word *experience*, as a nice variation on the usual position. Note that the computer makes such stylistic changes a snap—you can cut and paste to your heart's content until your sentences say exactly what you want them to say and sound exactly like you want them to sound. For you as a college writer, knowing some of these grammatical and stylistic alternatives will serve you well as you take on more challenging essay assignments and as your writing style becomes more confident.

An Excerpt Showing the Stylistic Effect of Transitions

Read this excerpt from Andre Dubus's essay, "Digging," and circle all of the transitions:

> My imagination gave me a dual life: I lived in my body, and at the same time lived a life no one could see. All my life I have told myself stories, and have talked in my mind to friends. Imagine my father sitting at supper with my mother and two older sisters and me: I am ten and small and appear distracted. Every year at school there is a new bully, sometimes a new one, sometimes the one from the year before. I draw bullies to me, not because I am small, but because they know I will neither fight nor inform on them. I will take their pushes or pinches or punches, and try not to cry, and I will pretend I am not hurt. My father does not know this. He only sees me at supper, and I am not there. I am riding a horse and shooting bad men. My father eats, glances at me. I know he is trying to see who I am, who I will be.

Note that Dubus's liberal use of the common conjunction *and* joining simple sentences gives his writing a Hemingwayesque flavor. The passage is easy to read, because the words and phrases flow along, joined by these seemingly unimportant little words like *and*, *or*, and *but*.

The Paragraph as a Transition

Occasionally, an entire paragraph can constitute a transition from one part of an essay to another, particular in long, complex pieces. Here, for example, is an excerpt (one paragraph and the first two sentences of another paragraph) that comes midway in a chapter titled "Under Montana's Big Sky," from Jared Diamond's book *Collapse: How Societies Choose to Fail or Succeed*. In this chapter, first Diamond discusses the harmful environmental and social changes that Montana has witnessed in the last few decades. The chapter ends with a discussion of Montana's future in light of all these problems. This transitional paragraph serves as a signpost for the reader, essentially saying—here is a summary of what I have been talking about, and here is what is coming up next. Note that the paragraph begins with the transitional element *thus*, which also points to a summary.

> Thus, seemingly pristine Montana actually suffers from serious environmental problems involving toxic wastes, forests, soils, water, climate change, biodiversity losses, and introduced pests. All of these problems translate into economic problems. They provide much of the explanation for why

Montana's economy has been declining in recent decades to the point where what was formerly one of our richest states is now one of the poorest.

Whether or how these problems become resolved will depend on the attitudes and values that Montanans hold. But Montana's population is becoming increasingly heterogeneous and cannot agree on a vision for their state's environment and future.

—Jared Diamond, *Collapse: How Societies Choose to Fail or Succeed*

As you work through the assigned readings in Part 7, pay attention to how each writer uses transitions both as aids to your reading comprehension and focus and as models for your own writing. We begin with the Practice Essay by Barry Glassner on teen suicide.

PRACTICE ESSAY

Teen Suicide and the Culture of Fear

Barry Glassner

Barry Glassner is a professor of sociology at the University of Southern California. His 1999 book, *The Culture of Fear: Why Americans Are Afraid of the Wrong Things*, analyzes how the media not only shape the news but also instill exaggerated and unnecessary fear in viewers. Glassner argues that the media exaggerate isolated incidents and treats them as if they were trends and blow events like the Columbine school killings out of proportion. The book takes up such diverse subjects as road rage, airline safety, violence in the workplace, teenage suicide, and Internet sex crimes. In each section, Glassner shows how the media inflate isolated examples into "false crises," thereby exploiting our anxieties and instilling in us needless fear. You can see Glassner interviewed in Michael Moore's award-winning documentary, *Bowling for Columbine*. In this excerpt, Glassner discusses the issue of teen suicide. Glassner's most recent book is *The Gospel of Food: Everything You Think You Know about Food Is Wrong* (2007).

VOCABULARY ANALYSIS

The Suffix *-cide*

In English the suffix *–cide* means "killing of." In paragraph 2, Glassner uses two words with this suffix: *suicide* and *homicide*. *Suicide* is formed by adding the root *sui* ("self") to the suffix—killing of oneself. *Homicide* is formed by adding the root *homo* ("man") to the suffix—the killing of another human being. Other words ending with this suffix are *matricide* (killing one's mother), *genocide* (killing an entire race of people), and *pesticide* (an agent that kills insects). What do these words mean? Check a dictionary if you are unsure.

patricide ______________________________

parricide ______________________________

infanticide ______________________________

herbicide ______________________________

Teen Suicide and the Culture of Fear

Barry Glassner

1 America's children face far graver dangers than parents realize. Journalists, politicians, and advocacy organizations reiterate that conclusion incessantly. One way they reiterate it, as we have seen, is through stories about sexual predators in churches, schools and cyberspace. Another is by asserting that children face huge hazards that the public and policy makers have failed to appreciate.

2 A front-page article in the sports section of the *New York Times* told the story of young Scott Croteau of Lewiston, Maine, cocaptain of the football team and reportedly the most popular student at his high school. Possessed of good looks and straight-As, Scott was being recruited by Harvard and Princeton at the time he hanged himself from a tree and then shot himself in the head with a revolver. "Suicide," the *Times* reported, "has become one of the major causes of death among American teen-agers, following automobile accidents and homicides." What is particularly disturbing, said a public health expert quoted in the piece, suicide by young people "is a virtually unrecognized national public health problem."

3 Or consider a page-one headline in the *Washington Post:* "Prescription Error Claims Dad's 'Angel'—Mistakes on Rise, Pharmacists Say." The story told of little Megan McClave of Hampton, Virginia, who was given medication by her father upon her return home from having her tonsils removed, went to bed for the night, and never woke up. "Pharmacists say their jobs are becoming tougher, and mistakes more common," reports the *Post,* "because of the rapidly increasing number of medications hitting the market every year and the new generic equivalents for older drugs." At some large-chain stores and bulk prescription services pharmacists who fill hundreds of prescriptions a day may be overworked, and as in Megan's case, dispense the wrong pills.

4 Reading this stuff, most parents undoubtedly think *my child could be next.* But need they? On closer reading, the evidence journalists amass in support of the supposed trends seldom turns out to be overwhelming. "Medical experts

say that although a mistake as serious as the one that killed Megan is extremely rare, prescription errors are not as infrequent as commonly believed," was the best the *Post* could muster. The *Times* at least gave some scary-sounding statistics in its story about suicide: the incidence of teen and young adult suicides nearly tripled between 1952 and 1992, to 1,847 in 1992.

Connecting Grammar to Writing

Glassner interrupts the first sentence of paragraph 5 by moving *however* to the middle of the sentence and using commas to separate it. Where else in the sentence could *however* go?

5 Those numbers can be read, however, in a considerably less alarmist way. At the conclusion of a forty-year period during which increases in the divorce and poverty rates, decreases in investment in education and counseling services, and the advent of AIDS put more stress than ever on American adolescents, about 1 in 10,000 saw fit to end his or her life. I do not want to minimize their tragic loss, but the numbers pale beside statistics for other threats faced by teens. One in nine goes hungry for some part of each month, for instance, and the number of hungry young Americans increased by half between the mid-1980s and mid-1990s.

6 That suicide is the third leading cause of death for teens—a startling fact that the media repeat early and often in stories about kids who take their own lives—also warrants a moment's reflection. Adolescents are unlikely to die of cancer, heart disease, or HIV. Those leading killers of adults generally take years to progress. Fortunately, we live in a period and place where, unlike most cultures throughout history, the vast majority of people survive to adulthood. It is far from surprising that those young people who do lose their lives fall victim to immediate causes, which is to say, accidents, homicide, and suicide.

7 The trend in youth suicide actually has been moderately encouraging in recent years. Nationwide, an all-time high was recorded in 1988, and since then the rate has stabilized, even decreasing slightly in some years. In the 1990s some locales experienced substantial increases that were widely reported in their local media, while others enjoyed spectacular declines that went almost unacknowledged. In Los Angeles the news media barely took note when the teen suicide rate fell to its lowest level in three decades during the mid-1990s. They focused instead on three adolescents who leapt to their deaths from a cliff in 1996. The deaths, reporters told us, were "a reminder of how astonishingly fraught with danger the teenage years have become in America" (*Time*).

8 Even more illuminating than speculation about the perilousness of American society or the fluctuations in the numbers of teens who commit suicide is a well-documented change in *how* they end their lives. More kids succeed in suicide attempts these days than in the past because more of them—about 60 percent—use guns. As we have seen, the ready availability of guns also accounts for most teen homicides and many fatal accidents, the other two leading causes of death for this age group. Perhaps politicians, social scientists, journalists, and anyone else who reports on dangers to kids should install on their computers a screen saver that shows a revolver, and beneath it, in big letters: IT'S THE GUNS, STUPID.

EXERCISES

A. Determining the Main Idea and Writer's Purpose

Choose the best answer.

1. The main idea of the selection is that
   a. America's children face far graver dangers than parents realize.
   b. public health experts should be concerned about the public health problem resulting from teenage suicide.
   c. suicide is the third leading cause of death among American teenagers.
   d. the media have exaggerated the dangers to American teenagers, alarming parents unnecessarily.

2. The writer's purpose in the selection is to
   a. challenge and discredit the way the media cover dangers to teenagers' health and safety.
   b. argue that newspapers need to be more factual and objective in reporting stories.
   c. prove that teenage suicide rates have actually declined.
   d. discuss the leading causes of death among teenagers in the 1990s.

B. Comprehending Main Ideas

Choose the correct answer.

1. In the story about Scott Croteau, the Maine high school student who committed suicide, the *New York Times* reported that the leading causes of death among American teenagers are, *in this order,*
   a. automobile accidents, drownings, and suicides.
   b. homicides, automobile accidents, and suicides.
   c. automobile accidents, homicides, and suicides.
   d. drug overdoses, automobile accidents, and suicides.

2. According to Glassner, the case of Megan McClave, the child who died as the result of the pharmacist dispensing the wrong drug, is an example of
   a. why generic drugs can be dangerous.
   b. an error committed by overworked pharmacists who cannot keep up with the number of new drugs coming into the market every year.
   c. an error committed by the child's father, who failed to follow the directions for administering the drug.
   d. a rare prescription error by the pharmacist.

3. Glassner asserts that the statistical number of teenagers ending their lives (about 1 in 10,000)
   a. has been deliberately inflated by the news media.
   b. is a grave public health issue that needs to be addressed more strongly.
   c. is not as serious as the number of teenagers facing the more serious threat of hunger.
   d. has never been verified by any reputable governmental agency or health institute.

4. Since 1988, according to Glassner, the nation's teenage suicide rate has
   a. doubled.
   b. stabilized and even decreased in some years.
   c. stayed the same.
   d. exceeded the death rates from AIDS and other communicable diseases.

5. Glassner concludes the teenage suicide rates should be of concern to us, not because of the rates themselves, but because of
   a. the fact that guns are used in 60 percent of such cases.
   b. the lack of sufficient mental health and counseling services available.
   c. parents' lack of involvement in their teenagers' lives, further adding to their isolation and alienation.
   d. the gun lobby's opposition to control the easy availability of weapons.

C. Sequencing

The sentences in this excerpt from the selection may have been scrambled. Read the sentences and choose the sequence that puts them back into logical order. Do not refer to the original selection.

1. Journalists, politicians, and advocacy organizations reiterate that conclusion incessantly. **2.** *America's children face far graver dangers than parents realize.* **3.** Another is by asserting that children face huge hazards that the public and policy makers have failed to appreciate. **4.** One way they reiterate it, as we have seen, is through stories about sexual predators in churches, schools, and cyberspace.

a. 2, 1, 3, 4
b. 2, 1, 4, 3
c. 2, 4, 3, 1
d. Correct as written.

D. Interpreting Meaning

Where appropriate, write your answers to these questions in your own words.

1. In paragraphs 2 and 4, Glassner uses an example of a teenager who committed suicide, Scott Croteau, to make the point that
   a. suicide is a leading cause of death for American teenagers.
   b. the *Times* article should have included some speculation about why he committed suicide.
   c. some high school students suffer from mental health problems that go undetected by their parents or their teachers.
   d. the supposed national health problem posed by teenage suicide is exaggerated and unproved.

2. Read paragraph 3 again. Newspaper articles such as the one describing the reason for Megan McClave's death exaggerate the danger of incorrect prescriptions and also prey on parents'
   a. desire to keep their children safe.
   b. fear of terrible things that might happen to their child.
   c. inexperience in dealing with medical matters.
   d. inability to detect the exaggeration in these articles.

3. What is the primary objection Glassner makes in paragraph 4?
   a. The *Post* shouldn't have published a story about prescription errors because it just upset parents unnecessarily.
   b. The *Times* didn't explain why teenage suicide rates nearly tripled between 1952 and 1992.
   c. Newspapers in general don't offer sufficiently convincing evidence that prove isolated incidents are really trends.
   d. The newspapers don't hire experienced journalists.

4. Read paragraph 5 again carefully. First, identify Glassner's central claim.

   ____

   What information, if provided, would have strengthened this claim?

   ____

   ____

5. Look again at paragraph 7, in particular at Glassner's description of how the media has reported the decline in teenage suicide rates and

the story of three teenagers jumping from a cliff in 1996. Which of these is the most accurate inference that one could draw from that information?

a. The stories of the decline in suicide rates and the deaths of the teenagers were given equal treatment.

b. The news media focused on the story of the three teenagers because they were outstanding students and athletes in their communities and therefore of local interest for readers.

c. The news media deliberately inflated the rates of teenage suicide and used the three teenagers as a warning to parents.

d. The news media find it more profitable to publish dire statistics and tragic stories than to publish positive ones showing stable or declining rates.

6. This selection demonstrates two instances of cause-effect relationships. What is the implied reason that newspapers sensationalize and exaggerate news articles on subjects like teen suicide? Consider, in particular, paragraph 7.

____

____

Now explain the cause-effect relationship that is central to Glassner's conclusion.

____

In making this cause-effect connection, what is Glassner implicitly proposing?

____

____

E. Paraphrasing Exercise

1. Paraphrase Glassner's "reflection" in paragraph 6 about teenage suicides and why the numbers are not particularly surprising.

____

____

____

2. Paraphrase this sentence from paragraph 8: "Even more illuminating than speculation about the perilousness of American society or the

fluctuations in the numbers of teens who commit suicide is a well-documented change in *how* they end their lives."

____

____

____

F. Vocabulary in Context

Here are a few vocabulary words from the selection and their definitions. Study these definitions carefully. Then write the appropriate word in each space provided according to the context.

alarmist a person who needlessly alarms others by inventing or exaggerating rumors or of impending danger or catastrophe

generic describing a type of drug that is nonproprietary and that is sold under its chemical name rather than under its brand name

asserted stated confidently and positively

perilousness a state of grave danger (a variant of *peril*)

fraught filled with

1. One ________ newspaper account of a little girl's death suggested that the pharmacist was confused by the abundance of new ______ drugs. The *Post* ________ that even getting a prescription filled is ______ with danger and is another example of the __________ of modern American society.

grave extremely serious

reiterate to repeat, restate

advocacy support, a group that argues in favor of a cause or an idea

cyberspace the space where communication takes place via computers

2. Even ________ groups often ________ the _____ dangers that children face. One example of a dangerous place for children is _________

pale to decrease in importance

warrant to justify, require

fluctuations variations, rising and falling rates

illuminating enlightening, providing understanding

amassed gathered, accumulated

3. The evidence ________ in support of scary statistics turns out often to be not particularly overwhelming. In fact, Glassner argues that such articles ______ a closer, more critical look. It is more ________ to study statistics involving how teenagers end their lives than it is to study ________ in suicide rates. When one considers that about 60 percent of teenagers commit suicide with a gun, all other concerns ____ in comparison.

DISCUSSION QUESTIONS

1. Does Glassner prove his point sufficiently? Look through the essay and locate places in the selection that might have profited from more examples or explanations.
2. Glassner ends the selection by suggesting that politicians, journalists, and others should install a screen saver on their computers that says, in big letters: IT'S THE GUNS, STUPID. This phrase is a reworking of a campaign theme by Bill Clinton and his inner circle in 1992 during his first presidential campaign: "It's the economy, stupid." The slogan referred to the importance of Clinton's staying on message, suggesting that Americans were more concerned about the economy than with other issues. Clinton, of course, went on to win, and the 1990s witnessed an unrivaled economic boom. Beyond suggesting a screen saver with this motto, what else is Glassner suggesting in this allusion?
3. Choose an article from a major metropolitan newspaper that covers a public health topic—for example, AIDS, the avian bird flu epidemic, childhood obesity, or one of your own choosing. Examine the article carefully to see if it contains unsubstantiated claims, if it is intended to exaggerate the readers' fears, or if an isolated incident is presented as a trend.

EXPLORE THE WEB

How was Glassner's book received by the reading public? Is this a book you might enjoy reading? Look at the reviews for *The Culture of Fear: Why Americans Are Afraid of the Wrong Things* at this address:

www.amazon.com

Type in the book title in the search box, and then scroll down to the Amazon review and another by *Publishers Weekly*. Finally, click on "See All Editorial Reviews" to get a wider sampling of opinion.

Reading Selections

The Telephone

Anwar F. Accawi

Anwar Accawi grew up in the small village of Magdaluna in southern Lebanon. Because the town was isolated from the outside world, natural disasters served as a kind of calendar, whereby momentous events were remembered and passed down to younger generations. When a village resident proposed that the town get a telephone, the modern world intruded on the centuries-old traditions, and the lives of the residents of Magdaluna were never the same. This selection originally appeared in Accawi's memoir, *The Boy from the Tower of the Moon* (1999). It has also been included in *Best American Essays* (1998, edited by Cynthia Ozick) and in the textbook *Best American Essays* (2001, edited by Robert Atwan). Accawi now teaches at the University of Tennessee's English Language Institute.

VOCABULARY ANALYSIS

The Greek Prefix *tele-*

Meaning "at a distance," the prefix *tele-* begins a few English words, most of them technical. For example, the word *telephone* combines *tele-* and *phonos* ("sound"). Here are three other words beginning with *tele-* besides the obvious *television* and *telescope*, both of which mean "distance + seeing."

telegram communication transmitted by wire; from *tele-* + *graphos* ("writing")

telepathy communication through means other than the senses; from *tele-* + *pathy* ("feeling")

teleconference a conference held among people in different locations

Words from Foreign Languages

Accawi also uses some unusual words from other languages. Among them are these:

myopic [paragraph 3] nearsighted; from Greek *muopia*, originally from *muein* ("to close") + *ops* ("eye")

gendarme [13] a police officer; from French *gens d'armes* ("mounted soldiers")

concierge [18] a staff member at a hotel who assists guests; from French, but originally from the Latin word for "fellow slave" (*conservus*)

oasis [21] a fertile green spot in the middle of a desert; also a place of refuge from unpleasantness; from Coptic, an Egyptian language (*ouahe*)

The Telephone

Anwar F. Accawi

1 When I was growing up in Magdaluna, a small Lebanese village in the terraced rocky mountains east of Sidon, time didn't mean much to anybody, except maybe to those who were dying, or those waiting to appear in court because they had tampered with the boundary markers on their land. In those days, there was no real need for a calendar or a watch to keep track of the hours, days, months, and years. We knew what to do and when to do it, just as the Iraqi geese knew when to fly north, driven by the hot wind that blew in from the desert, and the ewes knew when to give birth to wet lambs that stood on long, shaky legs in the chilly March wind and baaed hesitantly, because they were small and cold and did not know where they were or what to do now that they were here. The only timepiece we had need of then was the sun. It rose and set, and the seasons rolled by, and we sowed seed and harvested and ate and played and married our cousins and had babies who got whooping cough and chickenpox—and those children who survived grew up and married *their* cousins and had babies who got whooping cough and chickenpox. We lived and loved and toiled and died without ever needing to know what year it was, or even the time of day.

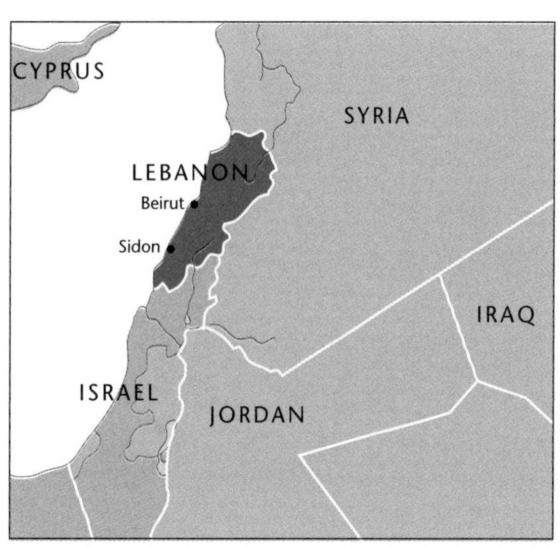

2 It wasn't that we had no system for keeping track of time and of the important events in our lives. But ours was a natural—or, rather, a divine—calendar, because it was framed by acts of God. Allah himself set down the milestones with earthquakes and droughts and floods and locusts and pestilences. Simple as our calendar was, it worked just fine for us.

3 Take, for example, the birth date of Teta Im Khalil, the oldest woman in Magdaluna and all the surrounding villages. When I first met her, we had just returned home from Syria at the end of the Big War and were living with Grandma Mariam. Im Khalil came by to welcome my father home and to take a long, myopic look at his foreign-born wife, my mother. Im Khalil was so old that the skin of her cheeks looked like my father's grimy tobacco pouch, and when I kissed her (because Grandma insisted that I show her old friend affection), it was like kissing a soft suede glove that had been soaked with sweat and then left in a dark closet for a season. Im Khalil's face got me to wondering how old one had to be to look and taste the way she did. So, as soon as she had hobbled off on her cane, I asked Grandma, "How old is Teta Im Khalil?"

4 Grandma had to think for a moment; then she said, "I've been told that Teta was born shortly after the big snow that caused the roof on the mayor's house to cave in."

5 "And when was that?" I asked.

6 "Oh, about the time we had the big earthquake that cracked the wall in the east room."

7 Well, that was enough for me. You couldn't be more accurate than that, now, could you? Satisfied with her answer, I went back to playing with a ball made from an old sock stuffed with other, much older socks.

8 And that's the way it was in our little village for as far back as anybody could remember: people were born so many years before or after an earthquake or a flood; they got married or died so many years before or after a long drought or a big snow or some other disaster. One of the most unusual of these dates was when Antoinette the seamstress and Saeed the barber (and tooth puller) got married. That was the year of the whirlwind during which fish and oranges fell from the sky. Incredible as it may sound, the story of the fish and oranges was true, because men—respectable men, like Abu George the blacksmith and Abu Asaad the mule skinner, men who would not lie even to save their own souls—told and retold that story until it was incorporated into Magdaluna's calendar, just like the year of the black moon and the year of the locusts before it. My father, too, confirmed the story for me. He told me that he had been a small boy himself when it had rained fish and oranges from heaven. He'd gotten up one morning after a stormy night and walked out into the yard to find fish as long as his forearm still flopping here and there among the wet navel oranges.

9 The year of the fish-bearing twister, however, was not the last remarkable year. Many others followed in which strange and wonderful things happened: milestones added by the hand of Allah to Magdaluna's calendar. There was, for instance, the year of the drought, when the heavens were shut for months and the spring from which the entire village got its drinking water slowed to a trickle.

The spring was about a mile from the village, in a ravine that opened at one end into a small, flat clearing covered with fine gray dust and hard, marble-sized goat droppings, because every afternoon the goatherds brought their flocks there to water them. In the year of the drought, that little clearing was always packed full of noisy kids with big brown eyes and sticky hands, and their mothers—sinewy, overworked young women with protruding collarbones and cracked, callused brown heels. The children ran around playing tag or hide-and-seek while the women talked, shooed flies, and awaited their turns to fill up their jars with drinking water to bring home to their napping men and wet babies. There were days when we had to wait from sunup until late afternoon just to fill a small clay jar with precious, cool water.

10 Sometimes, amid the long wait and the heat and the flies and the smell of goat dung, tempers flared, and the younger women, anxious about their babies, argued over whose turn it was to fill up her jar. And sometimes the arguments escalated into full-blown, knockdown-dragout fights; the women would grab each other by the hair and curse and scream and spit and call each other names that made my ears tingle. We little brown boys who went with our mothers to fetch water loved these fights, because we got to see the women's legs and their colored panties as they grappled and rolled around in the dust. Once in a while, we got lucky and saw much more, because some of the women wore nothing at all under their long dresses. God, how I used to look forward to those fights. I remember the rush, the excitement, the sun dancing on the dust clouds as a dress ripped and a young white breast was revealed, then quickly hidden. In my calendar, that year of drought will always be one of the best years of my childhood, because it was then, in a dusty clearing by a trickling mountain spring, I got my first glimpse of the wonders, the mysteries, and the promises hidden beneath the folds of a woman's dress. Fish and oranges from heaven . . . you can get over that.

11 But, in another way, the year of the drought was also one of the worst of my life, because that was the year that Abu Raja, the retired cook who used to entertain us kids by cracking walnuts on his forehead, decided it was time Magdaluna got its own telephone. Every civilized village needed a telephone, he said, and Magdaluna was not going to get anywhere until it had one. A telephone would link us with the outside world. At the time, I was too young to understand the debate, but a few men—like Shukri, the retired Turkish-army drill sergeant, and Abu Hanna the vineyard keeper—did all they could to talk Abu Raja out of having a telephone brought to the village. But they were outshouted and ignored and finally shunned by the other villagers for resisting progress and trying to keep a good thing from coming to Magdaluna.

12 One warm day in early fall, many of the villagers were out in their fields repairing walls or gathering wood for the winter when the shout went out that the telephone-company truck had arrived at Abu Raja's *dikkan*, or country store.

There were no roads in those days, only footpaths and dry streambeds, so it took the telephone-company truck almost a day to work its way up the rocky terrain from Sidon—about the same time it took to walk. When the truck came into view, Abu George, who had a huge voice and, before the telephone, was Magdaluna's only long-distance communication system, bellowed the news from his front porch. Everybody dropped what they were doing and ran to Abu Raja's house to see what was happening. Some of the more dignified villagers, however, like Abu Habeeb and Abu Nazim, who had been to big cities like Beirut and Damascus and had seen things like telephones and telegraphs, did not run the way the rest did; they walked with their canes hanging from the crooks of their arms, as if on a Sunday afternoon stroll.

13 It did not take long for the whole village to assemble at Abu Raja's *dikkan*. Some of the rich villagers, like the widow Farha and the gendarme Abu Nadeem, walked right into the store and stood at the elbows of the two important-looking men from the telephone company, who proceeded with utmost gravity, like priests at Communion, to wire up the telephone. The poorer villagers stood outside and listened carefully to the details relayed to them by the not-so-poor people who stood in the doorway and could see inside.

14 "The bald man is cutting the blue wire," someone said.

15 "He is sticking the wire into the hole in the bottom of the black box," someone else added.

16 "The telephone man with the mustache is connecting two pieces of wire. Now he is twisting the ends together," a third voice chimed in.

17 Because I was small and unaware that I should have stood outside with the other poor folk to give the rich people inside more room (they seemed to need more of it than poor people did), I wriggled my way through the dense forest of legs to get a firsthand look at the action. I felt like the barefoot Moses, sandals in hand, staring at the burning bush on Mount Sinai. Breathless, I watched as the men in blue, their shirt pockets adorned with fancy lettering in a foreign language, put together a black machine that supposedly would make it possible to talk with uncles, aunts, and cousins who lived more than two days' ride away.

18 It was shortly after sunset when the man with the mustache announced that the telephone was ready to use. He explained that all Abu Raja had to do was lift the receiver, turn the crank on the black box a few times, and wait for an operator to take his call. Abu Raja, who had once lived and worked in Sidon, was impatient with the telephone man for assuming that he was ignorant. He grabbed the receiver and turned the crank forcefully, as if trying to start a Model T Ford. Everybody was impressed that he knew what to do. He even called the operator by her first name: "Centralist." Within moments, Abu Raja was talking with his brother, a concierge in Beirut. He didn't even have to raise his voice or shout to be heard.

19 If I hadn't seen it with my own two eyes and heard it with my own two ears, I would not have believed it—and my friend Kameel didn't. He was away that day watching his father's goats, and when he came back to the village that evening, his cousin Habeeb and I told him about the telephone and how Abu Raja had used it to speak with his brother in Beirut. After he heard our report, Kameel made the sign of the cross, kissed his thumbnail, and warned us that lying was a bad sin and would surely land us in purgatory. Kameel believed in Jesus and Mary, and wanted to be a priest when he grew up. He always crossed himself when Habeeb, who was irreverent, and I, who was Presbyterian, were around, even when we were not bearing bad news.

Connecting Grammar to Writing

Good writers violate the old rule that one should never start a sentence with *and* or *but* all the time. Accawi begins the first sentence of paragraph 20 with *and*, which works well to emphasize the "bad news" he associates with the arrival of the telephone in his small village. Like any other stylistic effect, it's best not to overdo it.

20 And the telephone, as it turned out, was bad news. With its coming, the face of the village began to change. One of the first effects was the shifting of the village's center. Before the telephone's arrival, the men of the village used to gather regularly at the house of Im Kaleem, a short, middle-aged widow with jet-black hair and a raspy voice that could be heard all over the village, even when she was only whispering. She was a devout Catholic and also the village *shlikki*—whore. The men met at her house to argue about politics and drink coffee and play cards or backgammon. Im Kaleem was not a true prostitute, however, because she did not charge for her services—not even for the coffee and tea (and, occasionally, the strong liquor called arrack) that she served the men. She did not need the money; her son, who was overseas in Africa, sent her money regularly. (I knew this because my father used to read her son's letters to her and take down her replies, as Im Kaleem could not read and write.) Im Kaleem was no slut either—unlike some women in the village—because she loved all the men she entertained, and they loved her, every one of them. In a way, she was married to all the men in the village. Everybody knew it—the wives knew it; the itinerant Catholic priest knew it; the Presbyterian minister knew it—but nobody objected. Actually, I suspect the women (my mother included) did not mind their husbands' visits to Im Kaleem. Oh, they wrung their hands and complained to one another about their men's unfaithfulness, but secretly they were relieved, because Im Kaleem took some of the pressure off them and kept the men out of their hair while they attended to their endless chores. Im Kaleem was also a kind of confessor and troubleshooter, talking sense to those men who were having family problems, especially the younger ones.

21 Before the telephone came to Magdaluna, Im Kaleem's house was bustling at just about any time of day, especially at night, when its windows were brightly lit with three large oil lamps, and the loud voices of the men talking, laughing, and arguing could be heard in the street below—a reassuring, homey sound. Her house was an island of comfort, an oasis for the weary village men, exhausted from having so little to do.

22 But it wasn't long before many of those men—the younger ones especially—started spending more of their days and evenings at Abu Raja's *dikkan*.

There, they would eat and drink and talk and play checkers and backgammon, and then lean their chairs back against the wall—the signal that they were ready to toss back and forth, like a ball, the latest rumors going around the village. And they were always looking up from their games and drinks and talk to glance at the phone in the corner, as if expecting it to ring any minute and bring news that would change their lives and deliver them from their aimless existence. In the meantime, they smoked cheap, hand-rolled cigarettes, dug dirt out from under their fingernails with big pocketknives, and drank lukewarm sodas they called Kacula, Seffen-Ub, and Bebsi. Sometimes, especially when it was hot, the days dragged on so slowly that the men turned on Abu Saeed, a confirmed bachelor who practically lived in Abu Raja's *dikkan*, and teased him for going around barefoot and unshaven since the Virgin had appeared to him behind the olive press.

23 The telephone was also bad news for me personally. It took away my lucrative business—a source of much-needed income. Before the telephone came to Magdaluna, I used to hang around Im Kaleem's courtyard and play marbles with the other kids, waiting for some man to call down from a window and ask me to run to the store for cigarettes or arrack, or to deliver a message to his wife, such as what he wanted for supper. There was always something in it for me: a ten- or even a twenty-five-piaster piece. On a good day, I ran nine or ten of those errands, which assured a steady supply of marbles that I usually lost to Sami or his cousin Hani, the basket weaver's boy. But as the days went by, fewer and fewer men came to Im Kaleem's, and more and more congregated at Abu Raja's to wait by the telephone. In the evenings, no light fell from her window onto the street below, and the laughter and noise of the men trailed off and finally stopped. Only Shukri, the retired Turkish-army drill sergeant, remained faithful to Im Kaleem after all the other men had deserted her; he was still seen going into or leaving her house from time to time. Early that winter, Im Kaleem's hair suddenly turned gray, and she got sick and old. Her legs started giving her trouble, making it hard for her to walk. By spring she hardly left her house anymore.

24 At Abu Raja's *dikkan*, the calls did eventually come, as expected, and men and women started leaving the village the way a hailstorm begins: first one, then two, then bunches. The army took them. Jobs in the cities lured them. And ships and airplanes carried them to such faraway places as Australia and Brazil and New Zealand. My friend Kameel, his cousin Habeeb, and their cousins and my cousins all went away to become ditch diggers and mechanics and butcher-shop boys and deli owners who wore dirty aprons sixteen hours a day, all looking for a better life than the one they had left behind. Within a year, only the sick, the old, and the maimed were left in the village. Magdaluna became a skeleton of its former self, desolate and forsaken, like the tombs, a place to get away from.

Finally, the telephone took my family away, too. My father got a call from an old army buddy who told him that an oil company in southern Lebanon was hiring interpreters and instructors. My father applied for a job and got it, and we moved to Sidon, where I went to a Presbyterian missionary school and graduated in 1962. Three years later, having won a scholarship, I left Lebanon for the United States. Like the others who left Magdaluna before me, I am still looking for that better life.

EXERCISES

A. Determining the Main Idea and Writer's Purpose

Choose the best answer.

1. The main idea of the selection is that
   a. life in the small village of Magdaluna was slow, simple, and uneventful.
   b. the telephone brought many profound changes to Magdaluna, and in, turn, resulted in the town's near downfall.
   c. the telephone made it possible for Magdaluna to connect to the outside world.
   d. the telephone brought many positive changes to Magdaluna.

2. With respect to the main idea, the writer's purpose is to
   a. contrast life in his village before and after the telephone's arrival.
   b. show what life was like in a small rural Lebanese village.
   c. praise new technology for its role in modernizing his homeland.
   d. persuade residents of isolated villages that they should remain that way if they hope to preserve their way of life.

B. Comprehending Main Ideas

Choose the correct answer.

1. The residents of Magdaluna kept track of time and important events in their lives by means of a particular kind of calendar, specifically
   a. news of the outside world brought by itinerant visitors.
   b. a Muslim calendar.

c. natural disasters sent by the god Allah.

d. ancient time-keeping devices like sundials and stone columns.

2. Accawi and his friends especially enjoyed the year of drought when tempers flared and women fought with each other, allowing them to

a. have a day off from school to search for water.

b. peek at what was under the women's clothing.

c. be entertained by the spectacle of women rolling around in the dust.

d. make bets on who the victor would be.

3. Abu Raja, the owner of the *dikkan* or country store, proposed that Magdaluna get its own telephone and offered several reasons. Which one of these was *not* mentioned?

a. A telephone would bring much-needed extra income for the villagers.

b. A telephone was a symbol of progress.

c. The town would never be much of a town without one.

d. A telephone would link the town to the outside world.

4. After the telephone arrived, the village center shifted to Abu Raja's store, whereas before the telephone arrived, the men of the town had spent the evenings

a. at the home of Im Kaleem, who offered the men a place to relax and amuse themselves.

b. at the local bar and restaurant drinking, eating, and talking politics.

c. at home with their families.

d. praying in the town's mosques.

5. The most serious and long-reaching effect of the telephone on village life in Magdaluna was that its residents

a. became more interested in the outside world and neglected local affairs and customs.

b. realized that they had the best possible life right where they were.

c. began to demand more sophisticated kinds of technology to improve their lives.

d. became dissatisfied and left to search for a better life.

C. Sequencing

The sentences in this excerpt from the selection may have been scrambled. Read the sentences and choose the sequence that puts them back into logical order. Do not refer to the original selection.

1. It wasn't that we had no system for keeping track of time and of the important events in our lives. **2.** But ours was a natural—or, rather, a divine—calendar, because it was framed by acts of God. **3.** Allah himself set down the milestones with earthquakes and droughts and floods and locusts and pestilences. **4.** Simple as our calendar was, it worked for us.

a. 4, 1, 2, 3
b. 3, 2, 4, 1
c. 1, 2, 4, 3
d. Correct as written.

D. Making Inferences

Write your answers to these questions in your own words.

1. Look again at the details in paragraph 1. What point is Accawi suggesting about life in Magdaluna?

   ____

   ____

2. Again, in paragraph 1, why does Accawi say that the people of Magdaluna did not need to know what year or what time of day it was?

   ____

3. Accawi recounts the story some older men and his father told him about the heavens raining fish and oranges. Based on the evidence in the selection, do you think that story was true or not?

   ____

   What evidence leads to your conclusion?

   ____

   ____

4. Look at the last sentence of paragraph 10. Concerning Accawi and his friends, what does he mean to imply in the last sentence: "Fish and oranges from heaven . . . you can get over that"?

   ____

   ____

5. Accawi's friend Kameel didn't believe Accawi's account of the new telephone (see paragraph 19). What does this suggest about the telephone's significance to the larger community?

   ____

   ____

6. What does Accawi imply about his earlier life in Magdaluna from the last sentence of the essay when he writes, "I am still looking for that better life"?

E. Interpreting Meaning

Where appropriate, write your answers for these questions in your own words.

1. What is the purpose of the illustration in paragraphs 3–7 when Accawi's grandmother tells him how old Teta Im Khalil is? What point is her answer meant to reinforce?

2. Read paragraph 9 again. A good title for this paragraph is
   a. "The Year of the Drought."
   b. "A Fish-Bearing Twister."
   c. "How a Village Survived Without Water."
   d. "Allah's Milestones."

3. An *allusion* is a reference to something outside the text, and it is used to shed light on an idea by relating it to something that has gone before. Allusions can be from literature, mythology, history, or from a religious text like the Bible, among other sources. Paragraph 17 contains an allusion. First locate it and write it in the first space.

   Then explain why Accawi uses this allusion.

4. Consider carefully the changes that Accawi attributes [paragraphs 20 and 22] to the men who spent their evenings at Abu Raja's store. How did their conversations change?

5. Ultimately, what effect did the telephone have on these men and on their lives?

6. *Irony* is a discrepancy between what we might expect to happen and what actually does happen. Do you see any irony in what Accawi writes in paragraph 24?

____

____

F. Understanding Vocabulary

Write the dictionary definition for each underlined word in the phrases below.

1. We lived and loved and <u>toiled</u> [paragraph 1] ____________
2. floods and locusts and <u>pestilences</u> [2] ____________
3. it was <u>incorporated</u> into [8] ____________
4. women with <u>protruding</u> collarbones [9] ____________
5. <u>amid</u> the long wait [10] ____________
6. sometimes the arguments <u>escalated</u> [10] ____________
7. they were finally <u>shunned</u> [11] ____________
8. would land us in <u>purgatory</u> [19] ____________
9. the <u>itinerant</u> Catholic priest [20] ____________
10. my <u>lucrative</u> business [23] ____________
11. only the old and the <u>maimed</u> [24] ____________

DISCUSSION QUESTIONS

1. The telephone forever changed the lives of Magdaluna's townspeople. Go through the essay and locate each change as Accawi describes it.
2. Does Accawi's account of the desolation that befell Magdaluna after the arrival of the telephone seem believable? Can you detect any other forces that might have contributed to the town's becoming "desolate and forsaken"?

EXPLORE THE WEB

An interview with Anwar Accawi along with a list of his other publications is available at this site:

www.outreach.utk.edu/ELI/highlights/default.html

More Room

Judith Ortiz Cofer

Judith Ortiz Cofer was born in 1952 in Puerto Rico, where she spent her early years. Her father's military service eventually required the family to move to the United States, where they lived in Paterson, New Jersey. During her childhood and adolescence, the family moved back and forth between Puerto Rico and the mainland, and this dual cultural experience is reflected in much of her writing. A prolific poet, short story writer, and essayist, Cofer received the 1990 Pushcart Prize for *Silent Dancing*, a collection of poetry and autobiographical essays, from which this excerpt comes. Her work has appeared in several publications, among them *Glamour, The Georgia Review, Kenyon Review*, and *Southern Review*. Cofer is currently Franklin Professor of English and Creative Writing at the University of Georgia.

VOCABULARY ANALYSIS

The Greek Root *chron*

In paragraphs 2 and 9, Cofer uses two words containing the Greek root *khrnos* or *chron: chronology* and *chronically*. This root means "time," so the word *chronology* means the arrangement of events in time, and *chronically*, the adverb form of *chronic*, describes a condition that occurs over a long period of time or continuing, as in a "chronic cough" or a "chronic problem." Here are two others words containing this root:

chronological using time order

chronometer a mechanism for measuring time

What does the word *chronicle* refer to?

More Room

Judith Ortiz Cofer

1 My grandmother's house is like chambered nautilus; it has many rooms, yet it is not a mansion. Its proportions are small and its design simple. It is a house that

has grown organically, according to the needs of its inhabitants. To all of us in the family it is known as *la casa de Mamá*. It is the place of our origin; the stage for our memories and dreams of Island life.

2 I remember how in my childhood it sat on stilts; this was before it had a downstairs. It rested on its perch like a great blue bird, not a flying sort of bird, more like a nesting hen, but with spread wings. Grandfather had built it soon after their marriage. He was a painter and housebuilder by trade, a poet and meditative man by nature. As each of their eight children were born, new rooms were added. After a few years, the paint did not exactly match, nor the materials, so that there was a chronology to it, like the rings of a tree, and Mamá could tell you the history of each room in her *casa*, and thus the genealogy of the family along with it.

3 Her room is the heart of the house. Though I have seen it recently, and both woman and room have diminished in size, changed by the new perspective of my eyes, now capable of looking over countertops and tall beds, it is not this picture I carry in my memory of Mamá's *casa*. Instead, I see her room as a queen's chamber where a small woman loomed large, a throne-room with a massive four-poster bed in its center which stood taller than a child's head. It was on this bed where her own children had been born that the smallest grandchildren were allowed to take naps in the afternoons; here too was where Mamá secluded herself to dispense private advice to her daughters, sitting on the edge of the bed, looking down at whoever sat on the rocker where generations of babies had been sung to sleep. To me she looked like a wise empress right out of the fairy tales I was addicted to reading.

4 Though the room was dominated by the mahogany four-posters, it also contained all of Mamá's symbols of power. On her dresser instead of cosmetics there were jars filled with herbs: *yerba buena, yerba mala*, the making of purgatives and teas to which we were all subjected during childhood crises. She had a steaming cup for anyone who could not, or would not, get up to face life on any given day. If the acrid aftertaste of her cures for malingering did not get you out of bed, then it was time to call *el doctor*.

5 And there was the monstrous chifforobe she kept locked with a little golden key she did not hide. This was a test of her dominion over us; though my cousins and I wanted a look inside that massive wardrobe more than anything, we never reached for that little key lying on top of her Bible on the dresser. This was also where she placed her earrings and rosary at night. God's word was her security system. This chifforobe was the place where I imagined she kept jewels, satin slippers, and elegant sequined, silk gowns of heart-breaking fineness. I lusted after those imaginary costumes. I had heard that Mamá had been a great beauty in her youth, and the belle of many balls. My cousins had other ideas as to what she kept in that wooden vault: its secret could be money (Mamá did not hand cash to strangers, banks were out of the question, so there were stories that her mattress was stuffed with dollar bills, and that she buried coins in jars in her garden under rosebushes, or kept them in her inviolate chifforobe); there might be that

legendary gun salvaged from the Spanish-American conflict over the Island. We went wild over suspected treasures that we made up simply because children have to fill locked trunks with something wonderful.

6 On the wall above the bed hung a heavy silver crucifix. Christ's agonized head hung directly over Mamá's pillow. I avoided looking at this weapon suspended over where her head would lay; and on the rare occasions when I was allowed to sleep on that bed, I scooted down to the safe middle of the mattress, where her body's impression took me in like a mother's lap. Having taken care of the obligatory religious decoration with a crucifix, Mamá covered the other walls with objects sent to her over the years by her children in the States. *Los Nueva Yores* were represented by, among other things, a postcard of Niagara Falls from her son Hernán, postmarked, Buffalo, N.Y. In a conspicuous gold frame hung a large color photograph of her daughter Nena, her husband and their five children at the entrance to Disneyland in California. From us she had gotten a black lace fan. Father had brought it to her from a tour of duty with the Navy in Europe (on Sundays she would remove it from its hook on the wall to fan herself at Sunday mass). Each year more items were added as the family grew and dispersed, and every object in the room had a story attached to it, a *cuento* which Mamá would bestow on anyone who received the privilege of a day alone with her. It was almost worth pretending to be sick, though the bitter herb purgatives of the body were a big price to pay for the spirit revivals of her story-telling.

7 Mamá slept alone on her large bed, except for the times when a sick grandchild warranted the privilege, or when a heartbroken daughter came home in need of more than herbal teas. In the family there is a story about how this came to be.

8 When one of the daughters, my mother or one of her sisters, tells the *cuento* of how Mamá came to own her nights, it is usually preceded by the qualifications that Papá's exile from his wife's room was not a result of animosity between the couple, but that the act had been Mamá's famous bloodless coup for her personal freedom. Papá was the benevolent dictator of her body and her life who had had to be banished from her bed so that Mamá could better serve her family. Before the telling, we had to agree that the old man was not to blame. We all recognized that in the family Papá was as an *alma de Dios*, a saintly, soft-spoken presence whose main pleasures in life, such as writing poetry and reading the Spanish large-type editions of *Reader's Digest*, always took place outside the vortex of Mamá's crowded realm. It was not his fault, after all, that every year or so he planted a baby-seed in Mamá's fertile body, keeping her from leading the active life she needed and desired. He loved her and the babies. Papá composed odes and lyrics to celebrate births and anniversaries and hired musicians to accompany him in singing them to his family and friends at extravagant pig-roasts he threw yearly. Mamá and the oldest girls worked for days preparing the food. Papá sat for hours in his painter's shed, also his study and library, composing the songs. At these celebrations he was also known to give long speeches in praise of God, his fecund wife, and his beloved island. As a middle child, my

mother remembers these occasions as a time when the women sat in the kitchen and lamented their burdens, while the men feasted out in the patio, their rum-thickened voice rising in song and praise for each other, *compañeros* all.

9 It was after the birth of her eighth child, after she had lost three at birth or in infancy, that Mamá made her decision. They say that Mamá had had a special way of letting her husband know that they were expecting, one that had begun when, at the beginning of their marriage, he had built her a house too confining for her taste. So, when she discovered her first pregnancy, she supposedly drew plans for another room, which he dutifully executed. Every time a child was due, she would demand, *more space, more space*. Papá acceded to her wishes, child after child, since he had learned early that Mamá's renowned temper was a thing that grew like a monster along with a new belly. In this way Mamá got the house that she wanted, but with each child she lost in heart and energy. She had knowledge of her body and perceived that if she had any more children, her dreams and her plans would have to be permanently forgotten, because she would be a chronically ill woman, like Flora with her twelve children: asthma, no teeth, in bed more than on her feet.

10 And so, after my youngest uncle was born, she asked Papá to build a large room at the back of the house. He did so in joyful anticipation. Mamá had asked him special things this time: shelves on the walls, a private entrance. He thought that she meant this room to be a nursery where several children could sleep. He thought it was a wonderful idea. He painted it his favorite color, sky blue, and made large windows looking out over a green hill and the church spires beyond. But nothing happened. Mamá's belly did not grow, yet she seemed in a frenzy of activity over the house. Finally, an anxious Papá approached his wife to tell her that the new room was finished and ready to be occupied. And Mamá, they say, replied: "Good, it's for *you*."

11 And so it was that Mamá discovered the only means of birth control available to a Catholic woman of her time: sacrifice. She gave up the comfort of Papá's sexual love for something she deemed greater: the right to own and control her body, so that she might live to meet her grandchildren—me among them—so that she could give more of herself to the ones already there, so that she could be more than a channel for other lives, so that even now that time has robbed her of the elasticity of her body and of her amazing reservoir of energy, she still emanates the kind of joy that can only be achieved by living according to the dictates of one's own heart.

■ EXERCISES

A. Determining the Main Idea and Writer's Purpose

Choose the best answer.

1. The main idea of the selection is that Mamá, Cofer's grandmother,
   a. lived in a large and spacious house that resembled a chambered nautilus.

b. ruled the large household with many potent symbols of power that she kept in her chifforobe.
c. was forced to exile her husband from her bedroom so that she could achieve some personal freedom and fulfill her dreams.
d. was the victim of prejudice and unequal treatment because she was a woman.

2. The writer's purpose in the selection is to
   a. argue that women in Puerto Rico need to push for equal rights with men.
   b. explain the role of a typical and traditional Puerto Rican matriarch.
   c. reveal her memories and dreams of Puerto Rican life.
   d. tell about her grandmother's life, personality, and quest for autonomy.

B. Comprehending Main Ideas

Choose the correct answer.

1. Cofer writes that the heart of her grandmother's house in Puerto Rico was
   a. her grandmother's room.
   b. the kitchen.
   c. the parlor.
   d. the courtyard around which the rooms were arranged.

2. At the beginning of the essay, Cofer says that, to her, her grandmother's room resembled a "queen's chamber" and that her grandmother seemed like an "empress." These comparisons emphasize Mamá's
   a. extraordinary beauty.
   b. extraordinary power.
   c. political ambitions.
   d. royal pedigree.

3. Mamá's symbols of power were her
   a. large collection of makeup and cosmetics.
   b. furniture.
   c. exquisite wardrobe and elegant clothing.
   d. herbs, teas, and other curative substances.

4. Cofer thought that it was a privilege to spend the day with Mamá, even when she was sick, because she could
   a. listen to her grandmother's endless array of stories.
   b. eat the Puerto Rican treats that her grandmother made for her.

c. spend time with her many cousins.

d. look at the wonderful contents of the chifforobe.

5. Cofer offers several reasons to explain why her grandmother asked her husband to build a new room for him, as a way to prevent any more pregnancies. Which of the following was *not* included?

   a. Another pregnancy would harm her body and make her chronically ill.

   b. She needed her energy to take care of the family she already had.

   c. She wanted to control her own body and to exert her own personal freedom.

   d. She and her husband were experiencing marital discord.

C. Distinguishing between Main Ideas and Supporting Details

The following rewritten statements come from paragraph 11. Label them as follows: **MI** if the sentence represents a *main idea* and **SD** if the sentence represents a *supporting detail.*

1. ______ And so it was that Mamá discovered the only means of birth control available to a Catholic woman of her time: sacrifice.

2. ______ She gave up the comfort of Papá's sexual love for something she deemed greater: the right to own and control her body.

3. ______ She wanted to live to meet her grandchildren and to give more of herself to the ones already there.

4. ______ She wanted to be more than a channel for other lives.

5. ______ With time her body has been robbed of its elasticity and her amazing reservoir of energy.

6. ______ Still she continues to emanate the kind of joy that can be achieved only by living according to the dictates of one's own heart.

D. Interpreting Meaning

Where appropriate, write your answers to these questions in your own words.

1. Explain what Cofer means in paragraph 3 when she writes, "both woman and room have diminished in size, changed by the new perspective of my eyes."

   ____

   ____

READING

2. Read paragraph 5 again. A good title for this paragraph is
   a. "Hidden Treasures."
   b. "The Secrets of Mamá's Chifforobe."
   c. "A Test of Mamá's Dominion."
   d. "The Little Gold Key."

3. What is the central impression that Cofer conveys of Mamá in paragraphs 3–5?

____

____

____

4. Read the last two sentences of paragraph 6 again. What can you infer is the meaning of the Spanish word *cuento* in the second to the last sentence?
   a. a memento
   b. a type of medicine
   c. an object brought back from a trip
   d. a story

5. Read the beginning of paragraph 8 again. Why did Mamá's daughters precede their telling of the story about Papá's exile from Mamá's bedroom with the request that all listeners agree that "the old man was not to blame"?

____

____

____

____

6. From the information provided in paragraphs 9–11, why didn't Mamá just tell her husband that she did not want any more children? Why go to all the trouble of tricking him and having him build a new room that he assumed would be for another child?

____

____

____

E. Understanding Vocabulary

Look through the paragraphs listed below and find a word that matches each definition. Refer to a dictionary if necessary. An example has been done for you.

EXAMPLE: describing a living organism, something interconnected [paragraphs 1–2] organically

1. caused to experience, exposed to [3–4] ____________
2. bitter, sharp, harsh [3–4] ____________
3. pretending to be sick to avoid work [3–4] ____________
4. medicines that purify and cleanse the body [4 and 6—used twice] ____________
5. kept intact, forbidden to disturb, sacred [5] ____________
6. recovered, rescued, saved [5] ____________
7. bitter hostility, hatred [8] ____________
8. takeover, brilliant stratagem, triumph [8] ____________
9. kindly, caring [8] ____________
10. fertile, producing many children [8] ____________
11. expressed sorrow, regret, or grief [8] ____________
12. gave into, consented [9] ____________
13. famous, well known [9] ____________
14. considered, judged, regarded as [10–11] ____________
15. radiates, emits, sends forth [10–11] ____________

DISCUSSION QUESTIONS

1. Read paragraph 8 again carefully. Looking beneath the surface, you should be able to infer several things about the relationship between Mamá and Papá in particular and between Puerto Rican women and men in general. First, summarize what Cofer suggests here, for example, when she describes Papá as the "benevolent dictator of her body and her life" and when she describes the various activities that men and women engaged in during the extravagant celebrations held for special occasions.

2. Do you think that Mamá's decision to trick Papá into building her a new room was considered somewhat radical or extreme for that time?
3. How would you describe a Puerto Rican woman's "lot" during the time that Mamá was raising her family? What opportunities, if any, were available to her?

EXPLORE THE WEB

Do some research on social conditions for Puerto Rican woman both in recent history and today. Go to Google or to your favorite search engine and type "Puerto Rico" + "women" + "social conditions." One source to get you started is sponsored by the publisher Houghton Mifflin in its *Reader's Companion to U.S. Women's History*. The address is:

www.college.hmco.com/history/readerscomp/women/html/wm_013116_puertoricanf.htm

Long Walk to Freedom

Nelson Mandela

Nelson Mandela, former president of South Africa, was imprisoned for twenty-six years for his outspoken stand on apartheid—the policy of "separateness" established early in the twentieth century by South Africa's white-minority government. After his release in 1990, he continued to speak out against apartheid from his position as leader of the African National Congress (ANC). In 1994 South Africa held its first all-races election, and Mandela was elected president, ending white-minority rule in that long-troubled country. *Long Walk to Freedom* (1994) is Nelson Mandela's autobiography. In this selection, he explains the Xhosa tradition of circumcision, the ceremony whereby Xhosa boys become men.

VOCABULARY ANALYSIS

The Latin Prefix *bene-*

A *benefactor* is a person who gives help or aid to another. The Latin prefix *bene-* means "well," and it begins many so-called loan words from Latin, among them *benefit, beneficial, benevolence,* ("wishing well"), *benediction* ("good saying"); and *benign*.

What is a *beneficiary* of a life insurance policy?

Long Walk to Freedom

Nelson Mandela

1 When I was sixteen, the regent[1] decided that it was time that I became a man. In Xhosa tradition, this is achieved through one means only: circumcision. In my tradition, an uncircumcised male cannot be heir to his father's wealth, cannot marry or officiate in tribal rituals. An uncircumcised Xhosa man is a contradiction in terms, for he is not considered a man at all, but a boy. For the Xhosa people, circumcision represents the formal incorporation of males into society. It is not just a surgical procedure, but a lengthy and elaborate ritual in preparation for manhood. As a Xhosa, I count my years as a man from the date of my circumcision.

2 The traditional ceremony of the circumcision school was arranged principally for Justice—the rest of us, twenty-six in all—were there mainly to keep him company. Early in the new year, we journeyed to two grass huts in a secluded valley on the banks of the Mbashe River, known as Tyhalarha, the traditional place of circumcision for Thembu kings. The huts were seclusion lodges, where we were to live isolated from society. It was a sacred time; I felt happy and fulfilled taking part in my people's customs and ready to make the transition from boyhood to manhood.

3 We had moved to Tyhalarha by the river a few days before the actual circumcision ceremony. These last few days of boyhood were spent with the other initiates, and I found the camaraderie enjoyable. The lodge was near the home of Banabakhe Blayi, the wealthiest and most popular boy at the circumcision school. He was an engaging fellow, a champion stickfighter and a glamour boy, whose many girlfriends kept us all supplied with delicacies. Although he could neither read nor write, he was one of the most intelligent among us. He regaled us with stories of his trips to Johannesburg, a place none of us had ever been before. He so thrilled us with tales of the mines that he almost persuaded me that to be a miner was more alluring than to be a monarch. Miners had a mystique; to be a miner meant to be strong and daring, the ideal of manhood. Much later, I realized that it was the exaggerated tales of boys like Banabakhe that caused so many young men to run away to work in the mines of Johannesburg, where they often lost their health and their lives. In those days, working in the mines was almost as much of a rite of passage as circumcision school, a myth that helped the mine-owners more than it helped my people.

4 A custom of circumcision school is that one must perform a daring exploit before the ceremony. In days of old, this might have involved a cattle raid or even a battle, but in our time the deeds were more mischievous than martial. Two nights before we moved to Tyhalarha, we decided to steal a pig. In Mqhekezweni there was a tribesman with an ornery old pig. To avoid making noise and alarming him, we arranged for the pig to do our work for us. We took handfuls of sediment from homemade African beer, which has a strong scent much favored by pigs, and placed it upwind of the pig. The pig was so aroused by the scent that he came out of the kraal,[2] following a trail we had laid, gradually made his way to us, wheezing and snorting and eating the sediment. When he got near us, we captured the poor pig, slaughtered it, and then built a fire and ate roast pork underneath the stars. No piece of pork has ever tasted as good before or since.

5 The night before the circumcision, there was a ceremony near our huts with singing and dancing. Women came from the nearby villages, and we danced to their singing and clapping. As the music became faster and louder, our dance turned more frenzied and we forgot for a moment what lay ahead.

Connecting Grammar to Writing

Study the first two sentences of paragraph 6. Then underline and label the two dependent clauses they contain. Note, too, how they are punctuated.

6 At dawn, when the stars were still in the sky, we began our preparations. We were escorted to the river to bathe in its cold waters, a ritual that signified our purification before the ceremony. The ceremony was at midday, and we were commanded to stand in a row in a clearing some distance from the river where a crowd of parents and relatives, including the regent, as well as a handful of chiefs and counselors, had gathered. We were clad only in our blankets, and as the ceremony began, with drums pounding, we were ordered to sit on a blanket on the ground with our legs spread out in front of us. I was tense and anxious, uncertain of how I would react when the critical moment came. Flinching or crying out was a sign of weakness and stigmatized one's manhood. I was determined not to disgrace myself, the group, or my guardian. Circumcision is a trial of bravery and stoicism; no anesthetic is used; a man must suffer in silence.

7 To the right, out of the corner of my eye, I could see a thin, elderly man emerge from a tent and kneel in front of the first boy. There was excitement in the crowd, and I shuddered slightly knowing that the ritual was about to begin. The old man was a famous *ingcibi,* a circumcision expert, from Gcalekaland, who would use his assegai[3] to change us from boys to men with a single blow.

8 Suddenly, I heard the first boy cry out, "*Ndiyindoda!*" (I am a man!) which we were trained to say in the moment of circumcision. Seconds later, I heard Justice's strangled voice pronounce the same phrase. There were now two boys before the *ingcibi* reached me, and my mind must have gone blank because before I knew it, the old man was kneeling in front of me. I looked directly into his eyes. He was pale, and though the day was cold, his face was shining with

perspiration. His hands moved so fast they seemed to be controlled by an other-worldly force. Without a word, he took my foreskin, pulled it forward, and then, in a single motion, brought down his assegai. I felt as if fire was shooting through my veins; the pain was so intense that I buried my chin into my chest. Many seconds seemed to pass before I remembered the cry, and then I recovered and called out, "*Ndiyindoda!*"

9 I looked down and saw a perfect cut, clean and round like a ring. But I felt ashamed because the other boys seemed much stronger and braver than I had been; they had called out more promptly than I had. I was distressed that I had been disabled, however briefly, by the pain, and I did my best to hide my agony. A boy may cry; a man conceals his pain.

10 I had now taken the essential step in the life of every Xhosa man. Now, I might marry, set up my own home, and plow my own field. I could now be admitted to the councils of the community; my words would be taken seriously. At the ceremony, I was given my circumcision name, Dalibunga, meaning "Founder of the Bungha," the traditional ruling body of the Transkei.[4] To Xhosa traditionalists, this name is more acceptable than either of my two previous given names, Rolihlahla or Nelson, and I was proud to hear my new name pronounced: Dalibunga.

11 Immediately after the blow had been delivered, an assistant who follows the circumcision master takes the foreskin that is on the ground and ties it to a corner of your blanket. Our wounds were then dressed with a healing plant, the leaves of which were thorny on the outside but smooth on the inside, which absorbed the blood and other secretions.

12 At the conclusion of the ceremony, we returned to our huts, where a fire was burning with wet wood that cast off clouds of smoke, which was thought to promote healing. We were ordered to lie on our backs in the smoky huts, with one leg flat, and one leg bent. We were now *abakhwetha*, initiates into the world of manhood. We were looked after by an *amakhankatha*, or guardian, who explained the rules we must follow if we were to enter manhood properly. The first chore of the *amakhankatha* was to paint our naked and shaved bodies from head to foot in white ocher, turning us into ghosts. The white chalk symbolized our purity, and I still recall how stiff the dried clay felt on my body.

13 That first night, at midnight, an attendant, or *ikhankatha*, crept around the hut, gently waking each of us. We were then instructed to leave the hut and go tramping through the night to bury our foreskins. The traditional reason for this practice was so that our foreskins would be hidden before wizards could use them for evil purposes, but, symbolically, we were also burying our youth. I did not want to leave the warm hut and wander through the bush in the darkness, but I walked into the trees and after a few minutes, untied my foreskin and buried it in the earth. I felt as though I had now discarded the last remnant of my childhood.

14 We lived in our two huts—thirteen in each—while our wounds healed. When outside the huts, we were covered in blankets, for we were not allowed to be seen by women. It was a period of quietude, a kind of spiritual preparation for the trials of manhood that lay ahead. On the day of our reemergence, we went down to the river early in the morning to wash away the white ocher in the waters of the Mbashe. Once we were clean and dry, we were coated in red ocher. The tradition was that one should sleep with a woman, who later may become one's wife, and she rubs off the pigment with her body. In my case, however, the ocher was removed with a mixture of fat and lard.

15 At the end of our seclusion, the lodges and all their contents were burned, destroying our last links to childhood, and a great ceremony was held to welcome us as men to society. Our families, friends, and local chiefs gathered for speeches, songs, and gift-giving. I was given two heifers and four sheep, and felt far richer than I ever had before. I who had never owned anything suddenly possessed property. It was a heady feeling, even though my gifts were paltry next to those of Justice, who inherited an entire herd. I was not jealous of Justice's gifts. He was the son of a king; I was merely destined to be a counselor to a king. I felt strong and proud that day. I remember walking differently on that day, straighter, taller, firmer. I was hopeful, and thinking that I might someday have wealth, property, and status.

16 The main speaker of the day was Chief Meligqili, the son of Dalindyebo, and after listening to him, my gaily colored dreams suddenly darkened. He began conventionally, remarking on how fine it was that we were continuing a tradition that had been going on for as long as anyone could remember. Then he turned to us and his tone suddenly changed. "There sit our sons," he said, "young, healthy, and handsome, the flower of the Xhosa tribe, the pride of our nation. We have just circumcised them in a ritual that promises them manhood, but I am here to tell you that it is an empty, illusory promise, a promise that can never be fulfilled. For we Xhosas, and all black South Africans, are a conquered people. We are slaves in our own country. We are tenants on our own soil. We have no strength, no power, no control over our own destiny in the land of our birth. They will go to cities where they will live in shacks and drink cheap alcohol all because we have no land to give them where they could prosper and multiply. They will cough their lungs out deep in the bowels of the white man's mines, destroying their health, never seeing the sun, so that the white man can live a life of unequaled prosperity. Among these young men are chiefs who will never rule because we have no power to govern ourselves; soldiers who will never fight for we have no weapons to fight with; scholars who will never teach because we have no place for them to study. The abilities, the intelligence, the promise of these young men will be squandered in their attempt to eke out a living doing the simplest, most mindless chores for the white man. These gifts

today are naught, for we cannot give them the greatest gift of all, which is freedom and independence. I well know that Qamata is all-seeing and never sleeps, but I have a suspicion that Qamata may in fact be dozing. If this is the case, the sooner I die the better because then I can meet him and shake him awake and tell him that the children of Ngubengcuka, the flower of the Xhosa nation, are dying."

17 The audience had become more and more quiet as Chief Meligqili spoke and, I think, more and more angry. No one wanted to hear the words that he spoke that day. I know that I myself did not want to hear them. I was cross rather than aroused by the chief's remarks, dismissing his words as the abusive comments of an ignorant man who was unable to appreciate the value of the education and benefits that the white man had brought to our country. At the time, I looked on the white man not as an oppressor but as a benefactor, and I thought the chief was enormously ungrateful. This upstart chief was ruining my day, spoiling the proud feeling with wrongheaded remarks.

18 But without exactly understanding why, his words soon began to work in me. He had planted a seed, and though I let that seed lie dormant for a long season, it eventually began to grow. Later, I realized that the ignorant man that day was not the chief but myself.

19 After the ceremony, I walked back to the river and watched it meander on its way to where, many miles distant, it emptied into the Indian Ocean. I had never crossed that river, and I knew little or nothing of the world beyond it, a world that beckoned me that day. It was almost sunset and I hurried on to where our seclusion lodges had been. Though it was forbidden to look back while the lodges were burning, I could not resist. When I reached the area, all that remained were two pyramids of ashes by a large mimosa tree. In these ash heaps lay a lost and delightful world, the world of my childhood, the world of sweet and irresponsible days at Qunu and Mqhekezweni. Now I was a man, and I would never again play *thinti*, or steal maize, or drink milk from a cow's udder. I was already in mourning for my own youth. Looking back, I know that I was not a man that day and would not truly become one for many years.

---

[1]A ruler or governor.(Ed.)
[2]A South African word denoting either a rural village or an enclosure for livestock. Mandela probably uses the word in the second sense. (Ed.)
[3]A spear or lance used by South African tribesmen. (Ed.)
[4]Now a semi-independent area in southeast South Africa on the Indian Ocean, at the time Mandela was writing, it was a Black African Homeland. It received nominal independence in 1976. (Ed.)
Source: From Nelson Mandela, *Long Walk to Freedom*. © 1994, 1995 by Nelson Rolihlahla Mandela. By permission of Little, Brown and Company.

EXERCISES

A. Determining the Main Idea and Writer's Purpose

Choose the best answer.

1. The main idea of the selection is that
   a. all cultures conduct rituals to initiate boys into manhood.
   b. the circumcision ceremony marked the initiation of Xhosa boys into manhood.
   c. uncircumcised Xhosa males are not eligible to become leaders.
   d. a Xhosa boy must perform a daring exploit before the circumcision ritual.

2. The writer's purpose in the selection is to
   a. describe the actual circumcision he underwent.
   b. describe his emotional state before, during, and after the ceremony.
   c. honor the role this initiation ceremony plays in his culture.
   d. explain the tradition associated with the circumcision ceremony and his experience undergoing it.

B. Comprehending Main Ideas

Choose the correct answer.

1. In the Xhosa tradition, an uncircumcised male
   a. is allowed to remain intact only in certain extreme cases, for reasons of health.
   b. has no rights to inherit, to marry, or to take part in tribal rituals.
   c. is an object of ridicule and jokes among the tribespeople.
   d. is allowed to remain intact if his family rejects the tradition.

2. Bathing in the cold river waters before the ceremony was intended to
   a. test their endurance.
   b. purify them.
   c. baptize them.
   d. symbolically wash away their boyhood.

3. Flinching or crying out during the circumcision ceremony was considered disgraceful behavior because it
   a. ruined the ceremony for the other participants.
   b. showed disrespect for the elders and the circumcision expert.

c. made the participants' relatives anxious and tense.

d. caused disgrace to the entire family.

4. To symbolize the destruction of the young men's last links to childhood, the final step in the ritual was to

   a. burn the seclusion lodges and everything in them.

   b. bathe again in the river.

   c. paint their bodies with white chalk.

   d. chant traditional tribal songs.

5. Chief Meligqili, the main speaker of the day, warned the initiates that the promise of manhood was illusory and could never be fulfilled because black South Africans were

   a. not well enough educated to get good jobs.

   b. a conquered people with no control over their own destiny.

   c. too content to work for low wages and too afraid to fight for a higher standard of living.

   d. too timid to resist their oppressors.

C. Locating Supporting Details

For each main idea stated here, find two details that support it.

1. In Xhosa culture, the circumcision ceremony marks a significant step in a young boy's life. [paragraph 1]

   a. ____

   ____

   b. ____

   ____

2. Initially, Mandela was irritated by Chief Meligqili's remarks after the ceremony. [paragraph 17]

   a. ____

   ____

   b. ____

   ____

D. Making Inferences

For each of these statements write **Y** (yes) if the inference is an accurate one, **N** (no) if the inference is an inaccurate one, or **CT** (can't tell) if the writer does not give enough information to make an inference one way or another.

1. ______ Not all males in Xhosa culture become circumcised. [paragraph 1]
2. ______ The circumcision ceremony that Mandela describes has more symbolic than actual practical value in terms of a man's worth to the community. [paragraph 1]
3. ______ The circumcision ceremony was arranged principally for Justice because he was the son of a king. [paragraphs 2 and 15]
4. ______ The young black South Africans who ran away to work in the mines were well informed about the working conditions before they began their jobs. [paragraph 3]
5. ______ Some of the boys who were circumcised with Mandela went on to become great chiefs and advisers to kings. [essay as a whole]
6. ______ Although only 16 at the time he was initiated, Mandela was well educated and well informed about South Africa's political situation, and he understood clearly the white role in black oppression. [paragraph 18]

E. Interpreting Meaning

Where appropriate, write your answers to these questions in your own words.

1. Which of the following sentences from the selection *best* states the thesis?
   a. "When I was sixteen, the regent decided that it was time that I became a man."
   b. "For the Xhosa people, circumcision represents the formal incorporation of males into society."
   c. "As a Xhosa, I count my years as a man from the date of my circumcision."
   d. "At the end of our seclusion, the lodges and all their contents were burned, destroying our last links to childhood, and a great ceremony was held to welcome us as men to society."

2. Explain the fundamental irony that underlies paragraphs 3 and 16, concerning black South Africans working in the mines.

____

____

3. Write the sentence that represents the main idea of paragraph 9.

____

4. Look again at paragraph 12. A good title for this paragraph is
   a. "Concluding the Ceremony."
   b. "Becoming *Abakhwetha*."
   c. "Symbols of Purity."
   d. "How We Were Initiated."

5. Paragraph 18 contains a metaphor, an imaginative comparison. Locate it and explain its meaning.

____

____

6. In your own words, explain the main idea of paragraph 19.

____

____

____

F. Vocabulary in Context

Here are a few vocabulary words from the selection and their definitions. Study these definitions carefully. Then write the appropriate word in each space provided according to the context.

camaraderie good fellowship among friends

martial military, warlike

exploit a heroic act or deed

1. For Mandela and his peers, the __________ they experienced while undergoing the initiation ceremony was most enjoyable, especially when they performed the required ______, which in the old days was more of a ______ act than a practical joke.

clad wearing

flinched shrank back in fear

stoicism indifference to pain

stigmatized characterized or branded as disgraceful

2. It was considered unmanly, and a boy would be _________ if he ______ during the circumcision ceremony. The boys, ____ only in blankets after being purified, were expected to accept the pain with bravery and ______ .

remnants vestiges, remainders

quietude tranquility, peacefulness

initiates those who have been introduced to something new

3. For the ______ the period of ______ allowed them to prepare for the trials of manhood that lay in their future and to discard, both physically and symbolically, the ______ of their childhood.

heady exhilarating

paltry meager

dormant nactive, but capable of coming alive

squandering spending or wasting something of value

4. Although in comparison to Justice's gifts of an entire herd, Mandela's relatively _____ gift of heifers and sheep nonetheless gave him a _____ feeling; in addition, the chief's speech about the prospect of _________ illusory promises made to younger generations planted a seed that lay ______ for a time until he realized what lay in his future.

G. Annotation Exercise

Go through the article and put a star in the margin next to any information in the selection that supports this idea: *The circumcision ceremony is an important ritual in Xhosa society.*

DISCUSSION QUESTIONS

1. How would you describe Mandela as his character emerges from this autobiographical account?
2. What are some techniques that Mandela employs to help the reader stay on track and to follow his ideas?
3. What are the advantages of such a formalized ritual such as the Xhosa have devised to initiate young boys to take part in the larger community? What are the disadvantages?

EXPLORE THE WEB

Photos of South Africa are available at this site:

www.africaguide.com/country/safrica/photolib.htm

Here are two sites devoted to Xhosa culture:

www.questconnect.org/africa_xhosa.htm

webs.wofford.edu/mandlovenb/SAfrica/content/xhosa.html

A good introduction to the life and times of Nelson Mandela is available at The Mandela Page:

www.anc.org.za/people/mandela

The Many Layers of the Veil

Megan Stack

This article appeared in the *Los Angeles Times* in January 2005. In many Muslim nations in the Middle East, women are required to wear a head scarf or covering called a *hijab*. This requirement of Islamic law applies to women in public places and has engendered a great amount of controversy, both throughout the Muslim world and throughout Europe, which has a sizable Muslim population. For example, France, with a Muslim population of around 10 percent and which is rapidly growing, in 2004 prohibited Muslim schoolgirls from wearing the *hijab* and, in fact, prohibited all outward religious clothing, as a reaffirmation of its secular culture.

Megan Stack is the Cairo bureau chief for the *Los Angeles Times*. She has covered the U.S.-led wars in Iraq and Afghanistan, as well as the second Palestinian *intifada* (the recent uprising against Israel), and has traveled throughout the Arab world and Iran to write about regional changes since the terrorist attacks of September 11, 2001. She grew up in Glastonbury, Connecticut, graduated from George Washington University, and before joining the *Times*, worked for the Associated Press.

VOCABULARY ANALYSIS

The Root *crux*

Stack writes in paragraph 8 that the *hijab*, or head scarf, is "at the *crux* of cultural clashes—particularly since Sept. 11, 2001." Meaning a basic or supremely important point, *crux* is the root word embodied in the more common English adjective *crucial*, which describes something that is difficult

or severe, as in a *crucial* decision. In Latin, where this word derives, *crux* refers to "a cross." Christ was crucified because he died on a cross. And the *cruciferous* class of vegetables (brussel sprouts, cauliflower, and cabbage) are so termed because the leaves and stems are cross-shaped. (If you turn over a head of cabbage, you will see this cross structure clearly.)

Two Other Important Words

The words *secular* (paragraphs 10, 16, and 55) and *clerical* (paragraph 40) are important to your understanding of this article. Societies can be divided into two spheres—the secular or "worldly," that is, describing those not related to a religion or to a religious body—and the *clerical*, an adjective derived from the word *clergy*, describing those who are members of a particular religion. In the article, there is some discussion of the distinction between the two, particularly in Egypt, which has a secular government but a strong clerical or religious component both in private and public life.

Note, too, that the words *Islamic* and *Muslim* are interchangeable adjectives to describe someone who follows the religion of Islam.

The Many Layers of the Veil

Megan Stack

1 CAIRO—She was a 25-year-old journalist with a bare head and big dreams when things started to turn sour.

2 She got married and ended up divorced the same year. Then the stigma set in. Men knew she wasn't a virgin and stalked her as easy prey. She lost her job when the editor of her newspaper was jailed. Two years ago, lonesome and aimless, Hoda Abdel Wahab fell into a depression so deep she was afraid of becoming paralyzed.

3 "I thought, 'Nothing is worth it in this life, so I'll go to God,'" she says. Penniless, she sold her gold jewelry to buy a head scarf and *abaya*, or cloak.

4 Once she took the veil, the harassment stopped. On the streets, she gets only occasional murmurs from religious men: "Peace, sister."

5 She found a job, too, selling head scarves and flowing robes to wealthy women in a Cairo boutique. She swears that the transformation sank all the way into her soul. "The problems that really bothered me before disappeared from my mind," says the now 27-year-old Wahab.

6 She is one of millions of Muslim women who each day take a very visible side on the emotional, complicated question of the head scarf. Also known as *hijab*, a generic term for modest Muslim dress, the scarves look like simple runs of fabric but come layered with meaning.

7 The hijab is an expression of personal devotion to Islam, but critics decry it as an emblem of patriarchal repression. Covered heads can be powerful political statements or simply a fashion trend among teens.

8 Debate simmers in Islamic communities about whether the hijab is required for women, but the scarves appear increasingly at the crux of cultural clashes—particularly since Sept. 11, 2001.

9 Amid anger over the U.S.-led invasions of Afghanistan and Iraq and ongoing bloodshed in the Israeli-Palestinian conflict, the hijab has emerged in the Middle East with deep political significance. For some, the scarves express defiance of American aggression, silent protests against Arab governments that cooperate with Washington or a retort to Westerners' phobia of Muslims.

10 To many a wary eye, the hijab symbolizes the systematic degradation of women and provokes fear that Islamic fundamentalism will seep into Western societies. In France, which has struggled to assimilate its Muslim communities, the head coverings and other religious garb were banned from public schools last year. Officials cited a desire to defend the country's secular tradition.

11 Muslims around the world—even those who shun the hijab—poured into the streets in protest. Militants in Iraq threatened to behead their French hostages unless Paris reconsidered. But in Egypt, the nation's most powerful cleric scandalized his followers by preaching in favor of France's banning of the veil.

12 There are Muslim countries where women have no choice but to cover their heads. Religious police in Saudi Arabia and Iran hunt and even beat bareheaded women.

13 Yet in Turkey and Tunisia, there is the opposite pressure. The hijab is banned from public schools and offices, and veiled women complain of ridicule and abuse.

14 What is drowned out by the public outcry and political debate in many countries is the very personal nature of each woman's decision to cover, or bare, her head.

15 Some slip into head scarves at puberty without giving a thought to the controversial undertones. Others reach for the veil at a time of pain—marital strife, sudden unemployment or a midlife malaise. Some women say they covered their hair when they first sensed the inevitability of death, like a lapsed Catholic groping for a rosary on the sickbed.

16 In Egypt, where the government prides itself on its secular rule but Islam remains the most potent force in private and public life, the hijab is more or less a matter of choice. But on Cairo's bustling sidewalks, a naked female head has become a relatively rare sight. Schoolgirls bind their heads in white cotton, charwomen use fading polyester, businesswomen look demure in beige. The short, bright scarves of university students seem an afterthought over tight jeans, lipstick and scarlet nails.

Islamic Chic

17 A few decades back, when a young Omar Sharif heated up the black-and-white screen and Egypt shone as the Arab world's cultural vanguard, the veil was relegated to the poor. It began to reach the middle class with the Islamist revival of the 1980s and 1990s and has only recently been embraced by Egypt's wealthy women, who once sniffed at the notion of covering their coiffures.

18 Cairo's Al Motahajiba, a designer boutique for head scarves, is one of many luxury shops that have sprouted in the region as upper-class women join their poorer counterparts underneath the veil.

19 This is where Wahab works: among pink silk carefully shredded to resemble a feather boa and yellow silk delicately embellished with red embroidery. There is cashmere of midnight blue and "Saudi crepe," a new wrinkle-free fabric designed especially for veiled women. Silks are flown in from Qatar.

20 The air in the shop is rich with perfume, and high heels clatter across the hardwood floors. Gentle Muzak is piped in—"Never on Sunday."

21 "Not just anybody can afford these," murmurs one of the saleswomen, nodding at the shelves of brilliant chiffon and silk. "Only the rich come here."

22 Wahab nods and quotes one of Egypt's most popular preachers, a dapper Muslim televangelist widely credited with coaxing wealthy women to cover their heads.

23 "Amr Khaled says a woman on the street in hijab is the same thing as a Koran on the street," says Wahab, whose serious bespectacled face is rimmed by a black scarf. "He says it's protection and also a duty that God dictates."

24 Dalia Youssef is among one of the multitudes of women who regard the hijab as a Muslim duty. But the petite, bright-eyed George Orwell and T.S. Eliot enthusiast talks more about freedom than obligation.

25 She grew up in a household where her mother and aunts wore the hijab, and she perceived it as proud proof of maturity. When she turned 12, she covered her head. "It was childish," Youssef says now. "I wanted to show I was old enough."

26 In retrospect, the 26-year-old Egyptian admits that she was 15 before she came to understand the role of the hijab. It allows her to operate as an equal to men, she says, because it masks her sexuality.

27 "It's my evidence that I have a role in the public sphere, because there are a lot of challenges to Muslim women taking part. Maybe religion will be what liberates us. I don't see it as a burden."

28 From a sun-dappled office in Cairo, Youssef heads the Hijab Campaign at IslamOnline.net, a popular website created by young Muslims.

29 Her page tracks hijab law in all corners of the globe and gives a lesson on penning letters to the editor in protest of restrictions on wearing the veil. It also offers "psychological help"—advice for veiled women who are ostracized by friends or family, prevented from veiling at work or interested in fighting for their rights in their homeland.

30 "Sister, return curious glances with a saluting smile, return an insult here or there," the website counsels. "Then move on and thank Allah the Most High that you are holding firmly to your belief."

31 Convinced that globalization has endangered women's freedom to wear the hijab, Youssef has forged improbable ties with environmentalists, labor organizers and other anti-globalization activists around the world.

32 "You can't deal with hijab without all this." Youssef's voice trails off as she spreads her cupped hands into the air as if to encompass the whole city, the whole world. "It's loaded with political, cultural, religious contexts. It's not just a piece of cloth."

33 She's determined to use the hijab to teach Muslim women how to exercise their freedoms, she says, particularly in the West. The idea of a veiled woman in Egypt toiling to liberate her sisters from Europe's restrictions may seem odd to Westerners, but to Youssef, it's perfectly natural.

34 "This is the hidden or ultimate goal" of her page on the Internet, she says. "To make Muslims use the tools of civil society so they can be Muslims and citizens at the same time. We don't try to inject people with knowledge, as if we're superior [or] we're the ones with the *fatwas* [religious edicts]. No. We try to open their doors."

Interpreting the Koran

35 The origin of the hijab is hard to trace, twining back into long-standing debates over translations of sacred texts and the authenticity of the oral record of the

prophet Muhammad, as well as gender politics. But what's certain is that the tradition of veiling stems from three verses of the Koran, none of which mention the head or hair.

36 "O Prophet," reads one verse, "Tell thy wives and daughters that they should cast their outer garments over their persons when abroad, that is most convenient, that they should be known and not molested."

37 Another verse says: "And say to the believing women that they should lower their gaze and guard their modesty, that they should not display their ornaments except what [must ordinarily] appear thereof, that they should draw their veils over the bosoms and not display their beauty."

38 Finally, there is an order to men visiting the home of the prophet. "When ye ask [the wives of the prophet] for any article, ask them from behind a curtain; that is purer for their hearts and yours."

39 It is through those words, many Islamic clerics insist, that God has ordered women to cover everything but their hands and faces. The strictest clerics believe even those places are indecent for public exposure, and there are many Muslim women who wouldn't dream of stepping into the street without gloves and a *niqab*, or face shroud.

40 The Koranic commands to veil are buttressed, many clerics say, by a handful of *hadiths*, the recorded sayings and actions of the prophet relayed by his companions. But other scholars question the authenticity of some hadiths, which were passed orally for generations and are a perpetual source of clerical debate.

41 In 1994, an Egyptian judge named Said Ashmawi wrote a book that gathered all the religious arguments for the hijab, dissected them and concluded that Islam does not oblige women to cover their hair. His life hasn't been the same since.

42 Ashmawi studied at Harvard and rose to become a chief justice in Egypt. But now he is a pariah among Egypt's Islamists, confined to his home by death threats. A guard is posted in the lobby of his building, and Ashmawi refuses to give his apartment number over the phone.

43 He is afraid to wander into the city, and not without reason—novelist Naguib Mahfouz, a Nobel laureate and the dean of Egyptian literary circles, was stabbed and seriously wounded by Islamic militants on a Cairo street for espousing similar views.[1]

44 Isolated and defiant, Ashmawi passes his days in a dim sitting room crammed to fantastic overflow with golden candelabras, glass roses and ceramic apples.

45 "I don't want to ban hijab, but I'd like to explain to the people," Ashmawi says, fluttering plump hands during a recent meeting in his apartment. Islamists "are using their power to impose, and they are distorting our faith. I put legal arguments in the mouths of the people who read my books."

46 To like-minded people, the near-ubiquity of the hijab is evidence of a powerful patriarchal system that has imposed tribal traditions on women without religious justification. Ashmawi blames Islamist groups such as Egypt's Muslim Brotherhood for turning the head scarf into a "political badge."

47 The hijab is important to the Brotherhood, Ashmawi arguers, because it keeps up appearances in the streets. "Islamists have to prove themselves, either by beard or by veil," he says. "They say hijab is a duty. What duty? They want if somebody enters Egypt they will say, 'Oh, it's an Islamic country.'"

48 Asked about girls who choose the hijab for reasons of their own—religious devotion, asserting their Islamic identity, keeping up with a fashion trend—Ashmawi snorts: "What choice?"

49 "They are ordered, that's all. The father, the brother, he teaches her. They are forcing them," he says. "They are not free, not at all."

"To Him I Was Naked"

50 When Hala Dahroug decided to put aside the veil after wearing it for three years, she was knocked off guard by the response.

51 She was a 20-year-old Arabic literature student in the sleepy, Upper Egypt province of Beni Suef when her devotion to the head scarf began to soften. It was 1990, and she was intoxicated by the rush of politics, philosophy and leftist ideas that surged through campus.

52 One day she woke up, left her scarf behind and headed off to class with nothing on her hair but the sun.

53 The reaction came fast and hard. Students in the conservative Arabic department snubbed her. Her family implored her to go back to the hijab. "My uncle told me it didn't matter whether I was praying or not, but walking around without the veil meant to him I was naked," Dahroug recalls.

54 But she refused to back down.

55 Looking back now, she says she was young and in a "rebelling phase." Now 33, she works in television in Cairo and is the divorced mother of a 3-year-old girl. She remains secular and hopes fervently that her daughter won't grow up to take the veil. Still, Dahroug says, if her daughter wants to wear a head scarf, she won't stand in her way.

56 "What I care about is my daughter's mentality, not what she wears," she says. "Being unveiled doesn't necessarily mean you are more intellectual or smarter. I meet unveiled girls who've got nothing in their brains, and I meet veiled ones who care about the world."

57 Despite, or perhaps because of, her youthful struggles to bare her head, Dahroug turned up at the French Embassy in Cairo last year to protest Paris' ban on head scarves in public schools.

58 "The important thing here is freedom of expression and the freedom to practice whatever rituals you believe in," she says. "Women should choose to wear it or not."

---

[1]Mahfouz died in 2006 at the age of 95. He won the Nobel Prize for Literature in 1988.

EXERCISES

A. Determining the Main Idea and Writer's Purpose

Choose the best answer.

1. The main idea of the selection is that for Muslim women, the *hijab*, or head scarf,
   a. is a decision that involves a complicated, emotional, and multifaceted question.
   b. is a contemporary tradition with no basis in Muslim religious history.
   c. has become the focal point in the clash between religious clerics and secularists in all Arab countries.
   d. is a sign of patriarchal repression that is under attack in all Arab countries.

2. The writer's purpose in the selection is to
   a. defend Muslim women's obligation to wear the *hijab*.
   b. examine the controversy surrounding the tradition of *hijab* for Arab women.
   c. explore Westerners' and some Arab cultures' objections to the *hijab*.
   d. examine the way Islamic fundamentalism has changed Arabic cultures.

B. Comprehending Main Ideas

Choose the correct answer.

1. At the beginning of the article, Stack describes the experience of 25-year-old journalist Hoda Abdel Wahab, who, when she walked the streets of Cairo bareheaded, was
   a. branded as a heretic and arrested.
   b. greeted warmly by other feminists who applauded her courage.
   c. harassed by men following her as easy prey.
   d. recognized as a divorced woman with no prospects for remarriage.

2. Which of the following criticisms of the *hijab* was *not* mentioned in the article?
   a. It is a symbol of patriarchal repression.
   b. It is a symbol of systematic degradation of women.
   c. It is a way for Islamic fundamentalism to creep into Western secular society.

d. It is a fashion element only wealthy women can afford to enjoy.

e. It is worn by young girls as a symbol of maturity and identity.

3. The author strongly emphasizes that for Muslim women the decision of whether or not to wear the veil

   a. is a personal matter, one of personal choice.

   b. depends on one's social and economic class.

   c. depends on the country one lives in, since not all Middle Eastern countries require it.

   d. All of the above.

   e. Only a and c

4. For Dalia Youssef, a 26-year-old Egyptian woman, wearing the *hijab* is both a badge of maturity and a way for her

   a. to operate as an equal to men and hide her sexuality.

   b. to honor her parents who demanded that she wear the *hijab*.

   c. to be allowed to work outside the home and run an Islamic web page.

   d. to express her anti-Western ideals.

5. According to the writer, the tradition of wearing the veil to cover the hair and head

   a. dates back to ancient Egypt when the pharaohs commanded women to wear veils.

   b. is not specifically mentioned in the Koran or in the oral record of the prophet Muhammad.

   c. is a recent ruling prescribed by Muslim clerics after the terrorist attacks of September 11, 2001, and the American invasion of Afghanistan.

   d. is derived from the Muslim tradition of a woman not being allowed to appear in public with any male relative who is not her husband.

C. Distinguishing between Main Ideas and Supporting Details

The following sentences come from paragraphs 12–15. Label them as follows: **MI** if the sentence represents a *main idea* and **SD** if the sentence represents a *supporting detail*.

1. _____ There are Muslim countries where women have no choice but to cover their heads.

2. _____ Religious police in Saudi Arabia and Iran hunt and even beat bareheaded women.

3. _____ Yet in Turkey and Tunisia, there is the opposite pressure.

4. _____ The *hijab* is banned from public schools and offices, and veiled women complain of ridicule and abuse.

5. _____ What is drowned out by the public outcry and political debate in many countries in the very personal nature of each woman's decision to cover, or bare, her head.

6. _____ Some slip into head scarves at puberty without giving a thought to the controversial undertones.

7. _____ Others reach for the veil at a time of pain—marital strife, sudden unemployment, or a midlife malaise.

8. _____ Some women say they covered their hair when they first sensed the inevitability of death, like a lapsed Catholic groping for a rosary on the sickbed.

D. Making Inferences

Write your answers to these questions in your own words.

1. In paragraphs 1–5, Stack describes the experience of Hoda Abdel Wahab. What can you infer about the status of Egyptian women who go out in public without wearing a veil?

   ____

2. According to what Stack strongly suggests but does not say in paragraphs 7–10, do the critics of the *hijab* live in Middle Eastern countries or do they live in Western nations?

   ____

   ____

3. From what Stack implies in paragraph 9, how might the *hijab* actually be a symbol of rebellion and defiance?

   ____

   ____

   ____

4. From paragraphs 16–19, what inference can you make about the quality and style of veils for Muslim women?

   ____

   ____

5. Why does Dalia Youssef say that the *hijab* is "not just a piece of cloth"?

6. Stack suggests throughout the article that the decision to wear the veil is a matter of individual choice. From the experience of the Egyptian judge Said Ashmawi and the novelist Naguib Mahfouz, as described in paragraphs 41–49, how valid is this statement?

E. Interpreting Meaning

Where appropriate, write your answers to these questions in your own words.

1. What is the significance of the article's title? What does the word *layers* refer to?

2. What is the purpose of beginning the article with the experience of the Egyptian journalist Hoda Abdel Wahab?

3. Read paragraphs 7–10 again. A good title for this section is
   a. "The *Hijab* as a Means of Expression."
   b. "The *Hijab* as a Symbol of Oppression."
   c. "The Debate over the *Hijab* and Its Significance."
   d. "Why Women Wear the *Hijab*."

4. Why does Stack include the section from paragraphs 41–49, which summarizes the criticisms made by Said Ashmawi and Naguib Mahfouz against the veil?

____

____

F. Understanding Vocabulary

Look through the paragraphs listed below and find a word that matches each definition. Refer to a dictionary if necessary. An example has been done for you.

EXAMPLE: a mark of disgrace or reproach [paragraphs 1–5] stigma

1. descriptive of an entire group or class [6–9] __________
2. condemn openly, criticize [6–8] __________
3. the central point or feature [7–9] __________
4. reply in a quick or caustic manner [7–9] __________
5. a decline to a lower condition or quality [8–10] __________
6. struggle, quarrel, conflict [14–16] __________
7. general sense of depression or unease [14–16] __________
8. exerting strong influence, powerful [14–16] __________
9. modest and reserved in manner or behavior [16–17] __________
10. assigned to a particular class or category [17–20] __________
11. the leading position of a trend or movement [17–20] __________
12. excluded or banished from a group [28–30] __________
13. a garment that conceals or protects [39–40] __________
14. supported, reinforced, as of a claim [39–40] __________
15. a social outcast [42–43] __________
16. adopting or giving support to an idea [42–44] __________
17. apparent existence everywhere at once, omnipresence [46–47] __________

18. behaved coldly toward, deliberately slighted [53–55] ________________

DISCUSSION QUESTIONS

1. What information did you have about the Muslim requirement for women to veil themselves before you read this article? Has Stack's discussion changed your thinking in any way?
2. What is the writer's opinion of the *hijab*? Is there any evidence one way or another to show it? Does she present a balanced examination of the *hijab* and the issues it raises, or do you detect any Western bias?
3. What is your reaction to the *hijab* requirement and to Stack's discussion of the issues surrounding this article of clothing as it applies to Muslim women?

EXPLORE THE WEB

For several viewpoints on the requirement for Muslim women to wear the *hijab*, go to this site sponsored by a group called Islam for Today:

www.islamfortoday.com/women.htm

Click on "*Hijab* and Islamic clothing," and you will get several links pertaining to this controversial issue. For a look at how people in the Middle East see the Western world and for a different perspective on events in that part of the world, go to the website for Aljazeera, the primary television channel in the Arab world:

www.aljazeera.com

One unusual site allows American readers to eavesdrop on what foreign newspapers are writing about the United States. The site's editors, William Kern, formerly a copyeditor for the *International Herald Tribune*, and Robin Koerner, a British entrepreneur and business consultant, offer translations of articles written in six languages from a variety of foreign sources about the United States. Every day the pair search through 200 newspapers and broadcasts from Europe, Latin America, the Middle East, Africa, and Asia to find compelling stories that are then translated by a volunteer fluent in the language. The articles are published without commentary and thus are meant to be politically neutral. In these ways, this site is different from those offering English content sponsored by foreign outlets. The site is updated daily:

www.WatchingAmerica.com

Writing Cause-Effect Essays

CAUSE AND EFFECT—A DEFINITION

An essay developed by using the cause-effect pattern of development is primarily expository; that is, it serves to provide the reader with information concerning the reasons (the *causes*) that a problem or situation exists and its real or likely results or consequences (its *effects*). Before you continue with this section, you might want to review the discussion of the cause-effect pattern in the reading section at the beginning of Part 7.

To cite a real-world example and to make the relationship between cause and effect more understandable, I am going to diagram it:

Problem

- You work at a video store and ask your boss for a raise; he denies your request and justifies his decision with several reasons.

Causes (Reasons)

- Business has slowed.
- Fewer customers mean lower profits.
- The landlord just raised the rent, and utility bills have also increased.
- Other employees have been there longer and therefore deserve a raise more than you do.
- The market has changed; the owner had to replace the old VHS tapes with DVDs, creating an expense that cut into his profits.

After his refusal, you contemplate what no pay raise will mean to you as a struggling college student.

Effects (Consequences)

- Your landlord just increased your rent, and without a raise you will have to get a roommate.

- With the high cost of tuition and books, you might be able to afford to enroll in only three classes rather than the customary four.
- You will probably have to stop driving and use public transit because of the high cost of gasoline. You might even have to sell your car.

Further, your boss can ascribe more comprehensive reasons to account for the downturn in his video rental business: (1) Hurricanes Katrina and Rita caused energy prices to rise, so that people had less disposable income for luxuries like renting movies; (2) DVR recorders like Tivo are increasingly popular; and (3) online movie rental subscription services like Netflix and movies-on-demand offered by cable operators are convenient ways of watching movies at home. These are just three reasons that video rental businesses have been struggling. You will note that the more fundamental reasons cited here form a sort of subset to explain more generally why most video rental enterprises, and not just your boss's, are not as profitable as they once were.

For your part, a long-term effect or consequence of this situation is that it will take you longer to complete your undergraduate work, thus in turn delaying your entrance into the labor force full time.

WRITING TO IDENTIFY CAUSE AND EFFECT: ACADEMIC AND PROFESSIONAL WRITING

Understanding how cause and effect interrelate and learning to analyze causes and effects perceptively will lead you to understand more fully many aspects of your college subjects as well as many parts of your professional work.

Typical Academic Assignments Requiring Writing to Identify Cause and Effect

- For a sociology course, explain the effects of a particular natural disaster on the population of a designated area.
- For a health science course, explain the causes of a particular disease and how the understanding of those causes has changed during the past 100 years.
- For a business course, discuss the impact of e-mail in the workplace on the efficiency of workers engaged in a particular task.

Typical Professional Writing Tasks Requiring Writing to Identify Cause and Effect

- Explain the effects the purchase of a new piece of equipment will have on the productivity of your department.
- Explain why the increasingly high rate of employee absenteeism has led administrators to institute a new sick leave policy.

- Write a proposal for instituting new safety regulations and include a discussion of the cause and effects of recent accidents in your workplace.

ORGANIZING AND DEVELOPING A CAUSE AND EFFECT ESSAY

Writing a cause-effect paper requires the writer to achieve a sense of proportion, appropriate to the scope and length of the assignment. Depending on the topic, a writer might begin by defining the situation and then discussing and examining the *reasons* (causes) that the situation exists. Conversely, a writer might begin by defining a situation and examining the *effects* that it is likely to produce. In other words, the writer of a cause-effect essay need not worry about giving equal weight to both parts of the cause-effect pattern.

For example, if you are asked to write an essay discussing the changes brought about by the Internet, you do not need to dwell at any particular length on what the Internet is (the cause); you can assume that the reader is familiar with it or on how the Internet came to be. The introductory paragraph can provide some general remarks about the Internet's features, while each body paragraph might take up, in order, each of these ideas:

- The Internet has changed the way we locate and retrieve information.
- The Internet has changed the way we comparison-shop and purchase goods.
- The Internet has been responsible to some degree for increased social isolation.

Based on this short outline, you can see that the writer will focus on two positive effects and one negative one.

However, if your political science instructor asks you to write an essay in which you examine the reasons that the United States invaded Iraq in 2003, your introduction should provide a brief explanation of the situation in Iraq before the invasion, and the body paragraphs would focus on the reasons the government put forth in defense of its actions. But rather than merely reciting facts, you would need to find an insight that would tie your remarks together.

In the case of the Iraq invasion, the government's reasons for invading and for removing Saddam Hussein from power continually evolved as the war dragged on and as the death toll for American soldiers and Iraqi civilians increased. The first reason was to remove the threat of Hussein's weapons of mass destruction (WMDs). When it turned out that those weapons did not exist, the argument changed to the need to rid the Middle East of a tyrannical ruler whose legendary cruelty to his own people and a perceived threat to Israel justified "regime change," coupled with the goal of stabilizing the region and bringing democracy to the Middle East. Iraq would then serve as a beacon of democracy to the more autocratic regimes of Saudi Arabia and Syria. As the insurgency intensified, the argument changed once again. The Bush administration argued that Iraq was training terrorists and that fighting them in Iraq would keep us safe from terrorist attacks at home. The final argument presented was that terrorists were intent on establishing a "radical Islamic empire that spans from Spain to Indonesia."

What insight might you bring to bear on these shifting reasons? It's not enough just to recite them. Depending on your political worldview, your understanding of the situation, and the degree to which you accept or reject the government's motives, your thesis would identify and assess the significance of the government's media campaign. Here are two thesis statements, expressing completely different insights, on this cause-effect relationship:

> The Bush administration continually attempted to justify the American invasion of Iraq as being part of the larger war on terror, which made the war more palatable to the public.

Or

> The Bush administration's constantly shifting explanations for the American invasion of Iraq produced increased public cynicism for our government and distrust of its motives.

THE CAUSE-EFFECT CHAIN

When writers use the cause-effect pattern—at least with some topics—the discussion can form a sort of chain, with a single cause leading to one effect, which in turn leads to a second effect, which leads to a third effect, and so on. You saw this chain in a rather simplified form in the example of the video store's declining business fortunes at the beginning of this section. This chain is also evident in the following passage by Sallie Tisdale, who examines the reasons for the decline of the Asian elephant in its native habitat.

> There are between twenty-five thousand and forty thousand Asian elephants left in the world. Their gradual elimination in the wild is the result of a number of changes, most of them recent and a few subtle. The invention of the chain saw, for instance, made forest-clearing much easier and quicker work. But basically there is just not enough room in Southeast Asia for both elephants and people. The elephant's jungle habitat is being replaced by cropland, and many of the crops are delectable to the now homeless elephant.

> The elephant raids the millet and sugarcane, and is killed for his efforts, and kills in turn; in India, nearly a hundred and fifty people are killed by elephants every year. Wild elephants are found from India to Indonesia; most inhabit shrinking parks and preserves, in shrinking populations, separated from each other by human settlements as uncrossable as an ocean. Bulls, being more aggressive, are killed far more often than cows. Not only does this deplete the gene pool but the cows' opportunities to breed grow fewer, and as the birth rate falls their mean age increases. Because elephants will feed on the youngest, tenderest trees available, finding them the most appetizing, herds quickly denude small parks beyond the point of natural recovery. Several countries, notably Thailand and India, are attempting to conserve these insular environments and to confront the problems of the diminished gene pool and male-to-female ratio, but quite a few people in elephant biology wonder whether the wild elephant is past saving. There are estimated to be a million elephants left in Africa; however, their numbers are also dropping. Certainly its future, one way or another, resides in zoos.
>
> —Sallie Tisdale, "The Only Harmless Great Thing," *The New Yorker*

AVOIDING GENERALIZATIONS IN ASCRIBING CAUSES

One danger—perhaps *trap* is a better word choice—that student writers often fall into when writing cause-effect essays is generalizing. When examining a complex situation, students sometimes fail to account for other factors that produce a problem. It is tempting to target a highly visible cause for a complicated situation. But in real life, hardly any situation is the result of just one underlying cause. For example, let's examine this thesis statement:

> High school students who work part-time do so for frivolous reasons. These hours spent away from studying jeopardizes their GPA, their educational experience, and their chances of getting accepted into college.

This thesis sets up a cause-effect relationship, but one that relies on generalization and oversimplification. In the body of the essay, the writer then goes on to support his thesis by citing some frivolous reasons: buying CDs, buying tickets for rock concerts and clubs, paying for a new car and car insurance for that car, buying expensive designer jeans, and so forth. But is consumerism behind the motives of all high school students to take on jobs at the local video store or at the local Gap? Perhaps so for some students, but surely not for all. There may be other, more legitimate and justifiable reasons—and therefore less frivolous reasons—depending on the student and his or her financial situation.

In expensive cities like Boston, New York, and San Francisco, housing costs are so prohibitively expensive that some parents expect their children to contribute some of their earnings to household expenses or to rent or the mortgage. Many students work to save up for college expenses, if not for the tuition itself, then at least for books and living expenses. These clearly are not frivolous reasons for working while studying.

How can you avoid generalizing, then, when ascribing the causes of a situation? First, you can concede at the beginning of your essay that your thoughts are based on personal observations that you have made in *your* particular community and among *your* particular group of acquaintances. Second, you can recast sentences so that they do not represent sweeping generalizations. Instead of writing, for example, "all students want to spend the money they earn on Diesel jeans," you can write, "When I was a student at Portland's Cleveland High School, I observed many students who . . . ." A final recommendation is to make a larger claim and then to support it with a specific example of one or two students who are meant to represent the type.

TOPICS FOR CAUSE-EFFECT ESSAYS

1. Identify a technological device that has changed your life significantly. (Resist the impulse to write about the ubiquitous television.) Explain using specific details exactly how this device has affected you, and perhaps your family as well. Come to a conclusion about whether or not the changes have been more for good or more for ill.
2. Although modern parents try hard to treat their children equally, inequalities and differing expectations according to gender are nearly impossible to avoid. In what ways have gender expectations demonstrated by your family, friends, and teachers made you the person you are today? Identify these expectations and assess their impact on your personality, your values, your interests, and anything else that seems pertinent to you.
3. An imbalance between the native organisms in an environment is a common problem in many areas of the country today. In Maine and Vermont, wandering moose have caused numerous roadway fatalities, and deer are a huge problem in the mid-Atlantic states. In California and other Western states, coyotes have invaded suburban backyards. In British Columbia and Alaska, marauding black bears can wreak havoc on automobiles and gardens. Investigate and report on an ecological imbalance or unwelcome animal presence in your community. Be sure to assess the causes and the effects of the situation you describe.
4. In the fall of 2005, Nelson Mandela announced the publication of a series of comic books based on his life. The project is intended to help promote literacy among South African youth. Do some research on this project and write a report summarizing the project, its aims,

the content of the comic series, and the ways in which they will be distributed throughout the country. Begin with these two sites:

www.media.bloggingbaby.com/entry/1234000517065605

www.allafrica.com/stories/200511010178.html

5. For Americans of all ages, but particularly for teenagers, blue jeans have become almost like a uniform. How does the near-ubiquity of blue jeans as a popular article of clothing compare to the *hijab* for Muslim women? Write an essay in which you examine the phenomenon of standardized dress—its cultural significance and its deeper meaning—using ideas from Stack's essay and observations of your own for support.

TOPICS RELATED TO THE READINGS

1. In "Teen Suicide and the Culture of Fear," Glassner asserts that the media overplay and unnecessarily scare people in the way they cover isolated or random events. In his book, Glassner takes up such topics as road rage, crime, campus crime, medical errors, plane crashes, and workplace violence. Choose a recent incident that you read about in the newspaper or saw on television pertaining to one of these subjects (or to one of your own choosing) and then follow the media coverage of it. Examine the coverage for inflated statistics, making dire predictions from a single incident, and so forth. Summarize your findings in an essay.
2. Anwar Accawi's account of the telephone's impact on his small Lebanese village is almost overwhelmingly negative. Can you think of a technological device or invention that has caused similar disruption in a community, one that has produced far-reaching and mostly negative changes? (To avoid boring your instructor who has likely read hundreds of essays on the evils of television, I suggest that you choose another subject—for example, iPods, electronic video games, cell phones, or the like,)
3. Accawi's essay nicely illustrates the phenomenon of unintended results. Another example is the voice-activated recording system, which President Richard Nixon secretly installed in the Oval Office. When the existence of the recording system was revealed during the 1973 Watergate hearings, it led to a protracted fight to suppress their contents, and when Nixon's complicity in the whole messy affair and the cover-up became evident, he became the first president in U.S. history to resign. What is another instance of a type of technology that had serious unintended consequences? Again, avoid the subject of television. Be sure to establish a clear cause-effect relationship in your thesis.

4. Nelson Mandela recounts in remarkably specific detail the initiation and circumcision ceremony and highly codified ritual that young Xhosa boys undergo before they are considered men. How are young American boys initiated into rites of manhood? Write a short paper in which you contrast the Xhosa circumcision ceremony Mandela describes with American traditions. Be sure to include in your discussion the ways in which American boys "prove" their manhood. What type of initiation rites do American boys undergo? How do they measure up against the more ritualized Xhosa rites?
5. Write an essay in which you contrast the two contrasting methods by which a young North America boy and a Xhosa boy in South Africa become men.
6. Write an essay in which you examine the issue of the *hijab*, the required head covering for women in much of the Muslim world. Maintain balance and objectivity as you write, and explain the various points of view Megan Stack presents in "The Many Layers of the Veil." Be sure to annotate the article carefully before you begin.

PART EIGHT

READING

WRITING

8

Part 8 takes up analyzing and evaluating argumentative prose and techniques for writing your own arguments. We begin with an explanation of the elements common to all persuasive writing—the argument itself (the claim), the evidence used in its support, bias, and the refutation. Two short editorials argue both sides of the question of whether drivers should be allowed to use cell phones. Annotations and evaluations help you see why one argument is more convincing than the other.

The next section presents editorials on a variety of contemporary issues. Topics include the ethics of using torture to extract information from suspected terrorists, the media's seeming indifference to violence in African American communities, and the modern tendency to undermine and trivialize the concept of heroism as an aftermath of the 9/11 attacks. The burdens associated with unskilled immigrants (opinion pieces and cartoons) and the problem of global warming (opinion pieces and a cartoon) illustrate how the same subject can be treated from multiple points of view. The accompanying exercises will help you understand the structure of editorials as a way to measure their effectiveness and ability to persuade. The accompanying website includes paired editorials on whether gays should have the right to marry and whether Intelligent Design should be taught in high school science classes.

The final section outlines the steps necessary to prepare your own argumentative essay, including how to organize your remarks by using a practice outline along with an extensive discussion of the refutation. Part 8 ends with a mix of writing topics, some relating to the readings and some giving you suggestions for writing an argument of your own devising.

Evaluating Argumentative Prose

In this last reading section of the text we discuss techniques for reading opinion pieces and argumentative prose. Understanding and applying some fundamental principles and reading a sampling of opinion pieces will help you to sharpen your evaluative skills, to understand the issues of the day, and to structure your own arguments. Developing this skill will have eminent practical and intellectual value in your college classes and in the real world.

THE PRINCIPLES OF ARGUMENTATIVE WRITING

Being informed is one basis on which our democratic society is built; it is an important part of becoming an educated citizen, both of the country and of the world. A significant part of good citizenship is to identify the issues of the day, to weigh the arguments for and against proposed policies, and to come to a decision of your own, not one that is imposed on you by someone else. Controversial issues are rarely just black and white, and the ability to see a controversy from many sides is part of the leading-out process education affords us. This is best accomplished by reading the opinion pages in daily newspapers and magazines and on Internet opinion websites. Through wide reading, you can eventually learn enough about an issue to make up your own mind.

This right to make informed decisions is one of the many rewards of living in a democratic country with a free press and the (generally) unhindered freedom to express oneself without fear of punishment, retaliation, or censorship, as occurs in repressive societies. A glance at recent news headlines from other parts of the world and at recent stories of attempts to constrain the American press in its criticism of administration policies both here and abroad bears out this observation. At the risk of sounding preachy, I believe that this freedom is precious; none of us should take it lightly or for granted.

Issues abound in our society. Some current issues include stem cell research and its uses, genetic manipulation of crops, global warming and ways to slow its progress, violent video games and the question of whether government should regulate their sale to minors, the teaching of Intelligent Design in high school biology courses, gay marriage, whether torture is permissible in a society with humanitarian ideals, whether the administration should be able to conduct warrantless wiretaps, and countless others. But controversies do not have to be so momentous.

Closer to home we might identify issues in our community—for example, whether the local high school should ban vending machines that dispense chips and cookies, whether tuition fees should be raised at the community college, or whether a stoplight should be installed at the intersection of Main Street and Alhambra Avenue.

The reading selections in Part 8 represent various styles of persuasive and argumentative writing on a variety of contemporary social questions. Reading them and working through the exercises will help you learn to read prose expressing a subjective opinion. Note that the exercises are markedly different from those you have encountered in this text thus far. The exercises ask you to identify the various elements that comprise arguments. These elements are explained one by one in the remainder of this section.

THE AIMS OF ARGUMENTATION

Although we use the term *persuasion* and *argumentation* interchangeably in this text, technically, there are differences—it seems to me more in intent than in substance.[1] *Persuasion* is the attempt to get someone to change his or her mind, often using emotional appeals or entreaty. *Argument* presents reasons and logical evidence in support of a particular position. In the exercises following each editorial, you will be asked to decide whether the writer appeals to reason, to our emotions, or perhaps to both.

Argumentative and persuasive writing aims to convince you to accept an idea, opinion, or point of view. Politicians do this all the time, when they try to persuade us that they are the best candidates for public office. Someone may try to convince you to change your thoughts or behavior, as when a missionary exhorts you to embrace a particular religion. Someone may try to persuade you to take action—to quit smoking, to protest against American involvement in the Middle East, to donate money to St. Anthony's soup kitchen—or simply to consider that another point of view has merit. All of these are common aims of both argumentation and persuasion.

[1]If you are curious, go to the website listed here, sponsored by the NCTE (National Council of Teachers of English), scroll down to "Instructional Plan—Resources," and click on the link "Argument, Persuasion, or Propaganda Chart": www.readwritethink.org/lessons/lesson_view.asp?id=829.

The Purposes of Argumentation

- To convince you to accept a particular point of view
- To convince you to change your thinking
- To convince you to take action
- To convince you to at least consider that another point of view has merit

HOW TO READ OPINION PIECES

When you read the opinion pieces in Part 8 and in other sources like your daily newspaper, Internet sites, or political blogs, you should first ask yourself what the writer's purpose is and what the aim of the opinion piece is. By definition, argumentative writing presents a controversial issue that is open to discussion. Also by definition, an argumentative piece presents a subjective opinion. But there is wide latitude in argumentative writing. Some writers present two or even three points of view and leave you to make up your own mind about where you stand. Other writers make more obvious attempts to get you to change your mind or to persuade you to adopt their position by resorting to bias, slanted language, emotional appeals, and other manipulative devices.

Whichever techniques the opinion writer uses, the most important step—and your starting point—is to determine his or her central *argument* (also called the *claim*), the proposition or idea to be supported and defended, which lies at the heart of the piece. Like the thesis statement in an informative or expository essay, the claim or argument in an opinion piece may be *stated* directly or it may be *implied*. Further, argumentative claims can be classified into three types: *claims of fact*, *claims of value*, and *claims of policy*. Identifying the type of claim in each piece of persuasive writing you read will help you read opinion pieces more intelligently and understand the evidence used in their support.

TYPES OF CLAIMS—FACT, VALUE, AND POLICY

Claims of Fact

Claims of fact can be verified, measured, tested, and proved.

- Smoking causes numerous health problems for long-term smokers.
- Genetically modified crops will help feed Third World nations.

- The Los Angeles Lakers will win the NBA title next year.
- Bananas contain more potassium than dates.

A claim of fact can be defended by citing factual evidence, the results of scientific research, or in the case of predictions of future events, by the passage of time.

Claims of Value

Claims of value involve matters of taste, morality, opinion, and ideas about right and wrong and therefore are more difficult to "prove" than claims of fact. Examples of such claims include:

- Community colleges offer students a good education at relatively little cost.
- Broccoli tastes better than spinach.
- The remake of *King Kong* by director Peter Jackson is too long and lacks the impact of the original 1930s movie.
- Current attempts by the administration and judicial systems to engage in surveillance of ordinary citizens without using warrants invades our privacy and constitutes a dangerous precedent.

The support would be in the form of reasons, examples, and personal experience.

Claims of Policy

Claims of policy argue for a course of action, propose a change, or identify a problem that needs a solution. Note that these types of claims typically include words like *should, must, ought to,* or *need.* Examples of claims of policy include:

- Because of overcrowded classes, Centerville Community College should raise its tuition so that more teachers can be hired.
- To combat the growing problem of childhood obesity, public schools nationwide should follow the lead of the Oakland school district and ban candy and soft drink machines on campuses.
- We ought to boycott movies that glamorize smoking and illegal drug use.

Claims of policy are typically supported by good reasons, facts and statistics, examples, or the testimony of authorities or experts.

THE STRUCTURE OF AN ARGUMENT

An argumentative piece must be clearly organized if the writer is to get the point across effectively and to convince the audience to adopt the particular claim. Not every argument you read will look exactly like the one in the outline below. Many writers, for example, prefer to save the claim for the end of the piece, after assembling sufficient evidence. Study this section carefully, because you can adopt the structure described here when you write your own argumentative essays. Generally speaking, a good opinion piece should contain these elements:

- An *introduction* in which the author provides background, introduces the subject, perhaps engages the reader with an anecdote. The introduction *may* contain the argument or claim.
- The *body*, which contains evidence to support or prove the claim.
- The *refutation*, a section that may be relatively short, in which the writer considers *opposing views* and offers a counterargument against them. Many editorials and opinion pieces do not contain refutations.
- Finally, a *conclusion*, which may contain the claim, recommend future action, give a warning about what will happen if the claim is not accepted, or state the seriousness of the problem.

When you read an opinion piece, first locate the *claim* and then identify the *supporting evidence*. You should try to separate the two, because some writers mix the claim and the evidence in the same sentence. For example, consider this sentence:

> Because obesity has become such a serious health risk for our nation's children (the government estimates that 11 percent of American children are obese), our public schools should encourage children to walk or ride their bikes to school and should eliminate candy and snack food machines from school grounds.

Which part of the sentence represents the claim and which part represents the evidence? Write the claim in the first space and identify its type.

Claim: ____

____

____

Evidence: ____

____

____

Separating the claim and the evidence helps you to see the relationship between the two and to see how the claim leads to a particular kind of support. In this case, the claim of policy is supported with a good reason and with statistics.

KINDS OF EVIDENCE

After you have located the writer's argument or claim, then you can identify and evaluate the *evidence* used to support it. Writers of opinion pieces may use a single kind of evidence or they may combine various kinds. The most common kinds of evidence include facts and statistics, such as may appear in scientific studies, research reports, government-sponsored investigations, census reports, clinical tests, and so forth. These may be published either in print form or on an official website.

Evidence can also be in the form of "good reasons"—rational, logical, and plausible reasons that justify the writer's point of view and that answer the question "why." Finally, another type of evidence might be examples and observations drawn from the writer's own experience, observation, academic study, or from his or her reading. Also common in supporting claims of fact and claims of policy are quotations and testimony from experts and people in a position of authority who are able to judge a particular issue.

Here is a brief summary of the various types of evidence:

Kinds of Evidence

- *Facts and statistics:* From scientific studies and research reports
- *Good reasons:* Rational explanations that answer the question "why"
- *Examples and observations:* From the writer's own experience in the world, from observation, or from reading
- *Quotation or testimony:* The opinions of experts

EXAMINING TWO SHORT EDITORIALS: THE GREAT CELL PHONE DEBATE

Let's examine a pair of editorials on the same question: Should it be illegal to talk on your phone while driving? Each writer states his position up front with a simple "no" and "yes," but the way that each supports his position is quite different. Your appraisal of their positions might be influenced by your own experience. However, whether you regularly use your cell phone while driving and think that the practice is safe or whether you have had been involved in near accidents caused by someone talking while driving, for this exercise it is essential that you temporarily suspend your own opinion. In this way you can examine each argument *on its own merits,* not according to whether he is preaching to the choir (writing to an already converted audience). So the question is: *Objectively* evaluate each editorial to see which does a better job of defending his position.

These two editorials were published, appropriately, in *Via*, a bimonthly travel magazine published by the California State Automobile Association and sent to AAA members in Northern California, Nevada, Utah, Oregon, and Idaho. As you read both editorials, study the annotations in the margin. Here again is the question: *Should it be illegal to talk on your phone while driving?*

1—States position; if we ban cell phones, other distractions should be banned, as well.

2—First reason: cell phones help the economy, according to a Harvard study. No real savings in medical bills & property damage if cell phone usage were banned.

3—Second reason: cell phones rank only eighth among driving distractions. Ends with claim of policy: *Let's wait and get more information before we pass a law.*

No. The roads are filled with distractions and drivers doing silly things. If we ban cell phones, we should also crack down on the guy who dunks a croissant in his cappuccino while steering with his knees.

I use my phone for emergencies and urgent business, and I'm not alone. Cell phones are vital instruments of commerce. A 2002 study by the Harvard Center for Risk Analysis placed the economic value of phone calls from cars at about $43 billion per year. A cell phone ban would cut down on medical bills and property damage but the net result would be an economic wash.

I know, I know. Several studies show that talking on a phone while driving raises the risk of crashes. But studies have also concluded that the risk is small compared to other distractions. In statistics released by the University of North Carolina Highway Safety Research Center in 2003, for example, cell phones rank eighth among distractions causing crashes. Do you know what was once considered a hazard? Windshield wipers. Let's wait until we have more information before we pass a law.

—Josh Sens

1—States position; begins with illustration of friend who is a danger on the road.

2—First reason: cell phone users more impaired than drunk drivers.

3—Second reason: cell phone drivers out of sync and don't pay attention.

4—Cites examples of states where it's illegal to drive using handheld phones. Ends with claim of policy: *Urge lawmakers to pass similar pending legislation in other states.*

Yes. I have a friend who likes to call from her car to pass the time during her long commute. It probably won't surprise you to learn that many of these conversations end with my friend swearing colorfully, dropping the phone suddenly, then recounting some catastrophe she narrowly avoided.

In a study published last year by the AEI-Brookings Joint Center, a team of researchers compared the effects of driving while yapping on the phone with driving while drunk. They concluded that drivers using cell phones exhibited greater impairment than intoxicated drivers.

A 2004 National Highway Traffic Safety Administration study found that at any given daylight moment, an estimated 1.2 million drivers in the United States are on the phone. Even when these drivers aren't doing anything blatantly illegal, they're out of sync with traffic. They're the ones who send pedestrians scrambling on city streets because they never use their turn signals—that would require taking the nonphone hand off the wheel.

New Jersey, New York, and Washington, D.C., have made it illegal to use handheld mobile phones while driving, and similar legislation is pending in other states. Call your lawmakers to urge them to help get it passed. Just don't do it from your car.

—Bruce Newman

Note: AAA advises not using mobile phones while driving unless absolutely necessary.

On balance, which writer—Josh Sens or Bruce Newman—does a better job of defending his claim? (Remember, not the one you happen to agree with!) Looking at them objectively, I would argue that Newman's editorial is more convincing. Here are some reasons that occurred to me: He begins with the example of his friend, an example we can all relate to. He cites two studies that show the dangers of driving while talking. We could look up these studies online if we wanted to get more information. He cites the precedent of two states and the District of Columbia that have already made it illegal to use a cell phone while driving; other states are following suit.

Sens's piece is not nearly as carefully thought out. He opens with a comparison of cell phones to drivers doing other silly things, but it does not address the question. Talking on a cell phone is not a necessary distraction. Citing the economic value of cell phone calls ($43 billion) while driving is an interesting interpretation but still unconvincing. We do not know the total cost of medical bills and property damage from accidents caused by careless talkers, so we have to take it on faith that "the net result would be an economic wash." The tone in the first part of paragraph 3 is a bit flippant ("I know, I know"), as if Sens is weary of the usual conclusions found in "several studies" and therefore does not need to address them.

Finally, the UNC study alludes to other distractions besides cell phones, but the windshield wiper one is irrelevant; he's comparing apples and oranges. Windshield wipers are a mandatory safety feature on American cars. The claim that we need more information is evident only because of the weak evidence *against* cell phone usage that he has cited. Newman at least cites two studies that we could look up if we had the time and the interest.

THE REFUTATION

The final step in reading persuasive pieces is to look for a *refutation*, a section where the writer deals with the opposing side. Note that many editorial writers do not include a refutation, but if there is one, it might look like this: First the writer *concedes* that there is some merit to the opposing side. (After all, every question has two sides, and often more. A defender who says that there is only one side—the writer's—has produced a weak piece of writing.) The writer then takes one or two of the opposition's major arguments and *refutes* them, offering counterarguments against them. Because the cell phone editorials are so short, there is not really room for a refutation, but in many of the opinion pieces you read in Part 8, you will find a refutation, however brief, and you should include one in your own argumentative essays.

A refutation can take many forms. The writer may agree that there is some merit to the opposition but that the issue is more serious or complicated than the opponent realizes. The writer may argue that the opposing argument is somehow flawed. Finally, and probably most effective, the writer may admonish the opponent by warning of the consequences of not acting.

Or the reverse might be appropriate. For example, when George W. Bush and many Republican supporters argued for going to war to remove the Iraqi leader, Saddam Hussein, many writers, scholars, and government officials argued for *not* acting because an attack would have severe political and economic consequences.

When you read persuasive pieces, look for a refutation. The best opinion writers anticipate their opponents' objections and offer a rebuttal.

BIAS

Last, when you read opinion pieces, look for evidence of *bias*—prejudice or unfair preconceived ideas. (Obviously, complete objectivity is not humanly possible, since we are all the products of our environment, ethnic and religious heritage, social class, and the like.) By definition, an opinion writer is going to be biased, yet a writer should not come across as having an axe to grind—a particular point of view that he or she bludgeons the reader with. You can ask yourself if the writer treats the issue fairly, whether there is sufficient evidence to support the argument, and whether the writer appeals to your sense of reason or to your emotions (or perhaps to both). There is nothing wrong with a writer's appealing to the emotions, as long as you are aware that it is going on.

One final comment: You are not being wishy-washy if you read an editorial and are unable to come to a conclusion about which side you favor. Complex issues require complex analysis. And complex issues produce plenty of argument but few workable solutions. Good readers do not necessarily become immediate converts to one side or the other. Before taking a decisive stance that agrees with your general outlook and perspective, you can read material expressing other points of view. Reading the op-ed pages of the daily newspaper and looking up information on the World Wide Web and in Internet newsgroups are important ways of getting more information about the serious issues of the day.

In sum, if you know what to look for when you tackle persuasive prose, your reading will be at once more critical and more intelligent; and this awareness will serve you well for the rest of your life.

The arguments that comprise Part 8 come from many sources (newspapers, magazines, and websites) and represent geographic variety and editorial viewpoints. Some issues are represented by a single opinion piece, for example, whether torture might be ethical under some circumstances, why the media ignores violent crimes against ghetto residents, and why the concept of heroism needs to be more narrowly defined. Some issues are represented by multiple opinion pieces. You have already read two editorials on the issue of driving while using a cell phone. Another issue represented by multiple points of view (two pieces of writing and two editorial cartoons) is the immigration dilemma: Do immigrants, especially those who are poor and unskilled, result in a net benefit to our society or not? Finally, the problem of global warming is also represented by two different writers, both expressing the same point of view but in very different ways. A third point of view is demonstrated in a newspaper cartoon. On the website you can read two conflicting opinion pieces on gay marriage and two editorials on the question of whether or not Intelligent Design should be taught in high school science classes as an alternate theory to evolution.

All the opinion pieces included here treat significant issues that thoughtful citizens must wrestle with. The exercises accompanying the opinion pieces ask you to identify and to classify the writer's claim, the type of evidence used, the appeal (to reason or to emotion), the refutation (if any), and the writer's solution, if one is provided. Although no vocabulary exercises accompany these readings, you should be sure to look up unfamiliar words so that you have a full and accurate understanding of the argument presented.

PRACTICE EDITORIAL

The Ethics of Torture: Real Life Is Lived on the Slippery Slope

George Friedman

George Friedman is chairman of Strategic Forecasting, Inc., and author of a book titled *America's Secret War*. This editorial was originally published in the *Jewish World Review* (www.jewishworldreview.com).

The Issue

The issue is whether a civilized nation should engage in torture of prisoners and suspected terrorists, which has been much in the news since the overthrow of the Taliban regime in Afghanistan in 2001 and the invasion of Iraq in 2003. After stories were published about torture in Iraqi prisons such as Abu Ghraib, the debate intensified. In late 2005 President George W. Bush signed a law sponsored by Senator John McCain of Arizona banning the torture, abuse, or inhumane treatment of prisoners held in U.S. custody around the world.

After he signed the bill, however, President Bush issued a signing statement that he would not be bound by the law if it limited his ability to protect the nation or if it would impede the war on terror. It has been widely reported that Americans in Afghanistan and Iraq have relied on psychological torture (sleep deprivation, sensory deprivation, playing loud music for hours on end, and so forth), which complicates the legal definition of torture. If no physical scars result, is it nonetheless torture? How does one define torture? To what extent is torture an effective method of getting useful information from suspects? And finally, is torture consistent with the principles of a democratic society?

The Ethics of Torture: Real Life Is Lived on the Slippery Slope

George Friedman

1 Torture, once something we expected to hear about in a Third World country, has become a critical policy issue in the United States. Senior government officials are writing memos on the subject. The kind of simplistic shouting we have come to expect on all sides of all issues has come to torture. There is something absurd in thinking about torture: It is impossible not to think about it—and when you do, it is never simple.

2 Some say that torture is never justified. But assume for a moment that it were discovered that a nuclear device was planted in an American city, due to detonate in 12 hours. Someone was arrested who certainly knew where the bomb was located. He wouldn't talk. It would seem to me that any course other than torturing the man would be the height of immorality. Making an absolute argument against torture would mean that the lives of tens of thousands were worth less than the rights of this one man. I personally couldn't accept that.

3 Consider another example. Assume that a person was arrested who did not know where the bomb was, but did know the location of the man who did know and wouldn't reveal it. Would that torture be acceptable? It's a little less clear, but the same principle would hold.

4 Assume that there were 10 people who might know the location of the person who knew where the bomb was. All claimed not to know, but one certainly did. Would torturing all 10 to get the truth be justified? If torturing one person to save tens of thousands is justified, why not 10?

5 Let's say that the number were 100, and let's say that it wasn't a nuclear device—but rather there was a rumor that a car bomb might have been planted. Would torturing all 100 people be justified to save several hundred?

6 Going further down the slippery slope, let's say that there was a group of terrorists who were thought to be planning a strike. Would torturing anyone captured to find others be acceptable?

7 In reality, the circumstances in which torture takes place are never clear-cut. Life is lived further down the slippery slope. The problem with the slope is that, eventually, you slide down it to become the monster you were supposed to be fighting. On the other hand, to simply assert that torture is never justified is morally absurd. Surely in the first case, torture is obligatory. If you are willing to let a city die rather than torture a single person, you have become a moral monster just as surely as if you were randomly torturing innocent people.

Connecting Grammar to Writing

The first part of paragraph 8 contains a series of four short independent parallel clauses. The repetition of "They have to . . ." is both pleasing to the ear and lends weight to his observations about the "slippery slope" he describes.

8 Those who are charged with keeping the United States secure live on that slippery slope. They have to make decisions. They have to act on uncertainties. They have to live in a world of uncertain facts and justified terrors. They know that whatever decision they make will be reviewed meticulously by others who did not bear that burden. It is easy to be moral when you have no obligations, no

responsibilities and no one depending on you. It is much more difficult to know how to make moral decisions in the real world of U.S. intelligence and security.

9 The debate over torture has developed a cartoon-like quality. On the one side, the view is, "Rip their guts out. If the detainees turn out not to know anything, they should be grateful to have served a just cause." On the other side, there are those who condemn torture in all its forms everywhere. I wonder if they would hold such a view if torture could save the life of one of their children.

10 In the philosophy class, the newspaper column and the coffee shop, these are interesting topics to discuss. Out in the war, where men and women make snap decisions that could affect all of our lives, things are more difficult and opaque. I would not like to be a man called upon to draft a memo on torture that others must follow. Nor would I care to be a man who had to make a decision on whether to torture someone. But I have little respect for the simplistic arguments—on both sides—that have framed the torture issue. Real life is much more complicated than that.

EXERCISES

A. Identifying the Claim

1. In your own words, write Friedman's central claim or proposition. Also indicate the paragraph(s) where the claim is located.

____

____

____

____

2. Then decide if the claim is a claim of fact, a claim of value, or a claim of policy. Remember that an argument may have a secondary claim as well.

____

B. Locating Evidence

1. One piece of evidence is listed for you. List three other major pieces of evidence that the writer uses to support the claim. Then characterize each piece of evidence according to whether it represents facts and statistics, good reasons, examples and observations, or quotation or testimony.

a. Torture might be justified to get information from a suspect who knows where a nuclear device is planted that might wipe out an entire city. [hypothetical example]

b. ______________________________

____

____

c. ______________________________

____

____

d. ______________________________

____

2. In structuring the argument, does Friedman appeal more to our reason, to our emotion, or to a combination of reason and emotion?

____

C. Identifying a Refutation and the Solution

1. Write the refutation, if there is one, in the space provided.

____

____

2. Does Friedman provide a solution to the problem of torture? If so, write it in the space provided. Be sure to use your own words.

____

____

DISCUSSION QUESTION

What is your opinion of the use of torture to keep the country safe? Are Friedman's hypothetical examples about saving a city from a nuclear attack by torturing one individual or ten individuals or 100 individuals compellingly realistic or not?

READING

Editorials for Evaluation

Black, Dead, and Invisible
Bob Herbert

Bob Herbert is a syndicated columnist for *The New York Times*, where this editorial was first published. The subject is the degree to which the media ignore violence against our youth in poor neighborhoods.

Residents of our cities' poor neighborhoods, especially the young, are so accustomed to violence and to the constant presence of death that they cannot dream about their future, assuming perhaps that they could themselves be a target at any time. Elsewhere, the media have been accused of obsessively airing stories about white victims who were either killed or missing (for example, JonBenet Ramsey, Chandra Levy, Laci Peterson, Natalee Holloway) while ignoring stories about similar tragedies that have befallen inner-city youth.

Black, Dead, and Invisible
Bob Herbert

1 I once had a young black girl, whose brother had been murdered, tell me she was too old to dream. She was 12.

2 I remember a teenager in South-Central Los Angeles a few years ago saying, in a discussion about his peers, "Some of us don't last too long."

3 Don't bother cueing the violins. This is an old story. There's no shock value and hardly any news value in yet another black or brown kid going down for the count. Burying the young has long since become routine in poor black and Latino neighborhoods. Nobody gets real excited about it. I find that peculiar, but there's a lot about the world that I find peculiar.

4 Tafare Berryman was born on Feb. 16, 1983, in Kings County Hospital in Brooklyn. He debuted at 9 pounds 7 ounces. His mother said he was perfect, and she was still saying it this week as she prepared for his funeral. Tafare grew, as they say, prodigiously. When he was murdered early last Sunday morning, just

five weeks short of his college graduation, he was six feet seven inches tall and weighed 240 pounds.

5 His massive size was no defense against the bullet that came out of the predawn darkness. It was like an instant replay of all the bullets over all the years that have ended so many young lives for no good reason whatsoever.

6 The fact that he had stayed out of trouble, and that his parents were strict, and that he'd graduated from high school in three years and was serious about his college work—none of that afforded him any protection, either. The fact that he was a popular basketball player at the C. W. Post campus of Long Island University, and that his classmates, teachers and coaches all swear he was a lovely person, counted for nothing. There are a lot of good kids who don't last too long.

7 The shooting happened on a street in Nassau County on Long Island. There had been a fight at a club, and a friend of Tafare's suffered a knife wound to the head. The two young men left the club in a car, with the friend driving.

8 After a couple of miles, they had to stop because the friend was bleeding profusely. As they were switching seats, with Tafare climbing into the driver's seat, a car approached. A shot was fired, maybe two shots, and Tafare's life was over. His friend was not hit. The police said they did not think that Tafare had been involved in the fight and that the gunman might have mistaken him for his friend, or someone else.

9 Tafare's mother, Dawn Thompson, who lives in Brooklyn, got a call about 6 o'clock in the morning. All she was told was that her son had been shot. She and three carloads of relatives rushed to Long Island. In the town of Long Beach, the family was given directions to the morgue.

10 "He was laid down with his eyes open and his mouth open, like he was saying, 'Oh, God!'" said Ms. Thompson. She began to sob. "He was just tall and stretched out. He's very tall, you know. And his eyes were open like he was looking for somebody. And I started crying. And I said: 'Yes, that's my son. That's my son. He's dead.'"

11 When I was growing up, I didn't worry about getting shot or getting stabbed, and, frankly, I thought I would live forever. But there have been many cultural changes since then. I've talked to hundreds of youngsters over the years who have either witnessed homicides or been very close emotionally to young people who had died violently.

12 Entertainers sing ecstatically of rape and homicide, and rappers like 50 Cent and The Game brag about the number of bullets their bodies have absorbed (at least 14 between them). Street gangs have spread from the cities to the suburbs and beyond, moving into those places in the hearts of young people that have been vacated by parents, especially fathers. Guns in some neighborhoods are easier to get than schoolbooks.

13 None of this is new. Two days before Tafare Berryman was killed, a 17-year-old freshman named Sequoia Thomas was shot to death outside Jamaica High

School in Queens, apparently by an acquaintance. Her last words were: "Help me. Help me."

14 The big shots have other things on their minds. In New York there's a football stadium that the power brokers want to build. In Washington, the focus of presidents of the United States, past and present, has been on who would get to go to the pope's funeral. In Los Angeles the other day, the black celebrity elite turned out en masse to profile at Johnnie Cochran's funeral.

15 Youngsters dead and dying? Nobody of importance is much interested in that.

EXERCISES

A. Identifying the Claim

1. In your own words, write Herbert's central claim or proposition. Also indicate the paragraph(s) where the claim is located.

2. Then decide if the claim is a claim of fact, a claim of value, or a claim of policy. Remember that an argument may have a secondary claim as well.

B. Locating Evidence

1. State three primary pieces of evidence that Herbert uses to support his claim. Then characterize that evidence according to whether it represents facts and statistics, good reasons, examples and observations, or quotation or testimony.

   a.

   b.

   c.

2. In structuring the argument, does Herbert appeal more to our reason, to our emotion, or to a combination of reason and emotion?

C. Identifying a Refutation and the Solution

1. Write the refutation, if there is one, in the space provided.

 ____

2. Does Herbert provide a solution to the problem of violence against urban youth? If so, write it in the space provided. Be sure to use your own words.

 ____

 ____

DISCUSSION QUESTION

If Herbert's contention that the media ignores stories of violence against black and brown youth is true, do you accept his argument that they do so because there is no shock value in these stories any longer and no one gets excited about these tragedies? Are there other reasons that might account for the media's lack of interest in such stories?

Hero Inflation

Nicholas Thompson

Nicholas Thompson has written articles on politics, technology, and the law for a variety of publications, and he has also been a commentator for numerous TV and radio stations including Fox News, MSNBC, CNN, NPR, and NBC's *Today Show*. This editorial was first published in the *Boston Globe*.

The Issue

In the aftermath of the September 2001 terrorist attacks, journalists and media pundits representing every segment of the political spectrum sought to interpret this terrible event and its many repercussions. One repercussion was application of the word *hero* to both the World Trade Center victims and their rescuers. Thompson discusses the concept of heroism and why it should not be applied to tragic victims.

Hero Inflation

Nicholas Thompson

1 Since Sept. 11, American has become a nation of heroes. Stevie Wonder, Willie Nelson, and Bruce Springsteen played a "tribute to heroes" that raised

$150 million for victims of the attacks. Firefighters and rescue workers have earned acclaim for heroism, but so has nearly everyone who directly suffered on that horrible morning.

2 "The fatalities of that day are all heroes and deserve to be honored as such," said Thomas Davis, a Republican congressman from Virginia, while successfully working to obtain a full burial plot in Arlington National Cemetery for the former National Guardsman who piloted the plane that crashed into the Pentagon.

3 The victims of the terrorist attacks deserve tremendous sympathy. They died tragically and often horrifically. But not all died in a way that people have previously described as heroic. And even the heroism attributed to the rescue workers stems as much from the country's needs in responding to the disaster as from what actually happened in the collapsing buildings.

4 It is long overdue that Americans appreciate their public servants. It is also necessary to honor those who died simply for being in America. But changing the definition of hero to accommodate tragic victims may actually weaken us by diminishing the idea of role models who perform truly extraordinary acts.

5 To the ancient Greeks, "heroes," such as Hercules or Odysseus, performed great deeds, frequently challenged the gods, and were immortalized after death. Heroes lived in times and realms halfway between gods and men and often were deemed to have brought prosperity to the people who praised them.

6 That definition gradually evolved in this country as Americans adapted it to the people most respected here. Heroes won that standing by courageously transforming the world—Martin Luther King Jr. or Mother Teresa for example. Or heroes could earn that title simply for incredible acts of bravery several steps above the call of duty—Oskar Schindler, a young girl who plunges into a dangerous icy river and saves a stranger's life, or maybe someone from battle such as Henry Johnson who fought off 20 Germans with a knife and a couple of hand grenades in World War I.

7 Roughly speaking, American heroes first needed bravery. But bravery is not sufficient because evil people can be brave, too. So, the second trait in American historical lore is nobility. Heroes must work toward goals that we approve of. Heroes must show ingenuity. Lastly, they should be successful. Rosa Parks wouldn't have been nearly as much of a hero if she hadn't sparked a boycott that then sparked a movement. Charles Lindbergh wouldn't have been nearly as heroized if the Spirit of St. Louis had crashed into the Atlantic, or if scores of other people had made the flight before.

8 Recently though, a fourth trait—victimhood—seems to have become as important as anything else in determining heroic status. Today heroes don't have to do anything; they just need to be noble victims.

9 For example, if J. Joseph Moakley was known at all nationally, it was as a hard-working Massachusetts congressman who almost always followed the Democratic Party line. But when he was stricken with leukemia, he became a national hero, earning praise from the president and seemingly everyone else in Washington. He

Connecting Grammar to Writing

In paragraph 8, Thompson separates the single-word appositive *victimhood* from the rest of the sentence with dashes. He could have used commas or even parentheses. Study this little useful saying and then explain why dashes best suit his purpose in writing: "Parentheses whisper, commas state, and dashes shout."

was cited from the balcony, traditionally the spot reserved for heroes, by President Bush during the State of the Union message. (This paper even wrote about a letter received at his house addressed simply to "Joe Moakley, Hero.") His death earned almost as much newspaper coverage as the death this year of the 98-year-old Mike Mansfield, a giant of the U.S. Senate who served as majority leader longer than anyone in history and initiated the Senate Watergate Committee.

10 But that shouldn't surprise us. Books about overcoming adversity clog the bestseller lists, and perseverance during illness—any illness—is grist for the heroic mill. If John F. Kennedy wanted to run for president today, he might constantly mention his struggle against Addison's disease as opposed to emphasizing his exploits on his PT boat in the Pacific.

11 Of course, victimhood hasn't completely eclipsed action in our national selection of heroes. The biggest heroes have many of the virtues of traditional heroes but also are victims—for example, the 350 firefighters who died in the World Trade Center and who now stand atop our national pantheon. These men have been honored everywhere from the current cover of *Sports Illustrated* to a recent best-selling comic book that makes them into superheroes. They even inspired thousands of Halloween costumes.

12 But although the firemen who died in the Trade Center bravely fought the flames and led the evacuation, they did so as workers doing the best they could in their jobs—people trained by the city to rush into buildings and save others. Firefighters chose a very worthy line of work, but to die while doing it isn't completely different from, say, the computer programmers who stayed in the Trade Center and perished while desperately trying to preserve the data backing people's financial portfolios. Just after Christmas, a New Bedford policeman carried a woman out of a burning building. "I'm not a hero," he said upon emerging outside. "I'm just a worker."

13 There were no doubt some unconditional individual heroes on Sept. 11, including some of the people on United Flight 93 who fought the hijackers and individual firefighters and police who went well beyond the requirements of the job, but most of the other people who died in the attacks were simply victims, much like the tens of thousands of innocent people killed in home fires, or on highways, every year.

14 They deserve our grief and their families and communities merit great sympathy. But it's time for a little more perspective when Congress almost unanimously passes a bill called the "True American Heroes Act" awarding Congressional Gold Medals—the highest honor that body can give—to every government official who died in the attacks, including Port Authority employees who were killed in their World Trade Center offices.

15 Of course, some of the hero-making is born of necessity. In the aftermath of the attacks, we needed to turn the narrative away from the horror of the images on television and our clear vulnerability. As soon as the buildings came down, we needed to build the victims up. It also helped to reclassify everyone on the opposing side

as incorrigibly demonic and everyone on our side as paragons of virtue. After the 11th, the first part was easy and the second park took a little bit of work.

16 That wasn't of course a wholly bad thing. The inflation of the heroism of Sept. 11 surely helped the nation recover and pull together. Moreover, America probably didn't have enough heroes. An August *U.S. News and World Report* poll revealed that more than half of all Americans didn't consider a single public figure heroic. Right before the attacks, Anheuser Busch planned an ad campaign titled "Real American Heroes" that, among other things, saluted the inventor of the foot-long hot dog.

17 But just because the sometimes false focus on heroism helped the nation salve its wounds doesn't make such attitudes wholly good either. Heroes often end up as role models, a task not well suited for victims. Moreover, by lowering the bar for heroism, we cheapen the word and, in some ways, the exploits of people who have earned the right to be called that in the past.

18 Finally, when people earn classification as heroes, those acting in their names often try to take it a step too far. Last month, for example, the federal government announced plans to disburse about as much money this year to families of attack victims as the entire international aid community has slated to give to Afghanistan over the next decade—and that money will come in addition to incredible amounts of charitable aid also already raised. Nevertheless, a spokesman for a victims' lobby group immediately dissented, demanding more. "We are exploring our legal options and lining up attorneys," he said. Almost no criticism could be found in response.

19 Emerson once wrote that "every hero becomes a bore at last." Well, at least their lawyers and lobbyists do.

Source: From Nicholas Thompson, "Hero Inflation," *Boston Globe*, January 13, 2002. Used with permission. www.copyright.com.

EXERCISES

A. Identifying the Claim

1. In your own words, write Thompson's central claim or proposition. Also indicate the paragraph(s) where the claim is located.

___

___

___

2. Then decide if the claim is a claim of fact, a claim of value, or a claim of policy.

___

READING

B. Locating Evidence

1. One piece of evidence is listed for you. List three other major pieces of evidence that the writer uses to support the claim. Then characterize each piece of evidence according to whether it represents facts and statistics, good reasons, examples and observations, or quotation or testimony.

   a. Applying the word *hero* to victims changes the definitions that have served us well since ancient Greece and throughout American history. A true hero in American culture has traditionally been a person who acted bravely to successfully change the world, who acted with nobility, and who showed ingenuity in his or her actions. Today we apply the word *heroes* to noble victims. [examples and observations]

   b. ______________________________

   ____

   c. ______________________________

   ____

   ____

   d. ______________________________

   ____

   ____

   ____

2. In structuring the argument, does Thompson appeal more to our reason, to our emotion, or to a combination of reason and emotion?

   ____

C. Identifying a Refutation and the Solution

1. Thompson intersperses refutations throughout the selection. Try to find three examples and write them in the space provided.

   a. ______________________________

   ____

   ____

   b. ______________________________

   ____

c.

2. Does Thompson provide a solution to the problem of calling people heroes? If so, write it in the space provided. Be sure to use your own words.

DISCUSSION QUESTION

Thompson argues that the term *hero* is used too loosely. What is your opinion on this issue? Can you think of a person who was designated as a hero who could be more accurately described as a tragic victim? Is Thompson's definition of a *hero* too narrow?

The Immigration Dilemma: Editorials and Cartoons

BACKGROUND READING ON THE IMMIGRATION ISSUE

Benefit and Burden

Sonia Nazario

Enrique's Journey, by *Los Angeles Times* journalist Sonia Nazario, is subtitled *The Story of a Boy's Dangerous Odyssey to Reunite with His Mother*. Nazario recounts a little-known aspect of immigration: increasing numbers of mothers from Mexico and Central America who leave their children with relatives and cross the border illegally to find work in the United States. The psychological impact on the children is enormous. Enrique, the boy referred to in the book's title, is from Honduras. When Enrique was 7 years old, his mother, Lourdes, left him and his sister and went first to Los Angeles and later to North Carolina to find work. At the age of 15, Enrique decided to find his mother, and after a dozen or so attempts, he finally successfully crossed the border and located her. This excerpt comes at the end of the book, in which Nazario objectively assesses the impact of immigration on American society—the benefits and the burdens—and comes to a conclusion about which is greater.

This material is intended for background reading only; no exercise material follows it. Read it carefully, as Nazario's discussion will help you analyze and evaluate the editorials and cartoons that follow it.

Benefit and Burden

Sonia Nazario

1 Some opposition to immigration is racism, a resistance to change, a discomfort with having people around who don't speak the same language or have similar customs. Yet some of the negative consequences of immigration are real, and are becoming increasingly evident as more women and children arrive.

2 Overall, the NRC[1] said, immigrants use more government services than the native-born. They have more children, and therefore more youngsters in public schools. This is especially true for immigrants from Latin America, whose households are nearly twice as large as those of the native-born. It will cost the government two and a half times as much per household to educate their children, the study found.

3 Immigrants are poorer, have lower incomes, and qualify for more state and local services and assistance. Immigrant women receive publicly funded prenatal and obstetric care. Their U.S.-born children are entitled to welfare, food stamps, and Medicaid. Compared to native households, immigrant families from Latin America are nearly three times as likely to receive government welfare payments.

4 Because immigrants earn less money and are less likely to own property, they pay lower taxes. Some immigrants receive their salaries in cash and pay no taxes at all. In all, immigrants and their native-born children pay a third less tax per capita than others in the United States, the NRC study found. Households headed by immigrants from Latin America pay half of what natives pay in state and federal taxes.

5 The fiscal burden to taxpayers is greatest in immigrant-heavy states such as California, where an estimated one in four illegal immigrants live, and where half of all children have immigrant parents. Local and state governments shoulder the biggest cost generated by immigrants: public education. An average nonimmigrant household in California paid $1,178 more in state and local taxes than the value of the services they received. Conversely, immigrant households paid $3,463 less than the value of the services they received, the NRC found.

6 The crush of immigrants has hastened the deterioration of many public services, namely schools, hospitals, and state jails and prisons. Classrooms are crowded. Hospital emergency rooms have been forced to close, in part because so many poor, uninsured, nonpaying patients, including immigrants, are provided with free mandated care. In Los Angeles County, jails have had to release prisoners early because of overcrowding caused, in part, by criminal immigrants. A 2001 University of Arizona study found that in the twenty-eight southwestern border counties of Arizona, California, New Mexico, and Texas, the cost of arresting, prosecuting, and jailing illegal immigrants who commit crimes amounted to as much as $125 million per year. The Center for Immigration Studies, which seeks reduced immigration levels, found that in 2002, nationwide, households headed by illegal immigrants used $26.3 billion in government services and paid $16 billion in taxes.

7 Those hardest hit by the influx of immigrants are disadvantaged native-born minorities who don't have a high school degree—namely, African Americans and previous waves of Latino immigrants. They must compete for the same low-end jobs immigrants take.

8 Wages for high school dropouts, who make up one in fourteen native workers, have dropped in recent years. Between 1980 and 2000, a Harvard University study found, the influx of immigrant workers to the United States cut wages for native workers with no high school diploma by 7.4 percent, or $1,800 on an average salary of $25,000.

9 Sometimes, whole industries switch from native to immigrant workers. In 1993, I looked at efforts to unionize Latino janitors in Los Angeles. Previously, the jobs had been largely held by African Americans, who had succeeded in obtaining increased wages and health benefits. Cleaning companies busted their union, then brought in Latino immigrant workers at half the wages and no benefits.

10 In 1996, I went to an ordinary block of two-bedroom homes in East Los Angeles to understand why nearly a third of California Latinos had supported Proposition 187, a voter initiative to bar illegal immigrants from schools, hospitals, and most public assistance. The measure passed and was later struck down by the courts.

11 For residents of the block, support for Prop 187 wasn't a nativist reaction or scapegoating in tight economic times. They said ill feelings toward illegal immigrants were grounded in how the newcomers had affected their neighborhood and their lives. For them, the influx had meant not cut-rate nannies and gardeners, but heightened job competition, depressed wages, overcrowded government services, and a reduced quality of life.

12 The newcomers who moved into the neighborhood were poor. Residents estimated that the block's population had tripled since 1970; up to seventeen immigrants were jammed into one small stucco house. Some lived in garages without plumbing, using lawns to relieve themselves. The second- and third-generation Latinos on the block felt it was their working-class neighborhoods that bore the brunt of a wave of impoverished, unskilled workers. Immigrants were arriving at an unsettling pace, crowding them out of jobs and lowering wages. Immigrants weren't just taking jobs natives didn't covet; they competed for work as painters, mechanics, and construction workers.

13 In the 1980s, the RAND Corporation, a Santa Monica think tank, found that the benefits of immigration outweighed the costs. By 1997, they had reversed course. The economy wasn't producing new jobs for high school dropouts, an increasing proportion of whom—roughly half—were unemployed. RAND said some native adults had become unemployed because of immigrant competition. They recommended the country slash legal immigration to 1970s levels.

14 Some immigration experts question whether it makes sense to allow so many immigrants with low levels of education from poor, underdeveloped countries when the United States needs to compete globally in industries requiring high levels of education, creativity, and know-how. Mexican immigrants arrive with an average of five to nine years of education.

15 Other experts focus on how adding more than a million immigrants a year to the United States' population affects overcrowding of parks, freeways, and the environment. Immigration accounted for more than half of the 33 million new U.S. residents in the 1990s. With nearly 300 million people, the United States has almost five times as many residents as when Ellis Island welcomed new arrivals.

16 In Los Angeles County, the surge in immigrants helped cause the poverty rate to nearly double, to 25 percent, between 1980 and 1997. The effect, at least in the short term: a sea of poor and working-class neighborhoods amid islands of affluence.

Schizophrenic Policies

17 In the end any calculus of the benefits and burdens of immigration depends on who you are. People who own businesses and commercial interests that use cheap immigrant labor benefit the most from immigrants like Enrique and Lourdes. They get a ready supply of compliant low-cost workers. Other winners are couples who hire immigrants to care for their children and drive them to school, tend to their lawns, clean their houses, and wash their cars.

18 High school dropouts have the most to lose. So do residents of immigrant-heavy states such as California, where an estimated third of illegal immigrants live, because services immigrants use disproportionately, such as public schools, are funded with local and state taxes.

19 Polls show Americans in recent years have hardened their views of immigrants, particularly those who are in the country illegally. A growing proportion—two thirds, compared with half in the mid-1970s—thinks the government should reduce immigration from current levels.

20 Many immigration observers believe U.S. officials have pursued a purposefully schizophrenic immigration policy. The government has added Border Patrol agents along the nation's southwestern border and walled off seventy-six miles of that divide. Politicians talk tough about catching illegal immigrants. Meanwhile, critics say, efforts to enforce many of the nation's immigration laws are weak to nonexistent.

21 Labor-intensive industries—agriculture, construction, food processing, restaurants, domestic help agencies—want cheap immigrant labor to bolster their bottom lines. Whenever immigration authorities make even cursory attempts to enforce a 1986 law that allows employers to be fined up to $10,000 for each illegal immigrant they hire, businesses—onion farmers in Georgia, meatpacking firms in the Midwest—bitterly complain. Fines on businesses and raids by immigration enforcement agents have gone from sporadic to virtually nil. Similarly, a pilot project allowing some employers to check the immigration status of job applicants via telephone has never expanded nationally and remains voluntary.

22 In essence, politicians have put a lock on the front door while swinging the back door wide open. A crackdown on the U.S.-Mexico border, begun in

1993, was designed to shift immigrant traffic to more remote parts of the border, where Border Patrol agents have a tactical advantage. Since the buildup began, the number of agents patrolling the border and the amount of money spent on enforcement have both tripled, according to a 2002 study by the Public Policy Institute of California (PPIC). Yet there is no evidence, the PPIC concluded, that the strategy has worked. In fact, the number of immigrants in the United States illegally has grown more quickly since the border buildup began.

23 Many outcomes of the new strategy have been unintended—and negative, the PPIC says. More illegal immigrants now use smugglers (89 percent, compared to 70 percent before). Immigrants, particularly those from Mexico, once returned home after brief work stints in the United States. Today, the increasing difficulty and cost of crossing means more come and stay. The new strategy has also resulted in more than three hundred deaths each year, as migrants are forced to cross in areas that are less populated, more isolated, and more geographically hostile.

24 Some priests in Mexico whose churches are located near the rails are so sure the flow of Central American migrants will be neverending that they have recently built their own migrant shelters. As long as the grinding poverty such as Enrique's mother lived in exists, priests in these churches believe, people will try to get to the United States, even if they must take enormous risks to get there.

25 In the United States, many immigration experts have concluded that the only effective strategy for change is to bolster the economies of immigrant-sending countries. Hondurans point out a few things that would help bring that about. Forgiving foreign debt would allow more of their country's resources to go into development. Implementing U.S. trade policies that give a strong preference to goods from immigrant-sending countries would help spur growth in certain industries, such as textiles, that employ women in Honduras. Others believe the United States, notoriously stingy among industrialized nations in per capita gifts of foreign aid, should boost donations. Individuals, Hondurans note, can support nongovernmental organizations that encourage job-creating small businesses or improve the availability of education in Honduras, where 12 percent of children never attend a school.

26 Most immigrants would rather stay in their home countries with their extended families. Who wants to leave home and everything he or she knows for something foreign, not knowing if he or she will ever return? Not many.

27 What would ensure that more women can stay home—with their children, where they want to be? María Isabel's mother, Eva, says, simply. "What would it take to keep people from leaving? There would have to be jobs. Jobs that pay okay. That's all."

---

[1]National Research Council.

Can You Say, "Bienvenidos"?

Eugene Robinson

Eugene Robinson is an associate editor of the *Washington Post.* He writes on the *Post's* opinion page, chiefly about politics and culture. Robinson wrote this editorial during the spring of 2006 when thousands of immigrants—both legal and illegal—demonstrated in American cities to be recognized and protested against tough proposals to curb illegal immigration. Among the proposals were plans to build a fence several hundred miles long at the U.S.-Mexico border, branding illegal immigrants felons and shipping them home, or declaring immigrants "guest workers," which would allow them to work for a limited time before being required to return home. There are currently an estimated 11–12 million illegal immigrants now living in the United States.

Can You Say, "Bienvenidos"?

Eugene Robinson

1 White Americans, and black Americans too, are going to have to get used to sharing this country—sharing it fully—with brown Americans. Things are going to be different. Deal with it.

2 The most important legacy of the histrionic debate over immigration reform will not be any piece of legislation, whether enlightened or medieval. It will be the big demonstrations held in cities throughout the country over the past few weeks—mass protests staged by and for a minority whose political ambition is finally catching up with its burgeoning size. In the metaphorical sense, Latinos have arrived.

3 In the physical sense, of course, Latinos have been arriving for many years, and in huge numbers. In some cities they have sought and achieved political power—if there were such a thing as "the capital of Latin America," arguably it would be Miami. As a presence in national politics, however, Latinos have been much less influential than their weight in the population would suggest.

4 That just began to change.

5 Half a million people marched in Los Angeles, another half-million in Dallas, and hundreds of thousands elsewhere last week. The fact that so many undocumented immigrants came out of the shadows, giving up their anonymity to denounce legislation threatening their interests, wasn't the most remarkable thing. More significant was that so many fully enfranchised Latino citizens joined them.

6 What happens next won't look like the civil rights struggle that African Americans waged—the nation's two biggest minorities have different histories and face different issues, and anyway it's a different era. I doubt that any single Latino leader will emerge, or even any single leadership group. And the advance

won't be linear or continuous, because much of the Latino population lacks full citizenship and thus can't vote.

7 When I was in Phoenix two weeks ago, I talked to advocates of a round-'em-up, kick-'em-out policy on illegal immigration who predicted the protests would spark an Anglo backlash. Maybe it will, but everyone should remember that demography is destiny: Given the youthfulness of the Latino population, xenophobes could construct an Adobe Curtain along the length of the Mexican border next week (they'd probably use Mexican labor) and the political strength of Latinos in the United States would still continue to grow.

8 There are economists, I realize, who argue that illegal immigration—mostly from Mexico—has depressed wages for unskilled labor, to the detriment of low-income, native-born African Americans and whites.

9 Other economists disagree, and in any case the effect is somewhere between negligible and small. There's no reason employers can't be required to pay a living wage to every janitor, whether his name is John or Juan.

10 But I don't think the immigration debate is about economics anyway. It's about culture and it's about fear.

11 Among other things, it's about this voice-mail message: "*Para continuar en español, oprima el numero* 2. To continue in Spanish, press 2."

12 Many Anglos in Phoenix and elsewhere were surprised by the size of the protests three weeks ago, but the demonstrations were coordinated and publicized in the open, on Spanish-language radio. Latino immigrants in this recent wave, whether they intend to stay permanently or just work for a while and go home, are learning English but also keeping their Spanish—and the fact is the United States now has a de facto second language. That seems to frighten a lot of people.

13 Some academics, such as the Harvard University political scientist Samuel P. Huntington, have warned that unchecked Latino immigration is bringing with it alien cultural values—that somehow the Anglo-Saxon-ness of the country is threatened. But that ignores the fact that America has been shaped by successive waves of immigration going all the way back to the Pilgrims, and to the first African slaves. The country has proved that inclusiveness, adaptability and change are the keys to unparalleled success. Why on earth pull up the drawbridge now?

14 Maybe the real fear is more visceral than that. Maybe it's that you don't have to extrapolate immigration and fertility rates very far into the future to see an America in which minorities—Hispanic, African and Asian Americans—are a majority. To put it another way: an America in which whites join the rest of us as just another minority. That's already the case in our two most populous states, California and Texas, according to the Census Bureau, with others including New York, Arizona and Florida likely to follow soon.

15 Don't freak out, folks. It's not the end of the world. You might ask your black neighbors for advice on how to cope.

EXERCISES

A. Identifying the Claim

1. In your own words, write Robinson's central claim or proposition. Also indicate the paragraph(s) where the claim is located.

___

___

___

2. Then decide if the claim is a claim of fact, a claim of value, or a claim of policy.

___

B. Locating Evidence

1. One piece of evidence is listed for you. List three other major pieces of evidence that the writer uses to support the claim. Then characterize each piece of evidence according to whether it represents facts and statistics, good reasons, examples and observations, or quotation or testimony.

   a. Millions of undocumented workers who demonstrated in American cities were joined by legal immigrants, which is a testimony to their growing political and economic influence in American life. [fact, observation]

   b. ___

   ___

   c. ___

   d. ___

   ___

   e. ___

   ___

   ___

2 In structuring the argument, does Robinson appeal more to our reason, to our emotion, or to a combination of reason and emotion?

___

C. Identifying a Refutation and the Solution

1. Write the refutation, if there is one, in the space provided.

____

____

____

2. Does Robinson provide a solution to the problem of torture? If so, write it in the space provided. Be sure to use your own words.

____

____

____

____

____

Conspiracy Against Assimilation

Robert J. Samuelson

The winner of many journalism awards, Robert J. Samuelson writes a weekly column for the *Washington Post,* and he serves as a contributing editor to *Newsweek* as well. He writes on a variety of political, economic, and social issues.

Conspiracy Against Assimilation

Robert J. Samuelson

1 It's all about assimilation—or should be. One of America's glories is that it has assimilated many waves of immigrants. Outsiders have become insiders. But it hasn't been easy. Every new group has struggled: Germans, Irish, Jews and Italians. All have encountered economic hardship, prejudice and discrimination. The story of U.S. immigration is often ugly. If today's immigration does not end in assimilation, it will be a failure. By this standard, I think the major contending sides in the present bitter debate are leading us astray. Their proposals, if adopted, would frustrate assimilation.

2 On the one hand, we have the "cop" school. It adamantly opposes amnesty and would make being here illegally a felony rather than a lesser crime. It toughens a variety of penalties against illegal immigrants. Somehow, elevating the

seriousness of the crime would deprive them of jobs, and then illegal immigrants would return to Mexico, El Salvador or wherever. This is a pipe dream; the numbers are simply too large.

3 But it is a pipe dream that, if pursued, would inflict enormous social damage. The mere threat of a crackdown stigmatizes much of the Hispanic population—whether they're legal or illegal immigrants; or whether they've been here for generations. (In 2004 there were 40 million Hispanics, says the Pew Hispanic Center; about 55 percent were estimated to be native-born, 25 percent legal immigrants and 20 percent illegal immigrants.) People feel threatened and insulted. Who wouldn't?

4 On the other hand we have the "guest worker" advocates. They want 400,000 or more new foreign workers annually. This would supposedly curtail illegal immigration—people who now sneak into the country could get work permits—and also cure "shortages" of unskilled American workers. Everyone wins.

5 Not really.

6 For starters, the term guest worker is a misnomer. Whatever the rules, most guest workers would not leave. The pull of U.S. wages (on average, almost five times what can be earned in Mexico) is too great. Moreover, there's no general shortage of unskilled workers. In March, the unemployment rate of high-school dropouts 25 years and older was 7 percent; since 1996, it has been below 6 percent in only two months. By contrast, the unemployment rate of college graduates in March was 2.2 percent. Given the glut of unskilled workers relative to demand, their wages often lag behind inflation. From 2002 to 2004, consumer prices rose 5.5 percent. Median wages rose 4.8 percent for janitors, 4.3 percent for landscapers and not at all for waitresses.

7 Guest worker advocates don't acknowledge that poor, unskilled immigrants—whether legal or illegal—create huge social costs. Every year the Census Bureau issues a report on "Income, Poverty and Health Insurance Coverage." Here's what the 2004 report shows:

- Since 1990 the number of Hispanics with incomes below the government's poverty line has risen 52 percent; that's almost all (92 percent) of the increase in poor people.
- Among children, disparities are greater. Over the same period, 43 percent more Hispanic children are living in poverty while the numbers of black and non-Hispanic white children in poverty declined 16.9 percent and 18.5 percent, respectively.
- Hispanics account for most (61 percent) of the increase of Americans without health insurance since 1990. The overall increase was 11.1 million; Hispanics, 6.7 million.

8 By most studies, poor immigrants pay less in taxes than they use in government services. As these social costs have risen, so has the backlash. Already, there's a coalition of Mayors and Executives for Immigration Reform. It includes 63 cities,

counties and towns, headed by Republicans and Democrats, ranging from Cook County, Ill. (population: 5.3 million) to Gilliam County, Ore. (population: 1,817). Coalition members want the federal government to reimburse their extra costs.

9 We have a conspiracy against assimilation. One side would offend and ostracize much of the Hispanic community. The other would encourage mounting social and economic costs. The result either way is a more polarized society.

10 On immigration, I am an optimist. We are basically a decent, open and tolerant nation. Americans respect hard work and achievement. That's why assimilation has triumphed. But I am not a foolish optimist. Assimilation requires time and the right conditions. It cannot succeed if we constantly flood the country with new, poor immigrants or embark on a vendetta against those already here.

11 I have argued that our policies should recognize these realities. Curb illegal immigration with true border barriers. Provide legal status (call it amnesty or whatever)—first, work permits, then citizenship—for most illegal immigrants already here. Remove the job lure by imposing harsh fines against employers who hire *new* illegal immigrants. Reject big guest worker programs.

12 It's sometimes said that today's Hispanics will resemble yesterday's Italians. Although they won't advance as rapidly as some other groups of more skilled immigrants, they'll still move into the mainstream. Many have—and will. But the overall analogy is a stretch, according to a new study, "Italians Then, Mexicans Now," by sociologist Joel Perlmann of Bard College. Since 1970, wages of Mexican immigrants compared with those of native whites have declined. By contrast, wages of Italians and Poles who arrived early in the last century rose over time. For the children of immigrants, gaps are also wide. Second-generation Italians and Poles typically earned 90 percent or more compared to native whites. For second-generation Mexican Americans, the similar figure is 75 percent.

13 One big difference between then and now: Immigration slowly halted during and after World War I. The Italians and Poles came mainly between 1890 and 1915. Older immigrants didn't always have to compete with newcomers who beat down their wages. There was time for outsiders and insiders to adapt to each other. We should heed history's lesson.

EXERCISES

A. Identifying the Claim

1. In your own words, write Samuelson's central claim or proposition. Also indicate the paragraph(s) where the claim is located.

____

____

2. Then decide if the claim is a claim of fact, a claim of value, or a claim of policy.

B. Locating Evidence

1. One piece of evidence is listed for you. List three other major pieces of evidence that the writer uses to support the claim. Then characterize each piece of evidence according to whether it represents facts and statistics, good reasons, examples and observations, or quotation or testimony.

   a. There are too many illegal immigrants here already to make the tough "cop" approach workable. [fact]

   b.

   c.

   d.

   e.

2. In structuring the argument, does Samuelson appeal more to our reason, to our emotion, or to a combination of reason and emotion?

C. Identifying a Refutation and the Solution

1. Write the refutation, if there is one, in the space provided.

2. Does Samuelson provide a solution to the problem of immigration? If so, write it in the space provided. Be sure to use your own words.

DISCUSSION QUESTION

Having read the background material on the benefits and drawbacks of employing illegal immigrants and the changes—whether real or perceived—immigration has caused in this country, what do you think the government's policy should be toward illegals? How would you resolve the idea that our immigration policy is "schizophrenic"? That is, we deplore the presence of illegal aliens, yet American business relies on large numbers of low-paid workers to remain profitable. Finally, can assimilation work, and if so, in what specific ways?

TWO CARTOONS ON IMMIGRATION

Here are two cartoons on the subject of immigration. The first is by Mike Keefe, editorial cartoonist for *The Denver Post*; the second is by Walt Handelsman of *Newsday*, the leading newspaper of Long Island, New York. Identify the argument or central claim that each cartoon embodies. Then decide whether the claim is one of fact, value, or policy.

The Denver Post

Mike Keefe

Newsday Cartoon

Walt Handelsman

The Problem of Global Warming: Editorials and Cartoon

The Weather Where We Are: The Arctic

Margaret Atwood

Margaret Atwood is a Canadian writer best known for her works of fiction, in particular *The Handmaid's Tale* (1985), *Cat's Eye* (1988), and *The Blind Assassin* (2000). This opinion piece was published in the British magazine of new writing, *Granta,* as one in a series of short pieces called "The Weather Where We Are." Atwood's subject here is the Arctic.

The Issue

The issue in this piece concerns the Innuit (also spelled Inuit), the native peoples in the Canadian Arctic and Greenland. The Innuit have confirmed scientific evidence documenting the signs of global warming in this region—shrinking polar ice caps, the warming of the sea, the decline in the polar bear population—but the response by the world's industrial nations has been uneven. For example, the United States was the only major industrial nation that refused to sign the Kyoto Protocol a few years ago, which would have required countries to reduce the amount of fossil fuels burned; the U.S. argument against this was that to do so would stifle the American economy.

Scientists, too, differ in their opinions about what causes global warming. Some say that the universe has always experienced climate change, with periods of cooling and heating evident throughout geological history, and that fears of disaster are unwarranted. But more scientists argue that carbon dioxide is a "greenhouse gas," which means that it keeps the earth warm by trapping some of the heat that it radiates. This rise in carbon dioxide has been attributed to the burning of fossil fuels since the beginning of the Industrial Revolution.

The Union of Concerned Scientists sponsors an informative website for further exploration of this issue at www.ucsusa.org/global_warming/. In addition, in the winter of 2006, the *San Francisco Chronicle* published an extensive series on global warming by Jane Kay titled "Polar Warning—A Warming World: The Difference a Degree Makes." The series is well worth reading because it explains, in layman's language, exactly what global warming is, the environmental changes produced by rising ocean temperatures, its effect on marine life, and the certain impact on human populations. The series is available at www.sfgate.com. Once inside the site, type "global warming" in the search box. As well, former Vice-President Al Gore's 2006 documentary, *An Inconvenient Truth*, examines the issue with clear and convincing evidence.

The Weather Where We Are: The Arctic

Margaret Atwood

1 In the South—by this I mean any part of the earth with trees that grow up instead of sideways—it's hard to see the climate changing. A severe windstorm here, a warm winter or a drought or a flood there, but haven't there been severe windstorms and warm winters and droughts and floods before? Plants grow back, they regenerate after die-off, they cover over the scars. Species creep northward, but at least there are species. Things can't be that bad, you say, as you water your garden: Look how well the dandelions are doing!

2 In the Arctic it's different. Everything is so visible. Everything—except the rocks—is so fragile. There are trees, but they don't convert the limited sun-energy available to them into wood. They spider along the ground, two hundred years old and only a foot wide. Kill one and it won't be back soon. It's the same with the ice.

Connecting Grammar to Writing

Good writers try to achieve sentence variety. Notice how Atwood effectively mixes short and longer sentences in paragraph 3, for example. The short sentences express major points, while the longer ones represent examples and explanations.

3 Arctic ice is life-giving. Small organisms grow on the undersides of floating ice pans and icebergs, fish eat the organisms, whales and seals eat the fish, polar bears eat the seals. Ice gets into the sea in two ways: it falls in from calving glaciers, or it forms during the winter. Both kinds are spectacular, and both are essential. But the Arctic ice is dying. You can see it happening. There's no cover-up.

4 My partner and I have gone up there now over a four-year span—"up there" being the eastern Arctic, on the Greenland side and also the Canadian side, at lower altitudes, middle altitudes, and upper-middle altitudes. We go because we love it, and because we love it we worry about it. Everywhere it's the same. The Greenland ice cap is still calving into the North Atlantic, the icebergs still travel north to the top of Baffin Bay, then turn south and make their way past Newfoundland. But in the summer of 2004 there were almost no floating ice pans. Other glaciers are in retreat: we could see the rock valleys they used to fill, we could see the line they'd reached even a few years before. The shrinkage has been rapid.

5 Inuit told us stories about how hard it's become for polar bears and hunters to get out on to the ice, the only reliable place to catch seals. The ice was forming later and later every fall, melting earlier and earlier every spring. When you can't depend on the ice, what can you depend on? It would be as if—down south—the highways were to melt. And then what?

6 The canary in the mine used to be our warning signal: it keeled over and men knew they were in danger. Now it's the polar bears on the shore, dying of starvation.

7 The Arctic is an unbelievable region of the earth: strikingly beautiful if you like gigantic skies, enormous landforms, tiny flowers, amazing colours, strange light effects. It's also a region that allows scant margins of error. Fall into the ocean and wait a few minutes, and you're dead. Make a mistake with a walrus or a bear, same result. Make the wrong wardrobe choice, same result again. Melt the Arctic ice, and what follows? No second chances for quite some time.

8 You could write a science fiction novel about it, except that it wouldn't be science fiction. You could call it *Icemelt*. Suddenly there are no more small organisms, thus no fish up there, thus no seals. That wouldn't affect the average urban condo dweller much. The rising water levels from—say—the melting of the Greenland and Antarctic ice caps would get attention—no more Long Island or Florida, no more Bangladesh, and quite a few islands would disappear—but people could just migrate, couldn't they? Still no huge cause for alarm unless you own a lot of shore-front real estate.

9 But wait: there's ice under the earth, as well as on top of the sea. It's the permafrost, under the tundra. There's a lot of it, and a lot of tundra as well. Once the permafrost starts to melt, the peat on the tundra—thousands of years of stockpiled organic matter—will start to break down, releasing huge quantities of methane gas. Up goes the air temperature, down goes the oxygen ratio. How long will it take before we all choke and boil to death?

Connecting Grammar to Writing

The first "sentence" in paragraph 11—"What kind of story indeed?—is actually an intentional fragment used for emphasis.

10 It's hard to write fiction around such scenarios. Fiction is always about people, and to some extent the form determines the outcome of the plot. We always imagine—perhaps we're hard-wired to imagine—a survivor of any possible catastrophe, someone who lives to tell the tale, and also someone to whom the tale can be told. What kind of story would it be with the entire human race gasping to death like beached fish?

11 What kind of story, indeed? And who wants to hear it?

EXERCISES

A. Identifying the Claim

1. In your own words, write Atwood's central claim or proposition. Also indicate the paragraph(s) where the claim is located.

____

____

____

____

2. Then decide if the claim is a claim of fact, a claim of value, or a claim of policy.

____

B. Locating Evidence

1. One piece of evidence is listed for you. List three other major pieces of evidence that the writer uses to support the claim. Then characterize each piece of evidence according to whether it represents facts and statistics, good reasons, examples and observations, or quotation or testimony.

   a. In the Southern hemisphere, it's difficult to see evidence of global warming because there have always been storms, droughts, and floods, but in the Arctic, the signs are visible everywhere. [facts and observations]

   b. ____

   ____

   ____

   c. ____

   ____

   ____

   d. ____

   ____

   ____

   ____

2. In structuring the argument, does Atwood appeal more to our reason, to our emotion, or to a combination of reason and emotion?

____

C. Identifying a Refutation and the Solution

1. Write the refutation, if there is one, in the space provided.

____

____

2. Does Atwood provide a solution to the problem of global warming? If so, write it in the space provided. Be sure to use your own words.

Is It Warm in Here?

David Ignatius

David Ignatius writes a twice-weekly column on global politics, economics, and international affairs for the *Washington Post*. He has won the Edward Weintal Prize for diplomatic reporting and the 2000 Gerald Loeb Award for Commentary. Like the preceding piece by Margaret Atwood, this opinion piece takes up the problem of global warming but treats it in a completely different manner, both in content and in style. To access Elizabeth Kolbert's report on global warming from the *New Yorker* (mentioned in paragraphs 8 and 9), go to this website: www.newyorker.com. In the search box, type in "Elizabeth Kolbert" + "global warming." Kolbert wrote several articles in 2005 and 2006, and all are available in the *New Yorker* archives.

Is It Warm in Here?

David Ignatius

1 One of the puzzles if you're in the news business is figuring out what's "news." The fate of your local football team certainly fits the definition. So does a plane crash or a brutal murder. But how about changes in the migratory patterns of butterflies?

2 Scientists believe that new habitats for butterflies are early effects of global climate change—but that isn't news, by most people's measure. Neither is declining rainfall in the Amazon, or thinner ice in the Arctic. We can't see these changes in our personal lives, and in that sense, they are abstractions. So they don't grab us the way a plane crash would—even though they may be harbingers of a catastrophe that could, quite literally, alter the fundamentals of life on the planet. And because they're not "news," the environmental changes don't prompt action, at least not in the United States.

3 What got me thinking about the recondite life rhythms of the planet, and not the 24-hour news cycle, was a recent conversation with a scientist named Thomas E. Lovejoy, who heads the H. John Heinz III Center for Science, Economics and the Environment. When I first met Lovejoy nearly 20 years ago, he was trying to get journalists like me to pay attention to the changes in the climate and biological diversity of the Amazon. He is still trying, but he's beginning to wonder if it's too late.

4 Lovejoy fears that changes in the Amazon's ecosystem may be irreversible. Scientists reported last month that there is an Amazonian drought apparently

caused by new patterns in Atlantic currents that, in turn, are similar to projected climate change. With less rainfall, the tropical forests are beginning to dry out. They burn more easily, and, in the continuous feedback loops of their ecosystem, these drier forests return less moisture to the atmosphere, which means even less rain. When the forest trees are deprived of rain, their mortality can increase by a factor of six, and similar devastation affects other species, too.

5 "When do you wreck it as a system?" Lovejoy wonders. "It's like going up to the edge of a cliff, not really knowing where it is. Common sense says you shouldn't discover where the edge is by passing over it, but that's what we're doing with deforestation and climate change."

6 Lovejoy first went to the Amazon 40 years ago as a young scientist of 23. It was a boundless wilderness, the size of the continental United States, but at that time it had just 2 million people and one main road. He has returned more than a hundred times, assembling over the years a mental time-lapse photograph of how this forest primeval has been affected by man. The population has increased tenfold, and the wilderness is now laced with roads, new settlements and economic progress. The forest itself, impossibly rich and lush when Lovejoy first saw it, is changing.

7 For Levejoy, who co-edited a pioneering 1992 book, "Global Warming and Biological Diversity," there is a deep sense of frustration. A crisis he and other scientists first sensed more than two decades ago is drifting toward us in what seems like slow motion, but fast enough that it may be impossible to mitigate the damage.

8 The best reporting of the non-news of climate change has come from Elizabeth Kolbert in the New Yorker. Her three-part series last spring lucidly explained the harbingers of potential disaster: a shrinking of Arctic sea ice by 250 million acres since 1979; a thawing of the permafrost for what appears to be the first time in 120,000 years; a steady warming of Earth's surface temperature; changes in rainfall patterns that could presage severe droughts of the sort that destroyed ancient civilizations. This month she published a new piece, "Butterfly Lessons," that looked at how these delicate creatures are moving into new habitats as the planet warms. Her real point was that all life, from microorganisms to human beings, will have to adapt, and in ways that could be dangerous and destabilizing.

9 So many of the things that pass for news don't matter in any ultimate sense. But if people such as Lovejoy and Kolbert are right, we are all but ignoring the biggest story in the history of humankind. Kolbert concluded her series last year with this shattering thought: "It may seem impossible to imagine that a technologically advanced society could choose, in essence, to destroy itself, but that is what we are now in the process of doing." She's right. The failure of the United States to get serious about climate change is unforgivable, a human folly beyond imagining.

EXERCISES

A. Identifying the Claim

1. In your own words, write Ignatius's central claim or proposition. Also indicate the paragraph(s) where the claim is located.

____

____

____

____

2. Then decide if the claim is a claim of fact, a claim of value, or a claim of policy.

____

B. Locating Evidence

1. One piece of evidence is listed for you. List three other major pieces of evidence that the writer uses to support the claim. Then characterize each piece of evidence according to whether it represents facts and statistics, good reasons, examples and observations, or quotation or testimony.

   a. Stories about butterflies changing their migration habits and declining rainfall in the Amazon are not considered news by most of us because they do not touch us personally and because we cannot see these changes in our personal lives. [fact, observation]

   b. _______________

   ____

   ____

   ____

   c. _______________

   ____

   ____

   d. _______________

   ____

   ____

e. ____________________

2. In structuring the argument, does Ignatius appeal more to our reason, to our emotion, or to a combination of reason and emotion?

C. Identifying a Refutation and the Solution

1. Write the refutation, if there is one, in the space provided.

2. Does Ignatius provide a solution to the problem of global warming? If so, write it in the space provided. Be sure to use your own words.

DISCUSSION QUESTIONS

1. What measures can you personally take to avert the catastrophe that Atwood warns about in her conclusion? What changes could you make in your lifestyle that, together with changes of millions of other people, would make a difference?
2. Which of the two editorials on global warming is, in your opinion, more effective at alerting us to the dangers associated with global warming that are inevitable if significant changes are not made? Which writer does a better job of alerting the readers to the seriousness of this issue? Explain your choice.

Washington Post Cartoon

Tom Toles

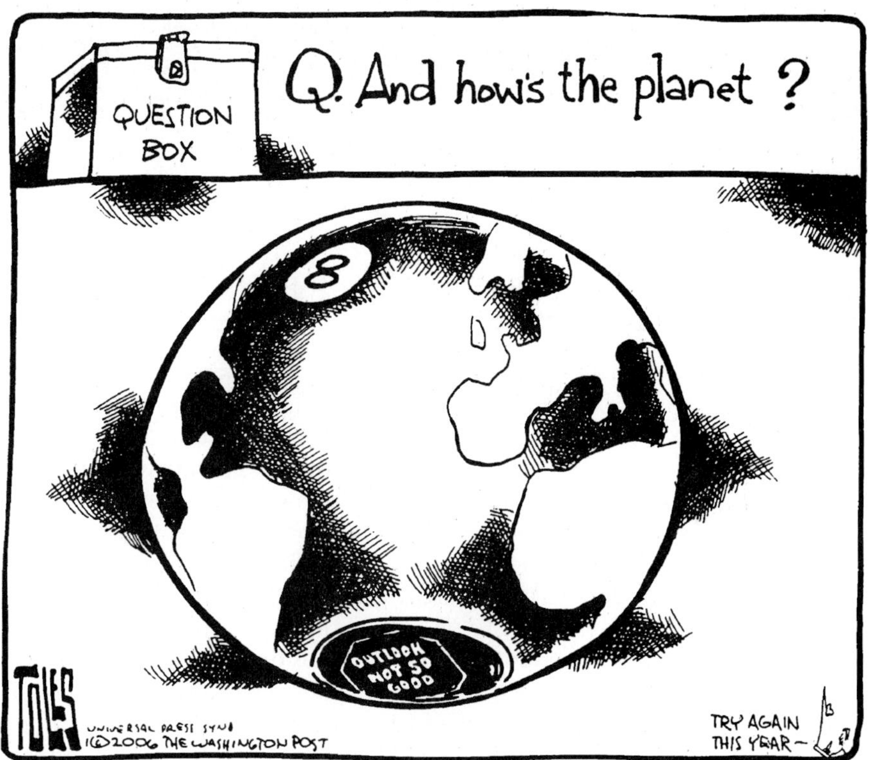

DISCUSSION QUESTIONS

1. A Magic 8-Ball is a toy that allows the user to ask it questions. If you shake the ball and turn it upside down, an answer to the question is revealed. Sample answers are "Better Not Tell You Now," "It Is Certain," "My Answer Is No," and so forth. Why is using the idea of the Magic 8-Ball appropriate for asking the question, "And how's the planet"? What is Toles implying about our awareness of the problem with this image?
2. Look carefully at the bottom right-hand corner. What is represented here?

Writing an Argumentative Essay

ARGUMENT AND PERSUASION IN THE REAL WORLD

The art of persuasion is a worthwhile skill to develop to sharpen your thinking ability and to put into effect in the world outside the classroom. Let's say that you have been working at your current part-time job for a year, you think you have done a good job, you take on new responsibilities willingly and without complaint, you come on time, and you do not fool around on the job. But you have not gotten a raise. How would you approach your boss to ask for a higher salary? What reasons would you give in support of your request? You might point to the fine qualities listed above. You would certainly wait to make sure that he or she was in a good mood and not stressed out about meeting deadlines or dealing with grumpy customers. You would point out your loyalty, your dedication to the job, and other stellar traits. And if you were lucky, you might succeed in getting that raise. This real-life example shows that implementing the finer points of persuasion can yield practical rewards.

Understanding persuasive techniques has far-reaching application in the real world beyond the raise-request example. You might, for example, use argumentative techniques in the following situations: You need to buy a car, but you hope to convince your parents to put some money toward the purchase; you want your best friend to take a weeklong backpacking trip with you; you want to get your roommate to stop once and for all borrowing your clothes without asking; you hope to convince your anthropology professor to accept an answer on your recent quiz that she marked wrong if she will just listen to your reasoning.

WRITING TO ARGUE: ACADEMIC AND PROFESSIONAL WRITING

Understanding how to argue logically and how to persuade readers to give serious consideration to your point of view will be an essential skill for academic writing as well as for professional writing.

Typical Academic Assignments Requiring Writing an Argument

- For a medical ethics class, argue for or against the proposition that left-over embryos from the in vitro fertilization process should be used for medical research.
- For a political science class, argue for or against the proposition that the decriminalization of marijuana would be a positive step for the criminal justice system in the United States.
- For a sociology class, argue for or against the proposition that interracial adoption is primarily a positive experience for both the children who are adopted and the adoptive parents.

Typical Professional Writing Tasks Requiring Writing an Argument

- Write a grant proposal, arguing that funds for a particular project should be given to the agency for which you work.
- Write a request on behalf of people who work for you, trying to persuade management to consider allowing them to "telecommute" from their homes one day a week.
- Write a memo to your immediate supervisor arguing that your department needs to add a new position to handle the heavy workload you have been experiencing.

STEPS TO WRITING AN ARGUMENTATIVE ESSAY

The readings in Part 8 give you ample examples of opinion writing. Each writer represented uses various strategies and appeals to get the reader to accept—or at least to consider seriously—his or her point of view. You may be asked to respond to one of the opinion pieces assigned by taking the opposite, or perhaps a different, point of view from the writer's, or you may be asked to write an opinion piece of your own on another subject. Whichever assignment you do, follow the suggestions given below to produce a successful essay.

When you are assigned to write an argumentative essay on a subject of your own choice, think carefully before you settle on one. Unless you are an experienced writer (or simply very brave), I recommend writing a paper on a claim of fact or a claim of policy, as claims of value are generally more difficult to support. Unless you are assigned a specific issue, I recommend also that you choose a subject that you know something about firsthand. Look around at your community or your campus, read the newspaper, watch the news. There are dozens of good issues out there to write about. For this assignment, I like students first to complete the practice outline on page 561 as a way of organizing their ideas and clarifying their thinking about the issue.

Before You Begin

- Choose a subject and fill out the practice outline on page 561. You might need to do this a couple of times, so make two or three photocopies of the page.
- Review the discussion of argumentative and persuasive techniques at the beginning of Part 8 to see how opinion pieces are structured (claim, evidence, refutation) because you will need to impose that pattern on your own paper.

Writing the First Draft—The Parts of the Essay

- Like any other writing assignment, your essay should begin with an introduction that whets the reader's interest, establishes your credibility, and states your reason for writing. By credibility we mean that you should establish your interest in and knowledge of the subject at hand. For example, in Margaret Atwood's opinion piece about global warming in the Canadian Arctic, she writes:

  My partner and I have gone up there now over a four-year span—"up there" being the eastern Arctic, on the Greenland side and also the Canadian side, at lower altitudes, middle altitudes, and upper-middle altitudes. We go because we love it, and because we love it we worry about it.

  These sentences tell the reader that Atwood has extensive firsthand experience in the Arctic and therefore is qualified to write about her observations. The introduction should also include your thesis—the claim or central argument.
- The body of your essay should include a minimum of *two* paragraphs giving evidence to support your thesis. The evidence might include examples, facts, good reasons, past precedent, observations from the real world, or to a lesser extent, personal experience or narrative. As you saw in both the section at the beginning of the text, "An Overview of the Writing Process" and at the end of Part 5, "Writing an Analysis and a Synthesis Essay," each body paragraph must be tied to the thesis and each should begin with a clear main idea to assure clarity and coherence for the reader.
- You should include a one-paragraph refutation, in which you deal with the most persuasive of the *opposition's* arguments. The refutation section will be discussed in more detail below.
- A short conclusion, which might include a warning or a recommendation. Do not merely rehash or summarize your supporting ideas.

Practice Outline for an Argumentative Essay

Subject:

Your interest in the subject (to establish your credibility):

Tentative thesis (your claim):

Three reasons or pieces of supporting evidence:

1.

2.

3.

The refutation: Find two reasons that an opponent would identify against your position. Then choose the *stronger* of the two reasons to refute:

1.

2.

The conclusion: This could be a warning for the future, a recommendation, a pertinent quotation, or, less effectively, a summing up.

SPECIAL CONSIDERATION: THE REFUTATION

The refutation section is probably the most challenging part of an argumentative essay. Remember that a refutation involves a *concession*—an admission that the opposing side has merit. But you cannot just let that concession stand. You have to show why your idea is better—in other words, a counter-argument. A real-life example will help you understand this process in more detail.

Let's say that you live near a dangerous intersection, Main Street and Alhambra Avenues, where several major accidents involving injuries to pedestrians have occurred while they were trying to cross the street. You and your neighbors request a meeting of the municipal transportation and safety board at which you explain the problem, give evidence that the problem is serious, and offer a solution: The intersection is so dangerous that it needs a stoplight.

The safety director counters your proposal by saying that the city's budget is tight, that a new light will cost $100,000, and that the community has more pressing needs. For example, the city has just committed the same amount of money to an after-school program for disadvantaged boys and girls. Hard to argue against that! Still, you and your neighbors are convinced that your position is right. You prepare your refutation, and at the next community meeting you come up with these counterarguments:

1. An after-school program for disadvantaged youth is surely a worthy cause (your concession), but the board needs to reexamine its priorities. Saving the lives of pedestrians is more important. Also, a stoplight is the city's responsibility; an after-school club is not. It would be more appropriate to seek funding for the club from private grants and charitable foundations. This is your first counterargument, representing good reasons and appealing to reason.
2. Your second counterargument appeals to the board's conscience: If a stoplight is not installed, more injuries will occur, and someone might die. Although $100,000 might seem like a lot of money for a single stoplight, it will be money well spent. A human life is more precious than the $100,000 saved by not installing one. How many people must die or be seriously injured before the board decides that a light is necessary? These two counterarguments appeal to one's reason.
3. Your third counterargument appeals to the emotions: It is unconscionable that the board is willfully ignoring traffic hazards.
4. Finally, you offer some hard evidence to refute the board's contention that the town does not have enough money in its budget for the project: Recently, the local newspaper ran a series of articles criticizing some recent frivolous expenditures at City Hall. For example, the mayor redecorated her office at taxpayer expense, buying leather couches, matching chairs, an expensive Persian rug, and installing a bar; she also requisitioned a new limousine. Surely pedestrians' lives are more important than an elegant office and a fancy car for the town's mayor.

Your refutation might work, or it might not, but at least you have dealt with your opponent's primary objections to spending this money.

TOPICS FOR WRITING AN ARGUMENTATIVE ESSAY

1. Look through the readings throughout Parts 2 through 7 and write an argumentative essay on an issue or controversy that appeals to you. For example, with regard to Eric Schlosser's discussion of fast food restaurants ("Fast Food Nation: Behind the Counter"), you might argue that fast food establishments actually contribute to a community's economy because they offer jobs to entry-level workers and a convenient way for poor people to eat inexpensively, or whatever other benefits you can come up with. Another example: Anwar Accawi's

essay, "The Telephone," presents a sobering look at how his native village underwent rapid change, and not for the better, after the installation of the town's first telephone. Write an argumentative essay on the negative effects of a new piece of technology in this country. Some possibilities for subjects are iPods, cell phones, PDAs, and hard-drive TV recorders like Tivos.

2. Choose one of the opinion pieces in Part 8 and write an essay on the same subject but expressing an entirely different opinion. For example, concerning the issue of global warming, you might defend the U.S.'s refusal to sign the Kyoto Protocol requiring developed nations to reduce the amount of fossil fuels burned. Another example would be to argue that during this time of serious threats to our national security, torture is an acceptable way to elicit information from suspected terrorists.

TOPICS RELATED TO THE READINGS

1. The discussion questions following the editorials serve as a springboard for an argumentative essay on one of the issues represented in Part 8.
2. Write an argumentative essay in which you take the opposing view from the one expressed in a particular selection. For example, concerning Bob Herbert's editorial, "Black, Dead, and Invisible," you might argue that the media is right to downplay violence against youth in urban areas. The body of your essay could be supported with good reasons, personal observations, or perhaps a combination of the two.
3. Nicholas Thompson in "Hero Inflation" challenges the contemporary practice of labeling tragic victims as heroes. In October 2005, British police killed a Brazilian immigrant, Jean Charles de Menenzes, in a London subway station, mistaking him for a potential suicide bomber. De Menenzes was working legally in England as an electrician. After his death, his body was returned to Brazil, where he was given a hero's funeral. Using Thompson's criteria as the basis for your discussion, write an essay in which you take a position on whether a victim of a police shooting, like de Menenzes, should be accorded heroic status.
4. Write an argumentative essay in which you debate two (or three) sides of an issue discussed in the paired readings and come to a conclusion of your own. This assignment will require you to write a combination synthesis-argumentative essay using paraphrase, summary, and quotation from the selections. For example, on the question of whether Intelligent Design is a legitimate subject to study for high school science students (see the accompanying website), explain the

arguments for and against and then defend your own position. On the question of why the immigration issue has become so worrisome, examine the various points of view expressed by Eugene Robinson and Robert J. Samuelson and come to a conclusion of your own.

5. Concerning the issue of global warming, write an opinion piece in which you persuade ordinary Americans to take a series of practical and specific measures to prevent further global warming. To get them to accept your recommendations, you will need to convince the reader that the issue is sufficiently serious to warrant individual, and not just government, action.

PART NINE

A Brief Guide to Grammar and Usage

Basic Grammar

I have tried to keep the grammatical explanations throughout this text to a minimum; however, a reasonable grasp of some fundamentals of grammar is essential to an understanding of many of the principles of usage. For example, it is impossible to explain to someone who can't distinguish between a subject and an object when to use *he* in a sentence and when to use *him*. (Your ear is not always reliable.)

So, prepare yourself for a concise tutorial in matters grammatical.

RECOGNIZING SUBJECTS AND VERBS

If you are able to recognize subjects and verbs with ease, recognizing objects, adjectives, adverbs, and the other parts of speech; identifying the five sentence patterns; and distinguishing clauses from phrases will be relatively simple.

Learning grammar is much like learning how to play the piano, or tennis, or almost anything else: it seems difficult at the beginning but gets easier as you go along. And, believe it or not, you might even discover you are enjoying the ride.

Verbs

The verb is the very heart of the sentence. It is what is happening. For example, in the sentence "*Humbert rides a bike to work,*" *rides* is what Humbert is doing. In the sentence "*In the late afternoon Heather always walks her dog along the beach,*" *walks* is what Heather is doing. So, one could say with certainty that verbs indicate action.

Some verbs, however, do not. They indicate what most books call *state of being*. Think about this sentence: "Emily is perhaps the laziest person in the class." There is no action involved here. Emily is, apparently, a particularly inactive individual. She, at least in the classroom, simply exists, and in this sentence the word that indicates that existence is *is*.

You will undoubtedly find some verbs that fall somewhere in the middle. In the sentence "Connie often becomes irritated at her mother," *becomes* doesn't really show any real action, yet it can't be said to describe a state of being either, for it reveals movement from one state to another. It is, though, clearly the verb.

Perhaps the message here is not to think about this too much. For example, blurt out the verb in this sentence: "Henrietta raises chickens."

The verb is *raises*, and, if life were simple, that would be all the explanation needed for the verb: It is the word in the sentence that shows action or state of being. However, for us to communicate the complexities of our existence in time, we need to add words to these basic verbs. Obviously, not everything happens in the present. Events have occurred in the past and will occur in the future; consequently we have what we call *tenses* to show these time differences. For example, maybe John's mother always gives him a ride to school but is sick, so John has to dust off his bike and pump up the tires. We would then say, "John will ride his bike to school tomorrow." To indicate a future action, we add a word, generally called a *helping verb*, to the main verb. In this sentence, the complete verb is *will ride*. Using some form of *have* as a helping verb, we can also indicate something that has occurred or began in the past and is still occurring. For example, "Before John finally passed his driver's test, he *had* ridden his bike everywhere he went." John rode his bike in the past but no longer does so because he can drive.

Paul Roberts, a grammar teacher I greatly admire, said that the verb is the hardest concept to define because it is the starting point. He felt the best way to approach the problem was by simply pointing out verbs. In other words, if a child didn't know what a horse was, telling him a horse was a solid-hoofed quadruped probably wouldn't do him much good. But pointing out a few horses would clear up the matter. So, rather than enumerate the eighteen tenses, I will offer a few sentences to see if pointing out the verbs will solve whatever problems you might have.

EXERCISE

Underline the verbs.

1. Sophie sells sandwiches at the local deli.
2. Ben is considering a career in law enforcement.
3. Laura has given her pet turtle to her new boyfriend.
4. Benny and Alfred have been good friends for many years.
5. George will often practice his bagpipes for hours.
6. By this evening George will have driven his neighbors crazy.
7. Louis played in the band and sang in the choir.
8. Will you have studied your grammar before you play your video games?

Answers

1. sells (What is Sophie doing?)
2. is considering (What is Ben doing?)
3. has given (What has Laura done?)

4. have been (What has been going on with Benny and Alfred?)
5. will practice (What is George going to do?)
6. will have driven (What will the insensitive George have done?)
7. played and sang (What did Louis do?)
8. Will have studied, play (What will you have done, hopefully, before you do something else?)

There is a group of words called *modal auxiliaries* that, when used with the principal verb, suggest necessity, obligation, permission, possibility. They are always verbs, but, because they do not behave like ordinary verbs, are considered a separate group. They are *can, could, may, might, must, shall, should, would*.

So, in the sentence "I might go to the movie with you this afternoon," the helping verb is *might* and the main verb is *go*.

It is also worth mentioning that in English we use some form of the verb *do* to form questions and create emphasis. In Spanish, for example, if you want to form a question, you simply put the verb before the subject. So, if you want to know if a boy likes baseball, the English equivalent of the Spanish question would be "Likes he baseball?" Obviously we do not do this in English. We say, "Does he like baseball?" The past would be "Did he like baseball?"

We also use some form of *do* for emphasis. If your teacher asks you if you did your homework, instead of simply saying "I did my homework," you would say, to show your strong objection that he would believe for a second you hadn't, "I *did do* my homework." The point being that *do* and *did* are always verbs.

EXERCISE

Underline the verbs.

1. The dog might have run away.
2. It does not matter.
3. John should have given Jeannine a ride.
4. Could that old man be the president of the company?
5. Do you know the answer to that question?
6. Would you mind holding the door for me?

Answers

1. might have run
2. does matter
3. should have given
4. Could be
5. Do know
6. Would mind

The secret to success in learning your verbs is to practice them. Look at the sentences in the sections you are reading in this book and underline what you think are the verbs. Then ask your teacher if you are on the right track. She or he will be more than happy to help a student genuinely interested in learning.

Subjects

Now that you know how to recognize verbs, finding the subjects should give you no trouble at all. All you have to do is ask Who? or What? and read the verb. The answer is the subject. For example, in the first sentence of the verb exercise on page 568 "(Sophie sells sandwiches at the local deli)", *sells* is the verb. Who sells? Sophie sells. *Sophie* is the subject.

If you look at all the sentences in that exercise, you will find the subject without much thought. For example, in sentence 2, who is considering a career in law enforcement? Obviously Ben. *Ben* is the subject.

As you might have suspected, though, these are the easy ones. There are a few minor complications worth noting:

1. Sometimes the subject comes after the verb. In the sentence "On the counter is a large spider," the verb is *is*. If you ask yourself what is on the counter, you say "spider."
2. Often a word, words, or a phrase (a group of words that doesn't contain a subject and a verb) comes between the subject and the verb. For example, "The girls, laughing hysterically, were sent to the office." The verb is *were sent*. Who were sent? The girls were sent, so *girls* is the subject.

   In the sentence "The passengers on the last flight ran down the runway," the verb is *ran*. Who ran? The passengers ran. The phrase "on the last flight" has nothing to do with the running; it simply describes the passengers.

   Think about this sentence: "One of the players has been suspended." Who has been suspended? The players haven't been suspended; only one has been suspended. The subject is *One*, not players. (Besides, "The players has been suspended" sounds wrong.)
3. Sometimes the word *There* begins the sentence, holds the place for the subject, which always shows up sooner or later. For example, consider the sentence "There is a wart on the end of his nose." What is on the end of his nose? A wart. In the sentence "There might be a light at the end of the tunnel," what is at the end of the tunnel? A light.
4. In imperative sentences, sentences used to express a command or a request, the subject is omitted but understood. For example, in the sentence "Take it easy," the verb is *Take*, but there seems to be no subject. If you think about it for a minute, though, you will realize that the subject is *you*. Someone is always telling or asking someone to do something, and that someone is always you, either singular or plural. Your mother might say, "Clean your room." Whom is she talking to? Unfortunately, she is talking to you. The teacher says, "Stop that

whispering." Whom is she taking to? She is talking either to you in particular or to the class as a whole, which, in either case, is a *you.*

EXERCISE

Underline the subjects once and the verbs twice.

EXAMPLE: The cat was cautiously entering the room when she saw the dog.

1. The lawyer, along with his client, rode to the banquet in a limo.
2. One of Mary's friends ran out of the room in tears.
3. At the end of winter quarter many students rush home for the holidays.
4. A brief stop for lunch at the deli became an unexpected ordeal.
5. Have you given your assignment much thought?
6. Don't drop your clothes on the floor.
7. For years my father has been planning on buying a boat.
8. There was hardly a dry eye in the house after Amanda finished her speech.
9. Do you think that Edna will be happy with her grade?
10. Could you see if there will be space in the theater for one more person?

Answers

1. lawyer rode
2. One ran
3. students rush
4. stop became
5. Have you given
6. (you) do drop
7. father has been planning
8. eye was, Amanda finished
9. Do you think, Edna will be
10. Could you see, will be space

PARTS OF SPEECH

There are eight parts of speech. We have already discussed one of them: the verb. Here are the others.

Nouns

The simplest description of a noun, the one you have undoubtedly heard many times, is that it is a person, place, or thing. For example, in the sentence

"The boy from Arizona had a bad attitude," it should be clear that *boy* is a person, *Arizona* is a place, and *attitude* is a thing.

You might also note that adding an *s* to a noun creates a plural and that a noun usually has an article (*a, an,* or *the*). If you look at this last sentence, you will see that *s, noun, plural, noun,* and *article* are all nouns.

Pronouns

A pronoun stands for (takes the place of) a noun. For example, in the sentence "Claudia couldn't find her hat so I gave her mine," the two *hers* are pronouns standing for Claudia, *I* is a pronoun, and *mine* is a pronoun standing for a hat. In the sentence "John forgot his homework, so the teacher ignored him," *his* and *him* are both pronouns standing for John. For future reference, the word the pronoun stands for is called the *antecedent*. (*John* is the antecedent for *his* and *him*.)

If we didn't have pronouns, we would have to say "John forgot John's homework, so the teacher ignored John," which is slightly confusing and more than a little awkward.

EXERCISE

Underline the nouns once and the pronouns twice.

1. The boy gave his aging grandmother a kiss on the check.
2. Happiness is a state of mind that many people seek but few find.
3. Our problem was simple: We couldn't give them any of our horses.
4. The absence of money in my wallet bothers me.

Answers

1. The boy gave his aging grandmother a kiss on the cheek.
2. Happiness is a state of mind that many people seek but few find.
3. Our problem was simple: We couldn't give them any of our horses.
4. The absence of money in my wallet bothers me.

Adjectives

There are only two parts of speech that describe or modify: adjectives and adverbs. An adjective modifies (describes) a noun or a pronoun. Here is an example: "The arrogant, young boy on a rusty bike swerved off the gravel path and crashed into a garbage can." The words *arrogant, young, rusty, gravel,* and *garbage* are all adjectives describing their respective nouns (*boy, bike, path,* and *can*).

In the sentence, "She was tired," *tired* describes the pronoun *She*.

Adjectives answer the questions Which one? How many? What kind? Also, you can add *-er* or *-est* to many adjectives. So, in the sentence "The saloon door had five bullet holes in it," *saloon* tells which door, *five* tells how many holes, and *bullet* tells what kind of holes.

■ EXERCISE

Underline the adjectives.

1. The red, white, and blue bird sitting in the tall tree looked rather patriotic.
2. The *Dick Van Dyke Show* was one of the most popular TV shows of the early 1960s.
3. The nasty weather caused the shore birds to find shelter in small caves in the cliffs.
4. The last few fireworks were spectacular.
5. Bill, tired and depressed because he had just lost his best friend, headed for the nearest bar.

Answers

1. The red, white, and blue bird sitting in the tall tree looked rather patriotic.
2. The *Dick Van Dyke Show* was one of the most popular TV shows of the early 1960s.
3. The nasty weather caused the shore birds to find shelter in small caves in the cliffs.
4. The last few fireworks were spectacular.
5. Bill, tired and depressed because he had just lost his best friend, headed for the nearest bar.

Adverbs

Adverbs modify verbs, adjectives, and adverbs. Let's look at some examples:

- "The newspaper arrived late." In this sentence *late* modifies the verb *arrived.*
- "That crate is very heavy." The adverb *very* modifies the adjective *heavy.*
- "The snake moved too quickly." The adverb *too* modifies another adverb *quickly.*

Most adverbs answer the questions How, When, Where, and Why. For example, in sentence 1, *late* tells when the newspaper arrived. In sentence 2, *very* tells how heavy the crate is.

■ EXERCISE

Underline the adverbs.

1. Not every student who studies hard will receive an "A."
2. He will probably invite you to dinner very soon.
3. There will be a concert there tomorrow.
4. My neighbor doesn't like children all that much.

Answers

1. Not every student who studies hard will receive an "A."
2. He will probably invite you to dinner very soon.
3. There will be a concert there tomorrow.
4. My neighbor doesn't like children all that much.

Clauses and Phrases

This seems to be the moment, before we launch into a discussion of prepositional phrases, to explain the difference between a phrase and a clause, the two word groups that comprise our language.

A *clause* is a group of words that contains a subject and a verb. So, "Denise plays tennis" is obviously a clause, as is "When Denise plays tennis," the first being independent, the second dependent, a distinction we will ponder a little later.

A *phrase* is a group of words that does not contain a subject and a verb. In the sentence "The bank having been robbed, a group of townspeople decided to form a posse," the phrases are "The bank having been robbed," "of townspeople," and "to form a posse." You will notice that there is not a subject and a verb in any of those groups of words. The entire sentence, of course, is a clause: It has a subject, *group*, and a verb, *decided*.

Now, let's proceed to the consideration of prepositions and prepositional phrases.

Prepositions

Prepositions are words that connect. They show a relationship between the words in a prepositional phrase to other words in the sentence. Consequently, they are almost impossible to define; they must simply be learned or intuited. And, since there are so very many of them, it is much easier to intuit them than it is to memorize an extremely long list.

It should be noted that every preposition must have an object (called the *object of the preposition*), and the preposition and its object are called a *prepositional phrase*. For example, *around* in the sentence "Jeanne ran around aimlessly" is not a preposition; it is an adverb telling where she ran. But, *around* in the sentence "Jeanne ran around the track three times," is a preposition: It has an object, *track*, and connects the track to the verb, *ran*. So, "around the track" is a prepositional phrase.

It is also worth noting that the function of a prepositional phrase is to modify: They are either adjectives or adverbs. For example, in the sentence "The old man with the spiked hair pushed into the front of the line," "with the spiked hair" is a prepositional phrase modifying *man*. It tells which man we are talking about, so it is used as an adjective. The phrase "into the front" modifies the verb *pushed*, and since it tells where he pushed, it is an adverb. And "of the line" modifies a noun, *front*, and tells which front we are talking about (the front of the line), so it is an adjective.

Like verbs, prepositional phrases are more easily seen than explained. After someone points out that this and this and this and this are prepositional phrases, you should find that they just pop right up in front of your very eyes.

Let's try a few sentences:

1. The musician in the pink tuxedo was staring at the woman in the red dress with a plunging neckline. (four)
2. After losing his very last dollar at the crap table in Harrah's, Rudy pulled a gun from the pocket of his suede jacket and, to everyone's horror, shot himself in the foot. (seven)

In sentence 1 the prepositional phrases are "in the pink tuxedo," "at the woman," "in the red dress," "with a plunging neckline." In sentence 2 they are "After losing his very last dollar," "at the crap table," "in Harrah's," "from the pocket," "of his suede jacket," "to everyone's horror," "in the foot."

You might notice that although the prepositions are different, the prepositional phrases all sound quite similar. Don't think about it too much, and you should have no trouble identifying them.

EXERCISE

Put parentheses around the prepositional phrases.

EXAMPLE: The leaves (of the tree) (in our backyard) were heavy (with dew).

1. In the corner of the room was a cat staring at a ball on the end of a string.
2. Within a few minutes of the call to the police, Abigail heard sirens in the distance.
3. The man watched in horror as his car rolled slowly down the hill and into the ravine.
4. Inside the cabinet was a glass figurine of an unusually grotesque animal standing on its hind legs and a live mouse with a long tail and quivering whiskers.

Answers

1. (In the corner) (of the room) was a cat staring (at a ball) (on the end) (of a string).
2. (Within a few minutes) (of the call) (to the people), Abigail heard sirens (in the distance).
3. The man watched (in horror) as his car rolled slowly (down the hill) and (into the ravine).
4. (Inside the cabinet) was a glass figurine (of an unusually grotesque animal) standing (on its hind legs) and a live mouse (with a long tail and quivering whiskers).

Conjunctions

Conjunctions are words used to connect or join other words, phrases, or clauses. There are only two main types of conjunctions: coordinating and subordinating. Correlative conjunctions are considered by some to be a third group, but they are really just another kind of coordinating conjunction.

The **coordinating conjunctions** are *and, but, or, for, nor, so, yet*

Coordinating conjunctions are used to connect equal grammatical elements: nouns to nouns, verbs to verbs, phrases to phrases, clauses to clauses, and so on. For example, in the sentence "Ingrid and Sven liked to laugh and play, but their parents didn't approve," the first *and* joins two nouns, the second *and* joins two verbs, and the *but* connects two clauses. In the sentence "He knows who is naughty and who is nice," the *and* connects two clauses.

Correlative conjunctions are a combination of the words *both, not, either,* and *neither* with the coordinating conjunctions *and, but, or,* and *nor*— For example, "Neither Dick nor Brandon wants to take the first solo." *Not only . . . but also* is another combination. For example, "Not only Mariellen but also Henry was involved in the project." It is clear that correlative conjunctions, like coordinating conjunctions, combine equal elements, and it is important to make sure the elements being combined are equal. For example, in the sentence "Josie likes not only to play music but also dancing the samba," the elements being combined are not equal: Josie likes *not only to play music but also to dance the samba* or *not only playing music but also dancing the samba.* We will explore this issue in more depth when we discuss parallelism.

Subordinating conjunctions will be discussed when we cover dependent clauses.

SENTENCE PATTERNS

There are only five sentence patterns in the English language, five ways words can be organized to form sentences. There can, of course, be any number of clauses and phrases within a sentence, but each sentence can be reduced to one of five fundamental patterns.

1. Subject-Verb (S-V)

Every sentence must contain a subject (S) and a verb (V), whether expressed or not. For example, "Birds fly" is a sentence. We can, and usually do, add modifying elements to the simple sentence. For example, in the sentence "Some birds fly south in the winter," we have added an adjective (*some*) and a prepositional phrase ("*in the winter*"). But, stripped of its modifiers, we have simply a subject and a verb. The verb in these sentences is called an *intransitive verb,* which means it is not followed by a direct object (a term you will learn in a very few minutes).

2. Subject-Verb-Subject Complement (S-V-SC)

A subject complement (SC) is a word that follows a verb and either renames or describes the subject. Here are some examples:

- "That plant is ivy." The subject is *plant* and the subject complement is *ivy.* The noun *ivy* renames *plant.*
- "Ivy is invasive." The adjective *invasive* describes *ivy.* It, too, is called a subject complement.

A subject complement, then, can be either a noun or an adjective.

The verb in these sentences is called a *linking verb* because it links the subject complement to the subject.

EXERCISE

Underline the subject complement.

1. That green stuff in the back of the refrigerator is too old to eat.
2. Ellen became a high school principal.
3. His phone is always busy.
4. After our long walk, the iced tea tasted great.
5. That freshly baked apple pie smells so good.

Answers

1. That green stuff in the back of the refrigerator is too old to eat.
2. Ellen became a high school principal.
3. His phone is always busy.
4. After our long walk, the iced tea tasted great.
5. That freshly baked apple pie smells so good.

3. Subject-Verb-Direct Object (S-V-DO)

In the sentence "Sarah plays the trumpet," *trumpet* does not rename *Sarah*; these are two entirely different things. We are talking about something Sarah, the subject, plays. In the sentence "Billy hit Ellen," we are talking about something the subject did to someone else. That someone or something else that is being played or hit is called the *direct object* (DO). In other words, the direct object receives the action of the verb.

The verb that introduces a direct object is called a *transitive verb. Transitive* comes from the Latin word meaning "to go across," the idea being that the action goes from the subject across the verb to the object.

To find either the subject complement or the direct object, simply read the subject and the verb and ask yourself What or Who(m). If the answer is the same as or describes the subject, you have a subject complement; if it is different, you have a direct object. Here are examples:

- "That old man soon became a nuisance to his neighbors." The subject is *man* and the verb is *became*. So, if you ask yourself, The old man became what? you say, without hesitation, a nuisance. Are the man and the nuisance the same person? Yes, they are. Consequently, *nuisance* is a subject complement.

- "The terrified witness identified the killer from the police photos." The subject is *witness* and the verb is *identified*. If you ask, The witness identified whom? "killer" pops right up. Are the witness and the killer the same person? Not likely. Therefore, *killer* is the direct object.

EXERCISE

Underline and label the complements.

1. After winning the lottery, Laurel bought drinks for the house.
2. The band received a standing ovation from the appreciative crowd.
3. Kevin finally became an accountant.
4. Sally had never felt so alive.
5. Has anyone seen my glasses?

Answers

1. drinks (direct object)
2. ovation (direct object)
3. accountant (subject complement)
4. alive (subject complement)
5. glasses (direct object)

4. Subject-Verb-Indirect Object-Direct Object (S-V-IO-DO)

Often there are two objects following a verb. For example, in the sentence "Elaine gave her son a bicycle," both *son* and *bicycle* are objects. One is an indirect object (IO) and the other a direct object. Generally speaking, the indirect object is the receiver of the direct object. In the example, "Elaine gave her son a bicycle," which is the direct object? (Elaine gave what? A bicycle.) *The son* is the receiver of the bicycle and is the indirect object.

There are a few other clues that may help you determine which object is which. First, in American English the indirect object always precedes the direct object. Second, the indirect object can be omitted, and the sentence still makes sense. Third, the indirect object may be expressed as an object of a preposition: "Elaine gave a bicycle to her son."

EXERCISE

Underline and label the direct and indirect objects.

1. Alfred told his brother a sad story.
2. Write me a letter sometime.

3. The coach gave the team a rest after John complained.
4. She showed Keith the way to go home.
5. You shouldn't give it a second thought.

Answers

1. brother (IO), story (DO)
2. me (IO), letter (DO)
3. team (IO), rest (DO)
4. Keith (IO), way (DO)
5. it (IO), thought (DO)

5. Subject-Verb-Direct Object-Object Complement (S-V-DO-OC)

The object complement (OC) renames or describes the direct object, and it completes the meaning of the sentence, much like the subject complement renames or describes the subject. Consider this sentence: "The agent made his client a star." The agent made whom? (his client, the direct object) a star. It is clear that *star* renames client and is necessary to complete the meaning of the sentence. ("The agent made his client" doesn't make sense.) The object complement functions just as the subject complement, but instead of renaming or describing the subject, it renames or describes the direct object.

- Example: "Fred considered his brother a fool." (*brother* is the DO, and *fool* is the OC)
- Example: "The student thought the homework a waste of time." (*homework* is the DO, and *waste* is the OC)

The difference between sentence pattern 4 and sentence pattern 5 is clear: the two objects are completely different or they are linked. For example, in the sentence "Antoinette fed the crowd cake," *cake* and *crowd* are two entirely different things. In the sentence "The horse considered his jockey a jerk," the *jerk* and *jockey* are linked. The two words refer to the same person.

Think about this sentence: "Therese called her friend a cab." Did Therese say to her friend, "You're a cab"? Or, did she pick up the phone and call the cab company? If Therese called her friend a name (*cab*, in this case), then *cab* is an object complement and *friend* is a direct object. If she called for a taxi, then *cab* is a direct object and *friend* is an indirect object.

EXERCISE

Underline the object complements.

1. I called him a liar.
2. General Patton considered naptime the high point of the day.

3. We thought it a great idea at the time.
4. Quincy found his front door locked.
5. The judge called it a breach of contract.

Answers

1. I called him a liar.
2. General Patton considered naptime the high point of the day.
3. We thought it a great idea at the time.
4. Quincy found his front door locked.
5. The judge called it a breach of contract.

APPOSITIVES

An appositive is a noun that renames another noun. For example, in the sentence "Tahiti, once an unspoiled island paradise, is now overrun with tourists," the noun *paradise* renames *Tahiti* and is, consequently, an appositive.

Although an appositive doesn't have an effect on the five sentence patterns, it is a very valuable stylistic tool in combining ideas and, for lack of a better place, I am mentioning it here at the end of this section.

EXERCISE

Write a sentence containing an appositive using these sentences taken from biographical information in some of the head notes accompanying the readings in this text.

Here is an example: Megan Stack is the bureau chief for the *Los Angeles Times*. She has covered the U.S.-led wars in Iraq and Afghanistan as well as the second Palestinian intifada. The term *intifada* refers to the uprising against Israel.

If you want to emphasize that Megan Stack has covered the Middle East, you would put the information about her job in an appositive phrase:

> Megan Stack, the Cairo bureau chief for the *Los Angeles Times*, has covered the U.S.-led wars in Iraq and Afghanistan as well as the second Palestinian intifada. The term *intifada* refers to the uprising against Israel.

To tighten the sentence further and to add some complexity, you could change the third sentence and substitute another appositive, like this:

> Megan Stack, the Cairo bureau chief for the *Los Angeles Times*, has covered the U.S.-led wars in Iraq and Afghanistan as well as the second Palestinian intifada, the uprising against Israel.

There are a number of ways you can arrange information. Generally, what you mention last is what is emphasized, what the reader takes with him.

EXERCISE

Combine these sentences into a single sentence using an appropriate appositive.

1. Mark Edmundson was an underachieving student at Massachusetts's Medford High School. He had never read a book in his life that hadn't been about football.
2. Bill Bryson is the best-selling author of several nonfiction books. He is best distinguished, perhaps, by his characteristic self-deprecating humor and wry perspective on human folly and frailty.
3. K. Oanh Ha is currently a reporter for the *San Jose Mercury News*. She received her B.A. in English from UCLA.
4. Nelson Mandela is the former president of South Africa. He was imprisoned for twenty-six years for his outspoken stand on apartheid.

Answers

1. Mark Edmundson, an underachieving student at Massachusetts's Medford High School, had never read a book in his life that hadn't been about football.
2. Bill Bryson, the best-selling author of several nonfiction books, is best distinguished, perhaps, by his characteristic self-deprecating humor and wry perspective on human folly and frailty.
3. K. Oanh Ha, a recipient of a B.A. in English from UCLA, is currently a reporter for the *San Jose Mercury News*.
4. Nelson Mandela, the former president of South Africa, was imprisoned for twenty-six years for his outspoken stand on apartheid.

EXERCISE

Label **SC** over subject complements, **DO** over direct objects, **APP** over appositives, **IO** over indirect objects, and **OC** over object complements.

1. Mike, the breadwinner in the family, is an architect.
2. I wrote Jan a recommendation.
3. Mr. Ed called Wilbur a fool.
4. Carol is writing her memoirs.
5. Alice sounds happier every day.

6. Charlotte, a public relations specialist for the wine industry, is constantly busy.
7. Those chickens have discovered a way to escape from the coop.
8. Most people consider health care a necessity.
9. Someone should tell Henry the story about the boy who cried wolf.
10. The mouse who ate the cheese was particularly fat.

Answers

APP SC
1. Mike, the breadwinner in the family, is an architect.

IO DO
2. I wrote Jan a recommendation.

DO OC
3. Mr. Ed called Wilbur a fool.

DO
4. Carol is writing her memoirs.

SC
5. Alice sounds happier every day.

APP SC
6. Charlotte, a public relations specialist for the wine industry, is constantly busy.

DO
7. Those chickens have discovered a way to escape from the coop.

DO OC
8. Most people consider health care a necessity.

DO DO
9. Someone should tell Henry about the boy who cried wolf.

DO SC
10. The mouse who ate the cheese was particularly fat.

DEPENDENT CLAUSES

A dependent or subordinate clause is exactly what its name implies: It is structurally dependent upon the main clause and expresses an idea that is not as important as the main thought.

There are three types of dependent clauses—adjective, adverb, and noun—and they function just as single-word adjectives, adverbs, and nouns.

Adjective Clauses

Like single-word adjectives, adjective clauses tell you which one. They modify and/or describe nouns and pronouns.

For example, in the sentence "The surprising victory stunned the fans," *surprising* is an adjective modifying *victory*. In the sentence "The victory, which was surprising, stunned the fans," which was surprising, also modifies *victory* and since it is a clause (it has a subject and a verb), it is an adjective clause.

There are restrictive adjective clauses and nonrestrictive adjective clauses. Briefly, a *restrictive adjective clause* is one that is needed to identify the word it modifies.

For example, in the sentence "The person who took my seat is in big trouble," we need the adjective clause "who took my seat" to identify the person we are talking about. We do not put commas around anything that is important for identification.

However, we do put commas around an adjective clause that we do not need for identification, that is simply added information.

For example, in the sentence "George Martin, who took my seat, is in big trouble," we know who took my seat: George Martin. We do not need "who took my seat" to identify him.

Note: Use *that* in restrictive clauses and *which* in nonrestrictive clauses.

For example, we could say either "The book that I read yesterday was absorbing" or "The book I read yesterday was absorbing." But, we cannot say "*War and Peace,* that I read yesterday, is absorbing."

Note: The difference between restrictive and nonrestrictive elements is discussed in the "punctuation" section on page 606.

EXERCISE

Underline the adjective clauses and put in necessary commas.

1. The person who sold me the bridge left town the next morning.
2. Our family always celebrates St. David's Day which is Nov. 1.
3. My Australian Cattle Dog whose name is Katie is a wonderful companion.
4. The bird that nests above our back porch wakes us up every morning.
5. The John Smith who met us at the airport turned out to be a stranger.

Answers

1. The person who sold me the bridge left town the next morning.
2. Our family always celebrates St. David's Day, which is Nov. 1.
3. My Australian Cattle Dog, whose name is Katie, is a wonderful companion.
4. The bird that nests above our back porch wakes us up every morning.
5. The John Smith who met us at the airport turned out to be a stranger.

Adverb Clauses

An adverb clause is a clause that generally functions as a single-word adverb. For example, in the sentence "The class started late," *late* is an adverb modifying the verb *started*. It answers the question When.

In the sentence "The class started when the teacher arrived," "when the teacher arrived" is a clause that modifies the verb, and it also tells When. Obviously this is an adverb clause.

Most adverb clauses, just as most single adverbs, answer the questions How, When, Where, or Why. Some adverb clauses, however, don't. Clauses of concession, for example, do not answer any particular question. These are clauses that state that two things are mutually true. For example, "Even though Dave likes to play golf, he has hasn't played in six months." The material in the adverb clauses is something conceded. Some of the words that introduce these clauses are *although, though, even if*, and *even though*.

Clauses of condition also fail to answer one of our handy questions, but they are adverb clauses, nonetheless. For example, "If I were you, I wouldn't answer the phone." The idea in the adverb clause is a condition.

Clauses of comparison also don't tell How, When, Where, or Why. Fortunately, they are very easy to recognize. Here is an example: "That sunflower is taller than any other plant in the garden." The sunflower is being compared to the other plants.

EXERCISE

Underline the adverb clauses.

1. The poor Boswell sisters have no pets because they are allergic to animal hair.
2. Although Mary had a cute little lamb, she wasn't allowed to bring it to school.
3. When Chet stood up to play, he tripped over the microphone cord.
4. That tennis player will never be as happy as he is at this moment.
5. Whenever her dog Bosley started to whine, Mariellen would put down her books and take him for a walk.

Answers

1. The poor Boswell sisters have no pets <u>because they are allergic to animal hair</u>.
2. <u>Although Mary had a cute little lamb</u>, she wasn't allowed to bring it to school.
3. <u>When Chet stood up to play</u>, he tripped over the microphone cord.
4. That tennis player will never be as happy <u>as he is at this moment</u>.
5. <u>Whenever her dog Bosley started to whine</u>, Mariellen would put down her books and take him for a walk.

Noun Clauses

A noun clause is a clause that functions as a noun. For example, in the sentence "Ron eats sushi," *sushi* is the direct object. (Read the subject, *Ron*, the verb *eats*, ask What? and you have the direct object.)

In the sentence "Ron eats whatever is on his plate," Ron eats what? "Whatever is on his plate." The clause is the direct object. Therefore, it is a noun clause.

Here is another example: In the sentence "Celia is a good cook," *Celia* is obviously the subject. (Who is a good cook? Celia.)

In the sentence "Whoever made that sushi is a good cook," who is a good cook? "Whoever made that sushi." This time the noun clause is used as the subject. It is possible to replace any noun or pronoun with a noun clause.

In the sentence "The minor earthquake gave the natives a scare," *natives* is an indirect object. It is possible to replace it "with whoever was on the island."

EXERCISE

Underline and identify the dependent clauses in the following sentences. Example: The birds started singing when the sun rose over the hill. (adverb)

1. I imagine that we will hear from him soon.
2. The weather in Tahiti is what we thought it would be.
3. We passed the park where I used to play.
4. She was the joy of my life, until I met Grace.
5. The idea that tomatoes are poisonous was once widely believed.
6. I'll give whoever finishes first a small prize.
7. The dogs barked at whatever dogs bark at.
8. After a parking lot was built on the meadow, the creatures that lived there had to find a new home.

Answers

1. I imagine that we will hear from him soon. (noun, direct object)
2. The weather in Tahiti is what we thought it would be. (noun, subject complement)
3. We passed the park where I used to play. (adjective)
4. She was the joy of my life, until I met Grace. (adverb)
5. The idea that tomatoes are poisonous was once widely believed. (noun, appositive)
6. I'll give whoever finishes first a small prize. (noun, indirect object)
7. The dogs barked at whatever dogs bark at. (noun, object of preposition)
8. After a parking lot was built on the meadow, the creatures that lived there had to find a new home. (adverb, adjective)

VERBAL PHRASES

As we learned earlier, the words in English are grouped together into phrases and clauses. To review, a clause has a subject and a verb and a phrase doesn't. There are two types of clauses, dependent and independent, and five types of phrases. We have already covered prepositional phrases, so there are only four left: the verbal phrases. This is the last of the grammar (for those of you who believe this may go on forever).

A verbal is a verb form used as something else in the sentence. For example, in the sentence "Dean is playing," *playing* is a verb. However, in the sentence "Dean enjoys playing," *playing* is the direct object; it is what Dean enjoys. So, by definition, *playing* in the second sentence is a verbal: It is a verb form used as something else. (For a more detailed explanation of present and past participles, see page 620.)

Participial Phrases

A participial phrase is a phrase beginning with a present or a past participle that is used as an adjective. Here are a few examples:

- "We made fun of the boy sucking his thumb." ("sucking his thumb" modifies "the boy")
- "The grizzled old miner, dying of thirst, crawled up to the bar and ordered a glass of milk." ("dying of thirst" describes "the miner")
- "We comforted the little girl stung by a bee in her own backyard." ("stung by a bee in her own backyard" describes "the girl")

EXERCISE

Underline the participial phrases.

1. Seeing a robin hovering overhead, the worm quickly burrowed into the soft earth.
2. We had to remove a magnificent but diseased elm planted the year I was born.
3. We were out of breath, having had to climb up eight flights of stairs.

Answers

1. Seeing a robin hovering overhead, the worm quickly burrowed into the soft earth.
2. We had to remove a magnificent but diseased elm planted the year I was born.
3. We were out of breath, having had to climb eight flights of stairs.

Gerund Phrases

A gerund is a present participle used as a noun. For example, in the sentence "John hates writing term papers," *writing* is a gerund, a present participle introducing the phrase "writing term papers," which is used as a noun (a direct object, in this case). Here are a few examples:

- "Ignoring the boss is rarely a good idea." ("Ignoring the boss" is the subject of the sentence)
- "The tiger enjoyed eating the villagers." ("eating the villagers" is the direct object)

- "He was tired of waiting for the streetcar every morning." ("waiting for the streetcar every morning" is the object of the preposition *of*)

EXERCISE

Underline the gerund phrases.

1. Franklin loves watching the sunset from his porch.
2. The best part of making a cake is licking the bowl.
3. Finding a good job was her top priority.

Answers

1. Franklin loves watching the sunset from his porch. (direct object)
2. The best part of making a cake (object of preposition) is licking the bowl. (subject complement)
3. Finding a good job was her top priority. (subject)

Infinitive Phrases

An infinitive is the simple form of the verb and is usually preceded by the word *to*, which makes most infinitive phrases easy to identify. Infinitive phrases can be used as nouns, adjective, or adverbs. Here are a few examples:

- "His goal is to become a fireman." ("to become a fireman" is used as a subject complement)
- "I am willing to discuss a compromise." ("to discuss a compromise" is an adverb modifying the adjective *willing*)
- "The athlete to be inducted into the Hall of Fame stood quietly behind the speaker." ("to be inducted into the Hall of Fame" is an adjective modifying the noun *athlete*)

EXERCISE

Underline the infinitive phrases and tell how they are used.

1. To dine at Hawthorne Lane is to dine well.
2. Elmer had the courage to stand up for his rights.
3. The poor, maligned bus driver just wanted to get through the day without a hassle.
4. The student went to New York to continue her education at Columbia.

Answers

1. To dine at Hawthorne Lane (subject) is to dine well. (subject complement)

2. Elmer had the courage to stand up for his rights. (adjective)
3. The poor, maligned bus driver just wanted to get through the day without a hassle. (direct object)
4. The student went to New York to continue her education at Columbia. (adverb)

Absolute Phrases

An absolute phrase, sometimes called a *nominative absolute,* is a phrase containing a participle and a subject for that participle. They are called *absolute* because they don't really modify anything in the main sentence. They seem connected, yet remote, like many absolute monarchs.

Look at these two sentences:

- Giggling happily, Ellen opened her birthday presents.
- Ellen giggling happily, we were sure her birthday present was a huge success.

In the first sentence, "Giggling happily" is a participial phrase modifying *Ellen,* which happens to be the subject of the sentence. In the second sentence, "Ellen giggling happily" is an absolute phrase; *Ellen* in now a part of the phrase, is, in fact, considered the subject of the phrase.

Absolute phrases are quite distinctive. They are very useful in attaching thoughts that are descriptive but not connected to any particular part of the main idea.

EXERCISE

Underline the absolute phrases.

1. The alarm system finally in place, we all felt much safer.
2. The team wanted to get plenty of rest, tomorrow's game promising to be a tough one.
3. They walked into the stadium, their heads held high.
4. The horses having been stolen, the townspeople formed a posse.

Answers

1. The alarm system finally in place, we all felt much safer.
2. The team wanted to get plenty of rest, tomorrow's game promising to be a tough one.
3. They walked into the stadium, their heads held high.
4. The horses having been stolen, the townspeople formed a posse.

Usage

Now that you have an understanding of basic grammar, you should have little trouble with the explanations in this section. I think you will be amazed as the familiar red correction marks on your papers begin to disappear, as if by magic. (Of course, it isn't magic at all; they are disappearing because of the effort you will have devoted to learning the principles of what is considered correct usage.) But perhaps the greatest difference you will notice is that you are gradually gaining confidence in your own writing—maybe not in what you have to say, which is another issue entirely, but certainly in the way you are saying it.

PRONOUN CASE

If one of your friends walks up to you and says, "Me and Bobby are going to the show," he is having a problem with pronoun case. How about a friend who says, "I am sorry you told Sally; that was just between you and I." Is this friend having a problem with pronoun case? (Yes, she is.) To a reasonably educated speaker, "me is going to the store" and "between you and I" are equally grating to the ear. So, since most people with whom you come into contact judge you initially on the way you speak, and, as you have discovered in your English classes, on the way you write, to avoid any embarrassment, it is rather important to come to some understanding of pronoun case.

There are three cases in the English language: subjective (nominative), objective, and possessive (genitive). The *subjective case* is used for subjects and subject complements, the *objective* case is used for objects, and the *possessive* case is used to show possession. It is obvious, then, that if you can recognize subject, objects, and subject complements, material that is covered on pages 576–579, almost all of the pronoun errors you make will instantly disappear. And, if you momentarily forget which pronouns are in which case, the following chart will refresh your memory.

Subjective Case	Objective Case	Possessive Case
I	me	my, mine
he	him	his
she	her	her, hers
we	us	our, ours
they	them	their, theirs
who	whom	whose

Most people have very few problems with pronoun case. Very rarely do you hear "Please give I the book" or "Him was sorry that me told she not to talk to we." We tend to make a clear distinction between pronouns used as subjects and those used as objects. For example, we say "He goes to the store," rather than "Him goes to the store." (*He* is the subject and is in the subjective case.) We say "She hit him," rather than "She hit he." (*Him* is the direct object and is in the objective case.)

But, as always, there are a few issues that give even well-educated people a moment's pause.

1. Appositives

An appositive is in the same case as the word or words it renames. Consider these two sentences:

- The class elected two girls, Cynthia and me.
- Two girls, Cynthia and I, were elected.

In the first sentence, *girls* is a direct object; hence, the appositives, "Cynthia and me," are in the objective case.

In the second sentence, *girls* is the subject; consequently, the appositives, "Cynthia and I," are in the subjective case.

2. Subject Complements

Subject complements and subjects are in the subjective case. The reasoning seems to be that since subject complements, when nouns, are the same as subjects "(John is a boy)," they should be in the same case. Unfortunately, in some cases this sounds better in theory than in practice. For example, when someone calls Jill on the phone, instead of saying, "This is me," she might, quite properly, say, "This is she" because *she* is a subject complement. If someone asked me if I was the one who was laughing at the president's grammar, I would answer, "It was I." These examples sound correct to an educated ear. However, some constructions, although grammatically correct, are rarely, if ever, uttered. For example, "It was we" sounds so strange almost no one would ever say it.

The problem here is that only a solid knowledge of the rules will give you the confidence to break them. Otherwise, you will continue to rely on your ear and will remain uncertain about your use of the language.

3. Comparisons *After, Before, Than,* and *As*

Think about these two sentences:

- My father stood before me.
- My father stood before I.

In the first sentence, *before* is a preposition, and the phrase means that my father stood in front of me.

In the second sentence, *before* is a subordinating conjunction. It introduces an adverb clause. What clause? you might ask. There is no verb. But there really is one; it is simply understood. What I am saying in the second sentence is that my father stood up before I did. The verb *did* (or *stood*) is understood.

Here are two other examples:

- You believe Mrs. Larney more than I.
- You believe Mrs. Larney more than me.

In the first sentence, you believe Mrs. Larney more than I believe her. I think she might lie every so often.

In the second sentence, you believe Mrs. Larney more than you believe me. To you, I am the unreliable one.

4. *Who* and *Whom*

Who and *whom* sound very much alike and therefore are often confused. Perhaps because they sound so much alike there is no reason to fret unduly about this difference. For example, which of the following is, grammatically speaking, correct? "Was it Sarah who I saw in the library?" or "Was it Sarah whom I saw in the library?" The difference in sound is slight. (The correct pronoun is *whom*. I saw *whom* in the library.)

It seems that *who* is gradually replacing *whom*, and perhaps one day *whom* will disappear forever from the language. But until that time, I think it is important for the careful writer to make a distinction between the two.

The solution is always the same: Ask whether the pronoun in question is in the objective or the subjective case. Once you know this, the problem is solved.

5. Possessive Pronouns with Gerunds

Think about these two sentences:

- Him jumping on the bed annoyed his mother.
- His jumping on the bed annoyed his mother.

The subject in both sentences is, without question, *jumping*. What annoyed his mother? The jumping. In the first sentence, *Him*, the objective form of the pronoun, clearly sounds odd. In the second sentence, *His* is the possessive form, and it obviously modifies *jumping*.

Let's look at a proper noun in the place of the pronouns:

- Alfred jumping on the bed annoyed his mother.
- Alfred's jumping on the bed annoyed his mother.

In the first sentence, *Alfred* sounds acceptable, but, again, the subject is *jumping*, so the question is, What is the function of *Alfred?* It isn't an object of anything, it isn't the subject, and it isn't an adjective. In the second sentence, *Alfred's* is indeed an adjective modifying *jumping*, and all is right with the world, or at least with this sentence.

It might be worth noting that if you put commas around "jumping on the bed" in the first sentence, it becomes a participial phrase modifying *Alfred*, which is now the subject of the sentence. Written this way, Mom is not annoyed with the jumping; she is annoyed with Alfred.

Think about these two sentences:

- The teacher hated me making faces behind his back.
- The teacher hated my making faces behind his back.

Did the teacher hate me or did she hate the fact that I was making faces behind her back? If she hated me, the first sentence is reasonable (except for a comma that I would put after *me*) because *me* is the direct object. If she thought I might be otherwise an OK person but hated my making faces, the second sentence is accurate, "my making faces behind his back" being a gerund phrase used as the direct object.

The secret to success here, and everywhere in the writing/speaking process, is to make sure you are saying what you mean. (I may have said this before and may say it again because these are words to live by.)

EXERCISE

Correct the pronoun errors. (Not every sentence contains a mistake.)

1. Could it have been him who had stolen the car?
2. Please address your remarks to Edith and I.
3. People like Allen and she will always find something to talk about.
4. Everyone except the parole officer and him was on time.
5. She thought the runaways might have been they.
6. The principal strongly objected to Tommy bringing a frog to school.
7. The salesperson smiled as the two girls, Alice and I, brought a big pile of dresses to the counter.
8. She wondered who I thought had lost the key.

9. Is it possible Koko, the ape, is smarter than he?
10. The jury decided to give the two defendants, Geri and she, the benefit of the doubt.

Answers

1. Could it have been **he** who had stolen the car?
2. Please address your remarks to Edith and **me**.
3. People like Allen and **her** will always find something to talk about.
4. correct
5. correct
6. The principal strongly objected to **Tommy's** bringing a frog to school.
7. correct
8. correct
9. correct
10. The jury decided to give the two defendants, Geri and **her**, the benefit of the doubt.

PRONOUN AGREEMENT

Agreement in Number

A friend says to you, "Dave likes his dog, Katie, because they were so loyal." You wonder, Who are "they"? Since Dave likes this one dog, it is confusing to refer to his dog as "they." The sentence should read, "Dave likes his dog, Katie, because she is so loyal."

The point is this: A pronoun agrees in number with its antecedent (the word to which it refers). Singular pronouns refer to singular antecedents, and plural pronouns refer to plural antecedents.

Consider the following sentence: "Carolyn and Monte were asked to bring their lunch." The antecedent for the plural pronoun *their* is Carolyn and Monte. Two people, two lunches.

Think about this sentence: "Every student who wants to be excused from gym must show their pass to the dean." How many students are we talking about?

Here are a few rules to help you avoid problems with this generally straightforward topic:

1. Use a singular pronoun when its antecedent is a singular indefinite pronoun (*everyone, everybody, anyone, someone, somebody*). Here are two examples:

    - Anyone who wanted a ticket was told he should be at the box office early.
    - Everyone should try his best.

In the first sentence, the indefinite pronoun *Anyone* is singular, and, consequently, the pronoun that refers to it, *he*, must be singular. In the second sentence, the antecedent for the singular pronoun, *his*, is also an indefinite pronoun, *Everyone*.

Although "*Everyone* should try their best" is quite common and sounds just fine to many speakers, it is wise to remember that the indefinite pronouns *everyone, everybody, anyone, someone*, and *somebody* are singular and should take singular verbs and singular pronouns.

The objection to the examples I have given is that the pronouns I used are masculine, and women have felt that using masculine pronouns exclusively reveals sexism in language. It does. However, fixing the problem has proven to be a rather difficult task. Using *his or her, him and her*, or *he or she* more than once becomes very tiresome and sounds affected. Another solution offered by one of my colleagues some years ago was *hisr* and *himr*. Needless to say, this never caught on.

I have always told my students that males should use masculine pronouns and females should use feminine pronouns.

2. If a compound antecedent is one person or one thing, the pronoun that refers to it should obviously be singular. For example,

   - Our father figure and hero fought his last battle last night. ("Father figure" and "hero" are obviously the same person.)

3. A compound antecedent preceded by *each* or *every* is considered singular:

   - "Every girl and boy was given an unpleasant task."

4. A pronoun referring to two or more antecedents connected by *or* or *nor* should agree with the nearest one. For example,

   - Neither the five pterodactyls nor the bellowing woolly mammoth was happy to find himself caught in the tar pit. (Notice that the verb, *was,* is singular because the closest subject is *mammoth;* consequently, the pronoun, *himself,* is also singular.)

5. Pronouns referring to collective nouns should agree with the number of the verb.

   Here is an example:

   - The audience rises to its feet. (The verb, *rises*, is singular, and so the pronoun, *its*, should also be singular.)

Agreement in Person

The term *person* refers to the speaker, the person spoken to, or the person spoken about. The person speaking (*I* or *we*) is called the first person, the person spoken to (*you*) is called the second person, and the person spoken about (*he, she, it,* or *they*) is called the third person.

What this means, in terms of agreement, is that you should keep your persons together. Think about this example:

- If a skater tries to catch a ride behind a bus, you can expect to get hurt. (Who is this mysterious *you*? Why not simply say, "If a skater tries to catch a ride behind a bus, *he* can expect to get hurt"?)

In other words, don't shift from one person to another without a good reason.

Finally, make sure your pronoun has a clear antecedent. Avoid vagueness. Consider this sentence:

- George played trumpet in the Stanford Band and decided to make it his life's work. (What does *it* refer to, exactly? Playing trumpet in the Stanford Band? Talk about the eternal student.)

And this one:

- Just five people showed up for the tennis match, which was due to the heavy rain. (What, exactly, does *which* refer to?)

And this one:

- At the deli section, they gave me a number. (*Who* gave me a number?)

The important things to remember when dealing with pronouns are to keep a clear relationship between the pronoun and its antecedent and to avoid shifts in person and number.

EXERCISE

Correct the pronoun errors.

1. Anyone who wants to enter the courtroom must leave their weapons at the door.
2. When one faces a difficult math problem, you should not hesitate to ask your instructor.
3. Many good surfers are attracted to big waves, which is why Mavericks is such a popular place to surf.
4. After I paid my money, they gave me a stamp on my hand.
5. Mike is an excellent golfer, although he never took lessons in it.

Answers

1. Anyone who wants to enter the courtroom must leave **his** weapons at the door.

2. When one faces a difficult math problem, **he** (or **she**, if you happen to be a woman) should not hesitate to ask **his** (or **her**) instructor.
3. Mavericks has the big waves that attract many good surfers. (One of a few possibilities.)
4. After I paid my money, I got a stamp on my hand.
5. Although Mike never took lessons, he is an excellent golfer.

SUBJECT-VERB AGREEMENT

Before you begin this section, you might want to review the explanation of basic sentence structure and the importance of being able to identify the subjects and the verbs. (See pages 567–571.)

Subjects and verbs agree in number. That means singular subjects take singular verbs, and plural subjects take plural verbs. To make this happen, you have to be able to recognize the subject and the verb in the clause, apply a few recognized rules, and use a little common sense. Here are two examples:

- A flower (s) blooms (v) in the spring.

The subject *flower* and the verb *blooms* are both singular.

- Many flowers (s) bloom (v) in the spring.

The subject *flowers* and the verb *bloom* are both plural.

- A hawk and a crow were fighting over a field mouse.

In the sentence two birds were fighting. The subject is plural and so is the verb.

Although writers generally have no trouble making subject and verbs agree—one doesn't hear "he are here" very often, if ever—there are a few troublesome areas that give even the most careful writer a moment's hesitation.

It might be prudent at this point to examine briefly the source of most of the errors that are made: the third-person singular form of the verb in the present tense. Think about this for a minute:

singular	***plural***
I play	we play
you play	you play
he, she, it plays	they play

Only the third-person singular form of the verb in the present tense takes an *s*. Consequently, most subject-verb agreement errors can be solved simply by asking if the subject is an "it," a "he," or a "she." If it is, put an *s* on the verb: if it isn't, if it is a "they", don't. Like all rules, this will work almost all of the time. For example,

- One of the janitors runs a computer repair business.

The subject *One* is a "he" (or a "she"), so the verb *runs* is singular.

- Fred and Henry run a computer repair business.

The subjects *Fred* and *Henry* are plural, a "they." No *s* on the verb.

Rules for Subject-Verb Agreement

1. Generally, phrases and clauses that intrude between the subject and verb do not affect the number of the verb. Consider this example:

   - One of my goldfish is dead.

   The subject is *One*, not goldfish. If in doubt, just ask yourself what is dead. One is dead; there may be others still swimming around, presumably healthy and happy. If you are still unconvinced, how do you like, "One of my goldfish are dead"?

   There are a few exceptions to this rule. Verbs with indefinite pronouns having to do with amounts—*many, half, all, some*, and *most*, to name a few—rely on the object of the preposition for their number. Think about this example:

   - Some of my money is missing.

   No problem here. The subject *Some* and the verb *is* are both singular. However, we do not say "Some of my dimes is missing"; we say "Some of my dimes are missing." It is obvious that in some cases the phrases that intrude between the subject and verb influence the number of the verb.

   As always, just be careful.

2. Many indefinite pronouns (*each, every, everyone, any, anybody*, and so on) take singular verbs, even though a word like *everybody* seems to represent at least more than one person. Look at the following sentence:

   - Everyone has at least one regret.

   The verb *has* is singular. How does this sentence sound?

   - Are everybody happy?

   Are is plural and obviously doesn't work.

3. If two subjects are connected by *either . . . or, neither . . . nor, not only . . . but also,* or simply *or,* the verb, in theory, agrees with the closer subject. Here is an example:

   - Neither John nor his brothers want to play that team again.

   The subject *brothers* is closer to the verb *want* than the subject *John.* Consequently, the verb is plural.

   However, this rule may lead to a slightly strange-sounding sentence. Consider the following:

   - Either the termites or I am leaving.

   If you don't like the way a sentence sounds, reword it. For example:

   - Either I am leaving, or the termites are leaving.

4. Collective nouns are nouns that refer to a group. For example, the *jury,* the *audience,* a *band,* a *herd,* the *committee* are all collective nouns. The consensus of opinion seems to be that if the particular group is acting as one, as a unit, the verb should be singular; if the members of the group are acting independently, the verb should be plural. Consider these examples:

   - The audience rises as one to applaud the performance.
   - The herd of cows grazes lazily on the green grasses of the meadow.

   These are obviously groups acting as a unit—singular subjects, singular verbs.

   However, when the members of the group act individually, the plural verb often sounds strange:

   - The jury are arguing about the verdict.
   - The band are not in tune.

   American English seems to favor the use of singular verbs with collective nouns. However, when in doubt, it is probably better to rewrite the sentence to avoid peculiar-sounding constructions. For example,

   - The members of the jury are arguing about the verdict.
   - The band members are not in tune.

5. The verb should agree with the subject, not with a word following the verb that is the same as (renames) the subject:

   - My favorite fruit is strawberries.

   In this sentence the singular subject *fruit* takes the singular verb *is.*

   - Strawberries are my favorite fruit.

   Here, the plural subject *strawberries* takes the plural verb *are.*

6. If the subject of a dependent clause stands for a noun or pronoun in the main clause, the number of that subject depends upon the number of the word it stands for (its ***antecedent***). Here is an example:

   - Sharon is a gorilla who likes to wrestle.

   The verb *likes* in the dependent clause "who likes to wrestle" is singular because its subject ("who") stands for *gorilla*, and *gorilla* is singular. The antecedent in the following example is *orangutans;* consequently, the verb in the dependent clause is plural:

   - Sharon, Alice, and Helen are three orangutans who like to wrestle.

   Finally, consider the following sentence:

   - Sharon is the only one of the orangutans who likes to wrestle.

   Now, only one of the orangutans likes to wrestle, so the subject in the adjective clause is singular, and so is the verb.

7. *The number* is always singular, and *a number* is always plural.

   - The number of e-mails I receive seems to increase every month.
   - A large number of e-mails are spam.

EXERCISE

Choose the verb that agrees with the subject in these sentences.

1. Every one of the boys (have, has) to take a test tomorrow.
2. Sheila may be one of those rare girls who (doesn't, don't) enjoy playing volleyball.
3. A number of my opportunities (was, were) wasted.
4. The number of rules (is, are) determined by the imagination of the players.
5. Half of the men on the rowing team (wants, want) to begin practice later.
6. Not only the assistant coaches but also the coach himself (feels, feel) 5:00 a.m. is a perfect time to begin rowing.
7. Doug and his friend Harry (tend, tends) to irritate their hapless science teacher.
8. Sally wrote one of the many petitions that (calls, call) for a stop to oil drilling.
9. Everybody in the classroom always (hate, hates) a visit from the vice-principal.
10. One of the many cars in his garage (was, were) given to charity.
11. The subject of accounting and the theory of economics (confuse, confuses) me.

12. Henrietta is the only one of the candidates who (understand, understands) the issues.
13. In a corner of the square (stand, stands) a small statue of Johnny Mercer.
14. Neither the doctors nor the medicine man (believe, believes) Trevor will recover.
15. Stephanie, along with her friend Jennifer, (take, takes) the dog for a walk every day.

Answers

1. has
2. don't
3. were
4. is
5. want
6. feels
7. tend
8. call
9. hates
10. was
11. confuse
12. understands
13. stands
14. believes
15. takes

PUNCTUATION

Punctuation marks function in one of two ways: They either separate or enclose.

The result is that they communicate the relative importance of a writer's ideas and represent, as best they can, the pauses and voice inflections used in speech.

Like words, punctuation marks depend upon mutual agreement. In other words, in English, the word *table* brings to mind a four-legged object at which people sit. There is nothing to connect the word to the object except mutual agreement. And so it is with punctuation. If, for example, a writer uses a colon when almost everyone else uses a comma, he defeats his own purpose (if that purpose is to avoid confusion).

Punctuation is an immeasurably valuable tool because it offers the writer the opportunity to inject into his prose, at least to some degree, the various pauses, voice inflections, facial expression, and body language that are lost when speaking is turned into writing. It is certainly the one element that, once learned, reveals a remarkable and instantly recognizable improvement in the writer's grasp of the craft. And, finally, it enables him to express his ideas with a newfound ease.

I have found that most students feel completely comfortable with the period, the question mark, and the occasional exclamation point. They are not so confident with the marks that occur within the sentence. Many students hesitate before using a comma, and some rarely, if ever, use colons, dashes, or parentheses. No wonder so much student writing sounds flat and lacks individuality.

What follows is a short review of these often mysterious marks that, when used properly, will add personality to a student's writing. I am limiting the review to the basic principles of separating and enclosing, to those rules that will allow students to organize their thoughts more effectively.

Marks Used to Separate

The following marks of punctuation are used to separate items within a sentence.

The Comma

Because the comma offers a slight, short pause, and since we are forever pausing in our speech, the question of whether or not to insert a comma when we are writing is often a tricky one. An examination of the basic rules and a few thoughts of my own should give you some insight into the seemingly gray area of the comma.

1. The most basic rule is the one covering the use of the comma between two independent clauses. If you learn this quite simple rule, you will never see the words "commas splice" on your papers again.

   Most books state that you use a comma between *and, but, or, for, nor, so,* and *yet* (the coordinating conjunctions) when one connects two independent clauses. If you do not have one of these words separating your two sentences, you must use a semicolon or a period.

   Although this is a good rule of thumb, it is more accurate to say that you *may* use a comma before a coordinating conjunction that separates two sentences, but you don't have to. You may use a semicolon, a period, or nothing at all. It depends on how you want to separate the two sentences.

   Let's look at four examples:

   - Jan ran and Peter walked.
   - It could have been worse, but it couldn't have been much worse.
   - I had waited an hour for the bus, tripped on the stairs, and spilled my coffee on my good pants; but then Tom asked me to marry him, so it turned out to be a wonderful day.
   - We hope Conrad is the man for the job. But you never know.

There are at least two independent clauses separated by a coordinating conjunction in each sentence. In the first one, there is no punctuation. The two sentences are more or less fused. No pause. You could, of course, put a comma before the *and*, but you don't have to if you want the sentences read as one.

The second sentence seems to call for a pause between *worse* and *but*. It creates a slight pause and, consequently, a slight emphasis on the second part.

The third sentence is long. It contains three independent clauses, and there are three verbs in the first one. The main break occurs between *pants* and *but*, and a semicolon makes that clear.

The fourth example contains two sentences. No matter what you may have heard, there is nothing wrong with starting a sentence with *And* or *But*. The effect of doing this is to set off the second sentence, to make it an entirely separate thought.

A comma, or commas, can also be used, sparingly, for emphasis. Consider the following two sentences:

- After finishing the marathon, George was tired but happy.
- After finishing the marathon, George was tired, but happy.

In the first sentence, *tired* and *happy* describe George's condition equally. However, in the second sentence, the slight pause between *tired* and *but* emphasizes *happy*.

The secret to success in this situation—in all situations where punctuation is used—is to hear in your head how you want the sentence to be read and then to punctuate it accordingly.

2. Use commas between items in a series.

A series consists of three or more items. For example,

- The dog learned to sit, stay, and come when called.

The dog learned three things, and they are separated by commas.

The items in the series can single words, phrases, or sentences. For example,

- Joey played with his toy tractor, Shane and Joe removed the tree stump, and Marian baked a pie. (three independent clauses)

Some people—notably journalists—leave out the comma before the last *and* or *or*. It seems wise to put it in to prevent possible questions about the closeness of the last two items. For example, how many items are in the following series?

- The captain wanted to supervise the boarding of the cargo, men, women and children.

Does the writer consider women and children one group or two groups? It is impossible to know unless the writer consistently adds a comma before the last *and* in the series. The argument that in a series the *and* before the last item takes the place of the comma has never made any sense to me. Here's another example:

- Samantha is inviting the twins, Rowan and Avery.

  How many people is Samantha inviting to her son's birthday party?

3. Use commas between coordinate adjectives that precede a noun.

   Coordinate adjectives are adjectives that modify equally. For example,

   - Last night I saw a scary, violent movie.

   The adjectives *scary* and *violent* modify the noun *movie* equally. You can easily test if they do by reversing them or placing an *and* between them and checking to see if the sentence still sounds okay. "Last night I saw a violent, scary movie" sounds perfectly fine, as does "Last night I saw a scary and violent movie."

   Therefore, the adjectives are coordinate, and you should separate them with a comma.

   However, think about this sentence:

   - Last night I saw a scary horror movie.

   Now the adjectives are *scary* and *horror*. If I reverse them the sentence becomes "Last night I saw a horror scary movie." This doesn't work, nor does "Last night I saw a scary and horror movie."

   If the adjectives are not coordinate, are not modifying equally, don't separate them.

4. Generally, use a comma to separate an introductory verbal phrase or a dependent clause or longish (a little vague, I admit) prepositional phrase from the sentence that follows.

   - To find the necessary items for the scavenger hunt, Richard rang at least 100 doorbells. (introductory infinitive phrase)
   - Feeling rather exhausted after the long ride, Lance decided to lie down. (introductory participial phrase)
   - After he told the boss to stuff the job, Johnny went home and told his wife the news. (introductory adverb clause)
   - Before starting the last page of her term paper, Ariel got up and poured herself a big glass of iced tea. (introductory prepositional phrase)

5. Use commas to set off parenthetical expressions.

   A parenthetical expression is either a word or a short group of words that interrupt the flow of the sentence but add nothing to the meaning.

Here are a few:

- Little Billy was certainly a brat, don't you agree?
- He was, however, Mama's little boy.
- To tell the truth, Billy got on everyone's nerves.
- His behavior at the dinner table, for example, was atrocious.

The Semicolon

Like most marks of punctuation, the semicolon has a rather well-defined purpose: It is used to separate structurally equal units.

Consider the following:

- I have lived in Denver, Chicago, and Reno.

This sentence contains three equal items in a series, and these items are separated by commas.

Now consider this sentence:

- I have lived in Denver, Colorado, Chicago, Illinois, and Reno, Nevada.

There are still three items in this series, not six. So, to make everything clear to the reader—always the goal—we punctuate the sentence this way:

- I have lived in Denver, Colorado; Chicago, Illinois; and Reno, Nevada.

Now the three items are delineated. The semicolon separates equal items, when needed; and it is needed in this sentence to separate city and state from city and state.

Here is another example:

- Hugh saw Fred, Harriet, and Matilda.
- Hugh saw Fred, who was looking at his watch; Harriet, who was bending over to tie her shoe; and Matilda, who was pretending she didn't see him.

The Colon

The colon is used at the end of a sentence to introduce a list or an explanation.

Here are a few examples:

- When Helen left the house, she had with her three things: her purse, her glasses, and her pepper spray.
- Harold had only one thing on his mind: finding the dog before his wife got home.

Consider these two sentences

- Vanessa had a wonderful idea; however, the boss vetoed it.
- Vanessa had a wonderful idea: She proposed we take tomorrow off.

Both sentences contain two independent clauses. In the first sentence they are separated by a semicolon because they are two different thoughts. In the second sentence that are separated by a colon because the second clause *is* the idea.

Used properly at the end of a sentence, the colon says, Here it comes, whatever *it* happens to be.

Do not think that because you have a list you automatically put a colon in front of it. Consider this sentence:

- Lou talked about his mother, his marriage, and the problems he was having.

Would you be tempted to put a colon after *about*? If so, fight the temptation. You certainly would not want to separate the objects of the preposition from their preposition.

Make sure you have a sentence before you decide to use a colon.

The Dash

The dash represents a break in thought. For example,

- The show begins at—now, when does the show begin?
- Open that Christmas present—no, not that one!
- A pencil, an eraser, and a dictionary—these were all we could bring to the test.

All represent a rather abrupt shift in thought. If, in the last example, the sentence was first and the list followed, you would put a colon after *test*, but when the list precedes the sentence, use a dash.

EXERCISE

Add the necessary punctuation.

1. A man I am told who is afraid of the dark will usually reach into a room to turn on the light before he enters.
2. Hoping for a treat the dog eagerly jumped through the hoops which were waist high ran up the ramp and crawled through the tunnel which was long and dark.
3. The large hairy spider crawled across the carpet then he moved slowly up Karl's pant leg.

4. It would be a pleasure to no on second thought it would not be a pleasure to see her again.
5. I have a great idea let's leave early and go swimming.

Answers

1. A man, I am told, who is afraid of the dark will usually reach into a room to turn on the light before he enters.
2. Hoping for a treat, the dog eagerly jumped through the hoops, which were waist high; ran up the ramp; and crawled through the tunnel, which was long and dark.
3. The large, hairy spider crawled across the carpet; then he moved slowly up Karl's pant leg.
4. It would be a pleasure to—no, on second thought it would not be a pleasure to see her again.
5. I have a great idea: Let's leave early and go swimming.

Marks Used to Enclose

There are only four ways to enclose words, phrases, or clauses: using commas, parentheses, dashes, and brackets. Only the first three are used with any regularity, so once you have decided to enclose something, you should have no trouble determining how you want to do it.

Commas

Commas are used to enclose nonrestrictive words, phrases, or clauses. *Nonrestrictive* is a term for a modifier that is not needed for identification, that does not limit the word it describes or renames. (Refer to adjective clauses, pages 582–583.)

Consider these two sentences:

- Everyone who ate the fish died.
- Eleanor, who ate the fish, died.

In the first sentence we need "who ate the fish" to tell us who died. Did everyone die? No. The only dead ones are those who ate the fish. The clause limits *Everyone* to those who ate the fish.

In the second sentence we already know who died: Eleanor. The adjective clause is not needed to identify her, so we put commas around it.

Because this is an important point, here is another example:

- The artist Paul Gauguin abandoned his family and moved to Tahiti.
- Paul Gauguin, the artist, abandoned his family and moved to Tahiti.

In the first sentence we need the appositive "Paul Gauguin" to identify the artist. ("The artist who abandoned his family and moved to Tahiti" doesn't tell us which artist we are talking about.) In the second sentence we don't need the artist to identify Paul Gauguin. The name *Gauguin* tells us exactly whom we are talking about; "the artist" is added, nonessential information.

EXERCISE

Put commas around the nonrestrictive elements.

1. Henry Mancini who wrote many wonderful tunes died recently.
2. The man who wrote many wonderful tunes died recently.
3. Hemingway's novel *The Sun Also Rises* was one of Stefan's favorite books.
4. He was born in a town known for its beautiful beaches.
5. He was born in Honolulu known for its beautiful beaches.
6. My brother Fred lost his leg in a boating accident. [I have three brothers.]

Answers

1. Henry Mancini, who wrote many wonderful tunes, died recently.
2. The man who wrote many wonderful tunes died recently.
3. Hemingway's novel *The Sun Also Rises* was one of Stefan's favorite books.
4. He was born in a town known for its beautiful beaches.
5. He was born in Honolulu, known for its beautiful beaches.
6. My brother Fred lost his leg in a boating accident.

Parentheses

Parentheses are used to enclose nonrestrictive words, phrases, and clauses that interrupt the flow of the sentence.

Here are a few examples:

- Josh (didn't he move to Nevada after his cat died?) was once a brilliant physicist.
- Jolene loved *film noir* (a genre of film that typically features dark settings, brooding characters, corruption, detectives, and the seamy side of the big city).

As you can see, parentheses are used to enclose information that has the feeling of an afterthought or that explains a term or idea. In the second example, it would be possible to put a comma after *noir,* but since there are commas in the phrase, the parentheses more clearly set it off.

Dashes

Since dashes indicate an abrupt break in the thought, they tend to emphasize what they enclose.

Think of these three examples:

- Carlos, who was my best friend in high school, hijacked a plane.
- Carlos (he was my best friend in high school, you know) hijacked a plane.
- Carlos—he was my best friend in high school!—hijacked a plane.

In the first example, the material within the commas fits nicely into the sentence. The commas add nothing in tone. In other words, the material enclosed is simply a statement of fact.

In the second example, the material within the parentheses does not fit smoothly into the sentence. You are, in fact, jamming an entire sentence inside another one. The parentheses indicate that the material is something that occurred to you about the time you wrote "Carlos" and were remembering he was your best friend, so you threw that in.

In the third example, you probably thought of the best friend idea about the same time you were poised to write "hijacked a plane," and you were saying to yourself, "Wow! He was my best friend in high school," so you stuck it in the sentence and used dashes for emphasis. Note: Question marks and exclamation points can be used inside dashes, and a question mark can be used inside parentheses. (Since parentheses tend to minimize the material, using an exclamation point would be confusing.)

Here are two examples:

- Hugh Villalta, (isn't he a psychology teacher?) has had back problems.
- Mac Swanton—what an incredible job he did on my fence!—is a truly great carpenter.

Apostrophes

There are two main uses for the apostrophe: to form the possessive case of nouns and to form contractions.

There are only a few things to consider when making a noun possessive. Think about these possibilities:

- The librarian has books.
- Three librarians have books.
- Spears has books.

We always put the apostrophe after the word we are dealing with. In the first sentence we are dealing with the singular noun *librarian,* so if we want to make that noun possessive, we put an apostrophe and an *s* after it: "the librarian's books."

In the second sentence we are dealing with the plural noun *librarians,* so we put the apostrophe after that word: "librarians' books." We do not put an *s* after the apostrophe because we do not say "librarianses."

In the third sentence Spears has books, so we put an apostrophe after *Spears*, and, since we say "Spearses books," we write "Spears's books."

Usage varies on this last point. Some people feel that even though you pronounce both *s*'s, the point is made with the apostrophe only. However, unless the word that follows the possessive begins with an *s*, thereby creating a lot of *s* sounds in a row ("Mr. Gomez's suspicious behavior was noticed by the cop on the corner"), I think it is wise to add the *s* if you pronounce it.

Apostrophes are also used to indicate that a letter is left out, in other words, in contractions.

- She'll be comin' round the mountain. (The first apostrophe replaces *wi* in *will*, and the second apostrophe takes the place of the *g* in *coming*.)
- It's a wonderful day, isn't it? (The first apostrophe takes the place of the *i* in *is*, and the second replaces the *o* in *not*.

EXERCISE

Add the necessary punctuation.

1. These were his goals in life money fame and power.
2. Money fame and power these were his goals in life.
3. Donald's unusual habit eating three breakfasts every day made him sluggish.
4. Only three candidates Kenny Dorham Republican Horace Silver Democrat and Anita O'Day Independent ran for office.
5. My mother can bandage that shes a trained nurse you know so that it wont hurt.
6. The men who concocted the scheme were soon identified and so left town on the very next train.
7. He told me can you believe it that I had won the lottery.
8. Writing in his dairy Drake made the following observation The sea is most unfriendly consequently most of us are depressed irritable and sick.

Answers

1. These were his goals in life: money, fame, and power.
2. Money, fame, and power—these were his goals in life.
3. Donald's unusual habit, eating three breakfasts every day, made him sluggish.
4. Only three candidates—Kenny Dorham, Republican; Horace Silver, Democrat; and Anita O'Day, Independent—ran for office.
5. My mother can bandage that (she's a trained nurse, you know) so that it won't hurt.

6. The men who concocted the scheme were soon identified and so left town on the very next train.
7. He told me—can you believe it?—that I had won the lottery.
8. Writing in his dairy, Drake made the following observation: "The sea is most unfriendly; consequently, most of us are depressed, irritable, and sick."

MISPLACED, DANGLING, AND SQUINTING MODIFIERS

Modifiers are words, phrases, and clauses that describe other words. They are either adjectives or adverbs. To use them effectively, all you have to do is to make clear what word is being modified.

Misplaced Modifiers

A misplaced modifier is one that is in the wrong place. You wouldn't say, for example, "The man took off his bald shirt." Presumably, the man, not the shirt, is bald, so you place the adjective next to *man* to make clear what word is being modified.

Here is another example:

- I saw a beautiful Victorian mansion walking down the street.

Needless to say, no mansion is ever going for a stroll. The modifier "walking down the street" does not modify *mansion*; it modifies *I*.

- Walking down the street, I saw a beautiful Victorian mansion.

Although it is wise to keep the modifier close to the word it modifies, it is not always necessary. For example:

- John introduced me to his girlfriend, not realizing that I would be smitten by her beauty.

The adjective phrase "not realizing that I would be smitten by her beauty" obviously modifies *John*, but it works at the end of the sentence.

Single-word modifiers can often give an unwary writer a problem. Think about these two sentences:

- The poker player lost almost all his money.
- The poker player almost lost all his money.

In the first sentence the gambler walked away from the table with very little of the money he started with. In the second sentence he walked away with all his money after almost losing it.

As always, be careful.

EXERCISE

Place the misplaced modifier in a position that makes more sense.

1. Ernie came by while I was feeding the pigs in his new car.
2. Dr. Coskey nearly earned $1000 for his treatment of a sick hippo.
3. They skipped merrily along the path that had been made by cows with a song in their heart.
4. Professor Cunningham has almost taught 18,000 students.
5. We had dinner at a little place where the waiters dress as Greek dancers on our night out.

Answers

1. While I was feeding the pigs, Ernie came by in his new car.
2. Dr. Coskey earned nearly $1000 for his treatment of a sick hippo.
3. With a song in their heart, they skipped merrily along the path that had been made by cows.
4. Professor Cunningham has taught almost 18,000 students.
5. On our night out we had dinner at a little place where the waiters dress as Greek dancers.

Dangling Modifiers

The dangling modifier is missing a word to modify. Consequently, it modifies an unintended word, generally with laughable results.

Consider these sentences:

- Flying low over the meadow, cows could be clearly seen.
- An ardent advocate of the rights of rodents, Mary Honker's struggle to criminalize the use of rats in laboratory experiments began in 1977.

In the first sentence, "Flying low over the meadow" modifies *cows*, but cows don't fly.

In the second sentence, "Honker's struggle" isn't an ardent advocate of the rights of rodents; Honker herself is.

The first sentence could read, "Flying low over the meadow, we could clearly see cows." (I have added a word, *we*, that the phrase can clearly modify.)

The second sentence could read, "An ardent advocate of the rights of rodents, Mary Honker struggled since 1977 to criminalize the use of rats in laboratory experiments."

Squinting Modifiers

A squinting modifier is one that can modify one of two words, but it is impossible to tell which one. For example,

- Ariel told Betsy that she needs a haircut.

Who is *she*? There is no quick fix for this problem. "Ariel told Betsy that Betsy needs a haircut" is acceptable but a little awkward. "Ariel told Betsy that Ariel needs a haircut" is more than a little awkward. A possible solution might be "Ariel told Betsy that she (Betsy) needs a haircut."

When in doubt, rewrite.

EXERCISE

Correct the modifier errors.

1. Walking to his seat, his books fell noisily to the floor.
2. Studying for hours, my eyes felt tired.
3. Tom told Henry that if he didn't begin to study, he would fail.
4. Opening the door as quietly as possible, no one seemed to notice him.
5. After struggling to stay awake in class, his decision was to get a cup of coffee.

Answers

1. Walking to his seat, he dropped his book noisily on the floor.
2. Studying for hours, I felt my eyes becoming tired.
3. Tom admitted to Henry that if he didn't begin to study, he would fail.
4. Opening the door as quietly as possible, he was able to enter unnoticed.
5. After struggling to stay awake in class, he decided to get a cup of coffee.

PARALLEL STRUCTURE

Parallel structure refers to the use of similar grammatical constructions to express equal ideas. For example,

- Lizzie's ideas are always clear, interesting, and unusual. (Three adjectives describe Lizzie's ideas.)
- When Peter gets off works, he looks forward to going home, reading the paper, and having a martini. (Three gerund phrases are used as direct objects.)

Problems arise when the writer fails to keep this simple principle of structural equality in mind. For example,

- Swimming, listening to Bach, and to play tennis are three of Alice's favorite activities.

In this sentence the subject, a series, consists of two gerund phrases and one infinitive phrase. The items are equal (they are all subjects), but the grammatical constructions are not. A better construction is, "Swimming, listening to Bach, and playing tennis are three of Alice's favorite activities."

- George is temperamental, creative, and has an opinion about everything.

In the above example, again the series consists of unequal grammatical elements. A better sentence would be, "George is temperamental, creative, and opinionated."

EXERCISE

Correct the parallel structure.

1. The shopper enjoyed finding bargains and to catch the checkers in a mistake.
2. He is extremely gregarious and who seems to go out of his way to find a party.
3. I explained the problem and that he should do something about it.
4. My dog, Katie, is loyal, faithful, and a friend.
5. We sat by the fire and sharing our dreams of the future.

Answers

1. The shopper enjoyed finding bargains and catching checkers in a mistake.
2. He is extremely gregarious and seems to go out of his way to find a party.
3. I explained the problem and told him he should do something about it.
4. My dog, Katie, is loyal, faithful, and friendly.
5. We sat by the fire and shared our dreams of the future.

COMPARISON

The secret to success is to make sure the items you are comparing are, in fact, comparable.

Think about this sentence:

- My house is smaller than Alfred.

No matter how huge Alfred has managed to become, he couldn't possible be bigger than my house. So, add an apostrophe to *Alfred*, and his house is being compared to my house:

- My house is smaller than Alfred's.

Now the houses are being compared. Here is another related problem:

- My house is smaller than any on the block.

If you think about if for a moment, you will see that "my house" doesn't seem to be on the block. If my house is, in fact, on the block, I should say either, "My house is smaller than any *other* house on the block" or "My house is the smallest one on the block."

Common ESL Issues

Many of you are well and painfully aware of the problems you encounter when trying to express yourself verbally. If you weren't, you probably wouldn't be studying this section of the book. Fortunately for native speakers, most of these problems can be fairly easily isolated and solved. They have, after all, been speaking the language, more or less correctly, all their life.

The nonnative speaker, however, has to start from scratch. Vocabulary, grammatical principles, even the basic sentence patterns are new and perplexing. The problems ESL students face cannot be easily isolated and then solved: There are too many, and they differ from student to student. In other words, a student from China and a student from Russia will have different problems. Consequently, there is no way to offer more than a cursory look at some common issues that many ESL students have when trying to learn English. Here are some of the more common areas of grammar that ESL students encounter in their writing.

COUNT AND NONCOUNT NOUNS

Think about these two sentences:

- A tree grows in Brooklyn.
- Rice grows in paddy fields.

Tree is a count noun. *Count nouns* refer to particular individuals or things and usually have a singular and plural form (*a plumber, a hat, plumbers, hats*).

Rice is a noncount noun. *Noncount nouns* refer to abstractions or masses and usually do not have a plural form (*justice, integrity, traffic, concrete*).

There are three count nouns, which I have underlined, in the following sentence:

- A <u>donation</u> is an effective <u>weapon</u> in the <u>battle</u> against poverty.

Each of the count nouns can be made into a plural. There could be, for example, two donations, many weapons, three battles.

Poverty, on the other hand, cannot be pluralized. *Poverty* is a *noncount* noun. In the following sentence there are two noncount nouns:

- His conduct caused his parents much anger.

Which nouns are count nouns and which are noncount nouns in the following sentence?

- The cook put too much sugar in that recipe for my taste.

A noun phrase consists of a noun and its modifiers. For example, in the sentence, "My old friend sat down at the battered piano and played a familiar tune," there are three noun phrases: "My old friend," "the battered piano," and "a familiar tune." Each noun (*friend, Piano,* and *tune*) has two modifiers. Words like *my, old, the, battered, a,* and *familiar* are sometimes called *determiners.* Determiners signal that a noun is coming up soon. There are a few groups of determiners:

1. Articles

   We have three articles in the English language: *the, a,* and *an*. *The* is called the *definite article*; *a* and *an* are called *indefinite articles*. (We use *a* before a noun that begins with a consonant sound and *an* before a noun that begins with a vowel sound: *a* tuba, *an* accordion.) We use *the* to indicate something particular and *a* or *an* to indicate something general, for example, *the* book, *a* computer, *an* opera.

   Consider the following two sentences:

   - Mac saw the accident.
   - Mac saw an accident.

   In the first sentence, Mac saw a particular accident; in the second, he saw some undefined accident.

2. *This, That* (singular), *these, those* (plural)
3. Possessive adjectives: *my, our, your,* and so on
4. *whose, what, which*
5. Adjectives that quantify: *all, both, many, some, every, half,* and so on
6. Numerals: *one, two,* and so on

Every singular count noun must have a determiner. Consider the following sentences:

- The check is in the mail.
- Check is in the mail.

- My dog has fleas.
- Dog has fleas.

The second and fourth sentences are not considered acceptable English sentences. Singular count nouns must be preceded by a determiner.

Noncount nouns do not take an indefinite article. For example, we do not say, "A salt is on the table." We can say, "The salt is on the table," or simply "Salt is on the table."

Unfortunately, it is almost impossible to make many hard-and-fast pronouncements about these matters. For example, I see a possible slight difference in meaning between the last two examples. The sentence "The salt is on the table" means that the salt to be used for seasoning, the salt shaker, in other words, is on the table. The sentence "Salt is on the table" could mean the same thing, but it could also mean that salt has been spilled on the table.

Needless to say, the native speaker knows instinctively which determiner to use for which noun; the nonnative speaker finds this a very confusing issue. One solution is to consult the dictionary because count nouns will include the plural form. For example, if you look up *identity*, the plural form will be indicated as *-ies*. Of course, not all count nouns take a plural *s*. But it is a start. Another suggestion for the nonnative speaker is to watch movies and listen carefully to native speakers so that finally he can use this most fundamental speaking and writing skill without conscious thought. This will take a little time. Patience is required.

PHRASAL VERBS

The English language has seemingly thousands of phrasal verbs. These verbs consist of a verb and an adverb, a verb and a preposition, or a verb and both adverb and preposition. These combinations are often idiomatic. This means that the meaning of the phrase differs from the verb if it stood alone. For example, the phrasal verb "to run into" may have nothing to do with running. It can mean, depending on the context, to hit an object (as when a vehicle hits a tree) or it can mean to encounter someone accidentally (as when you run into your old roommate unexpectedly). Here are a few examples:

- to look after (verb + adverb: Henry looked after his aging mother.)
- to look across (verb + preposition: He looked across the street.)
- to put up with (verb + adverb + preposition: I won't put up with your nonsense.)

As you can see, the only one of these three sentences in which the meaning is clear from the verb itself is "He looked across the street." The other two are idiomatic. Henry looked after his aging mother means that he took care of her. I won't put up with your nonsense means I won't tolerate your behavior.

Obviously you can't just attach any adverb to the verb stem. Here are some common phrasal verbs beginning with the verb *run*. Note that none of them refer to the physical act of running.

- to run across (verb + adverb: to see something, for example, an item in the newspaper)
- to run through (verb + adverb: to cover a lot of material quickly)
- to run down (verb + adverb: to criticize, also to locate)
- to run up (verb + adverb: to spend a lot of money)
- to run by (verb + adverb: to get someone's advice about a matter)
- to run around (verb + adverb: literally to run all over the place, but also to be involved romantically with more than one person at a time)
- to run away from (verb + adverb + preposition: to flee, escape)

You will notice that for each of these phrasal verbs a more formal synonym exists. Write the synonyms for the following phrasal verbs:

to stand for ___represent___ to stand in for ___substitute___

to try out ___test, audition___ to hold up ___rob, delay___

to water down ___weaken___ to keep from ___prevent___

to turn down ___reject___ to turn up ___appear___

Consulting an unabridged dictionary or a dictionary of phrasal verbs, like the *Longman Dictionary of Phrasal Verbs*, will help you avoid idiomatic errors when you write.

VERB TENSES

Use verb tenses consistently and appropriately. When writing about reading material, students are often unsure about what verb tense to use. Most English teachers suggest that students write in the present tense when they are discussing the *ideas* in a piece of writing (an essay, an article, a short story, and so forth), although it is acceptable to switch to the past tense when describing a past event that actually occurred. For example, consider this sentence:

- Captain Ahab remembers the excruciating pain he feels when his doctor amputates his leg.

Needless to say, this sentence makes no sense. Ahab is remembering something that is happening at the moment. You can only remember something that has happened in the past: "Captain Ahab remembers the excruciating pain he felt when his doctor amputated his leg."

I read a long time ago that the Navajo language doesn't have any tenses. Events don't happen in the past, present, or future. The concept of time, as we know it, doesn't exist for them. If this is true, Navajos would have an entirely different way of perceiving time, and would, I imagine, have some difficulty with a language whose premise is that time flows as a stream from the past to the future. However, since English is such a language, it is wise for the nonnative speaker—and the native speaker, for that matter—to keep in mind that English tenses are designed to express when events occur and to make sure what he is saying or writing corresponds with that concept of the flow of time.

THE SIMPLE PRESENT TENSE VERSUS THE PRESENT PROGRESSIVE TENSE

The present tense shows that the action takes (or took) place regularly and perhaps over a course of time, whereas the present progressive tense stresses that the activity is occurring now. For example, consider these two sentences:

- Andre Agassi is playing tennis with Steffi.
- Andre Agassi plays tennis with Steffi.

The first sentence states that Andre and Steffi are playing tennis right now. The second indicates that Andre and Steffi play tennis, but they are not necessarily playing at this minute.

With this in mind, if you were writing an essay, for example, about Rose Castillo Guilbault's summer job working with her Mexican coworkers sorting tomatoes, which of these sentences would be the most logical in terms of verb tense?

- Guilbault is working in the tomato-sorting sheds this summer in the Salinas Valley although she is preferring a more glamorous job like working in a clothing store.
- Guilbault is working in the tomato-sorting sheds this summer in the Salinas Valley although she prefers a more glamorous job like working in a clothing store.

The first sentence indicates that Guilbault, who is working during this particular summer, is preferring another job at this particular time, whereas the second sentence indicates that Guilbault is working at this particular time but would prefer to have another job.

Here are two more examples:

- I am liking this class.
- I like this class.

In the first sentence—which Microsoft Grammar Check objects to—I happen to like this class at this particular moment. The second sentence indicates that I simply like this class. Both meanings are possible. I may not like the class, but at this moment I am liking it. Or, I generally like the class.

As always, simply be careful. Make sure you are saying exactly what you mean.

PARTICIPIAL ADJECTIVES

Participial adjectives come in two varieties: the present participle and the past participle. The present participle is formed by adding *-ing* to the verb. For example, *playing, exciting, yelling* are all present participles. The past participle is formed by adding *-ed* to the end of regular verbs. For example, *played, excited, yelled* are all past participles. Some verbs are irregular. For example, the past participle of *steal* is *stolen* ("He has stolen Helen's notebook"). If you are unsure of the past participle of a verb, consult the dictionary.

Generally, deciding which of the two to use poses no problem. "The yelling boy was sent to the dean" makes sense; "the yelled boy was sent to the dean" doesn't.

The verbs that cause confusion seem to be those that refer to feelings. Should one say "An exciting contestant ran onto the stage" or "An excited contestant ran onto the stage"? The difference between the two is easily explained: The present participle is used to describe the person or thing receiving the action or the feeling. In the first sentence, the audience finds the contestant exciting. In the second sentence, the contestant himself is excited.

The same rule applies to the adjective if it is used as a subject complement.

- The contestant is exciting.
- The contestant is excited.

Sometimes, I suppose, in a moment of uncertainty, a student will avoid the issue entirely: "The student is excite." This is never an option. Whenever I see this on a student's paper, I am distress (ha, ha).

GERUNDS AND INFINITIVES

As you know from your careful study of the grammar section, an infinitive is the simple form of the verb and is usually preceded by *to*. A gerund ends in *-ing* and is used as a noun.

Deciding which to use is a problem that often plagues ESL students. For example, why is it perfectly okay to say, "I enjoy taking out the garbage" but not "I enjoy to take out the garbage," yet "I like taking out the garbage" and "I like to take out the garbage" are both acceptable? It is a thorny question with no obvious answers.

One point can be made with certainty: An object of a preposition can never be an infinitive. For example, in the sentence "The fireman was honored for saving the child's life," "*saving the child's life*" is a gerund phrase used as the object of the preposition *for*, and it is a perfectly good sentence. An infinitive as an object of a preposition will never work: "The fireman was honored for to save the child's life."

Another point that can be made, with a little less certainty, is that either an infinitive or a gerund works as a subject, an appositive, and a subject complement:

- Working in a coal mine is not my idea of fun. (gerund phrase, subject)
- To work in a coal mine is not my idea of fun. (infinitive phrase, subject)
- Bill's idea, working in a coal mine, is not my idea of fun. (gerund phrase, appositive)
- Bill's idea, to work in a coal mine, is not my idea of fun. (infinitive phrase, appositive)
- Bill's idea was working in a coal mine. (gerund phrase, subject complement)
- Bill's idea was to work in a coal mine. (infinitive phrase, subject complement)

Real uncertainly seems to arise when the infinitive or gerund is used as a direct object. Let's look at a few examples:

- Julie hoped to get a teaching position.
- The alligator wanted to eat the annoying zookeeper.
- Hank quit playing tennis.
- The angry mob resumed taunting the police.

I read once that an infinitive is used to state intentions, expectations, or things that have not yet occurred, and a gerund is used to state facts. Think about these sentences:

- The birds start singing early in the morning.
- The birds start to sing early in the morning.
- I prefer eating alone.
- I prefer to eat alone.

All are facts, and all are acceptable.

Here is an intention and a expectation (well, more or less):

- Dorothy considered to give her red slippers to charity.
- Dorothy wished to go back to Kansas.

Although clearly not facts, only the second use of the infinitive is acceptable. So, we can not say it is always safe to use the infinitive for expectations, intentions, or future actions of any kind.

Perhaps we can say that it is always safe to use a gerund when stating facts. (It would be nice to be able to make at least one definitive pronouncement about the use of gerunds and infinitives in the direct object position.)

Let's see:

- The cat obviously wants coming in right now.

That is a fact, and the gerund doesn't work. ("The cat obviously wants to come in right now.") However, it is the only verb I can think of that states a fact yet doesn't take a gerund as its direct object. There may be more, but I believe it is fairly safe to say that you may use a gerund as a direct object to state a fact. It's a start.

As you can see, there are few hard-and-fast rules that will be of any help in determining whether to use a gerund or an infinitive. My suggestion, as always, is to consult the dictionary. *Collins Cobuild English Dictionary* contains a list of verbs that are followed by an infinitive and a list of verbs followed by a gerund. This might be a good place to start if you are having trouble.

Proofreading Exercises

Proofreading Exercise 1

This is the second draft of Luisa Hernandez's paper, the final draft of which you will recall reading in the section titled "Overview of the Writing Process" in Part 1. She realized that although she had her thoughts more or less in order, she should go back over her paper carefully and check for errors before turning it in.

Luisa found the following errors. See if you can find them too.

- two parallel problems
- a problem with setting off a phrase
- three subject-verb agreement errors
- two tense shifts
- a fragment
- punctuating a series error
- two missing apostrophes
- comma missing in a nonrestrictive phrase
- one confusing pronoun agreement problem
- one singular-plural inconsistency

I have been following some of the corporate scandals of the 1990s and think about their effect on American culture. For several months, the dominant story in the business media have been the financial mismanagement and accounting fraud of corporate executives at companies like Enron, Tyco, Health-South, Adelphia Communications, and WorldCom. In each instance, executives falsify their financial statements to keep their companies' stock prices high, while systematically looting the company's assets for its own personal profit. These criminal actions ruined lives, damaged reputations and endangered their employees livelihoods.

As the number of these sordid stories multiplied, it occurred to me that these scandals were just an extension of a trend that have been gaining strength over the past decade: Deception and cheating are acceptable ways to get ahead in life. While it might seem like an exaggeration to link the serious criminal activity associated with these accounting scandals with cheating on a quiz; still one does not become a criminal overnight. Just as its hard to eat only one potato chip, it's hard just to tell one lie. Also, small lies, if undetected, leads to bigger lies. One might speculate that some of these corrupt executives might have started on their path to criminality with smaller deceptions from their student days. I have observed that many classmates, like the corporate executives involved in the recent scandals routinely cheat and then justifying their behavior.

Answers

thinking (parallel structure) [line 2]
has (S/V agreement) [line 3]
falsified (tense shift) [line 7]
their companies' assets (singular-plural inconsistency) [line 9]
their (pronoun agreement) [line 9]
reputations, and (comma before last *and* in a series) [line 10]
employees' (possessive) [line 11]
are (tense shift) [line 13]
has (S/V agreement) [line 14]
quiz, still (fragment) [line 18]
it's (it is) [line 19]
lead (S/V agreement) [line 20]
scandals, routinely (necessary comma to enclose phrase beginning "like the corporate executives) [line 25]
justify (parallelism) [line 25]

Proofreading Exercise 2

At the end of Part 5, Pete Glanting was assigned to write a synthesis essay using the information from three or more assigned readings. This is the first draft of Pete's paper. He writes fast and knows he has made a number of errors, so he went over what he had written. He found twenty-two errors, listed below. How many can you find?

- a missing comma in a series
- use of a noun as an adjective
- two commas missing between coordinate adjectives
- confusion between a present and a past participle
- missing commas enclosing two nonrestrictive elements
- two parallel problems
- two subject-verb agreement errors
- incorrect punctuation introducing an appositive
- four missing apostrophes
- an inconsistency
- a pronoun agreement error
- two commas splices
- a tense shift
- a missing comma in a nonrestrictive phrase
- an instance of wordiness

While many of us perhaps might take pity on those who has so few options in life that he must labor at low-skill minimum-wage jobs, such jobs are not always as bleak as they might appear, some people deliberately seek out such work and learn a valuable lesson in the process. For Rose Guilbault, her annual summer job sorting tomatoes in the vegetable shed of the Salinas Valley paid her more than she could have earned babysitting. She swallowed her pride and takes the job so she can earn money for college. But she also learned an unexpecting life lesson from her immigrant coworkers. In "The Conveyer Belt Ladies," Guilbault describes the confidences her Latino coworkers revealed to her; sad stories of abuse, sickness, and having been discriminated against. She writes, "I was appalled and deeply move by these confidences, and the injustices they endured enraged me" (64). Working with her coworkers raised her consciousness. She felt helplessness as she listened to their stories about their suffering and hardship. She also learned humility, and eventually she became ashamed of her initial selfishness and feelings of superiority.

Low-wage jobs, however, do not always offer the consolations and compensations Guilbaults summer job did. In the case of Eliza Zamot whose typical workday Eric Schlosser describes in "Fast Food Nation: Behind the Counter" there seem to be no future for her despite her obvious diligence in performing her McDonald's job in Colorado Springs. She is 16 years old, yet she is leading an adult life. Every day consists of the same humdrum mind-numbing routine and at the end of the day, she barely has enough energy to lie on the couch and lift the TV remote. In Schlosser's essay, he writes that the fast food industry deliberately hires teenage workers, "instead of relying upon a small, stable, well-paid, and well-trained work force" (266). The industrys reasoning is this:

> Teenagers have been the perfect candidates for these jobs, not only because they are less expensive to hire than adults, but also because their youthful inexperience makes them easier to control. (266)

From Schlosser's description, the only entity benefiting from Zamot's hard work is McDonald's. At sixteen years of age she should be in high school, but I surmise she has dropped out making her the perfect fast-food outlet worker. Without an education or higher skills, her fortune is limited, while McDonalds benefits from having a worker who knows her place and wont make a lot of unreasonable demands for promotion, better pay or wanting to join the union.

Answers

have (subject/verb agreement) [line 1]
they (pronoun agreement) [line 2]
low-skill, minimum wage (comma between coordinate adjectives) [line 2]
appear; some (comma splice) [line 4]
summer job, sorting tomatoes in the vegetable shed of the Salinas Valley, paid (nonrestrictive appositive) [lines 4–7]
took (tense shift) [line 8]
unexpected (participle confusion) [line 9–10]
revealed to her: [line 12]
discrimination (parallelism) [line 13]
helpless (noun, adjective confusion) [line 16]
Guilbault's (apostrophe) [line 21]
Zamot, whose typical workday Eric Schloser describes in "Fast Food Nation: Behind the Counter," there (nonrestrictive adjective clause) [lines 22–23]
seems (S/V agreement) [line 24]
humdrum, mind-numbing (coordinate adjectives) [line 27]
routine, and (comma before last item in a series) [line 27]
Schlosser writes (wordy and awkward) (who writes?) [line 29]
industry's reasoning (apostrophe) [line 32]
At age 16, or change the "16" in line 25 to "sixteen" (consistency) [line 38]
dropped out, making her (nonrestrictive phrase) [line 40]
while McDonald's (apostrophe) [line 42]
won't (apostrophe) [line 43]
better pay, (comma in a series) [line 44]
or union representation (parallelism) [line 44]

Microsoft Word Grammar Check

Sometime, when you are writing a letter of application for a job, a personal statement for a college, a letter to your child's teacher, and you feel you need help with your grammar or your sentence structure, whom will you call? Chances are no one will pop to mind. If your next impulse is to consult the grammar check program on your computer, let me offer a few examples of sentences from this book that Microsoft Word's Grammar Check flagged:

1. It takes a lot of guess work out of the dating process. (Grammar Check recommended *guesses work* or *guess works*, neither of which makes any sense.)
2. Poachers value rhinoceros horns because they are thought to have curative value. (Grammar Check suggests *Poacher's*; however, *Poachers* is the subject)
3. If you are unsure of its meaning, look up the word *propaganda* in a dictionary. (Grammar Check says to consider changing *its* to *it's*. *It's* means "it is.")
4. Bryson's first best-selling book, *Mother Tongue*, (1991), focused on the quirks of the English language. (This sentence is *not* a fragment but was flagged as one.)
5. Phoenix is among the five fastest-growing metropolises in the country, and few places are as relentlessly suburban in character. (Grammar Check suggests moving *suburban* after *character*, creating this: "and few places are as relentlessly in character suburban.")
6. Now after a lifetime of embracing my assimilation into American life, I am traveling back in time to find out more about who we were before we were changed. (Microsoft says to use *whom*, even though *who* is the subject complement of the clause "who we were" and is, therefore, correct.)
7. Human skin cells are all dead and are constantly being sloughed off. (Grammar Check recommends putting a hyphen between *all* and *dead*. What does *all-dead* mean?)
8. The criteria we use to judge people may not be completely consistent, since we may alter the standards we use to judge people at the instant

of meeting them. (Grammar Check says to change the comma after *consistent* to a semicolon; however, what we have here is an independent clause followed by a dependent clause. The comma is correct.)

9. Swimming, listening to Bach, and to play tennis are three of Alice's favorite activities. (Microsoft ignores the problem of parallelism and says that the writer should change the verb to *is*.)
10. Teenagers have been the perfect candidates for these jobs, not only because they are less expensive to hire than adults, but also because their youthful inexperience makes them easier to control. (Microsoft Grammar Check suggests changing *their* to *they're*—a stunning mistake. The difference between *their, there,* and *they're* is fundamental to the language.

Many, many times you will be called on—and truly want—to write something you consider very important. In this, as in so many other aspects of your life, it is a great feeling to know you can do it yourself.

Credits

Text Credits

"Girls of Summer: Lazy Days from a Gen X Childhood," by Kristie Helms from *Utne,* July-August 2002. Reprinted by permission of the author.

"Sugar," from *The Blood of Strangers: Stories from Emergency Medicine* by Frank Huyler. Copyright © 1999 by The University of California Press. Reprinted by permission of Henry Holt and Company.

"The Conveyor Belt Ladies," from *Farmworker's Daughter: Growing Up Mexican in America* by Rose Castillo Guilbault. Copyright © 2005 by Heyday Books. Reproduced with permission of Heyday Books via Copyright Clearance Center.

"Refugee's Journey," by K. Oanh Ha from *San Jose Mercury News,* August 17, 2003. Copyright © 2003 by Knight Ridder Digital. Reproduced with permission of Knight Ridder Digital via Copyright Clearance Center.

"Being Prey: Surviving a Crocodile Attack," by Val Plumwood. Reprinted by permission of the author.

Dictionary pages, pp. 104–105: Copyright © 2007 by Houghton Mifflin Company. Reproduced by permission from *The American Heritage College Dictionary,* Fourth Edition.

"Did I Save Lives or Engage in Racial Profiling?" by Lori Hope from *Newsweek,* April 1, 2002. Reprinted by permission of the author.

"The American Man, Age Ten," from *The Bullfighter Checks Her Makeup* by Susan Orlean. Copyright © 2001 by Susan Orlean. Used by permission of Random House, Inc.

"Our Perfect Summer," from *Dress Your Family in Corduroy and Denim* by David Sedaris. Copyright © 2004 by David Sedaris. Reprinted by permission of Little, Brown and Co.

"The New Orleans That Was," by Curtis Wilkie from *San Jose Mercury News,* September 4, 2005. Copyright © 2005 by Knight Ridder Digital. Reproduced with permission of Knight Ridder Digital via Copyright Clearance Center.

"Making Up for Lost Time: The Rewards of Reading at Last," by Richard Wolkomir from *Smithsonian,* August 1996. Copyright © 1996 Richard Wolkomir. Used with permission of the author.

"How Mr. Dewey Decimal Saved My Life," from *High Tide in Tucson: Essays from Now or Never* by Barbara Kingsolver. Copyright © 1995 by Barbara Kingsolver. Reprinted by permission of HarperCollins Publishers.

"The Teacher Who Opened My Mind," by Mark Edmundson from *Utne,* January-February, 2003. Reprinted by permission of the author.

"Cells," from *A Short History of Nearly Everything* by Bill Bryson. Copyright © 2003 by Bill Bryson. Used by permission of Broadway Books, a division of Random House, Inc.

"Easter's End," by Jared Diamond from *Discover,* August 1995. Reprinted by permission of the author.

Excerpt from "The Hollow Men" in *Collected Poems 1909-1962* by T.S. Eliot. Copyright © 1936 by Harcourt, Inc., and renewed 1964 by T.S. Eliot. Reprinted by permission of the publisher.

"The Burden of the Feast," by Bobbie Ann Mason from *The New Yorker,* December 22, 1997. Copyright © 1997 Bobbie Ann Mason. Reprinted by permission of International Creative Management, Inc.

"Behind the Counter," from *Fast Food Nation: The Dark Side of the All-American Meal* by Eric Schlosser. Copyright © 2001 by Eric Schlosser. Reprinted by permission of Houghton Mifflin Company. All rights reserved.

"Pricing French Fries: A Lesson in Economics," by Shannon Brownlee originally titled "Portion Distortion – You Don't Know the Half of It." Reprinted by permission of Shannon Brownlee, Senior Fellow, New American Foundation.

"Facing Up to the Ultimate Taboo – Failure," by William Ecenbarger from *Los Angeles Times,* February 23, 2005. Reprinted by permission of the author.

"Culture Suggests Cheaters Do Prosper," by Kirk O. Hanson from *San Jose Mercury News,* May 6, 2005. Copyright © 2005 by Knight Ridder Digital. Reproduced with permission of Knight Ridder Digital via Copyright Clearance Center.

"A Slippery Slope," by C.W. Nevius from *San Francisco Chronicle Magazine,* October 19, 2003. Copyright © 2003 by San Francisco Chronicle. Reproduced with permission of San Francisco Chronicle via Copyright Clearance Center.

"Nickel-and-Dimed: On (Not) Getting By in America," by Barbara Ehrenreich. Copyright © 1999 by Barbara Ehrenreich. Reprinted by permission of International Creative Management, Inc.

Excerpts from *Windows* by Jeff Rackham and Olivia Bertagnolli. Copyright © 1993 by HarperCollins College Publishers. Reprinted by permission of Pearson Education, Inc.

Graphic: "Digital Dominates the Camera Market," by Todd Trumbull from *San Francisco Chronicle,* May 23, 2005. Copyright © 2005 by San Francisco Chronicle. Reproduced with permission of San Francisco Chronicle via Copyright Clearance Center.

"Polio's Enduring Legacy," by Susan Levine from *The Washington Post,* April, 2005. Copyright © 2005 The Washington Post. Reprinted with permission.

"Many Theories on Root of Strong Hurricanes," by Keay Davidson from *San Francisco Chronicle,* October 3, 2005. Copyright © 2005 by San Francisco Chronicle. Reproduced with permission of San Francisco Chronicle via Copyright Clearance Center.

"Hurricane Fuel: Warm, Moist Air Over Warm Ocean Water," by Keay Davidson from *San Francisco Chronicle,* September 22, 2005. Copyright © 2005 by San Francisco Chronicle. Reproduced with permission of San Francisco Chronicle via Copyright Clearance Center.

Hurricane Dynamics illustration by John Blanchard: From "Hurricane Fuel: Warm, Moist Air Over Warm Ocean Water," by Keay Davidson from *San Francisco Chronicle,* September 22, 2005. Reprinted by permission of San Francisco Chronicle, Hearst Communications.

"Passing Fancy," by Adam Goodheart, first published in *Utne,* January-February, 2001. Copyright © 2001 by Adam Goodheart. Reprinted by permission of The Wylie Agency.

"Shop Like a Man," is reprinted with the permission of Simon and Schuster Adult Publishing Group from *Why We Buy: The Science of Shopping* by Paco Underhill. Copyright © 1999 by Obat, Inc.

"Speed Dating," by Gautam Naik, originally titled "The Mating Game is a Three-Day Event for Moroccan Berbers" from *The Wall Street Journal,* September 10, 2003. Copyright © 2003 by Dow Jones & Company. Reproduced with permission of Dow Jones & Company via Copyright Clearance Center.

"What's Love Got To Do With It?" by Anjula Razdan from *Utne,* May-June 2003. Reprinted with permission from *Utne* magazine, www.utne.com.

Reprinted by permission of the publishers and the Trustees of Amherst College from *The Poems of Emily Dickinson,* Thomas H. Johnson, ed., Cambridge, Mass.: The Belknap Press of Harvard University Press, Copyright © 1951, 1955, 1979, 1983 by the President and Fellows of Harvard College.

"Throwing Like A Girl," by James Fallows from *The Atlantic Monthly,* August 1996. Copyright © 1996 by James Fallows. Reprinted by permission of the author, c/o The Atlantic Monthly.

"Teen Suicide and the Culture of Fear," from *Culture of Fear* by Barry Glassner. Copyright © 1999. Reprinted by permission of Basic Books, a member of Perseus Books Group.

"The Telephone," from *The Boy from the Tower of the Moon* by Anwar Accawi. First published in the *Sun.* Reprinted by permission of the author.

"More Room" is reprinted with permission from the publisher of *Silent Dancing* by Judith Ortiz Cofer. Copyright © 1990 Arte Publico Press – University of Houston.

Map of Botswana: From *Improving Reading Skills: Contemporary Readings for College Students,* 5th edition by Deanne Milan Spears. Copyright © 2004 by The McGraw-Hill Companies. Reprinted by permission of The McGraw-Hill Companies, Inc.

Excerpts from *Long Walk to Freedom* by Nelson Mandela. Copyright © 1994, 1995 by Nelson Rolihlahla Mandela. Reprinted by permission of Little, Brown and Co.

"The Many Layers of the Veil," by Megan Stack from *Los Angeles Times,* January 12, 2005. Reprinted by permission of Los Angeles Times.

Excerpt from "The Only Harmless Great Thing," by Sallie Tisdale was first published in *The New Yorker,* January 23, 1989. Reprinted by permission of the author.

"The Great Cell Phone Debate," published in *VIA,* May/June 2005. Reprinted by permission of the California State Automobile Association.

"The Ethics of Torture," by George Friedman, CEO Stratfor, from www.stratfor.com. Reprinted with the author's permission.

"Black, Dead and Invisible," by Bob Herbert from *The New York Times,* April 8, 2005. Reprinted by permission of *The New York Times.*

"Hero Inflation," by Nicholas Thompson from *Boston Globe,* January 13, 2002. Reprinted by permission of the author.

"Benefit and Burden," from *Enrique's Journey* by Sonia Nazario. Copyright © 2006 by Sonia Nazario. Used by permission of Random House, Inc.

"Can You Say Bienvenidos?" by Eugene Robinson from *The Washington Post,* April 11, 2006. Copyright © 2006 The Washington Post. Reprinted with permission.

"Conspiracy Against Assimilation," by Robert J. Samuelson from *The Washington Post,* April 20, 2006. Copyright © 2006 The Washington Post. Reprinted with permission.

"The Weather Where We Are: The Arctic," by Margaret Atwood. Copyright © 2005 O.W. Toad, Ltd. First appeared in *Granta 91,* published in Fall 2005. Reprinted by permission of the author.

"Is It Warm Here?" by David Ignatius from *The Washington Post,* January 18, 2006. Copyright © 2006 The Washington Post. Reprinted with permission.

Photo Credits

p. 2: © LWA-Dann Tardif/Corbis; **p. 38:** © Glenn Campbell/Icon SMI/Corbis; **p. 48:** Courtesy of Kristie Helms; **p. 55:** Courtesy of Lisa Hemstead; **p. 69:** Courtesy K. Oanh Ha; **p. 92:** © Peter Ginter/Bilderberg/Peter Arnold, Inc.; **p. 115:** © John Spellman/Retna Ltd.; **p. 130:** © Ralph Orlowski/Getty Images; **p. 151:** © Steve Ueckert/Houston Chronicle/AP Photo; **p. 152:** © Rob Carr/AP Photo; **p. 153:** © Richard Vogel/AP Photo; **p. 158:** © Aflo Foto Agency/Alamy; **p. 167:** © Sue Owrutsky; **p. 180:** © Associated Press; **p. 190:** © Tim Wright/Corbis; **p. 204:** © Rick Friedman/Corbis; **p. 240:** © Bill Lai/The Image Works; **p. 251:** Courtesy of Bobbie Ann Mason, Photo by Pam Spaulding.; **p. 264:** © Susan Van Etten/PhotoEdit; **p. 273:** Courtesy of Shannon Brownlee, Photo by David C. Levy; **p. 284:** Courtesy of William Ecenbarger; **p. 291:** Courtesy of Kirk O. Hanson; **p. 301:** Courtesy of the San Francisco Chronicle; **p. 313:** © Suki Dhanda/Camera Press/Retna; **p. 352:** © Lester Lefkowitz/The Image Bank/Getty Images; **p. 375:** © James Leynse/Corbis; **p. 386:** Courtesy of Gautam Naik; **p. 419:** © Paul A. Saunders/Corbis; **p. 421:** Courtesy of The Ad Council and National Center for Family Literacy; **p. 422:** Courtesy of The Ad Council; **p. 434:** © John Birdsall/The Image Works; **p. 448:** Courtesy of Barry Glassner; Photographer: Jennifer Leshnick; **p. 457:** Courtesy of Anwar F. Accawi; **p. 469:** Courtesy of Judith Ortiz Cofer, Photo by Sortino; **p. 477:** © Louise Gubb/Corbis SABA; **p. 489:** © Lynsey Addario/Corbis; **p. 510:** © Digital Vision/PunchStock; **p. 526:** © The New York Times/Redux; **p. 529:** Courtesy of Nicholas Thompson; **p. 540:** © Alex Wong/Getty Images for Meet the Press; **p. 543:** The Washington Post Writer's Group; **p. 549:** © Colin McPherson/Corbis; **p. 553:** © Alex Wong/Getty Images for Meet the Press; **p. 566:** © Neal Preston/Corbis

Index

B

C

D

E

F

I

J

K

L

M

N

O

P

Q

R

S

T

U

V